DIRECTING

THE
DOCUMENTARY

Fourth Edition

DIRECTING

THE
DOCUMENTARY

Fourth Edition

Michael Rabiger

ELSEVIER

AMSTERDAM • BOSTON • HEIDELBERG • LONDON
NEW YORK • OXFORD • PARIS • SAN DIEGO
SAN FRANCISCO • SINGAPORE • SYDNEY • TOKYO

Focal Press is an imprint of Elsevier

Focal
Press

Focal Press is an imprint of Elsevier
200 Wheeler Road, Burlington, MA 01803, USA
Linacre House, Jordan Hill, Oxford OX2 8DP, UK

Recognizing the importance of preserving what has been written,
Elsevier prints its books on acid-free paper whenever possible.

Library of Congress Cataloging-in-Publication Data
Application submitted.

British Library Cataloguing-in-Publication Data
A catalogue record for this book is available from the British
Library.

ISBN: 0-24-080608-5

For information on all Focal Press publications
visit our website at www.focalpress.com

04 05 06 07 08 10 9 8 7 6 5 4 3 2 1

Printed in the United States of America

For
Netta Hakak with love–
Here comes the next generation!

CONTENTS

PREFACE TO THE FOURTH EDITION

If you are interested in making documentary films, everything you need technically and conceptually should be here. Using a hands-on, project-oriented approach, this book takes you through the necessary steps in using the screen as a tool of inquiry and self-expression. It can take you from absolute beginner, if that's where you are, to advanced levels of competency. If you are a professional, you should find new ways of seeing and a greater wholeness and logic in the world of your work. Because so many people (myself included) are experiential learners and temperamentally unsuited to absorbing masses of untried information, the book is designed to accommodate more than one kind of user. Your profile may be one or more of the following:

- You want conceptual preparation before undertaking production work. For you, each production-related phase includes an introduction and graduated projects to help you develop skills, judgment, and confidence.
- You learn best from doing rather than from conceptual preparation. You can jump straight into the projects and use the rest of the book as a problem-solving manual as solid issues take shape in your work.
- You want to direct fiction but wonder if documentary skills might be a useful. There is a section on how documentary work develops the confidence to improvise, experiment, and capitalize on spontaneity, and how useful documentary coverage is as a developmental tool during fiction-film rehearsals.
- You are trapped in film or TV work that has become routine, and you long to direct. This book offers paths to get there.
- You cannot afford time or money for schooling, and you want to learn making documentaries anyway. This book will help you get there.

This edition has been thoroughly updated, revised, and expanded to reflect changing technology and the veritable explosion of documentary production. Luckily, the explanations and practices that come from my filmmaking and teaching also keep developing. I especially value the stimulus from workshops, seminars, and conferences, for they confirm that the needs and practices of documentary makers are fairly universal. They also show how much the documentary voice is needed and appreciated, especially in nations that are entering or leaving the airless embrace of authoritarianism. In a world wracked by hatred and warfare, the still small voice of humane conscience has never been more vital.

Because seeing enough documentaries remains a practical impossibility, this book cites mainly English language films, many made by American independents. *Directing the Documentary*'s practices and methods must, however, work in a range of cultural settings, for it has gone into several languages since it first appeared and seems to work for its users.

Changes to the fourth Edition include new chapters:

- Evidence and Point of View in the Documentary (Chapter 4). This likens making a documentary to compiling evidence in a court case for presentation to the jury, or audience. By reviewing the rules of evidence and likening them to testimony from a camera, recorder, or witness, this chapter advances guidelines for making more persuasive documentary. The court's summing up phase represents the way that evidence is structured in a film to exert maximum dialectical effect on the audience—the jury whose judgment determines credibility and therefore truth.

- Projects: Critical Writing (Chapter 9). These introduce methods of critical writing about documentary and encourage its practice as a method to discover and clarify your inherent values.

- Missions and Permissions (Chapter 17) brings together ethics, embedded values, and practical issues concerning permissions and informed consent.

- The Preproduction Meeting (Chapter 19). Mindful that the book may be used for projects of very different complexity, this edition includes the preproduction meeting as a forum for coordinating a large production.

- Location Sound (Chapter 22). Now that camcorders have more sophisticated sound recording facilities, more people use location mixers and wireless mikes, so there is a new chapter on location sound.

- Using Music and Working with a Composer (Chapter 35). As digital editing frees documentary from the straitjacket of realism and as sophisticated synthesizers permit the making of low-cost original scores, music is being used more extensively for atmosphere and comment. This chapter summarizes how to work with a composer.

A major change in the fourth Edition is that the Aesthetics and Authorship section is now rewritten and repositioned ahead of that on preproduction because film teachers needed a more linear textbook. I have tried to make the material more concise, more proactive in its advice, and more directly relevant to beginners whose sights may be fixed more on production than on premeditation.

The fourth Edition also includes

- A history section updated with many recent films. Being fair and representative is impossible, so I have cited the best films I have seen. Because this book is used beyond the Anglophone world, I have included international films of stature in the hope that readers may see them too. This combination of chance and choice in my method undoubtedly results in a view neither adventurous nor balanced, but it's plainly impossible to satisfy all constituencies, and it is better to reflect what I know. So be it.

- Expanded research chapters (Chapter 15 and 16).

- Updated equipment references and updated film references throughout the book.

- How making documentaries can prepare you to direct fiction and how the Iranian cinema shows the way for a fusion of documentary realism and poetic, allegorical storytelling.

- Outcomes Assessment forms for most projects gathered together in Appendix 1. For teachers' convenience they will also be posted in Microsoft Word format under the book's title on the Focal Press Web site (www.elsevier.com/inca/publications/store/6/7/5/9/6/6/index.htt). Assessing work by its outcomes facilitates

  - Teachers assessing students' work more objectively

  - Students assessing and discussing each other's work

  - Greater awareness of multiple layers in film work

  - Constructing similar criteria for your own work—existing and projected

- Greater emphasis on going beyond using film as simple denotation to use it connotatively and poetically to liberate ideas and feelings.

- Initial Research and the Draft Proposal (Chapter 15) now expanded to include defining point of view and style. It contains discussion of "raising the stakes"—deciding what, for participants and audience alike, is at risk for the central character(s) and what the director might legitimately do to intensify this.

- Interviewing (Chapter 24) reformatted to make it clearer and more prescriptive.

- Sound theory and camera handling theory (Chapter 14).

- The three-act structure made more prominent, with encouragement to use dramatic form in all stages of directing.

- Beats and dramatic units explained and made germane to directing. Recognizing dramatic units as they spontaneously unfold in life helps the director know when a documentary situation is going somewhere and when, conversely, it will remain stuck without directorial attention.

- A questionnaire on embedded values at the end of the research phase, positioned as the last consideration before shooting (embedded values are the unquestioned assumptions that permit us to accept things as "just the way they are" when we should, in fact, be critical of them).

- More overview guidance for those who use the book as a field guide, including bullet points at the start of each part and each chapter. There is also a Production Projects overview as an introduction in Chapter 28.

There are new exercises in

- Pitching ideas (Chapter 10)
- The family drama (Chapter 10)
- Critical writing (Chapter 9)
- Sound theory and recording (Chapter 14)

Most projects and exercises in this book come with individual assessment criteria and suggested topics of discussion. Teachers in an educational climate that demands objective proof that students are learning will find outcomes assessment extremely useful for several reasons. Their students, having multiple criteria by which a piece of work will be judged, know what is expected and can plan for it. When work is finished, the assessments serve as prompts for teachers and learners to see more deeply into each piece of work and to evolve shared values. Film teaching seems to be moving away from the traditional model of students apprenticed to a master in favor of using more rational, open practices related to theories and practices in the rest of the arts. In general, this book should reduce the burden of instruction so that teachers and their students can concentrate on the truly fascinating relationships that develop over their work.

Worldwide, the documentary is growing in quantity, stature, and accomplishments. With fresh approaches and new causes to champion, the independent documentary is stirring ever greater public interest. Digital, high-definition video equipment and desktop computer postproduction have revolutionized screen production and displaced film from its elite and excluding position as the medium of choice. Drama can greatly profit from non-professional actors, neo-realistic use of settings, and imaginative stories arising from local cultures. The future has never looked more exciting for cinema independents.

Over the years many people have contributed help and ideas to this book. My sincere thanks go therefore to Peter Attipetty, Camilla Calamandrei, Dr. Judd Chesler, Michael Ciesla, Dan Dinello, Dennis Keeling, Tod Lending, Cezar Pawlowski, Barb Roos, and her students at Grand Valley State University. Thanks to Bill Yancey for help with the text, Dirk Matthews and Milos Stehlik for pictures and pictorial sources, and Paul Ruddock for freely sharing his experience from using the previous edition. My grateful thanks to Dean Mary Schmidt Campbell, Ken Dancyger, and the film faculty and students at the Tisch School of NYU for giving me the rare privilege of working with them. As a friend, supporter, and doyen of the documentary, George Stoney, also of NYU, has alerted me to significant omissions. Most of the information for the chapter on working with a composer came from Paul Rabiger, a composer for film and television. Joanna Rabiger, a documentary film editor and researcher, saved me from falling too far in arrears with documentary development. Penelope Rabiger, a teacher whose master's degree was in learning styles, has greatly helped me understand my early difficulties with traditional education and why I took alternative paths. I must thank Doe Mayer, Jed Dannenbaum, and Carroll Hodge for the inspiring exchanges, formal and informal, preceding the publication of their work *Creative Filmmaking from the Inside Out* (New York: Simon & Schuster, 2003). I thank them for permission to summarize some of its ideas on the dangers of embedded values.

I owe a great debt of gratitude to Columbia College, which allowed me to implement so many of my ideas. Through the support and vision of Bert Gall and Caroline Latta, the Film/Video Department was radically rethought, expanded, and rehoused during my tenure as chair. Over the years, the college and the Film/Video Department, now under the able leadership of Bruce Sheridan, have shown great affection and trust. To my students, at Columbia and elsewhere around the world, I have this to say: Dear friends, both past and present, you are too many to name, but you showed me the way to writing and rewriting this book. Thank you.

The excellent Focal Press staff have consistently been a pleasure to work with and to know, and I must particularly thank Elinor Actipis, Acquisitions Editor, for her outstanding encouragement, practical support, and professionalism at every stage. Given Focal's mammoth book list, I count myself more than lucky.

Lastly, heartfelt thanks to my wife, Nancy Mattei, for her endurance, sharp proofreading, and unfailingly kind, constructive, and astute critical suggestions. With the quantity and quality of help given me, any mistakes are mine alone. Maybe I should add that I have no relationship of personal gain with any of the manufacturers, services, or institutions named in this book.

Michael Rabiger
Chicago, 2004

PART 1

INTRODUCTION, HISTORY, AND FUTURE

Part 1 looks at

- Becoming a documentary director
- What makes a nonfiction film a documentary
- Objectivity and subjectivity in documentary
- Showing evidence and complexity to your audience
- The documentary's influence in society and the responsibilities that go with it
- How you relate as a documentary maker to your audience
- How film language evolved and how the documentary was born
- Interventional and non-interventional approaches to participants and their worlds

- The role of technology and its effect on handling documentary subject matter
- Where changes in technology and audience expectations may be taking us

This book is for practical people who like making things that are useful. Documentaries are stories, and stories have always been vital to human life. Making them from the actual—real people living their real lives—becomes special whenever a work taps into meanings that run deep, such as those also expressed in myth, legend, and religion. The presence of **ancient values** such as these in the documentary shows that human life in the 21st century still takes place under similar and mysterious laws of the universe.

A documentary might be about the seasonal bird movements across whole continents, as in Jacques Perrin's *Winged Migration* (2001), or about the desperate work of an Italian doctor and English nurse who must amputate a young soldier's leg on a kitchen table, as in Fabrizio Lazzaretti and Alberto Vendemmiati's *Jung (War) in the Land of the Mujaheddin* (2000). These two works alone plunge you into the mystery of being. One, taking you inside a *V* of geese flying high over Canadian mountains, is made by an extremely professional team with a vast budget; the other confronts us with the madness and suffering of humans in armed conflict, and is made with minimal resources by two young and brave Italian documentary makers fresh from film school.

Everyone who sets out to practice an art form begins from the inspiration and achievements of others. Part 1 of this book examines briefly who documentary makers are, how the genre originated, what work it has elected to do, and what it may become—given that its identity remains entirely open to new influences and change. To give context and some flavor of its evolution, I have compressed documentary history into a single chapter of subjectively selected highlights. Here are some of the uses, developments, and outstanding personalities in documentary's first eight decades.

Whether or not you have yet made your first documentary, you hold the keys to the innovations and changes of the future. My job is to convey, as best I can, whatever you need to make a flying start. Some of this will be unavoidably technical, but the most important work will be in freeing up your mind to operate radically. There is a direct, human analogy for making a documentary: research is anticipation and inquiry; shooting is experiencing and memorizing; viewing the dailies is recall; and the edited film is memory reorganized and articulated so that you can share a vital experience with others. Whatever you do, read Chapters 39 (Education) and 40 (Getting Work) soon. They stress how vital it is to form long-term educational and career plans, beginning now. Otherwise what matters is that you remain close to what is human, to what your life has taught you to believe, and that you develop your own ideas and authorial voice. This book uses many analogies to free you from intimidation by the medium.

For further information on issues arising in Part 1, use the Index or go to the Bibliography.

CHAPTER 1

THE DIRECTOR'S ROLE

This chapter considers

- The attraction of documentary, what it is, and what it may become
- Aspects of factual film that make it documentary
- Objectivity, fairness, clarification, and simplification
- Documentary as a subjective construct and mislabeling
- The contract with your audience
- Corporations and editorial freedom
- What medium to shoot in
- Why bearing witness matters so much

Becoming a documentary director is like taking over any new job: suddenly you must try to look competent in a new capacity and a new world. Discomfort and occasionally terror go with the experience, as with all truly worthwhile new experiences. This chapter looks at the assumptions, expectations, and myths that you can expect to encounter.

WHAT IS A DOCUMENTARY?

If you go to a documentary festival or conference where the filmmakers are present, you will be struck by the convivial, cooperative atmosphere and the modest way that documentary makers take on the issues of their time. It's like being at a convention of Davids, each engaged in passionate struggle with their chosen Goliath. You will see that documentary is that rare medium in which the common person takes on large, important issues and shakes up society. Directing documentaries involves handling a modicum of power, and this brings ethical issues and moral responsibilities. Those you will hear debated too.

Get two documentarians together, and the chances are high that they will argue about what documentary is. Even though documentary has evolved continuously from its inception, its purview and methods remain ambiguous, and its parameters keep enlarging. Uncontested, however, is what remains central to documentary's spirit—the notion that documentaries explore the mysteries of actual people in actual situations. The disagreements arise over allied issues:

- What any given actuality really is
- How to record it without compromise and without injecting alien values
- How to honestly and truthfully convey something that, being more spirit than materiality, can only be discerned subjectively

Such crucial ambiguities are not a fault in the medium; rather, they reflect what besets us whenever we face issues that accompany fully awakened consciousness. To make documentary is to practice living your life existentially, as though each day were your last. People who make documentaries put a high value on the joy, pain, compromise, and learning that come from being completely *alive*. No wonder they make great company.

Documentary as the "creative treatment of actuality": Documentary's founding father, John Grierson—to whom we shall return—defined it as the "creative treatment of actuality." The idea that you bring your own inventive sensibility to the real is conveniently imprecise, for it embraces all nonfiction forms, such as nature, science, travelogue, industrial, educational, and even certain promotional films. But, as we shall see, films under these categories may not really be documentary in the full sense.

Documentary and time: Usually documentaries are set in the present or the past, but the genre never stays long inside any set boundaries. Peter Watkins' *The War Game* (1965) showed that documentary could project itself into the future. His film takes the awful facts of World War II bombings of Dresden, Hiroshima, and Nagasaki and uses them to hypothesize a major nuclear attack on London. Until someone invents a time machine, documentaries about the past or the future have to use actors. This means that fictional characters and scripts are not automatically excluded from documentary.

Documentary is socially critical: Documentary always seems concerned with uncovering further dimensions to actuality and at the same time implying social criticism. The better ones do not go in for hand-wringing nor do they promote a product or service. They may not even be concerned with objectively measurable facts. For instance, a factual film about the way workers manufacture razor blades would be an industrial film, but a film that shows the effect on workers of repetitive precision manufacturing, and that *invites the spectator to draw socially critical conclusions,* can only be called a documentary—however well it might also relay the physical process of manufacturing.

Concern for the quality and justice of human life lifts the documentary out of the purely factual realm and propels it into moral and ethical dimensions. There, it scrutinizes the organization of human life and attempts to develop a humane consciousness in its audience. The best documentaries are models of disciplined passion, showing the familiar in an unfamiliar way. They invite us to function at a keen level of awareness and even to follow this up by taking action. Sometimes documentaries literally argue a case, but more often the argument is implicit and conducted through showing us the conditions of somebody's life.

Documentary, individuality, and point of view: The French novelist Emile Zola said that "a work of art is a corner of Nature seen through a temperament." This is not far from Grierson's "creative treatment of actuality." Amend Zola's statement to read, "a documentary is a corner of actuality seen through a human temperament," and it's plain that a documentary examines the actual through the prism of human temperament. Memorable films present their characters and events through the lens of an identifiable, authorial persona, even though films are nearly always made collectively, not individually. In fiction and experimental film, this personal stamp is familiar from contemporary fiction or experimental film directors such as Chantal Akerman, Jane Campion, Peter Greenaway, Abbas Kiarostami, Baz Luhrmann, Penny Marshall, Sally Potter, Julie Taymor, and Lars von Trier, all of whom have their recognizable concerns and style. A clear authorial identity is also visible in the documentaries of Nicholas Broomfield, Barbara Kopple, Michael Moore, Errol Morris, Marlon Riggs, Trinh T. Minh-ha, Fred Wiseman, Nettie Wild, and many others. Each brings a fresh, special, and engrossing involvement with some aspect of the human condition. You feel it in their passionate and empathic engagement with a subject and in their commitment to presenting the roots of a reality on the screen.

To explore an issue and to use a medium to its utmost are the preconditions for becoming an artist. Artists make visible what is only at the edge of society's consciousness, and any art museum or gallery shows a great historical range of such visions. Like painters, documentarians are guided by conviction, conscience, ideology, and interest in form. They too seek to persuade.

Not all artists conform to the romantic ideal of the genius working alone. A 15th-century Italian painting attributed to Fra Angelico or Uccello was almost certainly made by a team. Each assistant handled details such as landscape background, hands, or drapery. Likewise in film, a team, not an individual, handles aspects of a film's vision. *Hoop Dreams* (1994), codirected by Steve James, Fred Marx, and Peter Gilbert, shows how superb screen authorship can arise from shared values (Figure 1–1). Given how collaborative a technological medium is, and that film is shown to a collective audience, this is hardly surprising.

Documentary is an organized story: Successful documentaries, like their fiction counterparts, tell a good story and have engaging characters, narrative tension, and an integrated point of view. These elements are fundamental to all stories, and are present in myth, legend, sagas, and folk tales—humankind's earliest organized narratives. The poet T.S. Eliot, considering where poetic narrative comes from, said that, "It is the function of all art to give us some perception of an order in life, by imposing an order on it." Documentary often points to an underlying organization by demonstrating causes and effects. By mobilizing a range of strong feelings it urges us to action. Michael Roemer in *Telling Stories*[1] shows how plot (that is, the situation and pressuring circumstances in a story) is really the rules of the universe, and vital characters are those who contest—often

---

[1] Michael Roemer, *Telling Stories: Postmodernism and the Invalidation of Traditional Narrative* (Lanham, MD: Rowman & Littlefield, 1995).

FIGURE 1–1

Superb screen authorship arising from shared values in *Hoop Dreams* (1994), codirected by Steve James, Fred Marx, and Peter Gilbert. (*Hoop Dreams* Copyright 1994, Fine Line Features. All rights reserved. Photo appears courtesy of New Line Productions, Inc.)

heroically but unsuccessfully—the way things are. A character may take on the rules of the universe out of ignorance, obstinacy, or a host of other reasons, but the struggle becomes his or her (and our) education.

All successful stories seem to center on some aspect of human development, no matter how minimal and symbolic, and they do this in order to leave us with some degree of hope. Watching actual people struggling with actual circumstances produces strong and moving documentaries, especially if you also see someone learn something as a result.

Documentary's range of forms: Imposing an order by demonstrating cause and effect can be accomplished any number of ways. A documentary can be controlled and premeditated, spontaneous and unpredictable, lyrical and impressionistic, or starkly observational. It can have commentary or no speech at all, interrogate its subjects, catalyze change, or even ambush its subjects. It can impose an order by using words, images, music, or human behavior. It can use literary, theatrical, or oral traditions and partake of music, painting, song, essay, or choreography. Deciding which of these to use in your film need never be a lonely matter because examples are always available in songs, plays, short stories, history, and literature.

Fidelity to the actual versus realism: There are no limits to the documentary's possibilities, but it always reflects a profound fascination with, and respect for, actuality. But what *is* actuality? To the materially minded it is something objective that we can all see, measure, and agree on. The wealthy TV network or funding agency, wary of lawsuits, wants a documentary to contain only what the documentary theorist Bill Nichols calls *historical reality*—that which can be seen, proved, and defended in court if need be. Not surprisingly, these organizations are much readier to produce informational films or controlled corporate journalism than they are true documentary, which is guided by conscience and results in a more individual and critical view of the world.

True documentary reflects the richness and ambiguity of life, and goes beyond the guise of objective observation to include impressions, perceptions, and feelings. Human reality under pressure becomes surreal and hallucinatory, as you see so memorably in Errol Morris' *The Thin Blue Line* (1988). Modern documentarians must be ready to represent not just the outward, visible reality of those they film but also their inner lives, because thoughts, memories, dreams, and nightmares are the inside dimension of their lives. Writers have always been able to shift levels between their characters' inner and outer dimensions, and have sometimes included the storyteller's perceptions as part of the rich resulting narrative. Film is finding out how to claim these freedoms for itself.

Documentary as unfolding evidence: The modern documentary differs from its earlier, more scripted forms because mobile technology allows us to record events and authorial consciousness *as they unfold.* This produces the sensation of spontaneous, living adaptation familiar from the heightened moments in our own lives. Take, for example, Nicholas Broomfield and Joan Churchill's fine *Soldier Girls* (1981). Ostensibly it shows how the U.S. Army trains its women soldiers, but it also reveals a great range of formal and informal moments, including sadistic training and humiliations that are all the more disquieting because they are imposed by authoritarian white men on minority women. The film delays confronting a central paradox until late: because warfare is brutal and unfair, a caring instructor cannot train soldiers to survive kindly, no matter what their gender. But this argument wears thin after what we have seen and leaves us disturbed by larger questions about soldierly traditions and military mentality—just as the film's makers surely intended. We share what moved or disturbed Broomfield and Churchill, but the film never tells us what to feel or think. Instead, *by exposing us to evidence that is contradictory and provocative* it jolts us into realization and inner debate.

Whenever a film exposes us to good though contradictory evidence, we become jury members arbitrating truth. A documentary of this type is thus a construct of evidences that are weak or strong, as you will see in Chapter 4 (Evidence and Point of View in the Documentary).

Documentary as a social art: As we have said, films are usually made collaboratively. This means that an authorial attitude arises and is collectively mediated by the individuals who shoot and edit the film. Another collective—the audience—then considers the resulting work. All film, and the documentary in particular, is a truly social art form in every stage of its evolution.

OBJECTIVITY AND FAIRNESS

Objectivity: People frequently assume documentaries are objective because factual television likes to balance out opposing points of view. This is supposed to ensure a fair, unbiased view of the events and personalities in question. Such balance is a tactic inherited from journalism, which sometimes must preserve the identity of sources that gave information on condition of anonymity. Political balance lowers the dangers to, and responsibilities of, the newspaper. Papers fear accusations of political bias or of being proved wrong, because this brings discredit and lawsuits. So part of a journalist's professionalism has always been to keep things looking objective. A newspaper will further this appearance by prescribing a uniform and faceless "house" writing style, and by camouflaging staff attitudes as the opinion or the conflicts of others.

In the 1930s this fixation with equipoise led reputable British newspapers to depict the trouble brewing in Germany as a petty squabble between Communists and Blackshirts whipped up by Red troublemakers. We see in hindsight that no responsible commentator could sit on the fence and report in this hands-off way. It was neither fair nor responsible when the Nazis had already begun acting on their genocidal intentions.

Reporters and documentary makers, then and now, must *interpret* events. This means that for each specific issue your film must imply where the cause of justice and humanity probably lies. To guide us there, you will often have to lead us through a maze of contradictory evidence and let us make our own determinations—just as you made yours. Interestingly, this is how a court presents evidence to the ultimate authority in a democracy—a jury.

Fairness: In a world of ambiguities the documentarian's responsibility is to be fair. If, for example, you are telling the story of a malpractice accusation against a surgeon, it would be prudent not only to cover the allegations from both sides but to cross check everything that can be independently verified. In this you follow the same practices as the good journalist and the successful detective. Because matters are seldom as they first seem, the accused is not always guilty, and the accuser is not always innocent. Being fair to countervailing points of view also guards your own interests: your film will have its enemies no matter whose part you take, and you will probably have to defend them, possibly in court. If your enemies can demonstrate a single error of detail they will try to use it to damn the whole work. This is how opponents tried to shoot down Michael Moore's first film, *Roger and Me* (1989).

Clarification, not simplification: What interests the documentarian is seldom clear-cut, but there is an ever-present temptation to render it so. Nettie Wild's *A Rustling of Leaves* (1990) is a courageous and sympathetic account of the populist guerrilla movement in the Philippines, but the partisan nature of her beliefs makes one feel guiltily skeptical throughout. She makes heroes of the left-wing peasants in their struggle against right-wing thugs, and though her sympathy is clearly justified, we know that armed resistance cannot long remain honorable. Soon both sides commit atrocities and the waters become too muddy for the story to remain one of moral rectitude. To be fair means not only relaying the protagonists' declared principles but also exposing the ugly and paradoxical aspects of liberation through violence. Wild does this, for instance, by showing the trial and execution by guerrillas of a youthful informant. But one doubts if there is much of a trial when the camera is not around.

A film may be accurate and truthful, but it may fail unless it is perceived as such. Handling your audience well means anticipating the film's impact on a first-time viewer every step of the way and knowing when justifiable skepticism requires something more built into the film's argument. The more intricate the issues, the more difficult it will be to strike a balance between clarity and simplicity on the one hand and fidelity to the ambiguities of actual human life on the other.

A documentary is a subjective construct: The alluring notion that a camera can ever record anything objectively disintegrates when you confront a few practical considerations. What, for instance, is an "objective" camera position, when inescapably someone must place the camera somewhere? How do you "objectively" decide when to turn the camera on and off? And when viewing the resulting material, how do you spot the "objective truth" that should be used? These are all editorial decisions. They are inextricably bound up with film art's need to take what is lengthy and diffuse in life and make it into a brief and meaningful essence.

Quite simply, filmmaking is a series of highly significant choices:

- What to shoot
- How to shoot it
- What to use in the film
- How most effectively to use it

If your film is to be perceived as fair and balanced, you will need a broad factual grasp of your subject, evidence that is persuasive and self-evidently reliable, and the courage and insight to make interpretive judgments about using it. Almost every decision involves ethical choices, many of them disquieting and leading to sleepless nights. However noble your intention, the medium plays a very big part in the message. Remember that you can never show the events themselves, only a *construct* of them with its own inherent logic, dynamics, and emphases. Only by doubting its shape and balance, and by checking every aspect of its impact on other people, can you become sure that your representation aligns with your intentions.

Documentary is often wrongly labeled: Anything nonfiction is routinely called a documentary, even when it may be factually based advertising sponsored by a branch of the travel industry or a pet care film whose hidden agenda is to prove how necessary Contempo Cote Conditioner is to man's best friend. True documentaries are concerned with the values that determine the quality of human life, not with selling a product or service.

Then, again, the language used about documentary is often confusing. Penetrating but fair-minded exposure of a subject's issues will be called "objectivity," yet the same word will be used for the fence-sitting so favored by those who contrive the appearance of balance in order to advance a political agenda. Worse yet, the artful ways that news and documentary practitioners use to disguise their own biases suggest that documentary itself is objective. Nothing could be less true. Documentary is a branch of the expressive arts, not a science.

THE DIRECTOR'S JOURNEY

Like many craftspeople, most screen directors operate from a gut recognition that is really a process of internalized logic. Working more by reflex than by conscious deduction, they recognize what "works" and what will be effective. Of course, this is maddeningly inaccessible to the novice and seems calculated to shut him or her out. Even professional crewmembers routinely nurture quite distorted ideas of the directorial process, especially the stages that come before and after shooting. They think that directors are a special breed and make decisions in some remote and arty compartment of their being. Because we tend to separate art from technology anyway, this cultural rift is especially inappropriate for documentary makers, whose work so often argues for wholeness and integration.

The documentary director is essentially someone who:

- Investigates significant people, topics, or aspects of life
- Does what is necessary to record whatever is essential and meaningful
- Lives to expose underlying truths and conflicts in contemporary life
- Has empathy for humankind and develops a humane understanding of each new world
- Orchestrates footage to make a story that is cinematically and dramatically satisfying
- Can deeply engage an audience in mind and feelings

Let's be clear. Directing is not a mystical process. If a director at work appears inscrutable, it's probably because a strenuous inner process monopolizes most of his or her energies. No film—indeed, no artwork of any kind—emerges except by mostly conscious and responsible decisions. Although viewing makes us feel we are in direct contact with the subject, the record is never unmediated reality. It is a constructed experience made by people who know that the audience is trained by experience to expect every aspect of every shot to carry meaning.

The conventions of the cinema thus place the director in a distinct role, that of selecting and interpreting, of relating cause and effect, every step of the way. This is an active engagement and interpretation, not the blanket recording of C-SPAN.

To direct well takes a highly evolved, triple consciousness. You must be critically aware of:

- All aspects of the world you are filming
- How your own perceptual and emotional processes evolve as you learn about this world
- The special properties of the medium through which you will represent your own learning journey through that world

You attain this multi-layered consciousness not by "talent" but by hard, sustained, and repeated practice, much as a musician masters the interpretation of scores with an instrument. Expect a long, demanding learning process, and that your first works will be clumsy and naïve. Be prepared to grow painfully from repeated mistakes or miscalculations, and know that when you feel defeated that it will take faith and persistence to pick up and go on.

The rewards of making documentary are great. By involving yourself in life's mysteries and traveling deeply into the unknown, you link up with wonderful travel companions. By trying to raise your own and others' consciousness, you won't have to doubt that you are attempting something honorable and useful, and using your one little life wisely.

THE "CONTRACT" WITH THE AUDIENCE

How a filmmaker engages with the audience often proceeds from deep and unexamined assumptions about who "other people" are and how in a film you should relate to them. These convictions usually arise from a lifetime of omnivorous film viewing, but what you decide will firstly affect your choice of cinematic language and secondly determine how well your film conveys its scope and perspective. There are different ways to respect an audience's intelligence, and whichever language you use will become part of the implied contract between communicator and audience. That language pivots on the kind of evidence you present to the audience and how you imply the argument representing your point of view.

The advertiser or propagandist, wanting to condition the audience, produces only evidence to support a predetermined conclusion. He or she will often use jokiness or sensation to coerce the audience into buying the premise.

Moving up the scale of respect, there is the "binary" communicator mentioned earlier, who gives "equal coverage to both sides" in any controversy, as though issues only ever have two sides. By showing a world of equally matched opponents, this type of film implies we need do nothing except stay tuned to those in the know. Here too the audience is considered a passive mass to be informed and entertained, but not challenged to initiate judgments.

At a higher level is a discourse—and this is equally valid for narrative fiction—that aims neither to condition nor divert the viewer but to share something in all its baffling complexity. Ira Wohl's deeply touching *Best Boy* (1979) is about an elderly couple uneasily yielding up their mentally handicapped son to an institution in preparation for the time when they can no longer care for him (Figure 1–2). Delicately but perceptibly, the film touches on all the regret, pain, and failure connected with the son's position as a handicapped member of a family.

A film like this does not set out to celebrate, sell, or convert, but rather to expand the viewer's mind and emotions. It does this by drawing us through a series of events fraught with emotion, meaning, and ambiguity. It lets us draw difficult conclusions about motives and responsibilities, and takes us along as accomplices in a painful quest for truth. A good film, like a good friend, engages us actively; it never patronizes or manipulates its subjects or its audience.

Intentionally or otherwise, every film signals its premise quite early and sets how it means to treat its audience. As a restaurant hands out an inviting and informative menu, the good storyteller sets terms in the opening moments so that

FIGURE 1–2

Best Boy (1979) by Ira Wohl. Pearl must let her "best boy" Philly leave home to enter a supportive institution. (Ira Wohl)

the audience anticipates something compelling. This you can consider the "contract" you strike with your audience.

THE FILMMAKER AND THE MEDIA

Nowadays documentary makers rely almost wholly on television or cable to show their work. For the executives who control these corporations, the notion that truth may reside more powerfully in the vision of two or three individuals rather than in the consensus of the boardroom is a prickly issue, suspended as they are in the web of myth and litigiousness generated by our mercantile democracy.

Corporations by definition are committed to audience figures, survival, and profits; they shape programming by subtracting what might offend a sector of the audience and hurt profitability. They are terribly sensitive to sponsors, politicians, and the self-appointed guardians of public morals. Dissenting individuals or groups are only safe to honor later as historical heroes, so getting dissident views on television takes unending struggle. Paradoxically, though, it has been philanthropic endowments, enlightened corporations, or embattled individuals within them whose commitments to free speech have kept the documentary alive and (by extension) its contribution alive to democratic pluralism.

Today, the diversification of television consumption through cable, satellite, the Internet, and video replay facilities—with production equipment becoming smaller, better, and cheaper—makes video presentations possible that were once prohibitively difficult and expensive. Distribution is evolving toward the diversity of book publication, so a need exists for truly diverse screen authorship. Lowered production costs and increased outlet possibilities should mean increased freedom for the individual voice—the kind of freedom presently available in the print media. If logic prevails (a very big "if"!), this broadening expression would mean a more democratic and healthy society. The present American government seems intent on altering the rules to allow fewer communications companies to own more news outlets, so matters may be less than hopeful.

FILM OR VIDEO?

At the risk of aggravating purists, I have termed a work in either film or video a *film*. This book covers the concepts and methodology behind directing documentary in any medium, and although I implore you to learn your ABCs using video, nothing of conceptual importance is exclusive to one delivery medium. Most of this book also holds true for other nonfiction forms, such as *industrial, nature, travelogue,* and *educational* films. It is even true for *fiction* filmmaking because all screen forms operate out of a common fund of techniques, use the common screen language understood by audiences, and rely on the same dramatic principles for their effectiveness. I will, however, assume that for economic reasons you are using video as you embark on the wonderful adventure of making a documentary.

Using even the simplest video equipment, extensive and fascinating study is immediately possible. With film, expensive and time-delaying laboratory work is necessary before you see your material, so there is a delay in assessing results. I personally care very little whether I work in film or tape. I get a superior image on film but must worry constantly about the amount of stock I am consuming. Film equipment is now larger, less portable, and little more reliable than video, and video editing of film is now universal. *Hoop Dreams* was actually made on analogue Betacam video and then transferred in finished form to 35mm film for theatrical release. Wim Wenders' *Buena Vista Social Club* (1999) was shot using a variety of video formats. It was transferred to 35mm film and had an enormously successful cinema run. But I doubt the cinema audience for either film knew or cared. High-definition video removes any remaining gap, and many established feature film directors have shot their latest work on it. George Lucas, after shooting *Star Wars: Episode II* (2002), said in an interview, "It changes the way you create on lots of different levels. It's as profound a change as going from silent to talkies and going from black-and-white to color. It gives artists a whole range of possibilities that they never had before. . . . I'm completely sold on digital. I can't imagine ever going back."[2]

---

[2] "Filmless Filmmaking," available at http://www.tps.com.pl/artykuly/Filmless_filmmaking.htm

For your economy and morale, shoot documentary on film only after you have performed extensively and successfully in video. At the time of this writing, you could shoot and edit a 30-minute broadcast quality video film in digital format for $400 or less in tape costs, whereas its 16mm film equivalent (negative purchase, developing, workprinting, release printing, sound processing charges) would cost upward of $20,000. Although other factors enter any calculation professionals make over which medium to use, the novice can expect to have the same successes, problems, and faults regardless of which medium is used. The bottom line (there is always one of those) is that one avenue of learning is 50 times more expensive than the other and much more labor intensive to edit.

Linear video editing: Some people may still have to use linear videotape editing, which is fine except for one huge drawback. Because it involves selectively transferring scenes onto one uncut piece of tape, the edit is accumulated in a linear fashion. This means that you can't go back and shorten or lengthen one scene without retransferring everything that follows. In practice, there are sometimes ways to wriggle out of this straitjacket, but the overall hindrance remains.

Nonlinear editing: Editing by random access in a computer is now ubiquitous. It restores the flexibility of editing film while dispensing with all the splicing and filing that made handling film such drudgery. In nonlinear postproduction, the film or video rushes (more often known as "dailies") are transferred to a high-capacity hard disk as a video version in compressed digital form. This permits the assembly and manipulation of any number of cut versions with the same speed and efficiency that one takes for granted in word processing. Since the first edition of this book, editing film in the world's high-tech production centers has virtually vanished, and nobody is weeping very loudly.

Digital desktop production: With the proliferation of digital camcorders (Figure 1–3) and desktop nonlinear editing, you can now learn filmmaking quite

FIGURE 1–3

Sony DSR-PD 150, a digital camcorder using DVCAM tapes that is much liked by documentary makers. Consumer models of digital camcorders now fulfill broadcasting standards. (Courtesy of Sony Electronics, Inc.)

rapidly and at low cost. Shooting and editing to online (broadcast) quality can currently be accomplished with a $10,000 package (digital camcorder; fast audio-visual computer with high-speed, high-capacity hard drive; video and sound editing software; and digital output).

BEARING WITNESS

If you have ever searched for your forebears in local records, you have probably found only names, occupations, births, marriages, and deaths, and little else about the genetic heritage you carry. I would love to know more about the Cheeks, a branch of my family who in the 19th century were village chimney sweeps just north of London. Only two pieces of information, evocative in their contradiction, have been handed down: the boys had saltpeter rubbed into their torn knees and elbows to toughen the skin for the brutal job of climbing inside chimneys, and the family believed itself illegitimately descended from Sir John Cheke, who was Queen Elizabeth I's educator.

How much is authentic I cannot say, but one universal fact stands out: ordinary people know virtually nothing about the lives and minds of their progenitors, most especially when they were poor and illiterate. The great mass of humanity has left nothing save what can be glimpsed in the records of their time, in their folk music and cautionary sayings, and in the marks they made on the landscape. Of humble individuals you can learn nothing unless they tangled with the law or did something remarkable. If their collective history was recorded at all, it was written for them by their masters, who were neither expert nor unprejudiced. We must use our skills responsibly and consciously if we are to avoid becoming yet another cadre of distorting chroniclers.

You and I as common people must not pass silently from life. Future historians must have our testimony as their resource. Documentaries are our grassroots visions, not just what was preserved by an elite and its minions. You and I can use cinematic language—the 20th century's great contribution to universal understanding—to create a record of family, friends, and surroundings; to pose ideas and questions; and to forcefully convey what we see and feel. We can propose the causes, effects, and meanings of the life that we are leading. We can bear witness to these times, reinterpret history, and prophesy the future. The consequences of all this for democracy, and for a richer and more harmonious tapestry of cultures, are incalculable. This is the art and purpose of the documentary film.

CHAPTER 2

A BRIEF AND FUNCTIONAL HISTORY OF THE DOCUMENTARY

This chapter covers

- The roots of documentary in other arts
- How the documentary was born and its relationship to newsreel footage
- Notable international films and filmmakers through documentary's history
- Technology that liberated the camera to follow life instead of arranging life for the camera
- Observational and participatory cinema
- The documentary moves to television, then to cable and satellite TV
- Recent trends
- Reality shows that blur the boundaries
- Where documentary is going
- An important films list

In a book like this it is only practical to look briefly at the documentary's development, so I claim no historical or geographical balance. Many of the less known films cited here came my way by chance because I happened to catch them at a conference or festival, or because someone gave me a copy while I was abroad. Seeing documentaries is still a catch-as-catch-can business. Part of the problem is that documentaries don't travel. More bound by the vernacular than their fiction counterparts, they seldom cross national and linguistic boundaries. This may improve when films can be seen on demand via cable or the Internet, but we will then need plenty of informed guidance about what is worth seeing.

The corollary is that documentary makers must labor harder than fiction filmmakers to raise their films' significance beyond the parochial.

OBTAINING FILMS

Though many of the films cited in this chapter are classics, they can be hard to find even in their country of origin. Video stores usually carry a few documentaries, but seldom rarer or older films. Public libraries are beginning to carry foreign and classic films. If you live near a university, they may let you view specialized films in their library.

Try your library service for an interlibrary tape or digital video disk (DVD) loan, or call your national film institute (every country seems to have one) for advice on locating copies. Many documentaries can be bought or rented by mail in North America from Facets Multimedia in Chicago (www.facets.org). Facets carries more than 30,000 special films of all kinds. Movies Unlimited in Philadelphia (3015 Darnell Road, Philadelphia, PA 19154) has similar holdings but is less scholarly in its Web site (www.moviesunlimited.com). The large bookstores reachable through the Internet, such as Barnes & Noble (www.barnesandnoble.com) or Amazon.com (www.amazon.com), also have large holdings of tapes and DVDs at competitive prices. If you live in a country with the PAL (phase alternating line) television standard, you can search one of Amazon.com's European branches and be sure of getting a copy that is compatible with your equipment.

Tapes bought abroad probably won't work in your native TV format (NTSC, PAL, or SECAM—for a full list of national standards, see www.vidpro.org/standards). A simple cure for incompatibility is to invest in a universal VHS player such as the Aiwa HV-MX100, which plays any VHS tape (in stereo too) into any TV. It also records in either NTSC or PAL, so you can trade tapes with just about anyone in the world.

DVD versions of many films are now available and usually include valuable supplementary materials. Though a computer can usually play a range of DVD zones, the player connected to your TV will probably only play disks made for your zone. Some players can be reprogrammed to become region-free. The Web site www.regionfreedvd.net/player/ gives known or suspected fixes for many machines.

FACTUAL FOOTAGE AND THE GROWTH OF AUTHORSHIP

Nonfiction cinema existed for two decades before the documentary form crystallized in the 1920s. The first moving pictures transfixed pieces of reality for the world's wonderment, such as workers leaving a factory, a baby eating a meal, a train arriving to disgorge its passengers, and a rowing boat going out to sea. These are deeply touching because they are the human family's first home movies.

Early fiction cinema includes staged comedy, historical re-enactment, magic illusions, farce, and melodrama. From its beginnings as a fast-buck optical trick, the fiction cinema quickly expanded its subject matter, following contemporary audience tastes in the direction of vaudeville, music hall, and popular theater. During all this the camera never stopped gathering factual footage for newsreels, always very popular. During the First World War from 1914 to 1918, vast amounts of footage recorded all phases of the hostilities. Film became an important medium of communication and propaganda for wartime governments and their populations. To us now, the early factual footage of that war is the most familiar. It is also the most obviously biased in its attitudes and omissions. The footage and its titles seem jingoistic and naïve in their posturing, with "our side" as heroes and "the enemy" as a malevolent and inhuman machine.

Are newsreels documentary films? Plainly they are documentary material, but because they are episodic and disjointed, they lack any comprehensive vision. Footage is event-centered, but the underlying meanings to the event, and its relationship to the larger context, all remain out of sight. More than sound track is missing from this early film documentation: absent is the organizing, interpretive vision already common in fiction work of the time.

Why was fiction cinema telling stories with complex moral dimensions while the nonfiction cinema could only hold out the travelogue as its most sophisticated product? Surely it was because the fiction cinema had many excellent role models in literary fiction. A filmmaker could, for instance, pick up Tolstoy's *War and Peace* and find a historical novel form being used to subvert all the common assumptions about the importance of kings, generals, and ambassadors in warfare. Tolstoy's experience as a soldier at Sebastopol told him that hunger, inadequate equipment, or mistaken ideas about the enemy could put an army to flight just as easily as poor leadership. He took the facts of the French invasion of Russia and viewed them not from an Olympian historical vantage but from that of an ordinary Russian. Tolstoy's largeness of view, his compassion for the humble foot soldier, and his respect for the coherence of family life make us see war as a sordid tragedy to be avoided at almost any cost.

Early actuality films entirely lack this kind of vision. Where might their makers have looked for help? There was no obvious form or body of work. Persuasive factual reporting normally came through government reports, specialized journals, or newspapers. The journalist Henry Mayhew's *London Labour and the London Poor* (published from 1851 to 1862) is much nearer the documentary form because it pioneers interviewing methods that allowed his subjects to speak with their own words and ideas (Figure 2–1), but it takes no note of a whole interconnecting web of injustices. Compared with the social campaigning of Dickens, the book is quite passive.

Possibly documentary's antecedents are in painting or caricature, for its core values and concerns are visible in the work of graphic artists such as Brueghel, Hogarth, Goya, Daumier, and Toulouse-Lautrec. Goya's searing vision of wartime executions and Daumier's unblinking eye on the squalor and hopelessness of the urban poor both see from an individual, holistic, and emotionally committed perspective. This is what the documentary film would need as it embarked on showing the suffering and beauty of the 20th century.

Newsreels contributed to public knowledge of World War I, but the factual context was created through newspaper and government reports, letters, eyewitness accounts, fiction, and poetry. Historians have repossessed that silent footage

FIGURE 2–1

Henry Mayhew interviewed London's poor. (Illustration from Mayhew's *London Labour and the London Poor.*)

and have reworked it to reveal other perspectives of the Great War. Each revision of outlook is formed with the benefit of hindsight, of course, but each emerges from a different political and social consciousness from that considered true at the time. The lesson here is that that the same footage can support different interpretations. This fact about film may have shifted the world's notions of truth, because its plasticity epitomizes how *all truth is relative*. As people find more or different information and new researchers uncommitted to earlier viewpoints reinterpret complex patterns of action and event, they propose new chains of cause and effect and produce more broadly embracing historical explanations.

That process happens to parallel how we mature as individuals, placing our life-experiences into an ever larger pattern of shape and meaning.

THE DOCUMENTARY FILM IS INVENTED

The documentary spirit is first evident in Russia with the Kino-Eye of Dziga Vertov and his group. A young poet and film editor, Vertov first produced educational newsreels intended to recruit followers during the 1917 Russian Revolution. He came to abhor the stylized fictional life presented by bourgeois cinema and to believe passionately in the value of what he called *kino-pravda*, a "film-truth" cinema of real life captured by the camera. He served as a leading theorist during the Soviet Union's period of great cinema inventiveness in the 1920s.

The term *documentary* was first applied to a nonfiction film by John Grierson, the Scots social scientist and specialist in the psychology of propaganda whose impact on the genre was to become huge. Reviewing Robert Flaherty's *Moana* in 1926, he said it was "documentary" in intention. Actually, it is Flaherty's earlier *Nanook of the North* (1922) that is now acknowledged as the seminal work in the genre. Flaherty was an American mining engineer who began shooting an ethnographic record of an Eskimo family in 1915 (Figure 2–2). While editing in Toronto, he inadvertently set fire to his 30,000 feet of negative. He still had a workprint, and having to keep showing it as he sought funds to reshoot made him understand how flat and pedestrian his footage had been. He saw that he must reshoot in such a way that he could tell a story.

Owing to the constraints of a hand-cranked camera, insensitive film stock requiring artificial light, and appalling weather conditions, Flaherty had to ask his subjects to do their normal activities in special ways and at special times. Nanook liked Flaherty and knew they were placing on record a vanishing way of life, so the Inuit and his family both provided and influenced the content. This enabled Flaherty to shoot his "acted" film as if it were a fictional story (Figures 2–2 and 2–3).

FIGURE 2–2 ——

Nanook warming his son's hands. From *Nanook of the North* (1922). (The Museum of Modern Art/Film Stills Archive)

FIGURE 2–3

From *Nanook of the North* (1922). A family to feed. (The Museum of Modern Art/Film Stills Archive)

Having gotten to know his "actors" over such a long period, Flaherty's relationship with them was so natural that they could continue their lives quite unself-consciously before his camera. The life of the film's *participants* (as I shall henceforth call the social actors in documentaries) seemed so patently authentic that the film transcended mere acted representation. Flaherty's unsentimental vision of Eskimo daily life makes us conscious of a much larger theme—that of mankind's ancient struggle for survival. Actually, Nanook's clothing and equipment come from his grandfather's time, so the film reconstructs a way of life already erased by the onset of industrialized society and its technologies. Generations of critics and filmmakers have argued the significance of this and other anomalies in Flaherty's work.

Distributors at first refused to accept that *Nanook* would interest the public, but they were proved wrong when it drew large crowds. Yet while audiences lined up to see the film, its subject died hungry on a hunting trip in the Arctic. One can imagine no sadder or more ironic endorsement of the underlying truth in Flaherty's vision.

With *Man of Aran* (1934) and other films made later in his career, Flaherty came under fire from Grierson, Paul Rotha, and others for creating lyrical archetypes rather than revealing the politically determined conditions of his subjects' lives. They protested that he had assembled his own family from assorted islanders, rather than film a real one, and that he had screened out the big house of the absentee landlord—the individual largely responsible for the islanders' deprivations.[1]

From *Nanook* onward, factual cinema was never free of controversy as it began to tackle not just reality but also reality's underlying meanings. By turning events into a balanced narrative, the documentary cinema was interpreting its subjects' choices and implying notions of social cause and effect. This was illuminating in other ways, for documentary invariably reveals a lot about its makers. Indeed, much documentary is really disguised autobiography.

Grierson, the charismatic thinker behind the British documentary movement and the man who started Canada's National Film Board (NFB), defined documentary as the "creative treatment of actuality." The actuality chosen for American documentaries often followed Flaherty's lead by centering on the struggle between man and nature. Pare Lorentz's works made for the U.S. government, *The Plow That Broke the Plains* (1936) and *The River* (1937), showed rather too effectively how ecological disaster could have its roots in government policy (Figures 2–4 and 2–5). So successful were they at indicting government policies that American documentary makers were soon cut loose from government funding.

There was much work for the early documentary to do in Europe. Grierson's self-proclaimed mandate as he worked for the British Government in the late 1920s was that "somehow we had to make peace exciting, if we were to prevent wars. Simple notion that it is—that has been my propaganda ever since—to make peace exciting." In 1920s Soviet Russia, with a revolution scarcely complete, the new government found itself responsible for a huge nation of peoples who could neither read nor understand each other's languages. Silent film offered the new republic a universal language through which it could apprehend its own diversity, history, and pressing problems. The government wanted the cinema to be both realistic and inspirational, and to shed its roots in the falseness and escapism of western commercial cinema. To this end they gave much thought to codifying the cinema's function. One outcome was a heightened awareness of the power of editing, and another was Dziga Vertov's articulation of Kino-Eye, a documentary cinema that aimed to record life without imposing on it.

Vertov's *Man with the Movie Camera* (1929) is an exuberant record of the camera's capacity to move, capture life in the streets, and even become reflexively aware of itself. By compiling a rapid and ever-changing montage of shots, Vertov believed that life itself would emerge freed of all viewpoints but that of the all-seeing camera. Aiming to produce a film free of ego, the chaotic profusion of imagery, humor, and tumbling catalogue of events and characters could only be Vertov's.

Though Sergei Eisenstein, the gray eminence of the Soviet cinema, never made a documentary, his historical re-enactments such as *Strike* (1924) and *The Battleship Potemkin* (1925) have a quality of documentary realism that makes them the precursors of *docudrama*. Both Eisenstein and Grierson believed art had a functional purpose in society. Berthold Brecht expressed this as "art is not a mirror held up to reality, but a hammer with which to shape it." The talented individuals whom Grierson collected around him were socialists, idealists com-

---

[1] Included with the DVD of *Man of Aran* is George Stoney and Jim Brown's *How the Myth Was Made* (1978). They went to Aran to investigate Flaherty's process with some of the film's surviving cast.

FIGURE 2–4

The Plow That Broke the Plains (1936). (The Museum of Modern Art/Film Stills Archive)

mitted to the idea of community and communal strength, so the British documentary became famous for revealing the dignity in ordinary people and their work. *Night Mail* (1936) and *Coal Face* (1936) recruited the composer Benjamin Britten and the poet W.H. Auden to collaborate on works now famous for celebrating the rhythms and associations of humble work.

European documentaries of the 1920s and 1930s, made in societies neither recently settled like America nor torn by revolution like Russia, tended to reflect 20th-century urban problems. In old European cities teeming with poverty-stricken populations, Joris Ivens, Alberto Cavalcanti, and Walter Ruttmann produced experimental films now labeled "city symphonies" (Figure 2–6). Made in France, Holland, Belgium, and Germany, their films are notable for an inventive, impressionistic style of shooting and editing. They treat the busy rhythms of daily life lyrically and empathize with those living in poor, cramped quarters. Ordinary people, in their worn and dirty surroundings, show the earthy vitality and humor of the medieval ancestors whose hands originally created the environment. It is as though Brueghel has returned with a camera.

FIGURE 2–5

The River (1937). (The Museum of Modern Art/Film Stills Archive)

FIGURE 2–6

Walter Ruttmann's *Berlin: Symphony of a City* (1927). (The Museum of Modern Art/Film Stills Archive)

THE NATIONAL FILM BOARD OF CANADA

In 1939 Canada invited John Grierson to become its first Film Commissioner and to set up a film-producing entity that would become the "eyes of Canada" (see the NFB's Web site www.nfb.ca/documentary). Like many nations threatened by larger or more powerful neighbors, Canada's patriotic brief to the NFB grew out of the need to define, preserve, and project its own identity. Given the presence of the behemoth to the south, this is more than justifiable.

It was a good opportunity for Grierson to expand on his taste for epic, socially concerned cinema. The NFB's subsequent output placed Canada squarely at the center of international culture, where it remains to this day. Through a national cinema Grierson wanted people to see "Canada whole; its people and its purpose." By providing a high-minded stable for filmmakers as he had done in Britain, Grierson set the stage for a succession of fine films. Internationally famous NFB filmmakers include Donald Brittain, Tom Daly, Allan King, Bonnie Klein, Wolf Koenig, Colin Low, Norman McClaren, Michael Rubbo, Cynthia Scott, and Peter Wintonick. The NFB instituted a Women's Unit to further feminist viewpoints and produced many stunning parables from its Animation Unit.

Most documentary, because of its involvement with the dispossessed, tends to come from a leftist perspective. Right-wing perspectives in documentary tend to be journalistic or historical in nature. The European movement toward co-financing documentaries between countries seems to help lift sights above national and linguistic boundaries.

NEW TECHNOLOGY AND ADVANCES IN FORM

Until well into the 1950s, bulky 35 mm cameras and huge, power-hungry sound recorders were all that was available, and documentaries remained tethered by the limitations of their clumsy technology. Though camera mobility and location sync sound were possible, budget limitations and the need to limit participants' physical movement too often made them into stilted actors. A late Flaherty film like *Louisiana Story* (1948) shows the uncomfortable subjugation of content and form to an inflexible technology (Figure 2–9). Even Jennings' excellent *Fires Were Started* (1943) has such self-conscious dialogue sequences that you have to remind yourself that the firemen and the wartime scenes that follow are actual footage.

Too often life was staged; too seldom was it caught candidly as it happened. The exceptions prove the rule: Lionel Rogosin's *On the Bowery* (1956), a precursor of docudrama, makes extraordinary use of a hidden camera (carried inside a roll of carpet) by an actor who passes as a bum amid the suffering and despair of alcoholics living in New York's Bowery. *The Savage Eye* (1959) by Joseph Strick, Sidney Meyers, and Ben Maddow also occasionally uses a hidden camera to chronicle a newly divorced woman in Los Angeles, a city made of "images of postwar greed, spiritual emptiness, and brutality."[2]

---

[2] Richard Meran Barsam, *Nonfiction Film: A Critical History* (Bloomington/Indianapolis: Indiana University Press, 1992), 294.

FIGURE 2–9 ————————————————————————————————————

Flaherty shooting silent footage for *Louisiana Story* (1948). Sound was impractical on location. (The Museum of Modern Art/Film Stills Archive)

Advances in technology were soon to make capturing actuality less challenging. One was magnetic tape sound recording in the mid 1950s, which allowed sound shooting with a relatively small, portable audio recorder. Another in the late 1950s came from Ricky Leacock and the Robert Drew group at Time Inc., in New York, who invented sync recording that needed no "umbilical" wire tying recordist and camera operator together. From France in 1963 came the Eclair NPR, a self-blimped (mechanically quiet) camera that allowed handheld sync filming and fast magazine changes.[3] At last the eyes and ears of the cinema were free to roam.

Soon these advances transformed every phase of location filming, from news gathering and documentary to improvised dramatic production. Because they triggered a revolution in the relationship between camera and subject, the outcome transcended mere mobility. A handheld unit operated by two people could not only follow wherever the action might lead, but the camera and crew could become active participants in any event. On the screen this registered as a new immediacy and unpredictability, and it led to character-driven stories rather than ones that looked scripted and manipulated.

———————————

[3] For a short history, see the Éclair enthusiast's Web site http://members.aol.com/npr16mm/.

DIRECT CINEMA AND *CINÉMA VÉRITÉ*

On either side of the Atlantic this mobility evoked opposite philosophies about the relationship between the camera and its subjects. In North America, the Maysles brothers, Fred Wiseman, Allan King, and others favored what they called *direct cinema*, an observational approach that kept their intrusion on participants down to a minimum. This, they felt, allowed them to capture the spontaneity and uninhibited flow of live events. They shot under available light and without evident preparations, like ethnographers waiting for significant events to take shape.

They claimed a certain purity for the method, but unless the camera is actually hidden—an ethically dubious practice—participants are usually aware of its presence and cannot help but modify their behavior. The integrity of observational cinema is thus more illusory than actual, because its onscreen appearance is sustained by eliminating any material where the illusion is broken, such as when participants glance at, or adapt to, the camera. Certainly it leaves the spectator feeling like a privileged observer, but seldom are we seeing life unmediated as such films lead us to suppose. The fact is that observational cinema (as direct cinema is now called) is at its most truthful when events claim most of the participants' attention. Authenticity declines as the camera becomes more prominent than those being filmed and they become conscious actors in their own story. Though this situation has a truth of its own, it is no longer life caught unaware.

The other approach, called *cinéma vérité*, takes account of the central problem by actively involving participants in the process. It originated in France with the ethnographer Jean Rouch. Documenting ways of life in Africa taught him that making any record always provokes an important relationship with participants. Like Flaherty with Nanook, Rouch thought that authorship could usefully and legitimately be something shared. Permitting and even encouraging interaction between the subject and director, his *cinéma vérité* ("cinema truth," a translation of Vertov's *kino-pravda*) legitimized the camera's presence and let the crew become catalysts for what took place on the screen. Most importantly, *cinéma vérité* authorized the director to initiate characteristic events and to probe for what Rouch called *privileged moments* rather than passively await them.

Eric Barnouw, in his excellent *Documentary: A History of the Non-Fiction Film* (London: Oxford University Press, 1974), sums up the differences as follows:

> The direct cinema documentarist took his camera to a situation of tension and waited hopefully for a crisis; the Rouch version of *cinéma vérité* tried to precipitate one. The direct cinema artist aspired to invisibility; the Rouch *cinéma vérité* artist was often an avowed participant. The direct cinema artist played the role of uninvolved bystander; the *cinéma vérité* artist espoused that of provocateur.

Notice that Barnouw thinks documentarians are artists, not social scientists. This acknowledges that subjective judgments are involved whenever the screen reveals documentary truths. Direct cinema found its truth in events observable by the camera, while *cinéma vérité* (now more often called *participatory cinema*) was committed to a paradox: that it may take artifice to expose truth. Flaherty acknowledged this when he said that "one often has to distort a thing to catch its true spirit."

Both approaches capitalized on the spontaneous, and their most striking moments were often completely unpredictable. Since neither could be scripted, documentary was freed from the tyranny of the script. Editors, faced with the prospect of reducing great masses of footage, set about inventing film language that, using freer and more intuitive forms, counterpointed voice and effects tracks, and flexuous, impressionistic cutting to abridge time and space. The fiction feature film was quick to adopt these poetic advances, as you can see in Nicholas Roeg's thriller *Don't Look Now* (1973).

Participatory cinema acts willingly on what is being filmed, and observational cinema does so unwillingly. Both have much in common. Their competing claims of fidelity to the actual are equally questionable because editing routinely abridges what was originally separated by time and space. Despite any appearance of objectivity and verisimilitude, the documentary, like the fiction film, is always being channeled through human points of view—of those in front of the camera as well as those behind it.

In the end, all documentaries must invoke, as best they can, the spirit rather than the letter of truth—and they are exciting because of this. A documentary's authenticity ultimately lies in its organizing vision rather than any mechanical fidelity to life.

When should one use participatory cinema, when observational? Most films allow each sequence's subject matter to determine the approach. Some kinds of actuality-related truth reveal themselves unaided, while others are best elicited by inquiry or reconstruction. This seems so natural on the screen because this is how we proceed through the world: sometimes we are an interested observer, and sometimes we actively probe for the truths we need to discover. To help you in your work, this book will propose that documentary is really a screen version of human consciousness doing its living work.

TRUTH CLAIMS

How can we assess a documentary's implicit claim to fairness and truth? Always supposing the film is authentic to fact, you can only determine the truth of a film's more esoteric claims by comparing them with your knowledge of life. You reach subjective decisions through your emotional and experiential judgment, and there is no other, independent arbiter.

Art exists to encourage us to do this work, to spur us into becoming mentally and emotionally active. Working at its highest levels, documentary art probes the roots of human life and human values, and treats its audience as equal partners in the quest.

IMPROVISATION IN DRAMA

In the United States of the late 1950s, the actor John Cassavetes used the new portable 16 mm equipment to shoot his first film, a fiction piece that capitalized on the power of Method dramatic improvisation. *Shadows* (1959) is grittily shot and difficult to hear, but undeniably powerful in its spontaneity. Most importantly, it presents Cassavetes' ground-breaking understanding—one still largely uncomprehended—that *personal identity is not fixed, but something made and discovered in vital negotiation with others*. All his films show this, as Ray Carney has perceptively pointed out in his study of Cassavetes.[4] Part of the dramatic tension in improvisational work is that we see how people undertake this negotiation and sense how "character" is really fluid and dependent on circumstances. Knowing this thoroughly will have important consequences if you ever direct actors.

THE DOCUMENTARY AND TELEVISION

By the 1960s, increased mobility was matched by improvements in color-stock sensitivity so that color documentaries could also be shot by available light. However, color greatly increased the price of filmmaking, and soaring stock budgets and lab costs became more of an obstacle to documentary production. By this time, television viewing had eaten into cinema box-office returns, and the cinema documentary was looking for a new home. It found one on television. Now the documentary existed courtesy of television corporations whose executives are often exquisitely sensitive to commercial, political, and moral pressure groups. Even the British Broadcasting Corporation (BBC), with its relatively liberal and independent reputation, drew the line at broadcasting *Warrendale* (1967), a Canadian film about a controversial treatment center for disturbed adolescents (Figure 2–10).

Likewise, Peter Watkins' chilling *The War Game* (1965) had to wait 20 years to be broadcast (Figure 2–11). Shot as a BBC docudrama founded on facts drawn from the firebombing of Dresden, it showed in awful detail what would follow a nuclear attack on London. It is hard to see the censorship that buried these films for so long as anything but blatant paternalism.

For better or for worse, the ever-insecure documentary maker now depended on the approval and good will of television companies for survival. Because documentaries tend to concentrate on problems, they remain a minority interest. Worse, individual films with individual lengths do not easily absorb into the cyclical patterns of an entertainment system that wants everything slotted into a series. Documentaries were often quite slow, made demands on the audience's concentration, garnered low ratings, and from the position of an anxious television executive were always dispensable. T.S. Eliot never said a truer word when he wrote in *Murder in the Cathedral* that "human kind cannot bear very much reality." That, however, depends on how it's shown.

IMPROVISATION IN LIFE

The intrepid Albert and David Maysles (Figure 2–12) cobbled their own equipment together to make, with Charlotte Zwerin, their landmark documentary

---

[4] See Ray Carney, *The Films of John Cassavetes: Pragmatism, Modernism, and the Movies* (New York: Cambridge University Press, 1994).

FIGURE 2–10

Disturbed children on the razor's edge in Allan King's *Warrendale* (1967). (The Museum of Modern Art/Film Stills Archive)

FIGURE 2–11

Peter Watkins' *The War Game* (1965), a frightening view of nuclear disaster that was kept from the public. (Films Inc.)

FIGURE 2–12

Albert and David Maysles—a complete film unit ready to go. (Wolfgang Volz)

Salesman (1969). Using observational cinema, it follows a band of hard-nosed bible salesmen on a sales drive in Florida's tackier backwaters. With sympathy and humor it shows salesmen tormented on the rack of aspiration and the lengths they will go to meet company-dictated quotas. It also proves how accurately Willy Loman in Arthur Miller's *Death of a Salesman* epitomizes the dilemma of the American corporate male. Few works of stage or screen expose the operating costs of the American dream with more deadly wit.

A fine (and neglected) French film that used the new mobility was Pierre Schoendoerffer's *The Anderson Platoon* (1967) (Figure 2–13). With his crew, Schoendoerffer, originally a French army cameraman, risked his life in Vietnam to follow a platoon of GIs led by a black lieutenant. We accompany the platoon for many days, experiencing what it is like to grapple with an invisible enemy, to fight without real purpose or direction, and to be wounded or dying far from home. Without ever romanticizing war, the film quietly honors the ordinary soldier; compassionately it watches and listens, moving on the ground and in the air with the depleted patrol. Making frequent use of popular music, the film achieves the eloquence of a folk ballad.

An American whose art developed out of camera mobility is Fred Wiseman. Originally a law professor, he was moved to make a film about an institution to which he normally brought his class. *The Titicut Follies* (1967) is a devastating view of life at Bridgewater State Hospital in Massachusetts, an institution for the criminally insane. Unaware of how they must look to the outside world, the staff

FIGURE 2–13

The Anderson Platoon (1967), a ballad of an unwinnable war. (Films Inc.)

allowed Wiseman to take a huge amount of footage, which he shot using minimal equipment and no special lighting. The result is a violently disturbing, haunting film. It shows scene after scene of institutionalized cruelties that you would imagine had ended in the 18th century. The film caused a furor and was immediately banned by state legislators from being shown in Massachusetts.

The Sorrow and the Pity (1970) is Marcel Ophuls' magnificently subtle analysis of the spread of French collaboration with the invader in World War II France. Using mainly interviews, it opened discussion in France of an era of deep shame. In the United States, Peter Davis' *Hearts and Minds* (1974) was an outspoken, hard-hitting work that located the roots of America's involvement in Vietnam in its own internal problems with racism and anti-communism.

Hollywood cinematographer Haskell Wexler has been involved with documentaries since the 1960s. He covered the 1965 March on Washington with *The Bus* (1965), filmed a personal journey through North Vietnam in *Introduction to the Enemy* (1974), and shot footage for Joseph Strick's *Interviews with My Lai Veterans* (1971). Capitalizing on the moral ambiguities of his own experience as a cameraman, he developed *Medium Cool* (1969) as a fiction film set among actual events at the 1968 Democratic Convention riots in Chicago. Portraying a news cinematographer jerked from the cocoon of his craft into a growing political awareness, the film crystallized the unease Americans were feeling at the governmental violence being perpetrated inside and outside their country in the name of democracy.

FIGURE 2–14 ————————————————————————————————————

Harlan County, USA (1976), a film showing real-life violence in the making. (Krypton International Corp.)

A landmark American documentary is Barbara Kopple's *Harlan County, USA* (1976), which follows the development of a Kentucky miners' strike and shows how the bad old days of company intimidation and violence are still with us (Figure 2–14). In the finest tradition of the genre, Kopple reveals the close-knit ties and stoic humor of this exploited community. No film has better spelled out the abusive side of capitalism or the moral right of working people to protect themselves against it. Her *American Dream* (1990) documents the divisions within another lengthy strike, this time at the Hormel meat factory. In an America now downsizing and hostile to organized labor, the workers were destined to lose this battle.

DOCUMENTARIES FROM THE 1980s ONWARD

There aren't many joyful documentaries, but two were made in the same year that happen to celebrate dance. Emile Ardolino's *He Makes Me Feel Like Dancin'* (1983) shows Jacques d'Amboise, principal dancer in the New York City Ballet, teaching kids how to really move and enjoy it. In Cynthia Scott's *Flamenco at 5:15* (1983) we see the polite, high-bred students of the National Ballet School of Canada being drawn into an elective class that immerses them in the passionate currents of flamenco. Both films happen to be masterpieces of shooting and editing.

As Latin American dictatorships folded, documentary has blossomed. Eduardo Coutinho, Brazil's foremost maker of documentaries, made *Twenty Years Later* (1984). It returns to an aborted film project about a murdered labor leader and traces the man's family, dispersed by the mother for their own safety. The children, now grown up, had seen neither each other nor their mother for two decades, and Coutinho's journey to inform and reunite them stands as a moving allegory for reconciliation after the ruin visited on the country by a criminally repressive government. Mexican-born Lourdes Portillo worked with Susana Muñoz in Argentina to produce *The Mothers of the Plaza de Mayo* (1986) and has regularly produced films ever since. Her *Señorita Extraviada—Missing Young Women* (2001) examines the human rights scandal of the 230 raped and murdered women in the Ciudad Juárez area of Mexico. An excellent film about the rebellion in Mexico's poorest area is *A Place Called Chiapas* (1998), made by Canadian Nettie Wild. Her goal is to interview the eternally hooded, pipe-smoking Subcommander Marcos, who makes canny use of the Internet to inform the world of the peasants' program of resistance.

In 1992 came *Manufacturing Consent*, a prophetic postmodernist essay by the Canadians Mark Achbar and Peter Wintonick. In it the linguist and dissident intellectual Noam Chomsky warns that global corporations are engineering public opinion to their own ends. A mining conglomerate is behind the injustices revealed in Jeff Spitz' *Navajo Boy* (2000), which began from Spitz trying to trace a Navajo family seen in a 1952 roll of film. He found they had been poisoned by uranium mining on their land and then dispersed, so family members were lost to each other. Spitz united them and ignited a political furor.

By the late 20th century, the documentary had shown it can be vitally dramatic. In a pluralistic society committed to free speech, it is unparalleled at conveying actuality and so plays a critically important role in informing public opinion. This does not mean it is commercially valued. Because documentary filmmakers generate no profits from advertisers, they must either get enlightened sponsorship or find out how to make documentaries that are more widely relevant and appealing. To this end, documentary is gradually becoming more personal, acquiring a sense of humor, and dropping some of its pompous, moral solemnity. And guess what? Documentary is slowly becoming more popular.

Between 1996 and 1999, the growth of nonfiction premieres on U.S. television jumped from 28 to 98.[5] Numbers do fluctuate according to the season, but the trend is unmistakable: lots and lots of new films are getting made and shown. New trends or changes of approach in the flood are harder to discern. One, the success of authorship by committee, was brought to my notice by the veteran documentarian George Stoney. The outstanding PBS civil rights series *Eyes on the Prize* (1987) came from the late Henry Hampton's company, Blackside Inc. (see www.blackside.com). Against all odds he kept his company afloat for three decades, concentrating all the while on films about black American history. It took him ten years to raise the money for *Eyes on the Prize*, and he had to mortgage his house to finish it. The series uses a vast array of archive footage, yet somehow makes the events of the civil rights era feel personally told and experienced. The same is true of Blackside's *The Great Depression* series (1993).

---

[5] Compiled from listings in the International Documentary Association journal.

Surely it can be no accident that Hampton firmly believed in creating diverse production teams.[6] At Blackside everyone saw and critiqued everyone else's work. Filmmakers and subject specialists were black and white, male and female, all working together in a system of checks and balances. It was a process like that in the Grierson stables in which a demanding visionary leads diverse and talented people.

History did well in the 1990s. There was Mark Kitchell's retrospective, *Berkeley in the 60s* (1990), and Ken Burns' monumental (if soporific) *Civil War* series (1991), made from contemporary photos and written materials. D.A. Pennebaker and Chris Hegedus' *The War Room* (1993) chronicled the making of the Clinton presidency. Patricio Guzmán told the story of the Chilean presidency's undoing in *Chile, Obstinate Memory* (1997) and *The Pinochet Case* (2001). These were the follow-up to his *Battle of Chile* (1976).

For a nation that is better at forgetting than remembering its past, the long-running *American Experience* series has covered important areas of American history, especially Vietnam and the American presidencies (see www.pbs.org/wgbh/amex).

Traditional biography was well served with Don McGlynn's *Triumph of the Underdog: Charles Mingus* (1997) and Wim Wenders' immensely popular lyrical tribute to Cuba's musical old guard, *Buena Vista Social Club* (1999). George Butler's *Endurance: Shackleton's Legendary Antarctic Expedition* (2000) made good use of archive materials and interviews with relatives, and brought the doomed 1914 to 1916 expedition alive. Terry Zwigoff, making effective use of R. Crumb's stream of consciousness artwork in *Crumb* (1995), profiles the extraordinary and prolific creator of the *Keep on Truckin'* and *Felix the Cat* comics, and his profoundly dysfunctional family. David and Laurie Shapiro's *Keep the River on Your Right: A Modern Cannibal Tale* (2001) centers on Tobias Schneebaum, a feisty old artist who revisits the site of his induction into homosexual and cannibal practices by a tribe in the Amazon Basin long ago. Thomas Riedelheimer's *Rivers and Tides* (2002) is a German work that lyrically explores the installation art processes used by Andy Goldsworthy, who works with natural materials and environments. After he has made a cairn or tree construction, he watches it erode by natural forces working over time.

Two other biographical films use unorthodox but highly imaginative methods to reanimate subjects lost to us through death. Chris Durlacher's *George Orwell: A Life in Pictures* (2003)—having no moving images or voice recordings of Orwell to draw on—resorts to the bold solution of using an actor, Chris Langham, who looks uncannily like Orwell, speaking the thoughts and observations that Orwell recorded in his writings. The film even creates fake home movie footage, but because it hews closely to Orwell's thoughts and utterances, the film never feels false. In fact, it gives an unusually powerful sense of how an artist's inner self develops from outward pressures and opportunities. Just as interesting, though ultimately less successful, is Mark Rappaport's *From the Journals of Jean Seberg* (1996). Taking an actress from Seberg's same small Iowa town, he imagines Seberg living beyond her suicide to comment on the various parts she

---

[6] See www.current.org/hi/hi313 for an article on Hampton's methods reprinted from *Current* for July 13, 1993.

was given to play. Her critique centers on the way she was used as an icon by manipulative male directors. Because no diaries or authentic words existed, Rappaport writes them for her. But the result—a playful meditation on the exploitation of stars—is so hypothetical that it is more about Rappaport's musing than it is about the unfortunate Seberg.

In 21st-century America, the World Trade Center disaster made compelling documentary. Jules and Gedeon Naudet were two French film students making, as they thought, a documentary about a rookie firefighter in Manhattan. Instead, they were sucked into the eye of the storm during an unfolding tragedy. *9/11* (2002), finished by CBS, was marred by some heavy-handed commentary and gratuitous host interviews, but nevertheless was seen by a staggering 39 million viewers. *WTC—The First 24 Hours* (2002) was a release of striking images from around the World Trade Center. Shot by many camera operators during the hours following 9/11, it was released with no commentary or other distractions.

No reference to this period would be complete without mentioning the satirical activism of Michael Moore. In *Roger and Me* (1989), Everyman Moore set out to corner the president of General Motors (GM) and confront him with the social disaster he was causing by sending GM manufacture abroad. In *Bowling for Columbine* (2002), Moore cruises the American hinterlands trying to understand the American gun fetish and why Americans kill each other more than any nation on earth. That he discovers more questions than answers is unimportant. We stare longest into the dark when we can laugh at it.

Two outstanding French films defy categorization. One is Claire Simon's *Récréations* (1992), which takes an observational camera into a playground and shows young children apparently playing, but in reality acting out life-and-death issues of acceptability in the eyes of their peers. It is an endless, nightmarish scrutiny that will spark your own worst memories of that age. The other film is Vincent Dieutre's *Lessons of Darkness* (2000), whose title alludes to a Couperin composition. The film uses classical music and much dramatic detail from Caravaggio paintings to outline two doomed, gay love stories during a visit to the three cities of Utrecht, Naples, and Rome. The film is about the deathly disillusion when falling out of love and the disparity that Dieutre finds between today's idea of erotic male bodies and the more earthy bodily presence of those by Caravaggio. These, he makes us understand, are far more compellingly and disturbingly beautiful. In their different ways these two French films are masterworks.

Hubert Sauper, an Austrian based in Paris, made perhaps the most extraordinary and passionate documentary I've seen in ages, *Kisangani Diary* (1998). Had modern cameras entered the Nazi death camps, this is what they might have brought back. Shot at the site of Conrad's *Heart of Darkness*, this jewel of a film confronts the unspeakable suffering of refugees being hunted down in the African jungle of the late 20th century. Although violently angry with the cruelties he finds, Sauper speaks in a language that is visual, poetic, and purged of ego. It is a tour de force of compassion and filmmaking.

The Iranian cinema goes from strength to strength, and three recent documentaries plucked from the cornucopia cover much ground in very different ways. Orod Attarpour's *Parnian* (2002) is about a family of archeologists losing their mother to a wasting disease. The father and son (who also suffers the same affliction) contend with the shortness of life by working obsessively and devotedly at uncovering the past, which includes the skeletal remains of a mother who died in childbirth thousands of years ago. Austere on its surface, the film has poetically interconnected layers of imagery and meaning. Mahnaz Afzali's *The Ladies'* (2003), shot in a ladies' washroom in a Tehran park, is an informal refuge for abused women, runaways, drug addicts, and prostitutes who commune in search of help, advice, and gossip. It gives an astonishing insight into women's culture in a struggling underclass. Bahman Kiarostami's *The Mourners* (2001) follows a band of professional mourners, the men who are paid to sing and weep at funerals. At a meeting with their leader, ritual performance rises to a hilarious furor, which you somehow understand is personally cathartic and sincere.

These three films alone are a lesson in how complex and different Iranian society is from anything we think we know. All documentary makers should also take note of its fiction cinema, one that has achieved a sustained, poetic fusion of non-professional actors and mythic stories influenced by the culture of real tribes, villages, steppes, or urban settings.

To my certain knowledge, great documentaries are also being made in China, Sweden, Finland, Spain, Argentina, Chile, Brazil, Australia, and New Zealand, but I have neither space nor expertise to adequately discuss them. What I do know is that the personal voice is everywhere gaining ground as the documentary changes from something wholly identified with a network or corporation and matures by moving ever closer to the texture of individually felt experience. There is a discussion of improvisational fiction cinema as a logical extension of the documentary director's skills in Chapter 6 under "Documentary as a Preparation to Direct Fiction."

WALLS COME TUMBLING DOWN

The spread of cable and satellite television, the ubiquitous video rental store, and video on demand via satellite, cable, or the Internet all promise developments that nobody can accurately predict. Significant things are happening at the grassroots level. Appalshop in Kentucky (www.appalshop.org), Paper Tiger in New York (www.papertiger.org), and the Amber Group in Northern England (www.amber-online.com) have all used media for a considerable time as a vehicle of social and political activism. But in Chiapas, the desperately poor Mexican province whose indigenous people are at war with the landowners (and, by extension, the Mexican government), they are making inventive use of the Internet as a propaganda tool. By so doing they have kept their cause under the eyes of the world, and the army has been unable to quietly crush them, as seemed likely. If you search the Internet (using *Chiapas, video, documentary* in various combinations) you can trawl through a wealth of political and social activity. Activists shoot video for protection and propaganda, as you can see at www.mediarights.org, where its uses are additionally listed as protection against police harassment, leverage for victims of violence, and undercover documentation of environmental abuses, extremist groups, and sweatshops.

Video and cyberspace have become important frontiers in the wars between the haves and the have-nots. The Internet provides a forum for discussion and fundraising and is an information exchange that so far has proved very difficult to bring under political control. These resources are being explored in relation to every area of tension in the world. Increasingly it is documentary footage that provides the crucial evidence, and part of the Chiapas Project has been to train indigenous filmmakers to make their own case, as is done worldwide by Ateliers Varan in Paris. The *New York Times* has argued that it is videotaped appearances by Osama bin Laden and Saddam Hussein after each had lost power that gave the illusion of new life and kept them current in the world's eye. Even someone who may be dead can achieve continuing and significant existence simply by appearing on television.[7]

In the United States, a nation long presumed disinterested in actuality, Nielson Media Research made the surprising discovery in 1998 that 85% of American households try at least one documentary per week. The familiar network control that allowed so little viewer choice has been replaced by a greater diversity of choice. Documentaries now appear not only on PBS (Public Broadcasting Service) but are shown (and sometimes even financed) by a slew of cable or satellite channels such as ABC Cable, Access, AMC (American Movie Channel), A&E (Arts and Entertainment), Bravo, Discovery, Documentary, Family, Fox Cable Health Network, HBO (Home Box Office), History, Independent Film, Knowledge Network, Life Network, National Geographic, Sundance, and Vision TV. The competition to get films on the screen is fierce, but many more documentaries are being shown. Importantly, international viewers see many of these channels.

With less optimism we must notice a couple of other developments. One is that documentarians everywhere report shrinking budgets and dwindling production schedules. This, of course, is the law of supply and demand at work. The other is that the public has an insatiable appetite for "infotainment" shows based on police recordings, accidents, and bizarre events captured in home movie clips. By no stretch of the imagination are they documentary, even though they often document how people react in trying situations. They do, however, use documentary observation and provide work for documentary crews. Perhaps they also help, in a roundabout way, to define what documentary is *not*.

Survivor (2000), a game show liberated from the TV studio, involved beautiful people vying over popularity, sexual allure, and other tests of fortitude. *The Restaurant* (2003) shows the grief and toil that go into starting an eating place, but viewers complained of an over-choreographed feel and the camera lingering on the carefully planted logos of the funding corporations. *Boarding House* (2003) sets you vicariously down among the guys and gals in Hawaii who surf all day and party all night. Under consideration are a show seeking gay country music stars and another that will cover a journey into outer space by Soyuz space vehicle where, no doubt, volunteers will face interesting challenges in the toilet compartment. For more, see www.realityblurred.com/realitytv/.

PBS broadcasts more highbrow reality shows, some of which are British offerings that place volunteers in historically accurate surroundings where they must live under the conditions of the time. There was *The 1900 House* (2000),

---

[7] Stephen Stille, "Cameras Shoot Where Uzis Can't," *New York Times*, September 20, 2003.

The Edwardian House (2003, repackaged by PBS as *The Manor House*), then *The 1940s House* (2001)—a *déjà vu* experience for me to see the clothes, appliances, hairdos, and ration books of my own English beginnings. My favorite is the Canadian *Pioneer Quest: A Year in the Real West* (2003). It dropped willing victims on the prairie in autumn, equipping them with an 1870s pioneer's complement of animals, tools, and clothing. The winter proved the coldest in a century. *Warrior Challenge* (2003) has men training as medieval warriors, Vikings, and Roman gladiators. *The Ship* (2003) puts modern adventurers in the rigors of an 18th-century sailing ship, while *Colonial House* (2003) sets the challenges in the early 17th century. *Quest for the Bay* (2002) has people trying to live as Canadian fur traders, and *Klondike Quest* (2003) has them rushing for gold.

Evidently there is no end to what can be reconstructed, and certainly it's a great way to explore historical realities from a modern perspective. These are not documentaries but documented historical experiments and human-interest stories. What they lack is the thematic focus and purposeful social criticism that we have come to expect from the documentary film.

Many established documentaries can now be found and purchased as DVDs. These offer a significantly enhanced viewing experience even when viewed on a standard (that is, low) definition television. Often they give a choice of language for subtitles and a range of supplementary information by participants or production company members. Unlike film release prints, DVDs are struck from pristine, first-generation film elements and sometimes reveal details that not even their makers have ever seen before.

Financing and distribution cartels are changing, and the tremendous cost of making documentaries has become a thing of the past. Digital camcorders costing $4,000 surpass the picture and sound quality of broadcast cameras costing 20 times as much a few years ago. An hour of color sync recording can now be made on a cassette costing no more than a hot meal. The professional models of high-definition (HD) camcorders, offering phenomenal picture and unprecedented image control, are being adopted for high-profile feature films because they offer low-cost, flexible production methods. Digital shooting not only saves time and materials, but it facilitates profound changes in filming's artistic process. Consider the CBS television series *Robbery Homicide Division* (2003), which is being shot much like a documentary. Using minimally lit, real-life locations, semi-improvised scenes, and grab shooting by two cameras, the fiction series translates its speed and improvisation into raw dramatic energy on the screen. Steven Soderberg and George Clooney produce HBO's *K Street* (2003), an improvised series about life in Washington that thrashes out contemporary issues with a handheld camera and a mixture of fictional and actual political celebrities. Politicians who receive invitations to appear have been too intrigued, and perhaps too hungry for publicity, to turn it down.

The significance of so many reality shows is that the need for greater spontaneity on the screen is making fictional and documentary approaches converge. Everything you learn from making documentaries will therefore prepare you to become a venturesome fiction director too, should that be an avenue you care to take in the future.

FIGURE 2–15

Final Cut Pro for Apple Mac allows full editing creativity in virtually any resolution or format, even high-definition video.

Sophisticated acquisition technology is matched by wildfire developments in nonlinear postproduction. Desktop computers now produce broadcast, even HD, output at relatively low cost (Figure 2–15). Generations of copies can be made digitally that are every bit (pun intended) identical to the original. With digital media, quality loss between generations is a thing of the past, and longer-lasting archiving is now in sight.

This brief survey of the documentary's history—little more than a sketch of its highlights—is meant to show how documentary began with a simple, personal relationship between camera and participants. With the introduction of sound in the late 1920s began a long period of high-cost, industrialized production that made participants subservient to the needs of the recording equipment. Now, with inexpensive high-quality video and equipment that needs few people and no great degree of technical knowledge to get professional results, we have returned to documentary's simple and personal relationships. This means that the genre is, more than ever, a medium for the individual, committed voice, and that fiction can borrow from documentary to advantage.

As in the silent days of *Nanook*, documentary filmmaking is again the sum of intimate relationships during a period of shared action and living, a composition made from the sparks generated during a meeting of hearts and minds. We can again make films as a way of meditating on the meaning of being alive and even of contemplating our powers of meditation.

THE DOCUMENTARY'S FUTURE

High-definition television (HDTV) gives a picture sharpness and sound fidelity formerly associated only with 35 mm film and offers a truly cinematic experience in the home. One can confidently predict that HDTV audiences will come to prize cinematic above journalistic values, so fine imagery will again become a priority. This alone will make a crucial difference to documentary conceptualization. With improved quality comes a resurgent importance of music and non-verbal sound as dramatic elements, and of more poetical, less literal or journalistic approaches to filmmaking in general. The documentary will need to be separated from its long reliance on television reportage and journalism if it is to exploit the cinematic qualities of the improved technology.

Digital technology is leading to a convergence between phones, music appreciation, television, the computer, the Internet, and home entertainment. This seems likely to drive the film/video industry as a whole toward the more flexible, venturesome publishing operation that has long been the norm in the book and music industries. Who or what will dominate and how the markets will shake out is anybody's guess.

Evolution for filmmakers will remain challenging because screen language has become complex, and any open form remains difficult to conceptualize in advance. Once only the lucky, the aggressive, or those born with a silver tea service in their mouths could even try. But just as magnetic recording unlocked the door to working class musicians of the 1960s, digital technology is democratizing who controls the windows to the world. The consequences are incalculable.

Watch out for a six-episode series by Lumieres Productions called *To Tell the Truth*, which is in production at the time of this writing.[8] Covering the history of the documentary from the invention of the cinema up to the 1970s, it will explore the development of the documentary through "a diverse group of artists' struggles to use film to better understand the times; and to effect policy and social change."

THE MISSION

Documentary makers have an ardent respect for the integrity of the actual, for the primacy of the truth in the lives of real people both great and small. The documentary maker's mission is not to change or evade destiny but rather to embrace it, to speak passionately of its presence in history, and to examine the choices available for making a more humane and generous society in the future. Experimenting with, and learning about, this noble mission has never been so widely popular as now. More people are making more documentary than ever before,

---

[8] See *American Cinematographer*, September 2003.

and I believe this is because more people realize how necessary a pluralistic democracy has become in a world with so many displaced people and so much interfactional strife.

Concurrently there is a movement toward the individual conscience and personal voice. It has grown ever stronger and more pertinent since ordinary people in the rebellious 1960s began writing their own history. The person in the street, long the subject of documentary, can now author it. However, overview history, and work that challenges political assumptions, is still usually kept within the establishment, always on the alert for a transfer of power in the political realm. But the work of Blackside Inc., and other independents of integrity, shows how fruitful such decentralization can be. The media seem a little more ready to accept independently produced work, probably because traditional television is boring audiences to death. The screen needs new products, new approaches, and new voices if the audience is to continue watching. So, your time has come!

TWENTY IMPORTANT FILMS TO SEE

Many of the films in this "must see" list are cited repeatedly in this book because they break new ground for their time, take special risks, or embody specially significant aspects of documentary language. Each handles significant subject matter too, and each will be a memorable experience.

1. Robert Flaherty, *Nanook of the North* (USA, 1922). The seminal documentary that seems like ethnographic observation but is in fact carefully staged throughout. Silent, but available with music. At least one version has a commentary; avoid it.

2. Dziga Vertov, *The Man with the Movie Camera* (USSR, 1929). The exuberant life of a movie camera in late 1920s Moscow as it penetrates every house, factory, and street in search of cinematic Truth. A humorous silent masterpiece of montage.

3. Luis Buñuel, *Land Without Bread* (Spain, 1932). Early sound film by the surrealist master that uses an ironic narration and romantic era Brahms to emulate a travelogue. The subject meanwhile is starving villagers living in abject poverty.

4. Basil Wright and Harry Watt, *Night Mail* (GB, 1936). British classic set on a mail train running overnight from London to Scotland. Most of the action was re-enacted in a railway carriage specially lit and rocked in a studio. Notable for Benjamin Britten score and poetic narrative by W.H. Auden—both capitalizing on the inherent rhythms of the train and the postal work.

5. Pare Lorentz, *The River* (USA, 1937). An influential ecology film about disastrous flooding in the Mississippi Basin and the abuse of the land causing it. Arresting imagery, superb montage, spare commentary, and Virgil Thomson's magisterial score.

6. Humphrey Jennings, *Fires Were Started* (1943). A single night with a single firefighting unit during the London wartime Blitz, "an astonishingly intimate portrait of an isolated and besieged Britain"[9] and the firemen who risked

---

[9] Georges Sadoul, *Dictionary of Films* (Berkeley/Los Angeles: University of California Press, 1972).

their lives fighting nightly blazes. Avoids fervid patriotism in favor of an ironi-cal, poetic gaze.

7. Alain Resnais, *Night and Fog* (France, 1955). Weaving together past and present, Resnais summons us through Jean Cayrol's narration to become an inmate in a nightmarish world of the Nazi extermination camps.

8. Fred Wiseman, *The Titicut Follies* (USA, 1967). Unforgettable "direct cinema" pure observational documentary. Life in an institution for the criminally insane borders on the surreal for the cruelty of the system toward the inmates.

9. Jean Rouch and Edgar Morin, *Chronicle of a Summer* (1961). The seminal participatory documentary in which the filmmakers ask Parisians in the street if they are happy, then turn the camera on their own process of inquiry.

10. The Maysles Brothers and Charlotte Zwerin, *Salesman* (USA, 1969). Classic handheld observational documentary about bible salesmen with profound things to say about the unreachability of the American dream for those on the fringes.

11. Werner Herzog, *Land of Silence and Darkness* (Germany, 1971). A (mostly) observational film that travels deep inside the experience of the deaf-blind and gives a stunning idea of what absolute solitude must be like.

12. Donald Brittain, *Volcano* (Canada, 1977). Vividly imaginative biogra-phy of Malcolm Lowrie, author of *Under the Volcano*, that takes us deep inside the lurid world of a heartbroken English alcoholic adrift in Mexico. The film has a wit and intensity that undoubtedly come from Brittain himself being an alco-holic like Lowrie and understanding his subject's frustrations intimately.

13. Ira Wohl, *Best Boy* (USA, 1979). A family is in crisis as the aging parents confront what to do for their 50-year-old handicapped son. A superb biographical film that is both tender and tough. Long, long moments of won-derful sustained observation.

14. Eduardo Coutinho, *Twenty Years Later* (Brazil, 1984). The story of a forbidden film project about a murdered labor leader and his family. One by one, Coutinho traces the family members, who were dispersed and lost to each other. Each encounter is an emotional confrontation; each story is the result of a gov-ernment's brutality toward its dissidents.

15. Michael Apted, *28 Up* (GB, 1986). A 21-year longitudinal study of a dozen or so 6-year-olds as they become adults. A participatory film composed mostly of sensitive, probing interview footage that adds up to a profound indict-ment of a class-determined social system.

16. Marlon Riggs, *Tongues Untied* (USA, 1989). Through a series of imag-inative, elliptical, and disturbingly urgent tellings and performances, Riggs, who died of AIDS, shows what it is like to be black and gay in a racist, homophobic society.

17. Errol Morris, *The Thin Blue Line* (1989). A formalist documentary *noir* using re-enactment, movie clips, and a gallery of Texan law enforcement types whom Morris faces with his unblinking interview style. Pursuing justice for a falsely imprisoned man, Morris's film uses a strongly visual style, a minimalist Philip Glass score, and meticulous re-examination of a few key details in a bid to uncover the actual murderer.

18. Michael Moore, *Roger and Me* (USA, 1989). Ambush journalism, hilar-ious satire, and leftist sympathy for the working class come together. Playing the

role of a simple-minded American worker, Moore tries to corner GM's chairman in order to ask why he's sending work abroad and laying GM's hometown to waste.

19.   Henry Hampton's Blackside, Inc., *Eyes on the Prize* series (USA, 1990). Civil rights history told by those who risked their lives to fight American racism. Using much wonderful archive footage, the series feels personally experienced and told.

20.   Chris Durlacher, *George Orwell: A Life in Pictures* (GB, 2003). A biography of George Orwell. Lacking any movie footage or recording of Orwell himself, the film boldly recreates Orwell by putting his written words in the mouth of an actor who makes us believe he *is* Orwell. The producers even recreated fake childhood footage. It all works when it shouldn't.

PART 2

AESTHETICS AND AUTHORSHIP

Part 2 deals with

- The purposes and components of film language
- Types of documentary and documentary discourse
- Documentary as evidence presented to a jury
- Evidence varying in type and credibility
- Whether the camera should observe or participate when shooting
- Point of view in storytelling, and its variations
- The three-act dramatic structure and its usefulness in documentary
- How the handling of time affects a film's narrative structure
- The relationship you strike with your audience
- Deriving form from content
- Authorship and control issues, and what limits your options
- The documentary author's point of view
- How documentary skills are useful to directing fiction
- Mixing fiction and documentary forms
- Resources available in documentary theory
- Projects and critical writing as a means of engagement

Aesthetics determine a film's form in relation to its content. They strongly affect how an audience receives your film and even whether the film succeeds in its purposes. Making a film is a concrete activity. Discussion of aesthetics is necessarily abstract, and, for some, such discussion before doing any shooting will seem premature and theoretical. Don't feel guilty if this is you, because everyone learns differently. I too prefer to start with the tangible before the theoretical. (It means I reluctantly open the operating manual when the new purchase won't work.) If you can do some filming first, read this part later when it becomes relevant to your own needs.

Some take action via theory, whereas others arrive at theory by active experiment and distilling experience. Nuclear physics does not fit the latter approach, but you will always need to experiment in making film art because finite relationships just don't exist between cause and effect. There is no single, right way to do things, and the juxtapositions and interactions we create have effects that are subtle and limitless. To experiment is to relive film history on your own terms, and this is far from wasteful because it helps you take ownership of the screen as a medium. That is why many film schools (my own included) start their students by making silent films. Covering some of the ground that the Lumière Brothers and Chaplin covered is not an indulgence, because it faces you with the screen's most fundamental problem: how do you tell a story cinematically? That is, how do you tell it in behavior and images rather than words, words, words?

If it is to become a good story, each of your documentaries will need not only good content but a form organic to its subject matter. This means choosing what cinema language to use before shooting and finding the optimal dramatic shape in postproduction. Understanding what options you have, and what affects those options, will greatly strengthen any film you make.

In this part, I argue that documentary and fiction are fraternal twins, and that becoming proficient in documentary will increase your chances of becoming equally proficient as a fiction director.

For further information on issues arising in Part 2, use the Index or go to the Bibliography.

CHAPTER 3

ELEMENTS OF
THE DOCUMENTARY

This chapter covers

- Film language and the audience's experience of it compared with literature
- The raw ingredients of a documentary
- Modalities and categories of documentary
- Documentary as a genre that has work to do in the world

ON THE LANGUAGE OF FILM

All art, including film art, exists so we can vicariously experience realities other than our own and connect emotionally with lives, situations, and issues otherwise inaccessible. Reacting within a new context, we open up to other people and their conditions, and experience other ways of seeing what once seemed familiar.

Because the film arrived so recently compared with the other arts, the potential of its language and effect is not completely understood, the more so because it is still in vivid evolution. At a cellular level, two film shots placed together form a suggestive juxtaposition that changes when their order is reversed, so we can be sure that relativity and comparison are the heart and soul of film language. To complicate matters, the factual content of a few documentary shots cut together communicates a lot more than what the material "is." Reacting to the order and juxtapositions chosen by the film's makers, we make further associations and interpretations, which are affected not only by our individual interests and experience but also by the cultural perspective of our place and time. This is the crucial difference between what a film passage *denotes* (is) and what it *connotes* (suggests by cultural association) to us.

Film language functions differently from the language we know best, that of speech and literature. Film is a medium of immediacy, while literature is one of distance and contemplation. Reading is pensive and lets the reader move at his or her own pace while creating the story in his or her head. Literature easily places the reader in the past or in the future, but film holds the spectator in a constantly advancing present tense. Even a flashback quickly turns into another ongoing present.

We can say, therefore, that watching *film is a dynamic experience in which the spectator infers cause and effect even as the events appear to happen.* Like music, film's nearest relative according to Ingmar Bergman, the screen grasps the spectator's heart and mind with existential insistency. Usually the audience never stops, slows, or repeats any part of the show and thus is unlikely to grasp the extent of its emotional subjugation or question the legitimacy of the means by which it was persuaded. Watching film is more like living or dreaming than is the meditative experience of reading. Many aspects of the viewing experience never rise into the viewer's consciousness at all unless he or she happens to be analytical and takes time to ponder what he or she saw afterward.

Film's ability to put an audience into something like a dream state is attractive, but it holds responsibilities for its makers, particularly in documentary. Though the fiction film is always and evidently a show, the realism of documentary lulls the audience into passively watching "events" as though real and unmediated by any authorship. Critical analysis, particularly of older documentaries, shows how much the genre contains of its makers and how little of the objectivity that people associate with the genre. No less than the fiction films they resemble, *documentaries are authored constructs.*

Today, with the movement toward films having a more obvious authorial "voice," films can directly consider the ambiguities and contradictions inseparable from any full account of human life. Digital equipment helps this evolution because filmmakers can easily filter, freeze, slow motion, superimpose, or interleave texts at will. By imposing a more subjective and impressionistic treatment on live action footage, these techniques unshackle the screen from the tyranny of real time and its byproduct, realism. They help the filmmaker comment, not merely reproduce.

Your job as a filmmaker is to refresh film language by journeying inward, recognizing your own emotional and psychic experience and finding its equivalency to use on the screen. Only in this way will you deeply impress us with other realities—those of your subjects, and those of yourself and your associates.

SIZING UP THE INGREDIENTS

Though embracing definitions of documentary are in short supply, there are a number of generalities we can look at, beginning with techniques and construction methods central to a documentary's aesthetic contours. Consider first how few are the ingredients from which all documentaries are made.

PICTURE

Action footage

- People or creatures doing things, carrying on their everyday activities, such as work, play, and so on
- Shots of landscapes and inanimate things

People talking

- To each other with camera presence unobtrusive, perhaps even hidden
- To each other, consciously contributing to the camera's portrait of themselves
- In interviews—one or more people answering formal, structured questions (interviewer may be off camera and questions edited out)

Re-enactments, factually accurate, of situations

- Already past
- That cannot be filmed for valid reasons
- That are suppositional or hypothetical and are indicated as such

Library footage—can be uncut archive material or material recycled from other films

Graphics, such as

- Still photos, often shot by a camera that moves toward, away from, or across the still photo to enliven it
- Documents, titles, headlines
- Line art, cartoons, or other graphics

Blank screen—causes us to reflect on what we have already seen or gives heightened attention to existing sound

SOUND

Voice-over, which can be

- Audio-only interview
- Constructed from the track of a picture-and-sound interview with occasional segments of sync picture at salient points

Narration, which can be

- A narrator
- The voice of the author, for example, Michael Moore in *Bowling for Columbine* (2002)
- The voice of one of the participants

Synchronous sound, that is, diegetic accompanying sound shot while filming

Sound effects—can be spot (sync) sound effects or atmospheres

Music

Silence—the temporary absence of sound can create a powerful change of mood or cause us to look with a heightened awareness at the picture

All documentaries are permutations of these ingredients, and it is the associations and traditions they call on, their structure, and the point of view imposed on them that summon shape and purpose.

DOCUMENTARY MODALITIES

Michael Renov in *Theorizing Documentary* (New York & London: Routledge, 1993) divides the documentary into four fundamental modalities. They are to

1. Record, reveal, or preserve
2. Persuade or promote
3. Analyze or interrogate
4. Express

As he points out, these categories are not exclusive; any film sequence can use more than one. A film in its entirety can use the full range while favoring perhaps two such modalities. Let's try assigning the commonest to a list of nonfiction genres that is by no means exhaustive.

Nonfiction film genres	Records, reveals, preserves	Persuades, promotes	Analyzes, interrogates	Expresses
1 Analytical (essay)			•	•
2 Anthropological	•			
3 Art (films on)	•		•	•
4 Biographical	•		•	
5 Cinéma vérité (documentary catalyzed by makers)	•		•	
6 City symphony	•			•
7 Combat (war)	•			
8 Committed (political or social activist)		•	•	
9 Compilation (interprets archive material)		•	•	
10 Cross-section (sociological survey)	•		•	
11 Current affairs		•	•	
12 Diary	•			•
13 Direct cinema (observational, non-interventional documentary)	•			
14 Docudrama		•		•
15 Educational		•		
16 Ethnographic	•		•	

Nonfiction film genres	Records, reveals, preserves	Persuades, promotes	Analyzes, interrogates	Expresses
17 Experimental (avant garde)	•			•
18 Historical	•	•	•	
19 Incentive		•		
20 Minority voice (feminist, gay or lesbian documentary)		•	•	•
21 Mockumentary (fake documentary)		•		•
22 Nature	•	•		•
23 Persuasive (exposé or thesis)		•	•	
24 Political (agitprop)	•	•	•	
25 Process	•		•	
26 Propaganda		•		
27 Romantic tradition		•	•	
28 Science		•		
29 Sociological	•			
30 Training	•		•	
31 Travel and exploration	•			
32 War (effects of)	•	•	•	

Whether or not you are familiar with all these genres, it's plain that trying to typify and categorize them is highly arguable. You could, for instance, make a case for all films belonging in the second column because all nonfiction films seek to persuade. And merely by their selecting something for our attention, you could say that all films seek to express (fourth column). To further confuse matters, most genres make use of multiple modalities according to how they fulfill their self-imposed task. With such permeable boundaries the usefulness of any method of deconstruction is limited, but in production and before it, it helps to know what modality you are currently using so you can deploy it more consciously and successfully.

Bill Nichols in his valuable *Introduction to Documentary* (Bloomington, IN: Indiana University Press, 2001) divides documentary into six categories. For each I have chosen just a single well-known example. His list evolves chronologically from (as he asserts) documentary's roots in Hollywood fiction, and for each category he lists a commonly perceived deficiency:

- *Poetic documentary* (1920s). Poetically assembles fragments of the world but lacks specificity and is too abstract. Example: Joris Ivens' *Rain* (Netherlands, 1926), which evokes all the aspects of a passing shower in Amsterdam (Figure 3–1).

- *Expository documentary* (1920s). Directly addresses issues in the historical world (that is, the world we all share and experience as "real"). Once sound became established, it adopted the classic "voice of God" commentary. Expository documentary suffers from being too didactic. Example: Frank Capra and Anatole Litvak's *Why We Fight* series made for the U.S. War Department (USA, 1942–1945).

FIGURE 3–1

Amsterdam under umbrellas in Joris Ivens' *Rain*. [© European Foundation, Joris Ivens-Joris Ivens Archives]

- *Observational documentary* (1960s). Observes things as they happen, without imposing commentary or using re-enactment. Inclined to lack context and historical background. Example: Fred Wiseman's *Titicut Follies* (USA, 1967).
- *Participatory documentary* (1960s). Interviews or interacts with its participants and uses archival film to retrieve history. Its deficiencies are intrusiveness, excessive faith in witnesses, and a tendency to produce naïve history. Example: Jean Rouch and Edgar Morin's *Chronicle of a Summer* (France, 1960).
- *Reflexive documentary* (1980s). Questions documentary form and conventions—how it represents things, not just what it represents—as an important part of its purview, but it is inclined to become abstract and lose sight of actual issues. Example: Chris Marker's *Sans Soleil* (France, 1982).
- *Performative documentary* (1980s). Describes human issues not in the abstract, disembodied way of Western philosophic tradition, but gives them weight by presenting them subjectively as "concrete and embodied, based on the specifics of personal experience, in the tradition of poetry, literature, and rhetoric." Example: Marlon Riggs' *Tongues Untied* (USA, 1989), which draws on memoir, performance, dance, and incantation to convey what it feels like to be black, gay, and angry in a racist and homophobic society. The dangers in this mode are an over-reliance on style and subjectivity, and that its films can too easily be sidelined as avant garde.

Erik Barnouw in his excellent *Documentary: A History of Non-Fiction Film* (New York: Oxford University Press, 1974) looks differently at nonfiction forms. He assigns 13 different roles to the documentary as it evolved historically:

- Prophet
- Explorer
- Reporter
- Painter
- Advocate
- Bugler
- Prosecutor
- Poet
- Chronicler
- Promoter
- Observer
- Catalyst
- Guerilla

These are proactive roles that assign the documentary a range of active social functions. Evidently Barnouw believes that documentary exists to act on society by changing the viewer's heart and mind. If so, it does this by presenting evidence in order to engage us with particular issues in a particular world. The quality of the evidence—the subject of the next chapter—has much to do with each film's effectiveness.

CHAPTER 4

EVIDENCE AND POINT OF VIEW IN THE DOCUMENTARY

This chapter compares the documentary speaking to its audience to the court process in which evidence is presented to a jury. It discusses the notion of the audience experiencing a film's events through a variety of points of view (POVs).

- How documentaries present evidence
- How evidence comes in varying degrees of credibility
- The court case as an analogy to the documentary "argument"
- Credibility of testimony and witnesses
- Testing evidence
- How the documentary presents all aspects and conflicting accounts to the jury
- How the camera and microphone are used in collecting evidence
- POV and its relationship to feeling and experiencing
- Single and multiple POVs
- Omniscience and historical views
- The development of the personal, reflexive, and self-reflexive POV

QUALITY OF EVIDENCE

The language that historians and critics so often use about documentary—witnessing, recording, testifying, evidencing—suggests that documentary is something presented to an audience for consideration, like evidence to a jury. This is a useful analogy to pursue because it suggests that the documentary audience may not find all the evidence we shoot equally persuasive.

Some types of proof are inherently more credible than others, and the rules of evidence used in court can help us distinguish them. Like most rules, they have been distilled over time and help set conditions favorable to assessing the credibility of an account and deciding where the truth lies. Of course, a court is an imperfect analogy for a documentary because there is no judge to oversee the court's conduct. Because the filmmaker represents prosecution, defense, and judge, it will be important, especially when you present complex and contradictory situations, that you represent all relevant information and viewpoints, not just those that support your own conclusions. That would be a kangaroo court, one rigged as in totalitarian states to arrive at a foregone conclusion. A factual film made in this way would be propaganda, because it unduly simplifies the issues.

To keep this discussion close to making documentaries, I have modified the legal conventions and ask you to apply the analogy broadly rather than literally. For instance, the witnesses in a documentary normally are people, but consider the camera and sound recorder like witnesses too, and the images, sounds, and speech they capture as testimony providing atmosphere, ideas, conditions, and appearances. What the camera and recorder produce is sometimes reliable, and sometimes enigmatic and unreliable. Because the jury cannot ask for elaboration, the filmmaker must anticipate when the jury needs context, confirmation, or interpretation. That said, let's see how well the analogy fits.

THE TRIAL ANALOGY

INTRODUCING THE ISSUES AND BUILDING A CASE

As in a trial's opening stages, a documentary must first introduce its characters, their special world, and what is at issue (the problem, or case). As it advances, the film must at salient points supply more background information. Perhaps the case concerns researchers in a scientific laboratory, one that runs according to conventions unfamiliar to most people. A good advocate knows that too much information (exposition) before it is relevant will numb the jury, but too little will leave them guessing. So:

- What world are we in and what does it feel like?
- What is this world's main condition, activity, or purpose?
- What is the minimal basic information we need to engage with the main issues?
- How does this world operate under normal conditions?
- What has gone wrong?
- What is at issue?

INTRODUCING THE PLAINTIFF AND DEFENDANT

When trials are dramatic it is because they are organized around a conflict. No drama (and no court case) can exist when conditions are normal and everyone is friendly and at peace with each other. Laudatory films are like this. They are boring and lack dramatic tension because everyone is happy and admirable; there are no active issues, and there is nobody under duress with whom we can identify. Therefore, *most documentaries feature people who are trying to get, do, or accomplish something.* This involves using willpower, planning and strategizing, encountering foreseen or unforeseen obstacles, struggling, and adapting to overcome each succeeding obstruction. This applies equally to Napoleon leading the French army, or to a shy 5-year-old enduring her first day at school. Keep in mind that *only where the individual is active and struggling is he or she interesting* to the jury. So:

- What is each main person's role?
- What are their issues (that is, what is each trying to get, do, or accomplish)?
- What or who is stopping them, and why?
- Who supports whom, and who opposes whom?
- What were the stages of the story, and what is likely to happen next?

CREDIBILITY

The rules of evidence help assure fair play and, by encouraging skepticism, help put everyone's veracity and credibility under scrutiny. This gives the jury the information they need to assess people's motives and to decide what "really happened" as they move to render each decision. So:

- What are the qualifications of each person to give evidence?
- What do they know from their own experience that is relevant to the trial issues?
- How credibly do they convey what they know?
- Are their allegations supported or undermined by demonstrable facts?
- What witness viewpoints may be skewed by loyalties, prejudice, or self-interest?
- What testimonials concerning a witness' conduct might alter, prove, or disprove their testimony?
- What character evidence is available for the witness that is relevant to the issues at stake?
- Is there anything demonstrable from the person's background that puts their motives, preparation, knowledge, and identity in a new light?
- What have the witness' habits been in relation to the issues at hand? (This can apply to the routine practices of a family or an organization too.)
- Is testimony being given from direct experience, or from hearsay only?
- Can an opponent interpret key testimony differently?
- How authentic and credible are the documents, pictures, memories, or records used in evidence (for instance, are documents originals or copies)?

WITNESSES

In the documentary we frequently use testimony by a range of witnesses to support or undermine key allegations.

Testimony should be

- Limited to
  - What witnesses have seen and heard themselves
  - Opinions and inferences based on their own perceptions
- Disallowed when
  - Testimony involves hearsay
  - Testimony involves specialization exceeding the witness' competency
  - The witness has heard the testimony of other witnesses

Expert witnesses

- Should be open to cross examination by any party involved in the case
- May get the facts during the hearing or before it (before shooting or during it and thus on-camera)
- Should only give an opinion when
  - They have sufficient facts or data
  - The facts or data are of a type normally relied on by such experts
  - They have reliable principles or methods with which to interpret those facts
  - They have applied these principles or methods reliably to the facts of the case

CROSS EXAMINATION

In a documentary as in a court case, you elicit testimony, set up discussions, or cross cut between dissident views not only to elicit information but also to subject everything questionable to contrary pressures. Like the cross examination in court, subjecting testimony to pressure allows the jury to ascertain how reliable and comprehensive each allegation is and how qualified the witness is to make particular allegations. Interviewing (cross examining witnesses) should be

- Direct, to the point, and respectful of the person
- Effective at catalyzing testimony important for each stage of the overall argument
- Concerned with determining the credibility of both person and evidence
- Free of harassment or of anything creating undue embarrassment
- Free of leading questions

Hearsay evidence usually is weak evidence, and hearsay within hearsay more so. Generally, hearsay evidence is only admissible if

- The witness was present at the time of the event or immediately afterward
- The witness is describing conditions as they then existed

- The event was of a startling nature and the witness made a statement while under the stress of excitement (in other words, reacted spontaneously and without a delay in which to premeditate reactions)
- Testimony is supported by evidence such as a memo or recording made at the time
- The evidence concerns regularly conducted activity that was occurring at the time. It may be significant that there was *no* activity when such activity was normal.
- The testimony comes from records or reports made on a regular basis (such as vital records, statistics, or religious or other organizational records)
- Testimony comes from family records, recollection, or reputation concerning family history or character
- Testimony concerns judgment within a family of someone's previous actions

ORDER AND SELECTION IN PRESENTING EVIDENCE

Like a prosecutor or an attorney for the defense, the documentary director must decide how best to present the evidence and under what conditions. Some evidence is so complete, self-explanatory, and compelling that it needs no commentary. Other evidence needs introduction, context, or commentary, and witnesses must be cross examined to elicit relevant supporting testimony. Because the director presents evidence sometimes for the prosecution and sometimes for the defense, he or she must decide how to make the best case for each side, what order to present the evidence, and how best to involve the audience in the issues at every stage.

All this is enacted in a fascinating documentary, Errol Morris' *The Thin Blue Line* (1989). In the style of a *film noir* it argues, subtly and ultimately successfully, that Randall Adams, a drifter convicted of murder in Texas by a corrupt justice system, was not the killer at all. It arrives at this conclusion by closely examining all the evidence and questioning all who played a major part in the trial. In a stunning coda, the real killer obliquely confesses, and Adams was eventually freed.

It is important to realize that a case or issue almost never proceeds like a tennis match, with adversaries tidily ranged on either side of an unmoving line. For instance, the fundamental issue in *The Thin Blue Line* is "who killed the traffic cop?" But before the film can arrive at this question, it must introduce its protagonists, law officers, and witnesses, each with their own biography, perceptions of key events, and function in the trial. Ultimately it is this very complexity, of course, that makes life (and the best documentary films) so intense and fascinating.

SUMMING UP

As we said, the final version of a film can be likened to the final stage of a trial when the main issues are summed up for the jury. The jury must decide whom do they believe, whom do they like, whom do they disbelieve? With whom do they empathize, and whose version of events squares most with their own experience of life?

The summing up stage places all that has happened in relation to these questions in context for the jury to consider. Films differ from this last, adversarial stage of a trial because they are dramatic entities rather than decision-making ones. An edited film usually has the texture of many voices and multiple POVs, with the most embracing being that of the storytelling itself, which is the underlying "voice" of the director and crew.

Another good film where you can see this analogy at work, one also having a murder trial at its heart, is *Brother's Keeper* (1992) by Joe Berlinger and Bruce Sinofsky. In it, Delbert Ward, who is one of four aged and semi-literate farming brothers, is accused of murdering, or mercy killing, his sick brother William. But the town, alienated by big-city police tactics, rallies to the defense of the formerly outcast family. The Wards are shown in all their reclusive squalor, but gradually you realize that Berlinger and Sinofsky are on their side, but to get there the film takes us through multiple other viewpoints.

Shortly we shall look more in depth at the notion of POV in filmmaking, but first we must look at the options the filmmaker exercises when using the camera to collect evidence.

DOCUMENTARY PRACTICE

COLLECTING EVIDENCE: OBSERVATIONAL OR PARTICIPATORY APPROACH

Every camera setup involves collecting evidence, and how you do it will convey different kinds of meaning to your audience, or jury. You must first choose between two major approaches outlined in the last chapter. One we said is strictly observational; the other is participatory and allows the crew to intercede. To quietly observe the aggression between children playing in a school yard is more telling than interrupting their spontaneous activities to ask them to play a competitive game and hoping they do it aggressively.

Whether you shoot observationally or you catalyze the action onscreen is thus something you decide both philosophically and pragmatically. Fred Wiseman, a former lawyer, uses no lighting, no directing, and no questioning, and only ever uses the camera observationally. He shoots a massive amount of footage and makes his distinguished films from the results. If you have a similar conviction about the worth of observational documentary or you are an ethnographer, you will want to capture only events that are uncompromised by you and your camera. However, if you film an interview, it means that merely by asking questions and leading the conversation, you participate in making the record—even if all the questions are edited out.

Using the camera to elicit documentary truth arose, as we discussed earlier, in Russia with Dziga Vertov's *kino-pravda*, or "cinema truth." In France the revival of this approach by Jean Rouch in the 1960s was given the equivalent name in French, *cinéma vérité*. However, because English speakers corrupted the

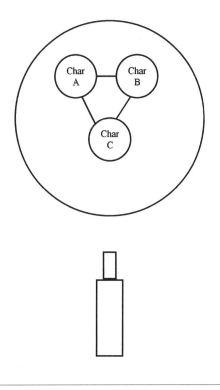

FIGURE 4–1 ————————————————————————————————————

Diagram representing direct or observational cinema, in which the camera records life and intercedes as little as possible.

term to connote spontaneous shooting, we now say that a documentary using these intercessional methods is *participatory*.

Whether to use intercessional or non-intercessional shooting is often a commonsense decision dictated not by dogma but by the situation in hand. Where 15 fire engines are hard at work putting out a fire, you won't need to exert any pressures by interceding. But if a naked man has chained himself to the Ministry of Agriculture's railing, you may want to question him if the filming is to go beyond a single enigmatic image.

Figure 4–1 represents symbolically how in observational cinema the camera and crew do their utmost to remain outside onlookers, minimizing their own effect on the proceedings. Figure 4–2 represents participatory cinema, in which camera and crew are avowedly present and inquiring, ready to catalyze, if necessary, an interaction between participants or between participants and themselves.

POINT OF VIEW

Although a *POV shot* will be a literal, physical viewpoint, the phrase *point of view* on its own usually denotes *the impression one gets, reading a story or watch-*

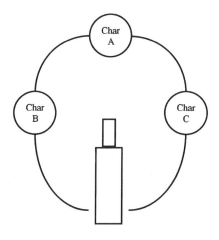

FIGURE 4–2

Diagram representing *cinéma vérité* or participatory cinema, in which the camera and crew may alternately be discreet onlookers or catalyze responses and situations.

ing a film, of the emotional and psychological point of view through which the story is being experienced. Sometimes, depending on context, it will refer to something like a Marxist or Freudian outlook being used as a tool of social or psychological analysis.

A documentary is a story whose "voice" and impact emerge, as in literature, from getting us to experience other people's realities and other POVs. How this works almost defies explanation, and plenty of filmmakers, if they understand it at all, do so more viscerally than conceptually. What is inescapable is that you will need to convey POVs other than your own in your films. It is hard to ever feel you are controlling them while you shoot, and it is hard to locate them in a finished film except in an intuitive way. Luckily, POVs seem to emerge on their own whenever the maker

- Has a clear purpose for telling the tale
- Relates emotionally to the story and each of its characters, and knows why
- Knows at every point how he or she wants to move the audience

POVs, your own as well as those of your participants, evolve and clarify during the marvelous voyage of discovery called the *artistic process*. From ideation (generating and developing the central idea) to creation (researching, writing, shooting, and editing), the film's POVs will develop and strengthen as your sense of the film's identity and purpose develops. This is especially so during editing.

Let me repeat, the clearer your attitudes to your subject and to the reason for making the film, the better. This is why this book insists on self-exploration as the foundation of creative identity and creative identity as the springboard to effective filmmaking. Following are categories of POV with film examples.

I have provided an explanatory diagram for each type of POV, but you will quickly realize from viewing any of the film examples that such a diagram is a simplified view of a subtle and complex range of realities. In practice most POVs incorporate other minor POVs, and the uniqueness and force of the major viewpoint depend on the contrast with minor ones.

The camera outline in the diagrams symbolizes a recording eye and ear, but to this you must add the human hearts and intelligences guiding their attention. The lines connecting the camera, director, and participants represent their awareness of, and relationship to, each other.

Single Point of View (Character in the Film)   As you can see from Figure 4–3, the film is being channeled through, or perhaps even narrated by, a main character. This person may be a bystander or major protagonist, and he or she may be observing, recounting, or enacting events. This kind of film may be a biography or, if talking in the first person, an autobiography.

The seminal work is Robert Flaherty's *Nanook of the North* (1922), which takes as its central figure an Eskimo hunter struggling to survive in the ultimate of hostile environments. Though shot silent and usually seen only with a musical accompaniment, it nevertheless creates a strong sense of intimacy with the hunter-gatherer Eskimo and his family. Many scenes were re-enacted for the camera, so we might classify the film as re-enacted observational cinema, if that isn't too

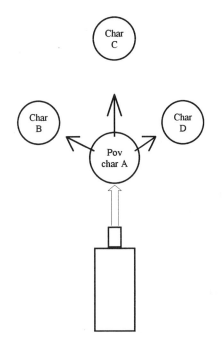

FIGURE 4–3

Diagram representing a single point of view (seeing through a character in the film).

contradictory. Yet the movie seems so true to life and made in such good faith that complaining about artifice seems ungrateful. In his later work, particularly *Louisiana Story* (1948), the passion in Flaherty's storytelling has become sentimentality and his dramatizing manipulative.

Werner Herzog's *Land of Silence and Darkness* (1971) has such a strange and fascinating subject that it can use non-intercession most of the time. It follows Fini Straubinger, a deaf-blind woman who lay in an institution for 30 years until she was taught the deaf-blind tactile language. She is on a journey to locate others as isolated and despairing as she once was herself. As the film progresses, her eerie, prophetic simplicity stresses how elemental is the need for human contact and how devastating is its absence or loss. She emerges as a gauche angel who personifies the love and nobility latent in the human spirit (Figure 4–4). Because the film includes interviews, it also uses participatory elements.

Taking a single character's POV limits a film's scope to what that person can legitimately know, understand, and represent. By making one person stand for a nation, as Nanook does, you may place too much thematic freight on a single representative. Flaherty's Nanook is an Eskimo archetype, and by using him to show man against nature, Nanook carries the burden of portraying his race as an endangered species. Having a strong historical sense of his people, Nanook

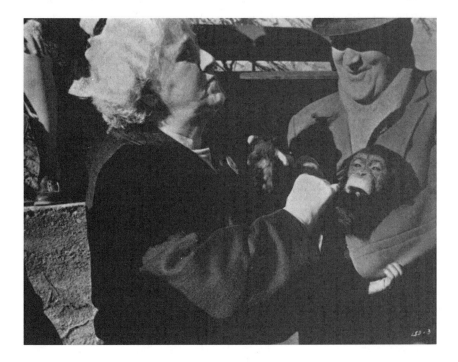

FIGURE 4–4

Through its character-within-the-film point of view, Werner Herzog's *Land of Silence and Darkness* (1971) shows that for the deaf-blind, contact with the rest of the world is by touch alone. (New Yorker Films)

surely collaborated in this. It was an equality of authorship that declined in Flaherty's later work.

The focus on a central character produces a hero, or sometimes an antihero. Too much emphasis on individualism can imply that destiny can be challenged and thwarted individually, and its corollary is that society victimizes the dissenting individual. Flaherty's romantic idealizations, uncomfortably visible in *Man of Aran* (1934), come under sympathetic examination in George Stoney and Jim Brown's *How the Myth Was Made* (1978). This documentary is included with a DVD version of *Man of Aran*.

A partisan viewpoint mainly routed through a central character does not have to lead to the distortions of idealizing. Just be careful to include broader insights. These will make for a stronger film.

Multiple Characters Within the Film.   The viewpoint represented in Figure 4–5 is of multiple characters, in which none tends to predominate. The combination of camera and editing may look *at* the other characters or *through* one person after another's consciousness of the others. Through what the seer sees, we empathically construct what he or she is feeling.

When each character represents a different constituency within the social tapestry, you build a texture of different, often counterbalancing, viewpoints like a Buckminster Fuller dome. This approach to POV is excellent for demonstrating a social process, its actors, and its outcome. This POV can be observational

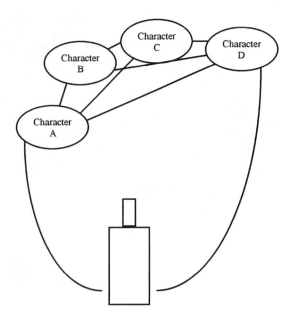

FIGURE 4–5

Diagram representing the multiple point of view. We may "see" anyone by way of anyone else's perspective.

or participatory, and is well suited to a "cross-section" film revealing cause and effect within a collective such as a family, team, business, or class of society.

Barbara Kopple's *Harlan County, USA* (1976) covers a strike by impoverished Kentucky coal miners (Figure 4–6). There are prominent characters but no ruling POV, because the central issue is exploitation and class conflict between workers and big business. Ironic protest songs carry some of the narrative forward, and these create such a powerful aura of folk tale and folk ballad that the film lives on afterward in one's memory. Shot mostly as observational cinema, there are moments—most memorably when the crew were shot at—when the filmmakers become participants in the events.

Michael Apted's *28 Up* (1986) introduces a sampling of British children across the class system and monitors how each person's view of him or herself develops over 21 years. Beginning with 7-year-olds, Apted returns thereafter every 7 years to press many of the same issues. The cool, empathic, incisive interviewing challenges even his wariest subjects to a touching scrutiny of their life's meanings. It is poignant indeed to see young people struggling with their beliefs and their demons, each wanting to believe they freely chose their destiny, yet many facing uncomfortable evidence of a path determined by their class origins. A *35 Up* and a *42 Up* followed, but in trying to cover ever more ground these films end up being less embracing. If you watch the later films and you *must* know what befalls the characters, it probably means you have come to love the characters like friends from your own youth. What more could you ask of a film?

FIGURE 4–6

Barbara Kopple's *Harlan County, USA* (1976). Music as an expression of suffering and protest adds to the many facets of the *multiple characters'* point of view. (Krypton International Corporation)

Omniscient.   The limitations of diagramming (Figure 4–7) suggest that omniscience is mostly free camera movement. Certainly the camera is no longer limited by what one character can see or know, and the eye of the omniscient story does indeed move freely in time and space. But omniscience carries with it an unfettered, all-knowing consciousness on the part of the storyteller, like the eye of God, who is said (reliably so far as I know) to see and know all. Here the all-knowing intelligence is that of the storyteller, who takes us to any place and time in pursuit of the story. This POV is by no means an impersonal mirror, for at its best it has an outlook and moral purpose for telling the tale.

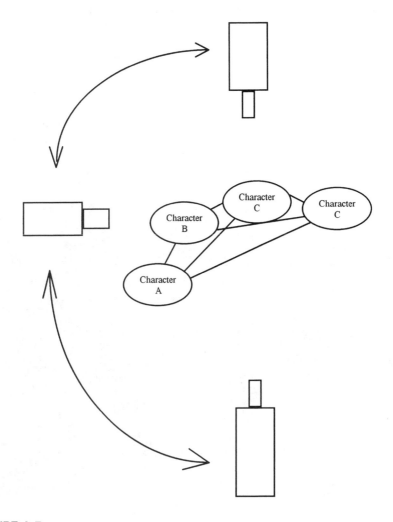

FIGURE 4–7

Diagram representing the omniscient point of view, in which the camera can move freely in time and space. The point of view isn't vested in any particular character and isn't fettered by any character's limitations or insight.

Typically narrated in the third person, the omniscient documentary will express a collective rather than a personal vision. The central organizing vision may be an institutional or corporate view or that of the filmmaker, who as storyteller need make no apology or explanation onscreen.

My feeling is that documentary inherited the omniscient viewpoint from the first genre of nonfiction, the travelogue, which in turn came from the 19th-century gentleman's slide lecture. To be modest, he presented his material non-egotistically, either as science or as ethnography, and avoided all references to the first person. Most older films take this position, though not always with humility in mind. Leni Riefenstahl's *Triumph of the Will* (1937) and *Olympiad* (1938) use omniscience to camouflage an intensely partisan view of Hitler and his Germany. Riefenstahl's masterly use of narrationless documentary seems to ascribe power and inevitability to her subject, but this should be taken as a warning of what "art for art's sake" can mask. All film seeks to persuade, but films that suppress their subjectivity and gloss over the paradoxes and conflicts in the world they reflect intend to condition more than enlighten.

Pare Lorentz's *The Plow That Broke the Plains* (1936) and *The River* (1937) use poetic narrations that turn each film into a long, elegiac ballad, a folk form that legitimizes the films' omniscient eye and seemingly egoless atmospheres. Their powerfully aesthetized imagery (Figure 4–8) and ironic montage set up a

FIGURE 4–8

Pare Lorentz' *The Plow That Broke the Plains* (1936). Stark imagery and ironic montage are used to set up a haunting vision with an omniscient point of view. (Museum of Modern Art)

unforgettable vision of a land plundered through ignorance and political opportunism. This is propaganda at its best, though my late friend and mentor Robert Edmonds, author of *Anthropology on Film* (Dayton, OH: Pflaum, 1974), would contend that all documentaries are propaganda because all seek to persuade. He liked to be provocative: all documentaries set forth an *argument*, but one that simplifies the evidence to make its conclusions unavoidable is seeking to persuade by conditioning, not argument. This is undoubtedly propaganda.

Few documentaries are set in the future, but Peter Watkins' *The War Game* (1966) appropriates a news program style to posit the nuclear bombing of London. The omniscient POV is sometimes used by an author who does not want to stand between the viewer and the film's subject. With grim impartiality, *The War Game* uses the facts of firebombing in World War II Germany to construct an infernal, incontestable vision of nuclear war and holds us mesmerized by its air of veracity. Passionately it seeks to persuade, but shunning heroics it avoids the personalizing found so often in screen treatments of disaster and forces us to include ourselves and our loved ones among the doomed. As a new parent when I first saw it, I found it nearly unbearable.

Omniscience can seem natural when a subject is complex and far reaching, such as war or race relations, where injecting an individualized storytelling POV would seem parochial or egocentric. Omniscient films put the viewer on guard whenever the film hides its credentials. This was not the case with *The War Game*, which cited all the sources for all its terrifying projections. The omniscient, all-knowing narrator who guides us through history is more worrisome, especially during those television history series that race over vast thematic and factual territory.

Powered from the resources of large corporations and using an army of production workers, the history series gravitates toward omniscience as naturally as royalty to saying "we." Thames Television's *The World at War* in the 1970s, WGBH's *Vietnam: A Television History* in the 1980s, and even Ken Burns' *The Civil War* (1990), which counterpoints contemporary accounts and photographs, all echo the textbook emphasis on facts rather than questions and issues. The ambitiousness, authorial impersonality, and apparent finality of such ventures make them suspect. Who is speaking to whom, for whom, and representing whom? Why do they suffocate historical curiosity when they should awaken it?

Not all ambitious screen history fails. *Eyes on the Prize* (1990), a PBS series from Blackside, Inc., chronicled the development of civil rights in America and managed to tread a fine line between omniscience and personal stories that spoke of passionate commitment. An openly critical film like Peter Davis' *Hearts and Minds* (1974) argues that the American obsession with sports lay behind the tragically mistaken U.S. involvement in Southeast Asia. Here the viewer is on a clearer footing and can engage with the film's propositions rather than go numb under a deluge of suspiciously uninflected information.

Personal.   Here the POV is unashamedly and subjectively that of the director, who may also narrate the film. A director's surrogate may still be in front of the camera as a "reporter" or catalyst, or the film may present its views in the form of a first-person or third-person essay. There are no limits to the personal POV beyond what the author/storyteller can demonstrably see and know. In

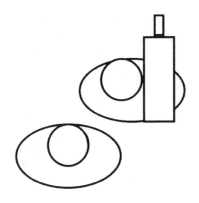

FIGURE 4–9

Diagram representing the personal point of view, in which the author/storyteller is the point of view character.

Figure 4–9 the director is behind the camera, but he or she can step forward into the visible world of the film.

Like his *Roger and Me* (1989), Michael Moore's *Bowling for Columbine* (2002) is a personal essay in which he again plays the rumpled, naïve Everyman just *trying* to get a few answers. In *Columbine* he sets out to comprehend American gun culture. His questions take him to gun stores, a bank that offers a rifle as an incentive for starting an account, and Charlton Heston (the president of the National Rifle Association). Along the way he compares shooting deaths in the United States to the far lower number in Canada, which has the same ratio of guns per capita, and ponders what cultural differences could possibly explain why Americans kill each other more often. By asking deceptively simple, provocative questions, Moore sparks a series of surreal, often hilarious encounters that leave you thinking afterward about all the paradoxes.

Barbara Sonneborn's *Regret to Inform* (1998) is a personal journey to the place in Vietnam where her first husband was killed when they were young. Undertaken as an exorcism, the 10-year journey to make the film put her in touch with both American and Vietnamese war widows, and the result is a searing examination of what war does to those left behind.

Reflexive. Reflexive documentaries are those acknowledging and even investigating the effect of the documentary process on its product. The anthropologist Jay Ruby, who uses anthropological insights to assess photographs, film, and television, says that

> To be reflexive is to structure a product in such a way that the audience assumes that the producer, the process of making, and the product are a coherent whole. Not only is the audience made aware of these relationships, but it is made to realize the necessity of that knowledge."[1] By sabotaging the traditional illusion

[1] Jay Ruby, "The Image Mirrored: Reflexivity and the Documentary Film," in *New Challenges for Documentary*, ed. Alan Rosenthal, 65 (Berkeley, CA: University of California Press, 1988).

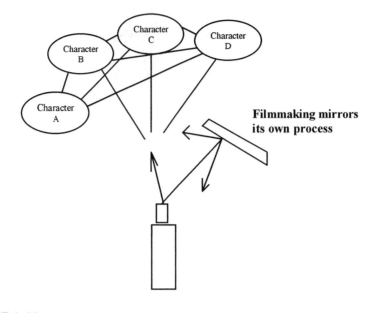

FIGURE 4–10

Diagram representing the reflexive point of view, one able to share salient aspects of the filmmaking process with the audience.

> that we are watching unmediated life, reflexivity signals that films are "created, structured articulations of the filmmaker and not authentic, truthful, objective records."[2]

The first radical investigation of documentary language is credited to Dziga Vertov, a poet and film editor in Russia of the 1920s. By seeking to show "life as it is" in *The Man with the Movie Camera* (1929), his Kino-Eye method laid the ground for *cinéma vérité* in France 40 years later. *The Man with the Movie Camera* portrays Moscow as a teeming spectacle of dialectical opposites. The exuberant camera, seemingly independent of human agency, alternately embraces the constants and contradictions of human life. Sometimes we see the camera and cameraman, sometimes we see them literally in a mirror, as in Figure 4–10. Vertov thought that the dynamics of camera and montage transcended human agency, and though we often see shots of the cameraman at work, he seems— like the dancer in *The Red Shoes*—more the camera's puppet than its master. For ideological reasons, Vertov denied personal authorship by claiming that film truth was vested in the apparatus itself—an ebullient mystification that he doesn't quite pull off. This is still a powerful belief in beginning film students, who assume that professional film equipment will make a professional-level film.

Figure 4–10 shows that the filming process includes the complex relationships between our friends, A, B, C, and D, and also lets directing, shooting, and editing acknowledge incidents in the filmmaking process itself. This I have symbolized, not too confusingly, I hope, by a mirror.

[2] Ibid., 74–75.

When a film exposes or analyzes the paradoxes of its own exploration, it draws the audience into the fact that major questions usually hang over every documentary. For instance, how often are we seeing not spontaneous life captured by the camera but something instigated by or for filmmaking itself?

The ethnographer Jean Rouch in his seminal *Chronicle of a Summer* (1961), made with Edgar Morin, first looked into this aspect of filmmaking when he posed the people of Paris with a fundamental question, "Are you happy?" By showing participants their own footage, he initiated a moving self-examination in his participants and a desire to go deeper. The results show Rouch's radical curiosity, his sympathy with the ordinary person's need to find meaning in life, and his willingness not only to question the medium but his own authority to use it.

Reflexivity allows the filmmaker to open doors and windows on filmmaking and to share thoughts about whatever ethical or other ambiguities have entered the process. Ethnographic filmmaking, in which the culture under study is supposed to be uncontaminated by the filmmaker's own cultural assumptions, is a prime candidate for such scrutiny. Explaining one culture for the benefit of another is inherently hazardous (if not ultimately impossible) and is fraught with lessons for all documentary makers about one person's right to represent another.

Aside from distortions, subjectivity, or misinformation there are other fascinating issues concerning the medium's boundaries. How, when, and why do we as an audience suspend disbelief? What deceptions does the medium practice on its makers? What may or may not be ethical? And so on. Plainly documentary is more of an emerging and imperfectly understood medium rather than a finished vehicle of information or advocacy for a "subject."

Self-Reflexive. The ultimate in reflexivity is self-reflexivity, in which a film can become a snake eating its own tail. Self-reflexive films reflect not only on their own process but incorporate their authors' thoughts, perceptions, and self-examination as well (Figure 4–11). For the filmmaker seeking self-administered therapy, this form can do what the pool did for Narcissus. It is a treacherous and difficult genre to pull off, but wonderfully rich when successful.

Michael Rubbo's *Sad Song of Yellow Skin* (1970) is an Australian/Canadian filmmaker's search to define Vietnam amid the flux of that country's paradoxes. By confining his attention mostly to city street kids and the young American dissidents working with them, Rubbo exposes us to the seamy side of a peasant civilization torn apart by a wealthy and technocratic occupying savior. Rubbo's ironic view of himself and the world saves his films from sentimentality.

Alan Berliner in *Nobody's Business* (1996) uses documentary to explore family history and dynamics (Figure 4–12). Approaching his crabby father to get a better understanding of his life, he is roundly repulsed—hence the film's title. Berliner senior insists adamantly that he is an ordinary man with nothing to say. Such visceral resistance drives his son to examine family film, photographs, and letters in search of the father he hardly knows. The film elaborates the strategies he uses to unravel his father's story as the son of an immigrant Jew. Along the way, the topics broaden out to include ethnicity, ethnic identity, and America as

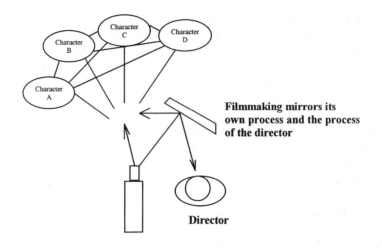

FIGURE 4–11

Diagram representing the self-reflexive point of view. This allows examination of both the film's process and that of its maker(s). However, treat this one carefully, for little separates self-reflexivity from self-indulgence.

the melting pot that failed to alloy its citizens into one culture. It is a larger view that more than justifies the means to get there.

IN SUMMARY

Each of these POVs represents a particular way of looking at people and their world. POVs are part of a storytelling strategy to be sure, but they are also a way to create the characters who see and feel the predicaments in which we find them. Though we see through other eyes, we retain our own values, and the double experience helps us define both the other and ourselves.

When we watch the materials of a film, we know each shot in each sequence is a step attempting to convince us of something: the beauty of a landscape in winter, the mendacity of a salesman, the alienation of children who live in the streets and sniff glue, the professional confidence of a tank commander as the convoy moves into Baghdad, the fake humility of a preacher asking the television audience to support God's work by contributing money, the willing intoxication of a young man in love. What makes us believe or disbelieve what we are being shown? Why should we believe this person rather than that? Why should we trust this expert rather than that one? Why should we care about this person and his or her issues? Why should I believe this film's assertions about tribalism and democracy among Papua and New Guinea tribesmen, when the film was made by non-natives? Why should I believe that this audience reaction shot is not a facile editing creation and really belongs with what the mayor just said at the City Hall microphone?

These are the skeptical thoughts of an audience member. Your job is to make it difficult for that audience member to doubt and yet expose him or her as fully as possible to the depth and complexity of the actual. You will have to edit your

FIGURE 4–12

Nobody's Business (1996) by Alan Berliner. A son challenges his irascible father to reveal himself. (**D. W. Leitner**)

footage and its POVs carefully and consciously, and you will need to guess where the audience's mind goes at any given moment in your edited film so that you can answer the audience's inner questions with further challenging and thought-provoking information. If that seems very difficult (and it is), then for now simply concentrate on examining what you shoot, how you shoot, whom you shoot, and how you authenticate them. For any particular project, try dividing up the evidence you have gathered and giving each piece a credibility rating. See if you can work in the upper third of that hierarchy, where the proof is most convincing. What do you have to arrange, say, or do to put a participant under test so that the next levels of truth are revealed? How can you raise the pressure so that there is more at stake?

Doing any of this will drive you to be more challenging and demanding of yourself and of your participants. This is what makes good documentary.

CHAPTER 5

TIME, DEVELOPMENT, AND STRUCTURE

This chapter explores the relationship between the chronology of documented events, their development in story form, and the way dramatic imperatives may lead you to reorganize the order of events to make a more effective story. This chapter deals with

- The uses of the traditional three-act structure in making documentary
- The use or reorganization of time in storytelling
- Types of documentary that preserve chronological time
- Types of documentary that reorganize the original chronology
- Lecturing your audience or stirring up a dialogue

THE THREE-ACT STRUCTURE

The classic *three-act structure* was developed in theater but is equally useful when applied to the contents of a single sequence or to a whole film. Here are the divisions.

Act I   Establishes the setup (establishes characters, relationships, situation, and dominant problem faced by the central character or characters)

Act II   Escalates the complications in relationships as the central character struggles with the obstacles that prevent him or her from solving the main problem

Act III   Intensifies the situation to a point of climax or confrontation, when the central character then resolves it, often in a climactic way that is emotionally satisfying

Note that when applied to sequences, the climax of a scene often leads to failure or the unexpected, which initiates a new round of problem, complications, escalation, climax, and resolution.

When you are covering re-created scenes or scenes where the participants tackle real issues between them for the camera, you should be able to tell where the situation is in relation to the three-act structure and whether to *side-coach* (make suggestions to participants in a low voice about possible action) to break the log jam when a situation has become hung up. You might even call "Cut" so that you can confer with your participants. This degree of intrusion presupposes a high degree of collaboration, of course.

My point is that once you accept how often drama falls into the classic three-act divisions, you will begin to find them in every aspect of life. The three-act structure applies to the long painstaking business of building a log cabin in the Life Television Canada series *Pioneer Quest: A Year in the Real West* (2003), where there are plenty of obstacles, and the resolution is shelter from the coldest winter for 120 years. The same divisions apply in miniature to a human problem such as opening a gate with your arms full or eating slippery noodles with chopsticks for the first time. Human life is composed of cycles. Every event is a cycle that breaks down into problem, intensification of complications, climax, and resolution.

TIME

Many elements influence how to structure a film you have shot, but deciding how to handle time will be paramount. Documentaries often have trouble giving an adequate sense of development, so the power to abridge, and to make comparisons between past and present, is important if you are to show that change is indeed taking place. In *Breakaway,* a BBC series I worked on, we preempted this problem by building change and development into the series formula itself. By focusing on individuals making a major change in their lives, we avoided the frustrating and familiar documentary that has no movement at its heart.

All satisfying stories need a sense of momentum, of going forward. This requires some organizing principle that usually can be found in the subject matter. A project about the Great Chicago Fire of 1871, for instance, can be confidently planned under predictable headings: how it started; how it spread; how people tried to stop it; how far the fire got before it waned; why it died down; and what the consequences were for people and the city. These groupings are inherent in the course of any extensive fire, and a lot of subjects contain the structural stages of any story about them in this way.

Other narratives, however, will tell their tale out of chronological order because there is a valid reason for organizing them differently, or because chronology is weak, absent, or unimportant to the angle of the story.

Following are some common documentary genres, gathered under the opposite polarities you can take in handling time—chronological time on one hand, and time fragmented and reorganized for some special purpose on the other.

TIME CHRONOLOGICALLY PRESENTED

The event-centered film: Here a significant event is the backbone of the film. It might be the launching of a ship, a rodeo, or the capture of a notorious criminal. Each event tends to have its stages, and into their forward movement you can plug in sections of interview, pieces of relevant past, or even pieces of the imagined future, such as a criminal might have as he says what he fears will happen while armed police are moving to surround him. The event may need more than one camera to cover it well, and you plan around the development and dynamics pegged out in advance by what is typical. Shooting with multiple mobile cameras without the cameras inadvertently shooting each other takes a quasi-military organization and timing.

Leni Riefenstahl's dark classic, *Olympia* (1936), follows the process of the Olympic Games in Berlin. With extraordinary, seductive virtuosity, it places Adolf Hitler, godlike, at the center.

Juan Francisco Urrusti's *A Long Journey to Guadalupe* (1996) centers on the yearly phenomenon of the mass migration to worship at the shrine of the Virgin of Guadalupe in Mexico City. First the pilgrimage is examined conceptually from an historical and cultural perspective. Then, charged up with ideas, we watch the mass migration itself, a spontaneous enactment by a poor and deeply religious people of their suffering, history, and faith. The latter part of the film concentrates, as only film can, on the actuality of the pilgrims' passion and shows how impossible it is to represent such cardinal human longings in words.

The process film: Most documentaries include many of life's processes (for example, making a meal, building a shed, taking a journey, or a court case). Documentaries usually are modular and present a succession of events in which each is a process having a beginning, a middle, and an end. Mostly they follow the sequencing inherent in the event (you can't put the roof on a house whose walls are only half built), but sometimes films use parallel storytelling by cutting between sequences that advance in parallel. A father may be at work in a factory while his daughter is in class at school getting the education that allows her *not* to work in a factory. Each sequence advances in steps, and the characters and their predicaments develop in a linear fashion. This lets you condense each sequence to essentials and thus helps with *narrative compression*.

Frederick Wiseman's *Titicut Follies* (1967) shows the inmate's every stage, from induction to burial, at an institution designed to warehouse the criminally insane. Memorable is one seemingly sane man's desperate efforts to extricate himself from its nightmarish embrace. The film's episodes, which lead the viewer progressively deeper into the surreal logic of the institution's personnel and their "treatment," are organized as side trips away from an ongoing show, the institution's annual review.

Les Blank's *Burden of Dreams* (1982) chronicles the shooting of *Fitzcarraldo* (1982), a Herzog feature about an opera impresario who contrived to bring a river steamer over the Andes (Figure 5–1). Through Herzog's own struggle in the jungle to get a steamer up a mountainside, Blank reveals Herzog's dictatorial obsessiveness and the risks to which he exposed his workers. By showing how realizing a cherished project can become more important than human life, Blank implies that totalitarianism can masquerade under the guise of art.

FIGURE 5–1

Werner Herzog and the boat he hauls up a hillside in Les Blank's *Burden of Dreams*. (Maureen Gosling)

The journey film: In the film industry they say that no film set on a train has ever failed. The journey's allure, with its metaphoric overtones, inbuilt rhythms of movement, and characters in transition who face tests and obstacles, is usually a natural choice for a documentary.

Basil Wright and Harry Watt's *Night Mail* (1936) shows the teamwork and camaraderie on an overnight mail trainrunning between London and Scotland. By revealing the postal workers' pride and confidence in performing their intricately phased operation, the film raises the dignity of the blue-collar worker, at that time usually seen on the screen only as a buffoon. Poetically it dramatizes how letters are the oxygen of ordinary lives. Though the movie has the look of poetic observation, it belongs with the Flaherty school of recreating reality and is artfully contrived at every level. If there is any central character it is the great steam train itself.

Ross McElwee's *Sherman's March* (1989) takes General Sherman's destructive journey during the American Civil War as its starting point and then, bored with his chosen subject, turns into a parallel journey by McElwee himself, encountering old girlfriends and new in a bid to end his status as a single man. McElwee discovers that the General is still with him, but more as an instructive metaphor for an ignoble end.

The historical film: All films reanimate the past, so all are to some degree historical journeys. Bill Nichols prefers to call actuality "the historical world,"[1] and this makes all the more sense when you consider that each film or video frame literally turns into history the moment it is recorded. Film ought therefore to be a good historical medium, but it seldom imparts a convincing relationship between events and time. Chronology, the essence of history, is also its enemy because histories must so often digress in pursuit of other chains of contributing cause and effect.

As Donald Watt and Jerry Kuehl point out, screen histories don't always satisfy their makers.[2] History films are beset with problems. They

- Bite off more than they can chew
- Force specific images to become backdrops for generalizations
- Skate hurriedly over large quantities of time or events simply because no archive footage exists
- Are unbalanced whenever particular coverage is not available
- Make TV executives terrified of making demands on the audience
- Try to sidestep controversy as school textbooks do
- Often fail to recognize that the screen is different from literature or an academic lecture
- Are often dominated by unverifiable interpretations

---

[1] Bill Nichols, *Introduction to Documentary* (Bloomington, IN: Indiana University Press, 2001), 5.
[2] Donald Watt and Jerry Kuehl, "History on the Public Screen I & II," in *New Challenges for Documentary*, ed. Alan Rosenthal, 435–453 (Berkeley, CA: University of California Press, 1988).

- Leave their audience unable to tell what strings come with funding or know how much any particular work is dominated by its maker's desire to build a monument

Then again, the screen, by its realism and ineluctable movement through time, discourages contemplation and diffuses whatever cannot be well illustrated. Because the meanings of history are abstractions, the screen seems like a singularly poor vehicle.

The incisive historical documentary usually takes as its focus a main issue, character, or thesis. Good examples are extremely diverse both in purview and language. Alain Resnais' *Night and Fog* (1955) leads us to confront the implications of Auschwitz. But it first takes us on a nightmarish journey, beginning from the bucolic, present-day images of the camp. We go back and forth in time, led by the evocative narration from poet and Holocaust survivor Jean Cayrol and the grimly gay music of Hanns Eisler. In imagination we become a hungry, terrified inmate, our life narrowed to surviving each mad, horrific day. The film leaves us looking over our shoulders for those among us capable of administering another such system.

Britain has produced some notable war series, such as *The Great War* (1964) and *The World at War* (1973–1974). America has produced its own blockbusters, such as *Vietnam: A Television History* (1983) and Ken Burns' *The Civil War* (1990). Compressed and heavily mediated by narration, these films deluge the viewer with facts. What he or she gains—a sense of virtue at having seen so much old footage, a sense of atmosphere and mood, patches of vivid and clearly remembered drama—is surely not the balanced and comprehensive understanding the producers imagined.

In France, Marcel Ophuls' *Sorrow and the Pity* (1972) and *Hotel Terminus: The Life and Times of Klaus Barbie* (1988) (Figure 5–2) and Claude Lanzmann's *Shoah* (1985) have concentrated on developing an understanding of fascism through drawing out the experience of its grassroots operatives.

An extraordinary historical evocation lies in the family history of the Havilio family, told by the Israeli director Ron Havilio in his 6-hour, two-part film, *Fragments: Jerusalem*. Told modestly and informally in home-movie style by the filmmaker, his wife, and three daughters, his family's 150 years of residency in Jerusalem encompasses much personal experience of the vast changes and upheavals in the city's often tragic history.

What elevates these films and makes them memorable is that they don't approach history in the textbook way—as bygone events requiring closure by consensus pronouncement—but as the light of human experience that can show the way ahead through dealing with contemporary predicaments.

The biographical film: Chronology also is important to the screen biography. Following a single character through time is in any case a variation on the hero's journey. Point of view plays a significant part because the central character's sense of events is often contradicted by others in his or her life. The sense of the main character getting older and meeting test after test also contributes to the kind of reliable momentum that easily allows sidebar excursions along the way.

The Kartemquin collective's *Golub* (1990), directed by Gordon Quinn and Jerry Blumenthal, tells the life of its socially conscious New York painter subject

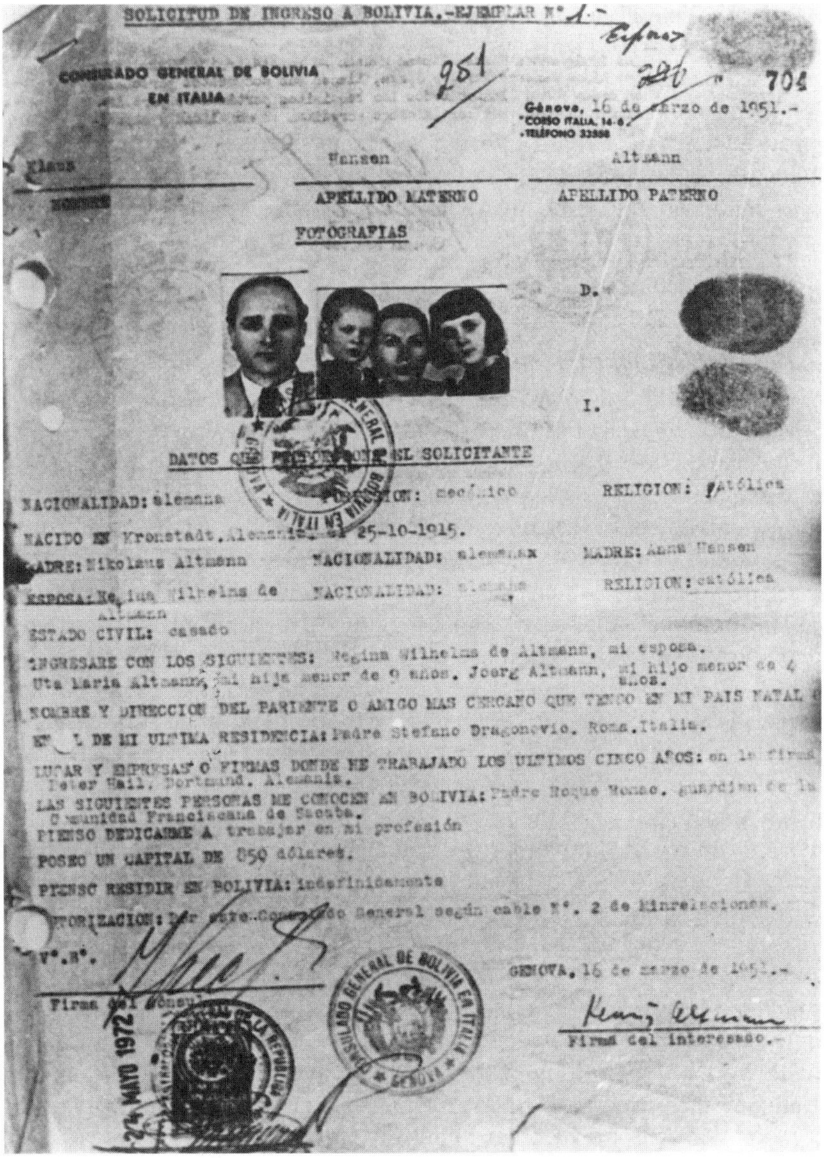
SOLICITUD DE INGRESO A BOLIVIA,-EJEMPLAR N° 1.-

CONSULADO GENERAL DE BOLIVIA
EN ITALIA

Génova, 16 de marzo de 1951.-
CORSO ITALIA, 14-6
TELÉFONO 32386

Klaus | Hansen | Altmann
NOMBRE | APELLIDO MATERNO | APELLIDO PATERNO

FOTOGRAFIAS

D.

I.

DATOS QUE PROPORCIONA EL SOLICITANTE

NACIONALIDAD: alemana PROFESION: mecánico RELIGION: católica
NACIDO EN Kronstadt, Alemania, el 25-10-1915.
PADRE: Nikolaus Altmann NACIONALIDAD: alemana MADRE: Anna Hansen
ESPOSA: Regina Wilhelms de Altmann NACIONALIDAD: alemana RELIGION: católica
ESTADO CIVIL: casado
INGRESARE CON LOS SIGUIENTES: Regina Wilhelms de Altmann, mi esposa. Uta Maria Altmann, mi hija menor de 9 años. Joerg Altmann, mi hijo menor de 4 años.
NOMBRE Y DIRECCION DEL PARIENTE O AMIGO MAS CERCANO QUE TENGO EN MI PAIS NATAL O DE MI ULTIMA RESIDENCIA: Padre Stefano Dragonovic, Roma, Italia.
LUGAR Y EMPRESAS O FIRMAS DONDE HE TRABAJADO LOS ULTIMOS CINCO AÑOS: en la firma Peter Wall, Dortmund, Alemania.
LAS SIGUIENTES PERSONAS ME CONOCEN EN BOLIVIA: Padre Roque Romac, guardian de la Comunidad Franciscana de Sacaba.
PIENSO DEDICARME A trabajar en mi profesión
POSEO UN CAPITAL DE 850 dólares.
PIENSO RESIDIR EN BOLIVIA: indefinidamente
AUTORIZACION: Por este Consulado General según cable N°. 2 de Minrelaciones.

V°.B°.

Firma del Cónsul

GENOVA, 16 de marzo de 1951.-

Firma del interesado.-

MAYO 1972

FIGURE 5–2

Incriminating document in *Hotel Terminus*—the false identity paper that allowed Klaus Barbie to enter Bolivia.

and incorporates elements of the process film by showing Leon Golub's artistic process as he develops a whole painting. The film is a well-developed argument for art that is responsible to the community and is politically conscious, something denigrated after Stalin initiated what Western critics called "tractor art."

Don McGlynn's *Mingus: Triumph of the Underdog* (1998) tells the main events of the jazz bassist and composer's life, but it goes further (as a biography surely must) by guessing at the complex roots of Mingus' lifelong frustration and feeling of outsiderdom. Being part black, part Swedish, part Chinese, and part German obviously had something to do with his feeling a misfit. Unforgettable, and painfully symbolic, is footage of the musical genius in deep depression, being evicted, and having his belongings heaped on the New York sidewalk by bailiffs.

TIME REORGANIZED

The poetic film: This type may want to render an atmosphere or put forth a thesis; it is less concerned with deriving its structure from events. Usually it relies on powerful imagery and uses verbal narrative sparingly. Often it will depict unfamiliar worlds, or familiar worlds seen in unfamiliar ways. A poetic first-person narrative like Vincent Dieutre's *Lessons of Darkness* (2000) structures the film by its maker's thoughts, memories, and feelings. In this case, a gay man is falling out of love while journeying between three European cities and finding solace in the erotic solidity of the men in Caravaggio's paintings. Other kinds of structure reflect how the film was made. Michael Rubbo's reflexive *Sad Song of Yellow Skin* (1970) investigates the impact of the American occupation on the Vietnamese. The film is driven more by the logic of Rubbo's contemplation than by considerations of space and time.

Wim Wenders' *Buena Vista Social Club* (1999) is not much ruled by chronology. To be sure, he has to find where the club once existed in Havana and locate the people who once played there, and then show them playing in different international venues. But once the music begins, the film can weave concerns with interviews and footage exploring the crumbling elegance of this most neglected of cities. There is no evident structure leading us from song to song, apart from the associations in the stories that each character tells.

The weakness in the poetic film is that it forgoes dramatic tension and forward movement for the delights of the moment, which is fine in principle but can make a film seem wandering and arbitrary if one wearies or is not caught up in the texture and ideas being fomented.

A favorite reorganization of time, one that feels far more secure, is to show an event and then backtrack in time to analyze the events and interplay of forces that led up to it, as in Joe Berlinger and Bruce Sinofsky's *Paradise Lost: The Child Murders at Robin Hood Hills* (1996). The film opens in West Memphis, Arkansas, with the terribly sad sight of the bodies of three murdered 8-year-old boys. The rest of the film follows the trial of the three local teenagers who were accused of killing them in a satanic ritual and casts much doubt on the validity of the evidence, much as the filmmakers did in their earlier film *Brother's Keeper* (1992), which was about some reclusive rural brothers accused of mercy-killing a sick sibling.

The walled-city film: Societies and institutions define their boundaries, close in upon themselves, and beget their own self-perpetuating code of conduct. The walled-city film usually investigates a microcosm in order to imply criticism on a much wider scale of the macrocosm. Its organization in time is often less rigorous than other structures because an organism, like a café, hospital, or park, has many activities that run simultaneously. Movement between activities can be thematically juxtaposed rather than straightened into the linearity of a chronology.

By concentrating on starving villagers in a remote Spanish village and by defining the various forces that prevent them from helping themselves, Buñuel's *Land Without Bread* (1932) angrily exposes the pattern of neglect afflicting the poor that was sanctioned by church, state, and landowners. Using a Brahms symphonic score and speaking ironically in the style of mellifluous travelogue, the narration guides us from one horror to the next as though hardly anything were out of place. Using montage governed by narration rather than any elaborate processes, the film has an unintentionally reflexive moment when a member of the crew steps into frame to examine the ulcerated throat of a dying child. Commendably humane sympathies sometimes turn observers into participants.

Any of Frederick Wiseman's films qualify as walled-city films, notably *Titicut Follies* (1967), *High School* (1968) (Figure 5–3), and *Hospital* (1969). Each implies a critical examination of mental health and normality, how we prepare the young for democracy, and how American society condones violence, both self-directed and that which is visited on others.

Two films by Nick Broomfield, *Soldier Girls* (1981) and *Chicken Ranch* (1982), also qualify as walled-city films but differ significantly in approach from

FIGURE 5–3

High School (1968) by Fred Wiseman. A walled-city film that looks at our attitudes toward preparing the young for democracy. (Zipporah Films, Inc.)

FIGURE 5–4

The ladies in Nick Broomfield's *Chicken Ranch* pose with their madam.

both the narrated and the direct cinema observational approach. One is about women soldiers doing basic training and the other about women and their customers in a brothel (Figure 5–4). Each shows how institutional life attempts to condition and control its inmates, and each leaves us more knowledgeable and critical, though neither film pretends to be neutral or unaffected by what it finds. By letting us see a discharged woman soldier embrace the camera operator or by including the brothel owner's harangue of the crew for filming what he wants kept confidential, both films admit where the filmmaker's sympathies lie and let us guess at the arrangements, liaisons, and even manipulation that made each phase of shooting possible.

The thesis film: This is any that sets out, like an essay, to educate, analyze something, or prove a hypothesis. Exposés or agitprop, experimental, or activist films are seldom structured by extended processes, but instead use montage to develop and assert ideas for the audience's consumption. For instance, if you want to convince the audience that, far from draining the local economy, poor immigrants to a large American city add economic value, then you must establish how and why the immigrants came, what work they do, what city services they do or don't use, and so on. You are building an argument and advancing the stages of a polemic so that you can convince even the skeptics in your audience.

Christine Choy and Renee Tajima's *Who Killed Vincent Chin?* (1989) chronicles the murder of a Chinese-American man outside a Detroit bar by a drunken white car worker. It seeks answers to how and why the self-confessed killer never served a day in prison, and its subtextual conclusion is that in America the lives of Asians are far less valuable than those of whites. This is not stated but revealed—through painstaking inquiry into the failures at all levels of the so-called justice system. Here, as in Errol Morris' *The Thin Blue Line* (1988), the film's structure, after introducing the murder, leads backward through layers of trial procedure and detection. Because we know the outcome, it is the miscarriage of justice that must concern us.

Pare Lorentz's *The River* (1937) is an essay film with a clearly defined beginning, middle, and end. Like a symphony, it has an inherent augmentation as, stage by stage, the film leads us from the beginning trickle all the way to the ocean. Along the way the river floods, and the film is memorable for its evocation of the powerful forces of nature sweeping away the flotsam of human homes, possessions, and lives. During the floods, only the amount of water and destruction determines where the shot belongs. There is no other marker, as there would be in a simpler process, to dictate where the shot should go.

TIME MADE UNIMPORTANT

The catalogue film: This is a documentary whose main and enthusiastic purpose is to examine something comprehensively rather than critically. A film about steam locomotives might organize their appearance by size, age, construction, or other logical classification. Unless the film takes the restoration through time of an old engine, say, as its backbone, then time won't play a centrally organizing role. Catalogue films usually are made by enthusiasts and seldom have much to say that is socially critical.

Les Blank's films, usually described as celebrations of Americana, are really catalogue films. There is *Garlic Is as Good as Ten Mothers* (1977), *In Heaven There Is No Beer* (1984), and the delightful *Gap-Toothed Women* (1987). All are good-natured forays into an enclosed world, and were they not so innocent they probably would be called voyeuristic.

The travelogue, the diary film, and the city symphony are frequently montage-based catalogue types.

When no time structure predominates: There may initially be no obvious time structure. For instance, a film about stained glass windows may have no discernible time structure in the actual footage. It could be arranged by historical dating of stained glass windows, by technical developments in glass, or by the regional origin and idiosyncrasies of the glassmakers. You decide which option to take by deciding what you want to say and what your material best supports.

Absurdist documentary: This is a rare form that is well suited to a playful handling of the outlandish or appalling. As her mother descends into Alzheimer's disease, Deborah Hoffmann's *Complaints of a Dutiful Daughter* (1995) uses dark humor to explore what would otherwise be a crushingly sad situation (Figure 5–5). What organizes the film's progression is the daughter's journey from early consciousness of her mother's growing eccentricity, to fearing that her mother

FIGURE 5–5

Deborah Hoffmann and her mother in *Complaints of a Dutiful Daughter* (1995). [Photo by Frances Reid courtesy of Deborah Hoffmann].

will turn into the pathetic shell of her former self, to realizing that her mother is actually becoming her more essentially humorous self.

MONOLOGICAL VERSUS DIALOGICAL FILMS

This brief review of documentary language and its uses suggests, I think, that the genre is becoming less monological and more dialogical. Still, old habits of disseminating improving tracts to the unwashed masses die hard, and far too much that circulates as documentary still has the aura of the classroom or the privileged traveler's slide lecture.

A new generation of filmmakers is dragging the documentary away from corporate bureaucrats and embracing the audience's eager longing for films that provoke an active inner dialogue. Slowly and surely, documentary is acquiring the complexities of language, thought, and purpose that once were confined to more mature art forms such as literature and theater. The old order is giving way to documentaries made by men and women who see the audience as equals and who are willing to investigate our inmost thoughts and feelings.

CHAPTER 6

AUTHORSHIP CHALLENGES AND OPPORTUNITIES

This chapter, concerned with difficulties and opportunities in form, control, and identity, will examine

- The relationship between subject and form
- The difficulties of authorial control over a world meant to be spontaneous
- How topics may be easy or difficult to film and the effect of this on the documentary's reputation
- How documentaries must be justified to participants and to funding sources
- How ethics are bound up with this
- How broadcasting handles the independent viewpoint
- How documentary language has influenced fictional forms

Trying to categorize the documentary confronted us in Chapter 3 with complex and circular relationships between its elements and modalities. Perhaps good documentaries succeed simply because someone found a way to turn particular footage into a compelling narrative. This would mean that good films are one of a kind and have a limited usefulness as prototypes. With this handicap in mind, let's examine some of the issues and contradictions in the documentarian's environment, for they influence what films get made. Some paradoxes lie in the medium, others in the ways that filmmakers have thus far used it.

CONTENT INFLUENCES FORM

A difficulty facing anyone making a documentary is that each film owes its credibility to acts, words, and images plucked from life, things that *lack central authorship*. In other art forms the creative artist has control over both the content and the form in which it is expressed. The documentary filmmaker is more like a mosaic artist whose freedom is curtailed by the idiosyncratic, chance-influenced nature of found materials. Unless the film is of the highly controlled essay type, the documentary author is at the mercy of whatever materials he or she manages to acquire. To those not obsessed with the need to control and who accept the dialectical, yin-yang nature of a world where everything is accompanied by its opposite, there is an enduring fascination in this subservience to actuality because it parallels so much else about our lives. We influence our fate but cannot control it. Instead we must harmonize and compromise with our destiny, and keep faith that something new and unforeseen will emerge—and it always does. Such is the nature of living and such is the nature of making documentary films.

FICTION AND DOCUMENTARY: AUTHORIAL CONTROL

Where the fiction filmmaker molds and compresses material during the writing stage to make the intended inner qualities visible and compelling, the documentary director must imply an authorial point of view later and in more indirect ways. Documentary compels you to work from behind the appearance of verisimilitude. Stamp your work with too much of your own viewpoint, and you imply a deficiency in the personalities and events you filmed. However, withdraw your own values from the tale, and the point of telling it vanishes.

The observational documentary, in particular, must strike a balance between tracts of autonomous, unfolding realism on the one hand and signs and portents that signal us to look beyond the literal on the other. That we are willing to do so seems spurred by three main factors, that the film's

- Subject is gripping and original
- Point of view is individual, flexible, and evident
- Language and conventions are used in a non-routine, stimulating way

Every director faces challenges in one or more of these areas, and the measure of your film's originality will be the energy and freshness with which you tackled the formal elements.

STYLE

The word *style* is often and confusingly interchanged with *form*. Godard said, "To me, style is just the outside of content, and content the inside of style, like the outside and inside of the human body—both go together, they can't be separated" (Richard Roud, *Jean-Luc Godard*, Indianapolis, IN: Indiana University Press, 1970).

The style of a film is really the visible influence of its maker's identity. This distinction is made messy by the fact that film authorship is collective. But the authorship of a Fred Wiseman or an Errol Morris film, even if you hate it, is immediately recognizable. Partly this is a characteristic choice of subject, partly it's the handling of the camera, and the characteristic forms each director chooses, and partly it's that their films have a consistent mark of individual personalities and tastes written all over them. It is this last, virtually uncontrollable, element that is properly style. A film's genre, its voice, and its style all tend to overlap and are impossible to separate. But in documentary there is a closer nexus between content and how content is articulated simply because stylizing actuality quickly leads to a forced look. The ultra fragmented, MTV camera-waving style applied to documentary, or the overcomposed look of Errol Morris' anecdotal biography of Stephen Hawking, *A Brief History of Time* (1991), each speaks of a dissatisfaction with their subjects and a decision to dress it up with a stylistic "statement" to camouflage something considered inadequate or uncinematic in the original.

Just as you can't choose your own identity at any meaningful level, so you should let your film style take care of itself. You can and should locate your film within a genre, and design its content and form to be an organic whole. If over the period of its creation you serve each controllable aspect of your film well, people will come to recognize in a succession of your films a continuity that is hard to pin down, but that will be called your style. From your audience and your critics you may even learn what it is—rather as (at considerable risk to one's equilibrium) one extracts a sense of one's character from the reactions of friends, enemies, family, flatterers, and detractors. Is it useful, once you've abstracted it? No, not very.

Setting out to strike a style or project an artistic identity, as students sometimes feel they must, leads to superficial and attention-demanding gimmickry. Far more important is to develop your deepest interests and make the best cinema you can out of the imprint left by your formative experience. Working simply, sincerely, and intelligently is what truly connects your work to an audience. Even then you must expect a long evolution while you internalize all the technical and conceptual skills.

LIMITS ON THE RANGE OF SUBJECTS

Getting the reader to notice a fragile and transient moment of significance is easily accomplished by a writer but is much harder to accomplish in documentary unless you are willing to use narration. This drives documentarians to play safe by resorting to sensational subjects. War, family violence, urban problems, eccentrics, deviants, demonstrations, revolts, and confrontations all promise something heightened. Less often do documentaries penetrate the heart of their subjects with the ease and precision we find regularly in literature. For the true feel of small-town life or for the authentic claustrophobia of a middle-class family, we look instinctively to fiction, not the documentary. This is not inevitable, but the documentarian wishing to buck the trend faces many difficulties, not least of which is raising money to budget a film about subjects considered minor.

Filmmaking of all kinds is a market commodity and thrives or dies according to audience figures. Complaining about this is futile and unproductive because there are plenty of other obstacles to discourage the fainthearted from working on a small canvas. Luckily, making a documentary no longer requires a huge budget, so now you can demonstrate what you mean with a film instead of with a written proposal only.

PARTICIPANTS' COOPERATION AND INFORMED CONSENT

Difficulties also arise in making the "ordinary-life" documentary because participants may not want to cooperate. How do you convince someone to let you earnestly film something that they themselves consider trivial? Fail to justify your purposes, and you fail to assure people of your underlying respect.

If, however, you make your interests clear and justifiable, many people will set aside their comfort or privacy because making the film seems important. A rape victim may sacrifice her privacy because she wants to raise public awareness of rapists and of how the courts process the raped woman's case. She does so wisely only *if you make her fully aware of the consequences*—which are not always predictable. When someone consents to film knowing all the circumstances of risk to themselves, this is called giving *informed consent*. If you secure consent and the person is unaware of negative consequences in the future, you have committed an ethical offense and later may do them actual harm.

RESISTANCE TO THE PERSONAL VIEWPOINT

A major obstacle to making films that look for the extraordinary in the ordinary has been corporate television's unwillingness to allow work expressing personal politics or beliefs—unless, of course, large viewing figures are assured. Television, for all its vaunted investigative journalism, generally avoids social criticism, no matter how well argued, unless it can be safely yoked to a famous name or a widely recognized movement. This not only serves to attract viewers, it dissociates the channel or station from responsibility for the opinions expressed.

Other kinds of resistance to the personal viewpoint may be cultural and harder to pinpoint. Mark Wexler's critically praised *Me and My Matchmaker* (1996) aroused a barely contained fury in a television buyer at a European festival, either because the film shifts focus between its women participants and Mark's changing relationships with them, or because documentary itself is still expected to suppress its maker's persona (Figure 6–1). The notion persists that television documentary is an objective public service and that all personal authorship is suspect. This may be particularly true when the buyer is European and the author unremorsefully American.

AN EVOLVING LANGUAGE

Documentary is a young genre in the young art of cinema and has only just begun exploring the limits of its potential. It no longer has to take the stance of objectivity or be a slave to realism. Its only limitation is that it relay aspects of actuality (past, present, or future) and implies a critical relationship to the fabric of social life.

FIGURE 6–1

Mark Wexler and his subject, Irene Nathan, in *Me and My Matchmaker* (1996). Autobiographical content, though popular with cinema audiences, is hard to get accepted by television. (Photo © Wexler's World.)

To engage and hold an audience, documentary uses narrative compression and draws on the wealth of storytelling techniques already in existence, as Flaherty recognized at documentary's inception. This may be uncomfortable for the ethnographer or for any purist for whom manipulation is always suspect. Marxist filmmakers, attempting greater respect for participants, tried to solve the problem by leaving uncut what they shot. Though this certainly made films look different (and much, much longer), it left the foundation of documentary unchanged. Inescapably, everything on the screen comes from choices and relationships; all of them reflect the makers' values and commitment to what matters, what is true, and what needs saying.

Here we return to the notion that a film must make a contract with its audience. It must promise something, deliver what it promises, and remain consistent while so doing. This is difficult stuff to control and everyone learns to do it slowly, given the extravagant time and effort it takes to complete (and therefore learn from) each project. A large public following exists for the right films, but you must find fresh approaches if you are to evade the dead hand of convention.

DOCUMENTARY AS A PREPARATION TO DIRECT FICTION

After the fiction film's innovative and experimental early days as silent film, it settled into a factory process that quashed most of the cinema's early immediacy and flexibility. This never really happened in documentary, which remained a handmade, improvisatory genre. When light sync equipment made freer filming possible in the 1950s, fiction improvisation too was reborn, notably in Britain by the proponents of Free Cinema, such as Lindsay Anderson, Karel Reisz, Tony Richardson, and others.

In France of the late 1950s and 1960s, a willingness to improvise and shoot on the run in the streets blossomed as the great films of the French New Wave. In America, Cassavetes, Altman, Jarmusch, and others pioneered the now thriving "indie" or independent filmmaking movement, developing imaginative films entirely outside the studio factory system.

Undoubtedly, by provided a demanding benchmark for screen realism, the documentary influenced fiction-directing relationships and styles of acting. Developments in theater, too, have made the actor/director relationship in film more intimate and demanding, more revealing of the actor's psyche. The traditional high-concept script, featuring stock characters driven by a stereotypical plot, has been in retreat before the onslaught of intensified, character-driven drama whose roots are in the actual. The most inventive directors are expecting, and getting, superlative creativity from their actors, and cinema worldwide has seldom been artistically or financially healthier.

The Iranian cinema consistently makes a documentary use of its many extraordinary cultures as settings for semi-mythic tales. Mohsen Makhmalbaf's *Gabbeh* (1996) brings to life the tale of a couple forbidden to love each other and sets it among a nomadic tribe famous for the carpets they weave. Jafar Panahi's *The White Balloon* (1995) is set in the city and tells of a little girl's determination to get what she wants—almost entirely without dialogue. Bahman Ghobadi's *A Time for Drunken Horses* (2000) is set among smugglers on the mountainous Iran/Iraq border and tells how some orphaned children contrive to get the money so their crippled sibling can have an operation. In each case, local people act in local stories, and the stories themselves carry a kind of poetic conviction and universality that usually is found only in masterworks or folk tale. There is a brief discussion of Iranian documentary in Chapter 2, under "Documentaries from the 1980s Onward."

THE DOGME GROUP AND SETTING LIMITS

In 1995 the founding members of the Danish Dogme 95 cinema group were Thomas Vinterberg, Lars von Trier, Christian Levring, and Søren Kragh-Jacobsen. In the next few years, group members produced such extraordinary fiction films as *Breaking the Waves* (Lars von Trier, 1999), *The Celebration* (Thomas Vinterberg, 1998), and *The Idiots* (Lars von Trier, 1999). They began by playfully setting up rules of limitation, rather as the photographers Edward Weston, Imogen Cunningham, Ansel Adams, and Willard Van Dyke had done in 1932 for their Group f/64. The photographers—tired of pictorialist work in which photography tried to make itself look like painting, charcoal sketches, or etching—proclaimed that photography would only be liberated to become itself if photographers rejected everything borrowed from other pictorial forms. So they concentrated on developing photography's own attributes.

Compare this idea with the Dogme Group's manifesto, which appears in various versions and translations. I have taken minor editorial liberties to render it into vernacular English as follows.

A VOW OF CHASTITY

- Shooting must be done on location. Props and sets must not be brought in, but shooting must go where that set or prop can be found.
- Sound must never be produced separately from the images or vice versa. Music must not be used unless it occurs where the scene is shot.
- The camera must be handheld. Any movement or immobility attainable by handholding is permitted. The action cannot be organized for the camera; instead, the camera must go to the action.
- The film must be in color. Special lighting is not acceptable. If there is too little light for exposure, the scene must be cut, or a single lamp may be attached to the camera.
- Camera filters and other optical work are forbidden.
- The film must not contain any superficial action such as murders, weapons, explosions, and so on.
- No displacement is permitted in time or space: the film takes place here and now.
- Genre movies are not acceptable.
- Film format is Academy 35 mm.
- The director must not be credited. Furthermore, I swear as a director to refrain from personal taste. I am no longer an artist. I swear to refrain from creating a "work," as I regard the instant as more important than the whole. My supreme goal is to force the truth out of my characters and settings. I swear to do so by all the means available and at the cost of any good taste and any aesthetic considerations.

Signed _____ (Member's Name)

The last clause is particularly interesting because it rejects a leadership hierarchy and personal taste, and strikes a mortal blow at the filmmaker's ego. Instead, it passes preeminence to the cast. Of course, in practice any number of contradictions will appear, but the group's work, and the high praise it called forth from actors, demands that one take the spirit of the vow seriously. Thomas Vinterberg, interviewed by Elif Cercel for *Director's World*, said:

We did the "Vow of Chastity" in half an hour and we had great fun. Yet, at the same time, we felt that in order to avoid the mediocrity of filmmaking not only in the whole community, but in our own filmmaking as well, we had to do something different. We wanted to undress film, turn it back to where it came from and remove the layers of make-up between the audience and the actors. We felt it was a good idea to concentrate on the moment, on the actors and of course, on the story that they were acting, which are the only aspects left when everything else is stripped away. Also, artistically it has created a very good place for us to be as artists or filmmakers because having obstacles like these means you have something to play against. It encourages you to actually focus on other approaches instead. (see http://stage.directorsworld.com)

Interestingly, these strictures belong with the improvisational spirit of documentary. Following this good-humored yet puritanical vow put Danish film for a while in the forefront of international cinema and induced the Danish government to increase state funding by 70% over the following 4 years. The moral? All undertakings profit from creatively inspired limitations. Some are inbuilt, some encountered, and the best are those you choose that will squeeze your own inventiveness. The Dogme Group's rules dethroned the mighty god Film Technique in favor of acting and were able to hand their excellent actors a rich slice of creative control. The actors responded handsomely.

So, what creative limitations will you set yourself?

MIGRATING FROM DOCUMENTARY TO FICTION

Taking the relatively small British cinema as an example, it's instructive to see who first worked in documentary before moving to fiction: Lindsay Anderson, Michael Apted, John Boorman, Ken Loach, Karel Reisz, Sally Potter, Tony Richardson, and John Schlesinger. Is this such a stellar list by chance? Now add those coming from painting, theater, and music, or who espouse improvisational methods, and more distinguished names appear, such as Maureen Blackwood, Mike Figgis, Peter Greenaway, Mike Leigh, Sharon Maguire, and Anthony Minghella. These are not all household names, but to me they indicate that eclecticism, improvisation, and a documentary sensibility are important to directing wherever fiction cinema is vibrant.

Recently, when chairing a panel discussion at an international film schools' conference on the utility of a documentary training for fiction directors, I made the following notes.

If you are an aspiring fiction director, experience in making documentary can

- Offer a rapid and voluminous training in finding stories and telling them on the screen
- Develop confidence in your abilities
- Show the rewards of spontaneity and adapting to the actual
- Demand intuitive judgments
- Develop your eye for a focused and truthful human presence

- Offer a workout in the language of film and demand that you find a means of narrative compression
- Offer the opportunity for fast shooting but slow editing, and time to contemplate the results (fiction, conversely, is slow to shoot but faster to edit)
- Require much inventiveness and adaptability in the area of sound shooting. Sound design can be quite intensive in documentary, and location sound inequities teach the preeminent importance of good mike choice and positioning.
- Show you real characters in real action. Character is allied with will or volition, and each is best revealed when the subject has to struggle with some obstacle. You will also see how individual identity is somehow developed in interactions between people and is not a fixed and formed commodity that functions the same in all circumstances.
- Face you with the need to capture evidence of a character making decisions. Gripping observational documentary usually deals with the behavior of people trying to accomplish things. Documentaries expose the elements of good dramatic writing by revealing these principles at work in life.
- Allow you to see how in active characters, issues flow from decisions, and decisions create new issues
- Demonstrate how character-driven documentaries are no different from character-driven fiction. Well-conceived documentary is thus a laboratory for character-driven drama.
- Show how editing must impose brevity, compression, and rhythm. In fiction this has to be injected at the writing stage. Thus, documentary teaches why the elements of good writing involve brevity, compression, and action.
- License a director and camera crew to improvise and spontaneously create
- Give directors advance experience of participants simply being, a crucial benchmark for knowing when actors have reached that state during the search for spontaneity
- Teach the director to catalyze truth from participants, so a fiction director can learn to do the same with actors
- Pose the same narrative problems as fiction, thus giving what is really writing experience
- Help the whole crew to see all human action as dramatic evidence
- Be shot in real time, when drama must be plucked from life. This accustoms directors to thinking on their feet.
- Establish that the risk/confrontation/chemistry of the moment are the stock in trade of both documentary and improvisational fiction

In the sister volume to this book, *Directing: Film Techniques and Aesthetics*, 3rd ed. ([Boston: Focal Press, 2003], 67–69), I advocate covering rehearsals for fiction film as if they were documentary material and suggest this is particularly useful for

- Discovering best camera positions
- Practicing camera framing and movements as something subservient to actors' movements
- Revealing performance inequities on the screen
- Demystifying the relationship between live performance and its results on the screen
- Seeing the need for rewrites based on the screen results
- Giving experience of working with non-actors or actors who are marginally experienced
- Helping to spot clichés, bad acting habits, and areas that are forced or false
- Helping prepare actors for the presence of the camera—thus lowering the regression that follows the introduction of camera when shooting begins
- Posing problems of adapting to a here-and-now actuality

Not so long ago, documentary was considered a lower form of filmmaking, a sideline for those not up to anything better. Now it is perceived quite differently— as a vibrant way to experience what the veteran Hollywood cinematographer Haskell Wexler calls "real filmmaking." Through experience in handling non-actors in an improvisatory genre and through using the full range of cinema skills to tell a story, a documentary director gets a supreme preparation for the greater artistic and industrial demands of fiction. These include writing, directing actors, leading a large crew, and spending a fortune each working day. Not everyone wants to give up documentary freedoms to become a latter day Napoleon, but make no mistake—the option to do so is now distinctly present.

CHAPTER 7

RE-ENACTMENT, RECONSTRUCTION, AND DOCUDRAMA

This chapter looks from a moral or ethical perspective at

- Re-enacting and truth claims
- Reconstructing or projecting situations
- Reconstructing subjectivity
- Fake documentaries as instruments of critique

A controversial aspect of the documentary is its conjectural ability, achieved by reconstructing bygone situations or even recreating an entire biography for someone no longer living. To take the former, less radical situation first, it sometimes happens that some important biographical event has passed before you begin filming—a crucial career interview, say, for a job that one's main character has already begun. If participants can credibly re-enact this scene, how important is it that you be totally truthful with your audience? There is no easy answer. Some films run a subtitle saying the scene is re-enacted, but this seems unnecessarily attention grabbing if the scene is only part of the exposition needed to get the film under way, and you are already using a distancing past-tense narration or voice-over. To pass the scene off as the real thing would, however, be highly misleading in a key evidence scene. You would be letting the audience think it was seeing a key piece of actuality rather than a reconstruction.

A while ago I saw an explosive documentary made in the Netherlands national film school, which turned out to have been wholly and masterfully fabricated—in fact, not a documentary at all. The audience (mainly, it must be admitted, of documentary teachers) was disturbed and even irate at being bamboozled, and this suggests how important it may be to keep the contractual relationship with the audience straight. We draw different inferences from documented actuality than from material that is acted and we feel manipulated when someone transposes the labeling. Indeed, it was to illustrate this very point that the film was shown.

The dividing line seems to be one of good faith; there is nothing controversial about showing how a character got her job, if we know she got one. But if instead our character says that the personnel manager tricked her, whether we see the actual interview or only a re-enactment becomes crucially important because someone's integrity is up for judgment.

To summarize, re-enacting important scenes that can be shown no other way is a useful and valid way to stimulate the audience's imagination and to fill what would otherwise be significant gaps in the narrative. If, however, the audience will be misled into making formative judgments from the re-enactment, it should be appropriately signified. Incidentally, when you direct a re-enactment, encourage your participants to approach their task not as acting, but as an exercise in reliving the spirit of what truly happened.

In large-scale reconstruction you definitely need clear labeling. Here a scene, several scenes, or even a whole film is reconstructed from available sources. These might be eyewitness memories, documents, transcripts, or hearsay. British television once showed an acted reconstruction directed by Stuart Hood of the trial of Sacco and Vanzetti. Adapted from the 1920s court transcripts of the famous anarchists' trial, it was intelligent, restrained, and austerely memorable. Although all who appeared were actors, the piece was factually accurate and can only be described as documentary in spirit because there was no central authorship. Each of the participants—the actors portraying the two anarchists, the judge, and the legal representatives—used the actual ideas and language preserved in the court records.

Even Peter Watkins' famous *Culloden* (1964)—an extremely hypothetical reconstruction of the 1746 Highlands battle in which Bonnie Prince Charlie and his Stuart cause were brutally put down by the English—is usually included with the documentary genre. Here historical accuracy is more than doubtful. The words of the officers and foot soldiers that Watkins "interviewed" are a modernist guess at what soldiers—had documentary existed—might have said at the time. Yet the attitude of the film toward its participants speaks of an overall respect and comprehension, not only toward the distant historical actuality but also toward the tragic human process by which such events recur in history. The film deals with power and politics, but its true concern is subjugation and the process by which the humble get used as cannon fodder in the ideological and turf struggles of their masters.

Where, then, is the dividing line between documentary and fiction? A short answer is that nobody knows, that any line is always being challenged, and that critics will challenge anybody who goes farther.

THE DOCUDRAMA

There is a yet more imaginative—some would say fanciful—use of the real, known as *docudrama* or *dramadoc*, and more common, it seems, in Britain than elsewhere. As its name signifies, it is a hybrid straddling two worlds, and two notable British examples must suffice. One is a dramatization of the plight of the newly homeless made in the 1960s, Jeremy Sandford's *Cathy Come Home* (1966). Working from case histories at a time when homelessness was new and shocking, Sandford and his wife, Nell Dunne, constructed a "typical" blue-collar couple that overspends and then encounters bad luck. The family—evicted, then homeless—plummets down the social scale until dismembered by the welfare state "for the good of the children."

Coming hard on the heels of the successful Conservative re-election slogan, "You never had it so good," the British public was at first stunned, then appalled, to find that the drama was true to life in all its particulars. The force of public feeling it aroused even contributed to some amelioration in the law, which is rare indeed for a film of any kind. *Cathy*'s effectiveness lay not only in its documentary basis but also in superb acting and presentation.

My other docudrama example is Anthony Thomas' *Death of a Princess* (1980), which set out to show how a member of the Saudi royalty could be publicly humiliated and executed for a sexual offense. It raised a storm of critical reaction on all sides. The film used actors to reconstruct the princess's life and death, and it seems to have taken altogether too many risks—first with the truth, which was insufficiently determinable, then with the authenticity of how it portrayed Islamic culture and assumptions, both plainly outside the producer's realm of experience. These uncertainties gave the film a contrived and speculative quality that left it successful neither as fiction drama nor as documentary. For myself, I was less repelled by the exposé of a barbarous punishment than by the film's self-congratulatory style. The surrogate for its director, who had undoubtedly researched among a range of weird and dubious characters to assemble a picture of the princess's death, was played by an actor directed to behave like a suave, James Bond-ish investigator. The performance was irritatingly upper class and self-involved, and this and the film's overall presentation seemed more concerned with entertainment values than with documentary fidelity. Too much drama and not enough doc.

Obviously the premise and style of a docudrama greatly influence how we assess and assimilate anything proffered as "true to life." If the premise seems unsupported or insupportable, we indignantly reject the film's pretensions to documentary authenticity. It is interesting to compare *Death of a Princess* with Jack Gold's well-received re-enactment of Ruth First's imprisonment in South Africa, *Ninety Days* (1966). Because First played herself, the program raised no question that it was an authentic account. It must have illuminated police-state methods rather too well, for she was later murdered in brutal reprisal.

SUBJECTIVE RECONSTRUCTION

Some works of reconstruction deserve notice because their language successfully creates a heightened state of imaginative identification with the subjects. The National Film Board of Canada's *Volcano* (1977), by the brilliant and quirky Donald Brittain, reconstructs the life of Malcolm Lowry, author of the novel *Under the Volcano*. Lowry (an alcoholic like Brittain himself) transmuted his own story into art by producing a novel of memorable depth out of a life of tragi-comic turmoil and self-destructiveness. In telling Lowry's life, Brittain uses some of the standard apparatus of screen biography, but the film uses no archive film and few photos of Lowry himself, concentrating instead on creating a sense of place and atmosphere akin to Lowry's own in contemporary Mexico. This is counterpointed against the novelist's words and ideas. Afterward you seem to have lived through a destructive addiction yourself—testimony indeed to the film's surreal effectiveness.

Errol Morris' *The Thin Blue Line* (USA, 1988) investigates the indictment and trial of Randall Adams, being kept on death row in Texas for killing a police-man many years earlier. Using minimalist music by Philip Glass and a camera that stares unblinkingly at a number of witnesses, each composed and lit as if for a feature film, Morris' tale gathers force as a formal work of intricate detec-tion. What really took place at the time of the murder? Morris re-enacts many versions of the killing according to each participant's testimony. The effect is like pondering a chess problem just as Morris, while groping for the truth, must have pondered that puzzle himself. The outcome is haunting: we see, from a prisoner's perspective, how he got caught in a real-life *film noir* web and how idiosyncrat-ically and unjustly Texas law can operate.

Marlon Riggs' *Tongues Untied* (1989) goes even further in creating an inte-rior world. Using Brechtian vignettes by the filmmaker and his gay associates, the film playfully and elliptically conveys what it is like to be black, gay, and invisible in a predominantly white heterosexual world. There is no obvious through-line of argument, only a series of forcefully stylish performances—every-thing from dance and body movement to inner monologue, street talk, and rap. The film defies description or analysis, except perhaps as a montage of moods, thoughts, ideas, and plaints when the tongue is untied by the imminence of death. Riggs died of AIDS, and the film is his last testament.

A lovely BBC biographical documentary is Chris Durlacher's *George Orwell: A Life in Pictures* (2003). There being no recording of Orwell's voice and no archive footage of him, the producers created their own facsimile using the superb actor Chris Langham. Importantly, he speaks only Orwell's words as written in novels, essays, letters, and diaries. Sections of interviews with people who knew Orwell are interspersed with interviews of the documentary's reconstructed Orwell. The effect is eerily authentic, and the sense of being in each period with the great anti-authoritarian author is increased by plentiful archive footage. Mixed in, and not at all intrusive, is a library of home movie footage created in authentic places with Langham. The effect is a sustained, imaginative portrait that you trust throughout, even though much of its material strictly speaking is questionable and even fake.

FAKE DOCUMENTARIES OR MOCKUMENTARIES

Mitchell Block's renowned short film about a female rape victim, *No Lies* (1973), shows how powerful a tool of inquiry documentary can be in the hands of an intrusively questioning filmmaker. We are appalled at the pressure he applies and fascinated by the revelations his filmmaker pries from the victim, then thoroughly disconcerted when the movie reveals that both are actors and that the exploitative relationship is a calculated performance.

The film was made to "cinematically . . . demonstrate and commit rape—and it does so in such a way as to make the experience of being the unwary, unprepared victim of an aggressive assault on one's person, on one's pride, and on one's expectations of and security in familiar activity in familiar surroundings a very real experience accessible to anyone of *either* sex who views the film."[1]

Ken Featherstone's *Baba Kiueria* (Australia, 1987) purports to be an Australian television documentary about how Aboriginal colonists discovered Australia back when the country was thinly peopled by primitive whites cooking meat in ritual places called "barbecue areas" (hence the film's title). Centering on a nervously compliant white family, it shows how they try to cooperate with the black colonizers and, because of their fecklessness, are split up by Aboriginal social workers for their own betterment.

By inverting predominant racial values in Australia and by making the film a comedy, this fake documentary uses irony and farce to show what it must feel like when liberal paternalism descends from one race to another.

Woody Allen's *Zelig* (1983) is a fictional fable in mock documentary style about a Depression-era Jewish celebrity with a penchant for assimilating himself, chameleon-like, into any situation. Through masterful image processing, Allen appears at Babe Ruth games and Hitler rallies, always adapting himself to the mood and identity of those around him. Like much comedy, it has an underlying critical purposes, one being to lampoon the pompousness of stereotyped documentary.

These films are Trojan horses that appropriate the documentary form to test the audience's credulity and to introduce doubts about the worth and trustworthiness of authoritarian documentary. They seem to warn us, "Beware blind trust!"

In this chapter I am indebted to enlightening discussions of docudrama and false documentaries led by Otto Schuurman and Elaine Charnov at the Sights of the Turn of the Century documentary conference at the Centro de Capacitación Cinematográfica in Mexico City, 1996.

The authority on docudrama, and tireless champion of its effectiveness, is the distinguished filmmaker and documentary historian Alan Rosenthal. His *Why Docudrama? Fact-Fiction on Film and TV* (Carbondale, IL: Southern Illinois Press, 1999) is a comprehensive survey of docudrama's history and possibilities.

---

[1] Vivian C. Sobchack, "No Lies: Direct Cinema as Rape," in *New Challenges for Documentary,* ed. Alan Rosenthal, 332 (Berkeley, CA: University of California Press, 1988).

CHAPTER 8

DOCUMENTARY THEORY AND THE ISSUE OF REPRESENTATION

This chapter concerns what discussion and help you can hope to find. It examines

- Documentary and wielding authority
- Theory and history resources
- Live issues concerning rights, veracity, politics, control, form, institutions, and history in documentary
- What is true documentary and its work?
- What is our true relationship to our subjects and do we actually do good?
- On what grounds can we make truth claims, and under what circumstances can we truthfully represent other people?
- Speaking with our own voices in a plural democracy

To wield a documentary camera is to exercise some degree of power. What that power is and how it should be used are issues that will dog your steps. It is not enough to believe you are right and doing good in the world—you must be willing to examine your motives and practices as you go, or have others do it for you in critical reviews of your work.

Those who make some of the world's nonfiction films are those with power whose aim is to instruct and pacify those who lack it. Some documentaries, however, are made by those without power who aim to get it. Institutional documentary often tries to occupy the middle ground, aiming to reason and mediate by representing those without a voice—a noble but potentially delusional role.

Power is never given, it is taken. In my experience, directors-in-training are attracted to the power vested in directing but are terrified of using it. Most will do almost anything to avoid the hot potato.

This chapter is a brief guide to useful film and documentary theory. The *Oxford English Dictionary* says that a theory is "a hypothesis that has been confirmed or established by observation or experiment." So you might echo Kurt Lewin's dictum that nothing is so practical as a good theory. But it is a curious fact that most film theorists come from history, psychology, sociology, anthropology, linguistics, or philosophy—everywhere, it would seem, except actual filmmaking. Their work is thus aimed not at making better or different films but at identifying the patterns and meaning in those already made.

FILM THEORY

For an excellent introduction to the often arcane language of film theory and for an overview of the knotty issues debated throughout the cinema's development, try Dudley Andrew's *Concepts in Film Theory* (New York: Oxford University Press, 1984). The book's chapter headings reveal its approach:

- The State of Film Theory
- Perception
- Representation
- Signification
- Narrative Structure
- Adaptation
- Valuation (of Genres and Auteurs)
- Identification
- Figuration
- Interpretation

Because documentary shares so much with fiction, don't be deterred by the fact that documentary receives little mention. At the end of the book is a classified bibliography.

HISTORY OF THE DOCUMENTARY

There are two standard texts, both very readable and updated from their 1970s original editions. Richard Meran Barsam's *Nonfiction Film: A Critical History*, 2nd ed. (Bloomington, IN: Indiana University Press, 1992) is particularly good on the earliest motion pictures. It surveys the genre's development by periods and geographical areas. Erik Barnouw's *Documentary: A History of Non-Fiction Film*, 3rd ed. (New York: Oxford University Press, 1993) is particularly interested in the evolving function of the documentary film. Both books contain stimulating portraits of the founders of the art form, including Cavalcanti, Dovzhenko, Flaherty, Grierson, Ivens, Jennings, Lorentz, Riefenstahl, Rotha, Shub, Storck, Vertov, Watt, and Wright—to name but a few.

A characteristic of the early practitioners, particularly those in the Grierson stable, is the great debates they pursued over documentary's identity, aesthetics, and function as a tool of social change. Today this critical tension has largely dissipated among established filmmakers, who seem to take a stance and then work out of it without any obvious further reflection. Except for women's and gay political issues, academics have taken over the arguments. Little about the original debates has ever been settled, and the documentary remains a minefield of temptations and possibilities, just as in the early days.

Most of the early figures either wrote autobiographies or have been written about, most notably Grierson and Flaherty. Grierson was never in doubt that the documentary could and should change the world. He was not wrong, for very slowly the world does change, and change always starts with the far sighted.

DOCUMENTARY ISSUES

Theorizing Documentary (New York: Routledge, 1993), edited by Michael Renov, is a valuable anthology of critical essays with a good bibliography and filmography. In a piece on the poetics of documentary, Renov proposes four basic tendencies for the genre:

- To record, reveal, or preserve
- To persuade or promote
- To analyze or interrogate
- To express

Brian Winston, whose innate iconoclasm is entertaining and sometimes brilliant, argues in "The Documentary Film as Scientific Inscription" (in *Theorizing Documentary*) that the credibility of documentary evidence, sustained thus far on a highly questionable "naturalistic illusion," is deeply at risk now that technology hands filmmakers ever more control over imagery. Winston has published a body of work questioning assumptions about media realism and documentary orthodoxy, as well as a critical biography of the poet of the British documentary movement, Humphrey Jennings.[1]

Philip Rosen, in examining what a documentary is or is not, places Grierson in the stormy waters of historiographical debate and demonstrates how docu-

---

[1] Brian Winston's books: *Lies, Damn Lies, and Documentary* (London: British Film Institute, 2000), *Media Technology and Society: A History from the Telegraph to the Internet* (London: Routledge, 1998), *Technologies of Seeing: Photography, Cinematography, and Television* (London: British Film Institute, 1997), *Claiming the Real: The Griersonian Documentary and Its Legitimations* (London: British Film Institute, 1995), and on Jennings, *Fires Were Started* (London: BFI Film Classics, 2000).

mentary representation, in trying to control mass perception of truth, is really a bid for political influence. He argues that the notion of "an organizing gaze as exterior to its objects" is an untenable idea. Trinh T. Minh-ha, in a review of stunning breadth and penetration, covers the arena of documentary assumptions and shows how inadequate, contradictory, or downright colonial most of them are, including the "scientific" ones dear to anthropology. Paul Arthur discusses how documentarians' claims to truth have not fundamentally changed in spite of postmodernism and new technology. Ana M. López argues that in the Brazilian series, *America*, it is the Brazilian outsiders whose "methods of post-modernism itself—pastiche, simulacra, images, gloss, and nostalgia" produce a critique that becomes a "fetishization of the image . . . [which] ultimately reduces the historical past invoked to a collection, the equivalent of a vast multimedia photo album with witty captions. And the affect produced is . . . curiously flat while simultaneously aesthetically sublime." Bill Nichols' essay on history, representation, and claims for truth is an authoritative survey of the boggy foundations on which so much of documentary's claim to representation rests. He suggests that "disembodied knowledge and abstract conceptualization" are inherently less trustworthy because they do not bring "the power of the universal, of the mythic and fetishistic, down to the level of immediate experience and individual subjectivity."

None of these writers makes easy reading, though Nichols, widely considered the guru of documentary theory, is more accessible here than elsewhere. His *Representing Reality* (Bloomington, IN: Indiana University Press, 1991) is considered the theorist's bible, and his *Introduction to Documentary* (Bloomington, IN: Indiana University Press, 2001) summarizes the earlier book's ideas in a more accessible style. Both books are analytical and philosophical and not prescriptive.

There are many anthologies that focus on a particular film, filmmaker, issue, or historical movement. Alan Rosenthal is a filmmaker whose production experience, clear writing, and long and scholarly commitment to documentary make his anthologies especially valuable. His mission has been to interview key critics and filmmakers. *The New Documentary in Action* (1971), *The Documentary Conscience* (1980), and *New Challenges for Documentary* (1988)—all published by the University of California Press—add up to a superb compendium of thought and documentary experience. *New Challenges for Documentary* is the most stimulating and provocative collection imaginable for anyone engaged in production. In upward of 600 pages its 35 writers grapple with an encyclopedia of documentary issues. The classifications here are my own.

Rights, Violations, and Veracity
- Protecting one's subjects from themselves
- Documentary ethics, the right of privacy, the prevalence of victimhood, and "using human beings to make a point"
- Truth claims based on arguments and evidence; vérité and the public's right to know

Politics and Control

- Women and minorities: raising consciousness; feminist documentary's theories and strategies; gay issues
- How impassioned, politically motivated films can fail through poor craft
- Political myths: how life and "politics" are inseparable
- How "the western world created image-producing technologies . . . to control reality by capturing it on film"

Issues of Form

- Legitimacy of drama documentaries; the dispute about how material is presented
- Traps and troubles in making the controversial series, *An American Family*
- Poetic documentary as opposed to talking-head loquacity
- Ethnographic filmmaking practices
- Exploitative cinéma vérité and audience voyeurism
- Documentary conventions that need to be abandoned

Issues of Authorship

- Reflexivity as "created, structured articulations of the filmmaker and not authentic, truthful, objective records"
- The filmmaker's own voice, and presenting one's own opinions rather than being a conduit for that of others
- The technologically produced image as a construct "of someone who has a culture, and often a conscious point of view"
- The conflict between the actuality of lives and the aesthetic needs of the portraying artist
- Wiseman as an analyst of American society
- Ivens and filming the Chinese cultural revolution

Institutional Issues

- TV: its "balance" within established structures, legitimizing prevailing interests and neutralizing conflict; its inability to provide context and passion in covering war
- Television's power to imply that a subject is guilty and then manipulate the viewer for entertainment purposes
- The Canadian Film Board

Documentary and History

- The compilation film and leftist history
- McCarthyism, censorship, and blacklisting
- Documentary, history, and the need to entertain; how "changes in documentary strategy bear a complex relation to history"
- Media research

Filmmakers, film theorists, critics, and historians have together acknowledged that intractable and possibly unanswerable questions lie at the heart of documentary practice:

- What constitutes true documentary, during its history and now?
- What work is the documentary meant to do?
- Are documentary's means (intrusions on and exploitation of ordinary people) justified by its ends (doing good, making a difference, etc.)?
- What is the underlying relationship between filmmakers and those on whose behalf we make our films?
- Under what circumstances can a filmmaker truthfully represent another person or group?
- On what grounds do we make truth claims?

If you reread the list substituting the words *religion* for documentary and *priest* for filmmaker, you can see what large parts ideology and belief play in documentary consciousness. The history of religion, and its handmaiden, colonialism, shows how the beliefs of those holding power tend to insulate them from grassroots reality and produce action that is neither moral nor just. For beginning filmmakers the fear of making "mistakes" or repeating history can be paralyzing. This is a pity, because the world badly needs the voice of passionate principle. Critics are important, but committed artists are more so. To become one means at first drawing on the traditions that best serve your needs as a vehicle for expression.

It is better in the end to be clumsily energetic than exquisitely correct—which is to say, silent. To verify and consolidate your commitment, you have only to start making a few short documentaries. Once you have a personal stake in the form, its history and present-day issues will come alive as the context to your own work. Make short films and then see what kind of dilemmas your forerunners faced and how they rationalized solving them.

IT COMES DOWN TO POINT OF VIEW

The works cited put forward fascinating ideas about how politicized the documentary is and how much it is class and culturally determined, both as a tool for social expression and as an art form. Much of the discussion revolves around the fissure that Brecht characterized when he distinguished between art as a mirror held up to society and art as a hammer acting on society to change it. Where you stand will involve your temperament, your background, the kind of change you want to effect, and how you want to go about it. In this, the issue of representation—who can speak for another—looms large. This is natural at a time when the West is moving tortuously toward a form of inclusive democracy that prefers a multiplicity rather than a hierarchy of voices.

Documentaries are, as I keep saying, a construct, and they reveal as much about their makers as they do about their ostensible subject. Like it or not, it is our own assumptions that we put on the screen. To make films intelligently means to examine and evolve who we are and what we believe, which has been this book's contention all along. In a just and open society, every group or motivated individual should be able to represent themselves rather than having to hire an "expert." Once the frontier was literacy (and still is, in too many places); the next frontier is truly democratic representation on the screen. We—whoever "we" are—have to become our own expert.

CHAPTER 9

PROJECTS: CRITICAL WRITING

This chapter is about critical writing as a means to study documentary in depth. It covers

- The benefits of writing and the way it helps you go farther
- Academic writing norms and how to write effectively
- A project for analyzing a film for its structure and style
- A research project in which you develop a point of view on a director's vision and how this connects with his or her life events

Analyzing a documentary and writing about what you discover makes you pay close attention to how every aspect works. In some strange way this lets you take possession of a film. To write is not just to report on what you know, but to set about discovering what it is that you *don't* know. Writing forces the mind to examine itself and then go farther. A friend used to say, "Nothing is real until I have written about it." She was right.

Your job as a critic is to illuminate and enhance a work. If the reader has already seen it, what and how you write should make that reader want to see it again. By writing, you not only travel outward into the film and its context, but inward toward your personal reactions, tastes, impressions, feelings, memories, associations, and biases. Critical writing will develop you as a director because you gain a more detailed and articulate grasp of your own values, and unconsciously you are making resolutions as you go. Small wonder that the French New Wave began as a movement by critics (such as Godard, Truffaut, Rivette, Rohmer) complaining in highly articulate articles about all that was wrong with French cinema of the time.

When you are viewing, be aware of your own interior processes because they are much like other people's and, used intelligently as a key to what you address, will help the reader decipher his or her own responses. Your writing should be in clear, direct, formal, active-voice prose that is well structured, develops your arguments logically, and supports each assertion with concrete examples from the work under review.

Scholarly work should reflect not only the writer's judgments and values, but put them in the context of what other scholars and critics have already said. You can take issue with other writers if you wish. Expect to write and rewrite multiple drafts before you have a "final." Let each draft sit for a day or two in a drawer, or you won't be able to read your work with fresh eyes.

Making a digest of available opinion is not sufficient because the goal is a publishable piece of writing and you must show evidence of original reaction and thinking. Be aware that it is academic theft to use someone else's ideas or observations without citing the author, publication, date, and page number.

Critical or analytical writing should follow scholarly norms, that is, it should

- Give detailed examples from the films or texts to illustrate your views, but doesn't assume the reader knows the films in any detail
- Seek support for its views from other critics but take issue with aspects with which you disagree
- Give citations, either as footnotes or endnotes, for any ideas you have borrowed or any quotations you have reproduced

PROJECT 9–1: ANALYZING A DOCUMENTARY FOR STRUCTURE AND STYLE

In this project you log the contents of a documentary, then write about the way its structure and style make its content available, what thematic statement it makes, and how choices of structure and style may contribute to this. The following should be covered in your essay, but not necessarily in this order:

1. Pick a documentary, preferably no longer than 30 minutes, whose subject you can show is a special interest of yours.
2. Using the Film Analysis Form in Appendix 2 or something similar, log the documentary, stopping after each sequence to record pertinent details. Define the beginning and ending point of each sequence, give it a tag description, and calculate its length in minutes and seconds.
3. Write a brief description of the documentary's content and what it handles.
4. Looking at the flow chart of sequences, describe the film's structure, pointing out what principle or factor seems to have determined the film's organization, and show how and where the film might be divided into acts (see Chapter 5, "The Three-Act Structure"). Consider the length of sequences in relation to what each contributes.
5. Discuss the film's style and what seems to have determined it.
6. Discuss the thematic impact of the film and its overall effectiveness. What made you care about its characters and their situations? What did it make

you feel? What did you learn from seeing the film? Should other people see it, and why?

Assessment: See Project 9–1 in Appendix 1. Be sure to check the assessment criteria before you start writing.

PROJECT 9–2: ASSESSING A DIRECTOR'S THEMATIC VISION

This project asks that you assess the themes of at least two films from a director's body of work and relate them to the director's emerging philosophic vision. If a director works in both features and documentary, you may want to compare films from both genres.

Pick a director whose output you either know or know by reputation and whom you find interesting.

1. View two or more films by the same director.
2. Note what feelings and thoughts the films evoked.
3. Do a bibliographical search and assemble photocopies and Web printouts of any relevant articles or essays by or about the films or the director.
4. View your chosen films again, this time making notes of each sequence's content so that you have a complete running order list. (A *sequence* is a block of material whose unity is determined by a location, piece of time, or subject matter.)
5. Research the director's biography and write a 7- to 10-page essay (typed in double spacing) assessing the themes of the two films and how they fit into the director's life and emerging philosophic vision. Demonstrate the connectedness of his or her themes and vision to two or more of the following, noting in your essay which of these parameters you have chosen:

A. The director's personal and professional history

B. The intention implicit in the films to change the audience's perspectives in a particular direction

C. The degree to which the films' "social awareness" component is (or isn't) revealed organically from within the subject

D. The degree to which the films correctly or incorrectly anticipate audience reactions, especially ones that are biased

E. Visual, aural, or other special considerations of cinema form that you find are successfully or unsuccessfully used

F. The way your own attitudes to the subject evolved as a result of seeing the films and writing the paper

Other (specify)

Assessment: See Project 9–2 in Appendix 1. Be sure to check the assessment criteria before you start writing.

PART 3

IDENTITY AND AUTHORSHIP

Part 3 covers

- Journeying inward in order to recognize your own deepest concerns
- Finding the marks your life has made on you and the themes, characters, and topics that flow from them
- Pitching a subject

- Setting subject, thematic, and social goals for your filmmaking
- Finding your path, losing it, and finding it again as part of the artistic process
- Privacy, competition issues, and dealing with the hostile environment
- Resources for finding documentary stories
- Testing a documentary idea
- Locating and raising story pressures
- Using the medium to stir your audience emotionally
- Testing an idea cinematic strengths
- Subject-driven versus character-driven films, and subjects to avoid
- Displacing your own story and finding its principles at work in others

Parts 1 and 2 outlined the world of the documentary. Now we turn to the interior world where documentary ideas originate. Here, in Part 3, we look at the internal drives influencing all the important choices each of us makes, with the aim of understanding those useful to storytelling through using the screen. This requires that you make a self-survey and from it a working description of your probable identity as an art maker. Please embrace the work in this chapter, for I think you will be glad afterward.

For some—the technically inclined in particular—an inward journey of this kind will seem intrusive or irrelevant. Perhaps they fear there is nothing to find or that it will somehow be embarrassing. This won't be so because you will remain in control throughout.

An artistic identity is, I am convinced, something that everyone naturally possesses, no matter how remote from the arts they may initially feel. "Art work is ordinary work," say the authors of *Art and Fear*, "but it takes courage to embrace that work, and wisdom to mediate the interplay of art and fear."[1]

For further information on issues arising in Part 3, use the Index or go to the Bibliography.

---

[1] David Bayles and Ted Orland, *Art & Fear: Observations On the Perils (and Rewards) of Artmaking* (Saint Paul, MN: Image Continuum Press, 1993), 117.

CHAPTER 10

PROJECTS: RECOGNIZING YOUR ARTISTIC IDENTITY

This chapter covers

- Questions to ask yourself as you seek to define your goals
- A project to take inventory of the marks you carry, the themes they suggest, and the kind of people with whom you empathize
- Your closest issues, finding their equivalencies, and displacing them outward into the world
- A project to locate your other selves
- A project to make use of your dreams and dream imagery
- A project to take stock of your artistic goals
- Sketching out your future path
- Losing and recovering your way, progress, and the artistic process
- Privacy, competition, and hostile environments

By nature, human beings are seekers. For those attracted to the world of the arts, the quest is to find meanings in life—a fundamental and noble human drive if ever there was one. Documentaries are a superb vehicle for this work, and making them will make you feel fully alive, not least because of all the good people you encounter on the road. First, some important questions for you to ponder:

- How should you use your developing skills in the world?
- What kind of subjects should you tackle?
- What are you avid to learn about?
- Do you already have an artistic identity, and can you articulate it aloud?

Do the work in this chapter, and even if you've never done anything you consider artistic before, you will find you have an artistic identity. By this, I mean *a drive to create a sense of order and emotional meaning, for yourself and for an audience, in connection with particular issues* in life. You probably know intuitively that you have this, but you cannot put yours into words. The temptation is to put this off until a better time because your beginning work will only be exercise projects. Most people handle these by taking a worthy subject and putting their effort into capturing it with the camera. This may not seem unreasonable, but something will be missing. You. You will be missing.

Every project, no matter how short or simple, is an opportunity to say something from the heart. "The only work really worth doing—the only work you *can* do convincingly—is the work that focuses on the things you care about. To not focus on those issues is to deny the constants in your life."[2] Marketa Kimbrell, the much-respected film directing teacher at New York University, says, "If you want to put up a tall building you must first dig a very deep hole." She means that a fine acting performance or a superb documentary is always rooted in a strong foundation of self-knowledge. In documentary your job, after all, is to get inside other people's realities and to see the world as they see it. You must become familiar with your own first.

If documentary is indeed "a corner of nature seen through a temperament," it is risky to look outward at "nature" and take no account of the temperament at the controls. If you are to have strong, positive ideas about the heart and mind making the choices, you cannot delay digging until faced with an important challenge. Such life-changing steps are not made at the throw of a switch when you need them: you have to take them incrementally as a series of small decisions, step by step—beginning now.

You will need to look non-judgmentally at whatever tensions, passions, and compulsions you carry, without labeling them "positive" or "negative," because that would be self-censorship. As an *hors d'oeuvre* to this process, here is a small quiz of mine for you to take in private. With complete honesty, rate how true the following statements are for you, with 2 points for "very true," 1 point for "fairly true," and zero for "not true."

	Not True (0 Points)	Fairly True (1 Point)	Very True (2 Points)
I avoid imposing my values on other people's lives			
I never pass judgment on friends and family			
I have taken more knocks than I have delivered			
I seldom see any need for confrontation			
I need people to think well of me			
Total . . . . _____			

---

[2] Ibid., 116.

If you

- Scored above 5, read what follows carefully
- Scored up near 10, read what follows *very* carefully
- Scored below 5, read what follows anyway, in case you are just good at passing tests

The quiz tests self-knowledge as it affects directing. Most people feel they know themselves intimately, but anyone who teaches screenwriting will tell you otherwise, for if this were true there would never be the universal problem of the *passive central character*. How can this happen? It seems that we are very sensitive to how people act on us but blind to how we act on others. As the hero of our own story, we see ourselves as acted upon, not ourselves acting on others. This could either be a psychological survival mechanism or a mindset left over from childhood when we felt very vulnerable.

Whatever the cause, a passive self-image is a huge disability in a storymaker. Trying to animate fictional stories with an inert central character is almost impossible. In documentary, it makes us blind to how our participants are actively making their own destiny. Instead, we see people as victims, which may be how the documentary came to have the "tradition of the victim."[3]

The quiz was meant to reveal how active and intrusive you are able to feel in relation to your surroundings. To begin seeing yourself (and those with whom you identify) as assertive may require changing the ingrown habits of a lifetime. This is some of the work it takes to dig that hole I mentioned earlier.

Creativity in the arts is fueled by active, sustained inquiry, both inward and outward. Acquiring better self-knowledge will always be a work in progress, and each film will be a stage (in both senses of the word) of your development. Selecting subjects, and approaches to subjects, seems easy for those marked by dramatic experience (say, of being an immigrant, of living in the streets, or of family turmoil) for they seldom doubt where their work must go. But for the rest of us, whose lives are less obviously dramatic, comprehending what motivates our sense of mission can be baffling. It's a conundrum; you can't make art without a sense of identity, yet identity is what you seek through making art.

Some choose the arts in order to express themselves, but what they probably want is the therapy of self-affirmation. Therapy is self-directed and aimed at acquiring a sense of normality and well-being. Nothing wrong with that. But making art is other-directed. It's about wanting to do useful work in the world and for the world. To prosper in documentary means contending for what you believe is true and valuable, and for this you need a definite sense of mission.

Documentary is a branch of drama, and for your drama to be original and authentic you will need to develop a dialogue—with yourself, and between yourself and your audience—through the conduit of the stories you choose to tell. You will do this best once you know your hot issues. Once you know them, they will offer endless variations. The work you are going to do and the work you have already done form significant patterns, and these are part of the dialogue too.

---

[3] See Brian Winston, "The Tradition of the Victim in Griersonian Documentary," in *New Challenges for Documentary*, ed. Alan Rosenthal (Berkeley, CA: University of California Press, 1988) 269.

Right now you need to establish what matters to you most, so you can do your best work. Actually, the key to this is already inside you and close at hand. It will reveal itself if—candidly and in private—you make the provisional self-profiles in the projects that follow. Some people will find confirmation of what they expected; others will be surprised (as I was) to discover that for years they have been overlooking the obvious.

FIND YOUR LIFE ISSUES

Finding your central issues begins with discarding everything outside a few strong emotional and psychological concerns. Whatever unfailingly arouses you to these strongly partisan feelings comes from a mark you've absorbed. The marks you carry, and the issues they bring, will be few and personal. Exploring them sincerely and intelligently through your films will deeply touch your audience and keep you busy for life. Unfortunately, filmmakers often seem willing to settle for a superficial understanding of these matters—far more so than writers or painters, for instance. Here are a few projects to help you begin the process of introspection.

PROJECTS

PROJECT 10–1: THE SELF-INVENTORY

To discover your issues and themes, and thus what you can give to others, start with a non-judgmental inventory of your most moving experiences. This should be straightforward, because the human memory retains only what it finds significant. If you already have a good handle on your underlying issues, take the inventory anyway—you may be surprised. Honestly undertaken, this project reveals life events that are key in your formation. Acknowledging them will urge you to work at exploring the underlying issues.

Here's what to do:

1. Go somewhere private and write rapid, short notations just as they come to mind of major experiences in which you were deeply moved (to joy, to rage, to panic, to fear, to disgust, to anguish, to love, etc.). Keep going until you have ten or a dozen.

2. Stand back and organize them into two or three groups. Name each group and define any relationship or hierarchy you can see between them. Some moving experiences will be positive (with feelings of joy, relief, discovery, laughter), but most will still have disturbing emotions attached to them, such as embarrassment, shame, or anger. Make no distinction, for there is no such thing as a negative or positive truth. To discriminate is to censor, which is just another way to prolong the endless and wasteful search for acceptability. Truth is *truth*—period!

3. Examine what you've written as though looking objectively at a fictional character's backstory. By seeing your formation a little objectively, you should find trends, even a certain vision of the world, attaching naturally to these experiences. Be bold and freely imaginative in developing this character's world

view, just as if you were developing a fictional character. Your object is not to psychoanalyze yourself or to find ultimate truth (those would be impossible): it is to fashion a temporary authorial role that you can play with all your heart. Because it's a role, not a straitjacket, you can change it, evolve it, and improve it as you go.

Now write notes that, without disclosing anything too private, will enable you to describe objectively and aloud to a group or class:

A. The *main marks your life has left on you* during formative experiences. Keep your description of the experiences to a minimum and concentrate on their effects, not their causes.

Example:

"Growing up in an area at war, I had an early fear and loathing of uniforms and uniformity. When my father came home after the war, my mother became less accessible, and my father was closer to my older brother, so I came to believe I must do things alone."

B. Two or three *themes* that emerge from the marks you carry

Examples:
"Separation breeds self-sufficiency."
"Someone taking what you value can motivate you to fight for your rights."
"Good work often starts out on the wrong foot."

C. Several *different characters for which you feel unusual empathy.* These can be people you know, types of people, or people who exist and whom you could contact.

Examples:

A friend from an orphanage who had to overcome difficulty with intimacy

A friend who vents his anger through anti-globalization protests

An older woman who fought to regain the job that her boss gave to someone younger

D. Two or three *provisional film topics.* Make them different but all focused on your central concerns. Displacing concerns into other areas of life avoids autobiography and lets you explore new worlds with authority. Choose worlds that reflect the concerns to which you are already committed.

Examples:

Anyone whose existence is complicated by having to keep their his or her secret (such as a gay person in the military)

Someone overcoming a situation where he or she is made to feel unacceptably different

Anyone forced into a lesser role and who finds ways to assert that he or she still has value

PROJECT 10–2: USING DREAMS TO FIND YOUR PREOCCUPATIONS

Keep a log of your dreams, because it is here the mind expresses itself unguardedly and in surreal and symbolic imagery. Unless you have a period of intense dream activity, you may have to keep a record over many months before common denominators and motifs begin showing up. Keep a notebook next to your bed, and awake gently so that you hold onto the dream long enough to write it down. When you get really interested in this work, you will automatically awake after a good dream in order to write it down. Needless to say, this will not be popular with a bedroom partner.

Dreams often project a series of forceful and disturbing images. By keeping track of the dream rather than going straight to an interpretation, you can return and reinterpret as you amass more material. Recurring images are often a key to your deepest thematic concerns.

PROJECT 10–3: ALTER EGOS

Some people believe we each have a single true self, others that we are made of multiple personalities, each evoked by particular circumstances. True or not, the latter view is convenient for storytelling, which is what documentary really is. In this exercise you uncover those characters or situations to which you resonate and supplement what you did in the previous project with an additional and different self-characterization.

1. List six or eight *fictional characters* from literature or film with which you have a special affinity. This becomes more interesting when you respond to darker and less tangible qualities. Rank the characters by their importance to you.

2. Do the same thing for any *public figures* important to you, such as actors, politicians, sports figures, etc.

3. Make a list of influential *friends or family,* people who exerted a strong influence on you at some time. Leave out immediate family (often too complicated because they are too close).

4. Taking the top two or three in each list, write briefly about any *dilemma or predicament they have in common,* and what *mythical or archetypal qualities* you can see they represent.

5. From what you discover from points 1 to 4, *develop an ideal authorial role* that you can describe to the group or class. To direct is to play a role, always. Develop one from your own qualities, but make the role more defined, passionate, and courageous. Don't hesitate to imaginatively intensify the role. The aim is to build a provocative and active role that you can try to uphold as you direct.

6. Describe either in the group or on paper *what kind of work this person should be doing.*

PROJECT 10–4: WHAT IS THE FAMILY DRAMA?

Prepare notes so that you can speak for around 4 minutes on

1. The *main drama in your family*. If there are several, pick the one that affected you most (examples: the impact of the family business going bankrupt, discovering that Uncle Wilfred is a cross-dresser, or the effect on your mother of her father wanting all his children to become musicians).
2. *What you learned* as a result of the way the family drama played out
3. What kind of *subjects you now feel qualified to tackle* as a result

PROJECT 10–5: PITCHING A SUBJECT

Funding agencies and commissioning editors who put support behind some film projects rather than others are extremely influenced by a good *pitch* (oral presentation) because they know how difficult it is to have all your thinking together. Prepare your ideas so that you can make a 4-minute *pitch* of a documentary idea to the group or class. Your words should be colorful and your enthusiasm should convey a clear, almost pictorial, sense of what the film will be like and why it should be made. Rehearse in front of a mirror so that you can make an appealing presentation that includes the following:

1. Outline of the
   A. Background to the topic
   B. Character(s) and what makes him or her (them) special
   C. Problem or situation that puts the main character(s) under revealing pressure
   D. Style of the coverage and the editing
2. Description of any changes or growth you expect during the filming
3. Statement of why it's important to make this film and why you are motivated to make it

Now listen to your audience's comments, take notes, and keep completely quiet! Your film has had its chance to communicate; now study its effect so that you can reconfigure it. This is the first chance to "show" a possible film to an audience and to get a first response.

4. Several days later, pitch your film again, taking into account all the critique that you found useful.
5. Pitch it a third time and see what your audience thought of the latest version. Even if the idea hasn't improved, your delivery of it probably has.
   Make a habit of pitching a new idea every week to anyone who will listen and respond. You will be amazed at how many good ideas you can come up with and how much you learn from doing this. You will only be afraid of having your ideas stolen if you have too few.

PROJECT 10–6: GOALS SUMMARY

To summarize your goals, finish the following prompts:

1. The *theme or themes* that arise from my self-studies are . . .
2. The *changes* for which I want to work are . . .
3. The *kinds of subject* for which I feel most passionately are . . .
4. *Other important goals* I have in mind are . . .

FINDING YOUR WORK'S PATH

The self-profiles with which you have been experimenting should bring you closer to an inner self that is searching for its own artistic path. Your life has given you special understanding of certain forces and the way they work in the world, and this inner force wants you to commit yourself to showing these forces at work and to express what you feel about them.

IF YOU LOSE YOUR WAY

Filmmaking has risks that arise from its social nature. To some degree we all depend on the approval of those we like and respect, so you can lose your own point of view in the face of the orthodoxies and criticisms coming from those around you. Because film is made and viewed collectively, you will need a strong sense of purpose if you are to hold on to the meaning of your own work. Never, ever alter more than small details of your work after criticism until you have had considerable time to reflect.

PROGRESS AND THE ARTISTIC PROCESS

When you engage in work, the work's process will release fresh dimensions of understanding. This is the creative process, something that is cyclical and endlessly fascinating, and brings us closer to others. In documentary the learning process is lengthy and demanding. At the beginning you get clues, clues lead to discoveries, discoveries lead to movement in your work, and movement leads to new clues and a new piece of work in which to evolve them. Work—whether a piece of writing, a painting, a short story, a film script, or a documentary—is therefore both the evidence of movement and an inspiration to continue.

Our work becomes both the trail and the vehicle for our own evolution. We get help at this in mysterious ways. Goethe said, "The moment one definitely commits oneself, then Providence moves too. All sorts of things occur to help one that would never otherwise have occurred." His wake-up call to the procrastinator is delightfully pithy: "Art is long, life short; judgment difficult, opportunity transient."

Finding and acting on the self-discovery material in this chapter means taking chances and trusting that it will lead somewhere. If you work closely with other people (as I hope you do), you will need to take chances, because having people listen and react to your story is vital to discovering and accepting it yourself.

PRIVACY AND COMPETITION ISSUES

The person who chooses to take the bull by the horns and work in the arts cannot logically remain private. In any group you'll see how the people of courage, even when they are shy by nature, go out on a limb while others who make a show of self-assurance are actually too afraid to show themselves. Telling your story to creative partners is important, for we cannot urge liberation on others unless we also work to liberate ourselves.

HOSTILE ENVIRONMENTS

The best school and work situations are nurturing yet demanding, and in them you see people flower and evolve over time. Some, however, do not support the kind of self-exposure I have been advocating. The personal chemistry is wrong, or the environment is dominated by intensely competitive personalities—usually because perquisites, patronage, or other advantages are being held out to favorites. These distortions are a common fact of life, deplorable but something you must find ways to circumvent. You cannot await ideal circumstances before getting down to what's important. Choose your work partners very, very carefully. With a good partner you can handle just about anything.

If you feel you are not making good progress as a film author, don't despair. Do production work for other people. It will keep you in situations of change and growth. Having something to say, and being ready to say it, more often emerges from times of conflict and struggle than it does from comfort and contentment. Overcoming dilemmas and hard times is vital to one's learning and development, something that for the active mind continues from film to film, relationship to relationship, role to role, and cradle to grave.

CHAPTER 11

DEVELOPING YOUR
STORY IDEAS

This chapter covers

- Observing and sorting what takes place around you
- Traditional stories as a source of inspiration
- Oral history as another fund of family stories
- The social sciences and fiction that is developed from actuality
- Testing your own investment in an idea
- Making best use of the medium and intensifying the story you choose

This chapter continues the work of idea development by examining the resources at hand so that you never have to wait for inspiration. In documentary, you can begin research almost anywhere and then confirm and amplify the idea you are developing. Making documentary and writing fiction have something in common. The first step is to find and develop an idea. Writers habitually change hats, and the two they wear most often are "story discovery" and "story development and editing." These modes use quite different parts of your mind. In one mode, you are looking for the subject or topic that will bring a "shock of recognition," and this means freely using imagination and intuition. In the other mode you take what you have initially written and subject it to analysis, testing, and structuring to see how it can be made into the best possible tale for the screen.

Let's first examine where documentary ideas are waiting to be found.

COLLECTING RAW MATERIALS

The seeker is the person committed to searching for meaning among the many baffling clues, hints, and details in life. If you are one, you are probably using some of what I'm about to describe—ways of collecting and sifting material for a story, *the* story you need to tell. When you examine your collection diligently, you will actually see the outlines of the collector, the shadowy Self that is implacably assembling what it needs to represent its own preoccupations, and nowhere more so than in a journal.

JOURNAL

Keep a journal and note anything that strikes you, no matter what its nature. This means always carrying a notebook and being willing to use it publicly and often. If you have a computer, try copying incidents into a simple database under a variety of thematic or other keys so that you can call up material by particular priorities or groupings. A computer isn't inherently better than, say, index cards, except that it lets you juggle and print your collection and experiment with different structures.

Rereading your journal becomes a journey through your most intense ideas and associations. The more you note what catches your eye, the nearer you move to your current themes and underlying preoccupations. You may think you know them all, but you don't.

NEWSPAPERS AND MAGAZINES

Real life is where you find the really outlandish true tales. Keep clippings or transcribe anything that catches your interest and classify them in a system of your own. Categorizing things is creative busywork because it helps you discover underlying structures, both in life and in your fascinations.

Newspapers are a cornucopia of the human condition at every level, from the trivial to the global. Local papers are particularly useful because the landscape and characters are accessible and reflect local economy, local conditions, and local idiosyncrasies. The agony columns, the personals, even the ads for lost animals, can all suggest subjects and characters. With every source, you have possible characters, situations, plots, and meanings to be found.

HISTORY

History doesn't happen, it gets written. Look at *why* someone makes a record or *why* someone writes a historical overview, and you see not objective truth but someone's interpretation and wish to mark or persuade. History is all about point of view—that's why they say that historians find what they look for.

The past is full of great and small figures that have participated in the dramas that interest you. In 1961 the playwright John Osborne explored in *Luther* the predicament of the anti-establishment rebel through the historical cleric Martin Luther. Alan Bennett in *The Madness of King George* (1994) investigated paternal authority as it veers over the brink of insanity. In 1993 Steven Spielberg brought Oskar Schindler alive in *Schindler's List* so that he could explore being Jewish in Nazi-dominated Europe. History is the full canvas of human drama, full of repetitions and thus full of analogs to contemporary situations. Around you there are millions of wonderful stories waiting to be told.

If history excites you, maybe your job is to tell the stories that have force and meaning for you. Do it well and you will move and persuade others to act a little differently ("those who forget history are condemned to relive it").

MYTHS AND LEGENDS

Legend is inauthentic history. By taking a real figure and examining the actuality of that person in relation to the legend, you can discover what humankind fashions out of the figures that catch public imagination. This is the subject of Mark Rappaport's *From the Journals of Jean Seberg* (1995), which uses a look-alike actress to play the part of a hypothetical Jean Seberg, who, instead of dying at 40, looks back questioningly at the parts she played through her life.

Every culture, locality, community, or family has icons to reflect its sense of saints, fools, demons, and geniuses. When you can find them or resurrect them, they make powerfully emblematic film subjects. Myth is useful because it expresses particular conflicts that humans have found enduringly insoluble and which therefore must be accommodated. The human truths in Greek mythology (for instance) do not lead to easy or happy resolution; instead, they leave the bittersweet aftertaste of fate and prove to be unexpectedly uplifting. Yes, we think, *that's* how it is! In Martin Doblmeier's biography *Bonhoeffer* (2001), for instance, we meet the intriguing German theologian who worked his way around to justifying an assassination attempt on Hitler and then was martyred when the attempt failed. The courage to overcome his inherent pacifism, and to weigh one evil against a larger one, makes him a mythical figure at this remove in time.

Each era generates its own myths or regenerates old ones to serve its needs, making them frame contemporary characters and actions that are otherwise unresolvable. This quality of paradox and the unanswerable is peculiarly modern. Virtually every character of magnitude in a documentary is re-enacting one or more myths, so finding out what mythical roles your characters represent is a powerful part of discovering what thematic thrust lies dormant and is waiting to be released in your documentary.

FAMILY STORIES

All families have favorite stories that define special members. My grandmothers both seem like figures out of fiction. One grandmother was said to "find things before people lost them." In all respects conventional, she had mild kleptomania, especially where flowers and fruit were concerned. At an advanced age, during breaks in long car journeys, she would hop over garden walls to borrow a few strawberries or liberate a fistful of chrysanthemums. How a family explains and accommodates such eccentricities is a tale in itself.

My other grandmother began life as a rebel in an English village, became an Edwardian hippie, and married an alcoholic German printer who beat her and abandoned her in France, where she stayed the rest of her life. Her life and those of her children are too fantastic to be credible in fiction, but they would make an interesting documentary. Family tales can be heroic or they can be very dark, but being oral history they are often vivid.

CHILDHOOD STORIES

Everyone emerges from childhood as from a war zone. If you did the creative identity exercise in the previous chapter, you surely wrote down several traumatic things that happened when you were a child and which have become thematic keys to your subsequent life.

One that springs to mind as I write this is when, at the age of 17, I overheard on the studio set a misogynistic comment about my editor. On returning to the cutting room, I naively repeated this to her as something absurd, but she flushed scarlet and sped out of the room to find the person who made the comment. I died several deaths waiting for what I felt sure would be murder and mayhem. What a lesson in the price of indiscretion.

The incident has rich thematic possibilities: we are sometimes spies, sometimes guardians, sometimes defenders, sometimes denunciators. When life hands us power, how should we use it? So many invisible influences direct our destiny. How far have you explored yours? What happened to blast you into a new consciousness?

SOCIAL SCIENCE AND SOCIAL HISTORY

Social science and social history are excellent resources for documentarians. If one of your themes happens to be the way the poor are exploited, you would find excellent studies of farm, factory, domestic, and other workers. With each will be a bibliography to tell you what other studies have been done. The more modern your source, the bigger the bibliography. Many books now contain filmographies too.

Case histories are a source of trenchant detail when you need to know what is typical or atypical. They usually include both observation and interpretation, so you can see how your interpretations compare with those of the writer. Social scientists are chroniclers and interpreters; their work can inform you because they usually are working from a large and carefully considered knowledge base. You can use their work also to tell whether your feelings and instincts in a particular area have support elsewhere.

FICTION

Don't separate and discard fiction because you are working with actuality. Works of fiction are often very well observed and can give inspiring guidance in a very concentrated form. Jane Smiley's *A Thousand Acres* is not only an excellent novel that reinterprets *King Lear* in a rural Midwest setting, it is a superbly knowledgeable evocation of farmers and farming. To read it in association with an intended work on, say, the depopulation of the land as big agribusiness takes over family farms is to be reminded at every level of what a documentary maker should seek.

TESTING A SUBJECT

Testing the power of a subject takes research (to find out what is there) and some self-questioning (to find out if it's for you). Most important is to ask, "Do I *really* want to make a film about this?" An absurd question? Look around and see how often beginners attach themselves to subjects for which they lack knowledge or any emotional investment.

Why do people take on subjects and later lose interest? Television has so conditioned us that we tend to do what's familiar by unthinking reflex. For Americans, "documentary" means those worthy, laudatory reports made to satisfy station licensing requirements that require some socially responsible programming. They often lack critical edge and present a closed, approving view that prevents the audience from making any judgments of their own. No matter how commendable the topic and the judgments, this is propaganda, not real documentary. Good documentaries go beyond factual exposition or celebration: they tackle areas of life that are complex, ambiguous, and morally taxing.

Making a documentary—I want to say this loud and clear—is a long, slow process. Be prepared for initial enthusiasms to dim over the long haul. You must wed yourself to more than a passing attraction. Try asking questions that dig into your own and the topic's makeup, rather as if you were choosing a spouse or a new country of residence.

- Is there an area in which I am already knowledgeable and even opinionated?
- Do I feel a strong and emotional connection to it—more so than to any other practicable subject?
- Can I do justice to the subject?
- Do I have a drive to learn more about this subject?

Honestly answered, these questions flush out one's level of commitment, and this is good, because if you search carefully enough there is a subject or idea that is just right, but you often have to search hard to find it. The drive to *learn* is a very good indicator that you will sustain interest and energy. Above all, do not bite off more than you can chew—a common impulse. Simple economics will keep you out of many topics because they are only open to large companies. For example, a biographical study of a movie actor would be impossible without corporate backing because the actor's work is only visible in heavily copyrighted works.

Another kind of inaccessibility may arise when you choose an institution as your subject. To film the police or the army, for instance, would be insurmountably difficult without very high-level approval. Even a local animal shelter may be hedged around with politics and suspicions. Most institutions have nothing to gain from letting in filmmakers who might dig up, or manufacture, damaging evidence. Some institutions make fascinating topics for films, but many don't because they are unremarkable. A film merely confirms what commonsense would expect, and what use is that?

Narrow your sights and pick a manageable subject area. You get no awards for failed good intentions, so treat yourself kindly and take on what matches your capabilities and budget. Not for a moment need this confine you to small or insignificant issues. If, for instance, you are fascinated by the roots of the war in Afghanistan but you have no access to combat or archival footage, there are always other approaches open to the inventive. You might find that the man who sells newspapers on your street corner is a Gulf War veteran with a fascinating and representative experience. You may then find that he has a network of friends who have snapshots, home movies, and mementos. Now you can make your tale about how Everyman goes to war believing he's defending freedom.

Ingenuity and being ready to reject the obvious is the way to refine good subjects. Be aware that your first and immediate ideas for a subject are generally those everyone else has already had, so to avoid clichés ask yourself the following:

- What is this subject's underlying significance to me?
- What do most people—people like myself—already know?
- What would I—and most people—like to really discover?
- What is unusual and interesting about it?
- Where is its specialness really visible?
- How narrowly (and therefore how deeply) can I focus my film's attention?
- What can I *show?*

Confronting the personal impact of a subject, instead of trying to see everything from an omniscient or audience point of view, usually takes you into new and exciting directions. Trying to discover the unexpected or reveal the unusual is vital if you are to produce a fresh view, and this always seems to involve narrowly defining what you want to show and conversely what you really want to avoid.

You might, for the sake of argument, want to make a film about inner-city life. But trying to cover too many aspects will lead to lots of thinly supported generalizations, which any mature viewer will reject. On the other hand, profiling a particular café from dawn to midnight might reveal much, and in very specific terms.

Think small. Think local. There are many good films to be made within a mile or two of where you live. Most people do not think of exploiting their own "turf." *Think small and local, and think short.* Try your skills on fragments at first, or risk being overwhelmed and discouraged.

LOCATING THE STORY PRESSURES AND "RAISING THE STAKES"

In every story there is something at stake for the central character or characters, those folks who are trying to do, get, or accomplish something. Raising the stakes might mean

- Sending canoeists through the banks of a river narrows where the water runs faster and more dangerously
- Reducing the rations for a long journey so that the travelers have less to carry but less margin for delay or accidents
- Seeing rain beginning to fall on mountain climbers

- A stock-market plunge for a business that is in danger of going broke
- An emotional setback for somebody taking an important exam
- The snowstorm for Nanook

You get the idea. Raising the stakes means considering (and sometimes contriving) what would make things more difficult for whatever person or group you are showing in struggle. A skilled storyteller always tries to figure out *what would make the central characters play for higher stakes*, a favorite Hollywood screenwriter's expression derived from gambling. The more there is at stake, the more the players care about succeeding, and the more compelling and important the game becomes for all concerned.

In Mohsen Makhmalbaf's semi-documentary *Kandahar* (2001), the Canadian/Afghan central character is trying to get to Kandahar by road to stop her sister from committing suicide. Every impediment she meets is an agonizing delay, and each puts her sister's life in more danger. The source of tension for the striking coal miners in Barbara Kopple's *Harlan County, USA* (1976) is over establishing the right to a union and bargaining for more human conditions. The stakes rise when company thugs snipe at the crew in the dark, eventually putting a bullet through one of the dissident miners. The tension in Jacques Perrin's *Winged Migration* (2001), in which birds fly through all weathers and temperatures, is the gamble the birds take to complete their migration and thus find food and climate to survive. Some do not make it, dying of exhaustion along the way—Mother Nature's pitiless test of competency.

In each case, new circumstances provide greater pressure, more hazards, more "tests" that the hero in folk stories must always face as he—actually he, she or it, of course—undertakes the epic journey.

As you plan a film, ask what might legitimately increase obstacles and raise the stakes for your central characters before our very eyes. Knowing this, you can figure out

- What obstacles your protagonist(s) will face
- Whether it will happen spontaneously
- What you may need to do if your camera is to be in the right place at the right time
- Whether you can legitimately arrange things to optimize your chances
- How to film appropriately and with the greatest credibility

Contriving things can sometimes get you into trouble. In John Schlesinger's lyrical *Terminus* (1961), a "city symphony" documentary about the events and rhythms in a great London train station, a small boy gets lost. His fright and misery are horribly credible as a policeman takes him to the stationmaster's office to await his mother. But this event was contrived, Flaherty style and with the mother's agreement. Afterward when the facts emerged, Schlesinger was strongly criticized for improving his film at a child's expense. Incidentally, Nick Hale, who had been the camera assistant, encountered the boy after he had grown into a man. He was amused that people had worried about this and was sure the experience had done him no harm!

If you believe that your job is to raise the dramatic temperature for the audience and to make them care about the characters and their issues, you must

- Set ethical lines that you won't cross, but not let this utterly inhibit experiment. Remember, you don't have to show everything you shoot.
- Search out situations, during research or while shooting, that build a picture of the pressures on the central characters and their situation
- Anticipate the audience's needs and questions and make sure you shoot whatever will answer them
- When important situations fail to develop or resolve, be ready to help things happen by contriving events or confrontations, *but only if it's ethical.*
- Raise the stakes only when you (a) have the permission of those involved or (b) can obtain their agreement afterward that your intercession was legitimate. Before it showed anything publicly, *Candid Camera* always sought written permission from the targets of its hilarious practical jokes.
- Try not to alienate participants or audience by injecting what is false. There may be no way back into favor.
- Don't let political correctness prevent your taking the occasional gamble. Nothing ventured, nothing gained.

USING THE MEDIUM TO STIR FEELINGS

WHY THE AUDIENCE MUST EXPERIENCE FEELING

Documentary should act on our hearts, not on our minds alone. It exists not just to inform us about something but *to change how we feel about it too.* For example, you can know that women's compositions are seldom played and that virtually no women conduct orchestras, and yet have no special feelings about this—after all, the world abounds with far worse injustices. *Antonia* (1974) by Jill Godmillow and Judy Collins will change that. The makers draw us into greatly liking and identifying with Antonia Brico, who has all the qualifications to conduct an orchestra except one: she is not a man. This is just one woman's heartbreak, but I think of her every time I enter a concert and look to see whether leadership roles are still unbalanced. Mostly they are.

THE SHOCK OF RECOGNITION

The veteran BBC producer Stephen Peet believes that the best documentaries deliver an emotional shock. This could happen in one memorable scene or it could be the sum of a whole biographical film, as in *Antonia*. To fully use documentary's potential means going beyond the vital facts and opinions and producing *evidence that will make a strong emotional impact.*

PRIMARY EVIDENCE

"What can I show?" is the key issue, for the screen really is different from other forms of persuasion. Film portrays people and situations by externals, by what can be seen in action. Descriptions of feelings or events do not move us to strong feeling as people seen living through them do. We want primary evidence, things seen in motion, not hearsay evidence at secondhand. Doing and feeling are more interesting, more inherently credible, than talk about doing or feeling. Can you position yourself to collect primary evidence? Can you press your participants to share their feelings and not just facts? Can you film material to tell a story with hardly any narrating speech?

LECTURING LACKS IMPACT

True, some subjects cannot be anything other than talking heads, and under the right circumstances a talking head film can be incredibly dramatic. But for many topics, that should be the option of last resort. Why do we so easily conceive ideas in terms of speech instead of action and image? Perhaps we are all too deeply indoctrinated with show-and-tell so that you begin from an abstraction and then reach for an image that will illustrate it. Imagine *Nanook of the North* made by journalists; the film would be based on narration, interviews, or a reporter, and it would use small pieces of action as cutaway illustrations.

TESTING FOR CINEMATIC QUALITIES

A tough discipline while developing a film idea is to *tell yourself that you must make a silent film.* Whether or not you have the action, behavior, and images to do this will reveal whether you are thinking like a journalist or like a filmmaker. To be cinematic you must chronicle and narrate using the camera rather than speech. *Behavior, action, and interaction on the screen invoke our thoughts, feelings, and judgments.* This is always more effective. It means you must comb living reality for ideas already symbolized and incipient. When your search is successful, the action of each shootable scene will impart a clear, strong feeling and will imply an idea. Mikael Wiström and Peter Östlund's *The Other Shore* (1992) returns after many years to visit Mikael's godchild, the daughter of a Peruvian couple he had photographed living on a rubbish tip. The appalling conditions of poor people and the recurring images of scavenging, ownerless dogs make description or corroboration in words unnecessary.

MOOD MATTERS

Good cinematography and good action tend to create a strong *mood.* This predisposes viewers to enter the movie wholeheartedly and opens them to a film's more abstract values. Once a film is freed from the tyranny of the interview peppered with what people call *B-roll* (illustrative footage), it can become more sensual, more lyrical, and more sensitive to atmospheres, lighting, and small but significant details. These build the strong aura of subjectivity that viewers will recognize from personally felt experiences of their own.

B-ROLL BLUES

Documentary units are often sent out to "collect B-roll," which means getting illustrative material for something that has been, or will be, said. Frankly, I loathe the term *B-roll* with a passion. It assumes that the function of images is to enhance something spoken. The B-roll idea belongs in the lecture hall, science lab, newspaper, Web site, classroom, hack TV show, and government agency, but it's alien to screen art. Besides, slotting words and pictures together smacks of facile TV, and the whole technique lacks credibility. It's so easily manipulated that we instinctively distrust it.

LOCAL CAN BE LARGE

Make films that are thematically large enough for the outside world and not just aimed parochially at capturing the approval of your locality or peer group. You can, however, take the most localized material and, if your eye is wise, reveal universal truths. This is not easy, and solutions come from developing ideas from what the situation suggests. Figuratively speaking, this is like starting out blind and willing yourself to see better and better. At any moment you always want to give up and say, "Hell, this is all that exists." But it seldom is. This, in fact, is only what you have seen so far. There is always more to see and farther to go.

SUBJECT-DRIVEN VERSUS CHARACTER-DRIVEN FILMS

One way to avoid the didactic film, which lectures or illustrates concepts, is to spurn messages altogether and look instead for characters of magnitude. By this I mean persons of spirit and energy who are trying to get or do something appreciable in the world. The essence of drama is effort and opposition. The lives and behavior of people with these qualities always suggest ideas and thematic meaning if you dig for them.

A strong character, one who is making waves in the world, always comes with strong issues. The issues may be connected with blood relations, regaining something, revenge, justice, redemption, letting go, taking back . . . anything. You have to find what the person's issues are and conceive a film that charts them in action, clarifies their nature, and suggests their meaning. A whole structured film can come from the imperatives of character.

The Swedish *Mods Trilogy* (1968–1993) by Stefan Jarl with Jan Lindqvist follows a group of Stockholm working class dropouts for a quarter century, concentrating eventually on Kenta Gustavson and Stoffa Svensson.[1] Their rebellious, pleasure-seeking lives are partly the fashion of the 1960s but are also, we gradually come to realize, the product of a Scandinavian drabness that goes hand in hand with puritanical values and refuge in booze. As the two characters lose control of their lives, we learn about their fractured, self-destructive families and the fatalism that makes the youths embrace the fate of their parents. Strangely but hopefully, Kenta and Stoffa's son and daughter have instead charted orderly, constructive lives for themselves and do not feel doomed by their parents' choices.

[1] *They call Us Misfits* (1968), *A Decent Life* (1979), and *The Social Contract* (993).

These three somber films are about character—individual, national, and generational—subsisting and protesting within the pervasive influence of streets, cityscapes, and working-class culture.

SUBJECTS TO AVOID

Many subjects come to mind easily because they are in our immediate surroundings or are being pumped up by the media. Stay away from

- Worlds you haven't experienced and cannot closely observe
- Any ongoing, inhibiting problem in your own life (see a good therapist; you won't find any solutions while trying to direct a film)
- Anything or anyone that is "typical" (nothing real is typical, so nothing typical will ever be interesting or credible)
- Preaching or moral instruction of any kind
- Films about problems for which you already have the answer (so does your audience)

DISPLACE AND TRANSFORM

After a period of careful inquiry and reflection, take your two or three best subjects and, even though they feel temporary and subject to change, assume they are your own real ones. If you are working directly from events and personalities in your own life, try to find others with similar situations so that you can *transform what's on the screen and move to a useful distance from the originals*. This has numerous benefits. It frees you from self-consciousness and allows you to tell all the underlying truths instead of only those palatable to friends and family. Most importantly, it allows you to concentrate on dramatic and thematic truths, instead of getting tangled up in issues of biographical accuracy.

Every film I have ever made has been about imprisonment and trying to escape. It was many years before I realized this. A colleague said that underlying all his films has been the search for a father (his own died when he was young). We are all marked in particular ways, and we are all deeply moved and motivated by this. Direct autobiography is usually inhibiting, but any of the analogs can be freeing and fascinating.

Research, development, and writing a proposal for a chosen subject are handled in Part 5: Preproduction.

FURTHER READING

Two other books of mine whose approach to story development may usefully complement the one above are:

- Michael Rabiger, *Developing Story Ideas* (Boston: Focal Press, 2000). Contains many resources and projects, and some nonfiction and documentary.

Describes the principles of drama, dramatic terminology, and critical methods.

- Michael Rabiger, *Directing: Film Techniques and Aesthetics*, 3rd ed. (Boston: Focal Press, 2003). This is the fiction counterpart to the book you are holding. Useful to a documentarian for making comparisons with the fiction process or if you are considering the move from documentary to fiction.

Highly recommended:

- Jed Dannenbaum, Carroll Hodge, and Doe Mayer, *Creative Filmmaking from the Inside Out: Five Keys to the Art of Making Inspired Movies and Television* (New York: Simon & Schuster, 2003). Considers the creative process under Introspection, Inquiry, Intuition, Interaction, and Impact. Contains interviews about their beliefs and approaches with prominent creative figures in both fiction and documentary. The book is particularly good on how filmmakers unconsciously include the values and ethics inculcated in them and which may be quite antithetical to their conscious intentions.
- Christopher Vogler, *The Writer's Journey: Mythic Structure for Storytellers and Screenwriters* (Studio City, CA: Michael Wiese Productions, 1992). Developed for filmmakers from Joseph Campbell's *The Hero with a Thousand Faces*, this shows how pervasive certain elements are in most of the stories that surround us, and this should help you see them around you as they are being lived in actuality.

Part 4 Contains

- An unconventional screen grammar that relates camerawork and editing to human processes of perception, observation, and memory
- Analysis projects in composition, editing, and lighting to help you master how other people's screencraft works
- Basic shooting projects to help you understand:
  - Sound in theory and practice
  - Camera handling in theory and practice
  - Tripod shooting
  - Handheld shooting

This part deals with the nuts and bolts of screen language and argues that film language is derived from evolving notions about human perception. Your filmmaking will benefit from seeing how everyday life is processed by your own consciousness and seeing how to translate this into film language, especially when you are handling or directing a camera. There follow a series of analytical and shooting projects, to reinforce theory with practice. Hands-on practice will help you internalize these as experience and will help make the necessary skills and reflexes available intuitively when you need them.

For further information on issues arising in Part 4, use the Index or go to the Bibliography.

CHAPTER 12

SCREEN GRAMMAR

This chapter covers

- The evolution of screen language, and how film truth is sometimes literal and sometimes poetic and nonliteral
- Juxtaposing shots and ideas, the basics of editing
- Different kinds of axes in a scene and your camera's relationship to them
- Passive and active forces in a scene and how this affects an observing camera
- Subtext—whatever important is at work below the surface
- Movement and direction on the screen
- Why multiple angles work in storytelling
- Subjectivity and abstraction, and how long we observe any scene
- Visible and invisible transitions between events

Don't bypass what follows here under the impression that it's just another screen grammar. It isn't. Rather, you'll find here a fresh and personal approach to film language. It will help anchor you in your own way of seeing and keep you from being swept into anonymity by the orthodoxies attached to film technique. Making films must always be about communicating with your audience members. They imbibe film as they do music, not for a demonstration of theories or technical virtuosity but to enter promising realms of experience, idea, and feeling. Film gives you the tools to take them there, and this chapter explains how much film language is really an analog for human perception, action, and reaction. Never let go of this idea, and your filmmaking will come from the heart as well as the head.

Like all languages, film has its own grammar and conventions. They began developing in the 1890s, when the early actors and cameramen (and eventually directors) competed to put simple stories before audiences. At first their films were naïvely simple, but within a couple of decades, and in spite of the absence of sound, they invented most of the screen language that we now take for granted. In the various filmmaking centers of the world, each group separately found out by trial and error what worked for audiences, with the Russians alone making a concerted effort in the 1920s to formulate what the screen could do. In fact, theory among working filmmakers is still notable for its absence. We should not be surprised, because spoken languages of great subtlety flowered long before anyone thought of philology.

Film language is a set of collectively generated conventions that enable us to tell each other stories through the orchestration of images, actions, sounds, and words. It exists because human beings of every culture share complex processes of perception and logic. Those in the time arts who routinely make creative decisions—at no matter what level of sophistication—focus most of their discussion on how each aspect of drama "works." Over and over again, the criterion applied to an action, a shot, a line, or a character's motivation is whether it "works."

The implication is important. Artistic decisions in film are made in the light of shared instincts of recognition. Were it otherwise, cinema and other time arts could not exist and still be less what they are, a universal language.

Most people learn film technique by copying other filmmakers. This is as natural and as risky as actors studying other actors. So heed Stanislavsky's warning that actors should search for the roots of their craft in life itself, not among other actors. Your ideas, feelings, and observations about life should be paramount. Make your screen techniques stay true to what you have lived and how you lived it. Do not mimic other filmmakers. Language exists to accomplish, get, or do what we need. My elder daughter's first sentence was "Meat, I like it." Language is a tool to do or get something (more meat), and film language is a tool to understand the world, then act on it (*give* me more meat).

From this rather fundamental perspective, let's look at the different units of film language.

THE SHOT

A shot is a framed image placed on record by someone to whom it holds some meaning. If you view someone else's *rushes* or *dailies* (i.e., footage straight out of the camera), you find yourself constantly trying to figure out what the makers (camera operator and director) were thinking, feeling, and seeking. You assess this not only from what is in the shot but also *from what it excludes*. A shot of a man staring offscreen may exclude what he sees and, in the process, focus us on how, rather than what, he is studying.

The more remote the film is in time and place, the easier it is to see filmmakers searching to construct meanings and to see how susceptible they were to the received wisdom of the day. Old films about rural workers or aboriginal peoples treat them like children who are unable to speak for themselves. We are apt to smile, secure in our knowledge that filmmakers are more sophisticated today. Then we may accept without question that some present-day footage is objective and value free.

But records, whether of actuality or of life enacted or re-enacted, are always *constructs*. Records are not given, they are taken, and the word warns how subjective is the heart and mind that do the taking. A movie record always invokes a triangular relationship between content, storyteller, and viewer. The storyteller *takes* from the documentary's "corner of nature" in order to *give* something to the audience.

Imagine you are hunting through archival shots in a film library, as I once did at the Imperial War Museum in London (www.iwm.org.uk). After you recover from the atmosphere of a place so packed with sad ghosts, you notice from the library stockshots that by today's standards their cameras and film stock were less developed. Even so, each shot in addition to its subject testifies to different kinds of involvement by its makers, that is, they evidence different emotions, emphases, and agendas.

Imagine you run a shot labeled, "Russian soldiers, vicinity of Warsaw, running into sniper fire." From the first frame you notice how emotionally loaded everything seems: it's shot in high contrast black-and-white film stock that accentuates the mood, and the air is smoky because lighting comes from behind the subjects. Though here, as elsewhere, filming is undeniably a mechanical process of reproduction, everything is polarized by the interrelationship of human choice, technology, subject, and environment, and all of these things are contributing to what you feel. The camera enters the soldiers' world because it runs jerkily with them instead of shooting from a sheltered tripod. You catch your breath when a soldier falls because the cameraman almost trips over his fallen comrade. The camera recovers and continues onward, leaving the wounded soldier to his fate. Then suddenly it plunges to the ground. The clockwork camera motor runs out while framing some out-of-focus mud. With slow horror you realize you have just accompanied a cameraman in his last seconds of work. Desolated, you replay his shot several times and notice that when you hold on particular frames, it seems as though time and destiny can be halted and replayed, re-entered, and relived. Back up, and your cameraman is still alive, still pressing forward, and then he dies—again. Even when you replay something and "know" what's going to happen, *film is always in the present tense.*

Now someone brings you a photo of a dead cameraman lying face down on the battlefield, his camera fallen from his hands. It's him. Your poor cameraman. You recognize the knob of mud from his last seconds of film. Left alone with him, you swallow hard and ponder what made him gamble his life to do this work. Who did he leave behind, and did they learn how he really died? You are alone with him as his witness, but you have also *become* him, taken on his destiny. He will always be with you, somewhere inside, informing your choices. You have grown and will always *be* him, somewhere in the recesses of your being.

Really, a shot's meaning can go very far beyond its subject.

SHOT DENOTATION AND CONNOTATION

If you can identify a shot's content you know what a shot denotes, but to grasp its connotations means looking beyond surfaces and interpreting how and why it might be used to imply more than it depicts. This speculation, in turn, prompts us to wonder about the heart and mind behind the shot's making. This is very obvious when a shot communicates the death of its maker, but much less so when we see calm shots of a flower or a hand lighting a candle. The shots *denote* a flower and a candle being lit, but depending on context, might *connote* "natural beauty," "devotion," or a host of other ideas. Connotation is a cultural activity in which the filmmaker tries to draw the audience along a path of metaphysical speculation.

SHOTS IN JUXTAPOSITION

When two images are juxtaposed, or cut together, we infer a meaning from their relationship. Table 12–1 gives some examples with explanations.

The examples in Figure 12–1 illustrate an engaging disagreement between two early Russian editing theorists. Examples 1 to 5 illustrate Pudovkin's categories of juxtaposition, in which exposition and building a story line are paramount. Examples 6 to 12 show some of the preferred categorizations of Eisenstein, to whom the essence of narrative art lay in conflict and dialectics.

His juxtapositions highlight contrast and contradiction, and argue as much as they inform.

Meaning and signification, like all communication, are culturally based and always in slow but inexorable evolution. The success of signification depends on a collusion between audience and communicator, a conversation via conventions. These have to be learned and agreed and do not always work. For instance, ethnographers have remarked, after projecting edited footage to isolated tribesmen, that their subjects understood the "story" until the film cut to a close-up. The tribesmen then lost concentration because they could not understand why the camera eye suddenly "jumped close." They would have to somehow absorb that a close-up does not collapse space so much as temporarily diminish the field of attention and clear away what surrounds and obscures the center of interest.

But *whose* center of interest? The technically oriented will answer, "the audience's." Our answer will be more complex and infinitely more useful to directing films because it proposes a storyteller role with influence over the audience's perceptions.

Perception by a camera is a mechanical process in which a focal plane is affected by incoming light. Perception by you and me is different because we are always developing intellectual and emotional frameworks within which to organize what our senses tell us. The convention of the internal monologue, or *voice-over*, verbalizes this process. For our purpose, let's say that *perception is the inner stream of ideas, feelings, and reactions that directs our interaction with what we see and hear.* I want to stress that this interior activity is not just passive reaction, for it directs our attention as we move to confirm impressions, hopes, fears, interests, and hypothetical explanations. The object of the oral or literary storyteller is to recapture, sustain, and modulate this vital activity as an entertainment for others.

Film, however, is always taking place in the present tense, so the film storyteller is a presence imperceptibly guiding our attention rather than a reteller who

TABLE 2-1 Pudovkin's Categories of Juxtaposition

	Shot A	Shot B	Shot B in Relation to Shot A	Type of Cut
1	Woman descends interior stairway	Same woman walking in street	Narrates her progress	Structural (builds scene)
2	Man runs across busy street	Close shot of his shoelace coming undone	Makes us anticipate his falling in front of a vehicle	Structural (directs our attention to significant detail)
3	Hungry street person begging from doorway	Wealthy man eating oysters in expensive restaurant	Places one person's fate next to another's	Relational (creates contrast)
4	Bath filling up	Teenager in bathrobe on phone in bedroom	Shows two events happening at the same time	Relational (parallelism)
5	Exhausted boxer takes knockout punch	Bullock killed with stun gun in an abattoir	Suggests boxer is a sacrificial victim	Relational (symbolism)

Eisenstein's Categories of Juxtaposition

	Shot A	Shot B	Shot B in Relation to Shot A	Type of Cut
6	Police waiting at road block	Shabby van driving erratically at high speed	Driver doesn't know what he's going to soon meet	Conflictual (still vs. dynamic)
7	Giant earth-moving machine at work	Ant moving between blades of grass	Microcosm and macrocosm coexist	Conflictual (conflict of scale)
8	Geese flying across frame	Water plummeting at Niagara Falls	Forces flowing in different directions	Conflictual (conflict of graphic direction)
9	Screen-filling close-up of face, teeth clenched	Huge Olympic stadium, line of runners poised for pistol start	The one among the many	Conflictual (conflict of scale)
10	Dark moth resting on white curtains	Flashlight emerging out of dark forest	Opposite elements	Conflictual (dark vs. light)
11	Girl walks into carnival	Distorted face appears in carnival mirror	The original and its reflection	Conflictual (original vs. distorted version)
12	Driver sees cyclist in his path	In slow motion driver screams and swings steering wheel	Event and its perception	Conflictual (real vs. perceived time)
13	Driver gets out of disabled car	Same image, car in foreground, driver walking as a tiny figure in distance	Transition—some time has gone by	Jump cut

Eisenstein's Categories of Juxtaposition

	Shot A	Shot B	Shot B in relation to shot A	Type of cut
6	Police waiting at road block	Shabby van driving erratically at high speed	Driver doesn't know what he's going to soon meet	Conflictual (still vs. the dynamic)
7	Giant earth-moving machine at work	Ant moving between blades of grass	Microcosm and macrocosm coexist	Conflictual (conflict of scale)
8	Geese flying across frame	Water plummeting at Niagara Falls	Forces flowing in different directions	Conflictual (conflict of graphic direction)
9	Screen-filling close-up of face, teeth clenched	Huge Olympic stadium, line of runners poised for pistol start	The one among the many	Conflictual (conflict of scale)
10	Dark moth resting on white curtains	Flashlight emerging out of dark forest	Opposite elements	Conflictual (dark vs. light)
11	Girl walks into carnival	Distorted face appears in carnival mirror	The original and its reflection	Conflictual (original vs. distorted version)
12	Driver sees cyclist in his path	In slow motion driver screams and swings steering wheel	Event and its perception	Conflictual (real time vs. perceived time)
13	Driver gets out of disabled car	Same image, car in foreground, driver walking as a tiny figure in distance	Transition—some time has gone by	Jump cut

FIGURE 12–1

Examples of juxtaposed shots or cuts.

recapitulates events that have passed. You can't retell the present, but you can observe, navigate, and even narrate it, interpreting its potential as it unfolds.

We are going to examine the way this perceptual process works in a notional figure I'll call the Concerned Observer. This person is an involved onlooker who, as he or she sees and hears, forms ideas and anticipations. At a later point we are going to make the Observer into the more directive and participatory Storyteller, whose function, though invisible, is absolutely central to conscious, integrated film directing.

I want to emphasize how constant and important perception really is. Because it is so routine in everyday life, we can be totally unaware of *how* or *why* we observe as we do. Even the word *observe* has misleadingly objective, scientific associations; in reality it is a highly active process and freighted with an intricate interplay of feelings, associations, and ideas—all leading constantly to actions.

THE SCENE AND CAMERA AXES

Next time you are near two people having an animated discussion, notice how your attention shifts from one to the other. Figure 12–2 represents A and B being watched by the observer O. It's useful to think of O as a child, because children are highly observant, have strong emotions, and are often invisible to their seniors. As the Observer, your eyeline moves back and forth, led from A to B and back again as they talk. Your awareness follows the line of tension between them, the active pathway of words, looks, awareness, and volition. This is called the *scene axis* and is really the subject-to-subject axis.

Every scene, in addition to having one or more subject-to-subject axes, has an Observer-to-subject axis. In my example it is at right angles to the scene axis between A and B. This is called the *camera axis* or *camera-to-subject axis*. The term is misleading because it makes it technical-sounding when really it is intensely human. The Observer (yourself watching the two people in conversation, for instance) has a strong sense of his own relationship to each person (his axis), to the invisible connection between them (their axis), and to what passes between them.

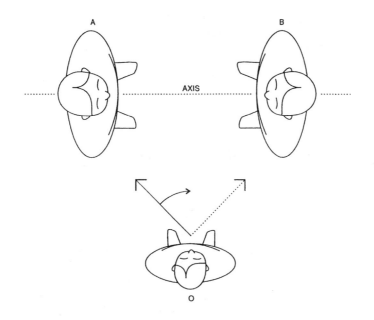

FIGURE 12–2

The Observer watching a conversation.

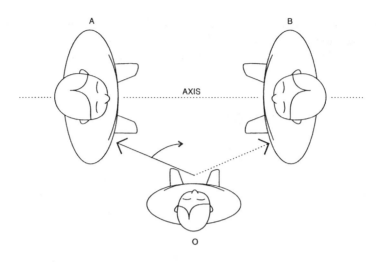

FIGURE 12–3

The Observer moves close to the characters' axis.

In turning to look from person to person, the Observer can be replaced by a camera *panning* (i.e., moving horizontally) between the two speakers. Now let's see in Figure 12–3 what happens when O moves closer to A and B's axis. To avoid missing any of the action, the Observer must switch quickly between A and B.

By blinking their eyes, human beings in this circumstance avoid seeing the unpleasant blur between widely separated subjects. To the brain this produces two static images with virtually no period of black in between. Cutting between two different camera angles taken from the same camera position reproduces this familiar experience. Historically this cinematic equivalent probably emerged when someone tried cutting out a nauseatingly fast pan between two characters. It "worked" because its counterpart was already integral to human experience.

THE ACTOR AND THE ACTED UPON

Listening to a conversation you sometimes merely turn to look at whoever speaks. Other times, when the talk becomes heated, you find yourself looking at the listener, not the speaker. What's going on here?

Any human interaction is like a tennis game. At any given moment, one player *acts* (serves the ball), and the other is *acted upon* (receives the ball). When a player prepares an aggressive serve, our eye runs ahead of the ball to see how the recipient will deal with the onslaught. We see her run, jump, swing her racquet, and intercept the ball. As soon as we know she's going to succeed, our eye flicks back to see how the first player is placed and how she will handle the return. The whole cycle has been reversed because our eye jumps back to the original player before the ball returns.

We monitor every human interaction of any intensity in the same way because we know that, consciously or otherwise, everybody is *constantly trying to get or do something*, no matter where, what, or who the people are. A tennis game ritualizes this exchange as a competition for points, but a heated conversation will be no less complex and structured.

Of course, we nice middle-class people hate to think of ourselves making *demands*. We imagine ourselves as patient, tolerant victims acted upon by a greedy and selfish world. Seldom do we see ourselves as acting upon others, except during our occasional triumphs. But the fact is—and you must take this to heart if you intend to work in documentary, which is a branch of drama— that *everyone acts upon those around them, even when they use the strategy of passivity.*

To the Observer, one person is the actor and the other is the acted upon at any given moment. Often the situation alternates rapidly, but it is via a person's habits of action and reaction that we routinely assess his character, mood, and motives.

Now look at how you watch two people conversing. Your eyeline switches according to your notion of who is acting upon whom. As in watching tennis, you'll find that as soon as you've decided how A has begun acting on B, your eye switches in midsentence to see how B is taking it. Depending on how B adapts and acts back, you soon find yourself returning to A. Once you understand this principle, most shooting and editing decisions will become obvious.

SUBTEXT

While you watch a conversation you search for behavioral clues to unlock the hidden motives and inner lives of the characters. Beneath the visible and audible surface, which we might call the *text* of the situation, lies the situation's *subtext*, or hidden meaning—something we are always seeking. Why do they say what they say, and do what they do? The underlying reasons are the subtext, something developed in drama by the director and the actors, and something continuously developing during rehearsal, shooting, and even in editing. It is the editor's job, in addition to putting the piece together, to liberate those subtextual possibilities that eluded everyone else.

HORIZONTAL MOVEMENT THROUGH SPACE

Dollying, tracking, and *trucking* are names given to any movement where the camera itself moves horizontally through space. In life we are sometimes motivated by our thoughts and feelings to move closer or further away from what commands our attention. We move sideways to see better or to avoid an obstacle in our sightline. Sometimes, in accompanying someone important, we look sideways at them. The point to remember is that camera movements all need *motivation*, either in response to the action or, more interestingly, as part of the strategy for revealing the story that has been adopted by the Storyteller.

VERTICAL MOVEMENT THROUGH SPACE

Craning up or *craning down* is a movement vertically up or down and is similarly motivated. The movement corresponds with the feeling of sitting down or standing up—sometimes as an act of conclusion, sometimes to "rise above," sometimes to see better.

SCREEN DIRECTION

Screen direction is a term describing a subject's direction or movement in a frame, or in a sequence when a subject's movement links several shots, as in a chase (Figure 12–4). An important screen convention is that *characters and their movements are generally observed from only one side of the scene axis.* Let's imagine you ignored this, and in a parade that is going screen left to right (L-R) you intercut it with another set of shots where the parade is going R-L. The audience would see two factions and wait for them to collide.

Now suppose you run ahead of the parade in order to watch it file past a landmark. In the new position, you would see marchers entering an empty street from the same screen direction. But in life you might cross the parade's path to watch it from the other side. This would be unremarkable because you initiated the relocation. But in film to simply cut to a camera position across the axis must be specially set up on the screen or the audience will become confused.

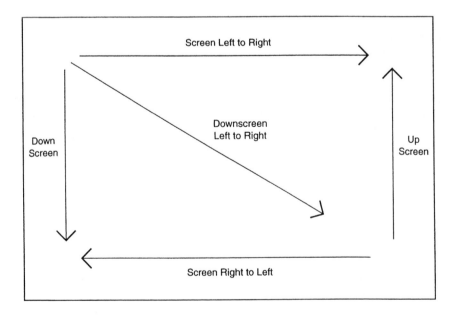

FIGURE 12–4

Range of screen directions and their descriptions.

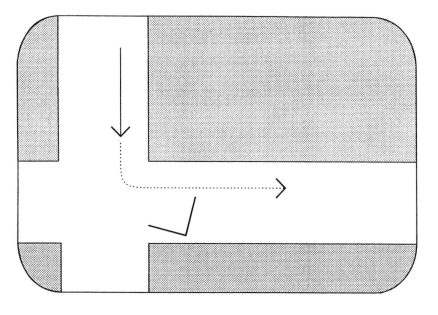

FIGURE 12–5

By shooting at a corner, a parade or moving object can be made to change screen direction.

CHANGING SCREEN DIRECTION

The screen direction of an ongoing event can be altered, but you must see the change onscreen. You can make a parade change screen direction by filming at an angle to a corner (Figure 12–5). The marchers enter in the background going R-L, turn the corner in the foreground, and exit L-R. In essence they have changed screen direction. If subsequent shots are to match, their action will also have to be L-R. Another solution to changing screen direction, during a gap in the parade, for instance, is to dolly so the camera *visibly* crosses the subject's axis of movement (Figure 12–6). Remember that any change of observing camera orientation to the action must be shown onscreen.

DIFFERENT ANGLES ON THE SAME ACTION

So far we have found everyday human correlations for every aspect of film language. But is there one to justify using different angles to cover the same action? We said earlier that cutting together long and closer shots taken from a single axis or direction suggests, by excluding the irrelevant, an observer's changed degree of concentration. But now imagine a scene of a tense family meal that is covered from several very different angles. Although it's a familiar film convention, surely it has no corollary in life. Ah, but wait. This narrative device—

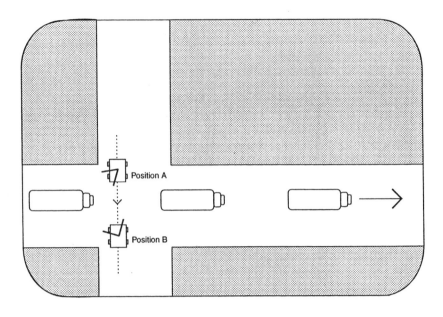

FIGURE 12–6

Dollying sideways between floats in a parade changes the parade's effective screen direction, but the dollying movement must be shown.

switching viewpoints during a single scene—was a prose convention long before film was invented, so it probably has rather deep roots.

In literature, multiple points of view imply not physical changes of location but shifts in psychological and emotional points of view. The same is true when this strategy is used onscreen. But film is misleading because, unlike literature, it seems to give us "real" events. So we must constantly remind ourselves that film gives us a *perception* of events, a "seeming" that is not, despite appearances, the events themselves.

Here's an example you can fill in from your own life. When you're a bystander during a major disagreement between friends, you get so absorbed that you forget all about yourself. Instead, you go through a series of internal agreements and disagreements, seeing first one person's point, then the other's. You get so involved that you virtually experience each of the protagonists' realities.

Screen language evokes this heightened subjectivity by using a series of privileged views. These correspond with the way an observer may identify with different people as a situation unfolds. His or her sympathy and fascination migrates from person to person as events unfold.

What's important in screencraft is that the *empathic shifts must still be rooted in a single "storyteller's" sensibility* if they are to have a naturally integrated feel. By the way, that state of heightened and embracing concentration is not one we normally maintain for long.

ABSTRACTION

The opposite of probing emotional inquiry is withdrawal into mental stocktaking or a state of abstraction. In this mode we alter our examination from the whole to a part, or from a part to the whole. Watch your own shifts of attention; you will find that you often do this to escape into a private realm where you can speculate, contemplate, remember, or imagine. Often a detail that catches your eye turns out to have symbolic meaning or is a part that stands for the whole. Thus, a car door handle near a swirling water surface can stand for a whole flood. This much used principle in film is called *synecdoche* (pronounced sin-eck-dockee). Often our eye is directed toward something symbolic, like the scale that represents justice or a flower growing on an empty lot that suggests renewal.

This act of abstraction can, of course, have different causes. It may not be withdrawal or refuge by the Observer, but rather looking inward in an intense search for the significance of a recent event. Selective focus is a device used to suggest this state. When an object is isolated on the screen and its foreground and background are thrown out of focus, it strongly suggests abstracted vision, as does abnormal motion (either slow or fast). These are just a few of the ways to represent how we routinely dismantle reality and objectively distance ourselves from the moment. We may be searching for meaning or simply refreshing ourselves through imaginative play.

SUBJECTIVITY VERSUS OBJECTIVITY

We experience a world full of dualities, oppositions, and ironic contrasts. For instance, you drive your car very fast at night. Then, stopping to look at the stars, you become aware of your own insignificance under those little points of light that have taken millions of years to reach your eyes. Human attention shifts from subjectivity to objectivity, from past to present and back again, from looking at a crowd as a phenomenon to looking at the lovely profile of a woman as she turns away. Screen language exists to replicate every aspect of an Observer's attention.

In your films, if you make the shifts in the stream of images consistently human, you will create the sensation in your audience of an integrated being's presence—that of our invisible, thinking, feeling, all-seeing Observer.

DURATION, RHYTHM, AND CONCENTRATION

Human beings are directed by rhythms that originate in the brain and control our heartbeat and breathing. We tap our feet to music or jump up to dance when the music takes us. Everything we do is measured by the beat, duration, and capacity of our minds and bodies. The duration of feature films is said to be based on the capacity of the human bladder! Screen language is (luckily) governed by other human capacities. The duration of a shot is determined by how much attention it demands, just as the decision when to cross the road is governed by how long we take to assess the traffic. The speed of a movement on the screen is judged by its context, where it is going, and why.

Speech has inherently powerful rhythms. The Czech composer Leoš Janáček was so fascinated by language rhythms that his later compositions drew on the pacing and tonal patterns of people talking. Films, particularly those with long dialogue scenes, are similarly composed around the speech and movement rhythms of the characters. Here screen language mimics the way an Observer's senses shift direction and reproduces the way we maintain concentration by refreshing our minds through search. These are the most difficult scenes to get right in editing because maintaining a consistency of subtext depends on orchestrating delicate nuances of performance and camera coverage.

Rhythm plays yet another important role in film viewing. Early and enduring stories, such as the Arthurian legends and Norse sagas, were composed in strict rhythmic patterns because it made memorization easier for the troubadours who recited them from court to court. Equally significant is the fact that when spoken language has strong rhythmic structure, audiences can better maintain concentration.

Film language makes use of every possible rhythm. Many sounds from everyday life—bird song, traffic, the sounds from a building site, or the wheels of a train—contain strong rhythms to help in composing a sequence. Even static pictorial compositions contain visual rhythms, such as symmetry, balance, repetition, and opposition—all patterns to intrigue the eye.

SEQUENCE

In life there is a flow of events, and only some are memorable. A story about a whole life only takes the significant parts of that life and bridges them together, as happens when one dreams. The building blocks are segments of time (the hero's visit to the hospital emergency room after a road accident), the events at a location (the high points of his residency in Rome), or a developing idea (as he builds his own home his wife loses patience with the slowness of the process). Because time and space are now being indicated rather than exhaustively played out, the transitions between the building blocks are junctures that must either be indicated or hidden, as the story demands.

TRANSITIONS AND TRANSITIONAL DEVICES

Most of the transitions we make in life—from place to place, or time to time— are imperceptible because we are preoccupied and can drive or walk automatically. Stories either replicate this by hiding the seams between sequences or, when necessary, by indicating or emphasizing them, to draw attention to time having passed. An *action match* cut between a woman drinking her morning fruit juice and a beer drinker raising his glass in a smoky dive minimizes the scene shift by focusing attention on the act of drinking. A dissolve from one scene to the other indicates (in rather dated screen language) "and time passed." A simple cut from one place to the next invites the audience to fill in the blank. However, a scene of a teenager singing along to the car radio during a long, boring drive, followed by flash images of a truck, screeching tires, and the teenager yanking desperately at the steering wheel, is intentionally a series of shock transitions. It replicates the violent change we go through when taken nastily by surprise.

Sound can be a transitional device. Hearing a conversation over an empty landscape can draw us forward into the next scene (of two campers in their tent). Cutting to a shot of a cityscape while the bird song from the campsite is still fading out gives the feeling of being confronted with a change of location while the mind and heart lag behind in the woodland. Both these transitional devices imply an emotional point of view.

All transitions are in fact narrative devices, ways of handling the necessity of moving, montage fashion, between discontinuous time and space. Each implies an attitude or point of view, either on the part of characters or the Storyteller.

SCREEN LANGUAGE IN SUMMARY

Note: The analytical projects in the next chapters are important because they ask you to investigate how screen language is actually used. You will connect ideas about screen language from this chapter with the actual handling of it in a film you respect. Even if you decide not to do the projects, do read through them carefully because they contain much useful information that you will come to need when you direct.

SOUL

Screen language is routinely misunderstood as some kind of professional packaging. Used as routine wrapping for events that an audience will consume, it can easily lack soul. But whenever, as viewers, we sense the integrity of a questing human intelligence at work, life onscreen becomes human and potent instead of mechanical and banal.

Imagine you go to your high school reunion and afterward see what another ex-student filmed with his little video camera. It is his eyes and ears, recording whatever he cared to notice. When you see what he shot, you are struck because his version of the events gives such a characteristic idea of his personality. You see not only who he looked at and talked to, but also how he spent time and how his mind worked. From his actions and reactions, you can see into his mind and heart, even though he mostly says nothing from behind the camera.

Likewise, a good fiction film's handling of its events and personalities creates an overarching heart and mind doing the perceiving.

ENTER THE STORYTELLER

Under the *auteur* theory of filmmaking, the perceiving intelligence behind the making of a fiction film is the director's vision. However, controlling how a whole film crew and actors create the perceptual stream is simply beyond any one person's control, so I prefer to personify the intelligence behind the film's point of view as that of the Storyteller. This is more than the simple "I" of the director or camera operator and more than the reactive passivity of the Observer. It is a fictional entity that is as proactive, complex, and dependent on artistic serendipity as any created by an actor or novelist.

This is also evident in documentary and, to a lesser extent, in other nonfiction forms. All are constructs, even though they may take their materials directly from life. At its most compelling, *screen language implies the course of a particular intelligence at work as it grapples with the events in which it participates.* People who work successfully in the medium seem to understand this instinctively, but if you happen to lack this instinct, simply pattern your work around the natural, observable processes of human perception, human action, and human reaction. You can't go far wrong if you are true to life. As you begin doing this, your film will somehow take on a narrative persona all its own, and this you should encourage.

To prepare yourself adequately for this responsibility, you could either read all of Proust and Henry James, or, if you don't have the time, simply adopt the habit of monitoring your own processes of physical and emotional observation, especially under duress. You will constantly forget to do this homework because we are imprisoned to the point of forgetfulness within our own subjectivity. In ordinary living we see, think, feel, and react automatically and notice so very little. Now compare this with what you are used to seeing on the screen. The camera's verisimilitude makes events unfold with seeming objectivity. Well used, it gives events the force of *inevitability*, like perfectly judged music.

Students often assume that the cinema process itself is an alchemy that will aggrandize and ennoble whatever they put before the camera. But the cinema process is primarily a framer and magnifier: it makes truth look more true and artifice more artificial. Small is big, and big is enormous. Every step by the cinema's makers relentlessly exposes their fallibilities along with their true insights.

Far from automatically delivering objective and inevitable cinema, the process delivers a metamorphosis of scale. Anyone present when something was filmed who later sees the film version has experienced how different it is from on-the-spot impressions. Not only has content been inescapably chosen and mediated by a string of human judgments, it has been transformed by the lenses, lighting, film stock, or video medium used, and even by the context in which one saw the movie (crowded cinema, motel TV, with your family, etc.).

To use the medium successfully you must become a masterly student of the human psyche. You need to know what your audience will make of what you give it. This is rooted not in audience studies or film theory, but in shared instincts about human truth and human judgments.

Let's say it again: a film delivers not just a filtered version of events but also, by mimicking the flow of a human consciousness at work, implies a human heart and mind observing and considering. Screen the world's first filming and the Lumières brothers are palpably present behind their wooden box camera, winding away excitedly at the handle until their handmade film stock runs out. It is through their minds as well as their cameras that we see workers leaving the factory or the train disgorging those passengers at La Ciotat, so unaware of the history they are making.

Film conventions mimic the dialectical flow of our consciousness as we follow something of importance to us. Our emotional responses play a huge part in this by literally directing our sight and hearing. You can test this out. Try noting down what you remember from a striking event you experienced. What most people recall of an accident, say, is highly visual, abbreviated, selective, and emotionally loaded. Just like a film!

CHAPTER 13

PROJECTS: SCREENCRAFT ANALYSIS

This chapter provides study projects and theoretical preparation to help you engage—closely and on your own terms—with prime examples of cinema art. This work will help you study

- The elements of static composition, visual rhythm, dynamic composition, and the compositional interaction between adjacent shots
- Editing, so you can use the conventions, abbreviations, and terminology of film language
- Construction of a whole film, its form and narrative structure, and the compositional elements of its sound track
- The floor plan and its uses
- Point of view (POV) and blocking (arranging camera in relation to the subject and subject in relation to its surroundings)
- Different kinds of lighting, lighting setup, and the effects they create

PROJECT 13-1: PICTURE COMPOSITION ANALYSIS

The object is to study

- How the eye reacts to a static composition
- How the eye reacts to dynamic composition
- Visual elements for composing more consciously

A highly productive way to investigate composition is in a group, but what follows can also be undertaken solo. I haven't found a need to formally log your reactions, although notes or sketches will reinforce what you discover if you are working alone. Help from books is not easily gained because composition texts tend to make the whole business intimidating and formulaic. Trust your eye to find what is there and your own nonspecialist vocabulary to describe it.

Equipment Required: Video or digital video disk (DVD) player, with freeze-frame and variable-speed scan functions. For the best sound, connect the videocassette recorder (VCR) sound output to a stereo, not the monitor. A slide projector and/or an overhead projector are useful but not indispensable.

Study Materials: Any visually arresting sequence from a favorite fiction movie (any Eisenstein movie is a good standby); a book of figurative painting reproductions (best used under an overhead projector so that you look at a big image); a dozen or more 35 mm art slides, also projected as large images (I find impressionist paintings ideal because they usually make an interpretation of a recognizably "real" scene, but the more eclectic your collection the better).

STRATEGY FOR STUDY

If you're leading the group, explain what is wanted more or less as follows:

> I'll put a picture up on the screen. First notice how your eye is drawn into the composition, then what course it takes as you examine the rest of the picture. After 30 seconds or so I will ask one person to describe how his or her eye behaved. Please avoid guessing what the picture is "about," even if it suggests a story. We're interested in how each person's perception worked.

Rotate through the class. Not everyone's eye responds in the same way, so there will be interesting discussions about variations. Out of the general agreement come ideas about visual reflexes and about those compositional aspects that the eye finds attractive and engrossing. After the group has seen enough pictures, ask members to formulate guidelines for framing images so that they lead the spectator's eye.

After the group has worked with paintings, I like to show both good and bad photos. Photography tends to be accepted more uncritically because it seems to have been made with fewer artistic choices. It's interesting to uncover just how much control goes into a photograph that at first seemed like a straight record. Now move the group on to more abstract images, even to completely abstract ones, and let them find the same principles at work.

STATIC COMPOSITION

Here are questions to help you see more critically. Apply them after seeing a number of images, or direct the group's attention to each question's area as it becomes relevant.

1. *Why did your eye go to its particular starting point in the image?* Was it the brightest point? The darkest place in an otherwise light composition? An area of arresting color, or a significant junction of lines that creates a focal point?

2. *When your eye moved away from its point of first attraction, what did it follow?* Commonly lines—perhaps actual ones, such as a fence or outstretched arm, or implied ones, such as sightlines between characters. Some-

times the eye simply moves to another significant area in the composition, jumping from one organized area to another, avoiding the intervening "disorganization."

3. *How much movement did your eye make before returning to its starting point?*

4. *What specifically drew your eye to each new place?*

5. *Are places in your eye's route specially charged with energy?* Often these are sightlines, such as between the Virgin's eyes and her baby's, between a guitarist's eyes and his hand on the strings, or between two field workers, one of whom is facing away.

6. *If you trace out the route your eye took, what shape do you have?* Sometimes a circular pattern, sometimes a triangle or ellipse, but perhaps many shapes. Any shape at all can point out an alternative organization that helps to see beyond the wretched and dominating idea that "every picture tells a story."

7. *How do you classify the compositional movement?* It might be geometrical, repetitive textures, swirling, falling inward, symmetrically divided down the middle, flowing diagonally, and so forth. Making a translation from one medium to another—in this case from the visual to the verbal—helps you discover what is truly there.

8. *What parts do the following play in a particular picture?*
   A. Repetition
   B. Parallels
   C. Convergence
   D. Divergence
   E. Curves
   F. Straight lines
   G. Strong verticals
   H. Strong horizontals
   I. Strong diagonals
   J. Textures
   K. Non-naturalistic coloring
   L. Light and shade
   M. Depth
   N. Dimension
   O. Human figures

9. *How is depth suggested?* This is an ever-present problem for the camera operator, who unless trained otherwise is liable to place human subjects against a flat background and shoot. Without something to suggest a receding space, the screen is like a painter's canvas and looks very much what it is—two dimensional. Depth can be created by angling so that the action takes place in depth instead of across the screen. It is created in composition and lighting by creating a foreground, middle-ground, and background. Those foreground tree branches in an exterior, or those foreground flowers in an interior, are placed to create a plane closer than the subject, which takes place in a middle-ground set against a background—maybe pools of light in a darkened space. Depth is never there unless created.

10. *How are the individuality and mood of the human subjects expressed?* Commonly it's through facial expression and body language, of course. But more interesting are the juxtapositions the painter makes between person and person, person and surroundings, people to the total design. The message here for documentary makers is that framing is arranged—as far as is legitimate—according to an interpretation of the subject's meaning, and composition helps define the subtext. The good camera operator is therefore the person who *sees in terms of relatedness* and uses that vision responsibly to further the ends of the film.

11. *How is space arranged around a human subject, particularly in portraits?* Usually in profiles there is more space in front of the person than there is behind him, as if in response to our need to see what the person sees.

12. *How much headroom is given above a person, particularly in a close-up?* Sometimes the frame cuts off the top of a head or does not show a head at all in a group shot.

13. *How often and how deliberately are people and objects placed at the margins of the picture so that parts are cut off?* By using a restricted frame in such a way, the viewer's imagination has to supply what is beyond the edges of the picture.

VISUAL RHYTHM

I have stressed an immediate, instinctual response to the organization of an image because this is how an audience must read a film. Unlike responding to a photograph or painting, which can be leisurely and thoughtful, the filmgoer must interpret within a relentless onward movement in time. It is like reading a poster on a moving bus; if the words and images cannot be assimilated in the given time, the message goes past without being understood. If the bus is crawling in a traffic jam, however, you have time to see it in excess and become critical, even rejecting, of it.

This analogy shows how there is *an optimum duration for each shot* depending on its content (or "message") and the complexity of its form (how much work the viewer must do to interpret the message from the presentation). Shot duration is conditioned by a third factor—audience expectation. We work fast at interpreting each new image or we work slowly, depending on how much time we were allowed to work on the shots immediately preceding.

The principle by which a shot's duration is determined—by content, form, and the expectation the audience develops from the previous shots—is called *visual rhythm.* As you would expect, a filmmaker can relax or intensify such rhythms like a musician, with consequences for the rate of cutting and the tempo of camera movements. Ideal for the study of composition and visual rhythm are films by Sergei Eisenstein, whose origins as a theater designer in Russia had made him very aware of the impact of musical and visual design on an audience. To this day, Eastern European films, even the documentaries, still show the influence of a strongly formal compositional sense.

Recent feature films incorporating a high degree of stylization, elliptical editing, and a powerful sense of design are Julie Taymor's adaptation from Shakespeare, *Titus* (1999), and Baz Luhrmann's *Moulin Rouge* (2001). These directors

...ir roots in theater and opera, and they show tremendous flair for design, color, movement, and costuming. Both take a zestful and eclectic approach to their stories. Such ebullient formalism is difficult in the documentary, but a strong sense of visual design distinguishes Godrey Reggio's apocalyptic ecology film *Koyaanisqatsi* (1983) and Errol Morris' "documentary noir" (his description) *The Thin Blue Line* (1988).

The *storyboard*'s origins are in designers' sketches and the comic strip. Storyboards are much used by ad agencies and the more conservative elements in the fiction film industry, to lock down what each new frame will convey. Trying to exert such control over the vagaries of the creative process seems rather totalitarian, and, as in politics, there may be a price to pay for making the trains run on time. Needless to say, there is little call for storyboarding in the more spontaneous documentary, which derives so much of its power and authenticity from accommodating the unpredictable. That means, however, that you need compositional and relational skills thoroughly internalized as you shoot. However, if you were to make a film about Chinese brush painting, you might want to match the formalism of your subject, and storyboard design techniques might be useful.

DYNAMIC COMPOSITION

When you work with a moving image rather than a still one, it becomes a *dynamic composition*. More principles come into play and new challenges emerge. For instance, a balanced composition can become disturbingly unbalanced if someone moves or leaves the frame. Even a movement by someone's head in the foreground may posit a new sightline and a new scene axis (about which, more later) and demand a compositional rebalance. A zoom into close shot usually demands reframing because compositionally there is a drastic change, even though the subject is the same.

To study this, use a visually interesting film sequence. A chase scene makes a good subject, and the slow-scan facility on your VCR or DVD player becomes very useful. Determine how many of the following aspects you can see.

1. *Reframing because the subject moved.* Look for a variety of camera adjustments.
2. *Reframing because something/someone left the frame.*
3. *Reframing in anticipation of something/someone entering the frame.*
4. *A change in the point of focus to move the attention from the background to foreground or vice versa.* This changes the texture of significant areas of the composition.
5. *Different kinds of movement (how many?) within an otherwise static composition.* Across the frame, diagonally, from the background to foreground, from the foreground to background, up frame, down frame, and so on.
6. *What makes you feel close to the subjects and their dilemmas?* This concerns POV and is tricky, but, in general, the nearer you are to the axis of a movement, the more subjective is your sense of involvement.
7. *How quickly does the camera adjust to a figure who gets up and moves to another place in frame?* Usually subject movement and the camera's compo-

sitional change are synchronous. The camera move becomes clumsy if it either anticipates or lags behind the movement.

8. *How often are the camera or the characters blocked (that is, choreographed) in such a way as to isolate one character?*

9. *What is the dramatic justification for zeroing in on one character in this way?*

10. *How often is composition more or less angled along sightlines, and how often do sightlines extend across the screen?* This often marks a shift from a subjective to a more objective POV.

11. *What does a change of angle or a change of composition make you feel toward the characters?* Maybe more or less involved, and more or less objective.

12. *Find a dynamic composition that forcefully suggests depth.* An obvious one would be where the camera is next to a railroad line as a train rushes up and past.

13. *Can you locate shots where camera position is altered to include more or different background detail in order to comment upon or counterpoint foreground subject?*

INTERNAL AND EXTERNAL COMPOSITION

So far we have dealt with *internal composition* that is internal to each shot. There is also *external composition*, which refers to the compositional relationship at cutting points between an outgoing image and the next or incoming shot. This is a concealed aspect of film language because we are seldom aware of how much it influences our judgments and expectations.

For example, a character leaving frame in shot A leads the spectator's eye at the cutting point to the very place in shot B where an assassin will emerge from a large and restless crowd. Here the eye is conducted to the right place in a busy composition. Another example of external composition might be the framing in two complementary close shots where two characters are having an intense conversation. The compositions are similar but symmetrically opposed (Figure 13–1).

FIGURE 13–1

Complementary compositions in which external composition principles call for balance and symmetry.

Use your slow-scan facility to help you assess compositional relationships at cutting points. Find aspects of internal and external composition by asking yourself the following:

1. *Where was your point of concentration at the end of the shot?* Trace with your finger on the monitor's face where your eye travels. Its last point in the outgoing shot is where your eye enters the incoming shot composition. Interestingly, the length of the shot determines how far the eye gets in exploring the shot—so shot length influences external composition.

2. *Is there symmetry and are shots complementary?* These are shots designed to be intercut.

3. *What is the relationship between two same-subject but different-sized shots that are designed to cut together?* This is revealing; the inexperienced camera operator often produces same-scene media and close shots that cut together poorly because proportions and compositional placing of the subject are incompatible.

4. *Does a match cut run very slowly show several frames of overlap in its action?* Especially in fast action, a match cut (one made between two different size images during a strong action) needs *two or three frames of the action repeated* on the incoming shot to look smooth because the eye does not register the first two or three frames of any new image. Think of this as accommodating a built-in perceptual lag. The only way to cut on the beat of music is thus to place all cuts two or three frames before the actual beat point.

5. *Do external compositions make a juxtapositional comment?* Cut from a pair of eyes to car headlights approaching at night, from a dockside crane to a man feeding birds with his arm outstretched, and the like.

COMPOSITION, FORM, AND FUNCTION

Because form is the manner in which content is presented, visual composition goes beyond embellishment to become a vital element in communication. While interesting and even delighting the eye, composition in the right hands can be *an organizing force that dramatizes relationships and projects ideas*. It makes the subject (or "content") accessible, heightens the viewer's perceptions, and stimulates critical involvement—like language used by a good poet.

How should one plan a compositional approach? One can first involve oneself with a subject and then find an appropriate form to best communicate that subject. Or, if you are more interested in language than subject, choose your form and then look for an appropriate subject. The difference is one of purpose and temperament.

PROJECT 13-2: EDITING ANALYSIS

The *object* is to

- Learn the conventions of film language so that they can be used with confidence
- Analyze a sequence using standard abbreviations and terminology

- Analyze how a whole film is constructed
- Consider a film's sound track as a composition

Equipment Required: Video or DVD player as in Project 13-1. Your monitor can be a domestic television set, but route the sound into the line input of a stereo system for better reproduction.

Study Materials: Any good live-action documentary—many are now available on tape or DVD at accessible prices. Compilation films (that is, films compiled from archive footage) make heavy use of narration to bind together otherwise unrelated material. They are mainly useful for studying how narration can be written and placed to make sense out of otherwise unrelated shots.

Making a documentary requires that you find a structure for the whole during the editing stage because there is no hard and fast blueprint in the beginning. Individual scenes are constructed—even contrived—out of available material, which may not cut together all that elegantly. The documentary maker's hands are often tied during the shoot by concern for the integrity of actuality, so there are many compromises. A feature recommended for documentarians to study is Carroll Ballard's *The Black Stallion* (1979). Ballard, originally a documentary maker, uses documentary shooting methods to cover free movement. The island scene, where the boy first tames the horse, is superbly lyrical and spontaneous. M. Night Shyamalan's *The Sixth Sense* (1999) also has many sequences worth studying because of the tension it generates and because of its sensitive portrayal of a child's POV.

FIRST VIEWING

Whatever film you choose, *first see the whole film without stopping* before you attempt any analysis. Write down any strong feelings the film evoked in you, paying no attention to order. Note from memory the sequences that sparked those feelings. You may have an additional sequence or two that intrigued you as a piece of virtuoso storytelling. Note these down too, but whatever you study in detail should be something that stirred you at an emotional rather than a merely intellectual level. Now see the film again, stopping to track down where the thoughts and feelings you had are rooted in the movie.

ANALYSIS FORMAT

Before you go ahead and analyze one of your chosen sequences, you may need to review standard film terminology (see Glossary) so that your findings can be laid out on paper in a form that any filmmaker could understand. What you write down is going to be displayed in split-page format, where all visuals are placed on the left half of the page and all sound occupies the right half (Figure 13–2).

It is better to do a short sequence (say, 2 minutes) very thoroughly than a long one superficially because your objective is to extract the maximum information about an interesting passage of film language. Make a number of shot-by-shot passes through your chosen sequence, dealing with one or two aspects of the content and form at a time. Your "script" should be written with wide line spacing on numerous sheets of paper so that there's space to insert additional information on subsequent passes.

Action	Sound
Fade in L.S. FARMHOUSE. EXT. DAY	Fade up birdsong, (music fades in.)
MS Farmhouse, burned out barn in B/G	Karen's V/O: "But I thought you said that whole business was being put off! When we last talked about it, you said..."
Cut to KITCHEN, INT, DAY CU Ted	Ted: "Everything's changed." K: "Everything's changed?"
2S Ted & Karen CU Karen, worried, shocked MS Karen moves L-R to stove MS Ted moves slightly after her	T: "We're not to blame. You know that." T: "There's a buyer . . . (Music fades out) someone's interested."
Karen turns sharply to face him BCU Ted, eyes waver & drop Cut to O/S on to Karen Cut to O/S on to Ted	K: "Ted, Ted! What are you telling me?" K: "You told me . . . (dog begins barking) . . . you promised me . . .
Cut to OTHER SIDE KITCHEN DOOR Anna, 4, clutching Raggedy Ann doll, looking frightened.	(V/O) you said you'd never let the lawyer swindle us out of this place...You said...." Ted's V/O: "The agent said it's now or never. We've got to make up our minds."

FIGURE 13–2

Example of split-page format script.

First deal with the picture and dialogue, shot by shot and word by word, as they relate to each other. The initial split-page script might look like Figure 13–2. Some of your notes, say, on the mood a shot evokes, will not fit into the script format, which must reflect only *what can be seen and heard*. Keep your notes on what the film makes the viewer *feel* as a separate entity. Once basic information is on paper, you can consider shot transitions, internal and external composition of shots, screen direction, camera movements, opticals, sound effects, and the use of music.

MAKING AND USING A FLOOR PLAN

For a sequence containing a dialogue exchange, make a floor plan (Figure 13–3) to determine what the room or location looked like in its entirety, how the characters moved around, and how the camera was placed to show this. Experience at doing this will help you with camera placement when you start shooting.

STRATEGY FOR STUDY

The action side of your split-page log should contain descriptions of each shot and its action. On the sound side note the content and positioning of dialogue, music start/stopping points, and featured sound effects (that is, effects that are more than mere accompaniment).

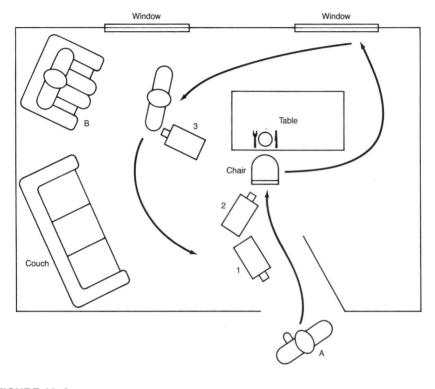

FIGURE 13–3

This floor plan shows the entry and movement of Character A within a room in relation to the seated Character B. The three numbered camera positions cover all of the action.

Scrutinize a film sequence according to the categories listed in the following. The categories are given in a logical order for inquiry, but reorder my list if something else works better for you. To avoid overload, concentrate on a few of the given aspects at a time. Find at least one example of everything so that you understand the concepts at work. If you feel overwhelmed, do only what is rewarding and interesting.

FIRST IMPRESSIONS

What progression of feelings did you have while watching the sequence? It is important to learn to read *from* film rather than read *into* it. Film is a complex and deceptive medium; like a glib and clever acquaintance, it can make you uneasy about your perceptions so that you accept too easily what "should" be seen or "should" be felt. Instead, recognize what you did feel and connect those impressions back to what can actually be seen and heard in the film.

Following are questions to help you round up important information.

DEFINITION AND STATISTICS

What determines the beginning and end points of the sequence?

- Is its span determined, for instance, by being at one location or by representing a continuous segment of time?
- Is the sequence determined by a particular mood or by the stages of a process?

How long is the sequence in minutes and seconds?
How many picture cuts does the sequence contain? Though shot duration and how often camera angles change are aspects of a director's style, they also may be driven by the sequence's content. Try to decide whether the cutting is determined by content or style.

USE OF CAMERA

What motivates each camera movement?

- Does the camera follow the movement of a character?
- Does it lay out a landscape or a scene geography?
- Does the camera move closer and intensify our relationship with someone or something?
- Does the camera move away from someone or something so that we see more objectively?
- Does the camera reveal significant information by moving?
- Is the move really a reframing to accommodate a rearrangement of characters?
- Is the move a reaction, panning to a new speaker, for instance?
- Is the move a storytelling revelation, motivated by an expectant POV rather than content?

When is the camera used subjectively?

- When do we directly experience a character's POV?
- Are there special signs that the camera is seeing subjectively (for example, an unsteady handheld camera for a running man's POV)?
- What is the dramatic justification?

Are there changes in camera height?

- To accommodate subject matter (for example, to look down into a stairwell)?
- To make you see in a certain way (e.g., to look up from child's POV at a stern teacher's face)?

USE OF SOUND

What sound perspectives are used? Does a particular passage of sound

- Complement camera position (near mike for close shots, far from mike for longer shots—replicating camera perspective)?
- Counterpoint camera perspective? (Altman films are fond of doing the opposite—giving us the intimate conversation of two characters distantly traversing a large landscape.)
- Remain uniformly intimate in quality (as with a narration or with voice-over and "thought voices" that function as a character's interior monologue)?
- Intentionally throwaway? (Films as divergent as Elia Kazan's *On the Waterfront* [1954] and Robert Altman's *Gosford Park* [2001] intentionally overload the sound track or let dialogue pass below the threshold of audibility.)

How are particular sound effects used?

- To build atmosphere and mood?
- For punctuation?
- To motivate a cut? (Next sequence's sound rises until we cut to it.)
- As a narrative device? (Horn honks, so woman gets up and goes to window, where she discovers her sister is making a surprise visit.)
- To build, sustain, or defuse tension?
- To provide rhythm? (Meal is prepared in a montage of brief shots to the rhythmic sound of a man splitting logs.)

EDITING

What motivates each cut?

- Is there an action match to carry the cut?
- Is there a compositional relationship between the two shots that makes the cut interesting and worthwhile?
- Is there a movement relationship (e.g., cut from car moving L-R to boat moving L-R) that carries the cut, or does someone or something leave the frame (making us want to see a new frame)?
- Does someone or something fill the frame, blanking it out and permitting a cut to another frame, which starts blanked and then clears?
- Does someone or something enter the frame and demand closer attention?
- Are we cutting to follow someone's eyeline, to see what she sees?
- Is there a sound, or a line, that demands that we see the source?
- Are we cutting to show the effect on a listener?
- What defines the "right" moment to cut?
- Are we cutting to a speaker at a particular moment that is visually revealing, and, if so, what defines that moment?
- If the cut intensifies our attention, what justifies that?

- If the cut relaxes and objectifies our attention, what justifies that?
- Is the cut to a parallel activity (something going on simultaneously)?
- Is there some sort of comparison or irony being set up by the juxtaposition?
- Are we cutting to a rhythm, say, of music?
- Are we cutting to the rhythmic cadences of speech?

What is the relationship of words to images?

- Does what is shown illustrate what is said?
- Is there a difference, and therefore a counterpoint, between what is shown and what is heard?
- Is there a meaningful contradiction between what is said and what is shown?
- Does what is said come from another time frame (for instance, a memory of one of the characters or a comment on something in the past)?
- Is there a point at which words are used to move us forward or backward in time?
- Can you pinpoint a "change of tense" in the film's grammar? (This might be done visually, as in the old cliché of autumn leaves falling after we have seen summer scenes.)

What is the impact of the first strong word on each new image?

- Does it clarify the new image?
- Does it give it a particular emphasis or interpretation?
- Is the effect expected (satisfying perhaps) or unexpected (maybe a shock)?
- Is there a deliberate contradiction?

Where and how is each music segment used?

- How is it initiated (often when the characters or story begin some kind of motion)?
- What does the music suggest by its texture, instrumentation, and so forth?
- How is it finished (often when the characters or story arrive at a new location)?
- What comment is it making (ironic, sympathetic, lyrical, or revealing the inner state of a character or situation)?
- From what sound does music emerge out of at its start?
- Into what other sound does it merge at its close? (Sound dissolves like these are each called a *segue* [pronounced "seg-way"].)

POINT OF VIEW

Here *point of view* means more than just whose eyeline we occasionally share; it refers to *whose reality the viewer most identifies with at any given time.* This is a complex and interesting issue because a film, like a novel, can present

- A main POV (probably through a "POV character")
- The multiple, conflicting POVs of several characters
- An omniscient, all-seeing POV
- An authorial POV

The authorial POV is implied rather than overt, except in documentaries narrated by their directors. Normally POV arises from the situations and how the characters emerge. A film's appearances can be deceptive unless you look very carefully. POV can migrate during a scene, and a multiplicity of viewpoints can contribute richness and variety to figures that, even when secondary or unsympathetic, nevertheless occupy the central character's world.

DEFINING POINT OF VIEW AND BLOCKING

Here are some practical ways of digging into a sequence to establish how it is structuring the way you see and react to the participants. A word of caution, though: you must consider the aims and tone of the whole work before you can confidently specify POV. Taking a magnifying glass to one sequence may or may not verify your overall hypothesis. How the camera is used, the vibrancy of the action, the frequency with which one person's feelings are revealed, and the amount of development the protagonist undergoes all play a part in enlisting our sympathy and interest.

Blocking is a term borrowed from the theater to describe how the participants and camera move in relation to the set. Who and how we see affect where our sympathies go, so blocking cannot be separated from POV.

1. *To whom is* **dialogue** *or* **narration** *addressed?*
   A. From one character to another?
   B. To himself (thinking aloud, reading a diary or letter)?
   C. To the audience (narration, interview, prepared statement)?
2. *How many* **camera positions** *were used?* Using your floor plan, show
   A. Basic camera positions and label them A, B, C, etc.
   B. Camera dollying movements with dotted lines leading from one to another
   C. Shots in your log, marked with the appropriate A, B, C camera angles
   D. How the camera stays to one side of the scene axis (the imaginary line between subjects in a scene) to keep characters facing in the same screen direction from shot to shot. When this principle is broken, it is called *crossing the line*. The effect is disorienting for the audience.
3. *How often is the camera close to the crucial axis between characters?*
4. *How often does the camera* **subjectively** *share a character's sightline?*
5. *When and why does it take an* **objective** *stance to the situation* (either a distanced viewpoint or one independent of sightlines)?
6. **Character blocking:** *How did the characters/camera move in the scene?* To the location and camera movement sketch you have already made, add dotted lines to show the participants' movements (called *blocking*). You can use different colors for clarity.

7. *What **point(s) of view** did the "author" engage us in?*
   A. Whose story is this sequence if you go by gut reaction?
   B. Taking into account the angles on each character, whose POV were you led to sympathize with?
   C. How many viewpoints did you share? (Some may have been momentary or fragmentary.)
   D. How much are audience sympathies structured here by camera angles and editing?
   E. How much are sympathies molded independently by the action or the situation itself?

For a more extended discussion, see Point of View in Chapter 4 (Evidence and Point of View in Documentary).

PROJECT 13-3: LIGHTING ANALYSIS

The object of this project is to

- Analyze common lighting situations found in both fiction and nonfiction films
- Understand what goes into creating a lighting mood

Equipment Required: VCR or DVD player as mentioned previously. At first, turn down the monitor's color control so that you can see light distribution in a black-and-white picture. Adjust the monitor's brightness and contrast controls so that the greatest range of gray tones is visible between video white and video black.

Study Materials: Any fiction or documentary film having a range of lighting situations, that is, interiors, exteriors, night shots, day-for-night, dawn, and so on. Errol Morris' *A Brief History of Time* (1991) or *The Thin Blue Line* (1988) have many elaborately lit interviews and interior shots.

LIGHTING TERMINOLOGY

Here the task is to

- Recognize different types and combinations of lighting situations
- Become familiar with the look and effect of each
- Be able to name them with the appropriate standard terminology

Unless you are specifically interested in color, turn down the color control on your monitor so that you see just *light* and not chrominance. Following is some basic terminology.

A *high-key picture* is a shot that looks bright overall with small areas of shadow. In Figure 13–4, the shot is exterior day, but the interior of a supermarket might also be high key.

FIGURE 13–4

A *high-key* image lighting style.

A *low-key picture* is a shot that looks overall dark with few highlight areas. These are often interiors or night shots, but in Figure 13–5 there is a backlit day interior that ends up being low key.

Graduated tonality shots have neither very bright highlights nor deep shadow, but mainly consist of an even range of midtones if they were viewed without color. This might be a rainy landscape or a woodland scene, as in Figure 13–6. Here an overcast sky is diffusing the lighting source, and the disorganized light rays scatter into every possible shadow area so that there are neither highlights nor deep shadows.

High-contrast picture shots may be lit either high key or low key, but there is a big difference in illumination level between highlight and shadow areas. This would be as true for a candlelit scene as it is for Figure 13–4. Figure 13–7 is a clearer example of a high-contrast scene because it contains a much more obvious area of shadow.

Low-contrast picture shots can either be high or low key but have shadow area illumination not far from the highlight levels. The country post office scene in Figure 13–8 and the woodland scene in Figure 13–6 are both low contrast.

Hard lighting describes light quality and can be any light source that creates hard-edged shadows (e.g., sun, studio spotlight, candle flame). The barn scene in Figure 13–7, with its sharply defined shadow, is lit by hard sunlight.

Soft lighting describes light quality from any light source that creates soft-edged shadows (e.g., fluorescent tubes, sunlight reflecting off a matte-finish wall, light from an overcast sky, studio soft light). Figures 13–6 and 13–8 both are illuminated by soft light and lack any defined shadows.

FIGURE 13–5 ——————————————————————————————

A *low-key* image lighting style.

FIGURE 13–6 ——————————————————————————————

A *graduated-tonality* image, illustrating lighting from a diffused source.

FIGURE 13–7

A *high-contrast* image, showing a big difference in illumination levels.

Key light is not necessarily an artificial source because it can be the sun. It is a light source that contributes the shot's intended shadows, and these in turn reveal the angle and position of the supposed source light. In Figure 13–7 the key light is coming from above and to the right of the camera, as revealed by the line of shadow. Like all lighting, this indicates time of day and helps to set a mood.

Fill light is the light source used to raise illumination in shadow areas. For interiors, it will probably be soft light thrown from the direction of the camera. This avoids creating additional visible shadows. Fill light, especially in exteriors, often is provided from matte white reflectors. In Figure 13–5, the girl would not be visible unless some fill light was being thrown from the direction of the camera.

Backlight is a light source shining on the subject from behind, and often from above as well. A favorite technique is to put a rim of light around a subject's head and shoulders to create a separation between the subject and background.

FIGURE 13–8 ————————————————————————————————————

A *low-contrast* image contains little range between levels of illumination.

You can see this in Figure 13–5, where the girl's arm and shoulder are separated from the background by a rim of backlight. Although Figure 13–9 is high key, the key light comes from above and behind, so the boy is backlit. This gives texture to his hair and makes him stand out from his background.

A *practical* is any light source that appears in frame as part of the scene (e.g., a table lamp, overhead fluorescent). The elderly couple in Figure 13–10 not only has practicals in frame (the candles) but is lit by them. Each candle tends to fill the shadows cast by the others, so the overall effect is not as hard as the light normally associated with a candle flame's point light source.

LIGHTING SETUPS

In the following figures, the same model is lit in various ways. The effect and mood in each portrait vary greatly as a result. In the accompanying diagrams, I have only shown key and fill lights, but most of the portraits contain other sources, including backlight, which is shown separately. In floor-plan diagrams such as these, one cannot show the *height* of the shadow-producing light sources, only the *angle of throw* relative to the *camera-to-subject axis*. Heights can be inferred from the areas of highlight and their converse shadow patterns.

Frontal lighting setups have the key light close to the camera-to-subject axis so that shadows are thrown backward out of the camera's view. You can see a small shadow from the blouse collar on the subject's neck. Notice how flat

FIGURE 13–9 ———————————————————————————

A *backlit* image can also be a high key picture, but with the light source behind the subject.

FIGURE 13–10———————————————————————————

A *practical* is any lighting source that appears in frame, no matter whether or not it is a functional source.

and lacking in dimensionality this shot is compared with the others (Figure 13–11).

Broad lighting setups have the key light to the side so that a broad area of the subject's face and body is highlighted. If you compare this shot to the previous one, you will see how skimming the key across the subject reveals her features, neck contours, and the folds in the blouse. We have pockets of deep shadow, especially in the eye socket, but these could be reduced by increasing the amount of soft fill light (Figure 13–12).

Narrow lighting setups have the key light to the side of the subject and perhaps even beyond, so that only a narrow portion of the woman's face is receiving highlighting. Most of her face is in shadow. This portion of the model is lit by fill. Measuring light reflected in the highlight area and comparing it with that being reflected from the fill area gives the *lighting ratio*. It is important to remember when you are taking measurements that fill light reaches the highlight area but not vice versa, so you can only take accurate readings with all the lights on (Figure 13–13).

Backlighting setups have the key light coming from above and behind the subject, picking out the body outline and putting highlights in the hair and profile. Some additional fill would make this an acceptable lighting setup for an interview. Backlight is a component in each of Figures 13–12 and 13–13, and helps to suggest depth and roundness. Figure 13–11 looks so flat because it lacks both shadow and highlights. Some backlight would put highlights around the edges and give it the sparkle and depth of the other portraits (Figure 13–14).

Silhouette lighting has the subject reflecting no light at all, so the subject shows up only as an outline against raw light. This lighting is sometimes used in documentaries when the subject's identity is being withheld (Figure 13–15).

STRATEGY FOR STUDY

Locate two or three sequences with quite different lighting moods and, using the definitions given earlier, classify them as follows:

A. Style   High key/low key/graduated tonality?
B. Contrast   High or low contrast?
C. Scene   Intended to look like natural light or artificial lighting?
D. Setup   Frontal/broad/narrow/backlighting setup?
E. Angles   High/low angle of key light?
F. Quality   Hard/soft edges to shadows?
G. Source   Source in scene is intended to be _____?
H. Practicals Practicals in the scene are _____?
I. Time   Day-for-day, night-for-night, dusk-for-night, day-for-night?
J. Mood   Mood conveyed by lighting is _____?

Among feature films, two classic, superbly lit black-and-white films are Welles' *Citizen Kane* (1941), with cinematography by the revolutionary Gregg Toland, and Jean Cocteau's *Beauty and the Beast* (1946), whose lighting Henri Alekan modeled after the interiors in 17th-century Dutch genre paintings such as those of Vermeer. More of Alekan's camerawork and lighting can be admired in Wim

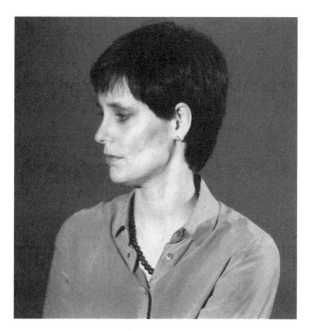

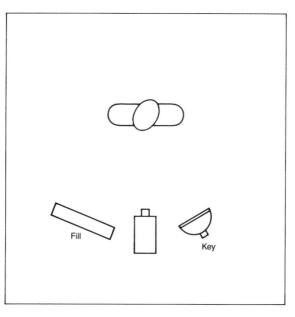

FIGURE 13–11

Example of *frontal lighting* and the setup diagram. (Dirk Matthews).

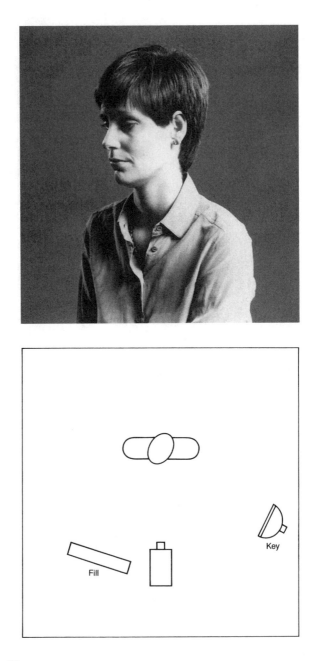

FIGURE 13–12

Example of *broad lighting* and the setup diagram. (Dirk Matthews).

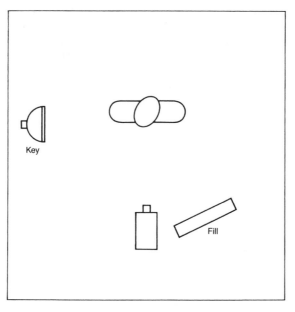

FIGURE 13–13

Example of *narrow lighting* and setup diagram. (Dirk Matthews).

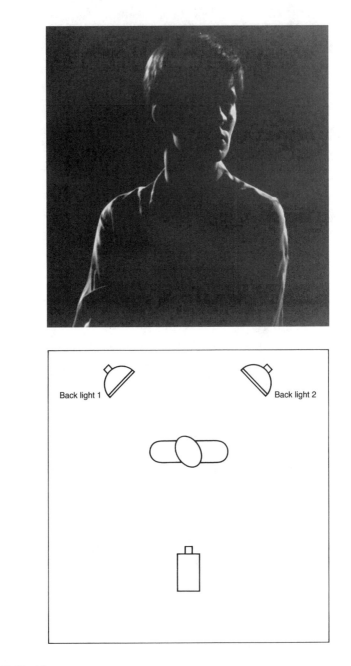

FIGURE 13–14

Example of *backlighting* and setup diagram. (Dirk Matthews).

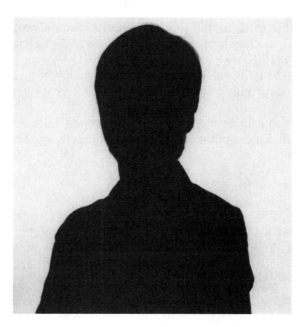

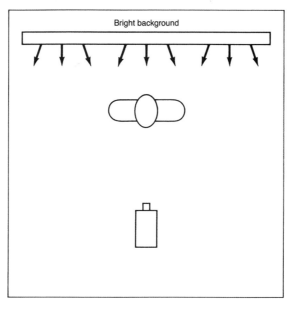

Bright background

FIGURE 13–15

Example of *silhouette lighting* and setup diagram. (Dirk Matthews).

Wenders' lyrical story about the angels over Berlin descending to earth, *Wings of Desire* (1988). Another lighting lesson is in Louis Malle's *Pretty Baby* (1978), a feature set in 1917 New Orleans and photographed by the great Sven Nykvist. Asked what he had learned over the years, Bergman's old cinematographer replied that is was mainly learning to work with increasingly simpler lighting setups.

Information on lighting and lighting instruments can be found in Chapter 21 (Lighting), which deals with the rudiments of lighting for the low-budget documentary maker.

CHAPTER 14

PROJECTS: BASIC PRODUCTION

In this chapter you will find

- Sound theory
- Voice recording projects, interior and exterior
- Sound troubleshooting chart
- Camera handling theory
- Basic camera handling projects that entail tripod shooting and handheld camerawork

Carrying out the projects in this chapter will equip you with a range of invaluable skills and awarenesses. Ahead in Chapter 28 (Projects: Advanced Production) are assignments demanding conceptual and authorial skills, but here your work will focus on gaining the prerequisite control over the tools and basic techniques. The sound experiments can often be combined with camera handling assignments. In a class it may be better if everybody does a different project so that all can learn from a wider pool of experiment. You will learn from other people's errors (and their successes, of course) as well as from your own.

SOUND THEORY

The object is to:

- Acquire basic understanding of how sound behaves
- Familiarize your ear
- Learn the necessities for successful voice recording

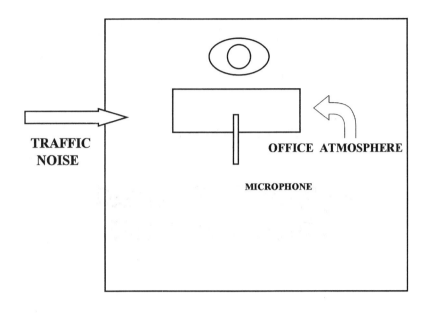

FIGURE 14–1

Diagram of typical sound situation involving a speaker covered by one microphone in a noisy office with traffic outside.

Film students tend to disregard sound, and they pay for it dearly later. Inconsistent or badly recorded sound is seldom the fault of the equipment but rather the way it is used. Some analytical experience will train you to recognize and correct a range of common failures. Let's look first at categories to be found in any location voice recording. Figure 14–1 is a diagram of a voice recording taking place in a noisy office that has busy street traffic outside. All sound recordings have four basic components that you can remember with the acronym *SARN*:

S = *Signal:* desired recording subject, in this case a speaker
A = *Ambience:* background sound inherent in the location (typewriter, phone nearby, and traffic)
R = *Reverberation:* secondary version of signal after it's bounced back from reflective surfaces
N = *Noise:* sound inherent to the sound system (hiss, hum, or interference)

Reverberative sound muddies the signal's clarity because reflected sound goes by a longer route after bouncing off reflective surfaces and arrives at the mike in varying degrees of delay.

FINDING THE PROBLEMS

One can evaluate a voice recording by posing these questions:

1. S:A. How Well Is the Signal Separated in Level from Ambience?   Think of our ambience (office atmosphere) competing with signal (the speaker) as a comparison, or ratio of signal to ambience, abbreviated as S:A. A high S:A is desirable because it means high signal to low ambient sound, which promises a good, intelligible speech recording. A low S:A would deliver a signal hardly louder than the ambience, putting undue strain on the audience and sabotaging intelligibility.

2. S:R. How Much Reverberation Is Muddying the Signal?   Location reverberation is S:R, that is, the ratio of the signal to its reverberant "reflections" returning from sound-reflective surrounding surfaces, such as the floor, walls, and ceiling. These prolong the signal by shuttling it back and forth in complex patterns that superimpose delayed versions on the original. Reverb does, however, have a function: it helps the audience identify with the mood of a particular enclosure—a large or small room, bare or furnished, high or low ceiling, and so on.
   There are, in fact, two kinds of reflected sound:

1. *Echo* is delayed sound you hear when the signal is reflected after a uniform delay (such as when you clap your hands some distance from a single tall building.)
2. *Reverberation* is reflected signal being returned by multiple surfaces and containing multiple delays. In a large space, such as an indoor swimming pool, the reverb delays are very long. Every signal is confused by a massive "tail" of reverb. In an average furnished room, delays are very short but their effect colors any recording.

The recordist makes a location *sound test* by loudly clapping hands just once. After the sudden *transient* of the hand clap (signal), its aftereffect (reverb) can be heard as either long or short, loud or soft. In the final mix, ambience or reverb can be added to a recording but never subtracted, so *dry* (nonreverberant) original recordings are always preferable.

3. S:N. How Much System Noise Is There?   Old sound amplification and recording systems had a low signal to noise (S:N) ratio, as old movie fans know well. Modern amplification systems are very clean, but analog recording (on VHS videotape or, worse, 16mm optical sound) is often anything but. Make the best possible original recording because each generation of copy augments and worsens noise levels. Digital recordings—both audio and video—can be copied for many generations without degradation.

4. How Cuttable Is the Sound?   This is a treacherous issue because inconsistencies only become obvious once sections are cut together.
   Inconsistency in S:A. Imagine a 2-hour interview shot in the back room of a restaurant. You want to cut together two sections that fit well together but that have utterly different S:A levels. The segment shot early has little restaurant atmosphere; the late one has a lot—a big but not insoluble problem. In the final mix you may be able to add a room tone to material with less ambience and make it match the noisy segment.

Inconsistency in S:R. This is virtually insoluble and occurs when complementary angles are cut together that have inconsistent miking. The result is that when cutting from a medium shot to a close shot, a voice changes wildly in quality because the longer shot is full of reverb. It cannot be "fixed in the mix." Needless to say, documentary shot on the run often suffers from these problems.

FINDING THE SOLUTIONS

When you take the role of recordist or mike operator, *always* wear headphones and concentrate not on what people say, but on sound quality as they say it. The golden rule is to place a mike as close to the signal source (the speaker) as the filming situation allows. This will give the highest signal amplitude and the best S:A and S:R. In film, the ideal is compromised by the need to hide the mike and allow subjects the freedom to move.

The recordist uses microphones with two main types of *reception pattern*. Each appears in various kinds of mikes, and each has its uses and drawbacks.

1. *Omnidirectional:* Usually giving better fidelity, the omni picks up sound equally from all directions and is useful for covering spontaneous group conversations. Lavalier (chest) mikes are "omnis" and are handy because they are small, easily hidden, and remain close to the speaker at all times. Lavaliers are often coupled with radio transmitters to give excellent sound and freedom of movement to wearers, but speech from someone in movement lacks all natural perspective changes. This is because the mike, unlike the camera, remains at a fixed distance from the speaker. The omni's big drawback is that it cannot be angled to help separate signal from ambient sound.

2. *Directional:* Often called a *cardioid* because of its heart-shaped pickup pattern, this mike type discriminates usefully against sound coming from off-axis. During a shoot in a noisy street, angling the mike toward the speaker and away from the traffic direction can enhance dialogue intelligibility and suppress off-axis traffic. *Superdirectional* mikes do not bring sound "nearer" or make it inherently louder; they simply discriminate more effectively against off-axis sound—but at some cost to fidelity.

Producing good sound means training yourself to hear sound coverage differences and to recognize the effect of a sonic environment. Editing your work together is important because sound inequities only show up when juxtaposition makes their inequities glaringly apparent. Listen to edited versions repeatedly and with your eyes closed. Learn to hear sound components like a conductor hearing the single instruments blended in an ensemble.

SOUND PROJECTS

PROJECT 14-1: VOICE RECORDING EXPERIMENTS FOR INTERIORS

Use a fairly large, minimally furnished room. Shoot a seated person reading in an even voice and holding the text so that it never gets between the mouth and microphone. A basic camcorder setup with headphones, equipped with both directional and omnidirectional mikes, is all you need.

1. *Hearing ambience.* In the barest room you can find, set up a wide shot about 12 feet from the reader. Station a radio playing music, as a source of constant ambient sound, near the camera. Using either an omni or directional mike near the camera, listen through monitor headphones and set the radio sound level so that it makes the reader difficult but not impossible to understand. Neither moving nor changing the voice and radio, now shoot 15 seconds each of wide shot, medium shot, and big close-up (BCU), using an appropriately changed mike position for each. Now edit the three shots together for a dramatic illustration of how S:A changes as the mike approaches the speaker. You wouldn't plan a shoot this way, but rushes shot by a moving camera can easily produce the identical effect.

2. *Hearing sound perspective changes and reverberation.* Repeat the experiment without the radio playing. Shoot wide-angle and close-up shots with appropriate mike positions, then reverse the logic by shooting a close-up picture with a wide-shot mike position, and a wide shot using close-shot sound. Edit the resulting footage together in different permutations. You will see that changing the mike positioning itself produces a sound perspective change and that close-shot sound is acceptable over a wide shot but not vice versa. Notice the hollow and "boxy" sound quality of the wide shot. Its recording contains a greater admixture of reverberant sound compared with that of the close-up.

3. *Hearing microphone axis changes.* Take a continuous medium shot of your reader with the mike in shot and directly before the speaker at a distance of about 4 feet. During a continuous reading, point a directional mike on axis (directly at the speaker's mouth) for 10 seconds, then rotate it smoothly and silently to a position 90 degrees from axis, hold this position for 10 seconds, then rotate it a further 90 degrees so it now points at the camera and away from the speaker. Hold this for a further 10 seconds. View/listen to rushes, then make an edited version that shows only the three static mike positions. *When sound is cut together one really hears the changes.* Notice, as the mike leaves the axis, how the voice quality becomes thinner and the reverberant component increases. You might try a blindfold assessment and, while listening, describe how the mike is situated at different times.

4. *Auditing the optimum speaker axis.* Speech, in particular the all-important consonants, comes out of a person's mouth directionally. Shoot a medium-close shot of the reader, taking 10 seconds of speech with a mike (preferably omnidirectional) handheld 2 feet in front of the person's face. Be careful not to introduce any handling noise. Keeping the mike at the same distance and always pointing toward the speaker, circle around to the speaker's side, holding steady there for 10 seconds. Finish by circling to the rear of the speaker, again holding for 10 seconds. View/listen to rushes, then edit the three positions together for an illustration of what happens to a voice's quality when the mike moves progressively away from the speaker's axis. Compare consonant clarity and the fidelity of other shots with the best (on-axis) recording, and note any changes in S:R.

Assessment: None, because this is an experiment.

PROJECT 14-2: VOICE RECORDING EXPERIMENTS
FOR EXTERIORS

Exteriors usually pose problems of background ambience and audibility.

1. *Hearing perspective changes.* In a quiet, open grassy space, use a directional or omnidirectional hand mike to shoot a speaker first in close, then wide, shot (camera about 20 feet or 7 meters distant). Edit back and forth between the two shots for an illustration of sound perspective changes that this time lack reverberant sound.

2. *Hearing S:A and camera distance.* Shoot in the open near some constant source of outdoor, ambient sound such as a highway, fountain, or playground. Using a directional hand mike, shoot a minute of interview with the camera and mike pointing toward the ambient sound's source and the speaker's back to it. Then turn the action around and shoot a minute with the mike at the same distance but with its axis, this time, away from the sound's source. Intercut the two tracks several times. Because there is virtually no reverberant sound, the mike's degree of discrimination will be readily apparent at the cuts.

3. *Hearing S:A and how it affects choice of microphone.* In the same noisy exterior setup, shoot an additional section for the interview in point 2 using a Lavalier mike. Intercut close-shot (CS) sound from point 2 with Lavalier sound to discover the differences between the two forms of mike coverage. Discuss the ratios of signal to ambience in your coverage.

Assessment: None, because this is an experiment.

SOUND TROUBLESHOOTING CHART

Sound Troubleshooting Chart

Problem Effect	Cause	Solution
Speaker obscured by high background noise	Lack of insulation or separation	1. Close windows to reduce exterior atmosphere 2. Move shoot away from source 3. Reduce ambient source
	Low S : A	1. Get mike closer 2. Use Lavalier for high S : A 3. Move directional mike so ambience is off-axis, signal is on-axis
Speaker's voice not clear	Lack of sibilants	1. Get mike on-axis to speaker 2. Mike from above, not below
Speaker's voice "edgy"	Overmodulating	1. Reduce recording level so peaks are contained below 0 dB
	Too much sibilance or sibs "popping"	1. Try moving mike progressively off axis 2. Experiment with mike in relation to reverb—it may be reinforcing certain frequencies

Sound Troubleshooting Chart

Problem Effect	Cause	Solution
	Two mikes picking up the same signal but out of phase	1. Cover situation with one mike 2. Move mikes closer to respective speakers so S : A ratio is higher 3. Rewire one mike or use phase-reverse switch if there is one
Feedback howl	Mike picking up headphone or speaker to create feedback loop	1. Greater separation between mike and secondary sound source 2. Move mike off-axis to secondary sound source 3. Reduce secondary source level
Speaker obscured by room acoustics	High location reverberation	1. Dampen reflective surfaces by carpeting floor, hanging sound blankets on off-camera walls 2. Move mike closer to source or use Lavaliers for higher S : R 3. Change location 4. Use tablecloth if there is a table, and don't place mike on or near highly sound-reflective surfaces
Sound inconsistent on cuts	Inconsistent ambience	1. Shoot presence track so you can boost quieter track to match louder 2. Angle mike to control S : A ratio
	Inconsistent voice quality	1. Try to use consistent mikes and miking 2. Keep mike at more consistent distance 3. Minimize mike changes when camera position changes. Close-shot sound can always be thinned to sound like long shot, but not vice versa.
	Inconsistent reverb	1. Minimize mike axis and position changes 2. Muffle reverberant surfaces as above 3. Improve S : R by using closer or Lavalier miking
	Inconsistent voice levels	1. This can be fixed in the mix 2. Watch recording level meter more carefully 3. Check rerecording procedures for workprint. A standard 0-dB tone on original is there to help standardize copy levels.
Unwanted noises in mike	Air currents	1. In windy location use blimp or windshield on mike 2. Alter miking if speaker's breath rattles mike diaphragm

Sound Troubleshooting Chart

Problem Effect	Cause	Solution
	Mike handling	1. Hold hand mike more carefully and monitor via headphones 2. Use mike shock-mount 3. Check that taut or dragging cables aren't transmitting handling noise 4. Consider using different type of mike
High system noise	Undermodulating or replay system at fault	1. Record at higher level. Sound should generally peak at 0 dB. 2. If original tape is OK make new workprint copies. 3. A sound head may need demagnetizing. A magnetized head partially erases the track, the top frequencies disappearing first.
Mike creating shadows	Positioning in relation to lighting	1. Mike from below frame instead of from above it 2. Keep mike still so shadow doesn't draw attention to itself by moving 3. Use wireless mikes so no boom is required 4. Try to get the director of photography to alter lighting(!)

CAMERA HANDLING PROJECTS

Over a number of assignments, your persistent strengths and weaknesses will emerge. Class members can rate each other's work because judging the work of others helps develop the quick and experienced eye you will need in the field.

Each of the following projects has suggested assessment criteria, to be found in Appendix 1. Be sure to examine the assessment sheet before you start the project, because the criteria are meant not just to assist in judging your end result but to serve as useful reminders of what to build into your work.

CAMERA HANDLING THEORY

Documentary camerawork can be divided into two different categories, tripod and handheld, each serving a different purpose.

Tripod   When camerawork is done from a tripod, it

- Usually is reserved for stable and relatively predictable shooting situations
- Makes possible very controlled transitions from subject to subject

- Makes possible very controlled image transitions
- Allows stable close-ups using the telephoto end of the zoom lens
- Conveys the cool, assured view familiar from studio television and feature films
- Is associated with an invulnerable, omniscient point of view
- Is associated with careful, elegant lighting.

Though invaluable for anything requiring a rock-steady camera, the tripod-mounted camera is virtually immobile and handicapped when it comes to covering spontaneous events. A subject in movement must be covered with multiple tripod-mounted cameras, or the action must be interrupted to allow moving the single camera to a new position. This limits coverage to subjects that can be made subservient to the needs of the camera.

Handheld.   The handheld camera

- Can be placed on the shoulder
- Can be held low, even at ground level
- Allows the operator to walk, stand, or sit while shooting
- Is most justified when motivated by events
- Can move under, over, or through obstacles as easily as a human being can
- Can react to events much as we do in life
- Implies a spontaneous, event-driven quest
- Must often cover action and reaction as they happen, with the operator making snap judgments
- Sometimes makes humanly imperfect movements and reactions
- Conveys a subjective, even vulnerable, point of view
- Is associated with shooting by available light
- Becomes increasingly shaky as the operator zooms in

Usually mounted on the operator's shoulder, the handheld camera can pan or track at will with the subject. During a protest march this could allow one to follow a single demonstrator throughout a day or to cover the main elements—speaker, marshals, police, contingents of demonstrators—that make up the event's totality. When events move with any speed, the operator, after being directed to "Roll camera," must make on-the-spot decisions about subject framing, camera moves, and whether to favor either action or reaction at any given moment. The challenge for the operator is to minimize any jerkiness or indecision because it unfailingly communicates through the camera handling to the audience. Sometimes this is dramatically right; other times it interrupts the audience's concentration. To minimize unsteadiness, use a Steadicam^{TM} body brace or keep your lens on wide angle, moving your camera physically close or distant from the subject as you require close or long shots.

PROJECT 14-3: (TRIPOD) INTERVIEW, ONE SUBJECT

Goals are to

- Produce a seamless, questionless, and "transparent" flow of onscreen statements
- Produce good sound with no mike visible and eliminate all trace of the interviewer's voice
- Have the interviewee seem entirely at ease
- Evoke expository information from interviewee
- Use wide shots for new subject matter but cover moments of intensity in close-up
- Zoom and recompose simultaneously and smoothly
- Produce compositional proportions that match on cuts between different-sized images
- Make interviewee's body position and expression match at cuts
- Restructure the interview to make it develop logically and meaningfully
- Edit to maintain natural speech rhythms of speaker
- Edit the story so it builds to a climactic or pivotal moment, arrives at a resolution, and is told with intensity throughout

Read the section on interviewing. Place the interviewer's head right under the lens. In this manner, the interviewer's presence is eliminated because the interviewee appears to directly address the viewer.

Action: For approximately 4 minutes of screen time, shoot an interview lasting 5 minutes with a seated subject. Use three image sizes:

- Wide shot (top of head down to knees)
- Medium shot (head and top of shoulders)
- Big close-up (forehead to chin)

Sound: A Lavalier mike is ideal for this setup. The interviewer shouldn't wear a mike because the questions are due for elimination during the edit.

Directing: Arrange a touch signal between the director/interviewer and camera operator so that you can request particular zoom changes. Image size changes must be considerable for compositions to cut together well.

Interviewing: Good short interviews onscreen require compact expository information, a center or focus that develops, some significant change, and an outcome or resolution. The speaker and interviewer must not overlap because eliminating the interviewer's voice (a prime object here) becomes impossible. If an overlap happens, immediately ask the interviewee to start again in the clear. Listen critically to ensure that no answer depends on your question. That is, make sure each answer comes out as a freestanding statement. To succeed at this, you must really listen, not think ahead.

Suggested Subjects:

1. How a special person helped the interviewee to resolve a major conflict in his or her life.

2. The worst period in the interviewee's life, how it came about, and how it ended

3. A pivotal event in the interviewee's life, how it happened, and what it helped decide

Editing: Use Project 38-1 guidelines in Chapter 38.

Assessment: See Appendix 1, Project 14-4 Assessment, and for editing, Project 38-1 Assessment.

PROJECT 14-4: (HANDHELD) TRACKING ON STATIC SUBJECT

Goals are to

- Handhold a camera while walking
- Make a smooth start to your tracking shot, and a smooth stop
- Produce a stable image that neither bobs nor sways
- Anticipate changes in the surface as you walk
- Use your non-viewfinder eye to see ahead or around

Action: Using the wide-angle end of your zoom, stand at 45 degrees to a brick wall and at 3 feet distance (Figure 14–2). Hold a static shot for 5 seconds, then move forward maintaining distance and angle. The bricks should slide past, neither bobbing up and down nor swaying nearer to and further from camera. You will only accomplish professional handheld camerawork by

- Making the camera into a solid part of your head and shoulders
- Walking with your legs a little bent so you can glide
- Making your footsteps fall in a straight line to eliminate swaying and transfer your weight smoothly from foot to foot without a pounding motion
- Drawing your leading foot over the ground surface ahead to help encounter obstacles or irregularities in time to accommodate them
- Using your spare eye to scope out where you are going by keeping it open part of the time while using your other eye to check composition through the viewfinder. This is a nauseating experience until you get used to it.

After 20 seconds of tracking, come to a halt and hold your composition steady, then cut the camera.

Assessment: Use Appendix 1, Project 14-4 Assessment.

PROJECT 14-5: (HANDHELD) TRACKING FORWARD ON MOVING SUBJECT

Goals are to:

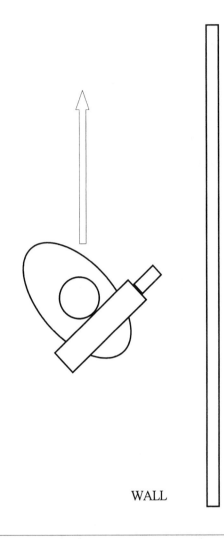

WALL

FIGURE 14–2 ————————————————————————————————————

Ground-plan sketch for handheld walking track exercise.

- Handhold a tracking shot in busy, unpredictable surroundings
- Reflect an awareness of the subject's changing background and its possible significance
- Be ready to recover from being discovered acting as a voyeur

Action: Walk behind a stranger in the street, staying about 8 feet distant and at 45 degrees to the person's forward axis. Keep your subject steady and appropriately composed in the frame. Feature the background meaningfully. Have something friendly to say in explanation if your subject becomes aware of you!

Assessment: See Appendix 1, Project 14-5 Assessment.

PROJECT 14-6: HANDHELD: TRACKING BACKWARD
WITH MOVING SUBJECT

Goals are to

- Handhold a camera while walking backward (with assistance)
- Experiment with relationship between a subject's eyeline and subject-to-camera axis
- Maintain consistent "lead space" ahead of walker from shot to shot
- Give subject mental work in order to reduce self-consciousness

Action (two versions):
   A. Arrange for a subject to walk facing you, as in Figure 14–3. The camera operator walks backward, guided through a light touch by an assistant

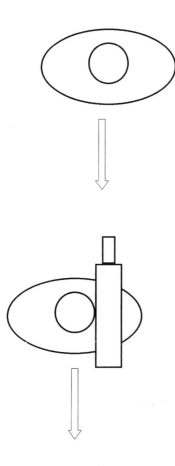

FIGURE 14–3

Subject following the camera.

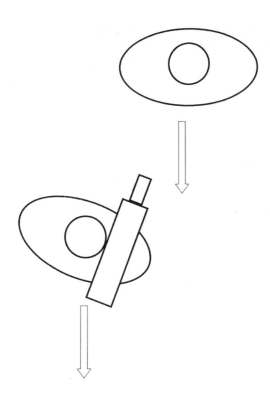

FIGURE 14–4 ⸻

Subject following camera with the camera on the subject's axis, but with the camera at 30 degrees to axis.

for safety's sake. Frame the subject in a wide shot, hold that shot for about 15 seconds, then let the subject gain on you until you have a medium shot. Hold this size shot for a while, then allow the subject to gain on you again, this time holding for about 15 seconds of big close-up. You may need to give your subject mental work to do so that he becomes less self-conscious.

B. Now do the same thing again but this time, as in Figure 14–4, with the camera shooting at about a 30-degree angle to the subject's axis. Experiment with the framing and background to find the most acceptable shot. Remember to include lead space (more space ahead of a moving subject than there is behind him) in the composition.

Editing: When cutting between different image sizes, be careful to preserve the footstep rhythm. Trying intercutting not just different image sizes but the different axis angles that you shot.

Assessment: Use Appendix 1, Project 14-6 Assessment.

Discussion: Which combinations of subject size, angle, and background seem to produce the smoothest shot? How much of a problem is it for the subject to have the camera in his or her eyeline? Can you intercut the on-axis and off-axis material at all elegantly?

Now you've covered some basics. The next shooting comes in the section of Production Projects in Chapter 28. Each of those projects represents a typical situation and genre of documentary. The work will require sophisticated handling of the camera and microphone, and poses a series of exciting authorial challenges. From this experience you will gain the broad experience of a working documentarian.

PART 5

PREPRODUCTION

Part 4 covers

- Definition of the preproduction phase
- From initial research to proposal, and organizing the materials for a proposal
- Writing a treatment, rough budget, and the prospectus (an invitation for potential investors)
- From draft proposal to more thorough research, and methods of researching
- An imaginary research case history that contains all the usual elements you are likely to encounter
- Deciding participants, preinterviewing, and assigning them metaphorical roles
- Developing final proposal and working hypothesis
- Refining research into a shooting plan
- Finding the dramatic components for scenes, dramatic curve, and three-act structure
- Beats and dramatic units as the tools of the director
- Handling facts and exposition
- Participants and getting informed consent to filming
- Ethical considerations, such as
  - Changing people's lives
  - Truth claims
  - Speaking on behalf of others

- Evidence credibility
- Perception changing reality
- Holding true to your mission
- Anticipating the shoot and its logistics; permissions and legal releases
- Developing a crew and defining responsibilities
- Crew job descriptions and common temperaments
- Making an equipment list
- A preproduction checklist for you to use in the field

This part deals with the important preparation you do after the initial idea and before the shoot. This includes initial research, forming a working hypothesis or premise for the documentary, performing research to locate the people and situations you might shoot, and writing a proposal.

The proposal, which communicates the film's purpose while you assemble funding or other support, is also a form of development in its own right. Writing it puts your ideas under a stringent test of logic and meaning. It helps you review the basic assumptions, develop imaginative variations, and look for stylistic or structural possibilities you would bypass if you went straight into shooting.

The crew you choose to work with and the permissions and understandings that you set up in advance are crucial. The preproduction phase is when you decide the who, what, when, where, why, and how of the documentary you mean to shoot.

For further information on issues arising in Part 4, use the Index or go to the Bibliography. Make frequent use of the Preproduction Checklist at the end of this part, and save yourself wasted time and energy.

CHAPTER 15

INITIAL RESEARCH AND
THE DRAFT PROPOSAL

This chapter handles

- An overview of preproduction and research
- Overview of steps in developing and refining the draft proposal
- Addressing aesthetic concerns
- Assembling plans, schedule, and crew
- Prior work with crew to assure communications and shooting standards
- Developing the final version of the proposal as a means of fine-tuning your directing intentions
- Getting support: creating the treatment, rough budget, and prospectus

ON PREPRODUCTION

A documentary's preproduction period follows research and covers all decisions and arrangements prior to shooting. This includes choosing a subject; doing the research; deciding who and what are going to be the subject of the film; assembling a crew; choosing what equipment will be necessary; and deciding the method, details, and timetable of shooting. It may also be a time in which you assemble final funding and distribution.

Seasoned filmmakers never rely on spontaneous inspiration because once you start filming, the pace and demand of the work are all-encompassing. Werner Herzog, questioned after a screening about "the intellectual challenge during shooting," replied caustically that "filmmaking is athletic, not aesthetic." Most filming, he told the startled audience, is so grueling that rarefied thought is all but impossible. François Truffaut makes a similar point in *Day for Night* (1973). Its central character is a director whose fiction movie runs into a thicket of problems and compromises. Played by Truffaut himself, the director confides that at the start he always thinks the film is going to be his best, but halfway through shooting he can only think about surviving until the finish. My own fantasy, which returns at least once every shoot, is to escape further filming by miraculously turning into the owner of a rural grocery.

The thought and planning you invest before shooting, and how thoroughly you anticipate problems, go far to ensure a successful and trouble-free shoot. Most importantly, they help ensure that the movie is a coherent entity. Directing a documentary, contrary to the impression of spontaneous *auteurism*, is always founded to some degree in preliminary conclusions reached during research. Depending on the kind of film you are making, this may mean that shooting is largely collecting evidence for underlying patterns and relationships already identified. Or, in less controlled situations, it is a solid preparation for what is normal so that, when an atypical event begins, you can react immediately to developments that would otherwise pass you by.

RESEARCH OVERVIEW

In summary, the purposes of research are to

- Assemble a context and basic factual information
- Get to know the whole scene so that you can narrow down to what is significant
- Become known and trusted by potential participants
- Communicate your motivations and purposes for making a film
- See a lot of characteristic activity so that you know what is normal and what is not
- Understand who represents what so that you can make representative choices
- See who will make a good participant and who won't
- Develop a proposal indicating intended content, theme, and style so that you can try out your ideas on other people and raise funds or other support
- Decide what the ultimate purpose of making the film should be
- Assemble all the human and material resources so that you can shoot

Let's assume you have chosen a subject and are starting the initial research phase that will culminate in developing a written proposal. No two people research alike, but some steps are fairly universal. Research methods hinge on the exigencies of the subject, so you must first be sure you have the makings of a film. No documentary can be made from good intentions, only from what can be captured with a camera. What film is possible?

Following are some recommended steps, which I will elaborate upon later. Often you will be forced by circumstances to take these steps out of any ideal order or to take several concurrently. Whenever you hit an impediment, turn and work elsewhere so that you don't waste time. Filmmaking demands lateral thinking; progress in one area affects what you have decided in another, making you constantly readjust your idea of the whole. This may be frustrating until you get used to it.

The following list of steps is for those doing exhaustive research, but because documentary makers usually have several irons in the fire, most proposals are written from partial rather than conclusive research. There is a Form and Aesthetics Questionnaire in Appendix 2 that will help you decide what stage you have reached. Even when research is rather complete, there is usually a fallow period while funds and sponsoring organizations are being sought, so you should always expect a last-minute hustle just before shooting begins.

Begin the initial stages:

1. *Define an off-the-top-of-your-head working hypothesis for the subject* (see Working Hypothesis and Interpretation section of the documentary Project Proposal organizer later). Don't reserve all judgments until you feel confident that you know enough. It will never happen, so get going with the imaginative work that begins an imaginative documentary.

2. *Begin site research.* That is, familiarize yourself with
   A. *People and situations* that you plan to film
   B. Find out what's *typical* in the world you are going to film
   C. Find out *what's unusual*, unexpected, and particular in the one you are looking at
   D. *Stay loose.* Keep any explanations broad and tentative so that you don't paint yourself into a corner

3. *Do background research*, that is,
   A. Use the resources of the *Internet* to pull up all the references and ideas you can find
   B. Study *publications* covering your subject, such as magazines, newspapers, professional journals, and even fiction, any of which may offer useful ideas and observations
   C. See the *films* on the the subject, but *not* if you feel vulnerable to their influence
   D. *Talk to any experts* who will share what they know. As a documentarian you routinely depend on others in this way. Your expertise rests in bringing a special world and its issues to a first-time audience, so being an ignorant outsider actually helps you decide what that audience needs, something that is beyond most experts.

4. *Develop trust.*
   A. *Communicate.* Make yourself and a broad version of your purposes known to everyone you may want to film. Let them question you if they need to find out your values and purposes.
   B. *Learn.* Put yourself in the position of learning from your subjects, because they are the experts.

    C. *Hang out.* Spending a period of time with your subjects is the most valuable thing you can do, both to absorb everything you need to know and to make yourself available so that people can develop trust in your character and purposes.

5. *Make reality checks* to ensure that
    A. You have *multiple perspectives* on each person, fact, or facet, especially when there are ambiguities (see the Form and Aesthetics Questionnaire in Appendix 2)
    B. *What you want to film is accessible*
    C. *People are amenable* and cooperative
    D. *Releases and permissions* will be forthcoming
    E. The *resources* you will need are not beyond your means

Develop the first draft of the proposal:

6. *List the action sequences* and decide how far action and behavioral material alone would make an interesting and coherent observational documentary. To envision making a coherent silent film is the litmus of how cinematic your film is and, conversely, how much it will need to rely on speech for narrative guidance.

7. *Preinterview*
    A. *Audition.* Using video very informally, interview those you're considering for the film. Ask no searching questions—reserve these for when you shoot.
    B. *Casting.* Watch the tape with a few trusted friends to see how potential participants come across. This is analogous to casting. Good quality audio can be used later as voice-over.
    C. *Don't push yet.* Avoid being intrusive or divisive. Discuss only the ideas your participants suggest and in nebulous terms that delay all decisions to the future.

8. *Rewrite the working hypothesis* as new information alters the basis for your intended film. Reworking the hypothesis (described later) is the best way to reconfigure your thematic purpose. Expect this to change as your knowledge grows. Avoiding this work will leave you unsure what or how to shoot, and you'll end up shooting everything that moves.

Refine the proposal:

9. *Narrow the focus, deepen the film.* Always seek the center of your film by assuming that you may not yet have it. Narrowing its scope always benefits a film because it makes you seek and expand its essence. Tightly focused films that go deep are always better than broad, generalizing films that skimp on specifics.

10. *List points your film must make* so that you forget nothing important as you direct. For instance,
    A. List *expository information* that the audience must have, and plan to cover it several ways
    B. List the *thematic or other goals* that you want your film to fulfill

    C. Make sure you shoot material so that you can *show what or who is in conflict*, and that you contrive to bring the antithetical forces together in *confrontation*.

11. *Develop your own angle* or point of view, defining what exactly you want to say and what emphasis you may need to impose so that you can collect the materials to do it.

12. *Write a three-line description.* If you can summarize your film and its purposes in three lines, and people react to it positively, you may be ready to direct it. If you can't, you aren't.

13. *Make necessary remaining choices*, that is,
    A. *Casting.* Decide finally which people and places you want to use, and define their rhythms, routines, and the imagery such as cityscape, landscape, workplace that is emblematic of their condition
    B. List *what's typical and atypical* to guide your filming when you are ready. You will want the best of both
    C. *Expunge clichés*, then list what can you show that is fresh, surprising, and different compared with other people's work
    D. Decide *central character* or characters (ask yourself from time to time whose story it is)
    E. Define *whose point of view* the various parts of the story should favor
    F. Define the essential *dialectics* of your film—the central point and counterpoint of its argument—so that you can be sure to collect all the materials you need

Address aesthetic concerns:

14. *Style.* Define
    A. The style that best serves *each sequence*
    B. The style that serves *your point of view*
    C. The *stylistic characteristics of the film* as a whole
    D. *Anything to avoid*

15. *Seek inherent myths, emblems, symbols, and key imagery* by deciding
    A. What *life-role* each person is likely to enact in the drama you are beginning to perceive
    B. What *images* you have seen or expect to see that convey the heart of what you have to say
    C. *Key actions* whose connotations have special meaning for the central purposes of your film
    D. *Which type of story yours is.* What is closest to it in the world's repository of stories? Any parallels that suggest archetypes, myths, or legends will strengthen your film by moving it toward the universal.

16. *Test your assumptions.*
    A. *Pitch* your ideas to anyone who will listen and solicit their reactions. Alter your pitch to maximize the audience response, and consider how these changes affect the film you intend making.
    B. *Ask people to read the proposal* and comment on what it makes them expect. Do they see the film that you see?

Getting near to shooting time:

17. *Make the final draft of your intentions.* Even if you have nobody to satisfy but yourself, work over all the considerations prior to shooting. Originality does not come from talent (whatever that is) but from the work of sustained, determined thinking. Writing makes you think. Check back with the Form and Aesthetics Questionnaire in Appendix 2.

18. *Make a rough budget* (see the Budget Planning Form later in this chapter).

19. *Write a treatment.* This is optional and consists of writing the film you see in your head after developing the research. A treatment and a sample reel may be necessities when you apply for money (see The Treatment).

20. *Obtain permissions.* Secure a commitment (preferably in writing) of time and involvement from those you intend to film. If you intend to shoot in non-public locations, secure written permissions for them beforehand. In many cities you now must have permission from the authorities to film in the streets or on public transportation.

Once shooting becomes definite:

21. *Secure your crew.*

22. *Make a shooting schedule* and build in options to deal with foreseeable difficulties, such as inclement weather or unavailability of a major element or participant.

23. *Do any necessary trial shooting* to
    A. *"Audition" doubtful participants*
    B. *Work out communications* with a new crew
    C. *Set standards for work* you are going to do together
    D. *Test new or unfamiliar technology*

THE DOCUMENTARY PROPOSAL

Everyone dreads writing the proposal, which is so necessary when you have to communicate your intentions, and particularly when it comes to fundraising. However, its most important function is forcing you to clarify the organizational and thematic analysis you have (or have not) developed during research. Then, as the time comes to *pitch* your film (that is, to seek support through making verbal presentations of it), you will be able to draw a clear and forcefully attractive picture of your intentions.

Another useful function is that the proposal helps prepare you to *direct* the film, that is, to shoot (capture and catalyze) materials that will really add up to something. Being unprepared leads to blindly collecting stuff that you hope can be beaten into shape during editing. It nearly always cannot.

The proposal also shows how well you intend to fulfill the conditions of documentary itself. Always depending on the kind of film you are making, it should

- Tell a good story
- Make human truths, both large and small, emerge through behavioral evidence, not just verbal description
- Present a personal, critical perspective on some aspect of the human condition
- Inform and emotionally move the audience

Like a gripping piece of fiction, the successful documentary usually incorporates

- Well-placed exposition of necessary information (facts or context placed not too early or too late)
- Interesting characters that are actively trying to do or get something
- Events that emerge from the characters' needs
- Dramatic tension and conflict between opposing forces
- Suspense—not people hanging off cliffs, but situations that intrigue your spectators and make them anticipate, wonder, compare, and decide
- Confrontation between conflicting persons, factions, or elements
- A climax in the tension between opposing elements or forces
- A resolution (happy or sad, good or bad, satisfying or not)
- Development in at least one major character or situation

These criteria may seem too much in bed with traditional fiction to fit documentary, but most of these points apply to stories of all kinds, even the most experimental. Look again at your favorite documentaries and see whether they incorporate these dramatic ingredients. I bet when you look closely they do.

Keep on writing and rewriting the proposal until it is succinct, free of redundancy, and effortless to read. A good proposal demonstrates how you expect to meet the implicit expectations of documentary and that you really understand the genre. Experienced funders know that thin or muddled writing will lead to thin or muddled filmmaking. Conversely, whoever can think and write clearly is on the way to excelling in the more demanding work of making films.

DOCUMENTARY PROPOSAL ORGANIZER

The Proposal Organizer following will help you write a proposal or develop a prospectus package as you search for financial support. Think of its categories like the pigeonholes in a mail sorting office. A well-researched film will have something substantial and different to put in most, if not all. If you find you've put similar material into more than one classification, go to further drafts until material is presented *only once and in its rightful place*. This is very important.

For simplicity the proposal organizer is geared toward a short and uncomplicated film, but it works well for something longer and more complex. Everything you write should be brief, because a completed proposal should not be longer than four or five pages. Use the Proposal Organizer as the first step toward the final version.

PROPOSAL ORGANIZER

Working title _____   Format _____

Director _____   Camera _____

Sound _____   Editor _____

Others (Role) _____   (Role) _____

1. WORKING HYPOTHESIS and INTERPRETATION. What are *your* persuasions about the world you are going to show in your film, the "statement" you want to emerge out of the film's dialectics? Write a hypothesis statement that incorporates the following wording:
   A. In life I believe that (your philosophy regarding the particular life-principle that your film will exemplify) _____
   B. My film will show this in action by exploring (situation) _____
   C. My film's main conflict is between _____ and _____
   D. My film's point of view, or its POV character, will be _____
   E. I expect my film's structure to be determined by _____
   F. The subject and point of view suggest a style that is _____
   G. Ultimately I want the audience to feel _____
   H. . . . and to understand that _____

2. TOPIC and EXPOSITION. Write a paragraph that includes
   A. Your film's *subject* (person, group, environment, social issue, and so on)
   B. *Expository information* (factual or other background information) so that the reader can see the enclosed world into which you are going to take us

3. ACTION SEQUENCES. Write a brief paragraph about any sequence that will show characters, an event, or an activity. (A sequence is usually delineated by being in one location, one chunk of time, or an assembly of materials to show one topic.) For each, describe
   A. The sequence's expected action
   B. What information or persuasion it contributes to the film
   C. The agendas or conflicts you expect it to evidence
   D. Any useful metaphors it will suggest
   E. Any special, symbolic, or emblematic imagery it will contain
   F. What structures the events (especially through time)
   G. What the sequence will contribute to the film as a whole

4. MAIN CHARACTERS. Write briefly about each main character, including
   A. The person's identity—name, relationship to others in film—and his or her qualities
   B. What he or she contributes to your film's story
   C. The metaphoric role you see this person occupying in relation to what else is in the film

    D. What this character wants to get or do in relation to the others or to the situation

    E. Any direct speech quotation that freshly and directly conveys what this person is about

5. CONFLICT. What is being argued or worked out in this film? Define
    A. What conflict the characters know they are playing out
    B. What conflict *you* see them playing out (of which they may be quite unaware)
    C. What other principles (of opinion, view, vision, and so on) you see at issue
    D. How, where, and when will one force confront the other in your film (the *confrontation*, which is very important)
    E. Possible developments you see emerging from this or other confrontations

6. SOCIAL SIGNIFICANCE. What will this film say about the lives it portrays, and what is the social significance of this? Why should people care to watch this film?

7. YOUR MOTIVATION FOR MAKING THE FILM. What, in your background and interests, impels you to make the film? This indicates whether you have the energy, passion, and commitment to stay the course and make an outstanding film.

8. AUDIENCE, ITS KNOWLEDGE AND PREJUDICES. A documentary should anticipate the expectations—both right ones and wrong—of its audience. Your film is in a dialogue with these prejudices and must extend, subvert, or endorse them. Complete the following:
    A. My intended audience is (don't write "Everyone!") _____
    B I can expect the audience to know _____ but not to know _____
    C. I assume positive audience prejudices are _____ and negative ones are _____
    D. Countervailing facts, ideas, and feelings that my audience needs to experience are _____

9. TO-CAMERA INTERVIEWS. Because "talking heads" have been overused they are now out of favor, but they do make good safety coverage. Also, a well-recorded track can be used as voice-over narration or interior monologue. For each intended interviewee, list
    A. Name, age, gender
    B. Job, profession, or role
    C. Metaphoric role in your film's dramatic structure
    D. Main elements that your interview will seek to establish

10. STYLE. Shooting or editing style that might augment or counterpoint your film's content. Comment on
    A. Documentary genre you are using, and how this affects the film's style
    B. Point of view and how this affects shooting and editing styles

C. Narration (if there is to be any, and by whom)
D. Lighting moods
E. Visual and other rhythms
F. Any intercutting or parallel storytelling
G. Intended juxtaposition of like or unlike materials to create comparison, ironic tension, etc.

11. TONE. Describe the progression of moods of the film as you see them, and the film's prevailing tone.

12. STRUCTURE. Write a brief paragraph on how you might structure your film. Consider
A. How you will handle the progression of time in the film
B. How and through whom the story will be told
C. What elements in the film (such as a process, journey, season, etc) that will probably structure the film
D. How important information will emerge
E. What will probably be the climactic sequence or "crisis" in your story, and where in the structure this might go
F. What other sequences will become the falling action after the "crisis"

13. RESOLUTION. Your film's ending is your last word. It exerts a strong influence on the film's final impact. Write a brief paragraph about how you imagine your film ending and what meaning you foresee it establishing for the audience. If the events could go in more than one direction, it is entirely realistic to hypothesize different endings.

THE PROPOSAL

The final proposal will probably be presented to a fund, foundation, or television channel—that's if they fund at the conceptual stage, which is rare today unless you have a stellar track record. You may be canvassing individual investors. Note that a good title for your film is an extremely important part of signaling your wares and attracting support.

Use the information you collected in the Proposal Organizer under the different headings, putting selected information in the order that will work best for the foundation, fund, or channel to which you are applying. Write compactly, informatively, and poetically so that the reader can "see" all the essentials of the film in the writing. This means summoning up the essence with maximum brevity. Expect to go through 10 to 20 drafts before you have something worthy of you.

Typically a proposal will include the following:

- Cover sheet (1 page)
- Program description (3 pages)
  - Synopsis of the project, maybe in 25 words or less
  - Treatment explaining background information, structure, theme, style, format (16mm film, DVCAM, Digital BetaCam, HDTV, etc.), voice, and point of view

- Target communities for the program and why this audience is presently unserved by television (television is usually trying to fill gaps)
- How you are known to (and trusted by) the community in which you propose filming.
- Why public television (for instance) is the right place for this program
- Current status of the project
- Production personnel (2 to 3 pages)
  - Applicants' full resumés
  - Key production personnel names, positions, short biographies
- Previous and present work samples
  - Previously completed sample work (either demo reel or completed film— see fund guidelines)
  - Work-in-progress (WIP) of perhaps 5 minutes minimum length
  - Written descriptions of prior work, applicants' creative contribution to it, its relevance to WIP, and what the WIP represents (rough cut, trailer, selects, or a clip)

Funding organizations that routinely solicit applications streamline their process to ensure that juries compare consistent documentation. They usually issue their own proposal forms, expect you to write in very specific ways, and want a specified number of copies with everything labeled in very specific ways. If you seriously expect support, you must fulfill what they expect, so check and re-check everything before you close up the package. A weary committee member sifting through a great pile of competing applications sees departures from the norm not as charming originality but indifference to the jury's task. You cannot afford to lose support at the outset through inattention to details.

The Independent Television Service (ITVS) Web site is a mine of information on how to apply and what independent films have recently been funded (see www.itvs.org and go to "For Producers"). The site gives valuable hints on writing a better application. Passion and innovation are high on the list of desirable attributes.

For information on the PBS series *POV* go to www.pbs.org/pov/utils/aboutpov_faq.html and to their call for entries Web site www.pbs.org/pov/utils/callforentries.html#callforentriesk. The guidelines of these program portals, through which many important American independent documentaries get made, are inundated with applications. Most documentaries must now be initiated by their makers rather than funded at the proposal stage. ITVS and POV ask producers to apply with a substantial amount of the footage or a long edited version.

Web sites that offer open access are normally a mine of information on all aspects of making documentaries for television. Read carefully, because everything you see is meant to parry the commonest mistakes and misunderstandings. Most documentary applications are abysmal. An ITVS regional jury on which I once sat for 3 days ended up unanimously considering only 6 out of 140 applications to be at all promising. Two of those we chose (which ITVS in the end failed to support) went on by other means to become quite famous independent films.

Note that when you propose a film to television, they expect you to be geared to their audience and to have plans for your film to function educationally in designated communities afterward. Documentaries are expected to have long and useful lives after their single showing on TV, and it's your job to figure out who will use your film afterward and in what way.

THE TREATMENT

The treatment, like the proposal, is more armament in the battle to get a film made and exists to convince a sponsor, fund, or broadcasting organization that you are uniquely prepared to make a film of impact and significance. Whereas the proposal presents its argument rationally via categorized information, the treatment evokes how an audience would experience the film on the screen. A treatment is therefore a short story narrative that excludes any philosophical or directorial intentions. To make one,

- Restructure the information you worked up in the proposal into a chronological presentation, allotting one paragraph per sequence.
- Write an active-voice, present-tense summary of *what an audience watching the film you expect to make will see and hear from the screen.*
- Write colorfully so that the reader visualizes what you see in your mind's eye.
- Convey information and evoke your characters wherever possible by using their own words in brief, pithy quotations.
- Never write anything that the reader will think you cannot produce.
- Keep within the specified page count.

BUDGET PLANNING FORM

Your final budget, or a budget summary sheet, should wherever possible be done using a budget software program. Here is an all-purpose form to prompt what you will need to cover by way of costs (Figure 15–1). Note that in this early stage, you may find it useful to compile for your own use both high and low figures as optimistic and pessimistic approaches, respectively. This should keep you from underestimation. A contingency percentage is always added at the end of a film budget to cover the unforeseen, such as bad-weather delays, reshoots, additions, or substitutions. Note that unusually low budgets are seen as a sign of dangerous inexperience and seldom attract support.

THE PROSPECTUS

This presentation package or portfolio communicates your project and its purposes to non-filmmaking funders, who may be quite task oriented. The League of Left-Handed Taxidermists wants to know how *Stuffing Badgers* will be useful to them, how much it costs, and why. A prospectus should be thoroughly professional and contain:

Brief Particulars for Project

Working Title:			Length ___ m ___ secs	
Crew Member	Address		Home phone	Work phone
(Director)				
(Camera)				
(Sound)				
(Editor)				
Format (circle all that apply):	DV/Betacam/Digital Betacam/HD Other _____		Film: B&W/color 16 mm/35 mm	
Schedule	Preproduction	Production	Postproduction	
From (date)				
To (date)				
Brief description of subject:				
Film's Working Hypothesis is:				

Preproduction

Item	*Low Estimate*	*High Estimate*
Director/researcher @ ____ per day for ____/____ days		
Travel		
Phone		
Photocopying		
Food		
Accommodation		
Tests		
Research (library, etc.)		
1: Preproduction SUBTOTAL		

FIGURE 15–1

Short budget estimate form. Note high and low estimate figures. A contingency percentage of the below-the-line costs is often added to the total to allow for the unforeseeable.

Production

Role	Daily Rate	Min Days	Max Days	Low Estimate	High Estimate
Director					
Camera Operator					
Sound Operator					
Gaffer					
Other					
2a: Production personnel SUBTOTAL					
Equipment					
Camera (film)					
Camcorder					
Magazines (film)					
Changing bag (film)					
Clapper board (film)					
Lenses					
Filter kit					
Exposure meter					
Color tem. meter					
Tripod					
Baby legs					
H-hat					
Tilt head					
Spreader					
Video monitor					
Nagra package (film)					
Headphones					
Mike boom					
Extra mikes					
Mixer					

FIGURE 15–1 *continued*

Role	Daily Rate	Min Days	Max Days	Low Estimate	High Estimate
Batteries					
Sun gun					
Lighting package					
Tie in cables					
Extension cords					
Other _____					
Other _____					

2b: Production equipment SUBTOTAL

Materials	Type	Cost per Unit	Min Days	Max Days	Low Estimate	High Estimate
Camera raw stock						
Nagra tape						
Develop negative						
Make workprint						
Sound transfer						
Sound stock						
Videocassettes						
Other _____						
Other _____						
Miscellaneous	Type	Per Day	Min	Max		
Insurance						
Transport						
Food						
Accommodation						
Location or other fees						
Other _____						
2c: Production miscellaneous SUBTOTAL						

FIGURE 15–1 *continued*

Postproduction

Role	Cost per Day	Min Days	Max Days	Low Estimate	High Estimate
Editor					
Assistant editor					
Narrator					
3a: Postproduction personnel SUBTOTAL					

Materials	Type	Amount	Min	Max		
Archive footage						
Time coding						
Window dub						
Offline editing equipment						
Music						
Titling						
Online (video)						
Sound mix						
Transfer mag master to optical (film)						
Conforming (film)						
First answer print (film)						
First release print (film)						
3b: Postproduction materials and processes SUBTOTAL						
Production office						
Legal						
Insurance						
Phone/fax, assistance, and other production office expenses						
Production manager						
Other _____						
Other _____						
4: Production office SUBTOTAL						

FIGURE 15–1 *continued*

Budget Summary

Phase	Category	Subtotal		Minimum Estimate	Maximum Estimate
Preproduction	1: Personnel and materials TOTAL				
Production	2a: Personnel				
	2b: Equipment/materials				
	2c: Miscellaneous				
	TOTAL				
Postproduction	3a: Personnel				
	3b: Materials/processes				
	TOTAL				
	4: Production office				
	FINAL SUBTOTAL				
	Contingency (add 12% of final subtotal)				
PRODUCTION GRAND TOTAL					

FIGURE 15–1 *continued*

1. *Cover letter:* This succinctly communicates the nature of the film, its budget, the capital you want to raise, and what you want from the addressee. If you are targeting many small investors, this may have to be a general letter, but wherever possible fashion a specific letter to a specific individual.

2. *Title page:* Finding a good title usually takes inordinate effort but does more than anything at this stage to arouse respect and interest. Evocative photos or other professional-looking artwork in the prospectus can do much to make your presentation persuasive.

3. *One liner:* A simple, compact declaration of the project. For example,
   - A theater director goes to live as one of the homeless so that she can knowledgeably direct a play about homeless people
   - Marriage as seen in the ideas and play of 7-year-olds from across the social spectrum
   - Three people, of different ages and from different countries, relive their near-death experiences and explain how profoundly their lives changed afterward

4. *Synopsis:* Brief recounting of the documentary's intended story that captures its flavor and style.

5. *History and background:* How and why the project evolved and why you feel compelled to make it. This is where you establish your commitment to

the people and story. This is very important because nobody finishes a complex project unless he or she has an emotional investment in it.

6. *Research:* Outline what research you've done and what it has shown you. Here you establish the factual foundation to the film, its characters, and its context. If special cooperation, rights, or permissions are involved, here is where you prove that you can secure them.

7. *Reel:* A 3- to 5-minute, specially edited trailer on VHS or DVD that proves the characters, landscape, style, and other attractions to which you lay claim. It may be a single sequence of great power or a montage of material. This is your chance to let the screen make your argument. Be aware that when there are 400 applications, reels must be of distinguished material that makes its point extremely rapidly. Include an overview list to help make viewing an alluring prospect.

8. *Budget:* Summary of expected expenditures. Don't understate or underestimate—it makes you look amateurish and may leave you asking for too little.

9. *Schedule:* Approximate shooting period (or periods, if shooting is broken up) and preferred starting dates.

10. *Resumés of creative personnel:* In brief paragraphs, name the director, producer, camera operator, sound operator, and editor, with summaries of their qualifications. Append a one-page resumé for each. Your aim is to present the team as professional, exciting, and specially suited.

11. *Audience and market:* Say whom the film is intended for and outline a distribution plan to show convincingly that the film has a waiting audience. Copies of letters of interest from television stations, channels, film distributors, or other interested parties are very helpful here.

12. *Financial statement:* If you have legally formed with others into a company or group, make an estimate of income based on the distribution plan and say if you are a bona fide not-for-profit company or working through one, because this may offer investors tax advantages they can claim against their contributions.

13. *Means of transferring funds:* Supply a letter for the investor to use as a model that makes committing funds to your production account easy.

Every grant application is potentially the beginning of a lengthy relationship, so your prospectus and proposals should convey the essence of your project and its purpose in a clear, colorful, individual, and impeccable way. Each prospectus you send out should be tailored to the particular addressee, but don't promise different things to different people because that could spell big trouble later.

At this stage you are what you write, so use all the facilities you can muster to give your work truly professional-looking graphics and typesetting. This is a tricky moment because you may have been unable to do more than basic research and must minimize your uncertainties. Once the project is deemed feasible and funds have been secured, then research and development can begin in earnest.

CHAPTER 16

RESEARCH LEADING UP TO THE SHOOT

This chapter deals with

- Research alone or with a partner
- A research "case history" to illustrate typical research strategies, deciding the action, casting the players, and the value of assigning metaphors and metaphorical roles
- How people alter in front of the camera and whether it matters
- Developing the film's thematic structure and double-checking your findings
- Developing your film's dialectics and a working hypothesis
- Pulling it all together into a dramatic plan with the three acts defined
- The dramatic components of successful scenes (beats, dramatic units)

Your proposal has received the green light, and now you are ready to embark on the next phase of research. This is the period of concentrated investigation and decision making that culminates in readiness to shoot. We are going to look at this period using an imaginary case history, one that contains just about everything typical.

RESEARCH PARTNERSHIP

An ideal way to research is in partnership with a second person, perhaps a key member of the crew. Film's strength lies in its collaborative nature, and you will appreciate how much richer your perceptions and ideas can become when you exchange them with a like-minded partner. Another benefit is having moral support when penetrating new places and confronting prejudicial attitudes. Together both partners can be relaxed, and the reassuring naturalness between you carries over into your participants' attitude to the camera, as you can see in the Maysles Brothers' *Grey Gardens* (1975).

A further benefit of partnership is being able to compare intuitions, particularly those of foreboding. There is much you detect only on the edge of consciousness, and it is all too easy to overlook an important early warning. Your peripheral vision may also pick up clues and hints that lead to greater things. Here, too, a partner can provide the vital endorsement.

A SAMPLE SUBJECT FOR DISCUSSION

Let us assume that you want to make a film about a local school band that you've been following for a while and that you find fascinating for particular reasons. You want to go further than merely showing how the band rehearses or how it absorbs new members, because that would merely illustrate what common sense alone would expect. Your purpose is to try and lay bare the fanaticism and quasimilitary discipline underlying the band's success.

Before shooting anything, find out whether such an idea is feasible. This is one of the prime purposes of research. By the way, if you work for television and must produce a film in a given time, it is a good idea to pursue the fundamentals of *several* possible ideas from the outset. Projects have a nasty habit of folding up. Permission to shoot might be a stumbling block, but sometimes during research you lose all conviction that any really meaningful film is possible. Recognizing this in time is somehow always easier when you have standby alternatives.

We are going to pursue the possibilities of this school band through the various stages of preproduction. Researching means initially surveying the general area to see if it is promising and beginning by making a "shopping list" of possible sequences. To do this you must start visiting for informal chats.

RESEARCH RELATIONSHIPS

Be purposely tentative when you tell people during research about the project you have in mind. Keeping to generalities lets you feel your way, indicates that you are open to suggestions, and allows participants a stake in determining the film.

To get to the bandmaster in our hypothetical school, you would start with the school principal. You might say that you live nearby and have been thinking about making a film on the school's marching band. If he asks for a full description of the project or a script to show to his board, this is a bad sign. It signifies fear, a bad precedent, excessive caution, a lack of authority, or all of the above. In all probability, he will be delighted and will tell the bandmaster to expect you. When you arrive, approval of your project is already implied because the signal has come from the top. In dealing with any kind of institutional structure, it is usually best to work from the top downward.

When you first make a research visit, take a notebook and nothing else. Explain who you are and what you have done previously. Present yourself in a friendly, respectful way and try to reassure those you meet about your motives. You are there to learn from experts; that is your role, and that is what you should project. It is a truthful presentation of your purpose (though not the whole truth perhaps), and it is a learning role to which most people respond appreciatively.

At this point you really do not know what your future film might contain, nor do you have more than a vague notion of what it will really be about. It is therefore both prudent and truthful to keep your options open and to parry questions with a request for *their* ideas. Often people ask to see a script. Explain that in modern documentary filmmaking, one films events that are real and spontaneous, so documentarians cannot make scripts.

Your role as an observer should be one of extremely wakeful passivity— watching, listening, and correlating what you perceive. Even the relatively suspicious come to respect a truly committed interest and gradually lower their barriers as they come to know you. This takes an investment of time on your part, but keep in mind that *documentaries are only as good as the relationships that permit them to be made.* Few relationships of trust are achieved quickly, so expect to proceed at your subject's own speed. This may mean you spend days, weeks, or even months getting to know your subjects and letting them come to trust you. People do not choose to be distrustful; they have learned to be that way, and unlearning it requires time and exposure.

TWO RESEARCH STRATEGIES

Two ways to elicit opinions without committing yourself to any particular point of view are to play the "student-of-life" role and that of devil's advocate. Instead of saying to the bandmaster, "I think you are tough and inflexible toward those kids," you probe in a more general and depersonalized way, no matter what your convictions may be, by saying, "Some of the people I've spoken to say you are pretty definite about what you want. Do you find there's opposition to this?" And perhaps later, you might hazard something like, "Your experience seems to have shown you that kids need a strong sense of direction." Without committing yourself to agreement, you have shown that you appreciate the bandmaster's convictions.

Many people assume that because you can accurately describe their convictions, you share them. While this is sometimes true, it is more likely a convenient misunderstanding, one it would be unproductive to correct.

Why does the student-of-life approach find such ready acceptance? Initially you will probably feel yourself trying to fake a confident, relaxed interest that you are too anxious to really feel. Do not worry; this is researcher's stage fright and always seems to accompany the initial stages of a new project, even for old hands. Yet you will be amazed at how readily your presence, and your right to ask all sorts of questions, is usually accepted. And then you will be eagerly passed on from person to person. Coming with a friend or colleague's recommendation always raises your trustworthiness several notches.

Have you stumbled upon exceptionally cooperative people? Probably not. Rather, you have uncovered a useful facet of human nature. Most of us seem privately to consider we live in undeserved obscurity, and that nobody properly recognizes our achievements or true worth. When someone comes along wielding the tools of publicity—the pen, microphone, or camera—it offers the fulfillment of a deep-seated yearning. Also, more people than you would imagine have a philanthropic desire to tell the world a few truths it should know. This, I think, helps explain why people may receive you with surprising enthusiasm and respond so gratefully to the recognition your attention confers.

With this comes an obligation on your part to act responsibly and to treat respectfully the lives you enter. More often than not, you will leave the scene of a documentary feeling that your participants have not only given you dinner but have shared something profoundly personal with you and your camera. You carry a strong sense of obligation not just to "the truth," which is an abstract thing, but to good people who gave you something of themselves.

This gets tricky when you feel similarly obligated to those whom you neither like nor approve. Making documentaries poses many awkward questions of moral obligation. One cardinal rule during the research period: *Never even hint you will film any particular scene or any particular person unless you are absolutely certain that you are going to.* Most people are longing to be interviewed or filmed working, no matter how cool they are on the outside. If you don't commit yourself, you will avoid disappointing people and making them feel you have rejected them. As long as possible, stress the tentative and uncertain aspects of your research. You may yet have to shoot certain scenes or interviews, just to keep someone happy. Diplomacy of this kind costs time and money and is to be avoided.

Another cardinal rule: *Never say you will show footage to participants, either cut or uncut, if you think there is the remotest possibility that pressure will be brought on you to make undesirable changes.* Participants in a film, whether documentary or fiction, are generally appalled by their own appearance and mannerisms. They are the worst people to help you make judgments about balance and content. If people argue over this, tell them that a reporter does not have to show her notebook to anyone before the article comes out in the newspaper and that documentarians are no different. You must avoid anything leading to loss of editorial control. This is ultimately in your participants' interest as well as your own, because their initial shock and embarrassment usually change later to pleasure and self-acceptance when an assembly of people is approving.

DECIDING THE ACTION AND CASTING THE PLAYERS

Earlier I suggested that you should start compiling a list of possible sequences. In the band project you have begun researching, you would spend time at the school getting to know the band's personalities and routine. You would start listing the possible action sequences.

- Auditioning for players
- Individuals practicing
- Group practice
- Marching
- Special performances
- Social activities between members either before or after sessions
- Social activities between members in times of waiting

As if for a fiction movie, you have been finding locations and pieces of action. Now you need to set about "casting players." You should begin making private, confidential notes on outstanding individuals. What kind of people are they? What does each represent in the whole? One may be the clown, another might be the diplomat, and another the uncertain kid who dislikes the band's militarism but likes being a member too much to leave. There may be senior kids who act as "policemen" and enforcers of the band's discipline. There may be a few eccentrics whose presence is tolerated because their playing outweighs their oddities.

THE VALUE OF ASSIGNING METAPHORICAL ROLES

It is extremely helpful to go beyond functional descriptions for your characters and give each a *metaphorical* characterization. All this, of course, is for your private use and not divulged to your subjects, as they might think you were mocking them. By producing a metaphorical vision of the group and their situation, you are compelling yourself to define each person's underlying and unacknowledged role. Fred Wiseman's *Hospital* (1969)—about all the human problems that find their way into a New York hospital emergency room—makes us think of purgatory, where souls are rescued or sent onward. Before our eyes the doctors, nurses, policemen, and patients become players in a renewed version of mythology. Echoes of mythology and archetypes underpin every successful documentary just as they do every arresting narrative.

Your obligation, as documentarian and artist, is therefore to more than just reflecting reality. A mirror does that, reflecting what it sees in a value-neutral and uninflected way that would be utterly banal in an artwork. You want your story to contain the characters, passions, atmospheres, and struggle proper to any human tale, but your film must reveal something more or different about your subject than people expect. The key lies in going beyond a sociological rendering. You must adopt the vision of the poet or dramatist who sees how the constants of myth and legend are regenerated in everyday life, and who looks for poetic meanings.

Giving a name to each of the metaphorical roles you see being enacted by the participants (for example, king, queen, jester, prophet of doom, diplomatic troubleshooter, sentry, earth mother) helps you do this. It gets you to recognize how, as in most established groups, your people have unconsciously set up a microcosmic society with its own roles, rules, values, and sanctions. With this golden key in hand, your film can go about compactly portraying this complete world in miniature.

Let us imagine that the band begins to look like a militaristic, patriotic, and authoritarian microcosm. It seems to say a lot about the ideology and background common to the teachers and students. Perhaps you now want to supplement with interviews the band activities, which suggest the contradictory values of both collaboration and dictatorship, because you see no other way to make these things accessible. Interviews, you hope, will give your audience access to the way the students and their teachers think. From chatting with people and absorbing many different points of view, you realize which individuals best represent the conflicting ideals you want to make visible. Certainly the bandmaster is a charismatic figure, and his power is accepted by most as a beneficial imposition. Talk to key instrumentalists and to other teachers, and casually cross check your own impressions by asking each for a view of the others.

THE PREINTERVIEW AND HOW PEOPLE ALTER IN FRONT OF THE CAMERA

During research you investigate the ramifications of your subject, but you also test the behavior of potential interviewees as they go on record. Someone with an unsuppressed yearning to "be famous" (which is what people associate with film and television cameras) may come across as a show-off or instead clam up from sheer nervousness. This could derail your shooting and you can't risk that.

So now it's time to take along a camcorder to do some preliminary interviews. I ask permission before turning on my machine and give some explanation of why I am doing an initial recording. When they begin, most interviewees are self-conscious and constrained. Soon they begin to speak more freely and with feeling, though some do not. Some instead become monosyllabic or show an accentuated tendency to digress or to qualify everything they begin to say.

Take your recordings and immerse yourself in them, letting thoughts and associations come to you on their own. Make scribbled notes of these. You are learning who will give you the most, who remains undistorted by character hang-ups, and who, on the other hand, cannot or will not deliver when he goes on record. Sometimes an interesting and likable person simply does not record well. His voice may be flat or uncongenial, or he does not construct verbal pictures in a logical, communicative way. Others prove to be monotonous or expressionless, and their affect negates whatever they say or do on screen. Even the voice quality itself matters greatly. Henry Kissinger's harsh voice, for example, may have been a major factor in his unpopularity.

For some reason, none of this is easy to see until you are out of the person's presence and can watch a tape, free of a sense of obligation. Recognizing now what does or does not work will save time, money, and heartache later. Often, of course, a recording confirms to the point of finality what you already suspected: Person A is a delight to watch and hear, and you are sure you want to use her. Person B, however, seems constrained and evasive by comparison, and you become sure that he cannot be in the film.

Your priorities are emerging, and the key participants—each representing different and probably opposing aspects in your underlying framework—have become a natural choice. These preinterviews can be used later as voice-over if you took care to record well, in a quiet place, and without letting voices overlap. You now have the unpleasant task of telling Person B that you won't need his services. Maybe there's something he can do for you on camera so that he doesn't feel completely rejected.

DEVELOPING THE FILM'S THEMATIC STRUCTURE

You have become convinced that the band, with its charismatic father figure at the helm, is a viable analog for a disturbing aspect of your country's political structure. This analogy is by no means farfetched. Peter Davis' *Hearts and Minds* (1974) repeatedly uses scenes of American sports and the team spirit atmosphere

to serve as an explanation and an analogy for the values expressed by supporters of the war in Vietnam. The film implies that the sports mentality conditions
young Americans to enter an ideological conflict under the tragically simplistic
notion of "our team" and "their team." Only in the field as they saw friends and
foes die did the young GIs begin to question what "playing for the team" actually meant. By such conditioning and metaphors in peacetime, the film suggests,
do we prepare our young people to suffer and die in the prosecution of grand
abstractions like "America," "freedom," and "my leaders, right or wrong." By
finding the embodiment of such paradigms, the documentarian draws attention
to the shadowy substructures of a whole society.

The documentarian's job is to point out the superficial and reveal deeper
truths. Suppose, in between the band practicing, the band members watch George
W. Bush in the nightly news exhorting the country to go to war again in the cause
of freedom and democracy. This, intercut with the bandmaster practicing tough
love as he conducts, might create a telling argument by analogy. It might prove
to be a cheap shot, but you won't know until you try it.

DOUBLE-CHECKING YOUR FINDINGS

During research, collect as many relevant viewpoints as you can. Your initial
judgments are often based on brief and persuasive exposure that later proves partisan, so testing your assumptions against the impressions of people whose lives
make them expert helps you sift out as much reliable information as possible. It
also helps you find the personalities and forces that are quietly ranged against
each other.

It is fascinating to discover how everyone, especially the visible and powerful, is perceived differently according to whom you question. Biases and prejudiced viewpoints are inevitable, and you need to develop ideas about what they
spring from. Cross checking different impressions of your major "characters"
enables you to avoid superficial judgments and lets you build into your film the
diversity of affinities and tensions that make any group of people vital and
fascinating.

You have become almost oppressively knowledgeable about the people and
practices that surround the school's marching band. You need to withdraw and
decide your priorities, because if you were to shoot now you would lack clear
direction.

FINDING THE DIALECTICS AND DEVELOPING
A WORKING HYPOTHESIS

Whatever your initial motives were for looking into the marching band, they
must now be reviewed in the light of your greater knowledge. Earlier I said that
a film qualifies as a documentary when it implies a critical attitude toward some
aspect of society. Here we face some problems inherent in film, because as
Richardson says in *Literature and Film*, "literature has the problem of making
the significant somehow visible, while film often finds itself trying to make the
visible significant." Film generally, and documentary in particular, has an over-
supply of the real. An unstoppable torrent of surface trivia often obscures deeper

meanings. It may not be enough to merely *show* something: we must also indicate where its significance lies. How is this achieved?

What we find significant—in issues as well as in individuals—exists because conflict is at work. It may be internal conflict in an individual who is torn between allegiances to class, generation, or a system of belief. It may be between individuals of different opinions, different convictions, or different ambitions. Or it may, like Nanook's, be between the individual and his environment as he struggles to adjust to harsh changes and to survive. A large proportion of people on the planet live, and have always lived, in dire insecurity—balanced between tenuous survival and annihilation by hunger, disease, or ideological enemies.

No human being, however free of threat from the outside, is without the internal conflicts that arise from conflicting needs, desires, or ambitions. Popularized versions of Freudian analysis suggest that every motive and every ill has its explanation in a few major principles, but Jean-Luc Godard was right to say that in drama as in life, we can never properly enter another's thoughts and feelings through psychological keys. Everything we learn about another person is suggestive, fragmentary, and pieced together from observing that person's behavior—particularly that which seems contradictory. Nor surprisingly, Godard's approach to revealing characters is simply to concentrate on their contradictions, because these invariably signal what is active and unresolved in their lives.

To show the pressing truths in human life, documentary must uncover the ambiguities and contradictions in its characters' "unfinished business" and focus on those most in flux. Poetry, says Billy Collins, "is a camping grounds for ambiguity and paradox." Documentary joins poetry whenever it plumbs the human psyche, for it finds contrary impulses and contradictory beliefs.

In your research, you now suspect that the band exemplifies how the country talks eternally about democracy yet hungers for "strong leadership" to sort out the misfits for their own good. But now you hit a snag. Although the bandmaster is an authoritarian of the worst kind, bands do need leaders, and a lot of the kids rather like him. Even more confounding is that, in spite of disagreeing with all his ideas, *you* find yourself liking him too.

What to do? Give up? Surely you have stumbled on a truly interesting subject, all the more so because you yourself have contradictory, ambivalent feelings toward benevolent dictatorship and toward the situation that he has projected around him. For your own clarity, you must now define the focus, the underlying and implicit concept of your film. This, which should not be shared with anyone outside your crew, is vital to determining the shooting to come. A helpful example comes to mind from a feature film. You may have seen *The Orchestra Rehearsal* (1979), a ribald Fellini movie shot for television about a fictitious orchestra in an opera house that rebels against its conductor and descends into anarchy. A comedy on the surface, it makes serious use of the orchestra as a metaphor for our complex, interdependent, and, of necessity, highly disciplined society. The conductor is the leader but can only fulfill his role if players cooperate by accepting his authority. Once they begin to assert autonomy, the music first becomes flawed, then discordant, and then completely chaotic. Eventually the opera house, under attack by unseen enemies, begins to fall down and out of sheer discomfort the orchestra reforms itself and returns to fulfilling its best potential.

An allegorical movie like this helps show how a band and its bandmaster might be a rather potent metaphor for the leader of a political unit such as a tribe or a nation. In fact, by dealing with charisma and authority, your movie could quite easily become a parable about power, nation, and the ideology that drives it.

Some in the social sciences will feel uneasy here and say, "But that's manipulation!" I would answer, yes it is. Film being a subjectively generated medium, the documentary can never be an ideal tool of social science. It cannot credibly postulate, as one can in print, the existence of such and such a phenomenon and reinforce its arguments with objectively gathered evidence. Rather, its purpose is artistic, to relay a way of seeing and feeling. At its best the documentary can take something apparently banal and unmeaningful, and give us a heightened, subtly argued vision that is charged with significance for our own lives.

So what meaning, what thematic structure, can we find in the band situation? You have discovered what you never believed existed: a benevolent despot who is valued and valuable, even though all his "subjects" see themselves as rugged individualists. It's a wonderful allegory for a "free" society that consents to march in lockstep in order to achieve supremacy, one that enthusiastically submits to a form of leadership that is the very antithesis of its democratic and individualist ideals. This is the kernel of your idea—this paradox below the surface that you "see."

Now all your sequences—the activities, interviews, and discussions you ask the kids to have between themselves for the camera—must create the contradictory parts. It is a complex vision and ultimately a nonjudgmental one that reflects little that you first expected to find. Instead it shows what was there, existing in the face of all logic and belief.

Though I invented this example, I experienced a similar conversion myself while making a film many years ago on an aristocratic estate in rural England. My film (A Remnant of a Feudal Society) reflected my inability to reconcile the contradictory nature of the estate, which operated in quite a feudal way until modern times. Some of the survivors remembered the estate community with nostalgia as a place of security and order—plenty of hard work but a great spirit of belonging. Others felt the regime was to some degree imprisoning, demeaning, and overdemanding. Not one person had clear, simple feelings because all had differing experiences and most had only arrived at tentative, qualified conclusions. The only predictable element was that those in the upper echelon recalled the old days with more nostalgia than those lower down, although everyone valued the place's safety and continuity.

Because of the rather monolithic view of history I'd absorbed in school, I had expected those who had served a feudal master to unite in condemnation. The reality was more human, complex, and interesting and showed me why my school history books had seemed dull next to real life.

THE WORKING HYPOTHESIS AS A NECESSITY

One never starts a journey without some direction and purpose. In documentary any hypothesis, even a frankly admitted prejudice, provides a more fruitful starting point than vacuity masquerading as scientific method. Had I not begun the feudal estate film from my own anti-authoritarianism, I probably would have developed no deeper vision of the place. The film would have been a tedious exercise in nostalgia, with colorful rustics and their masters remembering the good old days. Doing this is not directing but handing control over to your participants, who duly hand back whatever they think is expected. You see this all the time in the work of those who mistake critical tension for hostility. Critical vision is essential to being fully alive. Revel in it.

From the moment you are first attracted to an idea, write out *the minimum your film must express*. This, modified during research, will ensure a "bottom line"—something concrete that you intend to realize through the film. With thorough and focused preparation, the basic film is sure, barring accidents. You are freed during shooting from the terrifying gremlin that whispers in your ear, "Do you really have a film here?" From this solid base you will be able to see further and supplement or modify your original vision. Even within the pressures of shooting, you can easily keep the hypothesis in mind as the measure of everything you film.

Almost always, the working hypothesis is extended and enriched during the shooting into something far beyond the minimum you pegged out for an interesting film.

One gruesome fact about authorship must be stated emphatically: if you don't decide what your film's hypothesis will be, you will *not* find it during shooting. The demands of shooting preclude contemplation, so we might say that *a documentary only becomes a true inquiry when it starts from having something to say*. Go out with a crew expecting to naturally find "something to say," and all your energies will get burnt up keeping the crew busy and trying to fool them into thinking you know what you're doing. Back in the editing room, you'll find that the material has no focus and no vision.

Research is useless unless you turn your findings into specific, practical, concrete resolutions.

REFINING RESEARCH INTO A PLAN

THE NEED FOR DEVELOPMENT, CONFLICT, AND CONFRONTATION

Essential to any story is growth or change in the main character or situation. Here many documentaries fail by spending their time developing what turns out to be a static situation. This is a particular hazard during a short shooting time, because most human processes are rather long. You can avoid this, if logistics permit, by filming intermittently over a longer period so that change is inbuilt. A film that capitalizes magnificently on the passage of time is Michael Apted's *28 Up* (1986), which revisits a group of children at 7-year intervals from the ages of 7 through 28. Because so many eerily fulfill their earliest ideas about education, career, and marriage, this *longitudinal study* is haunting and raises important questions about how, and even whether, people make the choices that so deeply affect personal destiny. By now there is a *35 Up* and a *42 Up*, but I prefer the scope of their predecessor. Other longitudinal studies, inspired by the *Up* series, have been started in several countries.

Many documentaries shot in a restricted period leave the viewer disgruntled because nothing of importance changes. You can ensure development in your film by searching out where change is happening. This may be *physical movement* (e.g., new house, new job, journey) or *movement in time* (change of season for farmer, woman starts challenging new job, painter experiences first retrospective of his work), or it may be *psychological development* (ex-prisoner adjusts to freedom, teenager gets first paying job, adult illiterate learns to read).

Another way to ensure development is to make a film dealing with a short-term conflict that you can follow through enough stages to build up a sense of movement. This conflict might be within one character (a mother takes her child for his first day at school), between two characters (two social scientists with conflicting theories of criminality attend a key court case), between a character and the environment (an African farmer survives a drought from day to day), or thousands of other combinations.

Being able to show change comes from developing a sensitivity to people's issues and therefore anticipating how and where they face a crisis. You can help yourself by answering these questions: *What is this person trying to get or do? What does he want?* The question is valuable because it demands that you define a person in terms of movement and will. Volition cannot exist without opposition, you arrive quickly at the next important question: *What or who is keeping this person from getting what he wants?*

The elements of struggle, contest, and will are at the heart of dramatic tension in every narrative medium, documentary not excepted. A documentary without a struggle for movement is just a catalogue of expository episodes. You and I have yawned through a hundred such films.

While shooting your marching band film you can anticipate several kinds of development. One might be in a young contender auditioning to enter the band. Another might happen during a big competitive event that puts everyone under stress. Yet another might be after graduation, when the big man at school faces being a nobody searching for a job. With these processes covered, you have metaphorically encompassed a cycle of birth, life, and death in the band's ongoing existence.

You can define a conflict in your head, but it remains invisible and abstract unless you show it in action on the screen. Be sure, therefore, that you build the conflict's sides stage by stage, and be sure to arrange, if necessary, a *confrontation* between the opposing elements in your movie. If an instrumentalist has to pass a stringent test, be sure to shoot its key elements. If a young man must find a job, be sure to shoot him interviewing for one. It is always better to show struggle than to talk about it.

You may have to ensure that "the confrontation" happens; you might, for instance, arrange for two players with opposing views of the band to slug it out verbally or musically in front of the camera. If, in a film about a homeless shelter the key issue is whether strict rules are necessary, be sure to film clashes between inmates and those in charge. It may be necessary to ask either staff or inmates to initiate a typical episode or re-enact one if none happens spontaneously. This is the catalyst function that participatory cinema directors use and observational cinema exponents abhor. The poet and novelist Thomas Hardy said that "Art is the secret of how to produce by a false thing the effect of a true."

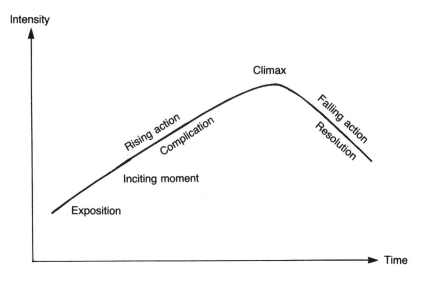

FIGURE 16–1

Dramatic curve. Variations of this apply to most narrative art, including documentary films. The same principle also is useful in analyzing a single scene.

THE DRAMATIC CURVE

It is never easy to forecast how documentary shooting will turn out in relation to your hopes. Applying the traditional dramatic curve (Figure 16–1) to your ideas, however, is useful during research and outstandingly useful as an analytical tool during editing, which is really the second chance to direct.

The concept of the dramatic curve is derived from Greek drama and represents how most stories first state their problem, develop tension through scenes of increasing complication and intensity, then arrive at an apex or "crisis." After this comes change and resolution—though not, let me say quickly, necessarily a happy or peaceful one. In Broomfield's and Churchill's *Soldier Girls* (1981), the crisis is probably the point at which Private Johnson, after a series of increasingly stressful conflicts with authority, leaves the army dishonorably but in a spirit of relieved gaiety. The film's resolution, once this major character quits the stage, is to examine more closely what soldiers need during training to survive battle conditions.

In the Maysles Brothers' *Salesman* (1969), most people think the story's apex is the moment when Paul Brennan, the salesman who has been falling steadily behind the pack like a wounded animal, unwittingly sabotages a colleague's sale. In the film's coda, his partners distance themselves as if deserting a dying man. The resolution is to leave Paul staring offscreen into a void.

Once you understand the idea of the apex or crisis, the rest of the dramatic convention arranges itself naturally in stages before and after the peak of the curve to make the classic three-act structure. Three categories precede the climax, and one follows. Let's examine the idea in more detail so that you can apply it to your research:

Act I

1. The *introduction or exposition* establishes the *setup* by laying out main characters and their situation and giving enough necessary factual information about time, place, period, and so on to get started. Modern drama often lacks a captive audience, so it cannot afford to delay the major committing action. The main conflict, or struggle between opposing forces, will probably be established early in the documentarian's "contract" with the audience. Signaling the scope and focus of the film to come, it aims to secure their interest for the duration.

2. The *inciting moment* is whatever sets in motion the opposition of interests. In the military, basic training sets in motion a battle between the homogenizing goals of the army and the self-protecting individualism of the recruit. The army aims to break down individual identity and replaces it with a psyche trained to unthinkingly obey. In *Soldier Girls* the inciting moment is when Sergeant Abing sees Private Johnson smirking after he has rebuked her. This signals the onset of a long and unequal struggle between them. Because a white male is imposing his will on a black female, the situation is replete with disquieting overtones of slavery and colonialism.

Act II

3. *Rising action* or *complication* usually shows the basic conflicts being played out as variations having surprise, suspense, and escalating intensity. In *Soldier Girls*, the army's expression of will and the misfits' expression of cowed resistance are repeatedly raised a notch to more serious and offensive levels. Seeing protagonists and antagonists engaged in such a revealing struggle, we come to understand the motivations, goals, and background of each, and during this period we choose sides. Our sympathies vacillate in the face of ambiguity.

4. In the final *confrontation* comes the *climax* or *apex* of the curve, a point of irreversible change.

Act III

5. The *resolution* or *falling action* is what the piece establishes as the consequence. This includes not only what happens to the characters but also what interpretation for the whole is suggested by the last scene or scenes. How you let the audience last see the characters in a documentary, as in other story forms, can alter the impact of an entire film.

Few documentaries fall neatly into this shape, but some memorable ones do. The formula is used with awful fervor in Hollywood, and some screenwriting manuals even prescribe a page count per act, with particular page numbers for "plot points" where the story lurches off at an interesting tangent. Documentary, thank goodness, is too wayward a form to attract such control fever, but it still needs to be dramatically satisfying, and this is just as true for essay, montage, or other forms of documentary, not just those of the narrative variety. Indeed, this escalation of pressure, crisis, then lowering to resolution is also found in songs, symphonies, dance, mime, and traditional tales, because it is as basic to human life as breathing or sex.

THE BEST SCENES ARE DRAMAS IN MINIATURE

What is fascinating is that a successful documentary scene is a drama in miniature; it follows the same curve of pressures building to a climax before releasing
into a new situation. During the shoot, the documentary director often sees a
scene develop, spin its wheels, and refuse to go anywhere. Then, perhaps with
some *side coaching* (verbal inquiry or prompts by the director from off-camera)
the characters lock onto an issue and struggle over it until something significant
changes. This fulcrum point of change, called in the theater a *beat*, is the basic
unit of any scene containing dramatic interchange. Even compilation montage
films that lack foreground characters, such as Pare Lorentz's *The River* (1937),
follow the same dramatic curve.

LOOK FOR BEATS AND DRAMATIC UNITS

When you see someone go through a moment of irreversible change of consciousness, such as realizing his love is recognized or that he is faced with incontrovertible evidence that he lied, you are seeing a *beat*. Other characters in the
scene may not notice anything, but that character (and the informed onlooker)
sees that moment of change and knows that he must now take a different course
of action.

A dramatic unit includes

- The initiation of a new issue
- Complications that escalate the pressures
- Apex of the confrontation
- The beat—a change of consciousness in one character that initiates a new
  issue and the onset of a new dramatic unit

A scene may have one dramatic unit or several. As you learn to recognize
dramatic units taking place in daily life and you see them unfold for you to
shoot, you know when to turn the camera on and later what portions of the documented scene to use. Being able to recognize this dramatic breathing action as
it takes place is the preeminent skill for actors and directors, in fiction or in
documentary.

A successful progression of beats contributes *dramatic tension*. It sets up
questions, anticipations, even fears in your audience. Never be afraid to make
them wait and guess. As Wilkie Collins, the father of the mystery novel, said,
"Make them laugh, make them cry, but make them wait." The need for dramatic
tension applies fully to the documentary.

EXPOSITION, FACTS, AND NARRATION

Before shooting, you should know what factual material you must gather so that
the audience can understand each situation. Nobody wants to use a narrator
if it can be avoided, so develop an ongoing list of facts that will be vital to an

audience's understanding of the material. These will include names, places, ages, dates, times, the sequence of main events, relationships, and so on. This factual information, or *exposition*, must emerge one way or another if the film is to make sense to a first-time audience. An important part of your role as director is to draw this material out of the participants and *in more than one version*. If you cover all your bases, you can probably avoid writing and recording narration. Images and characters may supply all vital information as it is needed.

CHAPTER 17

MISSIONS AND PERMISSIONS

This chapter addresses the following issues:

- Explaining your purposes and developing a foundation of trust
- Developing loyalties to those in your films and your obligations to "truth"
- When to warn participants of the consequences of being filmed
- Getting evidence that is convincing
- Truth claims in transparent and reflexive documentaries
- Your documentary as a catalyst of change in your participants' lives
- Accepting your incapacity for any ultimate truth or final word
- Authorship as looking both inward and outward at the world
- Being changed by your work
- Letting your last work prepare you for your next
- Location scouting, logistics, and scheduling
- Securing location and personal releases

Directing even the briefest documentary soon shows how loyalties and obligations develop between yourself and your participants and how authorship is inseparable from ethical dilemmas related to this. A single example: You are making a film about the victims of a housing scam who you get to know and like. You then gain the confidence of the perpetrators, who offer you hospitality. Because refusing might expose your judgment of them, you go out with them, eat an expensive dinner, and laugh at their jokes. When you next visit their victims, you feel thoroughly compromised, even a traitor.

Anyone working as a documentarian begins from a sense of values and mission. At first even the smallest decisions compel you to scared self-examination, but after a few years, particularly if you work in a news organization alongside older and cynical pros, you become more comfortable and risk becoming professional in the worst sense. That is, you are in danger of turning into a skeptical bystander or of using people to illustrate foregone conclusions. Belonging to a powerful corporation makes it seductively easy to overvalue your own importance and to undervalue those who let you into their lives. Following are some general guidelines for various common situations.

APPROACHING PARTICIPANTS

When you confirm that you want someone to participate in a project, you seldom have more than the sketchiest idea of who or what will be used in the film, what it will say, or how this individual, whom you don't know very well, will finally appear to the world. Given such shadowy outcomes, documentaries can only be made on a basis of trust. Indeed, you usually "cast" particular people *because* they are cooperative and show good will. Unfortunately, documentarians have been known to abuse this trust. When I worked at the British Broadcasting Corporation (BBC), a woman factory worker spoke candidly and trustingly in an interview about sexual morals among her female co-workers. Outraged when the film was transmitted, they beat her up the next day. The (male) director apparently knew this was a risk and gambled with her safety for the sake of a more sensational film.

For most participants, nothing comparable is at risk. To read them a standardized list of possible consequences would scare the hell out of them, and for no good reason. The case is different in investigative filmmaking; the very existence of an investigation should be fair warning.

In seeking permission, outright subterfuge is sometimes justified. When someone has just butchered 200 defenseless people, you can jettison all fine moral scruples. Such clarity is rare; usually you are not faced with black and white issues, but shades of pale gray. Such decisions take not less moral courage but more.

HOW THE SHOOTING PROCESS CHANGES THINGS

Altering reality: The fears many new directors express about "altering reality" surely come from believing that they cannot match the objectivity affected by so much on television. Leaving aside the invasiveness of cameras and equipment, it remains true that *every* set of relationships is changed according to whom is present and observing. A family picnic is altered according to who arrives; a 10-year-old child will make a different impact and result in less change to the atmosphere than a man in sunglasses who is silently taking photographs but whom nobody knows. If, however, the photographer first convinces the group that his interests are sympathetic and genuine, or if a trusted member of the group mediates his arrival, the newcomer will be welcomed. Your presence, with or without crew and camera, cannot help altering an event, but the changes can be large or small according to whom you film and how you handle the preparation.

Casting: Choose participants with care. Mistaken casting can mean waking up to find you have committed yourself to someone who resists, distorts, or even manipulates the process. To guard against this, defer decisions about who is to participate until the latest possible moment. The longer you give yourself to see people in action, the less likely you are to miscalculate. To lower the anxiety that distorts how people present themselves, be sure to tell participants that you shoot far more film than you use, so mistakes are unimportant, and avoid all comment about what is likely to survive into the final film.

When you get something other than you expect: Some mishaps and twists of fortune present both ethical and practical difficulties. Suppose the evidence you are getting does not support your hypothesis. Should you make a different film or stop shooting? Suppose somebody's basic situation changes? Suppose your lonely widow suddenly acquires a boyfriend. Do you collect materials to reconstruct the situation as it (interestingly) was, or do you alter your film to reflect the (less interesting) situation as it is now? The answers depend on what you have promised, what code of conduct you have set yourself, and what good story remains possible.

Temptations when interviewing: Interviewing poses ethical responsibilities. For instance, the thrill of the righteous chase can delude one into unfairly demolishing a person's defenses. Although there is a second chance in the cutting room to recognize and prevent this situation from becoming public, the damage to your relationship with your subject (and your co-workers) may remain. Especially if you don't have complete editorial control, you may be forced by your superiors to use something you regret shooting. Some documentarians even say, "If you shoot it, you'll use it."

Here is another interviewing dilemma. You take a participant up to an important, perhaps unperceived, threshold in his life. In a revealing moment, the interviewee crosses into territory never before penetrated. We see what Rouch calls a "privileged moment," where all notion of film as an artificial environment ceases for participant and audience alike. It is a wonderful moment, but it hinges on the revelation of some fact that should not become public. Can you now lean on the person to permit its inclusion in the film? Perhaps the participant is so trusting that you alone can make the decision whether or not it will damage him. Here wise and responsible co-workers can help you carry the burden of decision. But if it is best to suppress the revelation, can you carry on with the film as though nothing new had taken place? Again, only you, making use of your own values and knowledge of the circumstances, can finally decide.

Causing changes: The documentary often alters its subjects' lives merely by exposing them to scrutiny—their own and others. At first, participants will often maintain an "on the record" and an "off the record" relationship with you. Then the line becomes blurred as a participant develops a deepening trust and emotional dependency on you. One day you wake up to realize that you are not just directing a film but are responsible for directing a life as well. Once in a class of mine, there were several projects where this was happening. One was about a man who, as a teenager, narrowly missed being the victim of a multiple sex murderer; another was about a middle-aged gang member who was dying of acquired immune deficiency syndrome (AIDS) and wanted the film about him to become a posthumous message to his beloved daughter; another was about a young male prostitute whose activities existed through contempt for his own body; yet another concerned a *ménage à trois*. All the directors expressed anxieties about their responsibilities, and this needed considerable class discussion time. Invariably they needed support for their decisions more than they needed any radical advice.

PARTICIPANTS MUST LIVE WITH THE FILM'S CONSEQUENCES

Assessing risks: Most films change the lives they record, and it is our responsibility to help make the chemistry a positive one. For documentary participants, there is deserved and undeserved risk. Conceivably you may be told something that, were it to fall into the wrong hands, could lead to someone's injury or even death. This may be the time to stop the camera or to destroy footage. If you intend to broadcast revelations by someone in danger, make absolutely certain that the individual knows the risks and is ready to take them. Under some political regimes, something said confidentially and in passing to a camera crew can, once broadcast, lead to imprisonment or death. If you even suspect that someone will run such a risk in your film, discuss the possibilities with him or her or with the guardian if the subject is underage. Take particular care when the person is unused to being in the public eye.

Informed consent: To secure informed consent from participants means that you warn them that by publicly showing footage—though not necessarily by taking it—their reputation or even their life can be at risk, sometimes irreparably. Unlike the fiction filmmaker paying actors, the documentarian generally offers no financial compensation, and even if a substantial sum changes hands, there's little comfort in trying to settle moral obligations with cash. Checkbook documentary is still likely to be exploitation.

Where do your responsibilities lie? When do you owe loyalty to the individual and when to larger truths? Is there an accepted code of ethics? How much should you say to participants before they become too alarmed to permit filming? Only you and your advisers can decide. Usually your problems lie in the opposite direction, and you will expend much energy trying to convince people either that their fears are unfounded or that being in documentary will make neither you nor them rich and famous. Documentary exists entirely through the voluntary cooperation of participants, so take every care to avoid unnecessary exploitation. Consider what it will cost to do some good in the world, and decide *from your participants' vantage* as well as from your own whether a risk is worth it—a lonely calculation if ever there was one.

Pressures on the director to be ethical: Directing a documentary sometimes feels like being a doctor advising patients about the procedure, complications, and consequences of an irreversible operation. Some participants are not attentive or sophisticated enough to absorb all the implications, and although the signature on the release form discharges legal obligations, it doesn't meet those that are moral. In America during the 1970s, the Loud family consented to have their lives filmed (*An American Family*, 1973, PBS, 12 hour-long episodes). The exposure, first to the camera and then to savage criticism in the press (as though the family were performers) tore the family apart. Afterward the Louds said that the series' intentions were inadequately explained. Maybe so, but the open-ended nature of such undertakings makes comprehensive explanation virtually impossible.

Occasionally the filmmaker, using dubious practices to serve a larger purpose—as did Michael Moore in *Roger and Me* (1989)—can find his methods returning to haunt him. By simplifying and transposing some causes and effects, Moore handed ammunition to his film's many enemies. His later work, *Bowling for Columbine* (2002), which investigates the inanities of gun culture in America, is more careful and all the more effective. Because so few documentaries cross language and cultural frontiers, I was pleasantly surprised to find Moore's cheerful face advertising the film on a Madrid bus stop. It proves that satirical humor in the service of significant subject matter can get a documentary film shown all over the world.

EMBEDDED VALUES

All storytelling begins from assumptions about the way things are and about what will be familiar and acceptable to the audience. You only have to look back a few decades to see how many people, roles, and relationships in movies are represented in archaic or even insulting ways. Women are regularly secretaries, nurses, teachers, mothers, or seductresses. People of color are servants, vagrants, or objects of pity with little to say for themselves. Criminals or gangsters are ethnically branded, and so on—all this is very familiar and may seem like a problem that has passed. Not so.

These stereotypes come from what three film faculty members at the University of Southern California call *embedded values*, or values so natural to the makers of a film that they pass below the radar of awareness. Jed Dannenbaum, Carroll Hodge, and Doe Mayer of USC's School of Cinema and Television have an excellent book about making art, *Creative Filmmaking from the Inside Out: Five Keys to the Art of Making Inspired Movies and Television* (Simon & Schuster, 2003). Its examination of ethics is especially pertinent to documentary, where you can so easily make assumptions that silently guide the outcome of your film. *Creative Filmmaking* is mostly aimed at fiction filmmakers, but it poses some fascinating questions that I have adapted here. Embedded values, so easy to see in the next man's field, creep into your own work with surprising ease. The point is not learning to be politically correct, which is orthodoxy of another kind, but to avoid feeding into whatever is still considered normal and just shouldn't be.

Take a few steps back and consider how your intended documentary represents what is listed in the following and whether the world in your film will reinforce stereotypes or reflect instead the complexity and injustices of life as it is.

Participants:
- *Class:* What class or classes do they come from? How will you show differences? Will other classes be represented, and if so, how?
- *Wealth:* Do they have money? How is it regarded? How do they handle it? What is taken for granted? Are things as they should be, and if not, how will the film express this?
- *Appearances:* Are appearances reliable or misleading? How important are appearances? Do the characters have difficulty reading each other's appearances?

- *Background:* Is there any diversity of race or other background, and how will this be handled? Will other races or ethnicities have minor or major parts?
- *Belongings:* Will we see them work or know how they sustain their lifestyle? What do their belongings say about their tastes and values? Is anyone in the film critical of this?
- *Emblems:* Do they own or use important objects, and what is their significance?
- *Work:* Is their work shown? What does it convey about them?
- *Valuation:* For what do characters value other characters? Will the film question this or cast uncertainty on the intercharacter values?
- *Speech:* What do you learn from the vocabulary of each? What makes the way each thinks and talks different from the others? What does it signify?
- *Roles:* What roles do participants fall into, and will they emerge as complex enough to challenge any stereotypes?
- *Sexuality:* If sexuality is present, is there a range of expression, and will you portray it? Is it allied with affection, tenderness, love?
- *Volition:* Who is able to change their situation and who seems unable to take action? What are the patterns behind this?
- *Competence:* Who is competent and who not? What determines this?

Environment:
- *Place:* Will we know where characters come from, and what values are associated with their origins?
- *Settings:* Will they look credible and add to what we know about the characters?
- *Time:* What values are associated with the period chosen for the setting?
- *Home:* Do the characters seem at home? What do they have around them to signify any journeys or accomplishments they have made?
- *Work:* Do they seem to belong there, and how will the workplace be portrayed? What will it say about the characters?

Family Dynamics:
- *Structure:* What structure emerges? Do characters treat it as normal or abnormal? Is anyone critical of the family structure?
- *Relationships:* How are relationships between members and between generations going to be portrayed?
- *Roles:* Are roles in the family fixed or will they be shown developing? Are they healthy or unhealthy? Who in the family is critical? Who is branded as "good" or "successful" by the family, and who "bad" or "failed"?

- *Power:* Could there be another structure? Is power handled in a healthy or unhealthy way? What is the relationship of earning money to power in the family?

Authority:
- *Gender:* Which gender seems to have the most authority? Does one gender predominate, and if so, why?
- *Initiation:* Who will initiate the events in the film, and why? Who is likely to resolve them?
- *Respect:* How are figures with power going to be depicted? How will institutions and institutional power be depicted? Are they simple or complex, and does what you can show reflect your experience of the real thing?
- *Conflict:* How are conflicts negotiated? What will the film say about conflict and its resolution? Who usually wins, and why?
- *Aggression:* Who is being aggressive and who is being assertive, and why? Who are you supporting in this, and whom do you tend to censure?

In Total:
- *Criticism:* How critical is the film going to be toward what its characters do or don't do? How much will it tell us about what's wrong? Can we hope to see one of the characters coming to grips with this?
- *Approval/Disapproval:* What will the film approve of, and is there anything risky and unusual in what it defends? Is the film challenging its audience's assumptions and expectations, or is it just feeding into them?
- *World View:* If this is a microcosm, what will it say about the balance of forces in the larger world of which it is a fragment?
- *Moral Stance:* What stance will the intended film's belief system take in relation to privilege, willpower, tradition, inheritance, power, initiative, God, luck, coincidence, etc.? Is this what you want?

To make either documentary or fiction is to propose a version of reality. Films that entertain by dwelling on chain saw massacres or teenage shooting rampages gradually alter the threshold of reality for those attracted to such subjects, as a rash of international high school shootings has demonstrated. What do you want to contribute to the world? Are the elements you are using working as you desire?

These considerations are at the core of screen authorship, and *Creative Filmmaking from the Inside Out* has some very pertinent ideas in every area of screen creativity. Concerning embedded values, it asks that you know and take responsibility for the ethical and moral implications in your work.

GIVING AND TAKING

Any discussion of ethics makes the responsibilities of documentary sound very burdensome. But making documentary is not just taking, it is also giving. If "the unexamined life isn't worth living" (Plato), your documentary may endear you to your participants through the self-examination it brings them. Paradoxically, for those culturally unprepared for reflection or proactively solving their problems, your involvement can transform the very lives you may have wanted to record intact. So you face a conundrum, because filming can compromise, subvert, improve, or even create the end result. The answer may be to share the compromises with the audience rather than hide them. Today's audience is sophisticated, knows that filming is a complex artistic process, and is interested in what filming does to the situation under study.

TRUTH CLAIMS

Documentaries usually assert their validity as a truthful record in one of two ways. The traditional approach is to make a film that is honest to the spirit of your best perceptions and trust that the audience can infer the film's honesty. Consciously or otherwise, spectators judge any film against their own instincts and knowledge of life, so "transparent" films—films that purport to show life happening as though no camera were present—can still work very effectively.

In the reflexive approach, the director deliberately builds into the film whatever doubts and perceptions would not be adequately acknowledged through showing the material on its own. Such a film explores perception as well as what is perceived, and this may include some self-portraiture by the makers. Robb Moss' touchingly autobiographical *The Tourist* (1991) examines the two dominant and concurrent aspects of his life—his job as a documentary cameraman, often filming in third world countries where people have too many children, and his marriage to a nurse specializing in neonatal care, with whom he wishes to have children and cannot (Figure 17–1). Without falsely reconciling any of the open questions in his life, Moss chronicles the ironies that fate has dealt them. Finally, the film shows the joy of adopting a daughter.

How one sees, how one connects with others through making a film, is a Pandora's box that cannot be half-opened. Autobiography always omits or suppresses some truths and, by such subtraction, elevates others. As such, truth is always provisional and to some extent fictionalized. Either for economy or for self-preservation, we never tell all about ourselves, and in settling for telling some truths and for others partially told, we recreate ourselves as though we were figures in fiction.

BEHALFERS: SPEAKING FOR OTHERS

Speaking on behalf of others is almost a disease among documentarians, and (as I learned through Henry Breitrose, a fine writer on the documentary) they have earned a special word: *behalfers*. Behalfers make it their work to represent those without a voice, which in the end is everyone who cannot make films themselves. This should remind us how charity is dispensed by the privileged, how it can feel

FIGURE 17–1 ―――――――――――――――――――――――――――――――

Robb Moss examines his own image as cameraman and husband in *The Tourist* (1991). (Photo courtesy of Robb Moss.)

to the recipients, and how self-serving it can be to imagine you are promoting someone else's interests.

Offering your participants a share in authorship may be the only way to overcome the distrust that poisons relations between the religions and races, say, or between feminists and well-meaning males. For decades indigenous peoples were filmed like small children or zoo animals unable to speak for themselves. Missionaries ran roughshod over native populations because it was unimaginable to them that Africans or Aztecs could hold valid spiritual beliefs. The do-good impulse runs deep, so you must be awfully clear about its basis whenever you want to act on it. Belief is dangerous when it legitimizes superiority, and being an ethical filmmaker means treating other people, their values and their lives, with the respect and humility that you would want applied to your own.

As groups and individuals become more sophisticated about film's process and purposes and less trustful of those who elect to speak on their behalf, they become more discriminating about controlling the outcome. This represents not a loss of the filmmaker's rights but a maturing relationship that requires more depth from the filmmaker and that he or she acknowledge the right of others to control their own images.

EVIDENCE AND ETHICS

Another ethical concern should be with the standard of argument you put forward. Incontrovertible evidence is always more persuasive than opinion or hearsay. A documentary is always more powerful if its themes and ideas arise out of an unfolding life situation rather than if you plunder actuality to selectively illustrate a thesis. Interestingly, the same principle applies to fiction films; it is the difference between "signifying" a situation versus presenting it in the act of being. Once again, drama and the documentary share fundamentals.

You may have to take special care to show that a point in your film is not contrived. In the one I made about an English country estate, *A Remnant of a Feudal Society* (1970), a head groom spontaneously held out his deformed hand to demonstrate what happened (as he thought) to horsemen from holding reins at their master's pleasure in all kinds of weather. Because it was unclear what was wrong with the hand in the wide shot, the cameraman zoomed in close. I afterward kept the wobbly zoom. Removing it by making a cut between long shot and close shot, though more elegant onscreen, would have undermined the spontaneity of his action by making it look prearranged. A simple cut in the footage would have demoted its credibility.

To show the origin and authenticity of evidence and to acknowledge ambiguity, where it exists, are both ethical and practical considerations. They help you maintain a good-faith relationship with your audience.

WHAT DO YOU BELIEVE?

The two alternatives outlined earlier—transparency and reflexivity—can be described a little differently as either using the camera to look outward at the world (transparency) or using the world as a mirror in which to examine aspects of self evoked by that world. This difference is supposed to distinguish the classicist temperament from the romantic, but either can be valid and fascinating as long as you recognize at the outset your real purpose and priorities. Do you know what you believe? How will your beliefs guide and inform the way you see the world in your film?

Finally, of course, neither dimension is separable; there is no world without perception nor any perception without an object. Self and world are inextricably related, as I have argued all along. The decision about which route to take should arise from the subject and what you want to say about it. Often finding the right approach is a question of emphasis and of how, temperamentally, you function best as a storyteller.

How will you accommodate your human subjects when they make some adaptations for your camera? Do you trust your audience to make their own assessment of your relationship to truthfulness? Will you need to assist them, and if so, how?

The process of recording and interpreting needs to be justified to your participants. You need to be respected and trusted as you make your recordings. If the complexities of this relationship affect important truths, will you acknowledge this, either implicitly or explicitly? The recording process may be too intrusive to document some intimate occasions, or will seem so to the audience. Can you draw a line, and if so, where?

These are all very theoretical questions until they find application in the real world. Luckily, it is the real that helps us decide—not only what to do, but what we believe and who we are as we do it.

DOCUMENTARY AS EXPOSURE TO LIFE

Unlike some other arts, documentary is hard to make in retreat from life. Unless you make premeditated essay films, documentary is created by moving courageously into some area of life and by living with the consequences. Until you turn on the camera, many issues and aspects of personality (your own and those of your participants) will remain dormant and unresolved. Once you start, you may have to argue passionately for your rights as chronicler and critic. You will certainly be attacked for daring, as one person, to make an interpretive criticism of another. Are you ready to stand by your judgments?

Aesthetic and ethical decisions are seldom made from a position of cool intellectual neutrality; more often they are forged in discomfort and anxiety over conflicting moral obligations—to actual people who know and trust you, on the one hand, or to truths whose importance may transcend any individual's passing discomfort, on the other. One thought to keep in mind when making a documentary, one I find both comforting and liberating, is that my best efforts to make a film are still only what the French call *une tentative*—an attempt, bid, or endeavor that is no more than one little person's view at one little moment in time. In the end, it is delusional to take on responsibility for definitive truth. It is as irrational, as common, and as humanly foolish as wanting your children to be perfect.

MISSION AND IDENTITY

Luckily we already carry certain knowledge and certain convictions. To recognize this imprint is really to say, "This is what I believe and this is what I can pass on to others." If you feel the need to communicate it, you have the drive for authorship and to make art. To some, the maker of a "transparent" documentary negates his or her impact because this kind of film aims to present life on the screen with scarcely a trace of authorship. But it is still likely to be displaced autobiography, because rather than implying, "I have been the victim of a violent society, and look like what has happened to *me*," the filmmaker searches out others whose diversity and experience give universality to what the filmmaker has already discovered in his or her own limited but deeply felt experience.

Making documentaries is a way to put your convictions under test—by finding other people and other situations that somehow convey what you want to say. As such, it is how you see the world that you share with the audience, not yourself as subject. Your task is to identify the counterparts of your own experience floating unattached on life's stream and to catch and tether them in a structured statement that will mirror the truths that life has taught you.

A lot of what happens as you do this takes place at an unconscious level. Looking at someone else and trying to see through his or her eyes places useful restraints on indulging displays of ego. Seeking your most enduring preoccupations outside yourself, and in others, helps to create a product with overtones of universality. The discipline of such a process has its own rewards. With growing maturity you can identify the surrogates to your own values and temperament and allow them to achieve a life of their own in a film. Your work even alters the way you see the fundamentals of your own life—the very source from which your documentary process sprang. In this way, each project is midwife to the next.

ANTICIPATING THE SHOOT

SCOUTING THE LOCATIONS

During preproduction, the director of photography (DP), sound recordist, and director should check out locations for problems whenever possible.

Camera: The DP will want to know what problems the location may represent. If it is an exterior, the DP will want to see when available light is at its best. On overcast days, it is wise to carry a compass with you, so you can calculate the angle of the sun on a cloudless day. Is there enough electricity available for lighting, and where will lighting stands go so there's maximum freedom without getting them in shot?

Sound: The first thing a sound specialist does in a new location is to clap her hands, once and loudly. She then listens to what follows the *attack* of the handclap. Ideally it is an equally rapid *decay.* If the room is *live* (reverberant) there will be an appreciable comet's tail of sound reflected and thrown around the room. This will concern her greatly, and she may argue persuasively for an alternative venue.

Take such advice seriously, because the composition of surfaces in a location can make the difference between sound that is usefully *dry* or non-reverberant, and one unworkably live and reverberant (see Sound Theory in Chapter 14). Reverberation is multiplication of the original or *source* by sound ricocheting off hard, sound-reflective surfaces. A resonant room is one that has a "note" within the range of speech to which the room resonates. You'll know this phenomenon from singing in your shower and finding one or more note (or frequency) at which the room joins in, augmenting your song with a resonance of its own. Resonances are bad news to sound recordists.

When in doubt, audition dubious sound locations by shooting tests. Record some sample dialogue from representative microphone positions, then edit the results together. In no time at all, you have the measure of your problem. The sound recordist will be concerned with

- Reflectivity of ceiling, walls, and floor (drapes and carpet greatly reduce this)
- Whether there is, or can be, soft furniture or irregular surfaces legitimately introduced to break up the unwanted movement of sound within the space
- Alignment of surfaces likely to cause standing waves (sound bouncing to and fro between opposing surfaces, augmenting and cross modulating the source sound)
- Whether the room has intrusive resonances (this happens mainly in rooms with a lot of concrete or tile surfaces)
- Whether participants can walk and cameras be handheld in a quiet scene without the floor letting out tortured squeaks
- Ambient sound and sound penetrating from the outside

Typical intermittent sound intrusions from the surroundings come from being near to

- An airport flight path
- An expressway, railroad, or subway
- Refrigeration, air conditioning, or other noise-generating equipment that runs intermittently and will cause problems unless you can turn it off while shooting
- Construction sites. You scouted the location at a weekend, not realizing that come Monday morning, a pile driver and four jackhammers compete to greet the dawn. You have no hope of stopping them.
- A school. Schools have a large amount of hue and cry at certain times of day.

Interior dialogue shooting usually must be done with all doors and windows closed. In summer this can be trying, but part of checking a location is to ensure that you can get electric power cables in under the doors or through windows when they are completely closed during takes.

LOGISTICS AND THE SCHEDULE

Estimating how long each scene will take to shoot only comes with experience. In general, careful work takes much longer than you imagine possible. You probably should schedule only two or, at the most, three sequences in a day's work unless you are using available light and have good reason to anticipate that what you want is straightforward. Even a simple interview, lasting 20 minutes on tape, may take 3 hours to accomplish. You should also allow plenty of time for transport between locations, because tearing down equipment in the old location and setting it up anew is time consuming. A new film unit is usually a lot slower than it is 10 days later.

A 30-minute documentary can take between 3 and 8 working days to shoot, depending on (a) amount of travel, (b) amount and size of lighting setups, (c) the complexity of the necessary sound setup, and (d) the amount of randomness inherent in the subject matter. If, for instance, you are shooting in a school yard and want to film a spontaneous scuffle between boys during break, you may have to hang around in a state of exhausting readiness for days. On the other hand, if you simply want to film the postman delivering a particular letter, you can organize things to get it all done in 10 minutes.

Avoid the tendency to schedule optimistically by making best-case and worst-case estimates, and allotting something in between. One luxury peculiar to the independent filmmaker (and there are few) is that, like the nature photographer, he or she can shoot over a long period. As we have said, many documentaries show no real development because the economics of filmmaking make it prohibitive to reassemble a crew at, say, 6-month intervals for a period of 2 years. Yet only such extended observation is likely to capture real changes in people's lives. Independents tend to work as a group and on more than one project at a time, so they do not have to reconstitute a crew the way a commercial project does.

Whether you are shooting in a drawn-out or a compact way, make up a model schedule and solicit comment from all concerned. Well in advance of each day's shooting, *make sure everyone has a printed schedule.* Time spent planning and informing people is time, money, and morale saved later. A poorly informed crew waits passively for instructions and gives up taking initiative.

In the schedule include a phone contact number for each location. Whenever several people are meant to converge in an arranged place at an arranged time, count on someone getting lost or having car trouble. It is maddening to be incapacitated for lack of information, and unless everyone has a mobile phone, this is a constant threat on location. A low-tech solution is to have a *prearranged contact number* (one of the crew who has a mobile phone, your sister who works all day in an office, or a message service). Any number of people spinning in orbit can now make arrangements through the third party.

A schedule should also list special equipment or special personnel required in particular locations and give clear navigational instructions so everything and everyone gets there. Photocopies of a map marked up with locations and phone numbers can save hours of precious time. Not for nothing is filmmaking compared with special forces invasion.

THE PERSONAL RELEASE FORM

The personal release form is a document in which the signatory releases to you the right to make public use of the material you have shot (Figure 17–2). Some documentarians secure a record of agreement by asking participants to say they are willing to be filmed and that their name and address is such-and-such. They certainly can't subsequently claim they didn't know they were being filmed. A

Personal Release Form

For the $_____ consideration received, I give _____
Productions, its successors and assigns, my unrestricted permission to distribute and sell all still photographs, motion-picture film, video recordings and sound recordings taken of me for the screen production tentatively titled __.

Signed _____
Name (please print) _____
Address _____
_____

Date _____

Signature of parent or guardian _____
Witnessed by _____
Date _____

FIGURE 17–2

Typical personal release form.

signed document is better because people sometimes decide to pull out later, and a whole project can disappear down the toilet with a whoosh. Normally you won't have legal problems unless you allow people to nurture the (not unknown) fantasy that you are going to make a lot of money selling their footage. No one ever got rich making documentaries, so lose no time correcting any other notions.

Have personal release forms ready for participants to sign immediately after their filming is complete. No signature is valid without the $1 minimum legal payment, which you solemnly hand over as symbolic payment.

Because it is clearly impractical to get releases from, say, all the people in a street shot, one usually gets signed releases from speaking participants only. Naturally, use your judgment; securing the release is to prevent participants filmed under a verbal agreement deciding at the eleventh hour that they do not want to appear in your film. Forestall such problems by always obtaining the signed release immediately after shooting. Minors cannot sign legal forms themselves and will need the clearance of a parent or legal guardian.

PERMISSION TO FILM AT LOCATION FACILITIES

Conditions vary from country to country, but in general personal releases are signed immediately *after* the performance has been given, whereas location permission must be secured in writing *before* you start shooting. I was once held up for a year after getting permission to film an exhibition in a synagogue. Although I got permission for the building, the traveling exhibition's owner denied he had given verbal permission to film—and did this after hugely enjoying himself presenting exhibition items to the camera.

Anything unrestrictedly open to public view (such as the street, markets, public meetings) may be filmed without asking anyone's permission. All events on private property (which may include a city transportation system) must be cleared by whomever is responsible unless you care to risk being taken to court for invasion of privacy. This happens if you or your company seems worth suing or if someone wants a pretext for a court injunction to block a showing of your film. This is a great hazard to investigative journalism.

Most cities have restrictions on filming in the street. In practice this means you are supposed to get police permission and perhaps pay for a cop to wave away troublesome bystanders or to control traffic. Technically if you abandon a handheld technique and put up the tripod, you have crossed over from news gathering to the big time, but there may be nobody around who cares, unless of course you tie up traffic. Some big cities such as Chicago are film friendly, whereas in others such as Paris and New York the honeymoon is long over. Conditions are increasingly restrictive and usually to film at any urban location you must work through a special division of the mayor's office or state film commission to get permission to film. Tied in with this is a requirement to carry liability insurance to cover the many occasions when filming implies some risk to the public.

By tradition, documentary makers often shoot first and ask questions afterward, knowing if somebody takes exception, the combination of ideals and poverty will probably lead to nothing more hazardous than an irritable dismissal. This solution can be risky, particularly in non-democratic countries where cameras are often (and correctly) regarded as engines of subversion. Film or videotape, as the Rodney King episode testifies, can provide powerful evidence of wrongdoing in court. Because of a minute or two of footage shot by the alert owner of a camcorder, the Los Angeles police department went on trial before the entire world. Years of asserting police brutality had gotten black people nowhere until the evidence was inarguable. Therefore, anyone holding a camera is potentially gathering evidence these days.

CHAPTER 18

DEVELOPING A CREW

This chapter discusses

- Experienced and inexperienced crew, and how to handle each situation
- Assessing crewmembers' experience and temperaments
- Key crewmembers' roles and responsibilities defined
- Drawing up an equipment list

USING PEOPLE WITH EXPERIENCE

The title of this chapter speaks of "developing" rather than "choosing" a crew because even when experienced crewmembers are available, you should still do some experimental shooting together. This verifies not only how equipment is functioning, but also that you understand each other. It is quite usual to discover that one camera operator's close-up is another's medium shot. A brief and unambiguous language of communication will be vital if you are doing "run and gun" shooting, that is, making camera-position changes in response to a spontaneously changing situation. With no possibility for rehearsal or repeats, a wide margin exists for fatal misunderstandings.

Successful framing, composition, speed of camera movements, and microphone positioning all come about through mutual values, awareness, and adaptation. This happens best when people understand each other's signals and terminology. Expect while shooting exercise footage to discover a wide variance of taste and skill levels, as well as variations in responses, technical vocabulary, and interpretation of standard jargon.

DEVELOPING YOUR OWN CREW

Let us suppose, in a worst case scenario, that you live remote from centers of filmmaking, must start from scratch finding and training your crew, and need to work up your own standards. We will assume that you have access to a camcorder, microphone, and video monitor. How many and what kinds of people will you need? What are their responsibilities?

All the crew need to appreciate—or better yet share—your values. So before working together on anything so personal as a documentary, inquire into not only each person's technical expertise and experience, but also their feelings and ideas concerning documentary, books, plays, music, hobbies, and interests. Technical acumen is important, but a person's maturity and values are more so. Knowledge deficiencies can be remedied, but you are unlikely to change someone who dislikes your choice of subject or who disapproves of your approach.

CREWMEMBERS' TEMPERAMENTS ARE IMPORTANT!

A documentary crew is very small, two to six persons. A good crew is immensely supportive, not only of the project but also of the individuals in front of the camera, who usually are being filmed for the first time. The crew's interest and implied approval become a vital supplement to that of the director. Conversely, the presence of anyone detached or disapproving will be felt personally, by you and especially by participants, who are highly attuned in this new, unfamiliar work you are asking them to do.

Usually I was assigned wonderful crews when I worked for the British Broadcasting Corporation (BBC) but occasionally would get individuals with problems. Typically it was lapses in mental focus, but more than once I got someone actively subversive. Being under pressure and far from home unbalances some people or exacerbates latent insecurities and jealousies. This is hard to foresee and becomes an appalling liability in documentary, where good relationships are so vital.

If a potential crewmember has done film or other team work, speak to his or her co-workers. Filming is so intense that work partners quickly learn each other's temperamental strengths and weaknesses. In each crewmember look for

- Realism
- Reliability
- The ability to sustain effort and concentration over long periods and in discomfort
- A deep interest in the processes and purposes of making documentaries
- Knowledge and appreciation of films you particularly respect

In all film crew positions, beware of those who

- Have only one working speed (it's usually medium slow, and when faced with a crisis these people can slow up in confusion or go to pieces)
- Forget or modify verbal commitments
- Fail to deliver on what they've promised

- Habitually overestimate their own abilities
- Let their attention expand detrimentally beyond their own field of responsibility
- See your work as a stepping stone toward something more desirable

CLEARLY DEFINE THE AREAS OF RESPONSIBILITY

No crew functions well without clearly defined roles and responsibilities, which should cover emergencies such as a predictable absence. For example, the director of photography (DP) normally takes over when the director is absent or occupied. Crew should, in any case, be discouraged from taking any and every query to the director when the DP can handle the answers. A busy director should not have to decide whether someone should put another coin in a parking meter.

When you first work together, maintain a formal working structure in which everyone takes care of his or her own responsibilities and refrains from comment or action in areas of responsibility that belong to others. As you come to know and trust each other, formality can be relaxed. If, on the other hand, you start out informal and then need a tighter ship, the changes will be mightily resented.

A small film crew—director, camera operator, sound recordist, and production assistant—may also consist of prophet, visionary, scribe, and fixer. Someone will always assume the role of jester because every crew develops its own special dynamic and in-jokes. The pleasure that comes with working together well is the best intoxicant you can imagine and is headiest under pressure. And there is no hangover the morning after. Carefully selecting your partners makes anything possible, because a team of determined friends is unstoppable.

CREW ROLES AND RESPONSIBILITIES

Here is an outline of each crewmember's responsibilities and the strengths and weaknesses you might look for. Of course, in real life many of the best practitioners are the exceptions, so this list is fallible. Documentarians are beginning to use producers, so I have included a summary of the roles of both producer and director.

PRODUCER

As opportunities for independent documentaries have multiplied, so have markets and international co-production possibilities. Ironically, just as more sophisticated digital technology has allowed crews to shrink, so the business side of making films requires more and more attention. Today it is not enough to make and sell a good film, one must organize publicity, international showings, and even how the film will afterward lead a prolonged life serving as an educational tool to special interest groups. Markets have become more complex, so there is now a real need for specialized, entrepreneurial producers, and film schools are beginning to train them. This is fortuitous, because sales and business skills, and time to practice them, are all routinely lacking in most filmmakers.

Very little money is made in documentary, so any producer in need of a roof and regular meals will probably work with several directors and grow to resemble a literary agent. With five directors, there may be upward of 30 viable documentary ideas to shop around at any given time. The effective producer is therefore socially adept and highly articulate, and brings finished films along with their directors' follow-up film ideas to documentary marketplaces such as the Amsterdam International Documentary Festival. Here, commissioning editors from cable and television channels watch the latest work and listen to pitches (brief oral presentations of documentary ideas). Making their choices, the television representatives then compete to develop co-financing deals for the product they want.

Anyone with producing skills is therefore a combination of salesperson, production manager (if he or she works closely with productions), and accountant. He or she should know the changing world of documentary and its audiences and should be confident at discussing all aspects of documentary proposals and types of financing. The producer should be able to estimate the costs of making films, monitor those costs during production, and then ensure that the finished product gets full publicity, because good films will sink without trace if nobody publicizes their existence.

All this takes a special kind of temperament, and a producer should never be a wannabe director. The vice of producers is the secret belief that they have better ideas and are more efficient than those they have hired to make their films (if hiring is indeed what they do). Your producer should love documentary and nurturing production. Such people are uncommon. Anyone honest and reliable, who has good taste and a good stable of production groups, will, like a literary agent, become trusted and sought after by overworked commissioning editors, who look first to the best producers to find the most original new work.

DIRECTOR

The director is responsible for nothing less than the quality and meaning of the final film. He or she must conduct or supervise research, decide on content, assemble a crew, schedule shooting, lead the crew, and direct participants during shooting. Then he or she supervises the editing and finalization of the project. Because funds are always a problem, the film frequently has no producer, so the director must also assemble funding before shooting and hustle distribution afterward.

A good director has a lively fascination with the cause and effect behind the way real people live; has a mind that searches tirelessly for links and explanations; is social; and loves delving into other people's stories. Outwardly informal and easygoing, he or she is methodical and organized but quite able to throw away prior work when early assumptions prove obsolete. A good director has endless patience in stalking the truth; strong ambitions in doing it justice in cinematic terms; is articulate and succinct; knows his or her own mind without being dictatorial; can speak on terms of respectful equality with all film craftspeople;

and can understand their problems and co-opt their efforts into realizing his or her authorial intentions.

This paragon sounds impossibly idealistic, so here are some of the negative traits that make directors all too human. Many are obstinate, private, awkward, and even shy beings who do not explain themselves well, who change their minds, and who are disorganized and visceral. Most can be intimidated by bellicose technicians, have difficulty in balancing attention between crew and participants, and tend to desert one for the other. During shooting, sensory overload catapults many into a state of acute doubt and anxiety in which all choice becomes a painful effort. Some cannot bear to deflect from their original intentions and go catatonic or act like the captain who sinks at the wheel of the ship.

Directing frequently changes perfectly normal people into manic-depressives who suffer extremes of hope and despair in pursuit of the Holy Grail. If that is not enough to puzzle crewmembers, the director's mental state often generates superhuman energy that tests crewmembers' patience to the limit.

Directing an improvisation intended to crystallize life is a heady business. It means trying to live existentially, that is, fully and completely in the present and as if each moment were your last. The exigencies of directing often bring on this state, whether you like it or not, and particularly so after an initial success. Thereafter you confront failure and artistic/professional death every step of the way. But like mountaineers who feel most alive when dangling over a precipice, the director feels completely alive during the dread and exhilaration of the cinematic chase. Like stage fright for actors, this is a devil that never really goes away. But aren't fear and excitement the portents of everything worthwhile?

DIRECTOR OF PHOTOGRAPHY AND/OR CAMERA OPERATOR

In the minimal crew, the DP usually is called, less grandly, the camera operator. He or she is responsible for ordering the camera equipment, for testing and adjusting it when necessary, and for being thoroughly conversant with its working principles. Never begin important work without first running tests to forestall Murphy's Law ("Anything that can go wrong will go wrong"). The camera operator also is responsible for lighting, scouting locations to assess light and electricity supplies, and supervising setting up the lighting instruments.

The camera operator—if separate from the DP—is responsible for the handling of the camera, which means taking an active role in deciding camera positioning (in collaboration with the director), and controlling all camera movements, such as panning, tilting, zooming in/out, and dollying. If the production requires a lot of handheld camerawork, this is a special skill that all operators think they have and that few do well.

A good operator is highly image conscious and preferably has training in photography and fine art. You hope for a good sense of composition and design, and an eye for the sociologically telling details that show in people's surroundings. A good operator picks up the behavioral nuances that reveal so much about character. In "grab shooting" only the operator can really decide what to shoot moment to moment. While the director sees *content* happening in front of (sometimes behind) the camera, only the operator sees the action in its framed, cinematic form. The director may redirect the camera to a different area but must be able to place almost total reliance in the operator's discrimination.

For this reason a camera operator must be decisive and dexterous. Depending on the weight of the equipment, he or she may also need to be robust. Keeping a 20-pound camera on your shoulder for an 8-hour day or loading equipment boxes in and out of vehicles is not work for the delicate or fastidious. The job is dirty, grueling, and at times intoxicatingly wonderful. The best camera people seem to be low-key individuals who don't ruffle easily in crises, practical and inventive people who like improvising solutions to intransigent logistical, lighting, or electrical problems. Look for the perfectionist who will cheerfully try for the best and simplest solution when time runs short.

Many experienced camera personnel have an alarming tendency to isolate themselves in the mechanics of their craft at the expense of the director's deeper quest for themes and meanings. One such answered a question of mine with "I'm just here to make pretty pictures." He might have added, "and not get involved."

Though having a crew of frustrated directors is one problem, far worse is to have one of isolated operatives. The best crewmembers comprehend both the details and the totality of a project and see how to make the best contribution at any given moment. This is why a narrow "tech" education is never good enough.

GAFFER

The gaffer is a rare bird on a documentary in these days of declining budgets. He or she is an expert in rigging and maintaining lighting equipment and knows how to split loads so that lighting runs off light-duty household supplies without starting fires or plunging the whole street into darkness. Good gaffers carry a bewildering assortment of clamps, gadgets, and small tools. Resourceful by nature, they sometimes emerge as mainstays of the unit when others get discouraged. During a night shooting sequence in England, I once saw a boy stumble behind the lights and hurt his knee. Because he had been told he must be silent while we were shooting, he doubled over and clutched his knee in mute agony. The kindly electrician (as the gaffer is called in Britain) swooped silently out of the gloom and cradled him in his arms until the shot was finished.

Because the gaffer is usually the only person whose attention is free when the camera is running, he may be the only person with a whole and unobstructed view. Directors in doubt, therefore, sometimes discreetly ask how the gaffer felt about a certain piece of action.

Gaffers are usually chosen by the person responsible for lighting (the cinematographer or videographer), and the two will often work together regularly. An experienced gaffer gets to know a cinematographer's lighting style and preferences and can even arrive ahead of a unit to prelight. Teams of long association even dispense with spoken language.

GRIP

A grip fetches and carries (mostly electrical equipment) but also has the highly skilled and coordinated job of moving the camera support to precisely worked-out positions when the camera takes mobile shots. Grips should therefore be strong, practical, organized, and willing. On the minimal crew, they will help to rig lighting or sound equipment. A skilled grip knows something about everyone's job and in an emergency can do limited duty for another crewmember.

SOUND RECORDIST

Among students, sound recording is considered easy and unglamorous and gets left to anyone who says they can do it. But badly recorded sound fatally disconnects the audience. Sound training is improving, but still too many student films have characters talking through mashed potato in echoey bathrooms. Capturing clear, clean, and consistent sound is deceptively demanding and lacks the glamour to induce most people to try.

The recordist, who is responsible for checking equipment in advance and solving sound malfunctions as they arise, needs patience, a good ear, and the maturity to be low man on the totem pole. Lighting and camera position are determined first, so the sound recordist is expected to hide mikes, cause no shadows, and achieve first-rate sound quality. Shoots become a series of aggravating compromises that caring sound people tend to take personally. Many end up bitter that "good standards" are routinely trampled. But it's the disconnected craftsperson rather than the whole filmmaker who gags on compromise.

Because the sound recordist should listen not to words but to *sound quality,* you need someone able to hear the buzzes, rumbles, or edginess that the novice will overlook. The art of recording has little to do with recorders and everything to do with the selection and placement of mikes, and *being able to hear the difference.* No independent assessment is possible apart from the discerning ear. Only musical interests and, better still, musical training seem to instill this critical faculty.

The sound recordist, often kept inactive for long periods and then suddenly expected to "fix up the mike" in short order, needs to habitually make contingency plans. The least satisfactory is the person who comes to life at setup time and causes groans by then asking for a lighting change.

When shooting is mobile, the recordist must keep the mike as close as possible to the sound source, without casting shadows or letting the mike creep into frame. With a camera handheld and on the move, this takes skill, awareness, and quietly agile footwork.

PRODUCTION MANAGER

The production manager (PM) is a luxury on a minimal crew but is a necessity on a large, complex shoot. Among students there usually are people whose business background equips them to do this important job surpassingly well. The PM takes care of all the arrangements for the shoot. These might include locating overnight accommodations, booking rented equipment at the best prices, securing location or other permissions, making up a shooting schedule (with the director), making travel arrangements, and locating food near the shoot. The PM monitors cash flow, has contingency plans when bad weather stymies exterior shooting, and chases progress. All this lightens the load on the director, for whom these things are a counterproductive burden.

The good PM is of course organized, a compulsive list keeper, socially adept and businesslike, and able to scan and correlate a number of activities. He or she must be able to juggle priorities; make decisions involving time, effort, and money; and be unintimidated by officialdom.

CHAPTER 19

THE PREPRODUCTION MEETING

This chapter concerns final arrangements for equipment and logistics, and deals with

- Production meetings to determine final arrangements
- Scheduling and the factors that affect it, including bad weather coverage
- Budgeting, cost flow projection, and monitoring outgoings
- Equipment possibilities and decisions
- Decisions about formats and costs
- Forestalling Murphy's Law ("Everything that can go wrong will go wrong")
- The importance of shooting production stills
- Insurances and contracts
- The preproduction party

This chapter covers many aspects that will arise only on a large-budget production or series that may use union film workers and union actors and is in most respects shot like a feature film. Read it anyway, because there may be items to make you rethink aspects of your two-person shoot.

Typically there are a number of preproduction meetings, and the last is when everyone must OK the arrangements before the unit launches into action. Below are the main areas that a preproduction meeting must cover. All the principals must be present to represent their own concerns: director, director of photography (DP), sound recordist, and, if yours is a large unit, producer, production manager (PM), production secretary, electrician, and camera and sound assistants. Ideally, all principals have visited the intended locations and have accepted them as viable.

TROUBLESHOOTING

Anyone with a problem to be resolved brings it up at this meeting. Now is the time to coordinate everyone's efforts and to make corrections or changes if something has been overlooked or needs a schedule change.

DRAFT SCHEDULE

Preliminary budgeting will be based on the shortest schedule that is practicable. Everyone must check the logistics of travel, time to set up lighting, and so on. Some time will be built in for contingencies such as bad weather or breakdowns. See final scheduling factors listed later in this chapter.

DRAFT BUDGET

This is when everything must be final-checked in terms of its cost, so the meeting involves a rough budget based on known schedule, locations, equipment, crew, and artists (see Figure 15–1). It is good to consider the high figures and not just the lowest figures because the total, when higher figures prevail, can be a shock. Confront this while you can still make adjustments.

The budget is affected by many factors; the most significant is the number of locations, travel time needed, and days spent shooting at each. Simple software exists for budgeting, but the industry favorite is Movie Magic, an all-embracing (though expensive) package that provides well-proven tools. It will break down your intentions, turn them into a schedule, and arrive at a budget based on all the variables that you enter. The beauty of a relational database of this magnitude is that any change anywhere, such as in rates or scheduling, will immediately be reflected everywhere that matters. Your PM, if you have one, can use the software to keep tabs on daily cash flow so that no unpleasant surprises emerge from the accounts. You can see descriptions and reviews of a range of software for screenwriting, budgeting, and scheduling at www.writersstore.com, which also lists the tutorials and manuals to get the most out of the software. Such software is overkill for the average documentary but may be a lifesaver if you are working on a series that needs intricate scheduling. Most people will need something akin to a producer's training to make proper use of the software.

Budget issues are divided into *above the line* and *below the line* costs. The line is the division between preproduction and beginning production. So:

Above the Line costs: Story rights (if there are any)

Screenplay (if there is one)

Producer's fee

Director's fee

Principal actors' fees

Any other participants' remuneration

_____ "The Line"

Below the Line costs: Production unit salaries

    Art department
        Salaries
        Sets and models
        Props and costumes
    Artists (other than those above)
        Cast, stand-ins, crowd
    Studio or location facility rentals (with location and police permissions)
    Film or video stock
    Laboratories
    Camera, sound, and other equipment
    Power
    Special effects
    Personnel
        Catering, hotel, and living expenses
        Social security
    Transport
    Insurances
    Miscellaneous expenses
    Music
    Postproduction
    Publicity

Indirect costs include finance and legal overhead costs.
    The pertinent questions are as follows:

- How much does the production have in the bank?
- What is still to come?
- Using the projected shooting schedule, what will the film cost?
- Are there enough funds to cover projected costs?
- Are more funds needed?
- Can economies be made?
- Can any shooting be delayed until funds have been assembled?

Many factors lie behind locking down a budget and making a cash flow forecast, not least is the medium you are going to use, which may be 16 mm film, Super 16 mm, miniature digital video (DV or DVCAM), digital Betacam, or high definition (HD) video. This was probably a decision taken early, but the final word is cast at the production meeting. Be aware that most movie budgets include a *contingency percentage,* usually around 4% of the budget, added on to cover the unexpected, such as equipment failure, reshooting, and so on.

All filming in the developed nations will require liability and equipment insurance and some legal work, such as contracts with participants or with the funding and distributing agencies. Your budget should reflect this, which is sensible self-protection. We live in a litigious society, and there are always a small number of people who will, somewhere and sometime, try to profit from suing you.

DRAWING UP AN EQUIPMENT WANT LIST

Learn all you can about the technical requirements of your shoot so that you, your DP, and PM can decide what outlay is truly justified. Some extras turn out to be lifesavers; others sit in boxes and waste money. Keep in mind that human ingenuity makes good films, not just equipment.

How the film looks, how it is shot, and how it conveys its content to the audience are decisions that affect your equipment needs, but these decisions are about the form of the film and need to be made organically from the nature of the film's subject. Plan to shoot as simply as possible, choosing straightforward means over elaborate ones. With anything to be shot on film and edited digitally, your film negative must carry Keycode™ or the camera original cannot be conformed at the end of editing. Two good sources of information at every level are Kodak's student program, reachable through www.kodak.com/go/student and *DV Magazine* at www.dv.com for up-to-date information and reviews on everything for digital production and postproduction. Kodak, with every reason to want people to continue using film, provides superb guidance in its publications and Web sites. Their cyberspace is as prolific and labyrinthine as one would expect from an organization with so many divisions.

Testing and repair equipment: Never leave an equipment checkout point without putting all the equipment together and testing that everything, absolutely everything, functions as it should. Make sure you have spare batteries for everything that depends on a battery, and extra cables, which have a habit of breaking down where the cable enters the plug body. Carry basic repair equipment too: screwdrivers, socket sets, pliers, wire, solder and soldering iron, multimeter for continuity, voltage, resistance, and other testing.

ACQUISITION ON FILM

Major equipment needs hinge on what image format you will use to shoot. Using the traditional film camera means a fairly straightforward (if long and expensive) equipment list. Film captures the best image quality, has a usefully limited depth of field, can be shown in any cinema in the world, and can be transferred to any video format—at a truly chilling price. It requires heavy funding at the front end when you buy stock, and it will be expensive to process and make prints. Anybody experienced enough to light and shoot well in film probably will know where to get the equipment and how much it will cost to carry what you need for the days that you need it.

16 mm shoot: If you have quiet interiors, be sure to get a quiet camera. Old cameras can sound like coffee grinders, and it's a myth that they have a camera noise filter in postproduction. Be aware that the small format magnifies any weave or jiggle, and this shows up dramatically with any titles or overlays.

Super 16mm shoot: Find someone as a mentor who has recently and successfully completed the chain of production. Remember that Super 16 camera original has a different aspect ratio and runs on different sprockets in the lab, so not many labs can handle and print it. Are you going to strike workprints or have the camera original transferred to tape? Who's going to do it and for how much? Super 16mm's great advantage is that its 1.66:1 aspect ratio makes it an excellent format for HDTV's letterbox format of 1.77:1, sometimes expressed as 16 × 9 (see www.cinematechnic.com/super-16mm/super-16.html).

ACQUISITION ON VIDEO

One of the limitations of inexpensive digital cameras is that, having small imaging chips, they have a whopping depth of field. This produces the typically flat image in which all planes are in the same degree of focus. Miniature cameras are also hard to control and have sloppy lenses. Many features, such as white balance or sound recording level, can only be accessed by laboriously tapping your way through a menu, hardly an option if you are embedded in a tank that is heading into battle. Small camera menus also have a nasty propensity for getting changed without anyone noticing.

Another hassle is focusing the camera. Without manual control, you often are reliant on either setting a fixed distance in advance or letting the automatic focusing do what it will. This simply focuses whatever is in the center of frame, no matter what your compositional balance or where you want the audience to look. Manual focusing and manual sound level adjustment are important, and these feature are beginning to show up on prosumer cameras.

A professional camera is large and has setting knobs and switches instead of menus. The camera assistant can periodically eyeball the settings. Some professional cameras also have a slot for a *memory stick*, a solid-state memory smaller than a stick of gum that can hold all the camera settings that were used to get a particular look. From location to location this can save a great deal of time.

A choice you must make when shooting in National Television System Committee (NTSC) format is whether to use *drop frame* or *non-drop frame* timecode. Drop frame removes a digit every so often so that recorded timecode keeps in step with the advance of real time. Whichever you choose, you must stay consistent throughout the production because inconsistency can adversely affect editing. Digitally recorded sound is much more unforgiving than analog if you overmodulate during recording, which is another reason to use a professional camera if you can with its visible decibel (sound level) meters.

Medium of origination: Depending on how high your sights are trained, you may shoot with a modest DV camera, with digital Beta, or in HD video using the Sony or the Panasonic systems. A great advantage of shooting digitally is that you don't have to change film magazines every 10 minutes of shooting, as with film. Cassettes last anywhere between 30 and 120 minutes, keeping everyone focused for longer periods. Typically, digital feature-length documentaries take

FIGURE 19–1 —————————————————————————————————

Panasonic AG-DVX100. This manually controllable three-chip camera records at 30 or 24 frames per second, the slower frame speed being progressive scan frames that transfer well to film.

20–30% less schedule time than when using film. The camera runs longer, needs less maintenance (there is no film gate to collect dirt), is light and quick to move, and needs less overall light.

DV origination for eventual film transfer: For this you may use a tried and true Canon or Sony DV camera, or perhaps a switchable camera offering a choice of frame rates like the Mini DV Panasonic AG-DVX100 (Figure 19–1).

This manual or automatic control, three-chip camera can operate at either the video standard of 30 frames per second (fps) interlaced mode or at 24p (24 frames per second in non-interlaced or "progressive scan" mode) that transfers well to film. To explain this: the video frame normally is made up of two passes or scans, one recording the odd lines, the other interlacing the even ones. A progressive scan records the entire frame in one pass before moving on to the next frame. This is closer to the film imaging process and produces full-definition frames that are simpler to transfer to film. The camera also has two professional XLR sound input sockets at microphone or line levels, the usual IEEE1394 socket for digital transfer to and from a nonlinear editing (NLE) system, and a special function for shooting that emulates film gamma range. Most valuable are the large color viewfinder and the manual controls for audio volume, zoom, iris (aperture), and focus. There is also the 48-volt phantom power supply that some professional microphones require.

High-definition video: This video standard with its 16:9 aspect ratio gives nearly three times as many pixels (picture cells) per image as a standard NTSC video image.

NTSC Video Type	Aspect Ratio	Pixels Wide	Pixels High	Total Pixels per Screen
Standard definition (SD)	4:3	720	480	345,600
High definition (HD)	16:9	1,280	720	921,600

However, because of its interlaced nature, SD has a hidden deficiency that lowers its effective acuity on fast-motion subjects. Each interlaced frame is 1/60th of a second behind its partner, so each image the eye sees is actually a combination of two different moments in time. This is problematical when something in motion has appreciably moved position and may lower definition by as much as 30%. Progressive scan, on the other hand, builds the video frame in a single pass, so all its lines are defined from the single moment of exposure. See www.jvc.com/promotions/grhd1/what/main.html for a full explanation of this quite complex subject, with sample images for the two different standards.

The long and short of HDTV is that a consumer camcorder like the JVC GR-HD1 rivals 35 mm film in picture quality. The top of the line model, the Sony CineAlta HDW-F900, has four digital sound channels, can shoot interlaced or progressive scan, and has a variable frame rate that allows you to shoot fast or slow motion, something normally accomplishable in video only in postproduction. In common with all professional-level cameras, its features such as follow focus are as fully controllable as in a 35 mm camera. George Lucas, after shooting *Star Wars Episode II* using CineAlta cameras, said, "I think I can safely say I'll never shoot another film on film."[1]

Video to film transfers: Be aware that video to film transfers from 30 fps video (NTSC system) are very expensive. A timebase corrector has to combine the interlaced frames, then do a step-printing operation to render 30 fps of video as 24 fps of film. An NTSC 24 p or phase alternating line (PAL) 25 p video camera neatly obviates this.

PAL system compared with NTSC: By shooting in PAL video you gain some advantage in acuity because the PAL image has more lines of resolution. PAL also transfers its interlaced (or better, progressive scan) 25 fps more directly to film. However, when 25 fps is projected at 24 fps the 5% speed change raises the pitch of everyone's voice marginally and produces a 5% shorter film. Why do PAL and NTSC have different frame rates? Most countries have 220 to 230 volt with 50 cycles per second (hertz [Hz]) alternating current. PAL's frame rate of 25 fps is a straight division of 50 Hz. America and its followers are stuck with a 19th-century legacy of 110 volts. Thomas Edison set the national voltage at 110, and Westinghouse set the frequency of the alternating current at 60 Hz, so NTSC's 30 fps is a division of the USA's 60 Hz.

SOUND

Where will you record sound? In the video camera? In a separate digital audio tape (DAT) or analog Nagra recorder? If you shoot analog, how will sound be resolved and transferred for syncing up later with its video picture? How many channels will you need to record? How will you mike each different situation? If you are using wireless mikes, will you carry wired mikes as backup? What kind of clapper board will you use if you are shooting double system? What special thought has been given to sound design that the sound crew should be aware of? What sound effects or atmospheres are not obvious in the script and must be found or concocted during location shooting?

---

[1] For the full article, see http://www.sonyusacinealta.com/content/article_23.shtml

POSTPRODUCTION

Whatever origination you use will need the appropriate postproduction setup, from a $3,000 Mac with Final Cut Pro at the low end to a $225,000 Discreet Smoke HD or $300,000 Avid|DS HD postproduction rig at the high end. The length of the documentary, the amount of coverage, and whether there are any special effects will have a profound effect on the postproduction schedule. Don't forget the audio stage, when the film is put through a ProTools suite and the final track is mixed, possibly in a studio with a large theater costing hundreds or thousands of dollars a day.

CAUTION

If a software or camera manufacturer recommends particular associated equipment, follow the recommendation to the letter. There's a good reason. Before you commit to any of the links in a production chain, you must be 100% certain that all the links work together. For instance:

- Digital tapes shot on Sony equipment may not interface properly with other equipment. For example, Panasonic may not have identical recording specifications.
- If you shoot in PAL, check that your computer software is not limited to NTSC, or vice versa.
- It you edit in PAL in an NTSC country, or vice versa, you will need a multi-standard player and recorder (Figure 19–2).
- Your film lab may not be able to do a 25 fps transfer to film.
- You may have a problem transferring 25 fps sound to your 24 fps editing rig.
- If you mix and match equipment, each manufacturer or supplier will swear blind that the other fellow's equipment is to blame for the malfunction. Following one manufacturer's recommendations means you can expect to get his ear if anything goes wrong.
- For the same reason, always plan to have your processing lab conform the film prior to answer printing. If you use an outside service and the negative proves scratched, the lab will blame the conformer, and the conformer will blame the lab.

Know and understand each stage's process. For any problems you *must have definitive answers* before you commit. When you seek advice, follow the advice of those who have already done what it is you want to do, and then use exactly the recommended equipment and procedures.

EQUIPMENT LISTS

At the production meeting, everyone brainstorms over what they need. Make lists and do not forget to include basic repair and maintenance tools. Some piece of equipment is bound to need corrective surgery on location.

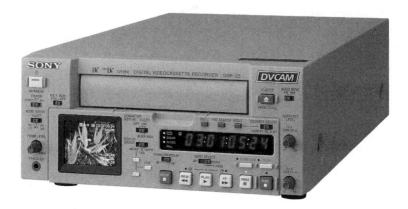

FIGURE 19–2

The Sony DSR-25 can record and playback PAL or NTSC formats using either DV or DVCAM cassettes.

Over-elaboration is always a temptation, especially for the insecure technician trying to forestall problems by insisting on the "proper" equipment, which always proves to be the most complicated and expensive. Early in your directing career you will be trying to conquer basic conceptual and control difficulties, so you probably have little use for advanced equipment and cannot afford the time it takes to work out how to best use it. At an advanced level, sophisticated equipment may actually save time and money. Expect the sound department in particular to ask for a range of equipment so that they can quickly adapt to changed lighting or other circumstances. This, within reason, is legitimate overkill.

If any in your crew is at all inexperienced, ask them to study all equipment manuals beforehand; these contain vital and often overlooked information. Make sure you carry equipment manuals with you on location. At the end of this book there is a bibliography to find more detailed information on techniques and equipment.

Do not be discouraged if your equipment is not the best. The first chapters of film history, so rich in creative advances, were shot using hand-cranked cameras made of wood and brass.

PRODUCTION STILLS

Someone should be equipped to shoot 35 mm production stills throughout the high points of the shooting. If time permits, the director and DP are the best people to take the stills because the pictures should epitomize the subject matter and approach of the film, and they act as a draw in a poster.

If the director and DP cannot take stills, then someone with intermittent duties who has an acceptable eye for composition should do so. Stills seem unimportant, but they prove vital when later you need to make up a publicity kit for festivals and prospective distributors. You'd be surprised, but for some quite famous contemporary documentaries there are no images—they forgot them!

SCHEDULING THE SHOOT

Scheduling is normally decided by the director and the PM and double-checked by principal crew members, particularly the DP. Excellent scheduling and budgeting software exists so that anyone with a computer can do a thoroughly professional job, as noted previously. Movie Magic is the film industry's choice of software package and will handle contracts, scheduling, and budgeting. You can see a range of software at www.filmmakingbooks.com/software.htm with a range of prices.

When scheduling, you will often have to make educated guesses because no film is ever quite like any other and there are few constants. Because time means money, your schedule must reflect your resources as well as your needs. Consider any or all of the following:

- Costs involved at each stage if hiring equipment, crew, or facilities (use Movie Magic or other reputable software, or see basic budget form in Figure 15–1)
- Scenes involving key dramatic elements that may be affected or delayed by weather or other cyclical conditions
- Availability of participants, actors (if you are using them), and crew
- Availability of locations
- Proximity of locations and thus amount of travel between them
- Availability of rented equipment, including props, and any special conditions attaching to them
- Complexity of each lighting setup, and total power requirements
- Time of day so that available light comes from the right direction (take a compass when location scouting!)

LOCATION ORDER

Normal practice is to shoot in order of location convenience, taking into account the availability of participants and crew. Lighting setups and lighting changes take the most time during a shoot, so a compact schedule avoids relighting the same location.

WEATHER OR OTHER CONTINGENCY COVERAGE

Schedule exteriors early in case your intentions are defeated by unsuitable weather. By planning interiors as standby alternatives, you need lose no time. Make contingency shooting plans whenever you face major uncertainties.

ALLOCATION OF SHOOTING TIME PER SETUP

Depending on the amount of coverage, the intensity of the scene in question, and the predictable or unpredictable nature of the scene, you might expect to shoot anywhere between 4 and 10 minutes of edited screen time per 8-hour day. Traveling between locations, elaborate setups, or relighting the same location all massively slow the pace. The expertise of the crew, especially of the DP in relation to lighting, can greatly affect shooting pace.

UNDER- OR OVERSCHEDULING?

This hardly affects the two-person shoot but becomes a serious issue with a large unit and actors. A promising film may also be sabotaged by misplaced optimism rather than any inherent need to save money. Consider the following:

- Schedule lightly during the first 3 days of a shoot. Work may be alarmingly slow because the crew is still developing an efficient working relationship with each other.
- You can always shorten a long schedule, but it may be impossible to lengthen one originally too short.
- Most non-professional (and some professional) units try to shoot too much in too little time.
- A crew and actors working 14-hour days soon lose interest in everything but surviving. Artistic intentions go out the window as a dog-tired crew and participants work progressively slower, less efficiently, and less accurately. Tempers and morale deteriorate.

The first half of the shoot may fall seriously behind if the assistant director (AD) and PM do not apply the screws and keep the unit up to schedule. Not only does the inexperienced crew start slowly and over days get quicker, it also tends to reproduce this pattern during each day unless there is determined progress-chasing by the DP and AD.

AGREEMENT ON BUDGET AND SCHEDULE

By the end of the meeting everyone should have agreed on equipment and schedule, and the PM can make a detailed budget and go to work preparing call sheets, which ensure that everyone takes the right equipment to the right place at the right time on the right day.

CAVEATS

Make "test and test again" your true religion. Leave nothing to chance. Make lists, and then lists of lists. Pray.

GOLDEN RULE NO. 1: EXPECT THE WORST

Imagination expended darkly foreseeing the worst will forestall many potentially crippling problems before they even take shape. That way you equip yourself with particular spares, special tools, emergency information, and first aid kits.

Optimism and filmmaking do not go together. One blithe optimist left the master tapes of a feature film in his car overnight. The car happened to be stolen, and because there were no copies, a vast amount of work by many people was instantly transformed into so much silent footage.

The pessimist, gloomily foreseeing the worst and never tempting fate, is tranquilly productive compared with your average optimist.

GOLDEN RULE NO. 2: TEST IT FIRST

Arrive early and test every piece of equipment at its place of origin. Never assume because you are hiring from a reputable company that everything should be all right. When you do, Murphy's Law ("Everything that can go wrong will go wrong") will get you. Be ready for Murphy lurking inside everything that should fit together, slide, turn, lock, roll, light up, make a noise, or work silently. Murphy relatives hide out in every wire, plug, box, lens, battery, and alarm clock. Make no mistake; the whole bloody clan means to ruin you.

COST FLOW AND COST REPORTING

On a complex film with many people participating, one goal of budgeting may be to make a cost flow projection. During production the PM prepares a daily cost report:

1. Cost for period
2. Accumulated cost to date
3. Estimated cost to complete
4. Final cost
5. Over or under budget by how much?

The object is to bring the production in on cost and in the agreed time.

INSURANCES

Depending on the expense and sophistication of a production, it may carry some or all of the insurances listed below. Even film schools, mindful of the litigiousness of John Q. Public, sometimes make their students carry insurance coverage. What should your production have?

Preproduction indemnity: Covers costs if the production is held up due to accident, sickness, or death during or before production

Film producer's indemnity: Covers extra expense incurred due to a range of problems beyond the producer's control

Consequential loss: Covers increased production costs due to the loss or damage to any vital equipment, set, or prop

Errors and omissions: Covers claims against intellectual property (copyright, slander, libel, plagiarism etc) or other mistakes

Negative insurance: Covers reshooting costs due to loss or any damage to film negative

Employer's liability: Mandatory insurance that may be required for protection of employees

Public or third party liability: Insures against claims for property damage and personal injuries

Third party property damage: Insures against claims brought against film company for damage to property in their care

Equipment insurance: Covers loss or damage to rented equipment

Sets, wardrobe, props: Covers costs resulting from their loss or damage

Vehicles: Coverage for vehicles, particularly specialized vehicles or those carrying costly equipment

Fidelity guarantee: Financial backer's requirement to guard against infidelity—the budget being embezzled

Union and other insurances: Film workers are often union members and their union stipulates what coverage is necessary when they are hired. Special insurances often are required when working abroad under unusual health or other conditions.

CREW CONTRACTS

Once all details have been decided for a large production, the PM sends out letters of engagement to secure the services of crew members. These describe the job, salary, working hours, and length of contract. As in any contract, there will be a number of clauses stipulating rights and expectations on either side. Any union requirements must be followed scrupulously if you want to avoid trouble later.

LEGAL

Michael C. Donaldson's *Clearance & Copyright: Everything the Independent Filmmaker Needs to Know* 2nd ed., (Los Angeles, CA: Silman-James, 2003) is the bible for anything concerning rights, copyright, public domain, personal rights, contracts and negotiation, copyright, chain of title, title clearance, insurances, rights to photograph, music clearance and rights, "fair use," rights to using film clips, registering copyright, copyright infringement, copyright and the Internet, and legal referral services. As with anything concerning the law, you are treading on eggshells, so read very, very carefully.

PRODUCTION PARTY

On a large production, once the crew is known, participants are chosen, and actors (if there are any) are cast, it is customary to have a production party. By bringing everyone together for the first time, this acts as an icebreaker. One of the pleasant aspects of working in the film business is that over the years you work with the same people every so often. Because everyone is freelance, everyone is happy to work. Production parties are therefore pleasant and constructive celebrations.

PREPRODUCTION CHECKLIST

During preproduction, remember:

- Logistical and mental preparation is the key to coherent moviemaking.
- Find a subject in which you can make a personal, emotional, long-term investment.
- A documentary shares a way of seeing and evokes feelings. It will become propaganda and not a documentary at all unless you invite the audience to weigh evidence and judge human values.
- Avoid situations where someone wants you to give up editorial control.
- Make requests sound natural and rightful, and you will often get the moon.
- Know before shooting what you want to say through the film. No plans lead to no film; the pressures of shooting prevent radical inquiry.
- Generalization is the enemy of art. Research knowledge will only communicate when you transform it into specific plans for shots, sequences, or questions.
- Make sure that conflicting values play out as onscreen confrontation with each other.
- Good documentary is good drama and shows people in struggle.
- In any good story someone undergoes some kind of change and development, however minimal and symbolic.
- Too often nobody develops in documentaries, making them static and pointless.
- Behavior, action, and interaction best show how people live.
- Given a camera and a sympathetic hearing, most people blossom.
- Treat the lives you enter with care.
- Expect to face many ethical and moral dilemmas. The greater good will often conflict with the obligations you feel to individuals.
- Documentaries are only as good as the relationships that permit them to be made (this applies to the crew as well as participants).
- Be ready throughout to supplement or modify your vision.
- Making documentary is long and slow, so be ready to go on working when enthusiasm wanes.

In preproduction, do not

- Bite off more than you can chew
- Make a film that confirms what anyone would expect of the subject

- Stretch your resources too thin or your subject too wide
- Be put off by participants' initial reservations and hesitancy. Keep explaining, and see what happens.
- Force people into situations or attitudes that are not their own
- Tell anyone you are filming anything until it is 100% sure
- Promise to show footage if by so doing you lose editorial freedom
- Act like you are begging favors, especially with officials

When searching for a subject,

- Maintain several project ideas on the back burner.
- Read avidly about what is going on, and keep a subject notebook and clipping file.
- Reject the obvious subject and the obvious treatment. You can do better.
- Only take on something that matches your capabilities and budget.
- Make a concerted effort to discover and reveal the unexpected.
- Define what to avoid as well as what to show.
- Think small, think local, think short. Do something contained and in depth.

When researching a particular subject,

- Expect filmmaker's funk, that is, stage fright.
- Take a research partner with you, and exchange impressions afterward.
- Be tentative and general when you explain your project.
- Be friendly and respectful, and signify that you are there to learn.
- Make a prioritized shopping list of possible participants and sequences.
- Define what each participant and sequence might contribute to your "argument."
- Keep your options open and make no impulsive commitments.

Once you have found a subject, ask yourself:

- Do I *really* want to invest part of my life making a film about this subject?
- In what other subjects am I already knowledgeable and opinionated?
- Do I have a strong emotional connection to this subject, more so than any other?
- Am I equipped to do justice to this subject?
- Do I have a drive to learn more about this subject?
- What is this subject's *real* significance to me?
- What is unusual and interesting about it?
- Where is its specialness really visible?

- How narrowly and deeply can I focus my film's attention?
- What can I *show?*
- What recent films am I competing with?
- What can I reveal that will be novel to most of the audience?
- What are my prejudices that I must be careful to examine?
- What prejudices will much of my audience hold toward my subject or my approach?
- What basic facts must the audience learn in order to follow my film?
- Who is in possession of those facts? How can I get more than one version?
- What change and development can my film expect to show?

When talking with possible participants,

- Assume you can be uncommonly curious and questioning.
- When participants ask about your ideas, turn the conversation so you learn about theirs.
- Advance at the participant's speed, or you will damage trust and spontaneity.
- Use a "student of life" attitude that invites the participant to take an instructional role.
- Use the "devil's advocate" role to probe risky areas without implicating yourself.
- Watch, listen, and correlate what you learn with what you have learned from other sources.
- Use networking and ask to be passed to the next person. It always helps to have been personally referred.
- Seek each person's view of the others as a cross check.
- Do some informal, nonaggressive interviews to see if being "on record" hinders participants' spontaneity.

When deciding what and how to shoot,

- Define what each participant represents or contributes as a character in your film.
- Assign each character a metaphorical role.
- Assign each event a metaphorical meaning.
- Define what microcosm your subject is, and what macrocosm it represents.
- Define what each sequence should contribute to the whole.
- Define what conflicts are at the heart of your drama.
- Decide how the forces in conflict will come into confrontation on the screen.

When defining the working hypothesis,

- What is the minimum your film must say?
- What are the forces in conflict that you must show?
- What are the telling contradictions in the main characters and their situations?
- What is each main character's "unfinished business"?
- What is he or she trying to get or accomplish?
- What are the major obstacles that prevent your main characters from getting what they want?
- If the film has a point of view character, who is it, and why did you choose him or her?
- What style or approach are you using, and how does it fit with your subject and what you want to imply?
- How do you want to act on your audience? What should they think and feel after seeing your film?

When scheduling,

- Discuss scheduling in advance with those affected.
- Schedule loosely, especially in the first day or two. The crew won't get up to speed immediately, and they will need food and rest even if you don't!
- Schedule the least demanding work first.
- List special equipment or requirements on the schedule.
- Take travel time into account.
- Give a typed schedule to crew and participants well ahead of time.
- Give clear navigational directions, plus photocopies of maps to drivers.
- Put mobile or other phone contact numbers in schedule in case anyone gets lost or delayed.
- Obtain signed location clearances well in advance.
- Have personal release forms and fees ready for shoots.

At the preproduction meeting,

- Make this the last troubleshooting session.
- Draft a schedule and budget for discussion.
- Decide what format you are going to use for acquisition and which for postproduction.
- Be aware of any difficulties that come with your particular TV standard.
- Decide whether to record sound in the camera or to record separately, bearing in mind that with the latter sound will have to be synched up to picture later.

- Follow manufacturer recommendations to the letter, and do not unnecessarily mix and match equipment made by different manufacturers.
- Make equipment lists conservatively—it costs money.
- Be sure to include a 35 mm stills camera for production stills—you'll need them later for the publicity kit.

When scheduling the shoot,

- Carefully check availability of locations, crew, participants and other personnel.
- Conserve on locations and setups, as this can extend equipment hire periods.
- Leave adequate travel time between locations.
- Factor in complexity of lighting or other arrangements at every location.
- Be aware of direction of natural light at the time of day you want to shoot—it may or may not be helpful.
- Be *very* cautious about equipment: set it up and test it before leaving its home base, and expect breakdowns in predictable ways. Optimism should never be vested in equipment.
- On big productions, use software to keep track of outgoings so you don't run out of resources.
- Carry enough of the right insurances, particularly if you have contracted to do so when hiring union personnel.
- Use formal contracts and formal arrangements when you can do so without causing offense.
- Throw a production party to bring everyone together in relaxed, enjoyable circumstances.

PART 6

PRODUCTION

Part 6 deals with

- Camera essentials for comfortable handling and control
- Monitoring what you are recording
- Lighting equipment essentials and power calculations
- Basic lighting coverage and participants' reactions to it
- Location sound recording

This part covers the responsibilities of the director during production. These include making sure that the production uses appropriate equipment, directing those in front of and behind the camera, and the intangibles of maintaining authorial control even when events stray far from what you expected.

As practice for building up a repertoire of specific skills, there is a chapter of production projects. These will give you experience at using the various aspects of documentary language.

For further information on issues arising in Part 6, use the Index or go to the Bibliography. Make frequent use of the Production Checklist at the end of this Part, and save yourself wasted time and energy.

CHAPTER 20

CAMERA EQUIPMENT AND SHOOTING PROCEDURE

CAMERA EQUIPMENT

Today there is so much usable equipment that this chapter can only alert you to better or worse features. Some models are overall better than others, but they usually are expensive. The important thing to remember is that good documentaries can still be made with modest equipment, especially when you are learning. This chapter covers

- Camcorder features and controls
- Lens characteristics
- White balancing and color temperature
- Batteries and power supplies
- Camera support systems
- Fundamentals of location sound recording equipment
- Monitoring picture and sound

CAMERA BODY

Because documentary often is shot handheld, the ideal documentary camera has a viewfinder at the side and a body balanced to sit on the operator's shoulder, as in the Éclair NPR film camera, the first workhorse of sync documentary (Figure 20–1). Its digital descendent is similar in layout and handling (Figure 20–2). The smaller digital camcorders often have the finder at the back of the camera, home movie camera style, and often have a color screen that folds out from the side. It can be faced back or upward for the operator, or forward so that you can frame yourself as you speak to-camera while making notes (Figure 20–3).

Small camcorders, however good their sound and image, are a little more difficult to control handheld, especially over a long period, because you cannot

FIGURE 20–1

Éclair NPR film camera, the first sync camera designed to sit on the operator's shoulder and capable of quick magazine changes. (The author shooting for a friend around 1980.)

steady the camera against your head and shoulder. Many incorporate image stabilization technology that is supposed to compensate for unsteadiness, but whoever operates the camera will have to practice long and hard to get professional-looking camerawork from anything you must hold out in front of your face.

LENS

A truly wide-angle zoom lens greatly simplifies handheld camerawork because the lens accepts a larger amount of the scene and enables moving camera shots that look steadier. Consider your camera's lens specifications. The range of a zoom lens is expressed in millimeters from shortest to longest focal length. Film camera lenses, unlike those fitted on consumer camcorders, are calibrated so that you can immediately size up their capabilities. In 16 mm photography, for example, a zoom may range from 15 to 60 mm. If the lower number (or "wide-angle" end of the zoom lens) is lower than 15 mm, you are in luck. Nine or 10 mm is especially useful, because it gives your camera a really wide angle of acceptance and allows you to cover a decent area in a small room. At the shorter focal length, you are also freed from making a lot of focus adjustments. A lens whose widest end is above 15 mm will present problems. You cannot shoot effectively in tight surroundings, will have problems achieving a steady handheld picture, and will find difficulty maintaining focus in low-light situations. Though

FIGURE 20–2

Chicago filmmaker Tod Lending and his Sony HDW-750, a state-of-the-art HD camcorder for shooting documentary.

supplementary lenses are available to alter a zoom's entire range, picture definition may suffer, particularly at the edges and in low-light situations.

Lenses on consumer camcorders have no standard calibration, so you will have to run tests to see how wide is the zoom's angle of acceptance. A visit to a video store will often allow you to make comparisons, and the manufacturer's literature may prove helpful too. Check whether automatic focus can be disengaged so that the camera doesn't hunt for focus every time picture composition changes. Never use the digital enlargement that some camcorders offer—it magnifies the pixel (picture cel) size and is an option for the unwary. Do, however, use the macro focusing that most camcorders offer. It allows you to

FIGURE 20–3 —————————————————————————————————————

Panasonic PV DV953, a typical small camcorder with a foldout screen. (Courtesy Panasonic Corporation)

focus down to inches, a really useful feature when you must shoot small objects or images.

Whether the camcorder sits on your shoulder or must be held away from your face, practice operating all the basic controls (sound level, exposure, focus, and zoom). Keep practicing until your hands naturally fall on each, as you need it.

EXPOSURE CONTROL

Examine your camcorder's lens and controls to verify that the *lens aperture* (or *f-stop* on a film camera) can be manually controlled. Most allow manual exposure control, which is good for achieving, say, an underexposed landscape to simulate sunset. The responsiveness of the control is important. Positive and immediate is good; floating and slow is not. Being able to choose then lock the exposure, so it doesn't drift, is very important. Exposure should hold steady even if a lady in a white dress walks across your frame during a street shot. Floating exposure happens because automatic exposure circuits react slavishly to brightness changes, with no regard for picture content. A manual control allows the user a degree of control vital to many kinds of lighting situations. Avoid using any automated controls if you can use manual ones.

COLOR BALANCE, PICTURE GAIN, AND AUTOMATIC CONTROLS

Video cameras have a *white balance* control that allows electronic adjustment of color rendition, so white is reproduced as white under particular light sources. Daylight, tungsten-filament bulbs, fluorescent, and other light sources all have different *color temperatures*, which means that they emanate a mix of colors in which some predominate. Unless you run a "white balance," your shooting under fluorescents, for example, will look unpleasantly greenish.

Manual white balance (done while framing a piece of white paper under the relevant light source) is always preferable to the presets that most camcorders offer (such as daylight, tungsten light, and fluorescent light) because these are approximations only. A useful feature is a white balance memory, which retains the white balance setting while the camera is off or its battery is being changed. Some need rebalancing after such changes, so check this too.

The ultimate reference in all color work is that flesh tones should look natural. Automatic white balance can, however, be valuable when you must track with a subject walking through different lighting zones in, for instance, an airport.

A useful feature found on many camcorders is a *picture gain* control. It allows you to shoot an enhanced image in low-light situations, but you pay with increased *picture noise* (electronic picture "grain"). A backlight control, if there is one, is supposed to compensate exposure for a subject whose major illumination is coming toward the camera and thus is backlit. Try everything out, and believe only what you see.

Other facilities usually found only on semi-professional or professional camcorders are built-in filters, black level control, gamma (color linearity), as well as truly manual exposure, focusing, and sound level settings, all of which can be locked. Consumer equipment tends to be automated, with variables achieved through tiny thumb wheels and menus that look like verb tables for a foreign language. Professional equipment is big because they give you proper controls, and there are a lot of them. Film equipment is all manually controlled with automation applied, if at all, to exposure and, in the case of sound recorders, to level control.

POWER SUPPLIES

Almost all film and video equipment runs off batteries rechargeable from 110- or 220-volt AC current, or even a car battery via the cigarette lighter socket. Chargers usually double as power converters so that you can run a camera or a monitor directly from an AC wall outlet. *Rechargeable batteries* never seem to run the equipment for long enough, especially if they have been incorrectly charged. Overestimate the number of batteries you need on location because manufacturers' literature tends toward optimism. Rechargeable batteries are inclined to be slow chargers, with 6 to 10 hours being normal. Never allow them to become completely exhausted, but work each nickel-cadmium (NiCad) battery to its useable limit and then completely recharge. Any other regimen may shorten the battery's "memory." Read the manual carefully in relation to conserving battery life.

A more conclusive solution to the dying battery problem is to buy or rent a battery belt, which has a much larger capacity than a battery and may power a camcorder for a whole shooting day. Many camcorders, however, are designed to work only with batteries of a particular interior resistance and shut down automatically when they sense a foreigner in their midst. Never, ever assume any departure from conformity will work without checking manufacturer's literature or finding the fruit of experience via the Internet.

CAMERA SUPPORT SYSTEMS

There's not much comfort here for the underfunded. The budget *tripod* and *tilt head* is a miserable piece of equipment indeed. It will work fine for static shots, but as soon as you try to pan or tilt, your wobbly movements will reveal why professionals use big tripods and hydraulically damped tilt heads. Shooting with a wide-angle lens will greatly improve any camera movement, and image stabilization in a camcorder sometimes helps, but believe nothing until you've tested it.

A *baby legs* is a very short tripod for low-angle shots, and a *high hat* is a hat-shaped support for placing the camera on the ground or on sandbags, which can be patted into shape to allow a degree of angling. A *spreader* or *spider* is a folding three-armed bracket that goes under the sharp legs of a professional tripod to stop the legs from spreading out and collapsing. It also permits the camera and tripod to be picked up as a unit and set down elsewhere. A spreader also guards against denting an expensive floor.

For a *dolly*, try a wheelchair. For exteriors, shoot backward out of the trunk of a car or station wagon. You can tie down a tripod inside a car and shoot out of a side window. For a forward shot, rope the camera securely to the hood. In all cases use a wide-angle lens to minimize road vibration. For superlative tracking shots with sync sound (dialogue, for instance), use a light car with partially deflated tires as a dolly and get several people to push it so that there's no engine noise to drown the dialogue.

A well-practiced, well-coordinated human being also makes an excellent camera support, especially if he or she is equipped with one of the low-cost Steadicam™ systems now available (see www.steadicam.com). Using one, Melinda Roenisch won awards for *Ruth's Journey* (1995), which lyrically explores the shell of a great lakeshore mansion. Here her grandmother hoarded a million collectibles rather than interact with her family.

MONITORS

A battery-operated monitor is indispensable on location for playback. It also makes a jumbo viewfinder when you shoot off a tripod. If you intend making do with a domestic television set, avoid going through the antenna circuitry. Instead use the TV's video and audio inputs, or an S cable input, if it has one. Truly reliable results with regard to color and framing are only obtainable by using a properly adjusted field monitor. This may be your only guarantee of color fidelity while shooting and the only double-check on the framing shown in the camera viewfinder, which can also be wrong. Monitors and television sets usually have abysmal sound quality. Bypass them during viewings by feeding camcorder, digital video disk (DVD), or videocassette player sound into a stereo system. The improvement in sound quality is truly dramatic.

SHOOTING PROCEDURES

Some of what follows will be needlessly complicated for a one- or two-person shoot using a camcorder (called a *single-system* setup). More elaborate procedures become necessary for the kind of scripted work you must do for docudrama or acted historical reconstruction. They do become necessary, however, if you use a separate sound recorder (called a *double-system* setup).

SHOT IDENTIFICATION

If you can, keep logs of important information as you shoot. Central to record-keeping is the ability to identify shots and *takes* (repeated attempts at a shot) as you shoot. The traditional marking system is the familiar wooden *slate*, or *clapper board*, with a closing bar on top.

There are many automatic film marking systems such as the Smart Slate, but my favorite is the exquisitely low-tech clapper board, which has only a piece of chalk and a hinge to go wrong. The clapper board ritual has three main functions:

- Visually it identifies the shot number and the production for the film laboratory.
- Aurally the operator's announcement identifies the track for sound transfer personnel.
- When sound and picture are recorded separately and must be synchronized later, the closing bar provides an exact picture frame against which to align the bang in the recorded track.

When video recording is single system (sound and picture on the one piece of tape) sync is not an issue. No clapper board is needed unless you shoot double-system sound (film or video picture, and sound recorded separately on a Nagra or digital audiotape [DAT] machine). For double-system productions, the clapper board is essential to precision sync.

In single-system shoots, you still need to log your material as you go by content and *timecode* (a unique time signature for every frame). Then, using log and high-speed scan, a chosen section can be rapidly located for viewing during production. This is invaluable on location when time spent reviewing tape is often stolen from much-needed rest.

On big documentary productions, clapper or numbering boards carry not only scene and take numbers but also a quantity of vital information for image quality-control experts in film labs or video online studio. These include a gray scale, white and black as a contrast reference, and a standard color chart. A color chart called *color bars* is also generated electronically by the camera and recorded for reference purposes as a standard procedure at the head of every camera original tape.

To summarize,

- For single-system (camcorder) video production, use a number board for the camera with announcement only. Under pressure you can dispense with this and log content and timecode afterward.

- For double-system shoots, treat the operation like film and use an announcement and a clapper board. Keep camera and sound logs.

Setup and Take Numbers   What information about the *setup* goes on the clapper board? The setup is the apparent position of the camera, which usually is altered by physically moving the camera to a new position. However, a simple lens change also counts as a new setup. There are two philosophies of numbering.

Method 1: The *scene/setup/take* system is favored in the Hollywood fiction film industry and might apply to a scripted dramadoc. All numbering is based on the script scene number, for example, "scene 104A, shot 16, take 3." Translated this means script scene 104A, setup 16, attempt number 3." Hollywood, making big highly supervised productions, needs lengthy factory part numbers. For the small, flexible production, this is unnecessary. The more elaborate a system is, the more susceptible it is to error and breakdown when people get tired or if you depart from the script.

Method 2: The *cumulative setup/take* system is used universally in documentaries and in European feature films. Shooting simply begins at slate 1-1. Each new setup gets a new slate number, and a second or subsequent attempt at the same setup will get a new take number, for example, "1 take 2" or 1–2). This system is preferred for the overstretched small crew because it requires no liaison to coordinate numbers with the script and no adaptation when the inevitable script departures come up. The disadvantage is that it makes life a little busier for the script supervisor, if there is one. Every setup number must be recorded against a scene in the master script or kept in a database.

SHOOTING LOGS

Shooting of any elaboration requires two kinds of log:

- A *camera log* (Figure 20–4) kept by the assistant cinematographer recording each cassette's contents by slate, take, and timecode readings. Each new cassette gets a new number, information that comes into play during editing.

- A *sound log* (Figure 20–5) kept by the sound recordist records slate and take numbers, and whether each track is sync or "wild" (non-sync voice or effects recording). The latter information is important to whoever digitizes into the computer from DAT or 1/4-inch master tape.

DOUBLE SYSTEM

Sometimes for reasons of quality or mobility, sound is recorded double system on a separate recorder and logged separately as it would be in a film shoot (Figure 20–5). Note that whenever sound is recorded separately, camera and sound recorder rolls do not stay in numerical step either because stock durations are different or because additional sound (wild tracks, sound effects, or atmosphere recordings) have been added to the sound master rolls as the production progresses. Sometimes, for speed, shots are taken silent. After sound has been

```
FILM CAMERA LOG    Production Title_____ Page_____

Operator_____ Camera #_____ Magazine #_____ Cam. Roll #____
Location_____ Film Type _____ Date ___/___/_____
------------------------------------------------------------------------------
Setup Take Comments                                                    Footage
  ____:____:_____:_____
  ____:____:_____:_____
  ____:____:_____:_____
  ____:____:_____:_____
  ____:____:_____:_____
  ____:____:_____:_____
  ____:____:_____:_____
  ____:____:_____:_____
  ____:____:_____:_____
  ____:____:_____:_____
  ____:____:_____:_____
  ____:____:_____:_____
  ____:____:_____:_____
  ____:____:_____:_____
  ____:____:_____:_____
  ____:____:_____:_____
  ____:____:_____:_____
  ____:____:_____:_____
  ____:____:_____:_____
  ____:____:_____:_____
  ____:____:_____:_____
  ____:____:_____:_____
  ____:____:_____:_____
  ____:____:_____:_____
  ____:____:_____:_____
  ____:____:_____:_____
  ____:____:_____:_____
  ____:____:_____:_____
  ____:____:_____:_____
  ____:____:_____:_____
  ____:____:_____:_____
  ____:____:_____:_____
  ____:____:_____:_____
  ____:____:_____:_____
Process Normal Yes/ No:_____      Total Shot :
------------------------------------------------------------------------:-------
Notes:

_____ Cam. Assistant:_____
```

FIGURE 20–4

Camera log for double-system recording.

```
SOUND RECORDER LOG Production Title_____ Page_____
Mike Op. _____ Recorder_#_____ Tape Type_____Roll #_____
Location_____ Date ___/___/_____
Setup Take Comments                                        Mike(s)  Sync?
____:____:_____:_____
____:____:_____:_____
____:____:_____:_____
____:____:_____:_____
____:____:_____:_____
____:____:_____:_____
____:____:_____:_____
____:____:_____:_____
____:____:_____:_____
____:____:_____:_____
____:____:_____:_____
____:____:_____:_____
____:____:_____:_____
____:____:_____:_____
____:____:_____:_____
____:____:_____:_____
____:____:_____:_____
____:____:_____:_____
____:____:_____:_____
____:____:_____:_____
____:____:_____:_____
____:____:_____:_____
____:____:_____:_____
____:____:_____:_____
____:____:_____:_____
____:____:_____:_____
____:____:_____:_____
____:____:_____:_____
____:____:_____:_____
____:____:_____:_____
____:____:_____:_____
____:____:_____:_____
____:____:_____:_____
____:____:_____:_____
Notes:




                              Recordist:
```

FIGURE 20–5 ————————————————————————————————

Sound recorder log for double-system recording.

digitized ready for editing, the cutting room assistant must synchronize each sound take to its picture before the editor can start work.

SINGLE SYSTEM

When shooting single system with a camcorder, the log (Figure 20–6) can be simpler because sound and picture usually are recorded side by side and on the

```
┌─────────────────────────────────────────────────────────────────────────┐
│                                                                           │
│   V I D E O   L O G  Production Title_____ Page_____   │
│                                                                           │
│   Cam. Operator_____ Camera_____ Date__/__/___    │
│   Location_____ Roll #_____     │
│                                                                           │
│   Counter Scene                                                           │
│   reading # and       Description                       Remarks           │
│   _____ take _____ _____        │
│                                                                           │
│   ... (ruled log lines) ...                                               │
│                                                                           │
│   Notes:                                                                   │
│                                                                           │
│                              Signed:                                      │
│                                                                           │
└─────────────────────────────────────────────────────────────────────────┘
```

FIGURE 20–6

Log for single-system video production.

same cassette (see flow chart, Figure 20–7). The camera assistant keeps a master log by timecode readings and keeps a record of content at the least, or preferably slate, take, and camera setup information if the material is being identified with a slate. The recorded cassette, containing both sound and action, goes to the cutting room for digitizing.

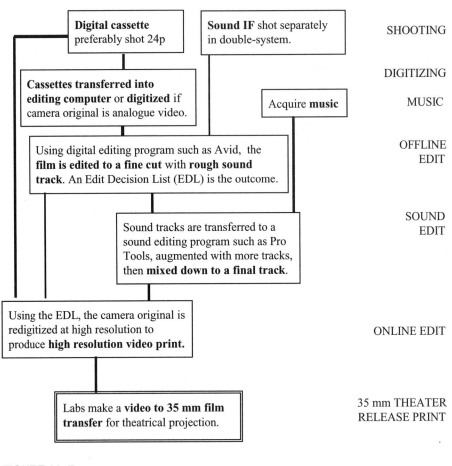

FIGURE 20–7

Flow chart for a production shot on digital video, with single- or double-system sound, resulting in a 35 mm release print for theatrical exhibition.

LOGS IN ACTION

Logs help the right material go to the right place when the content of camera and sound rolls must by digitized and synchronized. On an elaborate shoot with several cameras, a less obvious function of logs is to record (by serial number) which piece of equipment made which recording. Should a strange hum appear in the sound or a picture hue problem appear in a digital video recording, the offending equipment can be quickly identified and withdrawn for examination.

THE COUNTDOWN TO SHOOTING

When a double-system setup is used and a clapper board is being used as a marking system, there is an unvarying ritual at the beginning of each take.

1. The director calls "Stand by to turn over."

2. The clapper operator takes up a position holding the clapper board (also known as *clapsticks*) in front of the subject, at a height where it is clearly visible. The operator will sometimes direct its placement to ensure that the all important number and clapper bar are in shot.

3. The camera operator turns on the camera, says "Camera rolling," and calls out "Roll sound."

4. The sound recordist turns on the recorder, waits a few moments until its mechanism has reached a stable speed, then calls out "Speed."

5. The camera operator now says "Mark it".

6. The clapper operator calls out the scene and take number, closes the clapper with a bang, and immediately exits frame.

7. The director can now say "Action" as a cue for the action to begin.

STARTING WITHOUT A CLAPPER

Sometimes when shooting spontaneous material in the street, say, and not wanting to alert everyone that the camera is rolling, the director will simply signal to start the camera and sound recorder rolling. After the action is complete, the clapper board is brought in and filmed, but upside down. The clapper operator calls out the scene number, adding "Board on end" or "End clapsticks," then claps the bar, after which the director calls "Cut." In the cutting room the end-clapped material will have to be end-synced, then backed up for marking at the beginning.

CREW ETIQUETTE

During the scene, crew stand as still as possible and stay out of the participants' eyelines, not to distract them. Even if something funny happens, they must remain silent and expressionless. It is vital for a film crew not to behave like an audience, for that would turn the participants into actors. In any case, every member of the crew has something to monitor:

- *Camera operator* is watching through the camera viewfinder for focus, compositions, framing, and movements, and whether the mike is dangling into shot. Film cameras have an oversized viewfinder so that the operator can see something encroaching on the frame before it enters the filmed area.

- *Director of photography* (if there is a separate person) watches the lighting as participants move from area to area.

- *The director* is watching the scene for its content and emotional intensity. What is being expressed? Where is the scene going? Is it what I expected and does it deliver what I hoped it would deliver?

- *Electricians* are watching to see that all lights stay on.

- *Sound operator* listens for voice quality and any unwanted intrusions.

The scene proceeds until the director calls "Cut!"

WHO ELSE CAN CALL "CUT!"

There are some occasions when someone other than the director calls "Cut." The camera operator may abort the scene, having seen a hopeless framing mistake and knowing that it's useless to go on with the shot. The sound mixer may do likewise when getting unusable sound for some reason. Either may call "Cut!" if their right to do so has been established with the director. The idea is to save time and energy. Sometimes a participant, unhappy with what is being shot, will call "Cut!" You have no option but to cut the camera.

COMPLEMENTARY SHOTS

Once the master shot has been achieved in traditional tripod coverage, the camera will be moved in, or lenses changed, to get medium shots, close shots, over-shoulder shots, and so on. Each will count as a new setup, and each will get a new setup number, with each attempt being slated as a new take. Each camera position may use different lenses or different camera heights to alter the sense of space and perspective. The backgrounds may be cheated to contain enough of something significant in the frame as a juxtapositional comment. Lighting will also be cheated, because lighting for a wide shot only sets the general mood of the scene, and individual closer shots must often be adjusted for contrast or to achieve a better effect. The key lighting must still come from the same direction, and the changes cannot so alter the shot that it stands apart from the master shot, but within these parameters there is still plenty of latitude for poetic license.

SOUND PRESENCE

For each location the sound recordist must shoot a couple of minutes of sound presence. This supplies the cutting room with enough characteristic background, or ambience, to fill in spaces or make other adjustments.

GETTING THE SIGNED RELEASE FORM

Once a particular person's shooting ends, the director or an assistant will ask him or her to sign a legal release (see Chapter 17: Missions and Permissions).

IT'S A WRAP

When all the materials for a scene have been shot and everyone is satisfied that the editor has everything necessary, it is almost time to strike (dismantle) the set. But wait, the sound department must first shoot a presence track. Everyone stand still! In eerie silence everyone stands like statues for a couple of minutes, uncomfortably aware of their own breathing and of the little sounds in the room. "Cut!" calls the sound recordist. "It's a wrap!" says the director. Everyone moves to start their own winding-up responsibilities:

- Electricians lower all the lights and roll up cables while hot lighting fixtures cool down.
- Grips strike the set and collect up their clamps, stands, and boxes.
- Camera people take the camera off its support and start dismantling it and stowing gear in travel boxes.
- Sound equipment goes in its boxes.
- Whoever has the schedule for the next day's shooting hands it out to those affected.
- The director thanks participants or confirms the next day's arrangements, then thanks each person in the unit for a good day's work.
- The director checks that there is no damage to the location and that everything is left clean and tidy.

Doors open and close as weary people schlep the equipment out to the transport. The camera assistant is carefully labeling cassettes, while the recordist may be finishing up reports. Engines start up and the circus moves on its way, to reconvene the next day at the next location.

CHAPTER 21

LIGHTING

This chapter covers

- Common problems that make lighting necessary
- Lighting hardware and its power and safety issues
- Lighting terms, simple lighting methodology, and testing
- Consequences and human reactions to lighting

Comprehensive lighting instructions are far beyond the scope of this book, but here are some useful basic points. Video has an immense advantage over film in that you can see what a lighting setup looks like from the camera's viewfinder or a field monitor. By the way, I have no relationship with any of the manufacturers or services listed.

WHEN AND WHY YOU NEED IT

Color film often needs lighting, but with video cameras now able to register good images by candlelight, you would think that lighting for video was no longer necessary. However,

- An interior lit by daylight has bright highlight areas and impossibly dark shadow areas. (*Problem:* contrast ratio of key to fill light is too high. *Solution:* boost shadow area lighting.)
- An interior lit by daylight with pools of artificial light does strange things to skin tones when people move around. (*Problem:* they are passing through mixed color temperature lighting. *Solution:* filtering one source to make it consistent with others. Filter window light so that it matches interior lighting color temperature.)
- An exterior where you must shoot in heavy shadow has a sunlit background that burns out. (*Problem:* huge contrast ratio between sunlit and shadow areas. *Solution:* Use lighting or reflectors to raise light level in shadow area.)

Frequently lighting is needed because no video or film medium renders images like the human eye, which effortlessly evens out illumination and color inequities. Instead, cameras record within their limitations, and lighting is necessary to make an evening interior, for instance, appear as we expect it. Lens limitations also may dictate a higher overall light level. This is because when available light is low you must use a wide lens aperture, which in turn reduces depth of field and demands very precise focusing—difficult or impossible when camera and subject are on the move. By adding light you can use a smaller lens aperture, get a greater depth of field, and have fewer focusing problems. Use supplementary lighting when

- The scene is too dark to get an exposure
- A scene or an object does not look its best under available light
- Available light is too contrasty, creating "hot" (overbright) highlights and impenetrable shadows
- You are working under mixed color-temperature sources, that is, light sources having different color biases

AVOIDING THE OVERBRIGHT BACKGROUND

A truly aggravating problem when you shoot in small, light-colored or white spaces is the amount of light thrown back by the walls. The onscreen result can become a set of orange humanoid outlines moving against a blinding white background. The low-end video camera is especially vulnerable because exposure circuitry automatically adjusts for the majority of the image, letting the actual subjects go relatively dark. Color quality and definition all suffer.

CONTRAST PROBLEMS

Image recording limitations in film and video often require raising shadow light levels to reduce the disparity between the highest and the lowest illumination levels in the picture. By using *fill light* to boost shadow areas, you reduce the lighting ratio, that is, you reduce the range of brightnesses between shadow and highlight illuminations. Fill light may come from a lighting instrument or be provided by a *bounce card* (a silver or white cardboard reflector, white wall or ceiling). When you bring the range of brightnesses in the image within the (always limited) capacity of the recording medium, the screen reproduces the picture you wanted with enough detail in both highlight and deep shadow areas. Without lighting adjustments, this detail would have been lost. Currently film stocks reproduce detail over a wider range of brightnesses than video, but digital video keeps on improving.

COLOR-TEMPERATURE PROBLEMS

Color-temperature mismatches in source lighting are a big problem wherever daylight and artificial lighting are present together. Different light sources have different color biases, a problem that must be addressed if flesh is to look human rather than Martian. The eye effortlessly compensates for such mismatches and sees a white object as white under almost any illumination. But with film you must choose film stock and color filters for the camera according to their color temperature rating, if you are to render white as white onscreen. Electronic cameras permit immediate adjustment for an optimal color rendition.

Any camera can be balanced for *one* color-temperature source, but none can even out mixed light sources. Any unnatural lighting effects are particularly noticeable in close-ups, because our color judgments are made on how natural flesh tones look.

Imagine an interior setup lit by available daylight. You need to raise the exposure in the shadow, but color consistency problems arise when you try to boost blue-biased daylight by adding orange-biased tungsten light. If the video camera is adjusted to render daylight (5,400 K) as white light, the light coming from the tungsten light (3,200 K) will look, by comparison, noticeably orange. If you reset the white balance for the 3,200 K movie lighting, now the daylight-illuminated highlights look very blue.

The answer is to use a color-conversion gel over one or more of the light sources to adjust its color-temperature output to the majority lighting. We would probably filter the fill lighting to match the color temperature of the daylight and achieve consistent color temperature that way. Though this solves color imbalance, it lowers the light's output by as much as 50%, so now you may need twice as much light.

A simple interior can present a thicket of problems as the cinematographer faces contrasty, burnt-out walls, multiple shadows, and mike shadows—to mention just a few of the common difficulties. For specialized literature about such problems, see the Bibliography at the back of this book.

HARDWARE

LIGHTING INSTRUMENTS

Quite acceptable interior work can be done using only a 750-watt *soft light*. If you have plenty of current and space, you might use a *luminaire* (jargon for lighting fixture) with recessed bulbs and a very large, white-painted reflector (Figure 21–1). Or you might adapt a spotlight's output by diffusing it with a large square of silk or fiberglass. Another way to diffuse light is to bounce it off an aluminized umbrella or a white wall or ceiling.

Whichever method is used, the effect is of diffused light arriving from a broad area that throws very soft-edged shadows—shadows so soft that they are hardly noticeable. The terms *hard light* and *soft light* refer to the hardness or softness of any shadows cast. If you want the kind of hard light associated with sunlight or any other hard-edged shadows source, you will need *focusing lamps* or *spotlights* (Figures 21–2 and 21–3).

Open-face quartz lamps (Figure 21–4) are light and compact for travel. Quartz bulbs have a relatively long life, are small enough to provide fairly hard light, and remain stable in color temperature throughout their life. However, the

FIGURE 21–1

A 2K soft light. The bulbs are recessed so that light is diffused by the white reflector. (Mole Richardson Co.)

light from open-face lamps pours uncontrollably in every direction, making lighting a rather rudimentary exercise unless you at least have *barn doors* (adjustable flaps top and bottom). Anyone on a really stringent budget can find low-cost quartz work-lights at hardware stores that are quite usable as bounce light sources.

Warning: Movie lights, such as quartz bulbs, run *extremely* hot. Safety issues are as follows:

- Let lamps cool before disassembling them after shooting.
- Never touch quartz bulbs when you change them. Oil on your skin will bake into the quartz envelope and cause it to discolor or even explode the next time the bulb is turned on.
- Never turn on an open-face lamp with anyone standing in front of it. This is when bulbs explode, if they are going to.
- Never let water splash hot bulbs. Sudden cooling by water spots makes them explode.

FIGURE 21–2

Handy small spotlight. The fresnel lens produces hard light. (Mole Richardson Co.)

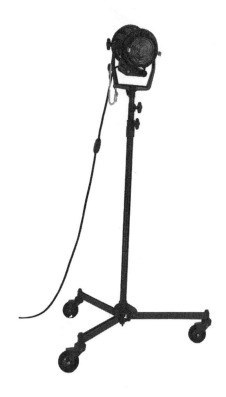

FIGURE 21–3

Larger spotlight. The stand allows the lamp to be rigged high or low, and to be wheeled rapidly into position. (Mole Richardson Co.)

FIGURE 21–4

Lightweight open-face quartz kit. Barn doors on lamps permit lighting spread to be restricted. (Lowel-Light Mfg.)

For fine-quality interior lighting, use directional lights such as *fresnel lights* (lensed studio lamps) with a tungsten filament rated at a color temperature of 3,200 degrees on the Kelvin scale (3,200 K).

POWER REQUIREMENTS

Movie lights are power hungry, consuming anywhere between 500 and 2,000 watts each. A decent soft light may draw 2 kilowatts (kW; or 2,000 watts). Because 1,000 watts is equivalent to 9.5 amps when run from 110 volts (or 4.5 amps when the supply is 210 volts), it follows that you cannot expect an American standard household circuit (110 volts at 15 amps) to power a 2 K lamp; you must search for a 20-amp power circuit.

To find power consumption in *amps* (rate of flow), divide your total desired *watts* (amount of energy consumption) and divide it by the *volts* (pressure) of the supply voltage. We can represent the common calculations as formulas:

$$\text{To calculate amperage (A): } W \div V = A$$
$$\text{To calculate wattage (W): } A \times V = W$$
$$\text{To calculate voltage (V): } W \div A = V$$

Keep any high-current requirements in mind when scouting locations for electrical supply, and be careful not to tap into a 220-volt supply by mistake. A cheap multimeter (combined voltage, resistance, and current meter) from an electronics store can help you check supply voltages and save a fortune in blown bulbs. It also can help you check that voltages under load have not dropped at the end of a long extension cord, which can markedly alter color temperatures.

Plan to bring heavy-load extension cables so that you can, if necessary, take each light's supply from a differently fused source and thus spread the load. The amount and type of lighting you need will depend on the size and reflectivity of the location space, how much (and what color temperature) the available light is, and what kind of lighting "look" you are aiming for.

Lighting is highly specialized, but later in this chapter you will find simple, basic setups that can get you through a lot, especially if you have a flexible lighting kit (Figure 21–5). If you were lighting for black and white, you would need great skill to give the viewer a proper sense of dimension, space, and textures. Color simplifies this task by separating tones by hue and thus requires less elaborate lighting strategies to give acceptable results.

BASIC LIGHTING METHODOLOGY

ADDING TO A BASE AND USING A KEY LIGHT

When you begin making documentaries and whenever you must work very fast, you can get away with a simple and reliable solution for lighting interiors. Called *adding to a base*, it means simply providing enough ambient light for an exposure, then adding some modeling with a key light.

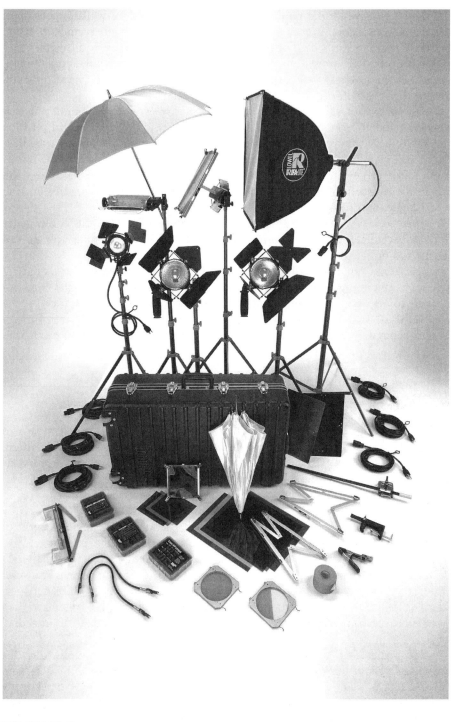

FIGURE 21–5

A lighting kit with great flexibility. A reflective silver umbrella converts any open-face (hard) light into a soft-light source. The frames carry diffusion material or gels. Everything packs into the suitcase. (Lowel-Light Mfg.)

Base light: Make the base by bouncing light off white walls and ceilings, which provides a good overall illumination. If there are no white surfaces to hand, bounce light off a white card or diffuse it with spun glass or other diffusion material that won't discolor with heat. Using only base light gives a dull and flat (comparatively shadowless) look, especially in longer shots. Now you must now add the key light, which should be logically *motivated*.

Key light: Motivated key lighting is the shadow-producing illumination that appears to come from a logical source. In a bedroom scene, you might position the key low and out of frame so that shadows are apparently cast by a bedside lamp. For a warehouse scene lit by a bare overhead bulb hanging into the frame, the additional key light would have to come from above. In a pathology lab where the source is a light table, the key would have to strike the subject from a low angle, and so on.

Cheating: You can substantially *cheat* the angle of the key for convenience and artistic effect, and to minimize shadow problems, providing you do not depart too noticeably from what seems likely.

Practicals: Any lamps that appear in the picture are called *practicals* but are seldom a functioning part of the lighting. They are adjusted for light output—enough to register as a light but not enough to burn out that portion of the picture. If a practical looks too orange, use a photoflood, but be careful of the heat it generates. Cut a practical's output by putting layers of neutral-density (ND) filter or layers of paper around the inside of its shade.

DEFINING SHADOWS: HARD AND SOFT LIGHT

The key provides highlights and throws shadows. The audience infers time of day, mood, and so on, mainly from the associations of a scene's shadow pattern. *Hard* and *soft* are terms for light quality that are indispensable to discussions about lighting and lighting style. *Hard light*, you may recall, is light that creates *hard-edged shadows*; *soft light* is light that creates soft-edged shadows or no discernible shadows at all.

Note that *hard* and *soft* have nothing to do with the strength of illumination. Thus, in spite of its dimness, a candle flame is a hard-light source because it creates hard shadows. Hard light comes from a small-area light source or from a source that is effectively small. This is because it is distant (the sun, for example) or because it is fitted with a lens (as in a fresnel spotlight). Light rays coming from effectively small sources are organized and parallel to each other and thus project a clear shadow image of impeding objects.

Soft light tends to come from a large-area source that sends out disorganized rays of light incapable of projecting clean-cut shadows. A fluorescent tube is such a source and is specially favored in everyday use as a relatively shadowless working light. The most bountiful source of soft light when you are shooting exteriors is an overcast sky. When you see huge lights used in feature film exteriors it is because available light is too soft to produce an adequate shadow pattern and so must be augmented with a hard-light source.

KEY LIGHT DIRECTION AND BACKLIGHTING

Folklore about taking photos with your back to the sun suggests that light must always fall on the subject from the camera direction. But this ensures a minimum of shadow area and removes evidence of the subject's third dimension—depth. Interesting lighting effects on the human face begin when the key light's angle of throw is to the side of the subject or even relatively behind it (see Chapter 13, Project 13-3 for pictorial examples and further discussion).

Key light can come from an open-face quartz lamp that is suitably backed off, or, like the fill, it too can be somewhat diffused to soften hard shadows. Using multiple key lights is a skilled business and without a lot of care can lead to that trademark of amateur lighting—ugly, multiple shadows.

Backlighting creates a rim of light that helps to separate the subject from the background. Achieving this separation is important in black-and-white photography but less so in color, where the varying hues help to define and separate the different planes of the composition.

TESTS

For shooting even small interiors with film, you will need three or more lamps of at least 750 watts each. For video, less power is necessary. Be forewarned that 3 or 4 kW of lighting goes nowhere in a large space or in a smaller room painted a dark tone. The only way to learn about film lighting is to shoot tests in the locations you intend using. Shoot 35 mm tungsten-balanced color slides on a fairly fast slide stock (say, 125 ASA at 1/50th of a second shutter time). Project them, and study your lighting triumphs or deficiencies in depth.

A lighting rehearsal can save you from costly electrical failures during the shoot. Long demoralizing delays are the penalty for taking chances. Check out where to find the location's fuses or breakers, which sockets belong on which circuit, and whether high-consumption, intermittent appliances, such as refrigerators and air conditioners, are going to kick in during shooting and cause a circuit overload. If you turn off a refrigerator during shooting, remember to turn it back on or you may have to replace the family frozen food supplies.

Try to shoot in spaces with dark or book-covered walls that absorb rather than reflect the light that you need to illuminate your subjects. When this is impossible, keep light off the background walls by angling and barn dooring your sources to raise illumination on foreground subjects. Keeping participants away from walls by "cheating" chairs, tables, and sofas several feet distant will help lessen shadow and illumination disparity problems. This helps cast shadows low and out of sight of the camera and seldom looks unnatural onscreen. Moving participants away from sound-reflective surfaces also improves sound quality.

LIGHTING: REACTIONS AND CONSEQUENCES

The discomfort caused by injudicious lighting will inhibit the nervous. Give your participants a chance to get used to unusual amounts of light pouring down on them, particularly in their own homes. Lighting equipment also creates heat, and when windows must be kept closed to reduce outside noise, interior shooting can become unpleasantly torrid. Participants whose faces sweat will need to be dulled down with a skin-tone powder. This is the only *make-up* ever used in documentary. Unless someone skilled handles make-up, it can look abominable. For objects producing overbright reflections, such as chromium chairs or glass tables, use a removable *dulling spray* obtained from an art supply store.

CHAPTER 22

LOCATION SOUND

This chapter covers

- Recording using different types of recorder
- Microphone types, power supplies, and pickup patterns
- Recording requirements and conditions
- How the recordist works during handheld shoots in relation to the camera operator
- Supplementary sound tracks that the editor will need
- Aesthetics of sound
- Dos and don'ts

Documentary, to be effective, depends on getting good, intelligible location sound. This takes forethought, skill, and willingness by the rest of the unit to accommodate the needs of the recordist. Knowledge of sound theory and practice will help you choose locations wisely and enable you to understand your sound recordist's problems. The component parts of sound recording are outlined under Sound Theory in Chapter 14. The sound Web site www.filmsound.org/ is a good resource for all sound information. By the way, I have no relationship with any of the manufacturers or services listed.

CAMCORDERS AND SOUND

Automatic sound level: Avoid camcorders having only automatic sound-level recording, because pauses during speech will get absurdly amplified while the automatic level control goes hunting for a signal.

Mike input sockets: Professional machines use *balanced line* mike cables that have sturdy XLR sockets and noise-canceling three-wire connections between mike and recorder. With these you can use much longer microphone cables without picking up electrical interference. When you must use a complex setup at, say, a concert, check all equipment ahead of time and preferably in the location, because there may be unforeseen problems.

In non-professional equipment you find the two-wire or *unbalanced* sound connections, made obvious by their mini-jack plugs. These sockets, soldered direct to circuit boards in the camcorder body, often become unreliable with extended use, and especially so when an external mike is used without a *strain relief* (anchoring a cable so that handling tensions are not transmitted to the plug and socket). A solution is to buy, or make up, a secondary input box with sturdy XLR sockets for the mike inputs and a mini-plug on a short lead. This transfers handling strains to a repairable external box securely mounted to the camcorder body.

Stereo: Most camcorders have stereo (two-track) recording ability that accommodates two inputs, *if* you can access them separately. Test first to ensure that peak sounds don't bleed into the adjacent channel.

Three or more sound tracks: Professional camcorders may have four sound tracks, but if yours only has two tracks and you need to cover an event using multiple mikes, you will need a location mixer and a camcorder with a "line input" socket that can take the mixer's line level output. Mackie makes good, low-cost mixers favored by documentary productions.

Sound level metering: Your camcorder's level metering is crucial because overrecorded digital sound distorts badly compared with its more tolerant analogue (older format) forerunner. Ideally, sound levels should be visible on meters mounted in the camera body so that the mike operator can check them while shooting, but sound level may only be visible as a moving bar graph in the viewfinder to the camera operator, who has other things to watch. An external mike mixer, however, gives the mike operator a visible recording level and the means to adjust it. The mixer's output must be adjusted so that its decibel meter parallels that of the camcorder. Now the recordist can keep the dynamic range well inside what's digitally allowable.

Single- or double-system recording: For a mobile camera shoot, the ideal solution is to record double system, with the sound operator carrying a discrete recording instrument whose recordings are synchronized to picture later.

DISCRETE SOUND RECORDERS

When recording double system, the Nagra brand of recorders is unparalleled for reliability and quality, either in analog or digital format. A digital audiotape (DAT) recorder such as those made by Tascam often is used on lower-budget productions. Some DATs record eight tracks on one machine, which allows you to record up to eight monophonic microphones, or four stereo, and worry about mixing a useable master track later. A recent trend is to record into a portable hard drive. The Zaxcom Deva II is a four-channel location mixer and recorder that can pack 60 track-hours of uncompressed recording into a tough and hermetically sealed hard disk (see www.zaxcom.com). The recorder has a 10-second sound buffer that can reclaim the 10 seconds of sound prior to switching on, which is very useful for spontaneous shooting or the odd missed cue because you know that the previous 10 seconds is included with the recording. A hard drive can be rapidly downloaded in the cutting room or even plugged directly into the computer. Having no open moving parts, the machine is immune from grit and dust, as well as temperature and humidity extremes. The conservative sound engineer may want to simultaneously record on tape too, just in case.

MICROPHONES

Film recording is done using a variety of microphones made by Sennheiser, Schoeps, Audio Technica, and other manufacturers. With microphones, as with so much else, you get what you pay for. A superbly informative sound Web site on this and other sound subjects is Fred Ginsburg's Equipment Emporium (www.equipmentemporium.com). This user-friendly organization sells a wide range of equipment and offers a wealth of good, down-to-earth advice for low-cost shooting solutions. You can download in portable document format (PDF) excellent articles on current equipment such as mixing panels for production sound, an introduction to timecode recording, production audio recording for digital video (DV) camcorders, reviews of editing systems, troubleshooting guides, and a host of other information.

Another site with useful basics on the effective placing of mikes is www.soundinstitute.com/article_detail.cfm/ID/135.

Camera-mounted microphones: Unless you must work alone, shun all camera-mounted mikes. They pick up camera motor sounds and handling noises transmitted by the camera body. They remain far from the sound source and are inflexibly pointed ahead of the camera when the main source may temporarily be out of frame. Instead use a separate mike, the most professional that you can afford, and have it handled by someone well versed in the imperatives of sound recording and wearing headphones.

Power supplies: Most mikes today require a battery to power them, and you should carry backup supplies of the alkaline type. These, on running down, do not exude the corrosive mess that the cheaper variety does. Some professional mikes need *phantom power*, which is a supply from the recorder delivered via the mike cable. Few non-professional camcorders supply phantom power, which may be why a shotgun mike mysteriously refuses to function with your camcorder.

Sound pickup patterns: Expertise in recording requires knowing about the sound pickup pattern of each type of microphone.

> *Omnidirectional mikes* give the most pleasing voice reproduction but tend to pick up more unwanted sound reflected by surrounding surfaces.

> *Directional mikes* (often called *cardioids* because of their heart-shaped pickup pattern) help cut down on reverberant sound and background noise. They accomplish this by discriminating against sound coming from unwanted directions, so their signal-to-noise ratio is better. Translated, this means that ambient and reflected sound is a little lower in relation to the desired source.

> *Hypercardioid* or *shotgun mikes* (so-called due to their shape and menacing appearance) do the best job of discrimination. Often used for documentary and electronic news gathering (ENG) work, they are very practical

in noisy situations. Their drawback is a slight loss of sound warmth and fidelity. More than most mikes, they need astute handling if they are to stay out of shot, not cast shadows, and point at the right speaker in a group. A British Broadcasting Corporation (BBC) news crew using a shotgun mike was astonished to find it had taken a prisoner during the Vietnam War.

Lavalier (or lapel) mikes are used for interviews or speech recording in noisy surroundings. They are very small, worn on or under a subject's upper clothing, and thus stay close to the signal (speech) source. They should be at least a hand's breadth away from a speaker's chin, otherwise sound levels will vary too much if the speaker turns his or her head. With Lavaliers you will need one for each speaker, so a location mixer often is necessary.

When clipping the mike in place, separately anchor its cord to give a free loop under the mike. Then, if the cord is touched or dragged, no handling noise will be transmitted to the mike. Lavaliers are prone to picking up clothing rustles and body movements, especially if the user is wearing man-made fibers. These generate static electricity, which sounds like thunder on a small scale. Warn participants to wear no man-made fiber; if they do, try placing some gaffer tape between the mike and the offending surface.

Sound perspective is entirely lacking from Lavalier mikes. Perspective is the aural sensation of changing distances that we get from a voice as someone moves around. These arise partly from changes of subject-to-mike distance and partly from the voice's changing relationship to its acoustical surroundings. The Lavalier, by remaining constantly close to the speaker and picking up so little reverberant coloration, removes all sense of the speaker's movement. Perspective changes might need to be emulated later in the mix.

Radio mikes are wonderful, when they work. A Lavalier mike worn on the body is connected to a personal radio transmitter, and the signal is picked up by a small receiver mounted on the camera. Radio mikes have a few peccadilloes. Cheap ones, like mobile telephones, frequently fade or pull in taxi and radio frequency (RF) interference in urban areas. Participants forget they are wearing them after the camera stops and embarrass the recordist by taking them to the toilet or making indiscreet remarks to confidants. A recording made inadvertently by some students was used in court to incriminate a duplicitous police chief.

Wired mikes: Wired (as opposed to wireless) lavaliers severely limit your subject's mobility. Usually the cable is hidden in clothing and emerges from a pants leg or skirt bottom. People forget they're wired and walk off—only to arrive at the end of their tether.

Boom: Documentary productions generally mount the mike on a short hand boom or *fish-pole*. This allows you to hold the mike out of sight below, above, or to either side of the frame.

Windscreens and shock mounts: Microphones should be suspended in a rubber *shock mount*. This prevents the mike from picking up boom handling noise. The mike itself should be guarded from air current interference by a *windscreen*. This can either be a rigid zeppelin type or a fuzzy fur mini-screen or windsock. Without such shielding, air currents shake the mike's diaphragm and produce the familiar wind rumbling noise. A cheap and practical solution is to wind many layers of cheesecloth around the mike and then hide this medical-looking abomination by pulling a black tube sock over it.

SPARES AND ACCESSORIES

A *smart slate* is a clapper board containing a crystal-controlled timecode display. The numbers move when the bar is opened and freeze when the clapper bar is closed. For double-system shooting this makes synching sound to its time-coded picture easy. Camera and recorder must be compatible with the smart slate, and their operators must "jam" (synchronize) the timecode generators every morning because they drift apart over a period of time. Carry a traditional clapper board if you fear this electronic gadget will break down.

Spares: Carry backup cables because breakdowns often occur in cables and connectors. Most mikes and mixers need batteries: be sure to carry the right spares. A basic toolkit of solder, soldering iron, pliers, screwdrivers, adjustable wrench, Allen keys, can of compressed air (for cleaning), and multimeter can get you out of minor trouble in the field.

RECORDING REQUIREMENTS

DIRECT AND REFLECTED SOUND

Some documentary subjects are not "run-and-gun" or grab shooting and may call for rather careful techniques. In any dialogue sequence, sound recordists aim to get clean sound that is *on mike*, which means recording dialogue spoken near a mike and into its most receptive axis. They want sound relatively uncolored by reverb reflected back from walls, ceiling, floor, or furniture surfaces. *Reflected sound*, bouncing off surrounding surfaces before finding its way to the mike, travels by a longer route and arrives fractionally after its direct, source sound. There is no way to clean such sound later of its accompanying reverberance. It will muddy the clarity of the original, something not apparent until you edit different mike positions together.

In a reverberant location, the mike positions have different sound characteristic, each determined by its different admixtures of reflected sound and different distances from the speakers. Mike position changes are mandated by the different camera positions necessary to any comprehensively covered sequence. Editing them together makes seams evident in what should sound seamless. There is more latitude for such inequities in documentary, but it's nice not to call on it.

Sound reflectivity in a location can be greatly reduced by laying carpet or blankets on hard floors and hanging blankets in front of any walls that are out of camera sight. To be fully effective, blankets must hang several inches away from the wall, not directly on it.

Getting mikes close to participants without causing shadows will take advance coordination between sound and camera specialists and the director. You may require more than one mike and may need to feed their inputs into a mixer. These, joined together, can produce a chaotic set of problems. To minimize mistakes while shooting, record into an eight-channel DAT recorder) and keep their contributions discrete. You can mix down from the most successful coverage in postproduction. If mixing must be done on the spot, the sound mixer really must know what he or she is doing because once mixed the omelet cannot be unscrambled. After the first mixed take, listen to the results through the headphones before proceeding.

SOUND SOURCE-TO-MICROPHONE DISTANCES

Keeping a mike close enough to participants on the move so that you can record well is a real skill. The boom operator's main task is to stay just out of frame at all times but also stay near the sound axis of each speaker. Not doing so means that sound levels decline as the mike-to-subject distance increases; however, ambient sound levels remain constant. Thus, the ratio of source to ambient sound can vary a lot. Cranking up the playback level afterward in the mix can compensate for the drop in source level and make the speaker's voice consistent in level from angle to angle, but at the expense of large changes in the ambience inherent to each angle.

The fundamental problem for sound is that film shoot procedures are optimized for photography. Sound recording fits around the needs of the camera and at the same time must keep its equipment invisible. The director can help by stabilizing speakers during a dialogue sequence or using creative set dressing so that a nice potted plant on a dining room table conceals a strategically placed microphone.

RELATIONSHIP OF RECORDIST TO CAMERA

Shooting handheld usually means the camera is on the move. Sound recordists position the mike just out of frame and prefer to place themselves to the left of camera, where they can be in contact with the camera operator, who will often carry a larger camera on his or her right shoulder. Keeping on the sound axis of moving participants, yet keeping the mike out of frame, requires that the mike operator constantly watch both camera and participants to anticipate who will move next, and in what direction. With experience, camera and sound people learn to work in perfect harmony and even to exchange eye or hand signals during the take.

Sometimes the mike is lifted to allow the camera to back away from the subject. Sometimes, because sound axes impose their own imperatives, the sound recordist will cross the shooting axis behind the camera by positioning the mike temporarily over the camera as she moves around the prevailing sound source. All the while she tries never to lose eye contact with the camera operator. It's a choreography that must all be managed in silence. A camera assistant will guide by hand touch so that neither camera nor sound collides or stumbles over objects, especially as they move backward. If there is nobody else to do this, the director may assist instead.

The ultimate challenge to the mobile documentary unit is a rapidly moving subject who jumps into a taxi after whirling through a street market—all the while talking uninterruptedly to the camera. Keeping all this nicely framed on the screen, and with no sign of the unit's frantic activity, will stretch a crew to its limits, particularly when three people silently cram themselves and their equipment around a surprised taxi driver.

NOISES OFF

AMBIENT SOUND AND PRESENCE TRACKS

What ambient sound is: Sound inherent to any location, whether interior or exterior, is called *ambient sound*. Examples include

- A playground has a distant traffic hum coming from one direction
- A riverside location has the hum and intermittent rumbling of a coal-fired power station a quarter mile off
- Every room in which you record has its own ambient sound noticeable only during silences. It may be a faint buzz from fluorescent fixtures, the hum of voices from an adjacent office, or birdsong and trees rustling from outside.

Procedure for shooting presence track: Before calling for a wrap at any location, whether interior or exterior, the sound recordist always records a *presence track* (also known as *atmosphere*, *room tone*, or *buzz track*). This is done in every location and every shooting day, because each has its own changing ambience. The procedure is simple:

- The recordist calls, "Everyone freeze: We need a presence track!"
- Nobody leaves the set and everyone stands completely silent.
- For a couple of minutes the recordist makes a recording of the ambient sound in the location.
- The recordist calls "Cut" and everyone jumps into action, wrapping up for that location.

Ambience in films: In a finished film, especially a documentary, your audience accepts some ambient atmosphere as part of each sequence's reality. The ear identifies the nature of the ambience then screens it out. That situation changes, however, when there are irrational changes from angle to angle. These the ear will find irritating and intrusive. To cure this, backgrounds have to be built and adjusted in editing to create something seamless.

How the editor uses presence tracks: Because postproduction can only add, never remove, background atmosphere in dialogue tracks, the editor must work to make every angle's background become consistent. The 2 minutes of presence recorded on the set, duplicated to make more, if needed, becomes the vital material from which to build. It will be used as

- Ambient sound to fill dead spaces in dialogue tracks. These might occur when, for example, you use a cutaway that was shot silent. In real life, ambient sound is constant no matter what happens, and we expect the same of films.

- Additional material to boost quiet atmosphere tracks. Tracks with quiet presence must match those in the angle having the loudest, if all angles are to end up having the same admixture of ambient sound.

LOCATION AMBIENCE PROBLEMS

Every location comes with problems, which you hope to have anticipated earlier (see Scouting the Locations, Chapter 17). Beautiful autumn leaves make the sound of swishing cornflakes when participants walk, and expressway sound that was minimal at two in the afternoon has become a dull roar by rush hour. Overhead wires turn into aeolian harps, dogs bark maniacally, garbage trucks mysteriously convene for bottle crushing competitions, and somebody starts practicing scales on the trumpet. The astute location spotter can anticipate some of these sonic disasters, but not all.

In each case, the choice of mike, the axis of directional mikes, and getting the mike in close to the desired signal can make a crucial difference. What would life be like without such challenges?

SOUNDS ON THE SET

During takes, the crew and any onlookers must be as stationary and silent as possible, and the camera must make no sound that the mike can pick up. Video cameras are mercifully quiet, but film cameras often are not. Their sound usually comes from the hollow metal magazines, which can be muffled with a soft, soundproof casing called a *barney*. If this expedient fails, sound may be passing down tripod legs to be amplified by a resonant floor. Placing carpet under the camera support should fix this. Fluorescents like to buzz, filament lamps can hum, and pets come to life at inopportune moments. Sound cables, placed in parallel with power cables, may produce electrical interference through induction, and sometimes long mike cables pull in cheery DJs via RF interference. Any large motor or elevator equipment can generate alternating current magnetic fields, and the most mysterious hum sometimes proves to come from something on the floor above or below. Every situation has some degree of remedy, once you have located the cause.

SOUND RECONSTRUCTION

To be true in spirit, some sound must be reconstructed. There is an exquisite nature center near where I live in Chicago. In its small space it has deer, wild flowers, some prairie, a lake with herons, and lots of wild birds. I have often considered filming a yearlong cycle of life there. But it's under the flight path for the busiest airport in America, and vehicle traffic is only two blocks away. Much sound would need reconstructing because I could not expect an audience to concentrate on lyrically backlit meadow grasses to the ominous whine of jetliners aiming at the airport. In film sound, you often have to provide what is logical and appropriate rather than what was actually present.

EFFECTS AND WILD TRACKS

Wild tracks: A *wild track* is any track shot independent of picture. When a participant flubs a sentence or some extraneous sound cuts across dialogue, the alert sound recordist asks for a wild, voice-only recording immediately after the director calls "Cut!" The participant repeats the obscured line as he just spoke it during the take. Because it's recorded in the same acoustic situation, the words can be seamlessly edited in and retakes avoided, thanks to that wild track.

Sound effects: An *effects track* (FX) or *atmosphere track* is a wild (nonsynchronous) recording of sounds that might be useful to augment the sequence's sound track later. The recordist might get a separate track of that barking dog, as well as other sounds, to help create a *soundscape.* In a woodland location this might mean getting up early to catch bird calls, river sounds of water gurgling, ducks dabbling, and wind rustling in reeds. A woodpecker echoing evocatively through the trees probably is best found in a wildlife library because getting near enough to one is hard. A sound recordist needs initiative and imagination, and a high level of tolerance for frustration.

ATMOSPHERE LOOPS

Often a short original atmosphere is made long by repeating or "looping" it. This can be perfectly acceptable unless recognizably individual sounds return at set intervals. A bus station with the same sneeze or cackling laugh every 6 seconds becomes a strange place indeed. When recording atmospheres, the recordist listens intently to make sure an appreciable amount has been recorded clear of such intrusions, so an effective loop can be made later. Of course, in nonlinear editing, you simply copy a sound section and repeat it, but the looping problem remains. By the way, atmospheres in sound libraries often are loops and often have those giveaway sounds.

AUTOMATIC DIALOGUE REPLACEMENT

Automatic dialogue replacement (ADR) in postproduction, sometimes called *looping*, is expensive and time consuming, and rarely used in documentary. Actors in a studio speak the words they spoke on the screen to produce a clean recording, working a section at a time. In fiction it mostly kills all dramatic credibility. The problem is that actors can never regain the emotional truth of a scene when they record one line at a time in a sound studio. Actors loathe doing it. ADR is misnamed: it is neither automatic nor any real replacement.

SOUND AESTHETICS

In a highly stylized documentary such as Errol Morris' dreamlike *The Thin Blue Line* (1988), the conventions set by the film itself allow great latitude for nonrealistic invention. Under such circumstances you could conceivably recreate dialogue in a *looping* or *ADR* session, but it is always expensive in terms of time and effort. Sound effects are a different matter, especially whenever an evocative atmosphere is required, so if you have a sequence in a swamp and just out of sight trucks are thundering past on a four-lane highway, it is prudent to reconstruct the swamp atmosphere and re-record footsteps in mud. This requires the atmosphere called for rather than what was technically present.

SOUNDSCAPES

A World Soundscape Project to research the acoustic ecology of six European villages began in 1975. Sponsored by the Tampere Polytechnic Institute in Finland, the goal is to document acoustic environments in change over many decades (see http://www.6villages.tpu.fi/). The Web site reveals the riches you discover when you set out to explore using your ears, something I started learning as a teenager in England from Brian Neal, a musician and great friend who is blind. Every place has its soundscape, and it takes critical listening skills to analyze what makes it individual and special.

To create with sound is to provoke imagination at a high level, much as music does. Usually the most memorable soundscapes come from simplifying and heightening rather than being literally true to everything in the location. In sound as in everything else, less is more. The doyen of Hollywood editors is Walter Murch, who is extremely sound and music conscious. He has written *In the Blink of an Eye* (Los Angeles: Silman-James Press, 2001) and has been interviewed at length about using sound (among much else) in a conversation with the novelist author of *The English Patient*, Michael Ondaatje in *The Conversations: Walter Murch and the Art of Editing Film* (New York: Knopf, 2002).

SOUND DESIGN

The most potent aspects of sound for film lie not just in faithful recording techniques but in *psychoacoustics*, a term describing how sounds are perceived and interpreted by an audience. The expert in this is Michel Chion, whose *Audio-Vision—Sound on Screen* (New York: Columbia University Press, 1994) explains ideas he has developed over 3 decades. Be warned that they are far from simple and require learning a specialized vocabulary.

Even the film industry relegates sound recording to a low priority, so it's no wonder that sound is invariably the neglected stepsister in low-budget or film school filmmaking. Yet sound, in documentaries as in fiction, is far more than accompaniment to picture or words issuing efficiently from a speaker's lips. Think of a movie sound track as an orchestral score, something that can be designed from the outset to further the aims of the movie you are making. In a fine article replete with information from feature films, sound designer Randy Thom contends that even fiction directors (whose control is more embracing) regularly lack any sound design consciousness. His article is at http://www.filmsound.org, which is an excellent Web site for all sound information.

As you develop your documentary proposal, make a design for the sound you expect to shoot. What kind of world are you showing? What are its special features? What will you need to record, and how? What kind of impact should the sound track make on the audience?

Remember what Bresson said in relation to sound: "The eye sees but the ear imagines."

DOS AND DON'TS

Never

- Leave the checkout point without putting all the equipment together and testing that everything, absolutely *everything*, functions as it should. Murphy (of Murphy's law) is never far from anything technical, and he's always waiting to get you.
- Accept "We can fix it in the mix." Sound cannot always be "fixed," especially if the film is a documentary and sound reconstructed risks losing all credibility.
- Take recordists for granted. Understand their problems and look for solutions.
- Wait, if you are a sound recordist, to ask for a lighting change at the last moment.

Always

- Carry spare batteries for everything that uses them.
- Carry extra cables. They often break down.
- Carry basic repair equipment.
- Warn participants to wear no man-made fiber clothing.
- Use a shock mount so that handling noise doesn't ruin recordings.
- Remind participants to turn off wireless mike transmitters when they don't want to be heard.
- Think ahead and have a mike placement strategy ready to roll.
- Design your sound track, don't just blindly collect it.
- Wear headphones always so that you know what you are recording.
- If you can, take a little longer and get it right.
- Try out complex sound setups in advance, if you can. You don't want to ruin a day's shooting by announcing there's something you cannot do unless you have more or different equipment.

CHAPTER 23

AVOIDING PROBLEMS

This chapter covers

- Keeping records and monitoring cost projections
- Shooting ratio concerns
- Guarding against breakdowns and power shortages
- Keeping alternatives ready
- Morale issues and leadership

LOGS AND BUDGET CONTROL

Either for documentary or a fiction on film, keeping picture and sound logs is important, though with today's two-person shoots using video, logging may have to be done at night or after shooting. Logs serve various functions. They

- Record special conditions and setups
- Keep a record of what is shot—a valuable adjunct to memory
- Keep a running total of stock consumption and thus indicate the state of the production budget
- Allow you to find the culprit when a camera or sound recorder proves to have produced damaged dailies
- Help trace and cross-reference material in the cutting room

Particularly when shooting film, a common beginner's mistake is to assess stock requirement for the total shooting and then to put it out of mind until dwindling reserves direct everyone's attention to the approaching famine. This results in liberal coverage for early material and insufficient coverage for later material. Keeping stock of all vital expenditures helps the low-budget filmmaker to mobilize precious resources according to rational priorities. The production manager (if you have one) rather than the director is the best person to carry this out. Monitoring outgoings

- Lets you compare your projected budget with the reality taking shape
- Gives early warning of impending crises
- Teaches you what to do differently next time around

WHERE VIDEOTAPE DIFFERS

Shooting on digital video is now so cheap compared with its film equivalent that it encourages you to shoot promiscuously and without keeping track. This is a pity. Sound and picture are all on one tape, so a log is easily maintained. A contents description (tape roll number, date, location, activity, personnel, digital counter reading) is enough to assist a quick replay during the shooting period. Keep logs and records simple on location. The more elaborate your bureaucracy, the more likely you are to abandon record keeping when pressure mounts, leaving you with no records at all. You can make a detailed log in peace and comfort when you review the *dailies* (also called *rushes*) at the start of postproduction.

SHOOTING RATIO

Shooting ratio is a handy way to express the amount of material shot to that used onscreen. It is quite usual for a half-hour film to emerge from upward of 6 hours of shooting; 25 hours is not unusual in today's video environment. These two figures would be a ratio of 12:1 or 50:1. To budget this ahead of time, add up what you expect to shoot and divide it by your intended screen time; the result is a projected shooting ratio. If you are shooting on film negative, your film stock, processing, and workprint will blow a large hole in the budget. Videotape camera stock, being cheaper, is hardly a concern—until you reach the cutting room and face the horrible reality of viewing and editing 70 hours of footage. This is learning the hard way that shooting coverage is not *directing* a film. Cheer up: We all do it at least once.

People frequently ask what a normal ratio is for a documentary. I answer, "How long is a piece of string?" It all depends on what you are tying up. A film of mine about Alexandra Tolstoy and her relationship with her parents (*Tolstoy Remembered by His Daughter*) was shot in only 3 hours. It consisted of one long interview, which I afterward slugged with many still photos, 1910 news film, and shots of documents. The shooting ratio was about 5:1. It was this low because my subject was 86 and I could not extend my questioning. It also was brief because Alexandra Tolstoy was an accomplished writer who spoke in beautifully succinct paragraphs. Virtually everything we shot was usable.

At the other extreme are the 90-minute observational films of Fred Wiseman for which he shoots 70 hours of film (yes, film). The high shooting ratio (46:1) comes from the long form's need for large themes and plenty of action to sustain development over such a long screen time. It also stems from Wiseman's strict policy of nonintervention, which prevents him from polarizing or influencing the events he films or from providing narrated guidance in the finished product.

You can roughly predict your shooting ratio by rating each sequence for its expected contents. If you want to catch certain kinds of unusual but highly significant behavior in children, you might need a 60:1 ratio. An interview with their teacher might, on the other hand, come in at 3:1 because she is concise about what she does. Ask yourself how predictable and repeatable is the material that you want and how long will it take to capture.

A good practice when shooting film stock is to project the smallest and largest figures for each sequence so that you can modify, as necessary, how you predict the ratio. During the shoot you can delegate someone to monitor actual consumption and predict what needs to be done to come in on target.

EQUIPMENT BREAKDOWNS

Many equipment failures result from inadequate checkout procedures in the first place. However "good" a rental house may be, no matter how "well" someone maintains a piece of rented equipment, nothing should ever leave its place of origin without a thorough inspection by the user and a *working test*. Expiring batteries for cameras, recorders, and mikes are frequent culprits.

Rechargeable batteries are picky about how much and how often they are put on a charge, and hire houses may unknowingly issue defective units. If you are shooting on a tripod, conserve batteries by running off a power line via the AC power converter whenever possible. Handheld shooting, however, can only be done from battery power.

Any parts that wear out, such as lamp elements, extension cords, and plugs, should have backup spares on hand. Wiring is especially vulnerable at its entry point to plugs and sockets. The crew should carry electrical and mechanical first-aid equipment to carry out spot repairs.

Equipment failures sometimes require replacements in double-quick time. Be ready ahead of time for emergencies on location by making a resource list for the area (or country) in which you will be working. This cuts down time lost in getting information. Once I had a camera cable for a new Hitachi camera die on location. No cable existed in all of Baltimore, but using the cheap test meter and soldering equipment I carried I was able sit down in a garage forecourt and trace the problem to a detached wire inside a plug—and to reconnect it. Prepare for the worst and you will seldom be disappointed.

HUMAN BREAKDOWNS

Human breakdowns happen, but any healthy crewmember who walks off a shoot soon finds out that nobody will ever use him or her again. Voluntary workers, even those wanting to "break into the industry," sometimes imagine they are immune from this law, thinking "I'm doing you a favor, so I'll come if I feel like it." Everyone in filmmaking, volunteers included, is drawn from that rare breed that honors commitments to the letter. A friend who runs a cinémathèque claims he only found reliable projection once he started employing born-again Christians. "They believe they go to hell if they break their commitments" he said by way of explanation.

The people you select should be those who understand with their heart and soul what commitment to a common endeavor means. And, of course, as their leader you must be an exemplary member yourself of that select band.

The most frequent breakdowns are the errors and omissions that escalate as people get tired. To guard against these breakdowns,

- Have a clear chain of responsibility. When duties are ill defined, two people may do some tasks, and nobody will think of doing others.
- Don't work your people into the ground.
- Keep checklists handy to help catch omissions when people are too tired to think straight. (Ready-made checklists are available as summaries after the parts entitled Preproduction, Production, and Postproduction in Chapters 19, 28, and 38.) Keep photocopies handy and look them over.)

A real disaster is when a participant withdraws or fails to appreciate how much is at stake when you plan a shoot. Some people assume that it's nothing to put off shooting by a couple of days, offering only that maddeningly evasive explanation, "Something has come up." To avoid this, stress the importance of your scheduling from the outset.

Even then, people drop out. In Paris I once had a couple of artists cancel 3 days before shooting. In the plane from London I had read about a sculptor and was lucky enough to secure him as an alternative subject in time for the crew's scheduled arrival. I then discovered that he spent much of each day under some migratory instinct wandering the streets. He did not always remember where (or whether) he had promised to meet us. It was so nerve wracking that I became certain that now I would be found out and would never get another film to direct. This conviction is to directors as dogs are to postmen.

HAVE ALTERNATIVES, STAY POSITIVE

Given the loyal presence of so many technical and human difficulties, it is always prudent to keep alternatives ready. Schedule exteriors that rely on a certain kind of weather early and keep interiors on standby as alternative cover. Shoot crucial sequences—those that decide the viability of the film as a whole—early rather than late in the schedule, and so on.

When a member of the crew (or anyone else for that matter) tells you that a particular thing cannot be done, ask for a detailed explanation and use lateral thinking to find any omissions in his or her thinking. Filming always depends on the coordination of multiple aspects, and when one is unfavorable, many people assume that the underlying intention cannot be carried out. Often by changing two of the aspects, rather than one alone, the original intention becomes viable again.

Assume everything can be accomplished with good planning and inventiveness, and you will nearly always be right. As a leader, your troops want you to remain positive in the face of all adversity. When they indulge in doom and gloom, they may be demoralized for some reason, or they may be testing you by handing you their fears to carry. To retain your authority, stay actively positive. Leave nothing to chance and do all your preparatory work, and you will have paid your dues. Presume the gods are on your side and they usually are. After a few small victories you become, in the eyes of your crew, the pilot who weathers the storm.

CHAPTER 24

INTERVIEWING

This chapter really deals with human interchange, which is at the very heart of the documentary process. It contains

- How most documentary is founded on interchange
- How directing need not be manipulative
- Liberating participants or endangering them
- The documentarian as witness
- Midwifing eloquence
- Research and interviewing partnerships
- The importance of the setting
- Group interviews and the effect of onlookers
- Street interviewing to create a Greek chorus
- Preparation and basic skills
- Using the camera to suggest relationship, and participation by the audience
- Controlling image size, and shooting for abbreviation in postproduction
- Framing questions and exerting control by insisting on specifics, not generalizations
- Right order for questions and crossing boundaries
- The director's authority, and giving and taking
- Concluding an interview and securing the legal release

Interviewing is at the heart of documentary, even though your film may not contain a single "talking head." By interviewing I mean not just eliciting on-camera information, but the skills and courage to conduct person-to-person exchanges at their deeper levels. This begins with the research interview; as an extended, trusting exchange, it is really the foundation to whatever you build, even for an observational film that has no interviews or narration. An audience will know whether a film is founded on a profound and trusting exchange. This kind of film is the most likely to build through exposition and specific emotional detail to a satisfying climax. The spectator is most likely to have the moving sense of seeing into human souls. With sensitive on-camera interviewing, this impression can be even more direct, and for the interviewees themselves the experience of emerging whole and into daylight can be so cathartic that they become able to make life-changing decisions.

To face another human being while making a documentary is to probe, to listen, and to obliquely reveal yourself by responding with further questioning. It can mean helping people to express the deepest events and meanings in their lives, to catalyze rare and important experiences, and to initiate changes.

None of this happens unless a skilled and empathic interviewer draws out what we see. Subtly or otherwise, the interviewer *directed* the participant by providing the necessary support, guidance, or challenge to help make visible something that would otherwise remain hidden. This does not mean manipulating the person into exhibitionism. Quite the reverse, it means providing the assistance and special occasion when the interviewee travels, perhaps for the first time, what is truly their own path. An important part of the creative process here is to provide resistance to the immediate and superficial when you sense that something profounder exists beneath the surface. Directing by interviewing is like narrowing and raising the banks of a river to make it run deeper and faster.

Here in making documentary we face a precarious duality. Interviewing can either create a liberating arena for discovery and growth or become intrusion and exploitation of the participant. But this is a risk in all human relationships. Some valuable and brave friendships seem complex and dangerous to onlookers. Others are kept safely limited or only move into areas of risk by mutual agreement and in great privacy. It's safe to say that the more there is at risk, the greater the potential for growth or harm. Naturally, you must find participants with whom you share values and aims, and who are looking for the kind of experience that you can offer while making a documentary.

The potential for harm exists because making a film is not a relationship of equality. The director arrives hoping to get access to another person's life and comes equipped with more power simply by having control over an instrument of history called a camera. There can be no film without access to people and their lives, so the danger of exploiting others is unavoidable. For this reason alone you must give as well as take, be sensitive yet assertive in the positive and creative sense. This takes unusual awareness and also courage.

You aspire to set up a partnership like the "poet as witness" that Seamus Heaney describes in a discussion of World War I poets. To Heaney, Wilfred Owen and other poets writing about the awful carnage in that war represent "poetry's solidarity with the doomed, the deprived, the victimized, the underprivileged." He might be speaking of documentary when he says, "The witness is any figure in whom the truth-telling urge and the compulsion to identify with the oppressed becomes necessarily integral with the act of writing itself."[1] Those who faced tanks in Tiananmen Square, who stood with Palestinian householders in the Occupied Territories, or were members of Voices in the Wilderness (who made

---

[1] Seamus Heaney, The Government of the Tongue (London: Faber, 1988), xvi.

themselves into human shields during their country's bombing of Iraq in 2003) are those who illuminate humane conviction at its ultimate. These are the people of conscience whom I was first privileged to meet as World War I "conchies" (conscientious objectors). Said one, a Quaker, "We felt very strongly that we would rather be killed than kill other people." This statement of values made so quietly and matter-of-factly still gives me the shivers—probably because I can hardly imagine what courage it takes to live by it. But I was able to appreciate it and to record for posterity what those people did, which is what Heaney would have us do.

Interviewing at its best is a form of displaced authorship. It is the midwifery of testimony and heartfelt eloquence, particularly by those unwilling to hazard the egotism of talking about their inmost lives. A good edited interview has all the elements of a successful oral tale, and you can improve your directorial skills from conducting them. Even when all the questions have been removed, the interviewer's ability as a catalyst, selector, and organizer remains written all over the screen.

By watching your dailies critically, you will see your few strengths—and a lot of weaknesses writ large on the screen. You can only reach for a level of interviewing that is truly yours by confronting the blind spots, artificiality, and egotism in your own behavior. There are spontaneous moments of humor, inspired questions, and well-judged pauses, but also persuasion tilting into manipulation, haste disguised as enthusiasm, and timidity masquerading as respect. What a rendezvous with the Self!

PRELIMINARY CONSIDERATIONS

WHO INTERVIEWS

Some documentary units include a researcher, who contributes greatly to the film by digging up facts and locating or even choosing the participants. In Jane Oliver and June McMullen I was lucky to have excellent researchers at the British Broadcasting Corporation (BBC). Some directors rely heavily on the experience and judgment of a particular researcher, who becomes a vital creative colleague. Such shared control seems to arise from a working relationship long and close enough to establish complete mutual trust.

During initial research it is important to refrain from pressing any questions to a conclusion if important areas are to be opened up later on camera. Then, when it's time to shoot, the question arises: Who is better equipped to conduct the interviewing, the researcher or the director? Each has possible advantages. If the researcher does the interviewing, he or she is continuing a relationship begun during the research period, and this continuity might be crucial for putting a hesitant participant at ease. If the director conducts interview, the interviewee may be more spontaneous because he or she is addressing a fresh listener instead of repeating himself to the researcher.

A researcher/director team can decide who will interview according to which combination is most promising. Sometimes you must be quite inventive to put a subject at ease. I made a film with the pediatrician and author, Dr. Benjamin Spock (*Dr. Spock: "We're Sliding Towards Destruction," "One Pair of Eyes"* series, BBC). Although I had done all the research with him, I found his to-camera manner had become stiff and unnatural. We stopped the camera and talked about it. He realized that as a pediatrician he was used to talking to women. Someone suggested I place our production assistant, Rosalie Worthington, in my position under the camera lens. Although I was still asking the questions, Dr. Spock addressed himself to Rosalie and his manner was relaxed and spontaneous. Had reflexivity been allowable (and had I had the imagination to exploit it), this biographically revealing information could have been included.

TYPES OF SITUATION

Setting: You can shoot interviews in almost any surroundings, but you must consider the likely effect on the interviewee. In settings such as home, workplace, or home of a friend, the interviewee is more at ease and will give more intimate and individual responses. In public places, such as streets, parks, or the beach, the interviewee is more likely to feel like one of many. Depending on the individual subject, this may be important. Other settings, such as on a battlefield or at the scene of an accident or demonstration, the interviewee will likely react to feeling in dramatic juxtaposition to events that were, say, beyond his or her control.

We are not fixed in whom we are. Each environment evokes a different "self" in the interviewee and makes him or her resonate a little differently. This is never entirely predictable, but if you use common sense and imagination and take into account the significance the person probably attaches to being filmed, you can usually guess what different settings are likely to contribute.

We are all—interviewers included—very much affected by our surroundings and tend to lower barriers (or erect them) according to our sense of circumstance. Filming may dignify a situation or render it embarrassingly public; it may offer a hotline to the world's ear, be the confessional box, or be good conversation with a friend. How the interviewee feels will depend on both the environment and the way you present your purpose. Remember that *a documentary film is the sum of relationships*, and the unseen relationships that you and your crew carry on with the interviewee are quite as influential as anything visible onscreen.

Presence of others: Another factor affecting interviews is the effect of someone present but off camera. If you are interviewing a gentle older woman whose peppery husband is always correcting her, arrange to have the husband otherwise occupied so that she can tell you her story. On the other hand, the relationship between the two may be an important and visible aspect of who they are or what they represent. I once shot an interview of a farm manager together with his wife. She interrupted and modified everything he said, and apart from being funny, this alerts the viewer to a larger dimension of modification and idealization in her account of the past.

Groups: Interviewing is not always one on one. A married couple, separately inarticulate through shyness, may with your help prod each other into action and reaction very well. Friends or work mates can likewise provide mutual support. Mutual antipathy may just as easily release inhibitions. Putting two people together who disagree, then interviewing them together, can be a highly productive strategy. You may interview a whole group, and do so by one of two ways:

- "Recognize" each new speaker from among those who want to speak
- Encourage them to begin speaking to each other

Usually when you start talking to a few people in a public place—say, at a factory gate—others gather to listen and join in. Unless the interviewer asserts control, it will turn into a spirited conversation or even a dispute, depending, of course, on how controversial the topic is. The interviewer is now on the sidelines but can step in at any time with a question or even a request, such as, "Could the lady in the red jacket talk a bit about the union's attitude toward safety precautions?" And talk she will. You can be unconcerned with maintaining control because people's thoughts and feelings are coming out. If something significant takes shape, you can remain happily silent because your role as catalyst has been accomplished.

Vox pops: There is a useful technique for street interviews. Called *vox pop* (short for *vox populi*, meaning "voice of the people"), it consists of asking a range of people the same few questions and then stringing the replies together in a rapid sequence. Entertaining and useful for demonstrating a Greek chorus of opinion, it can also show diversity or homogeneity, thesis or antithesis. Sections of *vox pop* can also provide lively relief from something sober and intense, such as an expository section explaining a complicated political development. They can function as a legitimate parallel action to which you can resort in times of need. In a film about the pediatrician and peace activist Dr. Spock, I had to compress the salient points of his 3-hour peace speeches into about 12 minutes. I did this by setting up a dialectical counterpoint between Spock at the podium and the ubiquitous man in the street. Each gave piquancy to the other, and virtue came from necessity.

PREPARATION AND BASIC SKILLS

No matter who does the interviewing, the same basic skills are needed. First and foremost, the interviewer must be prepared, and for this you need a hypothetical focus for your entire film. Though research will modify this, it gives a fundamental *purpose* to your directing, and you can then have a clear expectation of what each interviewee will contribute. I am not suggesting you prepare a script or even anticipate specific statements, because anything so confining would turn a participant into an actor. We will look at the dangers of this a little later.

Being prepared means knowing as much as possible so that you can ask the right questions. During research conversations, you often hear something that makes you think, "I must have this in the film." You write it down and then later prepare a question to elicit this statement as naturally as possible. Each interview will contain some "must have" material that you should approach in more than one way so that you get something as good as the original moment, or better.

Being prepared also means deciding who represents what. You have chosen people, or are considering people, for what they represent in your film's issues. During a labor fight with management, for instance, you will need representatives from each faction. There will be management, the union, and perhaps a sizable number of people who would like to stay out of a fight altogether. You choose people who will make the best case for each constituency. You also want them to represent what you think are the underlying values, humanity, greed, or other qualities that you find interesting and telling. So in effect you are casting and setting up archetypes to represent the forces in their universe. Analogies and metaphors help you see the nature of the situations at hand, and it helps to decide on an archetypal role for each significant person you meet who is a part of them. Whoever falls, clearly and strongly, into a definable role is probably going to carry an important piece of your film's argument.

Telling a story is really making an argument for a set of forces wielded by a set of personalities, each of whom plays a necessary role. Earlier we said that plot represents the rules of the universe, and among the characters is the protagonist, who usually is the person compelled to challenge those rules. This is a very useful way to think dramatically about those in your story.

CAMERA AND EDITING CONSIDERATIONS

INTERVIEWER AND CAMERA PLACEMENT

There are two approaches to camera placement when you are filming interviews, each reflecting a quite different philosophy of the interviewer's function. You can tell which is in use by examining the interviewee's eyeline onscreen. One approach (Figure 24–1) has the interviewee answering an interviewer who sits with his or her head just below the camera lens. This makes the interviewee appear to be looking directly into the camera. In the other approach (Figure 24–2), the interviewer sits to one side of the camera and out of frame, which makes the interviewee look off camera at an unseen interlocutor. These two approaches have different effects on the audience.

Audience in direct relationship to interviewee (on-axis interview): I prefer to edit out the interviewer altogether and to leave the audience in a face-to-face relationship with my interviewee. I organize shooting so that my subject speaks *on-axis* into the camera (as in Figure 24–1). I see my interviewing as *asking questions*

FIGURE 24–1 ————————————————————————————————————

Placement of the interviewer affects the subject's eyeline. With the interviewer's head immediately under the camera lens, the subject talks directly to the viewer.

FIGURE 24–2

With the interviewer to the side of the camera, the subject is evidently talking to someone offscreen.

that the audience would ask if it could. Once the interviewee is talking, my presence as catalyst and listener is irrelevant to the audience and even a distraction.

To clear away traces of my input from the process, I sit on something low with my head just under the camera lens. By talking to me, the interviewee talks directly to the camera and thus to the audience. Once my voice is edited out, the audience is left in direct relationship to the person on the screen.

Audience witnessing interview (off-axis interview): If you sit off-axis (that is, to one side or other of the camera-to-subject axis as in Figure 24–2), your interviewee is plainly talking to an offscreen presence—whether or not the interviewer's voice survives in the finished film. The farther away the interviewer is from the camera-to-subject axis, the more definite is that impression. Some filmmakers like this because it acknowledges there is an interviewer even though his or her voice is no longer present. My private thought is that some people who make films really want to be in them. Television journalists have no such ambiguity; when they interview, they expect to be in picture. Appearing onscreen is their career and is sometimes thoroughly justified. But unless the interviewer is a really active participant rather than an incidental catalyst, it seems redundant to see the occasional question being asked or to cut away conveniently to a nodding listener.

The most justification for having a questioner on camera is when there is a confrontation of some sort. Here the questioner's pressure and reactions become a highly relevant component of the exchange. Some television journalists are expert at these tactics.

If you must use off-axis interviewing (in vox *populi* interviews, for instance, it is virtually unavoidable), be careful to alternate equally the side from which you interview; otherwise, most or all of your interviewees will face the same direction.

AUDIENCE PARTICIPATION

The more indirect the spectators' relationship is to the characters on the screen, the more they are encouraged to feel passive and detached. As a spectator, someone onscreen who speaks directly to me challenges me to respond with a dialogue in my mind. This is much less so when an interviewee is plainly in conversation with someone offscreen and I am a witness rather than an interlocutor.

Watching film is inherently passive, so I think filmmakers need to mobilize the audience's active sense of involvement or else the viewer (particularly in television) is less likely to watch in an emotionally engaged and critical frame of mind.

SHOOTING FOR ELLIPSIS

During any filmed interview you are thinking how best to shoot for abbreviation in editing. Shooting in a one-size shot and then bridging the different sections together leads to the jump cut (Figure 24–3). In practical terms, this means that our subject's face suddenly changes expression, and his or her head is suddenly in a slightly different position. Today this has become not only acceptable but an implicit declaration of ellipsis. If, however, the film is generally transparent, that is, it hides evidence of the editorial processes under the guise of continuity, then jump cuts will violate that technique. You could cut away to reaction shots, but they usually make the interviewer look inane.

There may be something more relevant to which you can cut. For instance, if the interviewee is talking about the Dust Bowl era, you might cut to illustrative photographs, but this can be disappointingly literal. Another photo sequence might develop its own independent story in parallel. To do this, you would probably restructure the interview somewhat and resort to the speaker's face at moments of special animation. *Parallel storytelling*, as this is called, is useful because it allows the restructuring and telescoping of not just one, but both, story elements. By developing a counterpoint whose meaning must be sought and reconciled in the spectator's mind, it transcends mere illustration. This is a big advance over the deadly show-and-tell of the classroom or TV journalism.

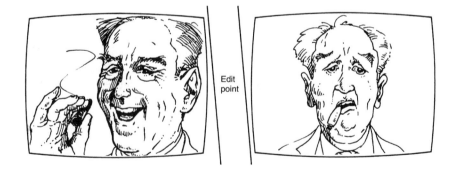

Edit point

FIGURE 24–3 ————————————————————————————————

A jump cut. When footage is removed from a static camera angle, the image may jump at the cut.

SHOOT ALTERNATIVES

In documentary you always *try to shoot each issue in several ways* so that you have alternative narrative strategies to try later. A political demonstration, for instance, would primarily be covered by footage showing how the demonstration begins, close shots of faces and banners, the police lines, the arrests, and so on. But it might also be covered through photographs, a TV news show, participant interviews, and perhaps an interview with the police chief. This would produce a multiplicity of attitudes about the purpose of the march and a number of faces to intercut (and thus abbreviate) the stages of the demonstration footage. Two vital purposes are thus served: you now have multiple and conflicting viewpoints; and the materials can be focused into a brief screen time.

Errol Morris in *The Thin Blue Line* (1988) shoots his interviews in one unblinking shot size but constantly cuts away to reconstructions that evoke the time, mood, or "facts" being recalled by the speaker. Somehow this heightens the subjective, dreamlike quality of the account and compels you to assess each speaker's world of unreliable memory and perception.

Suppose you want to shoot an interview for which there is no valid cutaway yet still achieve abbreviation and still restructure without using the pernicious jump cut. How can it be done? Try this yourself. During the interview have the camera operator use the zoom lens to unobtrusively change the image size. When you view the material, you see that the conventions of the screen allow you to edit segments together, provided that

- There is a bold change of image size, either larger or smaller
- The subject is in a similar enough physical attitude in the two shots
- Speech or other rhythms that flow across the cut are uninterrupted
- Action flows uninterrupted across the cut

Because of the bold change of image size between the two frames in Figure 24–4, minor mismatches will go unnoticed by the audience, especially because *the eye does not register the first three frames of a new image.*

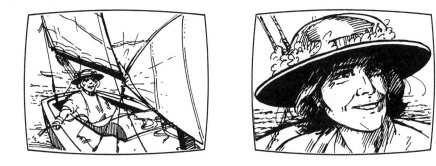

FIGURE 24–4

A match cut. By a bold change in image size, two shots can be edited together, if the images match.

BRIEFING THE CAMERA OPERATOR

When you go to interview, look through the camera viewfinder and agree with your operator on three standard image sizes particular to the shot. As you interview, signal changes between them using an agreed code of unobtrusive touches on different parts of the operator's foot. Typically this will be a

- Wide shot, used to cover each question
- Medium shot, used after the answer has gotten under way
- Close shot, used for anything particularly intense or revealing

During a lengthy answer I alternate between medium and close range until there is a change of topic, when I again signal for a wide shot. One place to change image size is when a speaker shows signs of repeating something. We do this in normal speech all the time, and the repeat version is usually more succinct. For ellipsis (editing for abbreviation) it can only be intercut with the first version if the image size is different or there are valid cutins or cutaways. Image size changing therefore allows

- Restructuring an interview and thus its abbreviation
- Eliminating the interviewer's questions
- Longer stretches of interview on the screen because the apparent camera movement, intensifying and relaxing scrutiny, answers the spectator's need for variation

More notes on camera placement appear in the Chapter 25: Directing Participants.

THE PROCESS OF INTERVIEWING

SETTING PEOPLE AT EASE

Research is, I have argued, to discover more or less what a person's potential contribution may be, while interviewing catalyzes it into being on film. To put the interviewee at ease and yet guard against digression, it is a good practice to *say which subject areas you want to cover and which you don't,* however dear to your interviewee they may be. Beginning directors are often too timid to set limits on the areas they want, and they allow their subjects to range far and wide. This ambiguity is ultimately unkind to the interviewee, who senses that he or she somehow isn't connecting.

Remember, you have the right and the obligation to say what you want. If someone is going to challenge this, you should have a reasonable explanation ready. You can only cover what you feel can be filmed well and what can be shown in depth within a reasonable screen time. Even if you feel apologetic about this, you'll have to make it sound reasonable, which of course it is.

You can lower the interviewee's anxiety by warning that you may occasionally interrupt or redirect the direction of the conversation. I usually say, "This is a documentary and we always shoot a lot more than we use. So don't worry if you get anything wrong because we can always edit it out. Also, if I feel we're getting away from the subject, I may suddenly interrupt, if that's all right with you." Nobody objects; indeed, interviewees seem reassured that I take responsibility for the overall direction of our conversation. Naturally, this only works if you have oriented the interviewee to the general content, thrust, and purpose of the film you are making in the first place.

Another way to reduce pressure on the interviewee is to make your first question deliberately relaxed or even bumbling. I like to imply that my expectations while shooting are nothing like the manic brightness people associate with television interviews, which too often are about manipulating ordinary people into performing. By example, I signal that no change of self-presentation is necessary just because a camera is rolling. If you want spontaneity, you must be natural yourself. You set the tone for the interview; if you are formal or uptight, your interviewee will be more so.

SETTING YOURSELF AT EASE

Because it is important not to bury your face in a page of notes, I prepare a list of questions short enough to go on an index card, which I keep on my knee. Having the questions there is a "security blanket" that releases me simply to have a conversation. I'm free to really *listen*, knowing I can always glance down if my mind goes blank (which it sometimes does). The mere act of preparing the questions usually ensures that I naturally and informally cover all my intended ground. It's also a checklist that allows me to be certain I have completed my agenda.

FRAMING QUESTIONS

Avoid closed questions: In phone company or other commercials masquerading as documentary, you see a pseudo-sincerity that reeks of manipulation. Some perfectly sincere documentary interviewers get the same effect because, out of anxiety or the need to control, they are signifying the reply they want. The interviewee, receiving a *closed question* (for example, "Do you think early education is a good thing?"), tries to fulfill the requirement, and this leads to acting rather than being. The result is a pervasive staginess and self-consciousness that devalues the whole film. The closed question boxes the interviewee into yes/no, black/white choices, and the classic one, incriminating however you answer it, is of course, "Have you stopped beating your wife yet?" An *open question* is one that is neutral and encourages a free reply (for example, "What do you feel about early education?")

Signify your area of interest: There is nothing unethical about signifying your interest in an exact area. Indeed, it gives clear and encouraging guidance. It should not, however, be confused with the *leading question*, which as we have said beckons the interviewee into a particular response rather than indicates a particular *area* of interest. "Did you feel angry coming home to an empty house?" is manipulative because it is fishing for a particular answer. The answer may anyway come as a "yes" or "no," which is useless. If you say instead, "Talk some more about the anger you mentioned when you came home to an empty house," you are in a completely legitimate area because you are asking for amplification of something already mentioned.

Rehearse your questions: Before an interview, work on the way your questions are phrased to make them direct and specific. Read each question aloud and listen to your own voice. See if it sounds direct and natural. See if you can interpret the question "wrongly." Sometimes certain wordings allow other interpretation; alter them until only the intended understanding is possible. Scrutinize your questioning for any signs of manipulation. Being a catalyst means initiating someone else's free process rather than inciting something that reflects particular values, though this will probably happen to some degree.

Focus your questions: Inexperienced interviewers often use general questions such as, "What is the most exciting experience you've ever had?" This signals that the interviewer is devoid of preparation or focus and is casting a big, shapeless net. Another common pitfall is the long rambling question with so many qualifiers that it ends up being a shapeless catalog of concerns. The confused interviewee only answers what she remembers, often the last thing said.

Focused questions are vital if you want to lead rather than follow your interviewee. Make questions specific and take one issue at a time.

Maintain eye contact and give behavioral feedback: During the interview, maintain eye contact with your subject, and give visual (NOT vocal!) feedback as the interviewee talks. Nodding, smiling, looking puzzled, and facially signifying agreement or doubt are all vital forms of feedback that sustain the interviewee in what might otherwise feel like an egocentric monologue. Errol Morris claims to get his extraordinary interviews by keeping expectantly silent and just letting the camera roll.

Aim to elicit feelings: Know what you want; use simple, conversational language; and deal with one issue at a time. A question such as, "You have some strong feelings about the fears suffered by latchkey kids?" will work well because it points the interviewee at a vital experience already mentioned during research and signals your interest in how he or she *feels*. Don't hesitate to turn the interview encouragingly toward feelings every time it veers off into objective fact and opinion, if you feel the interviewee is taking refuge from vulnerability.

Ask for the specific and ask for a story: Interviewees often give a general answer, for instance,

Q: What was your experience in the Marines like?
A: Oh it was all right, you know, nothing great.

This requires that you draw the speaker out. An older man, he is reared in the stoic tradition of not complaining and not drawing attention to his needs. What you need are the specifics, and when he answers, "Well, it was hard, and I didn't much like the leadership in my company," you need to ask for specifics. The easiest way to do this is to ask for a story that illustrates what he means. "Can you tell me a story to show that?" often brings excellent results.

Narratives need specific stories and instances. Many people (men particularly, I have to say) carry around not the stuff of experience but the conclusions they have drawn. They will report these rather than a clear sense of what the experience was. Emotionally loaded memories are buried deep in a filing cabinet, each one safely wrapped in a folder bearing a businesslike summary of its contents. Most of us will only discuss the names on the folders, not what the folders contain. The way to get inside is to keep asking for the specifics behind each generalization, and to ask for stories, stories, stories.

Thus, the interviewer's nightmare is the interviewee who gives only monosyllabic answers.

> Q: "I understand you weren't entirely satisfied when you moved into this apartment?"
> A: "Yep."

Every interviewer dreads this—someone who can't or won't talk. Try pressing for specifics: "Talk about what you remember." If the person doesn't respond to verbal prodding, it probably would be wise to abandon your attempt. He or she may be stonewalling or for whatever reason has resolved not to speak of this experience. An old and dear friend, a pilot at age 18 in World War II who suffered innumerable operations afterward, told me he has never spoken of his experiences. When I asked for some account, he sent me someone else's (excellent) published autobiography. Some experiences are such that people never speak of them. It was decades later, and with death looming, that many Holocaust survivors first spoke for a historical endeavor to record their experiences.

You can learn much from good interviewers, who are common in television and radio. In the United States I would single out Terry Gross and Scott Simon of National Public Radio. In documentary, excellent examples of formal interviewing can be seen in Michael Apted's *Up* series (*28 Up, 35 Up, 42 Up*), and Errol Morris' *The Thin Blue Line* (1988). Often, when someone in a documentary addresses the camera, he or she is doing so in reply to a question, although the questioning may have been entirely edited out. Terry Zwigoff's *Crumb* (1994) goes very far upriver into murky sexual territory, but his questions are very rarely heard. Claude Lanzmann's *Shoah* (1985) is a huge undertaking that uses the scalpel of voice-off interviewing to extract truth from those involved in all stages of the Holocaust atrocities. Mostly they do their utmost to evade and deny the past. Jeff Spitz' *Navajo Boy* (2000), which traces the irradiation of a Native American family by cynical industrial interests mining under their land, contains some remarkable exchanges that could only come from trust built over years of championing by the director. He even helps the family reunite after decades of separation—a most moving event.

When a person speaks from the heart, particularly for the first time, it can be magical. Here, speech *is* the action. Conversely, when an interviewee speaks routinely and without a sense of discovery, the result can sever our connection with the film. Talking head films must be intense and tell a good story, or they become hypnotically boring.

PREPARATIONS TO EDIT OUT THE INTERVIEWER'S VOICE

If the interviewer is offscreen and you intend to edit out all questions, you must prepare interviewees by telling them that they must include the information in your questions in their answer. Many people will look puzzled, so you will have to give an example: "If I ask, 'When did you first arrive in America?,' you might answer '1959,' but the answer '1959' wouldn't stand on its own, so I'd be forced to include my question. However, if you said, 'I arrived in the United States in 1959,' that's a whole and complete statement. That's what I need."

Most people understand, but they repeatedly forget to do it. Sometimes you even have to feed an interviewee the appropriate opening words to clarify by example what you need. You would say, "Try beginning, 'I arrived in America...'" As you interview, remember to listen at the beginning of every answer as though you are an editor. Every opening statement should be freestanding and non-dependent on the question. If it isn't, restart your interviewee.

THE IN-DEPTH INTERVIEW

A good general rule for interviewing is to start with factual questions and keep the more intimate or emotionally loaded material for later, when the interviewee has become more comfortable. If there is a delicate area you want to open up, there are a couple of ways it can be done. One approach is to use the devil's advocate approach; for instance, "Some people would say there's nothing special or frightening for a kid in getting home a couple of hours before his mother." The interviewee is being invited to discharge his or her feelings against all those too lacking in imagination or curiosity to have discovered what it's like to enter an empty house when you're a young and frightened kid.

Another way to initiate a sensitive topic is to first invite generalized, impersonal comment. For instance, you are almost certain that the woman you are interviewing has a suppressed sorrow because she ended up nursing a chronically ill mother instead of getting married. You really want to ask, "Didn't you resent your mother when you saw your fiancé marry someone else?" Your instincts warn that this is too brutally direct, so instead you start more generally and at a safe distance: "Our society seems to expect daughters more than sons to make sacrifices for their parents, doesn't it?" She has the choice of stopping at an impersonal opinion as an observer of life or of getting closer and closer to the injustice that ruined her life. When she ventures her opinions, simply ask for an example. By mutual and unspoken agreement, you steer toward the poignant testimony that both you and she want to put on record. You frame her situation as a sad injustice that overcomes women who are unaware of a societal trap, rather than inviting her to display any sense of personal victimization. The distinction is important: many people who are too proud or too realistic to complain will break self-imposed restraints only if doing so might save others from the same fate. Without this beautiful and generous human impulse, much documentary would be impossible.

The secret to good interviewing is to really *listen* and to press always for specifics and examples. Simple rejoinders, such as "How?," "Why was that?," and "How did that make you feel?," are the keys that unlock the sentient human being from the stoic observer. Occasionally it helps to ask the interviewee to take his time and only speak when he can see things in his mind's eye. Sometimes this elicits a new and better kind of telling.

ACHIEVING BREVITY

People often recount the same events in more than one way. When you pose an unexpected question, your interviewee will search and struggle to explain. This can be attractively spontaneous. But when this battle is directed toward, say, getting a few facts in order, it is tiresome to watch. Sensing this, an interviewee will often spontaneously repeat the explanation in a more orderly and rapid form. When this does not happen, you can ask, "Maybe you'd just like to go over that last explanation again as there were one or two stumbles." People are usually grateful for assistance and you benefit from getting alternative versions. In editing later, you can choose and may even combine the best of both.

Ask for a briefer version of any events for which you only need a summary. Most people enjoy collaborating in the making of a movie, and in playing the role of themselves they are no less sincere when doing something a second or third time.

CROSSING BOUNDARIES FOR THE FIRST TIME

Experienced interviewers deal first with what is familiar and comfortable, and only then steer toward new territory. A memorable interview invites the interviewee to take new steps and cross new emotional thresholds—large or small. This evokes the development that all stories need and delivers the emotional content—or even shock that I mentioned earlier—that we seek from dramatic art. It might come from getting someone to face the contradictions in her account of her mother and seeing her realize that she despises aspects of someone she wants to believe she only loved. Or it might be a man admitting to himself that he was unequal to a job in which he suffered a humiliating demotion. In both examples, the interviewee *is living out something important for the first time.* When this major breakthrough takes place, the suspense and sense of sharing a "privileged moment" are truly electrifying.

There are strange moments in interviewing when you sense there is more to tell but the person is unsure whether to risk telling it. A gentle "And?" or simply "Yes, go on" signals that you know there is more and that you support him or her in continuing. After this, do not be afraid to remain silent. *The expectant silence is the interviewer's most powerful encouragement to go deeper.* Used appropriately, a silence becomes a memorable and telling onscreen moment when the interviewee is visibly and dramatically grappling with a vital issue. The inexperienced or insensitive interviewer construes silence as failure to keep things going and comes crashing in with a new question, oblivious to missed opportunities. The underlying cause is *not listening properly and not listening for the unspoken subtext.* If you use the "security blanket" trick of keeping written questions on hand, you will be released to really listen and maintain eye contact. Remember, it's not live television. The material is going to be edited, so you take no risks by using silence and waiting.

THE RIGHT ORDER FOR QUESTIONS

Do not worry about trying to pose questions in their best order for your intended film. In editing you can reorganize the replies any way you want. The only logical order for an interview is the order that makes sense to the participant, who may wander associatively from topic to topic. If you want people to embark with the least sense of threat, start by asking about facts. Facts are safe, whereas opinions or feelings require more trust and a more confident, relaxed state of mind. So, keep the most demanding material for the end, when your subject has become used to the situation and is even enjoying it. Some people you cannot greatly influence, except momentarily. Accept this and see what you get.

Some people have sensitive issues that are difficult to approach. In a documentary I made with Alexandra Tolstoy, the 12th and most controversial of Leo Tolstoy's children, I learned during research that she was unwanted and in childhood had stumbled on the knowledge that her mother had tried to abort her. From her autobiography I saw how this grievous knowledge had affected not just her youth but probably her whole life. Hoping I would be able to touch on it but nervous of offending or hurting her, I delayed my most vital questioning to the end of the interview. Her reply patently came from the heart.

In editing I placed this section early because her contradictory feelings about her parents illuminate everything she says subsequently about herself. In my naïveté, I hardly supposed that an elderly lady of 86 could still feel the anguish of childhood so deeply. What emerges about a person's private pain always leads to deeper appreciation of their strengths. There would be no justification for intruding otherwise.

PRIVILEGED MOMENTS

The most impressive points in an interview come as detonations of truth—what Jean Rouch calls "privileged moments"—when someone on camera suddenly confronts something unfamiliar and important to him. It is like watching a mountaineer climb a challenging rock face, and seeing the danger of the climb intensify and the climber become only braver and more committed.

BELIEVING IN YOUR AUTHORITY

For the interviewer it takes close observation and empathy, not mystic powers, to spot areas of unfinished business in another person's life. It is easier in any case to see into another's life than into your own. If you have read a good mystery novel, you already know how to gather and collate the clues to patterns, personality, and motives. But novice directors are often too hesitant and self-conscious to act on their intuitions and fear rebuff. Remember that the role of making a record—as a writer or as a filmmaker—empowers you to be assertive and demanding in a way that is (wrongly perhaps) deemed invasive in normal life. You are making a record on behalf of an inquisitive audience, so most people accept that you are a seeker after truth and collaborate to a degree that is surprising and sometimes very moving.

YOU TAKE BUT YOU ALSO GIVE

When you have qualms about your authority to enter another person's life, remember that the ordinary person doubts his or her own significance and that your invitation to become part of a documentary record represents a confirmation that he or she not only exists but also matters. This is what you give, and what you give entitles you to a partnership that is seldom denied.

Why is this? It may be that the filmmaker—for reasons I can only guess at—is vested with the absolution powers of the priest or the doctor. Under the rubric of recording reality, you find you are allowed, even *expected*, to make incursions into your subjects' lives. Perhaps you are the village storyteller, who has the authority to reflect back and validate what each person really is. At first this is hard to believe and harder still to act on. You ask favors with an almost grotesque sense of apology and obligation, only to find that you are welcomed and assisted open-heartedly. You must treat such openness with responsibility, but you must resist having editorial decisions forged by a multiplicity of obligations. Sometimes this is very painful.

More often than not, a film crew provides a degree of support that allows people to make changes in their lives, even developments of which they never imagined themselves capable. Tod Lending's *Legacy* (2000) is about an African American family he followed for 5 years after the murder of a beloved family member. In a postscreening discussion, members of the family said frankly that they had worked their way out of the notorious Cabrini Green public housing in Chicago mainly because of the support from Tod and the filming. Filmmakers who imagine themselves witnesses often also function as believers and supporters, upholding their subjects' sometimes hesitant progress through an uncaring world.

CONCLUDING THE INTERVIEW

Before you conclude the interview, double-check with your topic lists that you covered everything you intended. While the camera is still running, I generally ask, "Is there anything else you want to say, anything we forgot to cover?" This hands the final word to the participant and makes a record of your having done so, should there be any dispute later.

After you cut the camera, thank the interviewee, making a point of acknowledging whatever was successful about the exchange. Keep everyone in place so that the recordist can shoot a minute or two of quiet atmosphere (also called *buzz track*, *presence*, or *room tone*). Later the editor uses this vital substance to fill spaces in the track. Without authentic presence as filler, the background atmosphere would either change or go dead, signaling where each of many edits took place.

When everyone rises to start dismantling equipment, give each participant a sum of money (often the minimum $1) and the *personal release form*, so you obtain for your records a signed permission form allowing you to use the material publicly. For the director this is always the most uncomfortable moment of all. I confess that when I could I gave this ghastly ritual to an assistant with instructions to carry it out as a necessary formality.

Very occasionally it happens that you want to curtail an interview because the interviewee is, for whatever reason, hopelessly unsatisfactory. Every director has at some time run the camera without film in order to escape without hurting the participant's feelings. Then again, to satisfy the man in the street wanting you to "take a picture of my store," the crew will, upon a prearranged signal, solemnly go through the actions of taking a shot without actually turning the camera on. It is a small price to make a complete stranger happy.

IN SUMMARY: GUIDELINES FOR EFFECTIVE INTERVIEWING

Here are some straightforward techniques that will help you maintain focus and intensity:

- Plan interview questions to produce responses covering specific areas.
- Because your audience has no prior knowledge, you must get comprehensive cover, especially of *expository information.*
- Cover expository information in more than one way and by more than one person so that you have alternatives in the cutting room.
- Don't be afraid to give direction to the interview.
- Expect most interviews, unless strongly controlled, to proceed nonlinearly and by association. This is fine because you will be editing and restructuring.
- Maintain eye contact at all costs.
- Keep your questions on a postcard on your knee, as a security.
- Never think about your next question because it will keep you from listening.
- It's your film and what it ends up saying is your responsibility, so don't give away all the control to your participants.
- Let the interviewee take control of the interview if by so doing he or she reveals something significant.
- Above all, listen for subtext, the unspoken meaning lying behind the words being used.
- Follow up your intuitions and instincts. Time and time again they are right.
- A subtle way to *steer* an interview is to summarize briefly what you have so far understood and ask the participant to continue. This consolidates interview and gives clear encouragement to build on it.
- Polite ways to *redirect* someone:

Say, "Can we return to . . ." and name the topic you would like to be amplified.
Repeat particular words the interviewee has used in a questioning tone, to encourage further exploration.
Courteously change the subject, "Could we move to . . . (new subject)"

- Listen for *leads* (that is, hints of further material), especially when suppressed feelings seem involved, and follow them up. You might say, "I was thinking you might have strong feelings about . . ." and then name what you have detected. Interviewees will often be grateful for your discerning encouragement.

- If your interviewee goes silent, respect the silence and wait for him to go on. If he needs encouragement, try repeating his last words in a questioning tone.

- Interviewing should be an exploration that leads to understanding, so make your interviewee *stay with a significant subject* until you feel it is exhausted.

- Keep exploring until you *reach complete understanding yourself*—both factual and emotional.

- Never settle for abstractions or generalities; always press for an example or a story to illustrate every worthwhile point. If you don't know what the interviewee meant, your audience won't either, so press for clarification.

- You have to *listen as if hearing everything for the first time* so that you can elicit whatever a first-time audience will need.

- Don't be afraid of interviewing people in crisis. You will soon know if someone truly wants to be left alone, but you'll never find out if you're too timid to ask. For most, crises are the time when you most need to talk. A truly satisfying exchange leads to a sense of release. If this is at all strong, you will feel it—and so will your audience.

- Giving testimony is a healing act, and so is listening to it.

- Offer the opportunity to add anything missing when you conclude the interview.

- If you can, check back with the interviewee the next day to see if he or she has had significant afterthoughts.

- Afterward, maintain humility by learning from your failures.

CHAPTER 25

DIRECTING PARTICIPANTS

This chapter deals with the psychological processes that make documentary participants quite like actors. It also deals, of course, with some of the physical processes of directing. It covers

- Issues concerning participants
  - Self-image and self-consciousness when under scrutiny
  - Action and doing as the remedy
  - Mannerisms and habits in participants
- Camera issues
  - More axis and other filming issues, as introduced in Chapter 12: Screen Grammar
  - Scene breakdown and making notes to help you function
  - Rationale for secure or insecure camera (handheld or tripod mounted)
- Social and formal issues
  - Making use of social breaks
  - Wrapping for the day
  - How few limits there really are to documentary

ISSUES CONCERNING PARTICIPANTS

IN SEARCH OF NATURALNESS

People often ask documentary makers, "How do you get people to look so natural?" Of course, you are tempted to shake your head sagely and say something about many years spent learning professional secrets. Actually, naturalness is much easier to achieve than is, say, a satisfactory dramatic structure, but it still takes some directorial skill. When all the participants are uniformly unnatural, as you sometimes see in a do-it-yourself show, it is the direction that is at fault. The key lies in the way you brief your participants, as we shall see.

Interviewing is just one way to direct a documentary. Overused, it leads to a "talking head" film. In an oral history work in which nothing but survivors are left to photograph, this may be the only film possible. Most directors, however, take great pains to show people active in their own settings, doing what they normally do. In part, this is to spare the audience from the hypnotic intensity of being talked at for long periods. We prefer to judge character and motivation not by what people say but by what they do and how they do it. Film is inherently behavioral, so actions speak louder than words. Having something familiar to do also sets participants at ease.

So you might want to shoot the subject of your film in his family life, at work instructing an employee, or in the neighborhood bar playing pool with cronies. But each situation will be stereotypical unless it contributes behavioral revelation about either the subject or his milieu. There is also another slight hitch. For most people, normality only exists when they don't feel watched. I once filmed in a glass-door factory, and one of the workers, who had spent years passing frames through a machine, completely lost her facility as soon as we turned on the camera. To her embarrassment the frames began to jam or miss the jet of rubber sealer solution. Why? Because she had begun *thinking* about her actions instead of just doing them.

When a person feels under intense scrutiny, his whole sense of himself can fragment. The implications are critical in documentary because we aim to capture people as they really are. Sudden attacks of self-consciousness wreck the process. The factory worker, feeling she must "act," lost automatic harmony with her machine, and there was nothing I could do except reassure her that this sometimes happens. So we waited until she managed a few rounds in her old rhythm. It was a striking example of the mind impeding the body's habitual function and shows that you must be able to help people stay inside their own normality.

THE MIND-BODY CONNECTION

The Russian actor and dramatic theorist Konstantin Stanislavski has important things to say about the mind's effect on the body. He says that every interior state has an outward and visible manifestation. In everyday life we discharge our actions and relationships quite unthinkingly, and we depend on a wellspring of assumptions about who and what we are and how we affect others.

Stanislavski points out that when an actor becomes self-conscious, he loses "focus" (that is, he stops experiencing the thoughts and emotions of his character), and the very visible effect is that he loses conviction in everything he says and does. It is the ability to focus, to shut out the anxious and critical "other" self, that is behind everyone's ability to function naturally. Through investigating what made some actors convincing and others not, Stanislavski realized that actors can perform naturally and believably only when their attention is fully occupied by the thoughts and actions of their characters. To this end, director and actor together generate "work" natural to the actor's role, because any opportunity for unstructured thought will let the ever-anxious mind take over.

Insecurity, of all kinds, even fear of losing focus, leads to a loss of focus, so trained actors stay in character by remaining mentally and physically occupied.

The paradox is that only by mental and physical focus is a person relaxed enough—whether acting or leading his or her personal life—to function emotionally and authentically. At such times the person has the bodily, mental, and emotional unity that comes from pursuing goals important to him or her. As a director you can, with an effort of will, tell from a person's body language whether he or she is focused or internally divided and troubled.

The key to directing actors, or to directing what Bill Nichols calls "social actors" (people "only playing themselves" in a documentary), is identical. Make sure that

- Any actors on camera have plenty to do so that they aren't stultified by self-consciousness
- Anything you ask them to do is organic to their life

If you ask a mother and daughter to let you film them washing the dishes at night, ask them to sustain a conversation as well. They start to discuss the next day, and now having so much familiar physical and mental activity to keep alive, they relax into obliviousness of the camera.

The least helpful thing to say is, "Just be yourself." It seems to set people worrying: What did he really mean? How does he see me? And which me does he really want? So,

- Do ask a participant to *do* something
- Do not ask him or her to *be* anything (natural, normal, etc.)

If you are shooting a scene of two brothers making dinner, ask what they would usually be doing. If they say "Talking," ask what they usually talk about, and pick a topic that relates well to your intended film.

One solution to keeping a participant engaged and natural during the unnatural situation of being filmed is to use the technique of reflexivity, that is, deliberately include the participant's relationship with those behind the camera as part of the movie. You might incorporate his or her questions, doubts, jokes, and even uncertainties about filming; however, this may backfire if the participant deals with his or her unease by throwing the initiative back on the film crew. A director, invited to become a character in his or her own film, will usually give only a modest and minimal response. Then a vacuum develops at the threshold that the director won't cross. In Nick Broomfield's hilarious *The Leader, The Driver, and the Driver's Wife* (1992), this threshold is justified. Broomfield uses boyish disingenuousness to draw out the South African white supremacist Eugene Terreblanche (sic) and we know full well why Broomfield holds back. But in other films of this type, it is the director's manipulation that stands uncomfortably naked, even at times in Ross McElwee's otherwise sophisticated *Sherman's March* (1989).

When you are making a nonreflexive, "transparent" film, tell participants

- That in documentary we shoot far more than we use, so they shouldn't worry about mistakes or silences because you expect to edit
- To ignore the crew's presence and *not look at the camera*. This prevents them from falling into the trap of "playing to the audience." The crew can help by concentrating on their jobs, avoiding eye contact, and giving no facial or verbal feedback.

When you are making a reflexive film, tell participants that

- They can talk to you or to the camera as they wish
- They can do anything or go anywhere as they need to in their work or other activity that is being filmed
- Nothing is off limits, and no thought or subject of conversation is disallowed
- The object of filming is to catch things as they happen, and that filming is part of the happening

Should participants feel that you are trying to manipulate or misrepresent them, even by cheerleading as an audience, they may become uncomfortable and uncooperative, or they may relish the appreciation, which will show on the screen.

If you establish justifiable and trustworthy reasons for making the film, participants usually take part with good will, naturalness, and spontaneity. This can be very revealing when an oppressive middle-aged couple, for example, falls into a recurring argument about what food the dog should have tomorrow. Domesticity of this kind happens on the documentary screen because participants become used to working with you and enjoy giving you who they are. Not infrequently people reveal their abiding passions. I once filmed elderly miners describing the bitter days of the 1926 General Strike in England. We filmed overlooking the mine in question, and the camera went within 2 feet of the miners' faces as they relived the greatest events of their lives. They lost all awareness of being filmed because they were reliving events that embodied the deepest and most divisive issues in their community. Our camera's attention lent the moment a special gravity and meaning, so their involvement was deeply emotional and left them no attention to spare for how they might appear to us or to the world beyond our camera.

I once saw the same thing during a drama improvisation when Aiden Quinn and a partner afterward had no memory of our roving camera's presence. They had been too involved in the improv to even notice it. Life being lived in the imagination and drama can be one and the same thing—consuming. People consumed by the moment are most deeply and revealingly themselves.

SELF-IMAGE AND SELF-CONSCIOUSNESS

The easiest people to work with are those who are oblivious of their effect on others. Old people and small children are natural because there is no ego, no internal censor at work. With this indicator in mind, you can predict who is going to present difficulties; those compulsively careful of their appearance or with many nervous mannerisms are least likely to be at peace in front of a camera. During a street interview I once had a lady completely lose focus. I was puzzled as to what had happened until, in mid-sentence, she began to remove the hair net she realized she was still wearing. The more "proper" someone feels he or she must look for the record, the less flexible, impulsive, and openly communicative that person is likely to be.

But because care and circumspection was this lady's stamp, her action was also wonderfully representative. Her friends, seeing the film, would smile in recognition. What we should note is that the pressure of the camera's presence did not make her behave uncharacteristically. People often say, "But the presence of the camera *must* change people." I think it only changes the aspect or degree of a person's response. Neither the camera nor any other form of observation can make anyone act out of character because nothing can change a person's underlying nature. That's why the camera sometimes catalyzes an honesty and depth of feeling seldom seen by a participant's closest friends. When the human craving for recognition is fulfilled, the floodgates may open wide.

One further observation that you should find liberating:

- Because you film something doesn't mean you have to use it, so there's no need to be unduly protective while shooting.

Later in the cutting room, you will have time and advisers to help you thoroughly consider the implications of the footage you have taken. Documentarians often decide, for one reason or another, not to use material. In rare cases, filmmakers have destroyed footage (shot in repressive or totalitarian countries, say, or revealing of a crime) when they realize that its very existence endangers someone's life. One exception here:

- Never shoot anything injurious when someone else has editorial control of your material. Some people go further and say, if you shoot it, you'll use it.

WHY YOUR MOTIVES FOR FILMING MATTER

You and your camera will only plumb the depths of someone's life if she senses that you and your crew personally accept, like, and value her. A *documentary is a record of relationships*, so success depends on what takes place before the camera is ever switched on. For this reason I avoid topics or participants for whom I feel little interest or empathy. Not always, though. I once embarked with very mixed feelings on a film about Sir Oswald Mosley and his 1930s British Union of Fascists *(The Battle of Cable Street)*. We set about tracing people who would admit to being followers, and in the end I interviewed Mosley himself. I felt apprehensive—not about the violence that surrounded those people and about the disgust I felt for their values but about their reputation for evil. As it happened, Hannah Arendt's phrase about the banality of evil fitted the situation better than any of my imaginings. The British upholders of the ideology that exterminated 11 million people were shockingly ordinary; no horns or cloven feet to be seen. They were anxious to present their case and even made a specious kind of sense. The only stance that researcher Jane Oliver and I needed to take was that of younger people wishing to learn history from its protagonists.

During the lengthy editing period, I found myself both fascinated and repelled by Mosley. An urbane, upper-class member of the establishment, he had ego-centrically distorted everything connected with him. I wanted to relay his version of the 1936 events and yet show what a self-delusion his version was. The film managed to satisfy the Left (who opposed the freedom Mosley was given to orga-nize racial hatred) and even Mosley himself, because he had expected to have his account distorted.

Part of creating trust is explaining plausibly why you want to shoot a par-ticular scene or topic. You can get a taxi driver to chat to the camera while he cruises looking for a fare because it is a central part of his reality and he enjoys sharing it. You may discreetly film a woman in her morning bath because it was in this very bath that she took the momentous decision to visit Egypt. You can film an old man feeding his dog and talking to it because he believes you too feel this is a special part of a special life. Organizations, especially those at the extremes, are far more likely to be paranoid than are individuals. At any time you may be told you must explain in writing why you are filming this topic or that scene, so you should keep explanations as simple and uncontroversial as you can. Your explanations should be consistent (because participants compare notes) but not so specific that you box yourself into a corner.

OBSTACLES: HABITS OF BEING

Particular jobs attract particular kinds of people, and some employment seems to generate mannerisms and self-awarenesses that are a liability in filmmaking, unless, of course, it is such characteristics that you want to show. Sometimes offi-cials, unused to making public statements and afraid of alienating superiors, will make excruciatingly boring and self-conscious contributions. Lecturers and politicians on camera will address invisible multitudes instead of talking one on one as they did so nicely during research.

The fact is that people under pressure or unusual circumstances fall back on habit, and ingrained habits of behavior are hard or impossible to change. Before you try to alter a participant's idea of how he or she should relate to the camera, estimate what is habit and what is only a misperception about filming. The latter you may be able to alter. For instance, the person addressing a large audience can sometimes be redirected by simply saying, "There is only one person, me, listening to you. Talk only to me." Another mistaken notion with horrendous consequences is the person's idea that he or she must project the voice. If the person cannot respond to direction, a little playback may do the trick. People are often shocked when first they see or hear themselves, so exposing an unsatis-factory "performance" should be a last resort, to be done privately and supportively.

Sometimes you will get someone whose concept of a film appearance is taken from commercials and who valiantly tries to project *personality*. This is still true to some aspect of the individual's character and assumptions: if you are making a film about stage mothers who want their children to learn acting for commer-cials, you could hardly ask for anything more revealing.

A person's response to being filmed may or may not be appropriate, but some thought beforehand can prepare you for what's likely. Choosing participants is "casting" as much as it would be for a fiction film. Documentaries are not truth itself but dramatic constructs made from found or catalyzed life materials. Who you use and what they do is what you end up saying on the screen.

CAMERA ISSUES

COMPROMISES FOR THE CAMERA

When shooting action sequences, you may need to ask people to slow down or control their movements because movement in general, once it has a frame round it, looks perhaps 20 to 30% faster. The operator's fanciest footwork cannot keep a hand nicely framed and in focus if its owner moves too fast.

How willing are you to intrude to get a result that is visually and choreographically accomplished? The ethnographer will want to intrude as little as possible into the life being documented, and the most intrusive documentarians still have a lot of the ethnographer in them. But as Jean-Luc Godard perceived, if you start out making a documentary, you are driven toward fictional techniques, and if you make fiction, you will be compelled toward documentary. Even in the most mechanized Hollywood drama shoot, there is always an element of improvisation and inventiveness that leaves the camera documenting a "happening." The rules of documentary are rules you make for yourself, and whatever you decide affects your relationship with the audience. It is something you must think through and decide through principle and experiment.

As the audience expects you to set the language of your film, so in everyday life people make allowances for a camera known to be documenting actuality. If you are shooting outdoors, especially in a public place or where there are crowds, do not be afraid to penetrate areas you normally would not enter. The camera is your passport, so use it to cross police lines, go to the front of a crowd, or squeeze between people looking in a shop window. In Western countries, the camera's right to do this is usually accepted as part of the freedom of the press. Of course, this is a cultural assumption not made in every culture. A colleague went to film in Nigeria and learned (through having stones thrown at him) that taking a person's image without asking first is regarded as theft. Merely holding a camera in a war zone, or staying in the wrong hotel, can get you killed, as journalists discovered in Baghdad. Every year, dozens of press corps personnel, of which you may become one, are injured or even killed while doing their jobs.

MAINTAINING SCREEN DIRECTION

Camera placement is one of the few areas where a little ignorance can produce irreversible confusion. Some theoretical knowledge can prevent all this. Because film presents the pieces of an artfully fragmented world, the audience is mentally assembling an image of the whole for each succeeding situation. Four partial angles of individuals in a room are enough for the film audience to conjure up an idea of the entire room and its occupants. To avoid confounding this useful process, the director should know the rules that maintain a sense of geographical consistency. Let us imagine you are shooting a parade. You must decide ahead of time (based on background or lighting factors) from which side of the parade you intend to shoot. By shooting from only one side, everyone in every shot will march across the screen in the same direction, say, screen left to screen right (abbreviated as "Screen L-R"). If you were to hop through the parade halfway and film from the other side, your parade onscreen would start marching in the reverse direction, screen right to screen left. Intercutting this material will cause the viewer to wonder: is this a counterdemonstration marching in from another direction? Or could it be another wing, marching away?

To maintain consistent screen directions, the camera must *stay one side of a scene axis or invisible line.* To do this, you first draw an axis between, say, two people having a conversation, as illustrated in Figure 25–1. As long as your camera stays to *one side of that line,* the character in black will always look left to right, and the character in white will always look right to left across the screen. Three different camera angles are shown in Figure 25–1: B is a two-shot, and A and C are over-the-shoulder shots. Look at the resulting frames. You can intercut any one with the others.

Should you take up position D, however, the camera has "crossed the line," and we have a problem. Compare frame D with its complementary shots. The

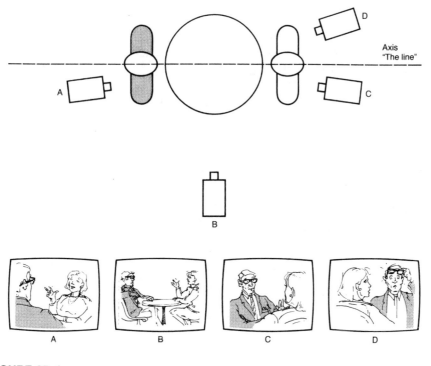

FIGURE 25–1 ————————————————————————————————

"Crossing the line." The three images produced from camera positions A, B, and C all intercut because the characters maintain their screen directions. Position D, however, produces a composition that reverses the characters' sightlines and would not intercut with the other angles. Position D has crossed the invisible line between the characters.

character in black is now facing in the same screen direction as the character in white. Cut them together, and one is talking to the back of the other's head. This makes no sense! This is the cardinal filmmaking transgression called *crossing the line*. Of course, there is no sin without redemption, so in fact you *can* cross the line halfway through the conversation, but you would have to dolly the camera sideways during the shot from position B to position D so that the audience sees the camera *moving to the new position*. From here onward, all new angles must be shot from the new side of the line to preserve the revised logic of screen direction.

In a situation like a parade, where you have people and objects on the move, you can cover yourself by taking direction-changer shots that show the altered direction onscreen. Figure 25–2 shows how the parade, after marching right to

FIGURE 25–2 ——————————————————————————————————

Changing screen direction. The procession starts right to left, then all in the one shot changes from left to right. This is a useful shot to keep in reserve because, in showing a change of direction, it allows you to shoot from both sides of the axis and still cut shots together in a logical flow.

left, turns a corner and now marches left to right. By including several direction-change shots in a day's shooting, you can shoot from either side of the parade and rest assured that it should all cut together in a logical flow.

When you shoot people at a garden party or in a museum, where they are free to move around, they will regroup and face in new screen directions during the scene. This means that early and late material probably won't intercut and that editing to give the scene a more logical development in content may be hard or impossible. Shooting cutaway reaction shots will help, especially if the subject's moving sightline indicates someone moving offscreen. Remember to shoot these to cover all likely directions of movement. You may even need to manufacture these shots by asking a bystander to follow with his or her eyes someone who is on the move.

These skills may be hard to learn theoretically, but they are easy enough to acquire through experience. Shoot a scene with a lot of people, and try editing it down to the best few minutes. You will encounter most of the problems of axis and motivation, and next time you shoot you will be editing in your head as you go. A lot of mental editing takes place as you direct.

MOTIVATION FOR CAMERA POSITIONING AND CAMERA MOVEMENT

Recommending camera positioning is difficult because every scene has its nature to be revealed amid the inherent limitations of its environment. These are usually physical: windows or pillars in an interior that restrict shooting to one direction or an incongruity to be avoided in an exterior. A genuine settler's log cabin might have to be framed low in order to prevent seeing, above the ancient trees, an ominous revolving sausage proclaiming the neighborhood hot-dog emporium. Making films, and especially making documentaries, is serendipitous and plans often have to be jettisoned to accommodate the unforeseen. Such limitations shape film art to a degree undreamed of by film critics but will be familiar to any student of Eastern philosophies, where the individual learns from an early age to harmonize with destiny rather than fight it. You will often feel challenged by the pull of roads not taken. So often your beliefs, values, and preparation face challenge from the gods of chance.

Sometimes serendipity participates in eerie ways. The British miners I mentioned earlier had sabotaged a scab coal train back in the 1926 General Strike. While we were in their area making the film, an express train derailed close to the original site. It happened during the night prior to interviewing a doctor who had participated in the 1926 incident. He knew we were coming the next day and thought he must be dreaming when he was summoned to a train crash in the small hours. After some soul searching about voyeurism, I altered our plans to film the wreckage because it brought home like nothing else the destruction the saboteurs had risked in their demonstration (Figure 25–3).

For some, adapting to the unexpected is frustrating, while for others it is the soul of existence and represents a challenge to their inventiveness and insight. The temptation is not to make plans at all, but you must, and sometimes plans even work out.

FIGURE 25–3

Be ready to adapt to the unexpected: an unforeseeable train wreck that occurred at the site while filming *The Cramlington Train-Wreckers.*

SCENE BREAKDOWN AND CRIB NOTES

The first step in filming any scene is to determine what it must establish and what you want it to contribute to the intended film. As always, list your goals so that nothing gets overlooked in the heat of battle. If, for instance, you are shooting in a laboratory, you might make a reminder, or *crib note,* on an index card as shown in Figure 25–4.

Less tangibly, you also might want to show that the lab workers are dedicated and even heroic. This is your bottom line; you cannot leave without getting shots that establish these things. Then, treating the camera as an observing consciousness, you must imagine in detail *how you want the scene to be experienced.* If you are to shoot a boozy wedding, it will make no sense to use carefully placed tripod shots. It's better for the camera to adopt a guest's point of view, by going handheld and peering into circles of chattering people. Then it can legitimately bump into raucous revelers, quiz the principals, and even join in the dancing. If you were going to shoot in a courtroom with its elaborate ritualized performances, the placing and amount of coverage by the camera would be quite different and certainly should not be unsteady and mobile. So how do you show lab workers as heroic? Probably the answer lies in studied shots that emphasize both the human vulnerability of each worker and the danger of the work the workers do. Perhaps you show a face next to a retort of boiling acid. Each person has his or her own world and risks destruction in order to investigate significant problems.

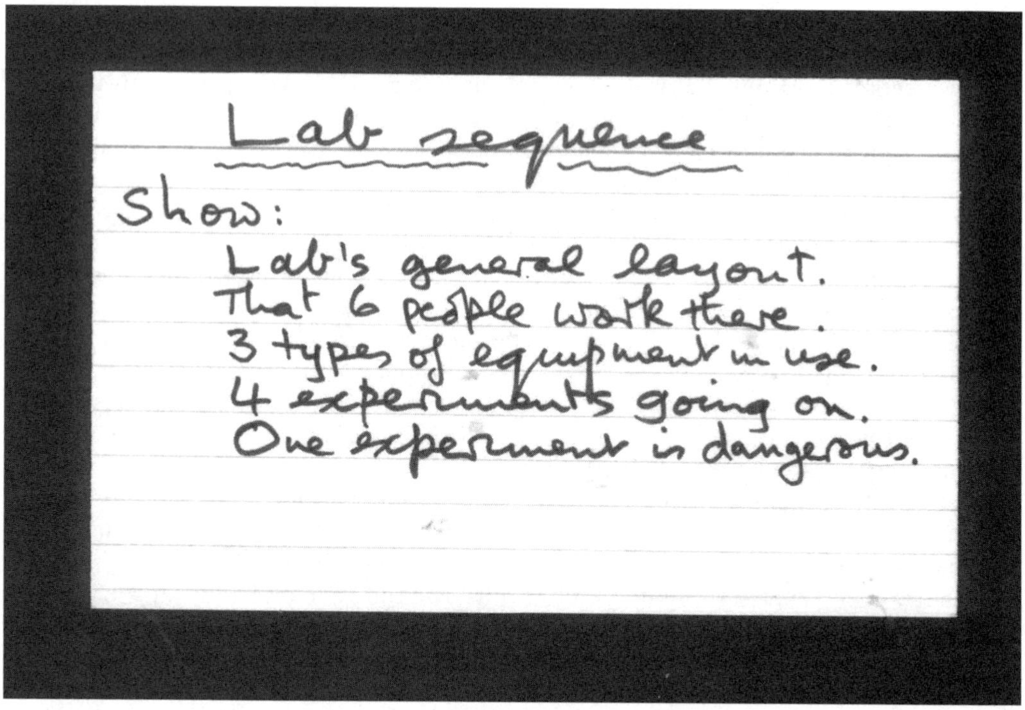

FIGURE 25–4

Crib note: goals for a laboratory sequence written on an index card.

Whatever the shooting situation, ask yourself the following:

- Whose point of view is the audience mostly sharing?
- Where does the majority of the telling action lie? (In the courtroom, for example, does it lie with judge, plaintiff, prosecutor, or the jury?)
- When is point of view likely to change, and to whom?
- What factual or physical details are essential to imply the whole?
- What will be each essential stage of development that I must cover?
- What signals the start and end of each developmental stage?

Camera positioning can change the implications of a piece of action. Isolating two people in two separate close shots, for instance, and intercutting them will have a very different feel than cutting between two over-the-shoulder shots. In the single shots, the observer is always alone with one of the contenders, but in the over-the-shoulder shots their relationship in space and time is shown, not manufactured through editing, so the viewer constantly sees one in relation to the other and senses himself in relation to the two of them.

There is no mystery here. Your guide to how an audience will respond always lies with the common experience and the common sense that make you and me alike, that make us react and understand similarly when sharing an unfolding situation. Where we are, what we see, in what order things unfold, affect us similarly; if not, cinema would not be the universal language that it *is*. *Knowledge of cinema, therefore, comes ultimately not from cinema but from a growing self-perception.* If learning this way is too slow or ambiguous for you, you can always "audition" different fiction and documentary approaches to situations similar to yours to see how others have done it. But remember that whenever you imitate the practices of others, you risk losing your authentic "voice." This is the risky side of film theory; by intellectualizing film language, it tends to cut you off from the very instincts that invented that language in the first place.

Another camera positioning issue lies in deciding how the background might comment on the foreground action. If a participant is in a wheelchair and the shot contains a window with a vista of people in the street, the composition will unobtrusively juxtapose her with what she is so poignantly denied.

Looking down on the subject, looking up at the subject, or looking at the subject between the bars of a railing can all suggest different ways of seeing—and, therefore, of experiencing—the action that makes the scene. *Don't leave the camera to be a passive recorder; make it into an instrument of ironic juxtaposition or disclosure.* True, revelation can be manufactured through editing, but so much more is accomplished by observation and juxtaposition that is built into the shooting. Exploit the location fully for its own signs and revelation, and make your camera respond to how participants' movements and actions convey the scene's subtext. The difference is between sharing the consciousness of someone intelligent and intuitive, who picks up the event's underlying tensions, and sharing the consciousness of an eye that swivels dully toward whatever moves.

Try answering the question, "How best to shoot my documentary?," by imagining how you would *inhabit* these events if you were functioning at a very high level of consciousness. Transfer this inhabiting to the screen, and you are on your way.

HANDHELD OR TRIPOD-MOUNTED CAMERA?

A tripod-mounted camera can zoom in to hold a steady close shot without crowding whoever is being filmed, but it cannot suddenly move to a better vantage should the action call for it. The handheld camera gives this mobility, but at the price of unsteadiness. Going handheld may be the only solution when you cannot predict the action or know only that it will take place somewhere in a given area. Some camcorders are equipped with image stabilizers that compensate (sometimes rather successfully) for the kind of operator unsteadiness that comes from the occasional need to breathe.

The two kinds of camera presence—one studied, composed, and controlled and the other mobile, spontaneous, and physically reactive to change—contribute a quite different sense of involvement, imply quite different relationships to the action, and alter the film's storytelling "voice."

The *tripod-mounted camera* is always "seeing" from a fixed point in space, no matter which direction the camera pans or tilts. Even when zooming in, the perspective remains the same, reiterating how much the observation is rooted in an assigned place. This feeling would be appropriate for a courtroom, because the positions of judge, jury, witness box, and audience are all symbolic and preordained by seating. Because no court would tolerate a wandering audience member, it is logical that the camera/observer also be fixed.

The *handheld camera* is a human intelligence on legs. Because using the close end of the zoom is impractical, the lens must be kept at wide angle and the camera physically moved through space if a long shot is to become a close shot. Changes in perspective alone make this dynamic relocation apparent. During a handheld conversation, the camera may reframe, reposition itself, and change image size many times to produce all the shots you would expect in an edited version: a long shot, medium two-shots, complementary over-the-shoulder shots, and big close-ups. Covering a spontaneous event with a well-balanced succession of such shots is a rare skill that calls for the sensibility of an editor, director, and camera operator all in one person. Because human life generates much redundancy, these shots can often be edited to approximate the feature film's elegant freedom of access to its characters. However, make the cutting too elegant, and your technique will cast doubt on the spontaneity of the scene.

Successful handheld work conveys something exceptional: the dramatic tension of a spontaneous, uncut event unfolding, and that simultaneously it is being assessed by a discriminating intelligence. This astute, comprehensive view is so formal as to be invisible in fiction filmmaking, but handheld documentary is manifestly a daring improvisation, something unfolding in the face of reality and on the run. Good camerawork is therefore a matter of acute concentration and acute sensitivity to underlying issues. Why else would a veteran Hollywood cameraman like Haskell Wexler call documentary "real filmmaking"?

SPECIAL PHOTOGRAPHY

Documentaries sometimes include material that must be shot under special conditions, such as graphics on a rostrum camera, mountaineering on a sheer rock face, coral reefs underwater, cities from a helicopter, or, if the subject includes insect life, through a high-power lens. At such times the director is in the hands of a specialist. The relationship may be pleasantly instructional, or it may be uncomfortable and confusing. Experts can after all use their knowledge to intimidate—as anyone knows who's gone shopping in a hardware store. Research the process and the personnel beforehand so that you remain in control of your filming. Bullying, subtle or blatant, is apt to take place whenever the pecking order is upset. A young director can expect some flak from older crewmembers, male subordinates will challenge a woman's authority, and a foreigner may feel pressure from the indigenous. All this is tiresomely human, so watch out!

SOCIAL AND FORMAL ISSUES

USING SOCIAL TIMES AND BREAKS

During production, when you are not shooting, remember to spend time with your participants. It is a mistake to retreat to the understanding company of the crew, however exhausted you may be. Without imposing, try to keep crew and participants together during meals or rest periods. Frequently, while lunching or downing a beer together, you will make discoveries that help your ideas evolve. Making a film together generates a higher consciousness in everyone and shakes out ideas, memories, and associations. You get a shared intensity of purpose and adventure, which binds everyone together. Conserved and encouraged, this excitement makes a more profound fellowship and communication becomes inevitable. This energizes even a jaded crew. An aware and involved crew acts as an antenna, alerting you to things said or done beyond your knowledge. While we were making a film about Dr. Spock during his anti-Vietnam War rallies, the sound recordist Roger Turner picked up a radio broadcast calling for demonstrators at a Christian pro-war rally. As a result, we changed our plans and went to Trenton, New Jersey, where we filmed proponents of the Vietnam War in full cry. This came at a time when I was overwhelmed with fatigue and was low on ideas. Crew initiatives can sometimes be gold.

WRAPPING

At the end of a day's shoot, make a point of personally thanking both the crew and participants. Be especially careful that all possessions and furniture have been replaced exactly as they were found. Attention to the details of someone else's home signifies your concern and appreciation, and it helps ensure that you will be welcome if you want to return. Reluctance to accept a film crew's presence is usually because of a horror story about what another crew did. You pave the way for other filmmakers as they did for you.

LIMITS TO THE DOCUMENTARY FORM

A predictable topic when documentary makers get together is always what is or is not documentary. Allegiance to fact is fundamental, but Grierson's "the creative treatment of actuality" is pretty good, and Zola's "A work of art is a corner of nature seen through a temperament" is even better. There are no rules in this young art form, only decisions about where to draw lines and how to remain consistent to the contract you set up with your audience.

Documentary film can also include acted reconstructions of events long before living memory, docudrama (a form of re-enactment mixing actors and real people), and re-enactment of previous events by the protagonists themselves. Ruth First, an African National Congress member formerly imprisoned in South Africa, acted her own story in reconstructed surroundings, with actors playing the parts of guards and interrogators. Is this documentary? I think it certainly can be, depending on its authorial goals and its fidelity to what was actual. Had First's experience included hallucinations from hunger or torture, these too could be recreated in the spirit of the truth. Ironically, her art must have done its job powerfully enough, because the racist oligarchy she unmasked made sure she was assassinated.

CHAPTER 26

DIRECTING THE CREW

Aspects to directing a crew in this chapter are

- Communicating the film's schedule and purpose before the shoot
- Ensuring that everyone knows (and keeps to) his or her area of responsibility
- Moment-to-moment communications during the shoot
- Encouraging the crew to act supportively toward the participants
- Encouraging solidarity and maintaining professionalism when there are internal disagreements
- Keeping the crew attuned to the project's larger dimensions so that they can make creative contributions beyond the confines of their own specialty

SCHEDULING AND COMMUNICATION

If you want professional reliability from your crew, you must first be a model of professionalism yourself. Day-to-day direction should begin from a comprehensive printed schedule with timely updates in cases of change. Include travel directions and a location contact phone number in case of emergency. *Everything of possible importance should be written down* because shooting is no time to test people's powers of recall.

At first be formal about the chain of responsibility, and then after incontestable proof of a person's trustworthiness, you can relax the traditional structure as appropriate. To instead start informally and then try to tighten up your regime is a recipe for mutiny.

Once the crew assembles at the location, quietly reiterate the immediate goals. These are in cinematic terms and you probably never share them with your participants. You might want a store to look shadowy and fusty, or you might want to emphasize a child's view of the squalor of a trailer park.

Confirm the first setup so that the crew can get the equipment ready. A clear working relationship with your director of photography will relieve you from deciding a myriad of details that might detract from your main responsibility, which is toward the participants and, thus, the authorial coherence of the film. Now get busy preparing the participants.

Beginning directors usually try to cover too much in a given time and end up shooting for very long hours. After a few grueling days, work gets sloppy and the crew becomes resentful and hypercritical. Err on the light side, because a crew in good shape is always ready to shorten a given schedule by working longer, while a crew suffering from terminal fatigue may rebel at the idea of an extra 2 hours. Treat your crew reasonably and they will rise to crises selflessly.

Here's something else to remember: when you direct, you are fully involved all the time and tend to overlook mere bodily inconveniences such as hunger, cold, fatigue, and bathroom breaks. If you want a happy crew, keep to an 8-hour working day and have meals and breaks built predictably into the schedule. A flask of coffee and packets of sandwiches produced at the right moment will work miracles on a weary crew's morale. On long shoots, crews need time off. When I first directed abroad, my producer advised that I allow time for my crew to sightsee and buy presents for their loved ones at home. As with everything Brian Lewis taught me, it proved excellent advice.

MAINTAINING COMMUNICATION

Ideally the crew has been involved in the evolution of the ideas for the film, but if you are shooting for television you will probably get an assigned crew. The director must first outline intended filming for the crew and then should keep them abreast of developments during the shoot—something I used to forget to keep up when the pressure mounted. During breaks away from participants, encourage the crew to discuss the production. One can learn much from mainly listening. At first you may be shocked by the crew's lack of all-around observation. The reason is simple: a good camera operator concentrates wholly on composition, lighting, shadows, framing, and camera movements. Only to a minor degree can he or she be aware of content. Likewise for the diligent sound recordist, words are less important than voice quality, unwanted noise or echo, and the balance of sound levels. Crewmembers monitor a restricted area of *quality*, each tending a particular vegetable patch and oblivious to the garden as a whole unless the director periodically invests time and energy in connecting them to the project as a conceptual entity. Some crewmembers will not appreciate your efforts. But if you want a farsighted crew, take pains to share your thinking on both local and global terms. Depending on the notion of industrialism prevalent in their home base, it may take special and sometimes unfamiliar effort for them to consider the work in hand from an authorial standpoint.

In film schools everyone gets used to working with people of similar sophistication to themselves. But in "the industry" you cannot assume that technicians have ever had a discussion outside their own area of expertise. They may at first be hesitant or hostile to your efforts. Persist.

Crew feedback should never go unacknowledged even when it is embarrassingly off target. Make mental adjustment for any skewed valuations and be diplomatic with advice you can't use. Above all, encourage involvement, and don't retreat from communicating.

MONITORING AND INSTRUCTING

Before shooting, always look through the camera to see if what you expect is really there. This is of paramount importance when you use film; it's too late to correct misunderstandings as you watch rushes days or weeks later.

Each time you start shooting, allow a minimum of 10 seconds of equipment run-up time before saying the magic word "Action" to your participants. Though most cameras hit speed almost instantaneously, good action immediately following a camera startup is not always usable because there may be color or picture instability problems as mechanical and electronic coordinations are stabilizing.

Always stand right next to the camera so that you see as nearly as possible what it sees. Relay minimal camera directions by whispering into the operator's ear, making sure, of course, that your voice will not spoil a recording. Be brief and specific: "Go to John in medium shot," "Pull back to a wide shot of all three," or "If he goes into the kitchen again, walk with him and follow what he does." If the camera is handheld, your sound recordist will adapt to the action and to what the camera does, but will probably shoot you meaningful glances now and then. Listening for quality, she will grow agitated at the approach of a plane or the rumble of a refrigerator that has turned itself on in the next room. Wearing headphones, she will have no idea which direction the interference is coming from and will look around in alarm. She may draw her finger across her throat (industry sign for "cut") and raise her eyebrows beseechingly. You are being asked to call "Cut!" Should you?

You have to make a decision and your head pounds from stress. You are supposed to be keenly aware of ongoing content and yet must resolve through glances and hand signals all sorts of other stuff—problems of sound, of shadows, of people who have done the unexpected, or of pets who have escaped bondage. At such times the director is blinded by sensory overload.

At the end of a shot, if the camera is on the tripod, be ready to look through the viewfinder to see the ending composition for yourself. Before allowing the crew to wrap, cast your mind back over the events you have just filmed and itemize *cutaway shots* or *inserts* (sometimes called *cut-ins*) to shoot in case you later need to shorten or cross-cut segments.

- A cutaway is a shot of something outside the frame, such as the wall clock that somebody looks at. You would shoot it from her eyeline as safety coverage.
- An insert shot is an enlargement of something in the main frame, such as the face of the watch that another character checks.

In one scene I directed of a carpenter in his workshop, I noticed that he folded and unfolded his rule below frame as he spoke to me. The cutaway we took of his hands at work enabled me to bridge together two separate sections of the interview and to visually explain the strange clicking noises coming from offscreen.

Many times you will use eyeline shifts to "motivate" cutaways. For instance, if someone says it is getting late and looks up, you would show the insert of the clock. If he looks moodily out of a window, you would do a cutaway of his point of view. Frequently a person will show a picture, refer to an object in the room, or look offscreen at someone, and in each case he directs our attention to a legitimate cutaway. In daily life, we are always looking where someone else looks, to see what it is that interests him or her. Eyeline cutting mimics this habit we have.

Sometimes a cutaway or insert shot will reflect an authorial attitude. For example, in the kitchen of a neglected elderly man, the tap drips incessantly. You film a close shot of it and of the dusty, yellowing photographs on his shelf in the background because it speaks volumes about long-standing disregard. Such shots, drawing the viewer's eye to significant detail, are motivated by narrative intentions rather than by action and can express an authorial point of view about the mood, the times, or whatever else.

After shooting two or more people in conversation, shoot *reaction shots* (listening, watching, or waiting close-ups) of each individual when he or she is not talking. These are worth their weight in gold to the editor. Never leave a scene, interior or exterior, without shooting a *presence track*, that is, an audio background filler shot with the same mike position, same recording level, and with everyone keeping silent and still for 2 minutes (also called a *buzz track* or *room tone*).

NEGATIVE ATTITUDES IN THE PROFESSION

Interestingly, the situation for the film crew is opposite to that of the participants. Whereas participants need a sense of purpose and work on which to focus, the crew has ready-made work, which can insulate them from responsibility to a larger purpose. Too often, a seasoned crew buries itself in technical or "company" concerns and signifies disconnection by their attitudes, remarks, or lack of involvement.

This is not malice but an exigency of the job. Unfortunately, working under pressure for large concerns with productivity goals will turn many a good person into a production-line operative. Because corporations are steered by competition and the profit motive, crewmembers feel like foot soldiers shunted cynically from pillar to post. Even the excitement of going to distant places wears off. Seriously jaded crews begin to rate the production solely by the level of hotels and restaurants organized for them. The terminally institutionalized know both company and union rules backwards, and they care not at all about filmmaking. They will lay down tools on the stroke of the clock and compute their overtime to the penny.

I do not mean to detract from the achievements of the craft unions in protecting their members from the gross exploitation that has bedeviled film technicians since the dawn of our industry. Huge profits still are made in entertainment, and it is absolutely right that those who create the product should share in the rewards. However, rules and restrictions become the refuge for the third-rate worker whose presence is adverse in any small, tight-knit operation.

The problem begins with the aptitudes and education (in the broadest sense) of the individual. Many working in film and television are inadequately or narrowly educated and as a result have built some defenses around themselves. Directors disassociate themselves from the technical problems of their sound and camera people and draw ill-informed and emotional conclusions; sound and camera personnel remain within tightly drawn compartments of technical operation and avoid acknowledging the conceptual problems inherent in directing.

Be sympathetic and interested in your crew's problems, and they will be generous when you want their help solving one of yours.

WORKING ATMOSPHERE

The transition into shooting should hide the excitement and tension you may feel and instead be a time of serious, focused attention. Shooting should take place in as calm an atmosphere as possible, and the crew should convey warnings or questions to you discreetly or through signs. For instance, the recordist or camera operator may hold up three fingers to indicate that only 3 minutes of tape or film is left. In potentially divisive situations, only the director should give out information or make decisions. Any disagreement or dissent among the crew should be kept scrupulously away from the participants. For them, a calm, respectful atmosphere is a necessity. The crew should preserve outward unity at all costs and should make no comment or observation that might undermine the authority of the director or of each other.

Filmmaking, although collaborative, is seldom democratic. A crew used to each other can be very informal, but there must be lines of responsibility respected on all sides if the unit is not to look foolish and discordant. The prime reason behind student film breakdowns is that each crewmember is apt to consider him or herself more competent than the person actually directing. As difficulties arise, well meant but contradictory advice showers down on the director. Any such disunity will soon propagate alarm and despondency in both participants and crew.

THE PROBLEM OF HAVING AUTHORITY

A major anxiety for the beginning director is the feeling that you lack competency and authority. Authoritativeness is not something a person can just assume, especially under what you imagine (not always wrongly) is hostile scrutiny by those you are supposed to lead. Therefore, choose co-workers carefully and, once you have started a collaborative relationship, work to reduce the misunderstandings and compartmentalization that grow like barnacles on any enterprise. Take time to understand your crew's concerns and problems, and make every effort to include them in the conceptual considerations of the film. This, in turn, invites suggestions that may or may not be practical and desirable. Unless everyone understands from the outset that only a director can decide ultimately what goes into a film, the director's openness may be misconstrued as an invitation to make the film by committee.

The balances involved in respectful collaboration are delicate but won't be a problem for the person who finds his or her function in the unit fulfilling. Not all groups behave so maturely and responsibly. Sometimes there are odd chemistries, and you must remain alert to the fact that groups react unpredictably to the pressure and intensity of filmmaking, though always in revealing ways. The director is at the center of all this and cannot necessarily control what transpires. Simultaneously an information center and parental figure, the director usually is found wanting somewhere, so prepare for sometimes having to tough it out and being unpopular. It goes with the territory.

That said, most who choose to work in documentary are fine, dedicated people. It is unwise to try to fool them or to make claims beyond your knowledge. Having authority really means being respected; it means having the humility to ask for help or advice when you genuinely need it and standing by your decisions and intuitions when you must.

A good way to develop mutual understanding is to see and discuss films together and to analyze the dailies of your own project. Television crews seldom see their own material, except on the air after editing, and thus are routinely denied the chance to learn from their mistakes. Ideally, the crew should be present at salient points during postproduction, when the growth and internal complexity of the film come under intense scrutiny. It is here, if anywhere, that the comprehensiveness of the director's work begins to show, and here too that crewmembers understand the contribution they have (or haven't) made.

As production becomes decentralized and increasingly the work of independent units specializing in particular types of subject matter, this integration of crews with the totality of authorship is increasingly common. Interestingly, this is a return to the intimate filmmaking of the early 20th century after a long period of industrialized production. For documentary, and probably for fiction too, it promises films made in a more human, individual way—which is surely a significant development.

CHAPTER 27

AUTHORSHIP

This chapter touches upon the planning process, setting expectations, and making sure you have the elements of drama. It also outlines the mysterious way in which a film assembles in your mind as you make it, disassembles itself, shifts, then reassembles in its own way and according to its own needs. This is the creative process as it applies to making films about actuality. This chapter covers

- The benefits and limits of scripting
- Defining your intentions and trying to bring them into being
- Measuring your authorial progress
- Going deeper and asking for more
- Ensuring cohesion by covering your story's needs and intentions in multiple ways
- The creative process as a mysterious spiritual journey in which your film becomes a separate entity rather than your creation

SCRIPTING

A modern documentary is an improvisation fashioned from real-life materials. To write a detailed script would rob the result of spontaneity and force participants into the role of actors. However, there are a number of nonfiction genres that involve some degree of preplanned relationship between words and images, such as the

- *Compilation* film, made from archive footage and achieving its continuity and meaning through narration, voice-over, and music
- *Nature* film
- *Science* or *medical* film
- *Travelogue*

- *Educational* film
- *Historical* or *social science* film
- *Biographical* film
- *Informational* film

Inquiry and spontaneity is not usually material to some of these genres because the factual film exists to convey information rather than open-ended inquiry, uncertainty, or ambiguity. Scripting can therefore be useful and time saving for some of these categories. Especially if you are working with given archive materials, you can plan out the film using the split-page script format shown in Figure 13–2. The script form is much favored by news, scientific, corporate, industrial, and educational sponsors, who often do not understand the more organic aspects of the creative process. Certainly it gives a highly detailed, if misleadingly final, idea of what a film will be like. The weakness of scripting is that it strives for didactic goals rather than capitalizing on the material's idiosyncrasies. Any good editor will confirm that one discovers the true potential of screen materials only after experimenting with the sound and picture materials themselves. This can greatly improve what was originally envisioned in the script.

Whenever an emotional significance arises from the interplay of words and images, as in Ken Burns' and other history films that are made from contemporary diaries, reports, photographs, and often interviews, you will always need to be guided in the editing room by the actual impact from the screen and be ready to make a myriad of significant adjustments.

In live-action documentary, scripting is limited to making a proposal and planning an intended structure to contain the materials you hope to get. You may even write a treatment to whet appetites. However, the documentary usually goes no closer to scripting than making a list of intended sequences and listing the contributions the director hopes each will make.

DEFINING AND FULFILLING YOUR INTENTIONS

The toughest demand for the director while shooting is to know whether you are fulfilling your intentions and "have a film." I want to stress that without the working hypothesis mentioned earlier to guide all aspects of your directing, you will surely be rudderless during the shoot. That carefully wrought definition of intent is *vital*.

Here is a sample of intended sequences for an imaginary film about Hans, a likable, impulsive engineer I knew who lost the battle against cancer. An overall statement would say, "These scenes must establish a German immigrant engineer's decision to sell all he has ever worked for in order to buy back his health and future."

Hans lived above his Chicago electric-motor workshop. His machine room was of staggering size and untidiness, containing many large metalworking and electrical machines. After talking with Hans and understanding his situation, a documentary director would make up a shopping list of shots and sequences annotated with their intended meaning:

Scene	Intended Meaning
Hans at shop counter, afternoon	Last normal day of business
Hans descending stairs from apartment, morning	Morning, a new day
Hans in greasy-spoon restaurant eating breakfast	Listless, sad, unresponsive to friends
He arrives at shop, walks through	Change of routine, ominous
Stands high above his silent workshop; begins to tour the metal shop; picks up one or two items	Making his last rites
Drawer with photographs emptied	Collecting, sifting through his past
Other clearing out, ending shots	Collecting, sifting through his past
Shock cut to auction: Hans stands impassively as machine after machine is auctioned	Hans stoic, numb, betrays no feeling
Check being signed	The price of his life's work
Torn papers in waste bin	Break with the past
Subjective shot, walking into building with "Mayo Clinic" sign	Feeling what it is like to enter as a frightened, sick person
Voice-over: receptionist greeting him, telling him his room is ready, etc.	

These ideas are based on what the director can reasonably expect Hans to do and feel. The list shows not just expected shots but what feeling and information are desired from each, and what impact the various brief scenes should have on the audience, both factually and emotionally, as the story builds. The Hans film, treated as a script, looks too rigid and locked down. But it's only a safety net, something to remind the director what to look for and what to expect, and to get a decent range of material. It is a resource, not a straitjacket.

MEASURING PROGRESS

Keep your intentions clear and handy so that you can make running checks. Keep nothing in your head that can be dumped onto paper. During the shoot, you generally suffer gnawing doubts just when you are supposed to be feeling "creative." This, of course, is nothing you dare show anybody. But if you define ahead of time what story points you must make and nail down what you need from each sequence, you are directing from a plan of campaign and can breathe easier. Now, at any juncture, you can assess whether you have won or lost the individual battles. This is made hard only because you are usually *under*whelmed by what takes place before the camera. Later, seeing the dailies, you usually find more in them than you imagined.

DIGGING BELOW THE SURFACE

When directing, it is important to delegate everything you can because if you micromanage your crew, you will be too involved in busywork to see "subtext" in each situation—the real meaning lying below the surface and hidden from all but the dedicated observer. Often, if not always, there are hints of something else imminent, some other unacknowledged truth just under the surface. Be alert and ready to back your instincts. Just leaving the camera running after the end of something may tip the balance and make it emerge. A few words of side coaching from you might steer the scene toward the confrontation you strongly sense wants to happen.

Side coaching means that you interpolate, at a static moment in the scene, a verbal suggestion or instruction, such as "Richard, try asking her what she really means." If your instinct is right, the real magic happens, and the genie comes out of the bottle. You can best trigger this by asking yourself the following:

- What life roles are these people playing?
- What dramatic characters do they remind me of?
- What human truth is being played out?
- What metaphor sums up what is happening here?

Metaphysical questioning makes you search for the more universal but invisible event in progress. In the Hans film, you see him selling his life's collection of tools and getting rid of memorabilia before entering a hospital. Sad but necessary, you think. But to go no deeper is to miss the point. What he is really doing is daring and desperate: betting everything in one last convulsive gamble. He is not letting go of his past but destroying it, as if to plead with the gods, "If I let go everything I've ever loved, will you let me live a little longer?"

A man is bargaining with the devil that clutches at his coat tails. As soon as you realize this, you know that he is a latter-day Dr. Faustus. Now you know what mood you want to create throughout, and how you will shoot his workshop machinery to show the power that he abandons for the white temple of regeneration.

The documentary director's enemy is the passive, uncritical habit of accepting life's surfaces as "what is." The person who best directs films is the person who treats life's superficialities as a cunning deception, a mask to be peeled away in the search for deeper meanings. We do this automatically when our lives are threatened with massive change or loss. Practice by treating each new event as a scene hiding a profoundly significant meaning that you must extract. It takes great effort to wrest meaning in this way, but anyone who has ever buried a loved one knows how much in life we let pass unexamined and unlived, and how it rears up when it's too late to change anything.

Making films demands that you live consciously. It requires that you think in terms of juxtaposition, irony, and comparison. This means that you actively create meaning around you instead of being a passive bystander. Because you are working in a highly allusive medium, your audience is already attuned by decades of film history to expect metaphorical and metaphysical overtones, so people are waiting to see what you can do. You must work overtime with your imagination to find the poetry behind the raw material of life, most particularly because the camera itself deals with externals and surface banality.

How do you get beyond recorded realism? As in poetry, you do it by juxtaposing materials and creating a provocative antiphony. First you do it mentally, and then you do it with the camera and editing equipment. Look for the contradictions in your subject and make sure his or her dialectics are well evidenced. By dialectics I mean the opposing polarities of action, opinion, and will that set image against image, person against person, movement against movement, idea against idea, and the parts of a person against himself. These are the spars—the pressures and tensions, often insoluble and irresolvable—that stand like bridge construction in a fog of banality.

COVER IMPORTANT ASPECTS MORE THAN ONCE

Be doubtful, and during shooting cover vital points in more than a single way so that later you can choose the best. When I filmed conscientious objectors from World War I, I thought I would find one man whose story could stand as an analog for them all. But it was a leaderless movement that downplayed its own heroism. I found no single person with more than fragments of the total experience, so I ended up doing detailed interviews with some 20 men and women to profile the movement and its underground support. No individual prevailed, so on the screen I gave equal voice to all. Because I shot several accounts of many incidents, I was able to choose the best, or combine them. It was a gamble that came off because the texture of voices, faces, and photographs was simple and appropriate for a leaderless, self-effacing movement.

RAISING THE STAKES AND ENSURING THE CONFRONTATION

Make yourself look at what the main characters have at risk, what it is they are trying to accomplish, get, or do. Do you have that properly covered? Without materially altering the situation, can you raise the stakes by ensuring that your protagonist confronts what he is trying to overcome?

Suppose your main character gets fired from his job. Does he confront the manager by seeking an explanation on camera or only talk about doing it? Can you legitimately suggest he go through with this? And if you know he will have the hardest time disclosing to his father that he was fired, can you shoot that too? Can you suggest that he dare to be assertive with his father—more so than usually? Can you ask him in an interview to search his own experience for the reasons he was let go?

There are ethical dilemmas in every situation in which you ask someone to sail close to the wind. Are you trying to document what he would do, were no film being made about him, or are you filming his best efforts at struggling with the actual issues in his life? Are you intensifying what he truly faces, or beginning to create a new set of issues entirely?

THE SPIRITUAL JOURNEY

Authorship sometimes requires not only judicious pressures to initiate what is waiting to happen but also its opposite—ceding control of the piece at certain points to an amorphous but vibrant sense of what is true. This happens most during editing. You feel a certain awe when an assembled piece begins insistently making its own demands, telling you, its creator, how it wants to be. Parents will recognize this situation. Like maturing children in relation to their parents, your films each turn out to have their own nature, idiosyncrasies, and integrity. Each will want to make its own decisions and to exist autonomously. It is a shock and a delight to see them take wing, each differently.

Some of this will happen while shooting. You will also find yourself occasionally in a state of wonderment and making a similar capitulation. A different truth than you expected is emerging about a certain character or a certain situation, and you must either ignore it or let it guide you into the unknown. For this reason, Marcel Ophuls limits research so he "will be surprised." He wants to shoot something open and developing rather than laboriously fulfill a blueprint of prior conclusions. Thus, documentary filmmaking sometimes embraces the mystery of existence. You put authority, identity, and career in jeopardy, but if you do not respond to those emerging, elusive truths, your crew (at least) will realize it and respect you less, and may ask you why you walked away from the challenge.

Committing to this search for deeper truth makes you a sort of Everyman undergoing a spiritual journey. A challenge may always prove to be the devil in disguise, throwing a seductive temptation to trip you up, or it may be the angel of truth, challenging you to follow her footsteps to an unknown destination.

As a documentarian, you search the world for the freestanding counterparts to your own experience. Finding them, you can communicate how life really is—without any need for self-portraiture.

CHAPTER 28

PROJECTS: ADVANCED PRODUCTION

Practically all the documentary techniques in use to record the human condition are covered by the few basic project categories in this chapter. Carrying out these assignments will build an excellent bank of experience to make you ready for more complex subject matter. They will also pose many of the ethical problems that face documentarians. These should form an important part of any discussion at your screenings.

Most filmmakers mix forms and methods of acquisition according to purpose, taste, and the situation in hand; however, these assignments confine you to relatively pure examples, so you gain experience with each approach separately.

AN INVITATION TO DEMONSTRATE AUTHORSHIP

Not all the practice projects support high authorial aims, but many can, so be inventive and use them to further your authorial interests. Make each project show some aspect of life that you care about, however small. Try to make it show something and say something that will surprise and touch the viewer.

To give yourself a running start, always first construct a working hypothesis for what you intend to shoot:

A. In life I believe that (your philosophy regarding life principle that your film will exemplify) _____

B. My film will show this in action by exploring (situation) _____

C. My film's main conflict is between _____ and _____

D. My film's point of view (POV), or POV character, will be _____

E. My film's structure probably will be determined by _____

F. The subject and POV suggest a style that is _____

G. Ultimately I want the audience to feel _____

H. . . . and to understand that _____

When the assignment permits, shoot material that does not just *denote* events but can be edited to *connote* poetic meanings. You will get ideas for special imagery, symbols, metaphors, and ironic juxtapositions through first making a concentrated, astute survey of the enclosed world your film is going to represent. By aiming for a poetic rather than flat, naturalistic reflection, you will begin to see the significant detail that you can heighten. This will take thoughtful and inventive camerawork, and directing with a strong sense of purpose. Such intentions, put into action while shooting, will have their rewards later—for unexpected possibilities—and new and telling juxtapositions will show up as you edit the final screen statement.

I want to emphasize the importance of handheld camerawork, with its emphasis on capturing spontaneity and making an effective dramatic analysis on the fly. Too many documentaries are foreclosed, take no risks, and end up being a demonstration of knowledge and containment. Exciting films emerge from a self-exposure to risk and real-life drama.

NEGATIVE LEARNING

Much learning in filmmaking is by negatives ("If only I had done . . ." or "Why didn't I think of . . ."). This is normal in a medium where so much is experimental. The process is long enough to allow you to have a better second idea before you have completed the first. People are apt to think this is some kind of failing, but all energy expended in experiment is forward movement. Of course, you will have your successes too, so be ready to contain yourself during the occasional attack of joy and amazement.

PROJECT OVERVIEW

Here is an overview of the assignments outlining the authorial purpose of each.

1. *Direct or Observational Cinema*
   Sometimes called the fly-on-the-wall approach, the camera intrudes as little as possible. Aiming to give us access to people and situations that is transparent and unobstructed, direct cinema makes us feel we are watching life uninterrupted and unmanipulated.
   A. Using a Tripod-Mounted Camera (gives a steady, settled, secure view of the action)
      Project 28-1: Dramatizing a Location
      Project 28-2: Three-Person Conversation (Interior)
   B. Handheld Camera (gives an inquisitive, adaptive, spontaneous, questing view of the action)
      Project 28-3: Covering a Process for Ellipsis Editing
      Project 28-4: Covering a Conversation (Exterior)
      Project 28-5: Mobile Coverage of Complex Action

2. *Cinéma Vérité or Participatory Cinema*
   In participatory cinema, filmmakers acknowledge that their presence is part of the subjects' reality, and they may question, challenge, and seek information or catalyze responses in a number of ways.
   A. Using a Tripod-Mounted Camera (gives a steady, settled, secure view of the action)
      Project 28-6: Interview in Depth
      Project 28-7: Two-Person Conversation with Conflict
   B. Handheld Camera (gives an inquisitive, adaptive, spontaneous, questing view of the action)
      Project 28-8: Five-Minute Story While Participant is Busy
      Project 28-9: A One-Shot Catalyzed Event
      Project 28-10: *Vox Populi* Interviews with Metaphoric Counterpoint
3. *Reflexive Cinema*
   The reflexive approach includes references to the filmmaking process in the film, and a stage farther is self-reflexivity, when you can even make the autobiographical experience of the filmmaker(s) central to the film. You can use archive footage, and during your own filming you can use either observational or participatory modes.
   Project 28-11: Self-Portrait
   Project 28-12: Observing the Observer
   Project 28-13: Story, Question, and Suggestion
4. *Compilation and Essay Cinema*
   These highly constructed and interpretative forms are common with any didactic film where the purpose is expository. What is interesting is seeing that you can use imagery and recordings in highly plastic ways. Your ability to write or speak a narration, or to construct one from letters, diaries, and other archival sources, will determine much of the film's final impact. If you enjoy writing, you will like this type of filmmaking.
   Project 28-14: Making History
   Project 28-15: National Anthem
   Project 28-16: Video Letter
5. *Eclectic Cinema*
   Because most films are a mix of techniques, the last classification is reserved for the ultimate film in your course and permits you to mix and match as you and your advisers judge necessary for your project.
   Project 28-17: Eclectic Cinema

PRODUCTION PROJECTS

The assignments that follow will be a easier and more rewarding experience if you review Chapters 3 to 8 in Part 2, Aesthetics and Authorship. The assessment criteria for all the projects are printed in Appendix 1. They can be used not only to assess a finished project but as reminder lists to help you remember all the aspects and layers that an audience expects. In Chapter 38, Projects: Post production, there are four editing projects that you simultaneously apply to the projects in this chapter. The appropriate one is noted under the Editing or Assessment headings below.

DIRECT OR OBSERVATIONAL CINEMA (TRIPOD)

Project 28-1: Dramatizing a Location   (Courtesy of Netherlands Film and TV Academy, Amsterdam)[1]

This 5-minute screen time assignment is shot silent but uses music and optional nonsync sound effects. Using a silent camera focuses makes you focus on the narrative, symbolic, or metaphoric possibilities of action and imagery.

Goals are to

- Conduct in-depth research and make extensive notes
- Define necessary exposition
- "Script" the film from research notes
- Practice unintrusive coverage of uncontrolled events
- Shoot to enable condensing a lengthy set of events
- Capture the unexpected and spontaneous
- Edit down to a brief version
- Use music
- Make a statement about human life through your film

Suggested subjects: Any well-populated locale with a cyclical life (train or bus station, restaurant kitchen, street market, construction site, market, café, plaza, hairdresser's shop)

Action: Using tripod camerawork, and only the lighting and sound indigenous to your location, shoot materials for a 5-minute film that compresses into shorthand form the feel and mood of the location over a time span of at least 4 hours.

Film example: Street scenes in Martin Bell's study of Seattle street children, *Streetwise* (1985) or most of Godfrey Reggio's environmental symphony about life out of balance, *Koyaanisqatsi* (1983)

Steps:

1. Pick a visually interesting public location with a strong cyclical life.

2. Spend at least a day just observing and listening. You might want to zero in on a single character associated with the place, or depict several. Make notes of everything that strikes you, paying special attention to expository detail (that is, what you must show to establish essentials of the location for your audience). You probably will be amazed by the number of evocative sounds you can use in a sound "score."

3. Work over your notes and select the best images and actions to show the life, people, and spirit of your location. From these, write a shot list "script" that

[1] This and other exercises attributed to European film schools can be found in Klaus Stanjek and Renate Gompper, eds, *Teaching Documentary in Europe* (Berlin: Vistas, 1995).

implies a structure and dramatic curve. Pay special attention to depicting the beginning, middle, and end of each cycle in the location's life.

4. Show your instructor or peer the script and discuss the music you have chosen as well as any intended sound effects. Do *not* use a song because its words will become a narration and short-circuit the test of your pictorial narrative skills. Aim to make the cyclical events of a period (usually a day) into a narrative that economically and wittily depicts character, time, and place.

5. Shoot your scripted shots plus any "gifts" that come your way.

Editing: See Project 38-4 for tips. Edit according to the script and the opportunities or limitations of your rushes. Show the rough cut to a trial audience for feedback, and make your fine cut exactly 5 minutes long.

Assessment criteria: See Appendix 1, Project 28-1

Discussion: How was the piece structured? Was there a build in intensity or other structuring device? Any characters evoked? What mood or emotion did the piece arouse?

Project 28-2: Three-Person Conversation (Interior) The challenge here is to stage-manage a conversation that looks spontaneous but is well structured and has high production values.

Goals are to

- Cover a group interaction from a single camera position, much as television does
- Block participants and light the setting for a natural look and pleasing compositions
- Use such smooth camerawork and editing that the audience is unaware of the filmmaking process
- Use the director's prerogative to shape and direct the conversation if it breaks down
- Shoot inserts and cutaways as editing coverage
- Shoot sound presence as filler for any gaps in editing
- Condense and restructure the conversation in editing
- Preserve natural speech rhythms and make conversation develop satisfyingly

Suggested subject: Find a topic of conversation that your three people can naturally drop into. It's useful if there can be some disagreement, as this provides some development, tension, and possibly resolution too.

Action: Here the camera must pan, recompose, and choose the appropriate shot size, which may include one, two, or three persons. How you set up the group will affect how natural they feel and look. The director will need to start the conversation going. Warn participants that you will side coach (give directions from offstage) and that they should not break focus and look at you if they hear your voice. If you want to preserve spontaneity, you may want to give them the discussion subject just before shooting. Use side coaching whenever you need to stimulate or redirect the conversation (example: "Susan, ask Warren why tourists in buses irritate him so much.").

Coverage: Shoot 10 to 12 minutes in preparation for a 4-minute final screen length. Shoot *plenty* of safety cutaways on each person listening to both of the others. To get these, let the conversation run past completion and signal the camera operator to shoot prearranged types of cutaway or reaction close-ups.

Lighting: Because this is such a controlled environment, try for a distinct lighting mood. Make lighting look "motivated," that is, natural to the setting.

Sound: Find a mike position out of frame that will cover all three speakers equally, or use a fish pole that can pan the mike just above or below the frame (watch out for telltale mike shadows). Don't forget to shoot presence track.

Film examples: The interior union discussions in Barbara Kopple's *Harlan County, USA* (1976) or the motel group scenes in the Maysles Brothers' *Salesman* (1968)

Editing: Use Project 38-2 Guidelines.

Assessment criteria: See Appendix 1, Project 28-2

Discussion: How natural were the participants in the discussion? How much editing was there, and how much did you think the discussion was restructured? How would you adapt this technique for your own use?

DIRECT OR OBSERVATIONAL CINEMA (HANDHELD)

Project 28-3: Covering a Process for Ellipsis Editing   Originally "ellipsis" was a literary expression signifying words omitted in a sentence. Applied to film it means abridging a long process to convey its essentials briefly, something fundamental in documentary because Life is often long and boring, and it must be abbreviated to become Art, which is supposed to be short and fascinating. The camera is handheld and responds to the situation, as an interested observer might.

Goals are to

- Shoot uncontrolled action with a handheld camera
- Cover the action with all appropriate camera angles to facilitate editing
- Shorten a 20-minute process (for instance) to exactly 3 minutes of screen time

Suggested subject, option 1: A car drives up and stops, and the driver gets out to inspect the tires. One of the tires must be defective because he or she changes the wheel. Driver gets back in and drives away. During the whole action, the driver does not look at or talk to the camera, and he or she must carry out actions as though nobody were present. The crew may not direct the driver in any way. This is a catch-as-catch-can exercise in which director and crew have no one control over the action.

Suggested subject, option 2: A game of skill and visible change such as Jenga®, in which two people build a tower of wood blocks, with the loser being the unfortunate one to make the move that brings the tower toppling. Lots of skill and tension.

Action: Walk through the likely actions, and then draw a ground plan showing the anticipated camera positions. Plan framings that reveal what is significant through relatedness, that is, *by juxtaposing major aspects of the situation* rather than framings that separate and isolate the elements so that you have to relate them through editing. Cover the action in *one unbroken take*, and shoot with editing in mind because this will be the material for a vital editing exercise. While shooting on the fly, make sure to get plenty of close-ups, cut-ins, and motivated cutaways.

Film example: Most of Ira Wohl's *Best Boy* (1979) is shot with long, unbroken takes because of the unpredictable nature of the subject, as is Joe Berlinger and Bruce Sinofsky's *Brother's Keeper* (1992).

Editing: Aim for a 2-minute edited result. See Project 38-3 for editing instructions.

Assessment criteria: See Appendix 1, Project 28-3 Assessment. You also can use Project 38-3 Assessment to evaluate the editing.

Discussion: What did you learn about covering an action in an unbroken take that is intended for severe editing? Did the filmmakers include incidental action that was funny or told us about the characters? How well would a first-time viewer understand the whole action from its abbreviated version?

Project 28-4: Covering a Conversation (Exterior)   Here the camera is an interested witness as two people wait for transportation and fill time in conversation. It will help if you can agree on a topic of conversation that has some tension in it. The camera must reveal the situation they are in and the characteristics of each person as they emerge during the exchange.

Goals are to

- Cover a spontaneous conversation between two people using handheld camerawork
- Relax them so that they speak naturally and in an unforced companionship
- Not intercede, and keep the camera running throughout
- Make each camera movement usable
- Provide a full palette of coverage to enable elegant editing
- Respond to conversation content with appropriately differing coverage
- Set the scene (waiting for bus/train/whatever) and make use of the setting and situation
- Edit to a brief version of the essentials
- Restructure in editing to make best use of any dramatic content

Suggested subjects: Any topic of mutual interest. Because they probably will be class or family members, a topic with some disagreement shouldn't be too difficult to find.

Action: Once the interchange begins, your continuously running camera must cover all aspects of the conversation and respond to its changing focus and implications. The speakers continue until the bus/train/whatever arrives. Using a handheld camera and wide-angle lens only; keep the audience at the conversation's psychological center. To capture material that edits well, pan from composition to composition, and relocate the camera position physically near or far from the subject to create sufficiently varied shots and image sizes.

Special points:

1. During preparation, sketch a ground plan to help you figure out what angles are necessary and what cutaways might be legitimized by POVs and likely eyeline shifts.

2. The camera footage should present an "edited" look that shows reactions, follows eyelines, and implies the conversation's subtext. Ideally you should be able to watch the unedited camera original with complete enjoyment.

3. When making a camera movement from one static position to another, decide first where you are going and then go there in one nicely executed movement. Create positive movements from one composition to the next, with appropriate periods of static "hold" on each. Commonly this is handled as a series of drifting, wandering movements (called *firehosing*) that communicate indecision to the audience and land your editor with an impossible task. We never observe like this in life—unless drunk.

4. Be sure to shoot an all-purpose "any sync" shot (an establishing shot, where mouth movements are either hidden or too distant to be properly seen). This you will hold in reserve to help you get around any unforeseen cutting difficulties.

5. Remember to show that your people are waiting for something. This should be established visually rather than verbally ("Ah, this is a chilly night for us to be standing here in our woolly hats waiting for the no. 92 bus.").

Try to shoot

- 8 to 10 minutes of continuous take; you can try more than one version
- Big close-up (BCU) single shots
- Two over-the-shoulder (OS) well-framed two-shots, one to favor each person
- One or two low-angle shots
- Smooth, usable transitions between all shots
- Transitions that respond to the speed and rhythm of exchanges
- Camera movements motivated by subjects' movements and eyeline changes
- Inserts, cutaways and/or reaction shots to help editing
- Sound according to mike operator's different priorities as he or she keeps out of frame

Film example: Any well-shot action documentary, such as Barbara Kopple's *American Dream* (1990), or any Fred Wiseman or Maysles Brothers film

Editing: Use Project 38-3 Guidelines **to edit into a smooth 4-minute sequence.**

Assessment criteria: See Appendix 1, Project 28-4, and for the editing use Project 38-3 Assessment.

Discussion: How natural were the two conversationalists? Could you understand what they were waiting for, and how they got there? Did each person emerge as a distinct character?

Project 28-5: Mobile Coverage of Complex Action   This is a challenging assignment that will need practice but should prove a rewarding demonstration of your coordination. The following instructions are addressed to whomever operates the camera, because it's impossible to direct this kind of subject-driven cinema.

Goals are to

- Learn to shoot coverage that is unstoppable and entirely subject driven
- Control the camera while navigating doors, steps, getting into a car
- Do a walking tracking shot, overtaking the subject to shoot as you walk backward
- Handle exposure changes resulting in going from interior to exterior then to interior of car
- Continue to shoot a subject no matter what he or she does
- Suppress all signs of difficulty in picture and sound shooting

Suggested subject: The continuous-take shooting follows a subject who talks to camera, starting indoors, then walking out of the front door and down some steps, along a path to a car, and continuing to talk as he or she starts up the motor and begins to drive.

Action (instructions for camera operator): Start inside building, with the camera static as your subject walks up. Pan with him or her, then start to follow as the subject walks through a door to the outside. As the subject walks down path, overtake so that we see his or her face while he or she walks toward a car. Then let the subject overtake you so that you are again following as the subject moves toward the driver's side of a four-door car. Keeping the driver framed, open the rear-passenger side door with your free hand and slide into the car as the driver gets in. By shooting over the car roof and sinking the camera as you both get in, you can completely avoid showing your own door opening and closing. Hold onto the driver as the car starts, then pan forward to show the road ahead. Hold for 15 seconds, then cut.

Coverage: If the action allows, shoot feet walking, POV of door knob opening—anything in addition to the specified camera angle changes that will facilitate ellipsis editing later.

Special points:

1. Open your non-viewfinder eye occasionally to see where you are going (or if you expect to fall over something . . .). Using both eyes for different purposes is a chameleon skill that dedicated camera operators acquire, but expect nausea at the beginning.
2. Walking backward means someone must provide safety guidance through hand touch to the camera operator. The director or mike operator can do this if there is no camera assistant.
3. Your subject should talk to the camera throughout. Suggested conversation subjects include an interesting challenge, a trial of skills, an accident, a worst moment, or a relationship that had to be abandoned (fits metaphorically with action).
4. Use onboard video camera mike, or, if you want real choreographic fun, use a mike operator.

Film examples: The beginning motorcycle sequence of Peter Watkins' classic *The War Game* (1965), the long mobile coverage of prison routines in Frederick

Wiseman's *Titicut Follies* (1967), or any of the home improvement programs on television, which often have stunning handheld coverage of action processes.

Editing: Use Project 38-3 Guidelines.

Assessment criteria: See Appendix 1, Project 28-5 Assessment. Use Project 38-3 Assessment for edited version.

Discussion: When was the camerawork driven by the action, and when were you aware of a camera struggling to keep up? Did any intrusions (such as gasping and curses) intrude via the sound track?

CINÉMA VÉRITÉ OR PARTICIPATORY CINEMA (TRIPOD)

This kind of documentary cinema acknowledges implicitly that filming is taking place and that truth sometimes is catalyzed during interaction between the participants and the director or the crew.

Project 28-6: Interview in Depth   This project is for developing on-camera interviewing skills, but informal interviewing can be used to generate an informal, natural-sounding narration or voice-over. People sound natural whenever they are working to inform or convince a listener.

Goals are to conduct an interview that will

- Stand alone in an edited version without the interviewer's questions
- Be well recorded with minimal ambience so that it can be used without picture as voice-over or interior monologue
- Evoke memories and feelings in the interviewee
- Provoke the interviewee into self-examination
- Take the interviewee over some personal threshold of realization that requires effort and courage in you both
- Be shot in different image sizes, allowing flexible editing later with minimal cutaways

Suggested subject and preparation: Tell your interviewee in advance only that you want to ask about a pivotal event in his or her life. If you preinterview, discuss subject matter only to the degree that you sense where to go, what is involved, and what is at stake. Concentrate on listening for the underlying issues, and be sure to keep probing questions until the interview proper. Set the interview in one of the person's own environments, such as a place of work, kitchen, study, or whatever else seems appropriate. Try to make the setting comment on the individual. Perhaps you can revisit the site of the pivotal event itself, and this will trigger feelings and memories for your participant. Brief the camera operator on three basic shot sizes and compositions and agree on a signal system so that you can direct camera changes.

Interviewing: Be sure to elicit whole statements; you will want to cut out your own voice later. Respond facially but not vocally, or you will interject your voice into the interview and make it hard or impossible to edit. Before you begin, tell the interviewee

- Not to worry about making any mistakes or corrections, because anything can be edited out
- That you may interrupt if he or she gets away from the subject or if you want more information
- That you want the information in your question included in the answer so that you can edit out questions

Steps and special points:

1. Make this a lit interior and place the participant in a revealing relationship to his or her setting.
2. Keep the participant away from walls to minimize unwanted shadows.
3. To experiment with the effect onscreen, interview either from under the lens or from beside the camera, but not both, unless you want to see how weird it looks to mix eyelines.
4. As the interviewer, listen for freestanding sentence beginnings and restart the answer if any requires the question to make sense. No overlaps are permissible between your voice and the response because they would force you to keep the interviewer's voice, which usually is unnecessary and intrusive.
5. Most interviewees will need repeated reminders to include the question's substance in their answer.
6. Most missed opportunities occur when the interviewer uncritically accepts generalizations instead of pressing for illustrative stories, examples, and specifics.
7. Listen not only for what you expect but also for the unexpected hiding out among the subtexts.
8. Remember to shoot sound presence.
9. After the interview and before you leave, prepare the ground for a return visit in case you later discover this is necessary.

    Film example: Michael Apted's *28 Up* (1984) or any Errol Morris film, because he relies heavily on interviews
    Editing: Use Project 38-1 Guidelines.
    Assessment Criteria: See Appendix 1, Project 28-6. Use Project 38-1 Assessment for the editing.
    Discussion: How deeply did this interview go? How much did the interviewer demand and how much did the subject give? Were the image size changes appropriate, and was the structuring of the interview satisfying? Was any important expository information missing?

Project 28-7: Two-Person Conversation with Conflict This is a conversation between two participants with the director's presence eradicated in the edited version. This is a little like Project 28-2: Three Person Conversation (Interior), except that here the director takes a more active and manipulative role. The idea is to provoke a conversation around the participants' own strong difference of perception or opinion and to get material that allows you to shape the conversation during editing around the emotional differences. Once the camera is running, the participants may self-consciously avoid the very issue they know you want them to discuss, so you may need to use side coaching to focus their attention. This is an ethically treacherous relationship because the director-as-catalyst can seem like the director-as-screenwriter to the participants.

Goals are to

- Find, catalyze, and present a human interaction
- Use ingenuity to film a conversation with conflicting viewpoints that, nevertheless, ends up looking spontaneous
- Use archive material such as family film or video, or news footage if disagreement is about a public event
- Shoot material that is elegantly lit, composed, and shot
- Shoot clean, faultless sound
- Portray a topic through an interaction that incorporates opposing and subjective viewpoints
- Impose your desire to put a spirited disagreement on film without forcing your participants into the role of actors

Suggested subject and steps:

- Locate and preinterview two people who know each other well, but avoid family members if they won't go along with the degree of manipulation this exercise requires.
- Get them to pick a shared event in their lives about which each feels very differently and for which there is visual documentation (news or TV footage, photos, home movie or video footage of a holiday, wedding, reunion, construction project, etc.).
- Note what topics this imagery might support so that you can direct their attention to particular subject matter for which visuals exist.
- Avoid catalyzing valuable interaction before the camera is present ("No, please don't talk about that now. Keep it till we have the camera present!").

After research and before shooting,

- Write up a working hypothesis
- Get feedback about it from an objective and critical colleague
- Use hypothesis to determine what expository information and what conflict your piece must evidence
- Determine how to direct them so that you best exploit the visual documentation
- When you've written the best, clearest statement of intention, shoot.

Because this is participatory, not observational, cinema, you must be ready to catalyze without violating credibility or your own code of ethics. Prepare the subjects to *focus on what they disagree about* and be ready to intercede and redirect them should they stray too far from what you want. Make sure they cover everything you thought significant during research. Aim to shoot a 15-minute interaction. You should

- Arrange the setting so that the frame is "packed" and interesting
- Light the set interestingly and credibly
- Place your subjects so that the camera can easily see either and is not forced to make awkward movements (example: sit the shorter person on a cushion so that both heads are at same level when you want to pan from one to the other)
- Do/say whatever is necessary to make their interchange become natural
- Make sure the known differences of emotion and perception emerge strongly, and be ready to intercede with side coaching if they do not
- Get them to *talk to each other* rather than to the camera
- Shoot from *one camera position only*, panning and zooming shoot different angles and image sizes on each person
- Direct the camera to follow the scene's psychological focus throughout
- Shoot enough natural-looking reaction shots on each person
- Cover any motivated cut-ins or cutaways after the main shooting
- Make videotape of any pictures, 8 mm film, graphics, or family video that would legitimately expand your interview's purview
- Take care to get good, clean sound with similar levels on both speakers
- Shoot sound presence to fill sound gaps during editing

Film examples: The doctor's office sequence in Ira Wohl's *Best Boy* (1979) or any of the group scenes in Joan Churchill and Nick Broomfield's *Soldier Girls* (1981)

Editing: Use the guidelines in Project 38-2 to edit down to a 5- to 6-minute piece, using inserts, reaction shots, and cutaways to help restructure and condense their interaction. Aim to produce a seamlessly clean sound mix with no bumps in level or quality. Because you are trying to shoot studio-quality sound, try using your editing software's equalization (EQ). This lets you set what are in effect tone controls for each track (containing all the, say, medium shot) so that unwanted differences in acoustical quality can more easily be made to match. Lay all sound sections from the same mike position on a single track, so any equalization you impose will apply to all that mike placing. If you have three mike positions, you will need three separate tracks.

Assessment criteria: See Appendix 1, Project 28-7 Assessment. Use Project 38-2 Assessment for the edited version.

Discussion: When did the discussion look natural, when contrived? How well was the topic of disagreement explored? How well was the discussion condensed and restructured? What did you learn about the character and issues of each participant?

CINÉMA VÉRITÉ OR PARTICIPATORY CINEMA (HANDHELD)

Project 28-8: Five-Minute Story While Participant is Busy This project capitalizes on the integrity of paying unbroken attention to someone while he or she is telling a story. It presumes that the environment and the participant's activity are an important counterpoint.

Goals are to

- Plan an approach and cover a storyteller in one unbroken take, with no recourse to editing
- Exploit the possibilities of an activity conducted in a meaningful location as revealing of the storyteller and a counterpoint to the story
- Use a true story, but give the participant freedom to tell it (even embroider it) according to taste

Research/preparation: Pick an articulate, interesting person with a story he or she can tell engagingly, but don't allow the story to be told in any depth until you shoot. Do a preinterview and work with the storyteller to find an appropriate and interesting space where you can shoot. Discuss what he or she could be doing while talking (laundry, making a meal, servicing a bike, laying out a dead body . . .).

Planning: Figure out

- Your working hypothesis
- Likely special areas or imagery that you want to highlight
- How much time you will allot for each intended stage of the story
- The likely image size changes, camera angles, and movements
- What you want to accomplish overall
- Special signals to be worked out with crew to cover exigencies

Shoot the story in one, unbroken 5-minute take, using an offscreen prompt to signal, say, "2 minutes left" as a countdown for the participant. Shoot more than one take to see what happens in different versions. This project explores collaboration between a participant and the film crew.

Film examples: Parts of Ross McElwee's *Sherman's March* (1989) and the rabbits section of Michael Moore's *Roger and Me* (1989)

Assessment criteria: See Appendix 1, Project 28-8 Assessment.

Discussion: When is this technique useful, and how much can be agreed in advance?

Project 28-9: A One-Shot, Catalyzed Event This project covers anything unexpected where the camera covers the POV character initiating events and includes ambush journalism.

Goals are to

- Plan and direct a complete event in a single take
- Think on your feet and make good use of the unexpected

- Prepare someone to improvise an interesting event or series of events for 7 to 10 minutes

Action: Using a mobile camera, record events in an unbroken 7- to 10-minute take. The POV character must be prepared to make things happen. For instance, during Project VISIONS (a European documentary workshop), a camera crew followed a woman into a conspicuously all-male Turkish café in Berlin and shot what happened when she asked why there were no women. To carry off this assignment, you will need a strong idea with plans to handle foreseeable contingencies. It requires the abilities both to improvise and to bring events to a conclusion in the allotted time span. The men in the café were, by the way, rather surprised at a film unit appearing, but they explained courteously that women were not forbidden, they simply "didn't want to go in such a place," which is why, they said, there were only men present. This could have been confrontational but was handled on both sides with tact and enjoyment.

Film examples: Jean Rouch's seminal *Chronicle of a Summer* (1961) and Werner Herzog's shattering and inspiring piece about the deaf blind, *Land of Silence and Darkness* (1971)

Assessment criteria: See Appendix 1, Project 28-9.

Discussion: What boundaries should you set for documenting intrusive action? When is it justified and when is it unethical? What are the practical difficulties? When is it most appropriate to documentary?

Project 28-10: *Vox Populi* Interviews with Metaphoric Counterpoint   This is a very challenging, participatory cinema assignment that requires you to think on your feet and have a good grasp of both technical and authorial skills. *Vox populi* (voice of the people) is a montage technique for creating a "Greek chorus" of faces and voices. By using it you can

- Broaden the cast of a film that is narrowly focused on a few people
- Demonstrate where a main character belongs in relation to mass opinion
- Remind your audience of the diverse character and opinion of the common person
- Demonstrate norms, received wisdom, or dissident voices just as you please
- Remind us how the individual exists fallibly within a web of prejudices and transient, socially conditioned norms

Topic: Pick a subject area in which you think public awareness is likely to be searching, divided, or prejudiced. Avoid topics made over-familiar by television unless you feel you can shoot something that exposes and critiques commonplace ideas.

Counterpoint: Plan to shoot a separate activity (not just cutaways) that, when intercut with *vox pop* footage, will act as a metaphoric counterpoint. Make sure your counterpoint story is visual and develops through a beginning, middle, and end.

Hypothesis: Decide the main conflict you expect to emerge, then write a hypothesis by filling in the gaps. Conflicts may exist between people, within the individual, or between the individual and some other force, such as Nature.

Interviewing: What one asks and how one asks it will exert a great influence on the replies you get. Confusing, unfocused, or unchallenging questions do not give the interviewee much to push against, but live issues presented from a provocative, devil's-advocate position can release a tirade.

Using *only four major questions,* be ready to probe the interviewee to get a satisfactory response to each. The key questions must be brief, directive, in the vernacular, and hard to misinterpret—even for the occasional person of limited intelligence. Your object is not to produce "balanced reporting" or to elicit a body of data by neutral questioning. It is, first, to tap into public feeling and opinion and, second, through responsible editing *to make an overall statement of your own* about the issues at stake.

Posing the same few questions often yields usefully predictable results, but sometimes you meet unusual and original responses or learn that your hypothesis was either wrong or incomplete. It is quite normal, as you learn from experience, to alter the questions or even the thrust of the whole undertaking in the face of what you discover. Because your edited presentation will have no reporter or introduction, you will need to elicit from your interviewees all necessary factual framework if your audience is to fully understand the issue at hand.

Because the street interview is immediate rather than built on a lengthy two-way relationship, it is open to unscrupulous manipulation during the interview or later in editing. This assignment raises a host of important issues about ethics and representation. How should general truths be represented? Whose POV will the audience judge them to be?

Shoot your interviews in at least two locations. One person armed with clip-board acts as the "catcher," stopping passersby to ask if they will participate. You will need a mike handler, a camera person, and of course the interviewer, whose job is to get people to really open up and be themselves. During the interviews,

- Stay informal and use the vernacular
- Pose the question again if you and your interviewee overlap, because you will want to edit out most questions
- Use only four questions, but be ready to refine or simplify them; you will learn as you go
- Listen for the subtext of each response and pursue it
- Capitalize on the idiosyncrasies of the interviewee by probing with further questioning
- Address at least two distinct socioeconomic groups
- Shoot without showing interviewer or microphone
- Use backgrounds that highlight the person's identity, if possible
- Vary backgrounds and compositions
- Using the lens at its wide-angle setting alone, move the camera to produce varying shot sizes within the interview
- Interview equally from either side of the camera to give onscreen variety
- Rotate crew members through all roles

- During the shoot, review how your hypothesis is working, and change it to match reality
- Refine and rephrase your questions as you need, or even reformulate them to evoke sharper responses

Film examples: The Emily Miller witness interview intercut with the clips from a Boston Blackie crime film in Errol Morris' *The Thin Blue Line* (1988) and the eviction sequence in Michael Moore's *Roger and Me* (1989) intercut with General Motors' celebration of Christmas, which is really parallel storytelling

Editing: Use Project 38-4 for editing guidelines. If each group member does his or her own edit, you will see how quite different sequences can emerge out of a shared experience, each expressing something of the editor. "Art," Jay Ruby has said, "contains and espouses the ideology of the artist." And, "Image makers show us their view of the world whether they mean to or not."[2] Find out for yourself!

Assessment criteria: See Appendix 1, Project 28-10 Assessment, and Project 38-4 Assessment for the editing.

Discussion: How skillfully did the interviews elicit a span of opinion and feeling attached to the chosen issue? How telling was the metaphoric material counterpointed against the interview material? Was there too much happening, or did the filmmakers keep a clear tension between the different planes of material?

REFLEXIVE CINEMA

Project 28-11: Self-Portrait   This is an autobiographical project that faces you with the problem of what to include and what to exclude. Constructing a self-portrait propels the autobiographer up to the frontiers of fiction and poses questions of balance and purpose that ought to be (and never are) equally as relevant when we portray others. Using a written narration and family records of your growing up, such as photos, film, or video, make a 5- to 8-minute self-portrait that

- Includes necessary facts concerning your growing up
- Includes a familial conflict that strongly affected you
- Reveals what is unusual about you and your family
- Ponders how you feel about your memories and the images of yourself
- Considers the values and dangers of self-representation

Even though you know your subject better than most, develop a full working hypothesis around the records you are going to use. Be prepared to narrow your film's focus because you are confined to whatever can be associated with the records your family happened to make. Records reveal the recorder quite as much as the person recorded, so be ready to explore the how and the why of the record, as well as what the record avoided or left out. Self-disclosure is difficult to do responsibly, and fascinating issues arise concerning risk, avoidance, and the distortions involved in profiling your own persona to an audience you must look in

---

[2] Jay Ruby, "The Ethics of Imagemaking," in *New Challenges for Documentary,* ed. Alan Rosenthal (Berkeley, CA: University of California Press, 1988), 308–318.

the eye. Making an autobiographical film, no matter how short, makes you more empathic to others because you subject yourself to what you expect of others when you interview them or invite them to participate in a film.

Film example: Nobody's Business (1996) by Alan Berliner and much of Deborah Hoffman's *Complaints of a Dutiful Daughter* (1995)

Editing: Use Project 38-4 Guidelines.

Assessment criteria: See Appendix 1, Project 28-11 Assessment, and Project 38-4 Assessment for the editing.

Discussion: With what ease or difficulty did the filmmaker tackle this challenge? What area of his or her life did the filmmaker choose to reveal, and what were you aware was being withheld? Did it matter? What was valuable about this project?

Project 28-12: Observing the Observer   This is a self-reflexive project in which you analyze the process of filming as you experienced it at the time, and with the benefit of hindsight.

Goals are to

- Analyze something you filmed for possible issues of ethics, manipulation, and filmmaker's responsibilities to fair play
- Construct a narration from an interview
- Develop your values concerning the abuse of power in documentary filmmaking

Take any extended human process you've covered as documentary and use it as the basis for a short film that inquires into how your input, and the camera's presence, affected what you filmed. You can freeze the action, run it in slow motion, and rerun salient moments to recreate the way a viewer might probe the screen record for cinematic insight. Instead of writing a commentary, have a perceptive friend interview you to evoke your spontaneous reactions and thoughts in relation to particular passages in the filmed material. Use this either as voice-over or as a to-camera interview. The resulting footage and verbal speculation should last 5 to 8 minutes onscreen.

Film examples: Michael Rubbo's *Sad Song of Yellow Skin* (1970) and Mark Wexler's *Me and My Matchmaker* (1996)

Editing: Use Project 38-4 Guidelines.

Assessment criteria: See Appendix 1, Project 28-12 Assessment, and Project 38-4 Assessment for the editing.

Discussion: How much depth did this inquiry achieve? What was expected and what was unexpected? How much did you learn about the filmmaker from his or her speculation about the ethical dimensions to the chosen work?

Project 28-13: Story, Question, and Suggestion   This 8- to 10-minute assignment is initially an interview you conduct as participatory cinema, upon which you build a second layer of self-inquiry and contemplation. In a third layer, you show your inner comments to the original storyteller, who then reacts to your reactions, questions, and comments.

Action: Because you probably don't have a couple of decades to try Apted's longitudinal study process (see film example following), here's a small, fast version. It should be a gold mine for connoisseurs of conceptualist humor:

1. Line up a willing participant who will answer a mildly self-revealing question that, for spontaneity, you will only reveal once the camera is running.

2. Set up equipment and participant, and ask for a true autobiographical story, 2 or 3 minutes long, that is somewhat testing of the participant's candor; for example, you might ask for a story about an occasion when the participant had to modify an undesirable aspect of his or her own personality, own up to a lie, or when he or she took something without permission.

3. View the resulting tape alone several times, develop your thoughts, then video record your questions, doubts, speculations.

4. Show both tapes to the participant and immediately afterward (or even while the tapes are running) elicit his or her reactions (making sure your voice can be edited out). Have a list of points so that you can prompt whatever significant material the participant forgets or avoids.

Film example: I know of no example with as many layers, but the seminal example is Jean Rouch and Edgar Morin's *Chronicle of a Summer* (1961). Rouch and Morin ask Parisians if they are happy, and the filmmakers and their subjects debate the making of the film as it is being made. There is also Michael Apted's masterful study of a dozen people's values, beginning when they are all 7 years old and continuing longitudinally through adulthood. The most famous version is *28 Up* (1984); in the following episodes, *35 Up* (1991) and *42 Up* (1998) participants revisit their own and Apted's earlier comments in a clear pattern of self-reflexivity.

Editing: Use Project 38-4 for guidelines. This film will collapse into a hall of mirrors unless you manage to keep the unfolding layers clear and consistent. It also can be hilariously funny. A suggested assembly is as follows:

First layer: Show your setup question, then the participant thinking of and telling the story, either in complete or abridged form. Cut to

Second layer: Reprise salient portions of the story, interpolating your comments and questions, perhaps using voice-over played on freeze frames. Cut to

Third layer: Show participant's explanations, justifications, and comments interpolated in abridged version of second layer.

Assessment criteria: See Appendix 1, Project 28-13 Assessment, and Project 38-4 Assessment for the editing.

Discussion: Seeing one person assess from a safe position the responses of another is familiar in documentary, but here there is two-way communication and accountability between them and an unusual parity as a result. Can you see applications for this process? How separable were the layers? How candid were the protagonists?

COMPILATION AND ESSAY CINEMA

Project 28-14: Making History This assignment gives you experience in making a historical film and lets you explore for yourself the didactic and expository power of film when applied to history. The aim is to take visual records, such as a series of photographs and/or news film from another era, and to put them together with a first-person reading of a contemporary letter, diary, or account that you find through research. Pictures and words should work together to make us imaginatively enter the spirit of the speaker and his or her time. Using judicious juxtaposition of word and image, you have great latitude to bend the apparent meaning and outcome, a facility that is close to propaganda.

Goals are to

- Find interesting visual records
- Find a contemporary letter, diary, or other account with which to interpret visual records
- Direct a reader so that the account sounds as natural as possible
- Explore the didactic and expository power of juxtaposition in compilation filmmaking
- Assess the use and abuse of the filmmaker's powers of distortion in presenting a historical account

Shooting: Check that your camera shoots what its viewfinder shows. Many do not, and there's no margin for error when shooting graphics. Within a single photograph or other image you can often find several more. Movements between these subsidiary compositions are hard but not impossible to do smoothly. Panning the camera on small subjects is too clumsy; try shooting down vertically onto a table and improvise a sliding platen so that a photograph can be slid between prearranged stops in any direction relative to the camera. Shoot movements at different speeds to accommodate any need later.

Narration: Directing a non-actor or even a trained actor to read so that it sounds like everyday speech is a big challenge. Usually the obstacle lies in the person's sense of occasion; he will project his voice or use "period" mannerisms. Sometimes you can help him focus by placing an attentive listener 3 feet away as someone real to concentrate on, or by having the reader imagine he's telling something to a nearby intimate. If you can figure out what's stopping naturalness, you probably can invent a strategy to unblock it. We become natural when we are no longer self-conscious and trying to be special.

Tip: Most screen history, like school history, is tedious stuff because television, which finances it, feels obligated to give panoramic overviews. Concerning itself with so many facts and exposition, instead of the questions of interpretation or present-day relevance, television makes history seem dull when it's really a vibrant source of human drama, profoundly mysterious in its ambiguities. See if you can bring human tensions and dilemmas alive, even if only briefly. As in any drama, the trick is to show someone experience a difficult change, however small and symbolic.

Film examples: Any television history, such as Ken Burns' *Civil War* (1990) series, that uses primary accounts; Alain Renais' trauma-inducing holocaust classic *Night and Fog* (1955), which has a masterful narration written by the poet Jean Cayrol, himself a survivor of the concentration camps; Pare Lorentz's classics *The Plow that Broke the Plains* (1936) and *The River* (1937).

Editing: Use Project 38-4 Guidelines.

Assessment criteria: See Appendix 1, Project 28-14 Assessment, and Project 38-4 Assessment for the editing.

Discussion: The genre is familiar, so how originally was it tackled? What was successful, and what was not? Were they interesting archive materials? Did the filmmaker manage to imply a burning issue rather than a presentation of facts and feelings?

Project 28-15: National Anthem[3]   This project experiments with music editing and the meaning of song words and ironic images counterpointed against them. Using a national anthem for your sound track, find or shoot images that contrast its lofty ideals with an alternative reality that might emphasize poverty, warfare, floods, or riots—whatever you feel makes an ironic counterpoint. This assignment is ripe for cheerfully subversive personalities, but please don't try it anywhere that they imprison critics.

Goals are to

- Use split-page script format as a planning medium
- Use found footage or shoot your own
- Edit to the beat points in music
- Design images to fit words and music
- Work with ironic juxtaposition

Steps:

1. Plan your film using split-page format scripting, with the anthem words written out and the cutting points and counterpointed images indicated on the picture side.
2. If you wish, use "found" images (newsreel, archive, stills, etc.) or make the film entirely of footage you shoot yourself.
3. Shoot and edit, placing any cut falling on a musical beat three or four frames *before* the beat point. Editors do this to compensate for our inbuilt perceptual lag on new images. This adjustment makes it look as if you have cut exactly in time with the music.
4. If your national anthem is in another language, include a translation as subtitles.

Film example: Barbara Kopple uses songs as ironic narration in *Harlan County, USA* (1976). Virgil Thompson's score in Pare Lorentz's *The Plow that Broke the Plains* (1936) makes ironical and highly atmospheric use of American folk songs, popular songs, and hymns in its orchestral score.

Editing: Use Project 38-4 Guidelines.

Assessment criteria: See Appendix 1, Project 28-15 Assessment, and Project 38-4 Assessment for the editing.

---

[3] I believe I heard this exercise from György Kárpáti, Academy of Drama and Film, Budapest. Apologies if I've attributed it wrongly.

Discussion: How inventive were the images? What kind of commentary did they make on the pomp and circumstance of the national anthem? To what other uses can you imagine putting this technique?

Project 28-16: Video Letter   This project explores the notion of film diary or film addressed to a particular constituency. In it you conceive and shoot a video letter that you send to documentary students either in your own school or one abroad. Foreign exchanges, where they can be arranged, are immensely exciting and invigorating, and sometimes begin from "correspondence" like this.

Goals are to

- Exchange ideas with people of similar interests
- Use documentary techniques and the correspondence tradition as the medium of communication
- Shape a piece for a particular audience
- Explain briefly but comprehensively the foundations of your own program for an audience you don't know

Starting: Consider whether you already have contacts in a particular country. If not, pick out one or two places that interest you from the list of foreign film schools at the end of this book, find the school's Web site address, and e-mail them a letter of inquiry. In it you could seek to find out

- Whether they have a documentary program, and who runs it
- Whether their documentary students are interested in a video letter exchange
- Whether they can play your DVD or VHS video standard (NTSC [National Television System Committee], PAL [phase alternating line], SECAM [Sequential Couleur Avec Memoire or Sequential Color with Memory]) and say what video formats your institution can play and record
- What they'd be interested in hearing about

Sending your video letter: Your addressees may live and learn in a very different environment, so you'll need to explain the basics of yours and its values. Expository clarity is a perennial need in documentaries and something very easy to overlook. How do you relay the essentials without going to excessive length? What kind of tone should you strike? In your tape you might

- Introduce the concepts, personalities, and contents of your course or program
- Explain what kind of place your institution is and how the education system works (the selection systems, for example, are quite different from country to country)
- Outline how particular personalities in your group came to be interested in documentary
- Discuss the assignments, mix of theory and practice, texts, etc. in your coursework

- Share what you most disagree about
- Include clips of the work you have been doing
- Talk about what particularly interests you
- Show what your homes are like or maybe a typical day
- Show what kind of economic juggling act you have to perform to actually go to school (how you have to wait tables, drive a cab, etc.)

Editing: Use Project 38-4 Guidelines.

Assessment criteria: See Appendix 1, Project 28-16 Assessment, and Project 38-4 Assessment for the editing.

Discussion: How well does the material lay out the basics of your study life for people in another culture? How well does it articulate the most interesting problems and issues you face? How do you think the other culture sees you and your circumstances?

ECLECTIC CINEMA

Project 28-17: The Final Project You should do this assignment after you have gained experience in the component parts of documentary language from earlier projects. If you are in a degree program requiring a thesis film or diploma film, this assignment could be a rehearsal using an allied or analogous subject.

Goals are to

- Mix forms of documentary language according to the needs of your subject, as most real-world documentaries do
- Direct a documentary that is between 20 and 30 minutes long (or to whatever length your documentary program demands)
- Consolidate your knowledge of the foundations and show you can now produce a film that successfully mixes documentary modes

Write a proposal: It would be better to avoid talking heads completely, if you can. If you cannot, then make your film *no more than one-third sync interview.* Writing a documentary proposal (see Chapter 15) will raise the thematic content developed during research to its ultimate clarity and help you make an organized, persuasive statement of your intentions. The goal of all proposal writing is to convince the reader beyond the shadow of a doubt that you can make a film of impact and significance.

Bear in mind that an effective documentary

- Tells a good story
- Changes us by evoking our emotions as well as by supplying a necessary framework of information and facts
- Usually takes a critical view of some aspect of the human condition
- Dramatizes human truths, both large and small, by showing them in action

- Usually needs you to supply the traditional dramatic ingredients—characters, exposition, building tension between opposed forces, confrontation, climax, and resolution
- Is made from a passionate involvement (which you often find as you go)

Steps:

1. Write a *subject description* and *working hypothesis* (see beginning of this chapter).
2. From your research, develop an *analytical draft* under capitalized headings (see Chapter 15, Documentary Proposal Organizer), structuring your material to demonstrate your research and analysis. Eliminate any repetition by deciding under which heading every particular idea and observation truly belongs.
3. Write a *treatment* (see Chapter 15, The Treatment) by reworking material from the analytical draft into a narrative. Remember to write in the present tense, using a new paragraph for each sequence, describing only what will be seen and heard from the screen. Quoting participants' own words from your preinterview session is a highly effective way to present characters on paper. Write evocatively, imagining where necessary what will happen so that the reader "sees" the attractive film that you hope and expect to make.
4. Make a *shooting schedule* to show your shooting dates and arrangements.
5. Make a provisional *budget* covering all phases to indicate how you will fund your film.
6. Obtain the permissions you need to shoot (location clearances, agreement with participants, etc.).
7. Shoot.
8. Edit first assembly.
9. Fine cut.
10. Show to one or more trial audience, evoke critiques, and make adjustments accordingly.
11. Finalize sound by mixing and equalizing tracks.
12. Show for evaluation.

   Film examples: You choose!
   Editing: Use Project 38-4 Guidelines.
   Assessment: See Appendix 1, Project 28-17, and Project 38-4 Assessment for the editing.
   Discussion: You decide!

PRODUCTION CHECKLIST

Before interviewing,

- Rehearse questions aloud and listen to see if there is room for misunderstanding
- Decide who is best equipped (director or researcher) to conduct interviews

- Consider putting people together to talk: people in couples or in groups sometimes give more
- Remember that antipathies and disagreements often stimulate good "talking" situations between people
- Have a clear expectation of what each interviewee can contribute to your film through prior research
- Decide the audience's relationship to interviewees, and plan on- or off-axis interviews as appropriate
- Decide whether the interviewer or her voice should ever be in the film
- Focus questions carefully on issues you want discussed
- Decide what setting will most productively affect the interviewee
- Remember that you must know in advance the minimum your film will say

When interviewing,

- Carry questions on an index card as a "security blanket"
- Make sure you have properly explained to participants *why* you are filming
- Ask interviewees' permission to interrupt or redirect conversation when necessary
- Coach interviewees to include the question's information in the answer
- Review who is present and whether they will negatively affect interviewee(s)
- Remain natural and unaffected when you interview—because you get what you give
- Ask factual, non-threatening questions first; hold back difficult or intimate matters until interviewee becomes acclimatized
- Listen to the beginning of each answer to be sure it stands alone without your question
- Be ready to jump in and ask for a new start
- Maintain eye contact with the interviewee
- Listen for subtext, not only for what you want to hear
- Give facial, but never verbal, feedback while the interviewee is talking
- Use the devil's-advocate role to advance "negative" questioning
- Ask *always* for specifics, examples, or stories to back up any assertion that is interesting
- Get a second version if the first, though spontaneous, was clumsy or too long
- Remain silent whenever you suspect there is something still to be said
- Remember the camera empowers you to go further and deeper than in everyday life
- Use "Can we go back to what you said about . . ." as a gentle redirection

- Use "And . . . ?" when you feel there is more to come
- Repeat interesting words or a phrase from what your interviewee said to stimulate him or her to continue the thought
- Make sure you have filmed the necessary confrontations inherent in your movie's system of issues

When interviewing, do not

- Forget to allow the camera at least 10 seconds of run-up before letting action begin
- Worry about the order of the interview—it will all be cut and reorganized
- Use vague, general questions
- Ask more than one question at a time
- Overlap your voice on that of an interviewee or allow his or her voice to overlap yours
- Make sounds of encouragement or agreement—use facial and bodily expressions only
- Hurry on to the next question or you risk quashing a "moment of truth"
- Allow correct choices or decisions to be swayed by a sense of obligation
- Be surprised by mannerisms accompanying a lifelong role held by the participant
- Forget to a shoot presence track for each interview location

When preparing to get action sequence coverage and to ensure variety,

- Make shopping list of sequences and shots, and *what feeling each must convey*
- Ask participants not to look at the camera
- Remember to shoot inserts, cutaways, and reaction shots
- Remember that *vox pops* are a great resource (the "person in the street" speaks)
- Show people active in their own surroundings
- Make each situation credible but also make it reveal something special about the participants through their behavior
- Make sure each participant has plenty to do to avoid self-consciousness
- Expect people in unfamiliar circumstances to fall back on habit

When shooting,

- Choose between a steady, immobile camera (tripod), and a subjective and mobile but unsteady camera (handheld) for each sequence
- Decide the size and framing of any static shot with the camera operator beforehand

- Stay next to the camera so that you see more or less what it is seeing
- Whisper directions into operator's ear or use touch signals (only if the camera is on a tripod, though)
- Make the camera into a conscious instrument of revelation and storytelling, not just a passive observer
- Whenever working off a tripod, look through the camera often to check framing, composition, and image size
- Decide whose POV the camera should sympathize with moment to moment and brief the operator accordingly
- Remain aware of where the center of significant action lies and monitor that your camera operator knows it too
- Exploit location as a meaningful environment rather than as a mere container or backdrop
- Always try to create a sense of depth in the frame by shooting down the axis of movement or subject to subject axis and by planning several planes in the shot (near, middle ground, background)
- Be alert to participants' changes of eyeline and be ready to follow them
- After the main shooting, use mental notes of where participants' eyelines went during the shot as reminders for shooting all possible safety cutaways

Use your social skills to

- Give individualized, positive reinforcement to participants and crew as you go
- Keep the group together during rest periods and meals so that the process of relationship continues informally
- Keep to meal breaks; do not overwork people
- Thank everyone personally at the end of each day
- Require that locations be left exactly as you found them and do your part to restore things to their proper places and conditions
- Insist that the director alone speak for the unit
- Keep dissent away from participants
- Let your crew know when you need advice or help, and when not.

Regarding crew and scheduling:

- Make sure there is a clear structure of responsibility for everything that may happen
- Provide the crew with a printed schedule, maps, and phone contact numbers
- Underschedule when in doubt
- When everyone is in transit, make sure there is a central phone number that anyone can call in the event of separation or breakdown

- Keep the crew involved and aware of developments in the picture's content and themes
- Be tolerant of the crew's incomplete grasp of subject development

Regarding authorship:

- Look for subtext in each situation and try to make its existence evident
- Consider using side coaching to impel something nascent into being
- Be aware of life roles that people fall into and be ready to make positive use of them
- Think of the dramatic characterizations each seems to have adopted
- Create a private metaphor for each person, situation, and activity to help you think poetically and metaphorically instead of materially and didactically
- Look for the dialectics in everything and therefore for any confrontations that you may need to assist into fruition
- Make sure expository material (facts, biographical and any other vital points) is covered in more than one way so that you have options later
- Periodically check your shopping lists to make sure nothing has been overlooked
- Remember that neither crew nor participants will have your demonic energy

PART 7

POSTPRODUCTION

Part 7 deals with

- The role and responsibilities of the editor and editing crew
- Overview of the process
- Viewings, their order and importance
- Preparing the material for editing
- Deciding a structure for the piece
- Viewing the first assembly and diagnostic approaches
- Text, subtext, and the audience
- Refining the cut and achieving a narrative flow
- Deciding whether narration is needed and methods of creating it
- Trial audience showings and moving toward a fine cut
- Working with music and with a composer
- Sound effects and dialogue replacement work
- Music recording and final mix
- Titling and subtitles

This part covers the vital postproduction phase, when raw materials are fashioned into a seamless tale. My purpose is not to discuss the merits of different software but to outline procedural steps in the creative process of editing and to discuss what you should expect conceptually as your work evolves. Advanced-level work should always be in the hands of an editor, not the director. So great is the contribution that an independent eye can bring that the documentary editor is rightly looked on as a second director. Rather than feel threatened by this collaboration, you should see it as liberating you to do better work because you can get away from the movie and regain relative objectivity.

The cutting room is the crucible of filmmaking. The experience of being present while your work is edited will teach you more about your directing than any other exposure possibly could. If you are editing digitally you will be able to incorporate transitions (what in film are called *opticals*) as you go, that is, you can freeze a frame, slow or speed up motion, apply color or optical filtering, dissolve between shots, or fade to black or to white. Overused, special effects can be gratuitous and annoying, but used tastefully they can elevate your film from pedestrian realism to a poetic, dreamlike condition that film achieves at its highest state. The 1988 "Voices and Visions" series, although made entirely using film, makes brilliant use of text and imagery techniques—as one would hope for in a series on American poets.

Now you can much more easily integrate text and, using an additional program, develop a range of composite imagery. For instance, I watched Mikel Wiström in Stockholm editing his film about a Peruvian family. In an introductory section he used black-and-white portrait vignettes in a landscape background that makes the screen look like a family photo album. One by one each image turns to color as the portrait starts talking and the image magnifies to fill the screen. Then it shrinks back into a monochrome image again as another family image comes alive. This might be showy in other hands or circumstances, but the photo album effect perfectly conveys the sense of his memory full of images from their 2 decades of relationship.

You have a full palette of techniques and a wonderful freedom. Such techniques are not new—film has always been able to do these things, but expensively and with a huge investment of time and energy in planning. Now you can imagine special ideas for your film and try them on your desktop.

For further information on issues arising in Part 7, use the Index or go to the Bibliography. Make frequent use of the Postproduction Checklist at the end of this part, and save yourself wasted time and energy.

CHAPTER 29

POSTPRODUCTION BEGINS

This chapter deals with

- The editor's role and responsibilities
- Postproduction overview for film and video
- Logs and note taking as part of preparing to edit
- Viewing dailies and making decisions
- Preparing to making a paper edit (for dialogue driven films) prior to first assembly

Most of the operations described in this chapter are the editor's responsibility, but a director must know postproduction procedures in order to get the best film from the editing stage. Editing is not just assembly to a plan but more like coaxing a successful performance from an imperfect and incomplete composer's score. This operation requires you to see, listen, adapt, think, and imagine as you try to fulfill something to the best of its emerging potential.

EDITING: ROLE AND RESPONSIBILITIES

Large-budget documentaries may use the editor from the start of shooting, so the unit's output can be assembled as fast as it is shot. With low-budget films, however, economics usually prevent cutting until everything is shot. The risk here is that errors and omissions may only surface when it is too late to rectify them. To guard against this, units try to see their work nightly so that any further shooting can be done right away before quitting the location.

Nowadays an editor often works alone on a low-budget documentary, but a large crew completes the postproduction of a large-budget documentary. There may be an editor, assistant editor, sound editor, sound mix engineer, and a composer if the production commissions original music. No matter whether the production is large or small, the number and complexity of the postproduction processes make editing central to the success of a documentary, both technically and creatively. Because editors deal with the structure and flow of a film, editing is the most common path to directing.

If the editing staff is hired after shooting, they are getting to know the director when the latter may be in a state of considerable anxiety and uncertainty. For the film, though shot, has yet to prove itself. Many directors suffer a sort of postnatal depression in the trough following the sustained impetus of shooting, and most, however confident on the surface, are in a state of morbid dread about their material's real or anticipated failings. If editor and director do not know each other well, both will usually be formal and cautious. The editor is taking over the director's baby, and the director often carries mixed and potentially explosive emotions.

The good editor is articulate, patient, highly organized, willing to experiment endlessly, and diplomatic about trying to get his or her own way. Assistant editors mirror these qualities.

CREATIVE CONTRIBUTION

The editor's job goes far beyond the physical task of assembly, and the good editor—really someone of undoubted author caliber who works from given materials—is highly aware of the material's possibilities. Directors are handicapped in this area through over-familiarity with their own intentions. The editor, not being present at shooting, comes on the scene with an unobligated and unprejudiced eye and is ideally placed to reveal to the director what possibilities or problems lie dormant within the material.

On a documentary or improvised fiction film, the editor is really the second director, given that the materials may be inherently interesting but lack design and so are capable of broad possibilities of interpretation. The editor must be able to make responsible subjective judgments. Editing is far more than following instructions, just as music is much more than playing notes in the right order. In fact, composing is a close analogy to the documentary editor's work, and many editors have music among their deepest interests.

PARTNERSHIP

Relationships between directors and editors vary according to the arcane chemistry of status and temperaments. Normally director and editor discuss the overall intention and likely structure of the film and then the editor sets to work making an assembly. This will be a first raw version of the film. The wise director leaves the cutting room and returns with a usefully fresh eye, but the obsessive director sits in the cutting room watching the editor's every action night and day. Whether this is an amenable arrangement depends on the editor. Some enjoy debating their way through the cutting procedure, but most prefer being left alone to work out the film's initial problems in bouts of intense concentration over their logs and equipment.

In the end, very little escapes discussion; every scene, shot, and cut is scrutinized, questioned, weighed, and balanced. The creative relationship is intense and often draws in all the cutting room staff, producer, and any nearby colleagues. The editor must often use delicate but sustained leverage against the irrational prejudices and fixations that at some time close like a trap around the heart of virtually every director.

DIRECTOR-EDITORS

In low-budget movies, under the rubric of economics, the director often becomes the editor. This is a dangerous economy. Often the real reason is a fear of sharing control and the conviction that no unified film will be possible. Such a personality will sometimes take criticism as an attack. Editing your own work, unless it is a limited or exercise film, is always a mistake, particularly for the less experienced.

Every film, being created for an audience, needs the steadying and detached point of view of an editor acting as first proxy for the audience. A good mind in creative tension with the director is an inestimable asset. A partner in the editing room guards the director against tumbling into the abyss of subjectivity and helps to question the director's assumptions and supply alternative ideas and solutions. The director who foregoes this tension never gets the necessary distance from the material. He or she either loves the material too much to cut anything or comes to so distrust the edited version that he or she keeps cutting it shorter until nobody new can understand it. He or she puts the film through every contortion in an attempt to cure all its imagined deformities.

The scrutiny of the emerging work by an equal and the editor's advocacy of alternative views both produce a tougher and better-balanced film than any one person can generate alone. You are the exception? Please, please think again.

EDITING: PROCESS AND PROCEDURES

With digital nonlinear editing (NLE), any part of an edited version can be substituted, transposed, or adjusted for length. This was emphatically not so with earlier linear video editing systems, which some people may still have to use. Here the edit is compiled by making a series of transfers from a source machine to a recorder. Subsequent work on the edited version is hampered because changing the length of a shot means either altering a following shot by the added or deleted amount or retransferring absolutely everything subsequent to the change. Using some workaround techniques, one can do perfectly sophisticated editing, but it is deathly slow and labor intensive.

Editing with NLE systems such as Avid, Final Cut Pro, Adobe Premiere, or Media 100 software has become ubiquitous. From video original, or from film camera original material scanned by a telecine machine, the material is digitally recorded in the editing computer's hard drive. Edits are compiled as a series of clips arranged on a timeline. As in computerized word processing, one may enter at any point and transpose, lengthen or shorten what is there.

The early established Avid system (Figure 29–1) remains the front-runner in performance and user friendliness, but it has been legendarily expensive to maintain because of its habit of requiring frequent, expensive updates. For Hollywood the price is small potatoes, but small potatoes are usually the documentarian's only potatoes. If you want to buy the industry leader, be warned that Avid got itself an unenviable reputation for arrogance toward smaller users and that its

FIGURE 29–1

Avid Media Composer, the film industry's preferred editing software. (Photo courtesy of Avid.)

undoubted excellence comes at a price. A clear advantage of Avid's low-end product is that the interface you learn remains the same throughout Avid's range, and this will be a benefit should good fortune take you up-market.

Among independent filmmakers, Avid has been losing ground to the Apple Computer Company's Final Cut Pro (Figure 29–2), a stable, very modestly priced program that now handles high-definition (HD) video. So flexible and capable is the program that Avid has been forced into competing in the lower-end market.

Adobe Premiere and Final Cut Pro are backed by large companies dedicated to serving large consumer markets, and their pricing and general reliability reflect a respect for the discriminating low-end user who wants professional features. There are a host of other NLE systems, but as always when you contemplate uniting your destiny with pieces of equipment, look long and hard before you leap. Check out a variety of comparable users' experience via professional journals and user groups on the Internet.

A POSTPRODUCTION OVERVIEW

Postproduction is that phase of filmmaking when sound and picture dailies are transformed into the film seen by the audience. Supervised by the editor, postproduction includes the following:

- Synchronizing sound with action (for double-system recording)
- Screening dailies for the director and producer's choices and comments
- Marking up the editing script (if there is one) according to what was actually shot
- Logging material in preparation for editing
- Making a first assembly
- Making the rough cut

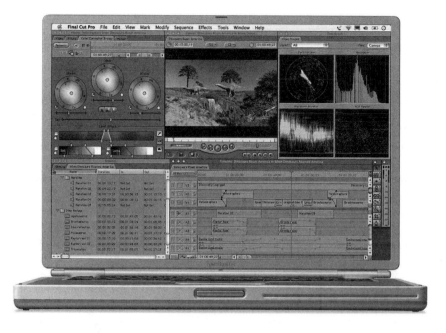

FIGURE 29-2

Apple Final Cut Pro editing software on a PowerBook portable computer. (Photo courtesy of Apple.)

- Evolving the rough cut into a fine cut
- Supervising the recording of any narration
- Preparing for and supervising any original music recording
- Finding, recording, and laying component parts of multi-track sound, such as atmospheres, backgrounds, and sync effects
- Supervising mix-down of these tracks into one smooth final track
- Supervising making of titles and necessary graphics
- Supervising the postproduction finalization processes

In film, the process subsequent to shooting involves the following film laboratory processes:

- Developing the camera original
- Making a workprint for larger-budget films to protect the negative from unnecessary handling
- Delivering to the cutting room either
  - A film workprint or
  - A tape made from a telecine scan of the negative or workprint for digitization in the editing system

It is now almost universal to digitize film dailies and edit on NLE software. This requires every negative image to have its own timecode (called Keycode™) because the resulting edit decision list (EDL) will be used to conform, or match edit, the camera original. There is no margin for error here in conforming; once the camera original is physically cut there is no going back.

There is one tricky aspect. With a system that transfers 24 frames per second (fps) of film to 30 fps (60 fields of interlaced video per second) of video, you end up with four film frames being represented by five video frames. The process may be complicated by PAL (phase alternating line) and NTSC (National Television System Committee) equipment that run at different frame rates and film cameras that run at either 24 fps or 25 fps according to whether the material was generated for NTSC, PAL, or SECAM (Sequential Couleur Avec Memoire or Sequential Color with Memory) TV systems. NTSC leaves you with phantom frames, and if you edit on one, it can only be approximated at the conforming stage. If your sound track has been completely prepared in the digital mode, a succession of phantom frames over a succession of cuts may lead to a mixed track that drifts out of sync with the conformed film.

Make sure the person coordinating the process is thoroughly aware of the need for clarity about pulldown mode in digitization and how to avoid the unwanted consequences described earlier. There is a good description of all this in Thomas Ohanian's *Digital Nonlinear Editing*, 2nd edition (Boston & London: Focal Press, 1998) in the chapter, "The Film Transfer Process" (pp. 279–281). If you think it looks like "how many angels can dance on the point of a pin," remember that ignoring the problem will be very, very costly.

Once editing arrives at a fine cut and sound mix, the lab uses either the edited workprint or the EDL to do the following:

- Make film *opticals* (optical effects such as dissolves, fades, freeze frames, titling) if they cannot be done at the final printing stage. Optical printing is an expensive, highly specialized, and fallible process that nobody should undertake lightly.

- *Conforming* (or *negative cutting*): The original negative is cut to match the workprint so that fresh prints can be struck for release. Conforming includes instructing the printing machine to produce simple fades, superimpositions, and dissolves. Conforming in the traditional method is simply matching negative to workprint in a synchronizer

- *Matchback conforming* follows a digitally edited film. An EDL of Keycode™ numbers compiled during digital editing is the sole guide to cutting the negative. This is risky business—see notes later!

- Making a sound optical negative from
  - The sound magnetic master in the case of traditional mixing
  - The sound program output in the case of a digitally edited film

- Timing (or color grading) the picture negative by the lab in association with the director of photography (DP)

- Combining sound negative with timed picture print to produce a composite or *married* print in order to produce the first *answer print* (or *trial print*)

- Making *release prints* after achieving a satisfactory answer print
- Making *dupe* (duplicate) *negatives* via a fine grain *interpositive* process. For films with a large release, too many copies would subject the original negative to too much wear and tear, so dupe negs are made. Rare indeed is the documentary that needs this!

From this point on, apart from the odd reference, I shall assume that postproduction is handled not in film but digitally, because virtually all documentaries are now shot and postproduced in the digital domain. If you need further information about the film process, a good source is Kodak's student program, reachable through www.kodak.com/go/student. Kodak has every reason to want people to continue using film and provides superb guidance in its publications and Web sites. These are as prolific and labyrinthine as you'd expect of an organization with so many divisions.

In digital or nonlinear editing, the camera original material is digitized, stored in a computer hard drive, and assembled as segments laid along a timeline. Multiple sound tracks can be laid opposite their picture and levels predetermined so that you can listen to a layered and sophisticated track even while editing. Many systems are now so fast and have such large storage that you can edit on a laptop computer at full resolution. This abolishes the need for the two-pass offline and online processes, with the extra time and expense. HD video may force some users into editing at low resolution (*lo res*) until it is once again cost effective to use high-speed, high-capacity computing at the editing stage. This retrograde step surely will be only temporary.

Depending on the features of the NLE system you use, postproduction will involve

- Digitizing a lo-res (inferior grade) image so that much material can be stored in a hard drive of limited capacity. Many systems now have the capacity to work at full resolution and at reasonable speed.
- Sound finalized in the *audio sweetening* process using sophisticated sound processing software such as DigiDesign's ProTools. Beyond simple level setting, such programs enable control over sound dynamics such as
  - Limiting (sound dynamics remain linear until preset ceiling, when they are held to that ceiling level)
  - Compression (all sound dynamics are compressed into a narrower range but remain equal in ratio to each other)
  - Equalization control (sound frequency components within top, middle, and bottom of sound range can be individually adjusted or preset programs applied)
  - Filtering: For speech with prominent sibilants, for instance, you can use a de-essing program
  - Pitch changes or *pitch bending* (this betrays ProTools' roots in music, but can be very useful for surreal sound effects or creating naturalistic variations from a single source)

- MIDI integration: This allows you to integrate a keyboard operated sampler or music setup.
- The EDL of the final edit is used to re-digitize only the selected material.
- The edit is reassembled by the computer at high resolution (*hi-res*).
- The hi-res version is output to tape and becomes the master copy for future duplication.

The facility of NLE for finding everything you want in a flash obviates the former need to search through out-takes and other material. Editors report that because they are no longer forced in their daily work to contemplate unused material, it is easy to miss diamonds in the rough. Because editing schedules have gotten shorter, the editor must make sure by the fine-cut stage that nothing useful has been overlooked.

Online edit: If offline editing has produced a low-grade picture and an EDL, the production is ready for online editing. A computer-controlled rig uses the EDL to assemble a high-quality version of the film from re-digitized camera original cassettes. This process is the video equivalent of the film process's conforming or negative cutting. Producing a video final print includes

- Timebase correction (electronic processing to ensure the resulting tape conforms to broadcasting standards)
- Color correction
- Audio sweetening as described earlier
- Copy duplication for release prints

DV Magazine at www.dv.com is excellent for up-to-date information and reviews on everything for digital production and postproduction.

SYNCING DAILIES

Digital picture and sound, when recorded separately, are synchronized by the same principle on the NLE timeline as they were physically with film. The picture (marked at the point where the clapper board bar has just closed) and the sound track (marked at the clapper bar's impact) are aligned so that discrete takes can be cumulatively assembled for a sync viewing.

VIEWING

CREW DAILIES VIEWING SESSION

At the completion of shooting, even though dailies have been viewed piecemeal, have the crew see all their work in its entirety. This lets everyone learn from their patterns and mistakes, as well as rejoice later in the successes that make it into the final edit. Screening may have to be broken up into several sessions, because 4 hours or so of unedited footage may be the longest that most can maintain concentration. The editor may be present at this viewing, but discussion is likely to be a crew-centered postmortem rather than one useful to the editor.

EDITOR AND DIRECTOR'S VIEWING SESSION

If nothing has yet been edited, editor and director should see the dailies together. A marathon viewing reveals the general thrust of the material and the problems you face for the piece as a whole. You begin to discover mannerisms that indicate, say, discomfort, in one of the participants. These must be cut around during editing if he or she is not to appear shifty. Or you might discover that one of your two main characters is more interesting or articulate and requires that you rethink your original premise.

Next view the material one scene at a time. With some labor, film dailies can be reassembled in scene order, but dailies that have been digitized can easily be seen in scene order. Run one sequence at a time, and stop to discuss its problems and possibilities. The editor will need the dailies book (see earlier) to record the director's choices and note any special cutting information.

GUT FEELINGS MATTER

Note down any unexpected mood or feeling. If, during the dailies viewing, you find yourself reacting to a particular person with, "She seems unusually sincere here," then note it down. Many gut feelings seem logically unfounded, and you are tempted to ignore or forget them. These are seldom isolated personal reactions. What triggered them remains embedded in the material for any first-time audience.

Any spontaneous perceptions you record will be useful when inspiration lags later from over-familiarity with the material. If you fail to commit them in some form to paper, they are likely to share the same fate as those important dreams that evaporate because you did not write them down.

TAKING NOTES

It is useful to have someone present at a viewing, taking dictated notes. If you must write during a viewing, make large, scribbled notes on many pages of paper so that you never stop watching the screen. You can easily miss important moments and nuances.

REACTIONS

When the crew or other people see dailies, there probably will be debates over the effectiveness, meaning, or importance of different aspects of the movie, and crew members may have differing feelings about the credibility and motivation of the participants. Listen rather than argue, because similar reactions may take place in your future audience. Keep in mind, however, that crewmembers are far from objective. They are disproportionately critical of their own discipline and may overvalue its positive or negative effect. They also develop subjective relationships with the participants and the filming situations. However, there is always much to be learned from their thoughts, feelings, and observations.

THE ONLY FILM IS IN THE DAILIES

The sum of the dailies viewing is a notebook full of choices and observations (both the director's and those of the editor), and fragmentary impressions of the movie's potential and deficiencies. Absolutely *nothing beyond what can be seen and felt from the dailies is any longer relevant* to the film you are making. Any documents such as the proposal or treatment are historic relics, old maps to a rebuilt city. Stow them in the attic for your biographer. The film must be discovered in the dailies.

Now you change hats. You are no longer the collector of the material: instead, you and your editor have become surrogates for the audience. Empty yourself of prior knowledge and intentions; your understanding and emotions must come wholly from the screen. Nobody in the cutting room wants to hear about what you intended or what you meant to produce.

PREPARING THE FOOTAGE

LOGGING THE DAILIES

In double-system filming, every new camera start receives a new clapper board number (see Chapter 20, under subsection "Shot and Scene Identification" for a fuller explanation of different marking systems). The clapper bar allows the editor to synchronize separately recorded picture and sound. With video, picture and sound are recorded alongside each other on the same magnetic recording medium, so scene numbers (and clapper boards) are not strictly necessary. Any log, however, must make it easy to retrieve material as you want it. A log of dailies should be cumulative, giving the new timing (or timecode) for each new scene or for each important action or event. Descriptions should be brief and serve only to remind someone who has seen the material what to expect. For example,

01:00:00	WS man at tall loom
01:00:30	MS same man seen through strings
01:00:49	CS man's hands with shuttle
01:01:07	MCS face as he works; stops, rubs eyes
01:01:41	His point of view of his hands and shuttle
01:02:09	CS feet on treadles (MOS)

The figures are hours: minutes: seconds. There is, of course, a frame count as well in timecode, but such hair-splitting accuracy is pointless. There are the usual shot abbreviations (see Glossary). Draw a heavy line between sequences and give each a heading in bold type. Note that the log records content, not quality; there is no attempt to add the qualitative notes from the dailies book. To do so would overload the page and make it hard to use.

Because the log exists to help quickly locate material, any divisions, indexes, or color codes you can devise to assist the eye in making selections will ultimately save time. This is especially true for a production with many hours of dailies.

Slapdash filing exacts its own revenge because Murphy (of Murphy's Law) loves to hide out in sloppy filing systems.

MAKING TRANSCRIPTS, AND A WORKAROUND SOLUTION

Tedious though it may seem, transcribing every word your characters speak will be invaluable to fully appreciating what your participants say. If you are making a film about testimony, the actual words people use will be paramount, and transcribing them is a necessity. Transcription is not as laborious as people fear: it saves work later and helps ensure that you miss few creative opportunities once the long editing process is done.

If you cannot endure the idea of doing this, you can log *topic categories*. This is a less arduous alternative that you can use as a workaround. Instead of writing down actual words, you summarize the topics covered at each stage of a discussion, filmed scene, or interview, and you log their timecode in- and out-points. This gives you quick access to any given subject. Then you make decisions during editing by auditioning whole sections and deciding which are best.

Not to make transcripts for a film being made from interviews is a "buy now, pay later" situation, because making content and choice comparisons without a transcript is hard labor of a different stripe. I should warn that using transcripts too literally also has some dangers. It can lead you to place too much emphasis on words and thus to making a speech-driven film. Words that look so significant on paper can sometimes prove anemic on the screen. If, for example, your film deals with teenagers producing an improvised play, it is hazardous to construct the film on paper from transcripts of what they say. The act of transcription always, to some degree, imposes an artificial and literary organization—especially if the original scene took place impulsively and chaotically. Particularly when voices overlap or people use special nuances or body language, transcripts often interpret and simplify reality. Remember, how something is said is quite as important as *what* is being said. What is lived and how it gets transcribed are often two different things with two different subtexts.

SELECTING TRANSCRIPT SECTIONS FOR THE FIRST ASSEMBLY

If your film is a journalistic or investigative film that is largely dependent on language, your first assembly will be constructed from long, loosely selected sections of transcript, so let us look at a method for carving up transcript copies and narrowing your choices into a workable form. Figure 29–3 is a flow chart illustrating this.

Step A: You have made transcripts (1) and from them a photocopy. Place the transcripts in a binder titled *Original Transcripts*, and keep them somewhere safe. You are going to work with the photocopy (2).

Step B: Run the material on a video cassette recorder or editing machine, and follow each speaker's words in the transcript photocopy (2). When you are struck by an effective section—for whatever reason—put a vertical "preference mark" in the margin as in (3). You are leaving a record of your responses. Some will be to a story graphically told; others to some well-presented factual information; still others will be in response to an intimate or emotional moment, be

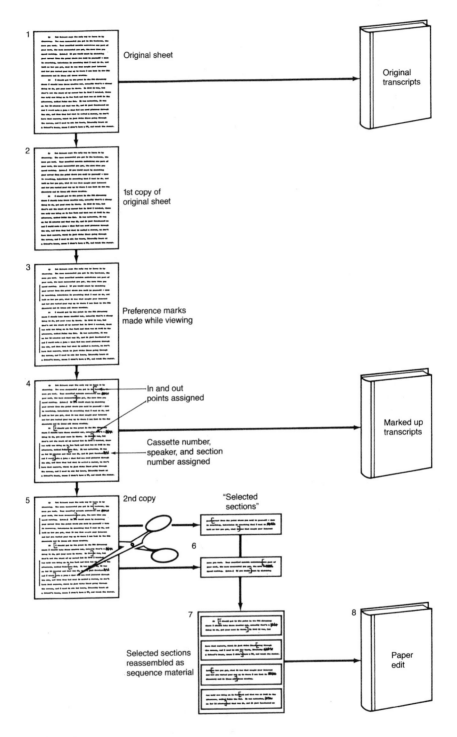

Original sheet

Original transcripts

1st copy of original sheet

Preference marks made while viewing

In and out points assigned

Marked up transcripts

Cassette number, speaker, and section number assigned

2nd copy

"Selected sections"

Selected sections reassembled as sequence material

Paper edit

FIGURE 29-3

Flow chart showing how to use transcripts to make a paper edit.

it humor, warmth, anger, or regret. At this stage just *respond*; don't stop to analyze your reactions. There will be a time for that later.

Step C: Once you have preference marks against all striking sections in the photocopy, study each and find a logical in-point and out-point, using two kinds of "L" brackets to show the preferred start and finish of the section (4).

In Figure 29–4, a chosen section has been bracketed at an in-point and out-point. However, only by returning to the recorded material can you determine whether verbal warmups (so common when people begin a statement) can be edited out as intended. Similarly, our intended out-point might need modifying if it forced us to cut away from Ted on a rising voice inflection that sounded strange and unfinished.

In the section's margin is the cryptic identification "6/Ted/3." This decoded means "Tape cassette 6, Ted Williams, section 3." These section IDs will later prove vital because they allow you to find the section in the full text and to locate the film section in its parent cassette. There is no set format for section identity codes, but as with all filing systems, *stick with one system for the duration of the project* and build improvements into the next project when you can start clean.

Returning to Figure 29–3, you now have photocopies (4) with selected sections marked, their in-points, out-points, and IDs, any or all of which might go into a finished film. You need to assign each section a description of its function, such as "Ted's descript. of Farmer Wills," as shown in Figure 29–4.

Step D: Now make a photocopy (5) of these marked sheets. The parent marked transcript photocopy (4) can now be set aside. File its sheets in cassette order in a binder titled *Marked-Up Transcripts*, with an index at the front so that you can quickly locate each character. Later, during editing, this file will be an important resource.

Step E: The photocopy of the marked-up transcripts (5) is cut up with scissors into selected sections (6), ready for sorting and grouping in pursuit of the paper edit. Because each slip is identified by subject or intended use, and

Q: What do you remember about the farmer?

Ted: What do I....?   Oh, well, you know, [he
was all right if you kept your place.   But if
you got smart, or asked too many questions,
he'd be after you.   "Where's that wagon load of
straw?   Why ain't them cattle fed yet?"   And
then he'd say there were plenty of men walking
the streets looking for work if I didn't want
to work.   The only thing you could do was be
silent, 'cos he meant what he said.]   Now his
wife was different.   She was a nice soul, you
know what I mean?   Couldn't see how she came
to marry him in the first place....

6/Ted/3

'Ted's descript. of Farmer Wills.'

FIGURE 29–4 —————————————————————————

Section of an interview transcript marked with in-point and out-point brackets, cassette/speaker/section ID, and margin description.

because it carries an ID, you know at a glance what it is, what it can do, and what its context is in the parent sheets, the *Marked-Up Transcripts*.

Now you are ready to go to the next chapter, which tells you how to construct a *paper edit*—really a detailed sketch for the first assembly. The selected sections (6) eventually will be stapled to sheets of paper (7) as sequences, and the sequences will be assembled into a binder (8) holding the paper edit or plan for the first assembly of your movie.

This procedure may sound unnecessarily complicated, but if you have a great deal of spoken material, time spent organizing at the outset (indexes, graphics, guides, color coding, and so on) is rewarded by disproportionate time saved later. I learned this the hard way when I was hired to edit the final game in a soccer World Cup documentary. There were 70,000 feet of 35 mm film (nearly 13 hours) shot from 17 camera positions. The only coordination was a shot of a clock at the beginning of each 1,000-foot roll. I spent a week with my assistant, Robert Giles, up to our armpits in film, making a diagram of the stadium and coding each major event as it appeared in all the various angles. The game had gone into overtime due to a foul, and it was my luck to eventually establish that, during this most decisive moment, *not one* of the 17 cameras was running. From sports reports and guided by Robert's far superior grasp of the game, I set about using an assortment of appropriate close shots to manufacture a facsimile of the missing foul. No one ever guessed we'd had to fake it.

The project was an editor's nightmare. Had we not first taken the time to invent a decent retrieval system, the men in white coats would have taken us away in the legendary rubber bus.

CHAPTER 30

THE PAPER EDIT:
DESIGNING A STRUCTURE

This chapter deals with

- Finding a structure for your film in the dailies
- The initial contract with the audience
- The need for development and change
- Action-oriented versus word-driven structures
- Beginning the paper edit

WHY A STRUCTURE MATTERS

You will need a narrative and thematic structure, no matter what genre of documentary you are making. If you were able to keep to your goals during the shoot, then structuring the assembly may now be straightforward. Usually it isn't. More often—because documentaries are mostly improvisations about people improvising their way through life—what you shot was not what you imagined. Your goals were frustrated or had to change, so now you need a first assembly planning process that will connect you to what you really filmed and let you make something imaginative out of it. Editing is your second chance.

TIME AND STRUCTURAL ALTERNATIVES

Structure and the "contract" with the audience: Identifying a structure for the footage you have shot means, first of all, deciding how to handle time, because progression through time is the all-important organizing feature of any narrative. You must decide in what order cause and effect will be shown and whether any dramatic advantages lie in altering the natural or chronological sequence of events. All this affects the contract you will strike with your audience.

Yes, consciously or otherwise, *your audience looks for a contract*, the manifestation of your story's premise, goals, and route. The contract may be spelled out in a narration or implied in the logic of the film's development. It also may be suggested by the film's title or in something shown, said, or done at the outset. However, one way or another, your audience needs a *sense of direction and an implied destination* in order to embrace the pleasurable prospect of a journey.

The structural types with film examples are laid out in Chapter 5: Time, Development, and Structure. The examples and discussion there can help you decide what limitations, and therefore what potential, lie in your dailies.

Story structures need to show development: A huge problem for documentary is that, unless you can shoot intermittently over months or years, human change and development may have to be implied rather than shown, because most human growth is slow and incompatible with an affordable shooting schedule. Here Michael Apted's *28 Up* (1986), and its successor films, is strikingly successful because it logs the same children's progress over decades, repeatedly exploring each individual's sense of goals and destiny. Actually, now that so many documentarians own their equipment, films shot over months or years are far more feasible than ever before. Longitudinal studies similar to the *Up* series have since been started in several countries.

How will your film imply that someone has grown or changed?

Microcosm and macrocosm: Sometimes a subject is large and diffuse, and as a macrocosm it must be implied through microcosmic examples. I worked on a series that attempted to show the contrasting values of Britain's nearest neighbors as Britain was reluctantly joining the European Common Market. Called "Faces of Paris," it showed aspects of the French capital by profiling some interesting citizens.

Here you confront a familiar paradox that goes something like this: In order to show France, I need to show Paris, but because "Paris" is too diffuse, I will concentrate on a representative Parisian so that my film will have some unity and progression. But how to choose a "typical" Parisian? To represent the universal, you look for an example of the particular, but particularizing on behalf of the general tends to demonstrate how triumphantly atypical all examples turn out to be and thus how absurdly stereotypical are your ideas about Parisians.

Do you have someone or something representative of someone or something larger? If so, how will you show where the parallels break down or misrepresent the wider example? The camera is relentlessly literal to its surroundings: it can only ever approach the abstract or metaphysical through the physical. Thus, the ideas it conveys most readily arise from what is visible and therefore superficial, rather than from what is underlying and much more significant. Film is handicapped compared with literature when it wants to convey compact generalizations or deal with abstract ideas. Making generalizations in film without resorting to the literary overview form of narration can be a real problem, and this may be a signal that you should bite the bullet and consider narration.

Writers faced, and solved, similar problems in previous centuries. One answer is to find a naturalistic subject that carries strongly metaphorical overtones. On the literal level, Bunyan's *Pilgrim's Progress* is a journey of adventure, but it also functions as an allegory for the human spiritual voyage. The Maysles Brothers' superb *Salesman* (1969) is like this—a journey film about a group of bible salesmen on a sales drive in Florida. During it we see the eclipse of Paul, once a star salesman, according to the measure by which he and his company determine success. Not only does the film show every phase of door-to-door selling—something the Maysles Brothers had done themselves at one time—but it establishes how moral compromise and humiliation are the price of competing as a salesman for a share in the American dream.

Another famous American repeatedly uses an allegorical "container" structure. Fred Wiseman will take an institution and treat it as a walled city, a complete and functioning microcosm of the larger society housing it. Through the emergency room doors in *Hospital* (1970), for example, come the hurt, the frightened, the wounded, the overdosed, and the dying in desperate search of succor. It conveys an apocalyptic vision of the self-destruction that stalks American cities. As a mirror of a society, or as a metaphor, the movie is terrifyingly effective. Yet the same "institution as walled city" idea applied in *High School* (1968) seems diffuse and directionless; the relationship between the teachers and the taught that Wiseman wants us to notice is too low key and too repetitive to build a sense of development. Because of his nonintercessional approach, because he rejects narration and interviews, his technique fails to develop and intensify what I presume is the key issue: whether an American high school can possibly prepare children to participate in a democracy.

Do not be fooled by the sophistication of today's technology into thinking that a storyteller's apprenticeship has changed. The help you need to structure your story lies in narrative traditions developed through centuries and in several disciplines. Your masters are in all the arts, and you belong with both Bunyan and Buñuel, and with Brecht, Bergman, Brueghel, and Bartók too. Take a keen interest in how fellow artists solve the problems you face, and you will learn fast.

DEVELOPING A STRUCTURE

To summarize this discussion,

- You must look for the best story in your dailies and the best way to tell it.
- Your approach to, and structure for, a particular subject must reach beyond the material world of cause and effect and imply a thematic and interpretive stance.
- All satisfying stories deal with change or the need for it. An interesting subject that lacks development in characters, theme, or emotion will fall short of being a fulfilling film.
- Literary, poetic, theatrical, and other disciplines have parallel examples to help you with the syntax of the story you are developing.

There are two ways to approach organizing the first assembly of material. Most people, unaware there are options, take the journalistic route and end up with a film that expresses itself in wall-to-wall words. The other method is image oriented and leads to an action-driven film. This makes better use of the screen as a medium. Which you use depends on knowing you have options, what you have shot, and how you want to relate to your audience.

FINDING AN ACTION-DETERMINED STRUCTURE

Early in my career while working on rapidly shot oral history films for the British Broadcasting Corporation (BBC), I got into the habit of depending too much on interviews and ended up making a lot of word-driven stories. A decade later, after shooting a Swedish community festival in Illinois with a sociologist friend, I found during editing that I had a great deal of action footage—that is, material in which people were busy doing things. So I assembled all the action footage first to make what was in effect an observational documentary that showed the course of Old Settlers' Day, as the Swedish reunion day is called. You see a buildup of people arriving at a prairie museum village, various activities prior to a parade, then the parade itself, which represents Bishop Hill's history since the 1840s. Intercut are the handicrafts, the Swedish food being cooked and consumed, an outdoor religious service, and a host of other scenes. There are also paintings from the 1880s by Olaf Krans, a celebrated naïve artist and native of Bishop Hill who documented key events and personalities. Finally I brought to the observational film selected voice-overs and interview segments to provide basic information, a historical backdrop, an explanation of how Bishop Hill's charismatic leader was murdered, and the commentary of a local historian who thinks that ordinary people are taking history into their own hands instead of letting academics do it for them.

Starting with imagery and action and then resorting to dialogue and intellectual information was a superior working method because it began from the visual and cinematic standpoint rather than one more literary and ideological. People's thoughts and ideas now arose out of what they were doing rather than their activities being used to illustrate their words. Not all documentaries have such a wealth of action material; many deal with ideas and processes (such as scientific discoveries) for which there can be little pictorial material. But when you have plenty of visual material and action sequences, try doing the following:

1. Put together an assembly using only observational material and view it without stopping. What does this material convey? Does it, for instance, tell a story, convey a mood, introduce a society, or set an epoch?

2. What time period do you know your material spans, and how well does the assembly convey that lapse of time? (It's always useful for events to happen in a set period of time.)

3. What memorable interchanges or developments did you capture on-camera? This, of course, is probably your strongest and most persuasive "evidence."

4. What would your film convey were it a silent film? (This is the acid test by which to see whether any film is cinematic rather than literary or theatrical.)

5. How many clear phases does the observational film fall into, and what characterizes each phase?

6. What verbal material do you have that adds new dimensions to the "silent film" assembly?

7. What does it add and what new dimensions does the original action- and behaviorally based film acquire? (Make a new working hypothesis.)

8. How little speech material do you need to further shift the film toward something you want?

By compiling visual and behavioral evidence you are letting imagery develop the story instead of words doing the job in a literary fashion. By bringing words in minimally, by using voice-over rather than "talking heads," you develop a film in which the characters seem to be speaking from their interior lives rather than addressing a camera.

FINDING A WORD-DRIVEN STRUCTURE (USING THE PAPER EDIT)

When the selected material of your film is mainly speakers, you can pre-edit transcripts and make what's called a *paper edit*. This makes use of shot descriptions and transcripts to design an effective first assembly. There is a special value to manipulating ideas on paper rather than editing footage at this stage. Handling descriptions enables you to consider content and subtext from a bird's-eye view and to concentrate on how each segment might function. If you try to do it from hours of footage, you get submerged in moment-to-moment action. Work on a paper edit is therefore a focused search for the *underlying structure and factual logic* that any film needs to be successful.

ASSEMBLING THE PAPER EDIT

To prevent your film from turning into solid speech, first deal with your action sequences, that is, those that show human processes with a beginning, middle, and end. Make a list of these sequences and design an overall structure that moves them logically through time. Be conservative with your first structure. If you have a film about a rural girl going to the big city to become a college student, stay true at first to the chronology of events (as opposed to the events unfolding according to their importance, say). Afterward, when you can better see how the material plays, you might intercut her high school graduation, conversations with a teacher, discussions with her father, and leaving home with the development of her first semester as a college drama student. You would now have two parallel stories to tell, one in the "present" and one in the "past." It would be very risky to assume you can accomplish this in one giant step.

First view the action or behavioral material in time sequence so that its narrative possibilities are firmly established in your mind. Now you can go on to plan a safe, linear version, beginning from a paper edit that includes speech.

To do this, take your chosen transcript sections, as discussed in Chapter 29 (see Figures 29–3 and 29–4). These slips of paper, coded ("Jane" for Jane's sequences) so you can rapidly turn to parent copies in the marked-up transcripts, might look something like this:

1/Jane/1	Graduation speech
1/Jane/2	Dinner with boyfriend's family
1/Jane/3	Conversation with English teacher
2/Jane/1	Conversation with Dad

Additionally, you have the many pieces of action made into a preliminary assembly, ready to accommodate the dialogue sections of the film. These are best represented as sequences rather than as individual shots, which would be too detailed and cumbersome. Three sequences would go on separate slips of paper, each with a cassette location (cassette number, minutes, and seconds):

1/5:30	Exterior school, cars arriving
2/9:11	Preparations at podium, Jane rehearses alone
4/17:38	Airport, Jane looking for bus

On the floor, or a large table if you have one, move the slips of paper around to try different orders and juxtapositions. Certain pieces of interview or conversational exchange belong with certain pieces of action, either because the location is the same or because one comments on the other. This "comment" may be literally a spoken comment or, better, it might be implied by an ironic juxtaposition (of action or speech) that makes its own point in the viewer's mind.

An example would be a scene in which our student Jane has to make a graduation speech before the whole school, an obligation that scares her. To make a literal comment, you would simply intercut the scene with the interview shot later in which she confesses how nervous she feels. A nonliteral comment might take the same rehearsal and intercut her mother saying how calm and confident she usually is. A visual comment might show that during the rehearsal she is flustered when the microphone is the wrong height and that her hands shake when she turns the pages of her speech.

What is the difference here? The literal comment is show-and-tell because it merely illustrates what Jane's thoughts and feelings already give us. The nonliteral comment is more interesting because it supplies us with conflicting information. Her mother rather enviously thinks she can handle anything, but we see the girl is under a lot of strain. Either the mother is overrating the girl's confidence or she is out of touch with her child's inner life. This alerts us to scrutinize the family dynamics more carefully. The purely visual comment gives us behavioral evidence that all is not well, that the girl is suffering. It is a privileged insight discreetly shared with the audience.

The order and juxtaposition of material, therefore, have potent consequences. The way you eventually present and use the material signals your ideas about the people and the subject you are profiling and reveals how you intend to relate to your audience. In essence, you are like a lawyer juxtaposing *pieces of evidence* in order to stimulate the interest and involvement of the jury, your audience. Good evidentiary juxtaposition provides sharp impressions and removes the need to do much arguing.

However, don't aim for too much refined control in the paper edit. Much of the final effect depends on the nuances of the material and can only be judged from how it plays on the screen. The mobility and flexibility of the paper edit system will reveal initial possibilities and get you thinking about what design these individual materials could make.

Do not be disturbed if your paper edit is vastly too long and includes repetitious subject matter. This is normal, because your more refined decisions can only be made from experimentally intercutting and screening the material.

Your slips of paper have been moved about like the raw materials for a mosaic. Once a reasonably logical order for the chosen materials has been found, you can staple the slips of paper to whole, consecutively numbered sheets, which you then bind into a file called the *Paper Edit*. Now you have a rudimentary story; you can rule lines between sequences and group the sequences into scenes and acts. From this master plan you begin making a loose, exploratory assembly in the editing computer.

CHAPTER 31

EDITING: THE FIRST ASSEMBLY

This chapter deals with

- Beginning the first assembly of the film
- Screening the film and seeing it as a first-time audience would
- Diagnostic questioning and deciding the film's ideal length
- Being a dramatist and finding subtexts
- Communicating with your audience

Using the film's action-driven structure or its word-driven structure found through the paper edit (if that's the route you took), you attempted to plan its themes and capitalize on your material. You can now put the material together roughly as planned without agonizing over the consequences of what you are doing. Leave everything long and do not worry about repetitiveness. You may need to see both men tell how the dam broke before you really know which to use or which to use most. Keep in mind that you cannot totally premeditate a film from knowledge of rushes any more than you can plan a journey to shore on a surfboard.

Putting the material together for the first time is the most exciting part of editing. You should not worry at this stage about length or balance.

I think it is important to *see the whole film as soon as possible in some long, loose form before doing any detailed work on any sections*. Once you have seen the whole ungainly epic, you can make far-reaching resolutions about its future development. Of course, you will be longing to go to work on a favorite sequence, but fixing details would be avoiding the need to first assess the film's overall identity and purpose.

During the first assembly, and certainly after it, your material will start telling you where and how to cut. This signals a welcome and slightly mysterious change in your role from proactive to reactive. Formerly you had to apply energy to get anything done, and now the energy starts to come from the film itself. Soon, all you have to do is to run the film, comprehend as an audience member, and act on what you understand. As your creation comes to life, this will be profoundly exciting.

SCREENING THE FIRST ASSEMBLY AND THE RETURN TO INNOCENCE

When you are about to see a first assembly of the film, you must deliberately set aside all foreknowledge or you will be unable to see the film with the eyes of a first-time viewer. The discipline of filmmaking requires that you regularly return to a state of innocence. This is never easy. But seeing as your audience sees is central to working effectively in an audience medium. Only by disciplining yourself to see like an audience can you construct a film that speaks satisfyingly to someone of your own intelligence who is seeing the film for the first time.

The same unobstructed, audience-like way of viewing is necessary *every* time you run your film. Though you use your familiarity with the source material to solve problems, this is only one of your identities. You must change hats every time you assess the film and *see it for itself, as a first-time audience would*. It helps to have one or two people present who have not seen the movie before. Although they may not utter a word, somehow their mere presence enables the makers to see the film from a fresh perspective.

If, on seeing your editor's new version, you experience a resistance in yourself because it is not what you expected, screen the new version again in order to see it more acceptingly, as an audience sees it, before you make any negative pronouncements.

AFTER THE FIRST VIEWING: DECIDING ON AN IDEAL LENGTH

That first viewing will yield some important realizations about the character, dramatic shape, and best length of the film. It may be that you have a particular length in mind. Television, for instance, usually has quite rigid specifications, with a 30-minute Public Broadcasting System (PBS) or British Broadcasting Corporation (BBC) "slot" requiring a film (including titles) of about 28:30 minutes to allow for announcements at either end. Almost all television documentaries are shown as part of a series because audiences only learn to watch, seemingly, when a time in the week becomes associated with a particular kind of film. This is why professional films are more often funded as packages and as co-productions.

If your movie is to be shown on commercial television, it will have to be broken up into segments of perhaps 5 minutes with so-called *natural breaks* to allow for commercials. Thus, the outlet for your film determines both length and structure. Classroom films are normally 10 to 20 minutes, whereas television uses 30-, 40- (in Europe), 60-, and 90-minute slots. Short films that say a lot have an immeasurably better chance of acceptance everywhere.

Look to the content of your film itself for guidance. Films have a natural span according to the richness and significance of their content, but the hardest achievement in any art form is having the confidence and ability to say a lot through a little. Most beginners' films are agonizingly long and slow; if you recognize early that your film should be, say, 40 minutes at the very most, you can get tough with that 75-minute assembly and make some basic decisions. Most of all, you need a structure to make the movie as gripping and comprehensible as any well-told tale. Bear in mind that a good plan does not guarantee a satisfying experience for an audience. Other criteria will come into play, arising from the emotional changes and development an audience will actually experience.

DIAGNOSTIC QUESTIONING

You are dealing with the film in its crudest form, so you want to elicit your own dominant reactions. To assess a likely audience response, question yourself after the first viewing.

- *Does the film feel dramatically balanced?* For instance, if you have a very moving and exciting sequence in the middle of the film, the rest of the film may seem anticlimactic, or you may have a film that seems to circle around for a long while before it really starts moving.

- *When did you have the definite feeling of a story unfolding, and when not?* This helps locate impediments in the film's development and sets you analyzing why the film stumbles.

- *Which parts of the film seem to work, which drag, and why?*

- *Which participants held your attention the most, and which the least?* Some may be more congenial or just better on camera than others.

- *Was there a satisfying alternation of types of material?* Or was similar material clumped indigestibly together? Where did you get effective contrasts and juxtapositions? Are there more to be made? Variety is as important in storytelling as it is in dining.

- *Does the audience get too much or too little expository information?* Sometimes a sequence "does not work" because the ground has not been properly prepared or because there is insufficient contrast in mood with the previous sequence.

- *Could exposition be delayed?* Exposition that is too much or too early reduces the will to concentrate by removing all anticipatory tension in the viewer.

- *What kinds of metaphorical allusions does your material make?* Could it make more? This underlying statement is the way you imply your values and beliefs. That your tale carries a metaphorical charge is as important as the water table is to pasture.

DEALING WITH MATERIAL THAT DOESN'T WORK

After seeing an assembly, scribble a list of memorable material. Then, by making and comparing a full sequence list, see what you *didn't* recall. Quite purposefully, the human memory discards what it doesn't find meaningful. You forgot all that good stuff because it failed to work, however great it looked on paper. This does not mean that it can *never* work, only that it is not doing so at present.

Here are a few common reasons why material misfires:

- *Two or more sequences are making the same point.* Repetition does not advance a film argument unless there is escalation. Make choices, then ditch the redundant.
- *A climax is in the wrong place.* You are using your strongest material too early, and the film becomes anticlimactic.
- *Tension builds then slackens.* Think of your movie as having a rising or falling emotional temperature; see if it is raising the temperature then inadvertently cooling it before an intended peak. If so, the viewer's response is seriously impaired. Sometimes transposing sequences will work wonders.
- *The film raises false expectations.* A film, or part thereof, will fail if the viewer is set up to expect something that never gets delivered.
- *Good material is somehow lost on the audience.* We read into film according to the context, and if this gives misleading signals or fails to focus the right awareness, the material itself falls flat.
- *Multiple endings.* Decide what your film is really about and get out the pruning shears.

THE DOCUMENTARY MAKER AS DRAMATIST

The earlier discussion looks like traditional dramatic analysis because this is really what it is. Like a playwright watching a first performance, you are using your instinct for drama to sniff out faults and weaknesses. It is hard because no objective measurements are possible. All you can do is dig for your own instincts through *feeling* the dramatic outcome of your material. If you called in some people whose reactions and tastes you respect, you will probably find some unanimity in their responses.

Where does the instinct for drama come from? It seems to be a human constant that resides in our collective unconsciousness, a human drive that has been present since antiquity. We have both a compulsion to tell stories and a hunger to hear them. Think of the variations on the Arthurian legends that exist. They come from the Middle Ages, yet they are still being adapted and updated and are still giving pleasure after a thousand years!

PLEASING YOUR AUDIENCE

As history personally felt and relayed, the documentary carries on the oral tradition. To be successful, it must connect with the emotional and imaginative life of a contemporary audience. The documentarian must be concerned not just with self-expression, which can be a narcissistic display of conscience or feelings, but with entertaining and therefore serving society.

Like all entertainers, the filmmaker has a precarious economic existence and either fulfills the audience or goes hungry. In *Literature and Film*,[1] Robert Richardson argues that the vitality and optimism of the cinema, compared with other 20th-century art forms, is due to its collaborative authorship and its dependency on public response. Of course, it would be absurd and cynical to claim that only the appreciation of the masses matters, but the enduring presence of folk art—plays, poetry, music, architecture, and traditional tales—should alert us to how much we share with the untutored tastes of our forebears.

The simple fact is that the "ordinary" person's tastes and instincts—yours and mine—are highly acculturated. In ordinary life we never have to discuss them in depth or use them to make art statements, so we lack confidence when it comes time to live by them. Making a documentary is exciting because you have to lay your perceptions and judgments on the line.

SUBTEXTS: MAKING THE VISIBLE SIGNIFICANT

In Chapter 5 of *Literature and Film*, Richardson goes to the heart of the problem filmmakers face compared with writers: "Literature often has the problem of making the significant somehow visible, while film often finds itself trying to make the visible significant."[2]

It is difficult, as we have said before, to drive the audience's awareness deeper than what is literally and materially in front of the camera. For instance, we may accept a scene in which a mother makes lunch for her children as simply that. "So what?," you ask; mothers make lunch for kids all the time. But there are nuances: one child has persistent difficulty choosing what she wants. The mother is trying to suppress her irritation. Looking closely, you see that the child is manipulating the situation. Food and eating have become their battleground, their frontier in a struggle for control. The mother's moral authority comes from telling her daughter she must eat right to stay healthy, while the child asserts her authority over her own body by a maddening noncompliance.

What we have here (as so often in film) is the problem of showing how a meal is more than food, of showing it as a battleground with a deadly serious subtext. If we first see child and mother in some other, more overt conflict over control, we probably would read the scene correctly. There may be other ways, of course, in which attention could be channeled, but without the proper structural support, the significance and universality of such a scene could easily pass unappreciated. Naturally, what you the filmmaker can see happening will not necessarily strike even the most perceptive of first-time viewers because they lack your commitment, your behind-the-scenes knowledge, and your repeated exposure to the situation that brings with it a deepening insight. However you evolved,

---

[1] Robert Richardson, *Literature and Film* (Bloomington, IN: Indiana University Press, 1969), 3–16.
[2] Ibid., 68.

you must now evolve your audience to the same point, but in 30 minutes instead of 30 weeks.

AFTER THE DUST SETTLES, WHAT NEXT?

After seeing the first assembly, fundamental issues really begin to emerge. You may see your worst fears: your film has no less than three endings—two false and one intended. Your favorite character makes no impact at all beside others who seem more spontaneous and alive. You have to concede that a sequence in a dance hall, which was hell to shoot, has only one really good minute in it or that a woman you interviewed for a minor opinion actually says some striking things and is upstaging an "important" contributor.

The first assembly auditions the best material and becomes the launching pad for a denser and more complex film. As a show, it is woefully inadequate because it is so long and crude, yet because of its very artlessness it can be both affecting and exciting.

In the coming stages, avoid trying to fix everything in one grandiose swipe. Wait a few days and think things over, then tackle only the major needs of the film. Forswear the pleasures of fine-tuning or you won't see the forest for the trees.

CHAPTER 32

EDITING: THE PROCESS OF REFINEMENT

This chapter covers

- Achieving a smoothly flowing narrative
- Editing to convey point of view (POV)
- Analogies to editing practices in music
- Keeping the audience challenged and occupied
- Disguising seams and mimicking consciousness shifts

THE PROBLEM OF ACHIEVING A FLOW

After you have run your first assembly two or three times, it will increasingly strike you as clunky blocks of material having a dreadful lack of flow. First you may have some illustrative stuff, then several blocks of interview, then a montage of shots, then another block of something else, and so on. Sequences go by like a series of floats in a parade, each quite separate from its fellows. How do you achieve the effortless flow seen in other people's films? Let's return to the way human perception functions and how it affects eyeline shifts.

HOW EDITING MIMICS CONSCIOUSNESS

Take the commonly dramatized situation of two people having a conversation. When inexperienced players act such a scene, they invariably lock eyes as they speak. This is an idea of how people converse, but reality is more subtle and interesting. Observe yourself during a normal conversation, and see how neither you nor the other person makes eye contact more than fleetingly. The intensity of eye-to-eye contact is reserved for special moments.

During any interaction we are either *acting* on the other person or *being acted upon*. At crucial points in either mode, we glance into the other person's face to see what he or she means or to judge what effect we have just had. The rest of the time our gaze may rest on some object or jump around the surroundings. At special junctures in our inner process, our eye returns to the other person. Developing ideas about how this works will greatly help you to decide camerawork and editing.

Now become the observer of two people talking and decide what makes your eyeline shift back and forth between them. Notice how often your eyeline shifts are triggered by shifts in *their* eyelines. Your consciousness is alerted by the significance of their shifts. As you watch, you will become conscious not only of a rhythm and motivation to their shifts of eyeline (controlled by the shifting contours of the conversation itself) but also that *moment to moment your eyes make their own judgment as to where to look.* Much of the time your center of attention independently switches back and forth, stimulated by the pair's action and reaction and their changes of eyeline.

Notice how often your eyes leave a speaker in midsentence to monitor his or her effect on the listener. Instinctively, from a lifetime's practice, we *"edit" according to our developing insight, trying to extract the most subtextual information from the scene.* This exercise explains how and why editing developed as we know it.

LOOKING AT AND LOOKING THROUGH

In my earlier example, a film would have to relay three different POVs: one for each of the participants and a third for the observer. The observer's POV is outside the enclosed consciousness of the two speakers and tends to look at them from a more detached, authorial vantage. According to choices made in editing, the audience can identify with either one of the characters or with the more removed perspective of the invisible observer—who in film is usually the storyteller. While character A talks, for instance, the observer (through whose eyes and mind we see) might look at either A or B in search of ideas that A has of B or vice versa. Or the film might allow the audience to look at both of them in long shot.

This flexibility of viewpoint allows the director not only to construe geographically privileged viewpoints but to share what the observer sees (and therefore feels) at any particular moment. This probing, analytical way of seeing is, of course, modeled on the way we unconsciously delve into any event that interests us. *The film process thus mimics the interpretive quest that both accompanies and directs human observation.*

Trying to put this in writing probably makes it sound unduly complicated. The best teacher is always going to be the movement of your own consciousness, that is, what you see, what you hear, what acts on your feelings, and what these make you think. Human beings are similar to each other (otherwise, there could be no cinema), and there are many nonverbal signs—in body language, eyeline shifts, voice inflections, and particular actions—to which we all ascribe similar meanings. A great benefit of documentary is that it's an excellent instructor in all this.

EDITING RHYTHMS: AN ANALOGY IN MUSIC

Music makes a useful analogy if we examine an edited version of a conversation between a grandparent and grandchild. We have two different but interlocked rhythms going. First, there is the rhythmic pattern of their voices in a series of sentences that ebb and flow, speed up, slow down, halt, restart, fade, and so on. Set against this, and often taking a rhythmic cue from speech rhythms, is the visual tempo set up by the interplay of cutting, image compositions, and camera movement. The two streams, visual and aural, proceed independently yet are rhythmically related, like the music and the physical movements in a dance performance.

When you hear a speaker and you see his face as he talks, sound and vision are in an alliance, like musical harmony. We could, however, break the literalness of always hearing and seeing the same thing *(harmony)* by making the transition from scene to scene into a temporary puzzle.

Here is an example. We are going to cut from a man talking about unemployment to a somber cityscape. We start with the speaker in picture and then cut to the cityscape while the man is still speaking, letting his remaining words play out over the cityscape. The effect is as follows. While our subject was talking to us about growing unemployment, we glanced out of the window to see all the houses spread out below us, the empty parking lots, and the cold chimneys of closed factories. The film version mimics the instinctual glance of someone sitting there listening; the speaker's words are powerfully counterpointed by the image, and the image lets loose our imagination as we ponder the magnitude of the disruption, of what it is like to live in one of those houses.

This *counterpoint*, of a sound against an unlike image, has its variations. One usage is simply to illustrate the actuality of what words can only describe. We might cut from a bakery worker talking about fatigue to shots taken through shimmering heat of workers in a bread factory moving about their repetitive tasks like zombies.

Another usage exploits discrepancies. For instance, we hear a teacher describing an enlightened and attractive philosophy of teaching, but then see the same man lecturing in a monotone, drowning his yawning students in a torrent of facts and stifling any discussion. This discrepancy, if we pursue the musical allusion, is a *dissonance*, spurring the viewer to crave a resolution. Comparing the man's beliefs with his practice, the viewer resolves the discrepancy by deciding that here is a man who does not know himself.

COUNTERPOINT IN PRACTICE: UNIFYING MATERIAL INTO A FLOW

Once a reasonable order for the material has been found, you will want to combine sound and action in a form that takes advantage of counterpoint techniques. In practice this means, as we have said, bringing together the sound from one shot with the image from another. To develop the previous example (the teacher with superb theory and poor performance), you could show this on the screen by shooting two sets of materials, one of relevantly structured interview and the other of the teacher droning away in class.

We edit these materials into juxtaposition. The conservative, first-assembly method would alternate segments as in Figure 32–1A: a block of interview in which the man begins explaining his ideas, then a block of teaching, then another block of explanation, then another of teaching, and so on until the point is made. This is a common, though clumsy, way to accomplish the objective in the assembly stage. After a little back-and-forth cutting, the technique and the message both are predictable. I think of it as boxcar cutting because each chunk goes by like boxcars on a railroad.

Instead of alternating the two sets of materials, it would be better to integrate them as shown in Figure 32–1B. Start with the teacher examining his philosophy of teaching and then cut to the classroom sequence, with the classroom sound low and the teacher's explanation continuing over it (this is called *voice-over*). When the voice has finished its sentence, we bring up the sound of the classroom sequence and play the classroom at full level. Then we lower the classroom atmosphere and bring in the teacher's interview voice again. At the end of the classroom action, as the teacher gets interesting, we cut to him in sync (now including his picture to go with his voice). At the end of what was Block 3 in Figure 32–1A, we continue his voice but cut—in picture only—back to the classroom, where we see the bored and mystified kids of Block 4. Now, instead of having description and practice dealt with in separate blocks of material, description is laid against practice and ideas against reality, in a much harder hitting counterpoint.

The benefits are multiple. The total sequence is shorter and sprightlier. Talking-head material is kept to a decent minimum, while the behavioral material—the classroom evidence against which we measure the teacher's ideas—is now in the majority. The counterpointing of essentials allows an interview to be pared down, giving what is presented a muscular, spare quality, usually lacking

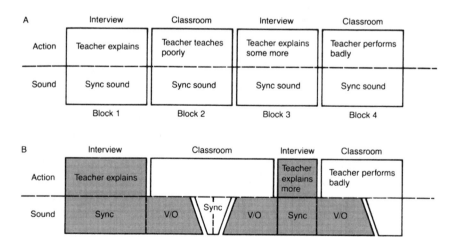

FIGURE 32–1

(A) First assembly of material through a block or "boxcar" approach compared with (B), an overlap edit, which allows a simultaneous counterpoint of idea and actuality.

in unedited reminiscence. There is a much closer and more telling juxtaposition between vocalized theory and actual teaching behavior. The audience is challenged right away to reconcile the man's ideas with what he is actually doing.

Counterpoint editing cannot be worked out in the paper edit, but usually you can decide quite confidently which materials could effectively be intercut. The specifics then can be worked out from the materials themselves.

THE AUDIENCE AS ACTIVE PARTICIPANTS

Significantly, this more demanding texture of word and image puts the spectator in a different relationship to the "evidence" presented. It encourages active rather than passive participation. The contract is no longer just to absorb and be instructed. Instead, the invitation is to *interpret and weigh what you see and hear*. The film now sometimes uses action to illustrate, and other times to contradict, what has been set up and what has seemed true. The viewer's independent judgment was invoked in the earlier example of the teacher and the classroom because the teacher is an *unreliable narrator* whose words cannot be taken as conventionally bland guidance.

But there are other ways for juxtaposition and counterpoint to stimulate imagination when the conventional coupling of sound and picture is changed. For instance, you might show a street shot in which a young couple goes into a café. We presume they are lovers. They sit at a table in the window. We who remain outside are near an elderly couple discussing the price of fish, but the camera moves in close to the window so that we can see through the glass how the couple talk affectionately and energetically to each other, while what we hear is the old couple arguing over the price of fish. The effect is an ironic contrast between two states of intimacy; we see courtship but we hear the concerns of later life. With great economy of means, and not a little humor, a cynical idea about marriage is set afloat—one that the rest of the film ultimately might dispel with hopeful alternatives.

By creating juxtapositions that require choice and interpretation, film is able to counterpoint antithetical ideas and moods with great economy. At the same time it can kindle the audience's involvement with the dialectical nature of life. If we are to interest people who normally turn away from the pedestrian nature of so much documentary, we must find ways to be as funny, earthy, and poignant as life itself. How else will we get audiences to willingly contemplate the darker aspects of life?

Counterpointing the visual and the aural is only an extension of what has been called *montage* since early in film's history. In editing, the juxtaposition of two dissimilar shots implies relatedness and continuity, and the audience's imagination is meant to supply the linkage between them or between sequences. The use of contrapuntal sound as a dialectical medium came relatively late and was, I believe, developed by documentary makers. In fiction filmmaking, Robert Altman's films from *M*A*S*H* (1970) onward show the most inventiveness in producing a dense, layered counterpoint in their sound tracks. Altman's sound recordist even built a special 16-track location sound recorder, which could make individual recordings from up to 15 wireless microphones. In documentary, Errol

Morris' *Mr. Death* (2003) is notable for its imaginative, if not surreal, atmosphere. Music and sound effects contribute much to the air of sustained hallucination that is Morris' version of Fred Leuchter's reality.

THE OVERLAP CUT: DIALOGUE SEQUENCES

Another contrapuntal editing device useful to hide the telltale seams between shots is called the *overlap cut* (also known as *lap cut* or *L cut*). The overlap cut brings sound in earlier than picture, or picture in earlier than sound, and thus avoids the jarring level cut, which results in boxcar editing.

Figure 32–2 shows a straight-cut version of a conversation between A and B. Whoever speaks is shown on the screen. This quickly becomes predictable and boring. You can alleviate this problem by slugging in some reaction shots (not shown).

Now look at the same conversation using overlap cutting. A starts speaking, but when we hear B's voice, we wait a sentence before cutting to him. B is interrupted by A, and this time we hold on B's frustrated expression before cutting to A driving his point home. Before A has finished and because we are now interested in B's rising anger, we cut back to him shaking his head. When A has finished, B caps the discussion, and we make a level cut to the next sequence. The three sections of integrated reaction are marked in Figure 32–2 as X, Y, and Z.

How do you decide when to make overlap cuts? It often is done at a later stage of cutting, but we need a guiding theory. Let's return for a moment to human consciousness, our ever-reliable model for editing. Imagine you are witnessing a conversation between two people; you have to turn from one to the other. Seldom will you turn your head at the right moment to catch the next

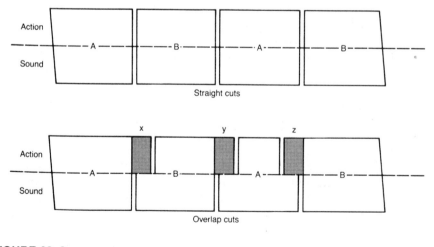

FIGURE 32–2 ————————————————————————————————————

Intercutting two speakers to make use of overlap cutting. Overlaps X, Y, and Z function as listening, reacting shots. Use this technique to reduce the sound gaps between speakers with no apparent speedup in pacing.

speaker beginning—only an omniscient being could be so accurate. Inexperienced or bad editors often make neat, level (and omniscient) cuts between speakers, and the results have a packaged, premeditated look that destroys the illusion of watching a spontaneous event.

In real life you seldom can predict when someone will speak next or even who it will be. So a new voice, after it has started, tells us where to look. If an editor is to convince us that a conversation is spontaneous, the observer/story-teller should mostly follow shifts, not anticipate them. The editor must replicate the disjunctive shifts we unconsciously make as our eyes follow our hearing, or our hearing focuses in late on something just seen.

Effective cutting always reproduces the needs and reactions of an involved observer, as if we were there ourselves. Listening to a speaker as she begins making her point, we often switch to consider the point's effect on her listener. Even as we ponder, that listener begins to reply. A moment of forcefulness causes us to switch attention to the listener, so without ceremony we glance away from her. The line of her mouth hardens, and we know she is disturbed.

Here we are receiving two complementary impressions—the speaker through our hearing and the listener through our vision, hearing the person who acts but looking at the person on whom she acts. When that situation reverses and our listener has begun his reply, we glance back to see how the original speaker is reacting. Unconsciously we are searching for visual clues—in facial expressions or body language—to the protagonists' inner lives.

This type of cutting allows the spectator to be engaged not just in hearing and seeing each speaker as he utters (which would be tedious) but also in *interpreting what is going on inside each protagonist* through seeing key moments of action, reaction, or subjective vision. In dramatic terms, this is the *search for subtext*, for what is going on beneath the surface.

For the aspiring editor the message is clear: be true to life by implanting the developing sensations of a critical observer in the audience. Do this, and sound and picture changeover points are seldom level cuts. Overlap cuts achieve this important disjunction, allowing the film to cut from shot to shot independently of the "his turn, her turn, his turn" speech alternations in the sound track.

THE OVERLAP CUT: SEQUENCE TRANSITIONS

In the same way, a transition from one sequence to another may also be a staggered cut. Imagine a scene where a boy and girl are talking about going out together. The boy says he is worried that the girl's mother will try to stop them. The girl says, "Oh don't worry about her, I can convince her." The next scene is of the mother closing the refrigerator with a bang and saying firmly "Absolutely not!" to the aggrieved daughter.

A level cut would mimic a fast theatrical scene change. More interesting would be to cut from the boy/girl scene to the mother at the refrigerator while the girl is still saying ". . . I can convince her." While she is still finishing her sentence, the picture cuts forward in time to show the mother slamming the fridge door and then saying her line, "Absolutely not!"

Another way to merge one scene into the next rather than make a staccato level cut would be to hold on the boy and girl, have the mother's angry voice say "Absolutely not!" over the tail end of their scene, and use the surprise of the new voice to motivate cutting to the mother's picture as the scene continues.

Either of these devices serves to make the "joints" between one sequence and the next less theatrical and noticeable. Sometimes you want to bring a scene to a slow closure, perhaps with a fade-out, and then gently and slowly begin another, this time perhaps with a fade-in. More often, you simply want to cut from one scene to the next and keep up the momentum. A level cut will often seem to jerk the viewer rudely into a new place and time. A dissolve can instead integrate the two scenes, but it also inserts a rest period between scenes. This dissipates the carryover of momentum.

The overlap cut is the answer. It keeps the track alive and draws the viewer after it, so the transition seems natural rather than forced. You have surely seen this done with sound effects. It might look like this: The factory worker rolls reluctantly out of bed, then as he shaves and dresses, we hear the increasingly loud sound of machinery until we cut to him at work on the production line. Here *anticipatory sound* drags our attention forward to the next sequence. Because our curiosity demands an answer to the riddle of machine sounds in a bedroom, we do not feel the location switch is arbitrary.

Another overlap cutting technique would be to make sound work the other way. We cut from the man working on the assembly line to him getting some food out of his home refrigerator. *Holdover sound* of factory uproar subsides slowly as he exhaustedly eats some leftovers.

In the first example, the aggressive factory sound draws him forward out of his bedroom; in the second, it lingers even after he has gotten home. In both cases, a psychological narrative is implied, because both sound devices suggest that the sound exists in his head as an awareness of how unpleasant his workplace is. At home he thinks of it and is sucked up by it; after work the din continues to haunt him.

By using overlap cuts we can not only soften transitions between locations but also suggest subtext and POV through implying the inner consciousness of a central character. We could play it the other way and let the silence of the home trail out into the workplace so that he is seen at work, and the bedroom radio continues to play softly before being swamped by the rising uproar of the factory. At the end of the day, the sounds of laughter on the television set could displace the factory noise and make us cut to him sitting at home, relaxing with a sitcom.

By using sound and picture transitions creatively, you can transport the viewer forward without the cumbersome (and in film, expensive) device of using optical effects, such as dissolves, fades, and wipes. You can also give important clues about your characters' inner lives and imaginations.

These cutting techniques are hard to grasp from a book. Look for them in the films you watch, and work out how they reproduce the habitual way our eyes, ears, and intelligence work together as they dig for subtextual meanings.

In summary, we have established that in life our consciousness can probe our surroundings either monodirectionally (eyes and ears on the same information source) or bidirectionally (eyes and ears on different sources). Our attention also moves in time, either forward (anticipation and imagination) or backward (memory). Film language can recreate all these aspects of consciousness and by so doing helps the audience to share the sensations of a shifting consciousness, either that of characters or that of the storyteller, or both.

HELP! I CAN'T UNDERSTAND!

If this is getting beyond you, don't worry. The best way to understand editing is to take a complex and interesting fiction sequence and, by running a shot or two at a time on a video cassette recorder (VCR) or digital video disk (DVD) player, make a split-page log of the relationship between the track elements and the visuals. In Chapter 13, Project 13-2, Editing Analysis, is an editing self-education program with a list of editing techniques for you to track down and analyze. Try returning to this section, and with examples in hand it should make a lot more sense.

CHAPTER 33

NARRATION

This chapter covers

- Reasons to use narration
- What to avoid
- Improvising a narration or using a text
- How to create narration and what to avoid
- Casting and directing a narrator
- Laying narration effectively

Today, and for good reason, it is unfashionable to use the disembodied, author-itative narration that is far too identified with older power structures. Today it is widespread only in journalistic documentary and history series. However, you may have directed a personal or anthropological film and want to use a perfectly justified narration to provide links or to supply context. Or you may be forced into using narration because expositional material is lacking and the film's story line needs help. Narration is always available as a recourse and need not be a dishonorable or detrimental one at that.

PROBLEMS THAT NARRATION CAN SOLVE

If during shooting you remembered to elicit all relevant expository information from participants, you can assemble the movie and see how it stands on its own feet. There are a number of common problems that indicate when you may need narration:

- Difficulty getting the film started (the *setup*, in the language of drama)
- Failure to establish background or historical context so that the audience can enter the movie

- Failure to identify the origin and therefore authenticity of material (it might be reconstruction, for instance)
- Film lacks momentum
- Audience wants to know more about a participants thoughts, feelings, and choices
- Complicated story line is incomprehensible
- Getting from one good sequence to the next takes too much explaining by the participants
- Lack of resolution to the film because the evidence never achieves a satisfying focus

Proof that you have information problems is when a lukewarm trial audience becomes enthusiastic because you add comments on the material. Because no film can rely on its maker's presence to be effective, whatever you added must now be built into the movie. It may be simple information, but narration probably is the only way to supply the succinct words that are missing.

DRAWBACKS AND ASSOCIATIONS OF NARRATION

Narration can get you out of tight spots, but it becomes one more element to shape and control. If narration is not first rate, it becomes so intrusive that it will hamper rather than advance your movie. The very existence of a narrator poses problems because the disembodied voice becomes a mediating presence standing between audience and the film's "evidence." This, of course, is the voice of *authority*, with all its connotations of condescension and paternalism. Audiences wait wearily to discover what product or ideology the film is touting. Such films force us into passivity because they insist that we either accept authority or tune out. The intelligent documentary aims to involve the viewer's values and discrimination, not just to invade his or her memory or colonize the subconscious.

Viewers take the narrator's voice as *the voice of the film itself*. They base their judgments about the film's intelligence and biases not just on what narration says but on the quality and associations of the voice. For this reason, finding a suitable voice is very hard. In effect, the search is for one that, by words and quality, can act as a surrogate for your own attitude toward the subject.

POSITIVE ASPECTS OF NARRATION

In spite of narration's inauspicious associations, it need be neither condescending nor intrusive. It can be a lifesaver, rapidly and effectively introducing a new character, summarizing intervening developments, or concisely supplying a few vital facts. Especially when a film must fit a lot into a short duration, time saved is time won for additional "evidence" footage. Acceptable narration

- Is limited to useful factual information
- Is nonmanipulative emotionally

- Avoids value judgments, unless first established by evidence in the footage
- Avoids predisposing the viewer in any direction, but may justifiably draw our attention to those aspects of the evidence—visual or verbal—whose significance might otherwise be overlooked
- Lets the audience draw its own conclusions from the evidence you show

A narration can, drawing on traditions in literature, ballad, and poetry, adopt a stylized "voice." Many films adopt special narrative strategies, such as

- Using the voice-over of one of the characters whose authority to have an opinion is never in doubt
- A historical view, as in countless films about immigration, war, or slavery
- Artful simplicity, as in the naïve reporter persona that Nicholas Broomfield and Michael Moore both adopt in their films
- A what-if suppositional voice, as in the poet Jean Cayrol's commentary for Alain Resnais' *Night and Fog* (1955). Cayrol's authority comes from being a Holocaust survivor himself
- Poetic/musical identification with the subject, as in Basil Wright and Harry Watt's *Night Mail* (1936). The poet W.H. Auden wrote the poem used as the narration
- Angry irony, as in Luis Buñuel's *Land Without Bread* (1932), which uses bland acceptance of the unacceptable to rile its audience
- A first-person writer's voice addressing a particular reader, as in the war letters used in Ken Burns' *Civil War* series (1990)
- A diary voice, as fabricated for Humphrey Jennings' *A Diary for Timothy* (1946)

TWO APPROACHES TO CREATING NARRATION

Any original writing for film, whether documentary narration or dialogue for actors, must use the direct, clear language of everyday speech or it will fail. Film moves relentlessly in time, so an audience either gets the narration or chokes on verbal obstacles. Following are two ways to create a narration.

Method 1: Read from a script. This, the traditional method, can work well if your film acknowledges that it is based on letters, a diary, or other bona fide text. Then the unavoidable tinge of formality in any reading makes sense. When you want spontaneity or a one-on-one tone of intimacy, written narration nearly always fails. Think how often narration is the single element that makes a film unacceptably dull or dated. Some common faults are

- Verbosity (a writing problem)
- Heavy or literary writing (a writing problem)
- Doubt over who or what the narrator represents (a question of the narrator's authority)

- Something distracting in the narrator's voice; it may be dull, condescending, egotistic, projecting, trying to entertain, trying to be liked, or have distracting associations (a performance or casting problem)

Recording a read narration is inherently risky. Do it well in advance and to picture (described later). Never assume it will be all right on opening night.

Method 2: Use some degree of improvisation. Improvised narration can strike an attractively informal, "one-on-one" relationship with the audience. Examples include

- When a participant serves as narrator
- When you use your own voice in a "diary" film that must sound spontaneous and not scripted
- When you want to create a composite poetic voice, say, of a Japanese woman carrying out a tea ceremony (a highly questionable "speaking for" ploy but formerly more acceptable)

Let's look at what's involved with each method.

THE SCRIPTED NARRATION

WRITING

First and foremost, a narrator must have a good text. Be prepared to write and rewrite upward of 20 drafts. A test of quality for any piece of writing, particularly narration, is whether you can effectively read it aloud to a group of listeners. Having listeners for some reason makes you acutely aware of everything that is wrong. There should not even be a redundant syllable.

Bad narration uses

- The passive voice (where the subject is acted upon—fatal in a genre already replete with victims anyway!)
- Signs of ego
- Sonorous, ready-made phrases and clichés
- Long sentences
- The syntax of writing or literary discourse
- Windy ornamentation
- Jargon or other language used to impress
- Over-information that robs the audience of time to imagine or guess (regularly inflicted in films for children)
- Description of what is already evident
- Assumed voices or other condescending humor

Good narration uses

- The direct, active-voice language of speech
- The right and simplest word for the job
- Fresh language, not stale
- The fewest words—as if you are writing poetry; pack the most meaning into the fewest syllables in language that is balanced and potent to the ear
- The active, not passive, voice (e.g., "Here immigrants *drive* the taxis" not "Here taxis *are driven* by immigrants")

As you edit and re-edit your film, hone your writing in search of the power of simplicity. Exult when you find a way to reduce a sentence by even one syllable.

THE TRYOUT

As you write, examine each film section and write what you think is necessary. Then read your words aloud against each section. Your narration should rhythmically match those of the outgoing and incoming sequences. What you write must sound right in relation to both outgoing and incoming speakers (if there are any), and it must be the right length so you don't have to speed up or slow down to fill the space. Ends and beginnings of scenes sometimes need adjusting to accommodate narration.

ADJUSTING SYNTAX TO MATCH SCREEN LOGIC

Sometimes it helps to invert the syntax so that the narration follows the audience's order of perception as it follows a sequence or shot. For instance, if you have a shot of a big, rising sun with a small figure toiling across the landscape, the viewer notices the sun long before noticing the human being. You might first write, "She goes out before anyone else is about." But this immediately sets the viewer looking for the "she." The viewer loses the rest of the sentence while searching the screen for "she," the subject. If you reconfigure the syntax to accompany perceptions (sun, landscape, woman), you would get: "Before anyone else is up, she goes out." This complements the viewer's perceptions instead of swimming against the tide.

ACCOMMODATING SOUND FEATURES

Another reason to alter phrasing or to break sentences apart is to open up spaces for featured sound effects, such as a car door closing or a phone beginning to ring. Effects frequently create a powerful mood and drive the narrative forward, so don't obscure them with talking. Effects also help to mask the bane of the documentary—too much talk or, to put it in the vernacular, verbal diarrhea.

THE POWER IN EACH FIRST WORD

Here's a fact not widely appreciated: the first word to fall on each new image exerts a major influence on how the audience interprets the whole shot. For instance, we have two shots cut together as in Figure 33–1. The first outgoing

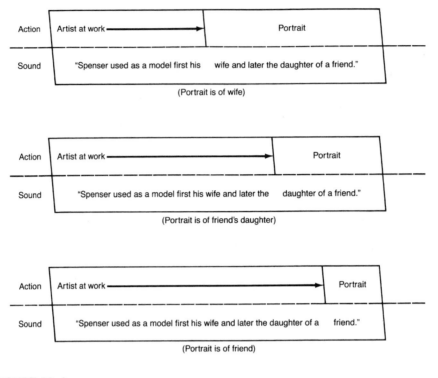

FIGURE 33–1

Three cutting points can convey three different meanings.

shot is a still photo showing an artist at work at his easel; the second incoming shot shows a painting of a woman. The narration says, "Spenser used as a model first his wife and later the daughter of a friend."

Different juxtapositions of words and images actually yield quite different meanings, and the crux lies in which word hits the incoming shot, as illustrated in the diagram. Using a single, unchanging section of narration we can in fact identify the person in the portrait three different ways depending on how it sits against the three images.

In another situation, illustrated in Figure 33–2, a simple shift in word positioning may alter only the emotional shading attached to an image rather than its basic identity. For instance, you see two shots, each of a piece of sculpture, and you hear the narrator say, "His later work was provocatively different."

By altering the relationship of narration to incoming image by a single word, the second sculpture can be made either just "different" or "*provocatively* different." Thus, writing skill and sensitivity to word positioning give you potent tools of communication.

OPERATIVE WORDS

Though I have talked about writing to images, you often face the reverse situation. Pictures must be edited to a preset narration or dialogue. There is a little

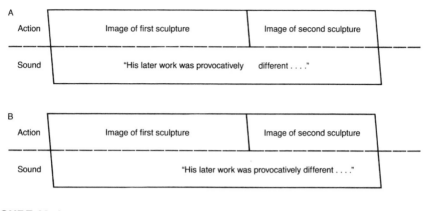

FIGURE 33–2 ——————————————————————————

Shifting word position against image can shade meaning. In (A) the second sculpture will be seen as an example of departure in the artist's work, while in (B) it is suggested more that the second sculpture (the "later work") elicited an excited critical reaction.

known key to doing this well: in any section of speech, there are strong places and weak places against which to make a picture cut. To decide this, examine the sentence. The speaker usually indicates dominant intentions by stressing certain syllables. Take something a mother says to a recalcitrant teenager: "I want you to wait right here and don't move. I'll talk to you later."

Several readings, each suggesting a different subtext, are possible, but a likely one is: "I want you to *wait* right here and *don't* move. I'll *talk* to you later. " Each of the stressed words represents an operative intention on the part of the speaker, so I call such words *operative words*. If we were to design how images would cut to this piece of dialogue, the split-page script would look like this:

Picture	*Sound*
Wide shot, woman and son	"I want you to . . .
Close shot, boy's mutinous face	**wait** right here and . . .
Close shot, her hand on his shoulder	**don't** move. (pause) I'll . . .
Close shot, mother's determined face	**talk** to you later."

On each operative word this script cuts to a new image: the mother's determination and the boy's stubborn resistance are reinforced by these placements, and each new shot punches in against a strong operative word. This dialogue principle pervades intelligent editing in both feature and documentary films. If you come across a sequence you like, study it in depth on your video cassette recorder (VCR) or digital video disk (DVD) player and decide what the thinking is behind the editing. This kind of work can greatly clarify how to direct and edit in documentary, though you may not want your documentary work to look so openly controlled, or your audience may feel that you are manipulating them.

A potent way to consider speech when editing is to listen to it as if you were a foreign musician. Not understanding the language, you listen for its meaning within the music that humanity makes as it communicates. What you begin to hear are rising and sinking tonal changes, rhythmic patterns in the stream of syllables like percussion, and dynamic variations of loud and soft. All this takes place in a single sentence, and once you become sensitive to this music, your editing, shot selection, and placement begin to take place inside a musical structure and forms a new, larger structure. Here film, music, and dance coincide.

Anyone interested in how orchestral music influenced by speech patterns can find examples in the late works of the Czech composer Leoš Janáček, particularly the middle movements of his *Sinfonietta*.

COMPLEMENT, DON'T DUPLICATE

When you write for film, avoid all temptation to describe what we can already see. Narration should add to the image, never duplicate by describing anything in the image's content. For example, you should never say that the child in the shot is wearing a red raincoat (blatantly obvious) or that she is hesitant (subtly evident), but you might well say that she has just celebrated her sixth birthday. This is information outside what we can see or infer.

TRYING IT OUT: THE SCRATCH RECORDING

Once you have written your narration, record a scratch (quick, trial) narration using any handy reader or your own voice. Lay in the scratch narration and watch it as dispassionately as you can three or four times. Improved versions of the wording will jump out at you, and the kind of voice you are going to need will be easier to imagine. Pacing and emotional coloration (if any) that will work best will also be evident. In some places, you see that the narrator has to hurry, so here you must thin the narration out; elsewhere the narration may seem too brief and perfunctory and in need of developing. Now you are ready to think about auditioning and recording the final narrator.

A SCRIPT FOR THE NARRATOR

The script prepared for the narrator should be a simple, double-spaced typescript, containing only what the narrator will read. Set blocks of narration apart on the page and number them for easy location. Try not to split a block across two pages, because the narrator may turn pages audibly during the recording. Where this is unavoidable, lay both flat during the recording so that no handling is required. Putting pages inside plastic page protectors will stop them from rattling.

NARRATION: AUDITIONING AND RECORDING

Writing well is one art, and finding someone to speak it effectively is quite another. Even professional actors can seldom read a commentary without making it sound canned. The fact is that speech and reading aloud are utterly different. When you speak to a listener, your mind is occupied finding words to act on him and ensure that he comprehends. Reading from a script turns you into an audience for your own voice. A few highly experienced actors can overcome this predicament, but they are very rare.

Now think of documentary participants; they are going to have even more difficulty speaking from a script than trained actors, even if the words or ideas were originally their own.

Because choosing a narrator is choosing a voice for the film, you will find yourself rejecting many types of voice due to their associations alone. The convention has been to use the deep, authoritative male voice, but today that signals either a sales pitch or a deeply tainted paternalism. For any number of reasons, most available voices simply won't sound right. As with any situation of choice, you should record several, even if you believe you have stumbled on perfection.

VOICE AUDITIONS

To test native ability, give each person something representative to read, then ask for a different reading of the same material to see how well the narrator responds to direction. Sometimes the reader focuses effectively on the new interpretation but is unable to hold on to what was previously successful. Another reader may be anxious to please and is capable of carrying out instructions, but lacks a grasp of the larger picture. This is common with actors whose only experience is commercials.

After you make audition recordings, thank each person and give a date by which you will get back in contact. Even when you think someone is just right, do not confirm until you first listen carefully to the others. Listening to a disembodied, recorded voice is often a lesser or different experience than you had in the actor's presence.

Your final choice must be independent of personal liking or obligation toward anyone who auditioned but, rather, made solely on what makes the best narration voice.

RECORDING AND DIRECTING THE NARRATOR

Show your chosen narrator the whole film and listen to his or her ideas about what it communicates and what the narration adds. Allowing the narrator to find the right state of mind has much to do with getting the words to sound right. When we speak, we speak from thoughts, experiences, memories, and feelings; invoking the whole person of the narrator gets better results than imagining that everything is on the page.

Record in a professional fashion, that is, with the picture running so that the narrator can key into the rhythms and intonation of other adjacent voices in the film. As you go to record each section, the narrator should cease watching the picture (that is the job of the editor and director) and be cut off from hearing track in- and out-points, which would be distracting. If you don't have access to a custom-designed studio, you can set up your own rig with video playback and original sound available to the artist via headphones. It will be more than worth the trouble.

To record *wild* (that is, shooting narration while not watching picture and without immediate regard for synchronization) is extremely risky because you can't be sure anything works until you fit the narration. By then the artist has been dismissed.

A good voice recording probably will be made with the artist about 1 to 2 feet from the microphone. Surroundings should be acoustically dead (not enclosed or echoey), and there should be no background noise. Listen through *good* headphones or through a speaker in another room. It is critically important to get the best out of your narrator's voice. Watch out for the voice trailing away at ends of sentences, for "popping" on certain sounds, or distortion from overloading. Careful mike positioning and monitoring sound levels all help.

The narrator should read each block of narration and wait for a cue (a gentle tap on the shoulder or a cue light flash) before beginning the next. Rehearse first and give directions, which should be phrased positively and practically, giving instructions on what feeling to aim for rather than why. Stick to essentials, such as "Make the last part a little warmer" or "I'd like to hear that said a bit more formally." Name the quality or emotion you are after. After rehearsing, record those blocks and then move on to rehearsing the next.

Sometimes you will want to alter the word stressed in a sentence or change the amount of projection the speaker is using ("Could you give me the same intensity but use less voice?" or "Use more voice and keep it up at the ends of sentences"). Occasionally a narrator will have some insurmountable problem with phrasing. Invite her to reword it while retaining the sense, but be on guard if this starts happening a lot. Sometimes narrators want to take over the writing. Let her do it only if you can hear certain improvement.

When all narration has been recorded, play everything back against the film so that you can check that everything really works. If there are one or two doubtful readings, cover yourself by making additional versions incorporating a variety of readings before letting the narrator go. These can be tried later and the best one chosen.

CREATING THE IMPROVISED NARRATION

A spontaneous and informal narration that sounds like one-on-one conversation, so difficult to create through writing, can be achieved quite easily through interviewing. Under these circumstances the speaker's mind is naturally engaged in finding words to act back on the interviewer—a familiar situation that unfailingly elicits normal speech. Here are some ways to create an improvised narration:

1. *Improvising from a rough script.* In this relatively structured method, briefly show your narrator a rough script or a list of ideas just before recording. You ask interview questions, and he or she then replies in character, paraphrasing because you have not allowed any learning of lines. Finding the words to express the narration's content reflects what happens in life; we know what we want to say, but we have to find the words on the spot to say it.

2. *Improvising from an identity.* This method develops a character or type of person for the narrator to "become." Together you go over who the narrator is and what that character wants the listener to know, then you "interview" that character, perhaps by taking a character role yourself, asking pertinent and leading questions. Replying from a defined role helps the narrator lock

into a focused relationship. This method might be used to create a historical character's voice-over.

3. *Simple interview.* From interviewing you can afterward extract a highly spontaneous-sounding narration in the cutting room. In the most common method, the director interviews the documentary's "point-of-view" character carefully and extensively. Probably it will be done in spare moments during shooting when the chase is on.

When you shoot sync interviews (that is, sound and picture on film or videotape) you can always cut to the speaker's image at critical moments; however, if overused, this can be the slippery slope to a "talking head" picture. You can also interview people while they are at their normal activities. *The House,* a 1996 series of films about London's Royal Opera house in transition, had wigmakers and set designers talking to the camera as they worked about the failings of the management. There is no more need to make transparent films. They pretended that the camera was looking in on real life as it happened and that no camera crew was present. Nowadays we happily share the whole reality with the audience. If you want to narrate your own film, get a trusted and demanding friend to interview you.

If you interview someone, you will have to listen carefully as you interview, to make sure you cover all your bases. Keep on hand a list of information that you must elicit so that nothing is forgotten, and get more than one version from more than one person so that you have lots of options later in the cutting room.

SUMMARY

All three methods produce a narration that can be edited down, restructured, and purged of the interviewer's voice. The results will be fresh and strike a consistent relationship with the audience. Of course, this takes more editing than a written narration, but the results more than justify the labor.

A film I once made on baby expert Dr. Benjamin Spock (*Dr. Spock,* "One Pair of Eyes" series) was covered by method 3. As the central, point-of-view character in a television essay, Dr. Spock was expressing his vision of human aggression and its contribution to the American political scene during the turbulent 1960s. Shot all over the Eastern United States, the film was due to be edited in England with no chance of return. In one day-long session, we interviewed him widely to ensure narration that would cover every eventuality—and it did.

Recording and then fitting the improvised narration to picture are editing procedures similar to those for the scripted narration, so read the next sections carefully.

RECORDING THE PRESENCE TRACK

Whether you are recording a scripted or an improvised narration, you will need to record some of the recording studio or location atmosphere. Later you will have the right quality of "silence" should the editor want to extend a pause or add to the head of a narration block. No two presence tracks (also called *buzz track* or *room tone*) are ever exactly alike, even in the same recording studio and using the same mike. Make it an automatic act after recording a scene, an interview, or a narration to ask everyone to remain where they are and to record a couple minutes of silence *at the same sound level setting*. To overlook this little ritual causes the editor grief.

FITTING THE NARRATION

Lay narration carefully against picture so that operative words hit each new image to maximum effect. You often need to make small picture-cutting changes to accomplish this, though adding to or reducing the natural pauses in the narration can sometimes stretch or compress a section of unsuitable length. Be very careful, however, not to disrupt the natural rhythms of the speaker. Pay attention to operative words and their potential, and you will see pictures and word patterns become receptive to each other, and that the two fall into mutually responsive patterns that are magically effective, driving the film along with an exhilarating sense of inevitability. Good editing is the art that disguises art.

CHAPTER 34

EDITING: THE END GAME

This chapter deals with

- Over-familiarity with your film and getting distance through making a flow chart
- Common problems you can expect that beset the documentary
- Holding trial showings and interrogating your audience
- Using criticism constructively
- Moving carefully so that you don't lose sight of your artistic intentions
- Dealing with changes that alter or disable your working hypothesis
- Responsibilities to truth in editing
- Your judgments made public at a showing and preparing participants for what they may consider "negative"

After considerable editing, a debilitating familiarity sets in. You lose objectivity and feel your ability to make judgments departing. Every alternative version looks similar, and all seem too long. This is most likely to hit director-editors, who have lived with both the intentions and the footage since their inception.

Two steps are necessary. One is to make a flow chart, or block diagram, of your film to gain an overview of its ideas and intentions; the other is to show the working cut to a trial audience of a chosen few.

DIAGNOSIS: MAKING A FLOW CHART

Whenever you need a new understand of something, it helps to translate it into another form. Statisticians, for instance, know that the full implications of their figures are not evident until expressed as a graph, pie chart, or other proportional image. In our case, we are dealing with the mesmerizing actuality of film, which, as we view it, embraces us within its unfolding present to the exclusion of much sense of overview. Luckily, a block diagram can give you a fresh and a more objective perspective of your work.

The Editing Diagnostic Form shown in Figure 34–1 makes a radical analysis of your film easy.

To use it,

- Stop your film after each sequence
- Write a brief description of the sequence's content in the box. A sequence might contribute
  - Factual information
  - Information on or introduction to a new character
  - A new situation and a new thematic strand
  - A location or a relationship that will be developed later in the film
  - A special mood or feeling
  - Almost anything else!
- Next to the box write what the sequence contributes to the development of the film as a whole
- Add timings (optional, but helpful when you must make length decisions)
- Give each sequence an impact rating of, say, one to five stars (this helps you see how strong material is distributed)

Now you have a flow chart for your film that can help you see, dispassionately and functionally, what is subconsciously present for an audience. What does the progression of contributions add up to? As with the first assembly, you will probably find many of the following:

- Lack of early impact or an unnecessarily pedestrian opening, so the film is a late starter (fatal on television)
- Duplication or redundancy of expository information
- Inconsistent supply of necessary information
- Holes or backtracking apparent in progression
- Type and frequency of impact poorly distributed over the film's length (resulting in uneven dramatic progression)
- Similar thematic contributions made several ways; choose the best and dump (or reposition) the rest
- A sequence or sequence grouping that does not contribute to the thrust of the film. Be brave and dump it. You have to kill your darlings.
- The film's conclusion emerges early, leaving the rest of the film as an unnecessary recapitulation
- The film has more than one ending. Three is not uncommon. Choose.

Each ailment, as it emerges from the analysis, suggests its own cure. Put these into effect, and you will feel the degree of improvement rather than be able to exactly account for it.

EDITING DIAGNOSTIC FORM

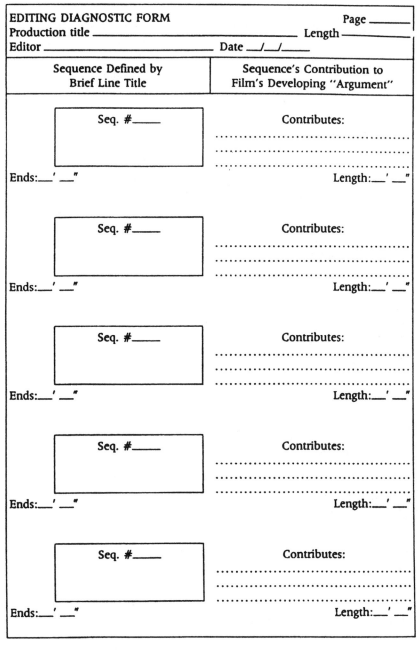

FIGURE 34–1

An editing diagnostic form that helps turn a film into a flow chart.

I cannot overstress the seductions film practices on its makers. After radical changes expect new problems to creep in during housecleaning. It is smart to make a new flow chart, even though you don't think it's necessary. It will certainly turn up more anomalies. Much of what emerges in this formal process eventually will become second nature to you and will occur spontaneously in the earlier stages of the cut. Even so, filmmakers of long standing invariably profit from subjecting their work to this formal scrutiny.

A FIRST SHOWING

Knowing now what every brick in your movie's edifice must accomplish, you are well prepared to test your intentions on a small audience in a trial showing. This audience should be about half a dozen people whose tastes and interests you respect. The less they know about your film and your aims, the better. Warn them that this is a work in progress and still technically raw. Itemize what may be missing, such as music, sound effects, and titles. Incidentally, it is a good idea to cut in a working title because this helps focus the film's purpose or identity for the audience.

Whenever you show the film, the editor should *control the sound levels*. Even experienced producers drastically misjudge a film when it is made inaudible or overbearing through sound inequities. Take pains to present your film at its best, or risk getting misleadingly negative responses.

Having prepared a flow chart makes one more big contribution because it gives you an agenda to explore through your first audience. You know the probable weak points, now you can find out.

SURVIVING YOUR CRITICS AND MAKING USE OF WHAT THEY SAY

After the viewing, ask for impressions of the film as a whole. Don't be afraid to focus and direct your viewers' attention, or someone will lead off a discussion that is superfluous to your needs. Soliciting feedback needs to be handled carefully, or it can be pointless. On the one hand, listen carefully, but on the other, retain your fundamental bearings toward the piece as a whole. Speak as little as possible, and at all cost don't *explain* the film or *explain* what you intended. Explanations at this stage are irrelevant and only serve to confuse and compromise the audience's own perceptions. A film must stand alone without explication from its authors, so concentrate on getting what your critics are really saying.

It takes all the self-discipline you can muster to sit immobile and take notes. For many, listening to reactions and criticism of their work is an emotionally battering experience. Expect to feel threatened, slighted, misunderstood, and unappreciated, and to come out with a raging headache.

Following is a suggested order of inquiry that moves from large issues toward component parts:

- What do audience members think is the film's theme or themes?
- What are the major issues in the film?

- Did the film feel the right length or was it too long?
- Which parts were unclear or puzzling?
- Which parts felt slow?
- Which parts were moving or otherwise successful?
- What did they feel about . . . (name of character)?
- What did they end up knowing about . . . (situation or issue)?

In fact you are testing what you wrote in the analysis form next to each sequence in the "what it contributes" description and testing your working hypothesis for the film. Depending on your trial audience's patience, you may be able to get feedback on most of your film's parts and intentions. If your audience begins squirming, you may only get to test the dubious areas. Write anything and everything down, or make a video recording for study later. Subsequently, you can look at your film with the eyes of, say, the three audience members who missed that the boy was the woman's son. You see that it is implied twice, but you find a way to put in an extra line where he calls her "Mom." Problem solved.

An irritation the director must often endure, especially in film schools, is the critic who insists on talking about the film he would have made rather than the film you have just shown. When this happens, diplomatically redirect the discussion. Dealing with audience critics means absorbing other points of view and, when the dust settles, looking to see how such varying impressions are possible. As far as you can, allow for the biases and subjectivity that emerge in your critics. Take notice when several people report the same difficulty, but otherwise don't rush to fix anything. Where comments cancel each other out, no action may be called for.

Make no changes without careful reflection. Remember that when you ask people to give criticism, they look for possible changes—if only to make a contributory mark on your work. *You will never, under any circumstances, be able to please everyone.* Nor should you be tempted to try.

Most importantly, hold on to your central intentions. You should never revise them unless you find there are strong and positive reasons to do so. You should meanwhile *only act upon suggestions that support and further your central intentions.*

This is a dangerous time for the filmmaker, or indeed for any artist. It is fatally easy to let go of your work's underlying identity and lose your sense of direction. Keep listening and don't be tempted by strong emotions to carve into your film precipitously.

It is quite normal by now to feel that you have failed, that you have a piece of junk on your hands, that all is vanity. If so, take heart. You might have felt this during shooting, which is worse. Anyway, the film as a work in progress is not at its best. Audiences are disproportionately alienated by a wrong sound balance here, a missed sound dissolve there, a shot or two that needs clipping, or a sequence that belongs earlier. These imbalances and rhythmic ineptitudes massively downgrade a film's impact to the non-specialist viewer. The polish you can yet apply has considerable influence on the film's reception.

DUBIOUS EDITING PRACTICES

There are more than a few dubious editing practices. One that can happen inadvertently is to allow acted or reconstructed material to stand unidentified in a film made of otherwise original and authentic materials. Make sure you identify the material's origin either by narration or subtitle if there is any doubt about how the audience will take it.

Most documentary editing involves compression, and a long statement can be unfairly reduced to serve the film but misrepresent the speaker's original pronouncement. Any participant who runs his own audio recording while you film (as happened to me when filming the leader of the British Union of Fascists, Sir Oswald Mosley) may be preparing to serve you up a legal challenge.

Apparent truths and bogus meanings can be manufactured by juxtaposing unrelated events or statements. What you have done may be invisible or insignificant to you and to a lay audience and yet may scandalize participants. Even the way you compress into three shots a long process, such as buying a house, may be attacked. Be ready to defend and justify every such device in your narrative flow.

Here's another situation you will encounter: you must deal with a participant's fear-fantasy when, after weeks of anguish, she wants to retract some innocuous statement that is vital to your film. You have the legal right to use it and you know it can bring her no harm, but should you go ahead and override the participant's wish? Your good name and career may suffer, and at the very least your conscience will prick you for violating someone's trust. Then again, a real risk to a participant may emerge only at the editing stage, and you must face up to the conflict between releasing a significant film that causes pain and danger to someone and removing something important to the film's effectiveness, not to mention retarding your career or even threatening your survival as a filmmaker.

Dilemmas do not lie in choosing between right and wrong, but between right and right.

PUBLIC SHOWING

When should a participant have the right to see and veto a cut? If you agreed from the outset that editing would involve feedback from participants, they obviously have such a prerogative. If you have not worked out a consultative agreement with your subjects, you are ill advised to embark on one without strong cause. If you must show your cut to participants, do so only after clearly explaining any limitation to their rights. If you are willing to be advised but not instructed, make this absolutely clear, or there will be much bad feeling.

Before a public showing, get legal opinion about anything that might land either you or your participants in legal trouble. Be aware that lawyers look on the dark side, as their job is to look for snags and to err on the side of caution.

If at a showing of your film a participant sitting in the audience may feel betrayed by something critical in your film, you should prepare that person in advance so that he or she does not feel humiliated in the presence of family and friends. If you don't, that person may henceforward regard you as a traitor and all film people as frauds. Avoid renegade behavior at all costs, but keep in mind that participants see themselves on the screen with great subjectivity. To adjust oversympathetically to this would be to abandon documentary work for public relations. Usually, having a general audience and a person's friends present can be an advantage, because their enjoyment and approval mitigate the subject's oversensitivity. All this is a matter of judgment.

THE USES OF PROCRASTINATION

Whether you are pleased or depressed about your film, it is always a good thing to stop working on it for a while and do something else. If this anxiety is new to you, take comfort: you are deep in the throes of the artist's experience. This is the long and painful labor before giving birth. When you pick up the film again after a lapse of days or months, your fatigue and defeatism will have gone away and its problems and their solutions won't seem so overwhelming.

TRY, TRY AGAIN

With a film of some substance requiring a long evolution in the editing room, you should expect to try the film out on several new trial audiences. You may want to show the last cut to the original trial audience to find out what progress they think you made.

As a director with a lot of editing in my background, I am convinced that a film is really created in the editing process. It is here that magic and miracles are wrought from the footage. Not even crewmembers know what really happens in the cutting room unless they have edited themselves. It is an alchemy unknown and unguessed by those who have not lived through it.

CHAPTER 35

USING MUSIC AND WORKING WITH A COMPOSER

This chapter deals with

- When and why you might use music in a documentary
- Copyright issues for music already recorded
- When and how to start work with a composer
- Using a guide track and developing music cues
- Misuse of music
- Keys, transitions, music sync points
- Recording live music
- Fitting music during postproduction

USING MUSIC

Music in any film can be misused as a dramatic crutch and in a documentary can seem manipulative. Too often filmmakers reach for music to reliably stir emotions that should arise from the film's content but doesn't. Music should not have to substitute for anything. It should complement action and give us access to the inner, invisible lives of the characters and their situations.

Good music can initiate emotional aspects of the sequence that the audience should investigate. Errol Morris makes excellent use of Philip Glass' minimalist score in his masterly *The Thin Blue Line* (1989). The bleak and beautiful repetitiousness of Glass' music underlines the nightmarish conundrum in which a man is caught on death row for a crime he didn't do.

How do you decide where to have music? Films usually provide their own clues about whether music is needed, and where. It often seems natural during journeys and other bridging sequences—a montage of a character driving to a new home, for instance. Transitional sequences of any kind can benefit from music, especially if the film needs lifting out of one mood into another. Music can highlight an emotional change when, for instance, an aspiring football player learns he can join the team or when someone newly homeless lies down for the first night in a doorway. Music is being used more freely as documentaries dare to become subjective and lyrical again.

Another use for music is to foreshadow an event and to inject tension—a favorite function in B movies but seldom legitimate in documentaries, unless a strong storytelling "voice" is established as part of the narrative strategy. Music can make a film modulate from realism to a more abstract point of view, as Godfrey Reggio does in his long and grandiloquent parable about the human rape of the natural world, *Koyaanisqatsi* (1983). It also can supply its own ironic comment or suggest alternative worlds, as Hanns Eisler's score does for Resnais' unforgettable Holocaust documentary, *Night and Fog* (1955). Instead of picture-pointing the deportation trains or the captured human artifacts with a tragic or poignant accompaniment, Eisler's score often plays against the obvious by using a delicate, ghoulish dance or sustaining a tense, unresolved interrogation between woodwind instruments.

In the best circumstances, music doesn't merely illustrate, it seems to give voice to feeling or an emotional point of view, that of either a character or the storyteller. It can function like a storyteller's aside that expresses an opinion or alternative idea, imply what cannot be seen, or comment on what can.

Be aware that film music (like debt or smoking) is easier to start than stop. Music is addictive, and we value it most keenly when it is removed. Ending a music section painlessly can be a real problem. The panacea is to give something in its place. This can be either a commanding effects track (a rich train-station atmosphere, for example, really a composition in its own right) or a new scene's dialogue or an inciting moment of action that lugs the spectator's attention elsewhere.

When using music not designed to fit your film, section ends can either be faded out or, better, come to a natural finish. In the latter mode, you would lay the music backward from the picture finish point and either fade up at the picture start or adjust the scene length to make the picture fit the music from composer's start to composer's finish. With music that is too long, you can frequently cut out a repeated phrase. Composers like to milk good musical ideas, so most pieces are replete with repeated segments.

If you are searching among commercially recorded classical music for something that will work, enlist the advice of a knowledgeable enthusiast. You won't know whether a piece really works until you play it against the sequence in question.

COPYRIGHT

The copyright situation for music is complicated and may consist of fees and clearances from any or all of the following: composer, artist(s), publishers, and record company. As a student you can often get written clearance for a manageable fee but only for use in festivals and competitions. If you then sell your film or receive rentals for showings, you may find yourself being sued.

Never assume that the recorded music you want to use will be available when you get around to inquiring. The worst time to negotiate with composers, performers, publishers, and performing rights societies is when your film has come to depend on a particular recording. You are now in the weakest position, and those with a nose for such things will capitalize on your vulnerability. Commissioning original music obviates the difficulty of getting (and paying for) copyright clearance on music already recorded.

WORKING WITH A COMPOSER

Composers are the last in the creative chain to be hired and in film generally have to work under pressured circumstances. The more time you can give them, the better. For most of what follows I am indebted to my son Paul Rabiger, who lives and works in Cologne where he makes music for television and film. Like many involved in producing music these days, he works largely with synthesizers, using live instruments as and when the budget allows. Software favored by composers includes Steinberg Cubase and Emagic Logic Audio. Programs like these permit many tracks, integrate MIDI (musical instrument digital interface) with live recording, and support video in QuickTime format so that the composer can build music to an accurate video version of the film.

WHEN THE COMPOSER COMES ON BOARD

If the composer comes on board early, he or she probably will read the screenplay and see the first available version of the edited film. An experienced composer probably will avoid coming in with preconceived ideas and will inquire what the director wants the music to contribute. The composer can then mull over the characters, the settings, and overall content of a film, taking time to develop basic melodic themes and deciding within the budget what instrumental texture works best. Particular characters or situations often evoke their own musical treatment or leitmotif (recurring themes), and this is always best worked out with some time in hand, especially if research is necessary because music must reflect a particular era or ethnicity.

WHEN THERE'S A GUIDE TRACK

Sometimes while editing, the editor may drop in sample music, called "temp" music, that nobody expects to keep but which helps assess the movie's potential. At the screening the composer may be confronted with a Beatles song or a stirring passage from Shostakovich's *Leningrad Symphony*. This certainly shows what a certain kind of music does for the scene and indicates a texture or tempo that editor and director think works, but it also raises an intimidating barrier because the composer must extract whatever the makers find valuable (say in rhythm, orchestration, texture, or mood) and then try to reach beyond the examples with his or her own musical solutions.

DEVELOPING A MUSIC CUE LIST

Once the content of the film is more or less locked down, it is screened with the composer, director, editor, and producer. The tape version given to the composer has a timecode burned into the lower part of the screen that displays a cumulative timing for the whole film (Figure 35–1). The group will break the film down into acts and where these occur on the film's timeline. They will discuss where music seems desirable and what kind seems most appropriate. Typical questions will center on how time is supposed to pass and whether music is meant to shore up a weak scene, as it often must. The composer finds out (or suggests) where each music section starts and stops, aiming to depart the discussion session with a music cue list in hand and full notes as to function, with beginnings and endings defined in timecode in- and out-points. Start points may begin with visual or dialogue clues.

If the editor generates the music cues, sections should be logged in minutes and seconds. If there are tightly fitting sections, then include the frame count and log to the nearest half second. Figure 35–2 shows what a composer's cue sheet logged to the nearest second looks like. Because music is easy to start but hard to end, cue endings will take careful planning. A rule of thumb is to conclude or fade out music under cover of something more commanding as it begins. You might take music out during the first seconds of a noisy street scene or just before the dialogue in a new scene. For best practice, study fiction films that successfully integrate music with the kind of action you have in your film.

The computer-savvy composer then gets a tape copy to compose to, either first creating a traditional score to be performed and recorded or working with

FIGURE 35–1

Video frame timecoded in hours, minutes, seconds, and frames.

Music Section 4

00:59:43	Begin music over long shot of Drottningholm palace
00:59:59	Medium shot actors crossing courtyard and entering theater building
01:00:22	Interior theater, long shot
01:00:31	Backstage, actors enter
01:00:40	Stage manager tests primitive wind machine (make space in music here)
01:00:51	Actors getting into costumes (bring music up between 00:54 and 01:05)
01:01:24	Curtains opening on dress rehearsal
01:01:34	Lose music under first lines from cast

FIGURE 35–2

Typical scene measurements for a music cue segment.

computers and MIDI-controlled synthesizers to make music sections directly. In the course of hands-on composing, music cues are occasionally added, dropped, or renegotiated when initial ideas meet actuality. Poorly placed or unjustified music may be worse than no music at all.

WHEN TO USE MUSIC, AND WHEN NOT

Though music is most commonly used as a transitional device or a filler or to set a mood, there are other ways to use it. Try never to use it to enhance what can already be seen on the screen. It is better to suggest what cannot be seen, such as a character's expectations, interior mood, or feelings that he withholds. The classic example is Bernard Herrmann's unforgettable all-string score for Hitchcock's *Pyscho* (1960), with its jabbing violin screams as the pressure within Norman Bates becomes intolerable. Music, so natural an element to melodrama, is perhaps hardest to conceive for comedy. Ethnic scenes in documentary pose some problems. The riskiest solution is to emulate Thai music for a scene in Thailand.

Music is often used to foreshadow events and build tension, but it should never give the story away, nor should it ever "picture point" the story by commenting too closely. Walt Disney was infamous for "Mickey Mousing" his films—an industry term for fitting scores like aural straitjackets around the minutia of action. The first of his "true life adventures," *The Living Desert* (1953), was full of extraordinary documentary footage but was marred by scorpions made to square dance and music that supplied a different note, trill, or percussion roll for everything that dared to move. Used like this, music becomes a smothering form of control.

A related mistake is to simply use too much music, thus burdening the film with a musical interpretation that disallows the audience from making its own emotional judgments. Many traditional documentaries of an older generation suffer from this, as they do from the omniscient narration. Luckily, fashions change, and today less is considered more. A rhythm alone without melody or harmony can often supply the uncluttered accompaniment that a sequence needs.

When its job is to set a mood, the music should do its work then get out of the way, to return and comment later. Sometimes a composer will point out during the screening just how effective, even loaded, a silence is at a particular point. The rhythms of action, camera movement, montage, and dialogue are themselves a kind of music, and you need not paint the lily.

Better than using music to illustrate (which merely duplicates the visual message) is to counterpoint the visible with music that provides unexpected emotional shading. An indifferent sequence may suddenly come to life because music gives it a subtext that boosts the forward movement of the story. In a story with fine shading, a good score can supply the sense of integrity or melancholy in one character and the interior impulsiveness directing the actions of another. Music can enhance not just the givens of a character but indicate the interior development leading to an action and imply motives not otherwise visible. Music can supply needed phrasing to a scene or help create structural demarcations by bracketing transitions in scenes or between acts. Short stings or fragments of melody are good if they belong to a larger musical picture. These conventions are well established in fiction but have to be used cautiously in documentary unless, as in Errol Morris' *The Thin Blue Line* (1988) the style of the film has been boldly set up to allow it.

Given that an intelligent film is a weave of scenes whose longitudinal relationships often need strengthening, a composer may color code his cues to help group scenes, characters, situations, or suchlike into musically related families. In a 60-minute film there may be many music cues, from a "sting" or short punctuation to a passage that is extended and more elaborate. He or she may want to develop music for a main plot but have musical identities for two subplots. Keeping these separate and not clashing during cross cutting can be problematical, so their relationship is important, particularly in key. Using a coding system keeps the composer aware of the logical connections and continuity that the music must underpin.

Because many factors are involved in producing an integrated score, it is important that music cues, once decided, not be changed later, or the film re-cut, without compelling reason.

KEYS, DIEGETIC AND NON-DIEGETIC MUSIC

An initial planning stage for the composer is to decide what progression of keys to use through the film, based on the emotional logic of the story itself. Especially when one kind of music takes over as a commentary upon another, the key of the one following must be related so that the transition is not jarring. This is true for all adjacent music sections, not just original scoring. A film may contain popular songs that the participants listen to in their car, and scored music must be appropriate in key.

Any sound that is a part of their world is called *diegetic* sound. Following may be the film's music, which of course the characters do not hear or react to, because this is part of the film's authorial commentary and addressed to the audience. This is called *non-diegetic* sound.

CONFLICTS AND COMPOSING TO SYNC POINTS

An experienced musician composing for a recording session will write to very precise timings, paying attention to track features such as the tire screech and dialogue lines. The choice of instrumentation must not fight dialogue, nor can the arrangement be too busy at points where music might compete with dialogue or effects. Music can, however, take over the function of a diegetic sound track that would otherwise be too loaded. Musical punctuation rather than a welter of naturalistic sound effects can produce something more impressionistic and effective. It's worth noting that an overloaded, over-detailed sound track takes energy on the part of the audience to interpret and is not well reproduced by the television speakers through which many people will hear your work.

If the composer must work around dialogue and spot effects, he or she should have an advanced version of the sound track rather than a simple dialogue track that may be used during editing. This is particularly true in any track that will be heard in a cinema setting. The sound system is likely to be powerful and sophisticated, and the film's track will come under greater audience scrutiny.

When a written score is recorded to picture, it is marked with the cumulative timing so that as the music is recorded (normally to picture as a safeguard), the conductor can make a running check that the sync points line up. Low-budget film scores often make use of MIDI computerized composing techniques. The composer builds the music to a QuickTime video scratch version of the film, digitized from a cassette, so that music fitting is done at the source.

HOW LONG DOES IT TAKE?

An experienced composer likes to take upward of 6 weeks to compose, say, 15 minutes of music for a 90-minute feature film, but she may have to do it in 3 weeks, with a flurry of music copyist work at the end if the recording session is live.

THE LIVE MUSIC SESSION

The editor makes the preparations to record music and attends the recording session because only the editor can say whether a particular shot can be lengthened or shortened to accommodate the slight mistimings that always appear during recording. Adjusting the film is easier and more economical than paying musicians to pursue perfect musical synchronicity. Be prepared for conductor, composer, and soloists to pursue a degree of perfection that is inaudible to anyone else.

POSTPRODUCTION

FITTING MUSIC

After the recording session, the editor fits each music section and makes necessary shot adjustments. If the music is appropriate, the film takes a quantum leap forward in effectiveness. In the feature world, some editors specialize in only cutting and fitting music. Paying for their expertise may be a lifesaver on a film about music.

THE MIX

The composer may want to be present at all mix sessions affecting the functionality of the music that he or she has composed. When music has been composed on MIDI, it is only a matter of a small delay to return to the musical elements and produce a new version incorporating musical changes or alterations in level.

CHAPTER 36

EDITING FROM FINE CUT TO SOUND MIX

This chapter deals with

- Importance of a movie sound track that stimulates the imagination
- Discussion of the implementation of sound design
- Post-synchronizing dialogue and the Foley stage for recording effects
- Sound clichés
- What the sound mix can achieve
- Preparing tracks and charts for the sound mix
- Premix strategy and tailoring differences
- Sound mix procedure
- Making safety copies, foreign versions music-and-effects tracks, and a transcript

Sound is an incomparable stimulant to the audience's imagination, and sound design only rarely gets its due. Ideally everyone is alert to sound compositional possibilities from the moment the documentary is conceived and keeps building on these concepts until postproduction ends. Opportunities and special moments arise in addition to those programmed in from the beginning, and this is part of everyone helping a work to assert its identity. It's important to keep track of every idea for sound that anyone has along the way and not leave it all to an "audio sweetening" session. That, by the way, is an expression I detest. It suggests that sound is sour and needs sugaring. Sound design, sound editing, and sound mix are more direct and respectful terms. Especially if you have monitored and directed the sound treatment throughout, the sound mix will be a special and even exhilarating occasion.

What happens when sound is left to fend for itself? Poor handling of dialogue tracks alone will disrupt the dreamlike quality that a good film attains, so it's worth learning how to handle sound.

Finalizing sound is another computer operation, usually using ProTools and a first-rate amplifier and speaker system to replicate a hypothetical cinema's sound environment. I say "hypothetical" because few cinemas approach the state of the art. Yet good sound, as Dolby cinemas have discovered, is good business, so sound may yet get its day. Most documentaries are viewed on television sets, so it's important to periodically view your evolving editing on a TV to make sure the small, cheap speaker isn't overwhelmed by too subtle and complex a track.

THE FINE CUT

With typical caution, filmmakers call the end result of the editing process the fine, not final, cut because there may still be minor changes and accommodations. Some of these arise out of laying further sound tracks in preparation to produce a master mixed track.

MAKE A FINAL CHECK OF ALL SOURCE MATERIAL

The editor should try to review all shot material to make sure nothing useful has been overlooked. At this point in editing, and especially if there is a lot of original material, this demand is skull-crackingly tedious and time consuming, but almost invariably there will be some "Eureka!" discoveries by way of compensation. If there aren't, you can rest easy that night.

SOUND

SOUND DESIGN DISCUSSIONS

If sound design has been a concern from the inception of the film, this part of the process will be one of finalizing. Mostly sound just evolves, and so an overview discussion at the end of editing is a good way to make sure you are dealing with the big picture. How and why music gets used needs careful discussion, as described in Chapter 35. Although sound is made of different elements—music, dialogue, atmospheres, effects—it is a mistake to put them on a hierarchy and to think of them separately at this, the ultimate compositional stage.

Before the sound editor goes to work reorganizing dialogue tracks and laying in sound effects, there should be a detailed discussion with the director to agree upon the sound identity of the whole film and how each sequence should be treated within this identity from the sound point of view. You should agree on the known sound problems and on a strategy to handle each. This should be a priority because dialogue reconstruction—if needed—is an expensive, specialized, and time-consuming business, and no film of any worth can survive the impact of having it done poorly, least of all a documentary.

Though documentary leads the way in narrative inventiveness, feature films use far more resources to develop their sound tracks, and documentarians can learn much from them. Walter Murch, the doyen of editors and sound designers, makes a practice of watching a film he is editing without the sound turned on, so he imagines what the sound might properly be. Among less usual functions of sound among many listed in Randy Thom's "Designing a Movie for Sound" (www.filmsound.org/articles/designing_for_sound.htm) are to

- Indicate a historical period
- Indicate changes in time or geographical locale
- Connect otherwise unconnected ideas, characters, places, images, or moments
- Heighten ambiguity or diminish it
- Startle or soothe

That Web site, www.filmsound.org, is an excellent source of information for all aspects of sound in film, by the way.

Any good sound editor will tell you that it's not quantities or complexity of sound that make a good sound track, but rather the psychological journey that sound leads you upon as you watch. This is the art of *psychoacoustics*, and usually sound is most effective when it is simple rather than complex, and specific rather than generic. The sound clichés alluded to later result from slavishly inserting sounds rather than thinking about and responding to the narrative needs of the movie.

POST-SYNCHRONIZING DIALOGUE

Post-synchronizing dialogue is very rare in documentary and means turning participants into actors who must create new speech tracks in lip sync with an existing picture. In fiction this laborious operation is variously called *dubbing*, *looping*, or *automatic dialogue replacement* (ADR). It is done in a studio with the actor or actors watching a screen or monitor and rehearsing to picture before they get the OK to record. A long dialogue exchange will be done in minute or half-minute increments.

The process is ardently to be avoided because newly recorded tracks invariably sound flat and dead in contrast with live location recordings. This is not because they lack background presence, which can always be added, or even finally because sound perspective and location acoustics are missing. What kills ADR is the artificial situation. The poor actor is flying blind as he labors to reconstitute every few seconds of dialogue. He is completely in the hands of whomever is directing each few sentences. However good the whole, it invariably drags down the impression of their performances, and actors hate ADR with excellent reason. Luckily, documentary audiences are tolerant of rough technique, which they understand to be inseparable from the challenge of capturing reality. Dialogue replacement should therefore be considered only if the original is incomprehensible. The usual solution is to supply subtitles for marginal recording.

THE FOLEY STUDIO AND RECREATING SYNC SOUND EFFECTS

Many sound effects shot wild, on location or in a Foley studio, can be fitted afterward and will work just fine. Some must, however, be manufactured, often because the genuine recording sounds nothing like you expect. To have a door closing in an otherwise stylish documentary that sounds like someone kicking a cardboard box destroys the level of illusion upon which all films depend. So, making sounds that sound right has become an art all of its own.

The Foley studio was named after its intrepid inventor, Jack Foley, who realized back in the 1940s that you could mime all the right sounds to picture if you had a sound studio with different surfaces, materials, and props available. It takes some invention to create a sound that is right for the particular shot. Baking powder under compression in a sturdy plastic bag, for instance, makes the right scrunching sound of footsteps in snow, and you may have to experiment with different types and fillings of bag to get a decent range of body punches for a film about boxing. Always the question must be: Does this pass as an authentic sound, and, if not, does the style of my film allow for a subjective or impressionistically experienced world of sound?

A Foley studio has a variety of surfaces (concrete, heavy wood, light wood, carpet, linoleum, gravel, and so on). Foley artists may add sand or paper to modify the sound of footsteps to suit what's on the screen. In a most forgettable Jayne Mansfield comedy, *The Sheriff of Fractured Jaw* (1959), directed by Raoul Walsh, my job was to make horse footsteps with coconuts and steam engine noises with a modified motorcycle engine. It was fun.

You usually can create repetitive sounds that must fit an action (knocking on a door, shoveling snow, or footsteps) by recording their action a little slower and then cutting out the requisite frames before each impact's attack, which is easy using a computer. More complex sync effects (two people walking through a quadrangle) will have to be post-synced just like dialogue, paying attention to the different surfaces that the feet pass over (grass, gravel, concrete, etc.). Surviving a grueling series of post-sync sessions makes you truly understand two things: one, how valuable it is when a location recordist can procure good original recordings, and two, how good top-notch location film sound and editing crews really are at their jobs.

On a complex production with a big budget, the cost is economically justified. For the low-budget filmmaker, some improvisation can cut costs enormously. What matters is that sound effects are appropriate (always difficult to arrange) and that they are in sync with the action onscreen. Where and how you record them is not important provided they work well. Sometimes you can find appropriate sound effects in sound libraries, but *never* assume that a sound effect listed in a library will work with your particular sequence until you have tried it against picture. By entering "sound effects library" in an Internet search engine, you will turn up many sources of sound libraries. Some let you listen or even download effects. Try Sound Ideas at www.sound-ideas.com/bbc.html.

A caution: most sound libraries are top heavy with garbage shot eons ago. Many effects tracks are not clean, that is, they come with a heavy ambient background or ineradicable system hiss. The exotic sounds, such as helicopters, Bofors guns, and elephants rampaging through a Malaysian jungle, are easy to use. It's the nitty-gritty sounds, such as footsteps, door slams, and small dogs growling, that are so hard to find in a usable version. At one time there were only *six* different gunshots used throughout the film industry. I heard attempts at recording new ones. They were awful and sounded more like ruptured air hoses—not at all what you expect. Expectation is the key to getting it right. Authentic sounds are nowhere next to those you imagine, and accept, as the Real Thing.

SOUND CLICHÉS

Providing sounds for what is on the screen can easily be overdone. Because a cat walks across a kitchen is not an excuse for a cat meow, unless the cat is seen demanding its breakfast in a coming shot. Do look up this Web site for a hilarious list of sound clichés: www.filmsound.org/cliche/. In it, all bicycles have bells, car tires must always squeal when the car turns, pulls away, or stops, storms start instantaneously, wind always whistles, doors always squeak, and much, much more.

WHAT THE SOUND MIX CAN DO

After the film has reached a fine cut the culmination of the editing process is to prepare and mix the component sound tracks. A whole book could be written on this preeminent subject alone. What follows is a list of essentials along with some tips.

You are ready to mix down tracks into one master track when you have

- *Finalized the content* of your film
- *Fitted music*
- *Split dialogue tracks*, grouping them by equalization (EQ) and level commonality
  - A separate track for each mike position used in dialogue recording
  - Sometimes a different track for each speaker, depending on how much EQ is necessary for each mike position on each character
  - *Filled in backgrounds* (missing sections of background ambience, so there are no dead spaces or abrupt background changes)
- *Recorded and laid narration* (if there is any)
- *Recorded and laid sound effects* and mood setting atmospheres
- *Finalized ProTools* timeline contents

The mix procedure determines the following:

- *Sound levels* (say, between a dialogue foreground voice track against a background of a noisy factory scene if, and only if, they are on separate tracks)
- *Equalization* (the filtering and profiling of individual tracks either to match others, or to create maximum intelligibility, listener appeal, or ear comfort; a voice track with a rumbly traffic background can, for instance, be much improved by "rolling off" the lower frequencies, leaving the voice range intact)

- *Consistent quality* (for example, two tracks from two angles on the same person speaking will need careful EQ and level adjustments if they are not to sound dissimilar)
- *Level changes* (fade up, fade down, sound dissolves, and level adjustments to accommodate sound perspective and such new track elements as narration, music, or interior monologue)
- *Sound processing* (adding echo, reverberation, telephone effect, etc.)
- *Dynamic range* (a compressor squeezes the broad dynamic range of a movie into the narrow range favored in TV transmission; a limiter leaves the main range alone but limits peaks to a preset level)
- *Perspective* (to some degree, EQ and level manipulation can mimic perspective changes, thus helping create a sense of space and dimensionality through sound)
- *Multichannel sound distribution* (if a stereo track or surround sound treatment is being developed, different elements go to each sound channel to create a sense of horizontal spread and sound space)
- *Noise reduction* (Dolby and other noise-reduction systems help minimize the system hiss that would intrude on quiet passages).

Be aware that when old manual technology must be used, changes at a manually operated mixing board cannot be done instantaneously on a cut from one sequence to the next. Tracks must be checkerboarded (meaning, they alternate from track to track) so that a channel's EQ and level adjustments can be set up in the section of silent sound spacing prior to the track's arrival. This is most critical when balancing dialogue tracks, as explained later.

SOUND MIX PREPARATION

Track elements are presented here in the conventional hierarchy of importance, although the order may vary; music, for instance, might be faded up to the foreground and dialogue played almost inaudibly low. When cutting and laying sound tracks, be careful not to cut off the barely audible tail of a decaying sound or to clip the attack. Sound editing should be done at high volume so that you hear everything that is—or isn't—there when it should be.

Laying digital tracks is much easier than in the old manual days because you follow a logic that is visible to the eye and can hear your work immediately. Fine control is quick and easy with a sound-editing program such as ProTools because you can edit with surgical precision, even within a syllable. The equivalent operation in manual film is not difficult, but you cannot properly hear the results until mix time. Traditional mix theaters nowadays are about as common as steam trains, and there is not much weeping over their loss. Getting dozens of tracks laid for a mix was a monumental task, and watching them churn to and fro in 30 dubbing players slaved to a film projector was stressful (my first job was cement splicing in a feature film studio). Twelve people worked a day or more to mix 10 minutes of film track. For battle sequences or other complex situations, you could multiply that period several times over. Some battles did not stay on the screen either.

NARRATION OR VOICE-OVER

If you lay narration or interior monologue you will need to fill gaps between narration sections with room tone so that the track remains live, particularly during a quiet sequence.

DIALOGUE TRACKS AND THE PROBLEM OF INCONSISTENCIES

You will have to split dialogue tracks in preparation for the mix. Because different camera positions occasion different mike positioning, a sequence's dialogue tracks played "as is" will change in level and room acoustics from shot to shot. The result is ragged and distracting when you need quite the contrary effect—the seamless continuity familiar from feature films. This result is achieved by painstaking and labor-intensive sound editing work in the following order:

- Split dialogue tracks (that is, lay them by grouping on separate tracks) according to the needs imposed by the coverage's mike positioning. For instance,
    - In a scene shot from two angles and having two mike positions, all the close-shot sound goes on one track and all the medium-shot sound goes on the other
    - With four or five mike positions, expect to lay at least four or five tracks
    - When tracks must additionally be split according to character, especially if one of them is under- or over-modulated in the recording
- EQ settings can be roughly determined during track laying, but final settings must be determined in the mix. The aim is to bring all tracks into acceptable compatibility, given that the viewer can expect a different sound perspective to match the different camera distances. These settings may now apply to multiple sound sections as they have been grouped according to EQ needs.
- Clean up background tracks of extraneous noises, creaks, and mike handling sounds—anything that doesn't overlap dialogue and therefore can be removed. Any gaps will sound like dropout unless filled with the correct room tone.
- If you have to join dissimilar room tones, do it as a quick dissolve behind a commanding foreground sound, so the audience's attention is distracted away from the change. The worst place to make an illogical sound change is in the clear.

Inconsistent backgrounds: Although manual and nonlinear sound mixing can handle many tracks, it is usual to premix groups of tracks and to leave final control of the most important to the last stage. The ragged, truncated background is the badge of the poorly edited film, where inadequate technique steals attention from the film's content. Frequently when you cut between two speakers in the same location, the background to each is different in either level or quality because the mike was angled differently or because background traffic or other activities had changed over time. Now is the time to use those presence tracks you shot on location so that you can add to and augment the lighter track to match its heavier counterpart. If an intrusive background sound, such as a high-pitched band saw, occupies a narrow band of frequency, you can sometimes effectively lower it by using a graphic equalizer. This lets you tune out the offending frequency, but with it goes all sounds in that band, including that part of your characters' voices.

Inconsistent voice qualities: A variety of location acoustical environments, different mikes, and different mike working distances all play havoc with the consistency of location voice recordings. Intelligent adjusting with sound filtering (EQ) at the mix stage can massively decrease the sense of strain and irritation arising from having to make constant adjustment to unmotivated and therefore irrational changes.

LAYING MUSIC TRACKS

It is not difficult to lay music, but remember to cut in just before the first sound attack so that its arrival isn't heralded by studio atmosphere or record surface hiss prior to the first chords. Arrow A in Figure 36–1 represents the ideal cut-in point; to its left is unwanted presence or hiss. To the right of A are three attacks in succession leading to a decay to silence at arrow B. A similar attack-sustain-decay profile is found for many sound effects (footsteps, for instance), so you can often use the same editing strategy. By removing sound between x and y we could reduce three footfalls here to two.

SPOT SOUND EFFECTS

Spot sound effects occasionally are used in documentaries and sync to something onscreen, like a door closing, a coin being placed on a table, or a phone being picked up. They need to be appropriate, in the right perspective, and carefully synchronized. Sound effects, especially tape library or disk effects, often bring problematical backgrounds of their own. You can reduce this by cutting into the effect immediately before a sound's "attack" (Figure 36–1, arrow A) and immediately after its decay (arrow B), thus minimizing the unwanted background's intrusiveness. Mask unwanted sound changes by placing them behind another sound: a doorbell ringing, for example, could mask an unavoidable atmosphere change. You can bring an alien background unobtrusively in and out by fading it up and down rather than letting it thump in and out as cuts.

Bear in mind that *the ear registers a sound cut-in or a cutout much more acutely than a graduated change.*

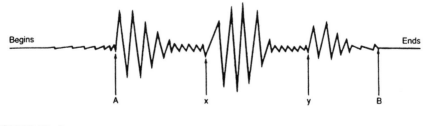

Begins   Ends

A   x   y   B

FIGURE 36–1

Diagram of sound attack and decay for a recording of three footsteps. Points A and B are ideal in- and out-cutting points. Points x and y are alternative in-points.

ATMOSPHERES AND BACKGROUND SOUND

Atmospheres are laid either to create a mood (birdsong over a morning shot of a wood or wood saw effects over the exterior of a carpenter's shop) or to mask inconsistencies by using something relevant but distracting. Always obey screen logic by laying atmospheres to cover the entire sequence, not just a part of it. Remember that when a door opens in an interior scene, the exterior atmosphere (children's playground, for instance) will rise for the duration that the door is open. If you want to create a sound dissolve, remember to lay the requisite amounts to allow for the necessary overlap and listen for any inequities in each overlap, such as the recordist quietly calling "Cut!".

TRADITIONAL MIX CHART

For traditional film mixes, you will need to fill in a mix chart blank (see Appendix 2) that reads from top to bottom, unlike a computer timeline, which reads horizontally from left to right. Anyone using computer software has a graphic representation to work from, with a cumulative timing available for the music cues.

In the completed sample (Figure 36–2) each column represents an individual track. By reading down the chart you see that

- Individual tracks play against each other, like instruments in a vertically organized music score.

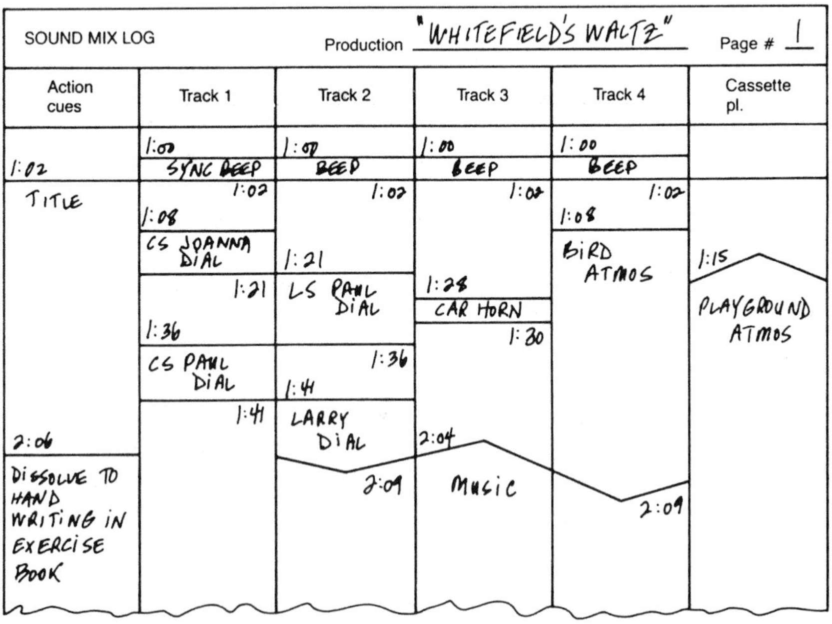

FIGURE 36–2

Specimen sound mix log for traditional film mix.

- The sync pip or "BEEP" at 00.30 is a single frame of tone on all tracks to serve as an aural sync check when the tracks begin running.

- Segment starts and finishes may be marked with footages or cumulative timings.

- A straight line at the start or finish represents a sound cut (as at 04:09 and 04:27).

- An opening chevron represents a fade-in (Track 4 at 04:10).

- A closing chevron represents a fade-out (Track 2 at 02:09).

- Timings at fades refer to the beginning of a fade-in or the end of a fade-out.

- A dissolve is two overlapping chevrons (as at 02:04 to 02:09). There is a fade-out on Track 4 overlapping a fade-in for the cassette machine. This is called a *cross fade* or *sound dissolve.*

- Timings indicate length of cross fade (sound dissolve), ours being a 5-second cross fade.

- When planning a dissolve, lay both tracks longer in case you want a longer dissolve during the mix session.

- You can lay up alternative sound treatments and choose during the mix.

Vertical space on the chart is seldom a linear representation of time. You might have 7 minutes of talk with a very simple chart, then half a minute of railroad station montage with a profusion of individual tracks for each shot. To avoid unwieldy or overcrowded mix charts, use no more vertical space than is necessary for clarity to the eye. To help the sound mix engineer, who works under great pressure in the half-dark, shade in the track boxes with a highlight marker.

SOUND MIX STRATEGY

PREMIXING

One sequence of a feature-length documentary may comprise 40 or more sound tracks. Because only one to four sound engineers operate a traditional mix board, it requires a sequence of premixes, and the same principle holds good for computerized mixes. *It is vital to premix in an order that reserves until last your control over the most important elements.* If you were to premix dialogue and effects right away, then a subsequent addition of more effects or music would uncontrollably augment and compete with the dialogue. Because intelligibility depends on audible dialogue, you must retain control over the dialogue-to-background level until the very last stage of mixing. This is particularly true for location sound, which is often near the margin of intelligibility to start with.

Note that each generation of analog (as opposed to digital) sound transfer introduces additional noise (system hiss). This is most audible in quiet tracks, such as a slow speaking voice in a silent room or a very spare music track. Analog video sound is the worst offender, because sound on VHS cassettes is in narrow tracks recorded at low tape speed, which is the worst of all worlds. The order of premixes thus may be influenced by which tracks should most be protected from repeated retransfer. Happily, digital sound copies virtually without degradation.

TAILORING

Many tracks, if played as laid, will enter and exit abruptly, making an unpleasantly jagged impression on the listener. This negatively affects how people respond to your subject matter, so it is important to achieve a seamless effect whenever you are not deliberately disrupting attention. The trouble comes when you cut from a quiet to a noisy track, or vice versa, but this can be greatly minimized by tailoring; that is, making a very quick fade-up or fade-down of the noisy track to meet the quiet track on its own terms. The effect onscreen is still that of a cut, but one that no longer assaults the ear (Figure 36–3).

COMPARATIVE LEVELS: ERR ON THE SIDE OF CAUTION

Mix studios sport excellent and expensive speakers. Especially for video work the results can be misleading, because low-budget filmmakers must expect their work to be seen on domestic TV sets, which have miserably small, cheap speakers. Not only does the luckless consumer lose frequency and dynamic ranges, he or she loses the dynamic separation between loud and soft, so foregrounds nicely separated in the mix studio become swamped by backgrounds. If you are mixing a dialogue scene with a traffic background atmosphere, err on the conservative side and make a deliberately high separation, keeping traffic low and voices high. A mix suite will obligingly play your track through a TV set so that you can be reassured of what the home viewer will actually hear.

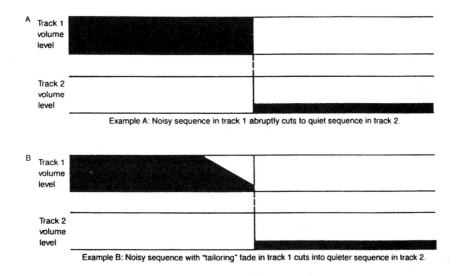

FIGURE 36–3

Abrupt sound cut tailored by quick fade of outgoing track so that it matches the level of the incoming track.

REHEARSE, THEN RECORD

If you mix in a studio, you as the director approve each stage of the mix. This does not mean you have to know how to do things, only that you and your editor have ideas about how each sequence should sound. To your requests, and according to what the editor has laid in the sound tracks, the mix engineer will offer alternatives from which to choose. Mixing is best accomplished by familiarizing yourself with the problems of one short section at a time and building sequence by sequence from convenient stopping points. At the end, it is very important to listen to the whole mix without stopping, as the audience will do. Usually finding an anomaly or two will reward your time.

FILM MIXES AND TV TRANSMISSION

The film medium is sprocketed so that tracks or a premix are easily synced up to a start mark in the picture reel leader. The final mix, whether it is made traditionally or digitally, will be transferred by a film laboratory to a sprocketed optical (that is, photographic) track and then photographically combined with the picture to produce a composite projection print. Television used to transmit films from double system; that is, picture and the magnetic mix were loaded on a telecine machine with separate but interlocked sound. The track was taken from the high-quality magnetic original instead of from the much lower-quality photographic track. Today television transmission is from the highest-quality digital tape cassettes, which are simpler, easier, and more reliable to use.

MAKE SAFETY COPIES AND STORE THEM IN DIFFERENT LOCATIONS

Because a sound mix requires a long and painstaking process, it is professional practice to immediately make safety or backup copies, which are stored safely in multiple buildings in case of loss or theft. Copies usually are made from the master mix in the knowledge that should it suffer damage or loss, backups exist.

The same principle should be followed for film picture or video original cassettes. Keep masters, safety copies, negatives, and internegatives in different places so that you don't lose everything should fire, flood, revolution, or act of God destroy what you might otherwise keep under your bed next to your shoes.

MUSIC AND EFFECTS TRACKS

If there is the remotest chance that your film will make an international sales, you will need to make a transcript of the whole film, so translators can do simultaneous translation, and a music and effects mix, often referred to as an *M & E track*. This is so that a foreign language crew can dub the speakers and mix the new voices in with the atmosphere, effects, and music tracks.

CHAPTER 37

TITLES AND
ACKNOWLEDGMENTS

This chapter deals with

- Titles, their form and content
- Rules for legible subtitling
- Copyrighting your film

TITLES

Although every film acquires a working title, its final title often is plucked late from an agony of indecision because it must be short, special, and epitomize the final version's identity. Remember that your film's title may be the only advertising copy your audience ever sees, so it should be informative and alluring. TV listings and festival programs rarely have space to describe their offerings, so the title you choose may be your sole means of drawing a potential audience.

Titles, especially when film rather than video is involved, are a minefield of trouble. Here's a short guide to avoid blowing yourself up.

Style: Form follows function. Emulate others by finding models among films of a length and budget commensurate with your own film and see which approach to titling you like. Documentary titles are usually plain and unfussy, but see examples on TV or for rent in the video store. Some of the most artistically ambitious films use brief and classically simple white on black titles. You could do a lot worse.

Font, layout, and size: Choose font for clarity and size and avoid small lettering. Anything too small or too fancy disappears on the television screen, where so much work is seen. The edges of the TV image are often clipped in poorly adjusted monitors and home TVs, so keep titling within the safe area.

Overladen titles: A sure sign of amateurism is a film loaded with an egocentric welter of credits. The same name should not crop up in multiple key capacities, and acknowledgments should be kept eloquently brief.

Contractual or other obligations: Because many favors are granted the makers of documentaries in return for an acknowledgment in the titles, be sure you honor your debts to the letter. Funding sources also may have a contractual obligation that you must acknowledge in prescribed wording, so this and all such agreements should be carefully checked and double-checked before titles are locked down.

Spelling: Spelling in titles and subtitles should be checked scrupulously by at least two highly literate and eagle-eyed checkers. The spelling of people's names should receive special care; a misspelling indicates for all time that you care too little for them or their work to give their correct name.

Title lengths: Decide the right duration for a title to remain onscreen by reading the contents of each screen *out loud one and a half times.* If you are shooting titles for film, be sure to shoot at least three times as much as you need. This allows for a title to be extended if needed. Long crawl titles must be run fast, or TV just chops them off.

Titles and quality: Good-looking titles usually are easy when you are postproducing digitally, but if your final is on film, reserve some of the budget to shoot the best titles you can afford. Professional-looking titles signal a high-quality film, and only high-quality films win festival awards. Here is the procedure:

1. Make up title cards ready for shooting. You will need to get adhesive letters and lay them out scrupulously on black card. This must be done meticulously, because even small inequities of proportion and straightness show up badly and make titles look amateurish.

2. Title cards are best shot on an animation stand with a known field of view.

3. If you shoot your titles using a regular camera:
   A. First do a viewfinder field test using a grid to check that what you see is what you are putting on film.
   B. If titles come up misaligned, suspect misalignment in your camera's viewfinder. Judging layout through a film viewfinder is hard anyway because the image is so small.

4. Shoot using high-contrast film, or black won't be true black but gray. Run tests with standard lighting to determine best exposure. Light titles on black are easy to overexpose, leading to a puzzling loss of definition that gives your lettering an out-of-focus look.

5. A/B roll titling—that is, shooting complete titles on film and then fading them in and out in the answer print stage before the film begins—is low cost and very serviceable. However,
   A. If you want lettering conventionally superimposed on an image for background, you can only superimpose black titles on that image when you use a negative-to-positive printing process. This is because black lettering produces white lettering on the negative, which lets though a fully exposing

light that prints black on a positive print. Few topics benefit from black titles unless you specialize in mortuary documentaries.

B. If you try to superimpose white titles using the negative-to-positive process, white lettering renders as black in a clear negative. Light then passes all *around* the titling, burning out the image meant to be the background.

C. For white titles on a moving background, the printing elements must first be converted into positive form and then contact printed on to a new negative, which then is cut into the appropriate place in the film-printing negative.

D. If you are making composite prints (one shot superimposed on another) be aware that registration in 16mm is none too steady, and expect some jiggle between lettering and background. Do a camera *steady test* first (shoot a grid, rewind the film, move the camera slightly and shoot the grid again, then process and project to see how much movement is apparent between the two passes).

E. Colored or fancy titles probably have to be shot using an optical printer. First-rate opticals are done in 35mm—at astronomical cost.

For elaborate film titling, you will have to talk with the customer representative at one of the few surviving film labs to see who specializes in making up and shooting titles. They may use either the traditional optical printer process or one that is computer generated. Because the bulk of such work is for feature films, check prices very carefully, preferably when sitting down in case you faint. If you go ahead, meet with the person who will be making them up and get all prices and everything else you discuss in writing. Be sure that any further charges you face for reshooting are fully defined.

Never leave film titles late in the process and assume that all will be right on the night. They are tricky to get right, especially if you are at all ambitious and want fancy effects. Titles, like troubles, are sent to try us, so give yourself plenty of time.

Titles for video: Most editing software comes with excellent titling capability, with a large array of typefaces; drop shadow, movement, crawl, and other exotic behaviors. Resist the temptation to exult in your new freedom; keep titling classically simple—unless of course your film's topic and treatment call for something more in keeping. The blessing with video is that you see immediately what you are getting, and can make changes until everything looks right. Superimposed lettering, whether colored or white, is more legible when you add a black outline, and this is especially true for subtitles.

FOREIGN MARKET: SUBTITLES AND TRANSCRIPT

Often when you submit your film to a foreign competition, the festival asks for a typed transcript of all dialogue in the film (for simultaneous translation) and a subtitled print in a particular language. Using nonlinear editing this is now easy (if time consuming) to do. Here are some guidelines:

1. Make an *abbreviated* transcription of the dialogue that you want to appear as a subtitle. Abbreviate dialogue exchanges down to absolute essentials—you don't want the audience so busy reading that they don't see your film.

2. Get the text translated by a literate, native speaker (not that friend who took several Spanish classes) and have it typed up with all the appropriate accents.

3. Pick a clear typeface in yellow with black edging. Your subtitles must be visible no matter how light or dark the background. Use a font size that can easily be read on a TV screen and place subtitles well into the TV safe area so that nothing gets lost on a poorly adjusted set.

4. Place every sentence within a continuous shot because we will read the title all over again if it overhangs the next shot. This is very irritating and unnecessary.

5. Break any long sentences into short sections, indicating anything that is run-on with triple periods (. . .), as in this example that is spread out over four shots:

How are you?	Shot 1
I feel OK just now . . .	Shot 2
. . . but am hoping you can . . .	Shot 3
. . . give me some advice.	Shot 4

Copyright: At the very end of the titles, remember to include your name and the © symbol, with the year as a claim to the copyright of the material. To file for copyright in the United States, look up the U.S. Copyright Office at www.loc.gov/copyright/ and follow directions for copyrighting. If you reside in another country, be sure to check out the correct copyright procedure with professionals. If and when you come to sell your film, any legal omissions can be costly or even paralyzing.

PRESS KIT AND WEB SITE

Once your film is completed, you can enter it in festivals. To give yourself the best chance, you will need to prepare a press kit to help you market your work. This usually includes a brief description of the film, quotations from any praise or reviews it has received, brief details on the careers of the makers, and good-quality photographs. You should also include your e-mail and Web site address (if you have one), plus phone, fax, and street address. When you go to festivals, go armed with press kits and business cards. You will be surprised what develops from the serendipity at screenings and conferences.

FESTIVALS

You can find festivals by using the Web sites listed in part 9, "Useful Websites." At last you get to experience the ultimate rite of passage: seeing your film in the company of your true masters—a paying audience. This can be a thrilling or a chastening experience. Whichever comes your way, it is the final reckoning, the last phase of learning, and represents closure of that project for the filmmaker.

Now what film will you make next?

CHAPTER 38

PROJECTS: POSTPRODUCTION

The projects in this chapter are editing projects and will vary according to the source material you choose. Each project highlights particular aspects of editing and can be well explored using material from the projects in Chapter 28, Projects: Advanced Production. However, the notes and Assessment Criteria (in Appendix 1) that come with the projects here are widely applicable, and one or other of them can be used to interrogate editing aspects of almost any project.

EDITING PROJECTS

PROJECT 38-1: INTERVIEW, VARYING IMAGE SIZES

Materials for this editing project can come from Project 28-6: Interview in Depth.
 Goals are to

- Shorten interview material shot with a single camera
- Restructure into most logical and best dramatic order
- Intercut three different image sizes
- Produce from an interview a continuous, *transparent* monologue. Transparent filmmaking minimizes evidence of time lapses and other spatial and temporal manipulations normal to filmmaking.

Recommendations

1. First restructure the interview. Like any story, long or short, you must find a storytelling structure that has a beginning, middle, and an end. Use transcripts and the paper edit method if the interview is extensive.

2. Eliminate all evidence of the interviewer's voice so that the interview stands alone.

3. Avoid all jump cuts or action mismatches in this exercise, which exemplifies the transparent style of filmmaking.

4. When editing, play sound loud so that you don't inadvertently cut into the middle of any low breathing sounds—they are part of normal speech and should be left intact.

5. Be careful to maintain the natural rhythms of the speaker's voice, and watch out that rising or falling inflections sound natural at the cutting points between shots.

6. Sometimes the least noticeable picture cut is one made after a sentence has begun. Using the null points between sentences, though logical, is often clumsy because it draws attention to the cut instead of burying it in a flow of words and movement.

7. Be careful that the speaker's head and body positions match as you cut from one image size to another. When this is a problem, remember that the more radical the change of image size, the less the audience will notice a mismatch.

Assessment criteria: See Appendix 1, Project 38-1 Assessment.

Discussion: If you were made aware of the camera or of the hand of the editor, what interrupted the otherwise "transparent" technique? How succinct was the interview? Were there any departures from the natural rhythms of the speakers? Did the editor manage to get all traces of the interviewer (including eyeline evidence) out of the edited final?

PROJECT 38-2: CONVERSATION, TWO OR MORE PERSONS

Materials for this assignment could come from Project 28-2: Three-Person Conversation (Interior) or Project 28-7: Two-Person Conversation with Conflict.
    Goals are to

• Edit coverage of a multi-person conversation to make it shorter and more compact

• Restructure conversation for maximum effectiveness

• Use the different angles, cutaways, and inserts to create a natural tempo and development

• Restructure lengthy material of uneven intensity into a sequence of appropriate length, logical development that is dramatically fulfilling to watch

All the comments in the previous editing project concerning rhythms and matching the action apply, but depending on coverage and the cutaways supplied, you can develop the reactions and inner life of the participant who is being acted upon as well as, or in place of, the one who is speaking. You can also use motivated cut-ins or cutaways to give more feeling of what the characters are seeing or thinking. (A *cut-in* or *insert* is a magnified detail in an existing frame; a *cutaway* is something beyond that frame.)

Assessment criteria: See Appendix 1, Project 38-2 Assessment.

Discussion: How natural did the conversation look? Were you aware of manipulation in the editing such as ellipsis or restructuring? How well were cutaways or inserts used? Were they motivated? Were there any departures from the natural rhythms of the speakers?

PROJECT 38-3: EDITING FOR ELLIPSIS

Materials for this assignment can come from Projects 28-3, 28-4, or 28-5.
   Goals are to

- Reduce a long life-process shot in real time to a brief screen time
- Jump cut time
- Reduce something long to informative essentials only
- Use contrasting or complementary angles
- Develop an elegant shorthand editing style to show just high points of a process

Often an editor is faced with lengthy material of a conversation or a process, such as changing a car tire or planting a tree, and must drastically shorten it to show only the salient stages. An alert camera operator covers such action by shooting reactions, inserts, and cutaways that can patch over ugly jump cuts. Even better, that operator will have covered the event from a number of logical angles. The editor can now compress essentials into a fraction of the original running time and has many options for maintaining "transparency," that is, keeping up the illusion that one is seeing real life rather than an edited film.

When a process is poorly covered, the hapless editor is often starved of sufficient angle changes or cutaways and must use great ingenuity to avoid an ugly, bumpy cut. Some comments:

- The odd jump cut in an otherwise transparent sequence disrupts attention by intruding an inconsistent narrative style, but several bold jump cuts can be a tasteful way of signaling time shifts.
- If you cannot create dissolves and have no parallel story line as a cutaway strand, there is another saving resource—sound. You can create the effect of an optical fade-out/fade-in by fading the outgoing scene to silence, then fading up the incoming one from the cut.
- Likewise, if the two scenes have contrasting sound tracks, you can create the illusion of an optical dissolve by overlapping them and making one dissolve (or segue) into the other. These sound strategies are classically simple and effective.

   Assessment criteria: See Appendix 1, Project 38-3 Assessment.
   Discussion: How concise but comprehensive was the edited coverage? Did you see all necessary stages of the action? Were there unexpected or unusual moments?

PROJECT 38-4: COMPLEX EDITING PROJECT

Materials for this assignment might come from Projects 28-1, 28-10, 28-11, 28-13, or 28-17, or from any film that uses a combination of materials and techniques.

Goals: In a complex scene you would expect to see

- Action match cutting
- Montage principles to render a mood, compress action, or create a sense of lyricism
- Cuts making use of movement by either the subject or camera
- Intercutting between complementary shots
- Overlap cutting where sound precedes its accompanying picture
- Overlap cutting where picture precedes its accompanying sound
- Exploitation of inherent verbal, visual, and musical rhythms
- Inserts or cutaways used as motivated point-of-view (POV) shots
- Development of subtextual hints and information
- Reaction shots used to indicate inner lives of participants
- Meaningful tension and counterpoint between words and images
- Figurative sound or visual devices used to create foreshadowing, analogy, irony, metaphor, repetition
- Music used intelligently

Creating tension between words and images usually means looking at the available visuals for their figurative (as opposed to merely illustrative) content. A young man's voice saying it was a pleasure to leave home can take on different meanings: playing the voice over a shot of a cat looking through a window at the street carries different implications than playing it over a saucepan in a sink filling with water then overflowing. There is unlimited poetic force at your fingertips when you start placing ideas against the unexpected image, always providing that the image is organic to the world under scrutiny and is part of an expressive scheme rather than being used incidentally and alone.

Assessment criteria: See Appendix 1, Project 38-4 Assessment.

Discussion: Did the edited project create a tension between ideas, between sound and image? How many of the listed techniques did it use? Were there any others that it could have used to advantage?

POSTPRODUCTION CHECKLIST

The documentary editor is

- Patient, organized, experimental, and diplomatic
- Really a second director and should be willing to make subjective judgments

Noteworthy aspects of editing:

- Film recreates aspects of consciousness to help the audience share a character's (or storyteller's) shifting consciousness.
- Interesting discrepancies of information urge the audience into an active, problem-solving relationship with the film.
- Every call to imagination or judgment is an acknowledgment of equality with the audience and an invitation to participate in discovery.
- Dramatic advantages can sometimes be gained from disrupting chronological time.
- Cross cutting between two stories can telescope or stretch time and heighten comparison and irony.
- The operative word falling on each new shot helps us interpret the image's meaning.
- Changing the juxtaposition of words and shots can imply different meanings.
- It is easier to shorten a film than to pump substance back into one prematurely tightened.
- If an edited version is very different from what you expected, see it again before commenting.
- As a director, stay away from the cutting process to preserve your objectivity.
- The film's structure and authorial voice are developed during editing.

Transcripts

- Do not reflect voice inflections, so don't assume that anything will sound as it is written
- Can be replaced by a summary of topics, each with its timecode location, as an index to finding important material quickly.
- Can be avoided but usually it's "live now, pay later"

Logging

- Liberates time and energy so you can be creative
- Never change to a better system in midfilm

Paper Edit

- Selecting Sections
  - Make a photocopy of transcripts to use as follows:
    - During a viewing, draw a line against any good transcribed section.
    - Bracket the in- and out-points.
    - Put ID (cassette, character/scene, section number, timecode) in margin.
    - Put a brief functional description in margin.

- Preparing for a Paper Cut
  - Make a photocopy of the marked transcript sheets to use as follows:
    - Cut selected transcript sections into slips.
    - On each slip write name and origin of each action sequence.
  - Paper cut structural considerations
    - Avoid the word-driven documentary by making an action-only paper cut first, and then bring in speech later.
    - How is your film to be structured in time?
    - What information must the audience get to understand the unfolding film?
    - What other organizing features does it have that can help you group material together?
    - How will your film reveal its purpose? (The "contract" must not be long delayed.)
    - Are there dramatic advantages to disrupting the subject's natural advance in time?
    - What can you tell as parallel stories to telescope or stretch time?
    - What special juxtapositions can you contrive to create comparison and irony?
    - How can you show development (which is so important)?
- Assembling the Paper Edit
  - Do your best, but remember a paper cut is only marks on paper representing film.
  - Exclude nothing workable if you are in doubt—leave choice of alternatives for later.
  - Make a simple blueprint; let complexities develop from film, not on paper or in your head first.

First Assembly

- Put a loose version of whole film together without working on any detail.
- Don't deal with embellishment until you know the film's entire identity and purpose.
- The order and juxtaposition of material have very potent consequences.
- You are presenting pieces of evidence, one at a time, to build a case in the audience's mind.
- Let your film begin telling you what it wants you to do.

Rough Cut

- Deal only with the film's major needs at this stage (there will be many stages).
- An early decision about maximum length helps face the inevitability of jettisoning certain material.

- It is easier to shorten a long film than to pump substance back into one prematurely tightened.

Viewing

- Try to see each new cut as an audience does, without prior conceptions or special knowledge.
- If a cut is very different from what you expected, see it again before commenting.
- Where is the film dramatically unbalanced?
- Does a graph of the movie's "dramatic temperature" make sense?
- Where does the film drag?
- What remains in your memory, and what has left no trace?
- Have you made the most of revealing contrasts?

Narration

- Try to make your film tell its own story without any narration.
- If narration is unavoidable, decide whether scripted or improvised narration will be best.
- Narration must be assimilated by the audience the first time or not at all.
- Narration must be in the simple, direct language of speech, not that of written discourse.
- Never describe what can be seen in the shot. Add to the image with words; do not duplicate.
- Be ready to invert syntax to fit the sequence of the viewer's perceptions.
- Leave spaces for featured sound effects.
- The first (or "operative") word to fall on each new shot has a major consequence for how the audience interprets the shot.
- Altering the juxtaposition of words and shots can imply different meanings.
- Unless it's a personal POV, use narration primarily to relay facts.
- Avoid predisposing your audience to any particular attitude with narration; they may resent it.
- The intelligent narration prepares the audience to make its own value judgments.
- Narration can accelerate your film's exposition and make brief, agile links between sequences.
- Any narration, especially if its poorly written or delivered, is an intrusion into the audience's relationship with the subject.
- Narration can focus your audience on aspects of the material you want them to notice.

Narrators

- The audience looks upon the narrator as the voice of the film.
- The narrator's voice quality and delivery must act as a surrogate for your own attitude to the subject.
- Try a scratch narration before recording to be sure that it works and that you have covered all your bases.
- Audition narrators cautiously, giving directions to see how the candidate responds.

Narration Recording Session

- Show the chosen narrator the film and explain what characteristics must be embodied in the narration.
- Give brief, positive, qualitative directions to a narrator.
- The narrator studies the script, and the director watches the picture while recording and listens through a speaker or headphones to ensure that delivery is appropriate and tempo is correct.
- Remember to record 2 minutes of narration studio presence track.

Music

- Music should not inject false emotion.
- Choice of music should give access to the inner life of a character or the subject.
- Music can signal the emotional level at which audience should investigate what is being shown.
- You cannot know if music choice really works until you try it against the picture.
- It is better to use no music than bad music.

Fine Cut

- Use overlap cuts to smooth transitions and to create interesting disjunctions between what is seen and what is heard.
- Know standard film lengths for likely distribution so that you can choose one.
- Aim to say a lot through a little.
- Good short films are welcome everywhere.
- Most people are prejudiced against the long, well-meaning film unless it has a very high thematic density to repay the investment of time it demands.

Evoking a Trial Audience Response

- Remember, you can't please everyone!
- Use sample audiences and careful, open-ended questioning to see whether your film is functioning as intended.

- In a trial showing, exert maximum control over sound—it affects audience responses disproportionately.
- Direct audience attention to issues on which you need information, but remember to ask open, nondirective questions, listening carefully for what people are really saying.
- Is your audience getting the main underlying meanings? If not, why not?
- Hang on to your fundamental intentions; let go of them only with very good reason.

Diagnostic Method

- Make a block diagram of the movie to spot invisible anomalies (see text for common ones).
- After re-editing to cure the latest round of difficulties, make another block diagram to see what problems the housecleaning introduced by the back door.
- Put the film aside for a week or two, and view it again before deciding if the fine cut is final.

Track Laying and Mix Chart

- Alternate ("checkerboard") dialogue tracks to facilitate equalization and level adjustments.
- Use correct presence track to fill holes in dialogue, narration, or scene.
- When presences are mismatched, lay in extra to bring the quieter up to balance the louder.
- Plan featured sound effects to go in dialogue gaps (or vice versa).
- Sync spot Sound Effects (FX) carefully.
- Mask unavoidable inconsistencies with a logical atmosphere track.
- Cut into music or FX just before attack and just after complete decay to avoid hearing studio or other ambience.
- Sound dissolves require an appropriate track overlap.
- Make a fair-copy mix chart that the eye can easily follow.

Sound Mix

- Premix, retaining control over the most important elements until last.
- Rehearse each section before recording.
- Soften ragged sound cuts by tailoring the louder to the quieter in a rapid fade-up or fade-down.
- When mixing foreground speech with background sound (music, FX, atmosphere, and so on), err on the side of caution and separate foreground well from background.
- Make a safety copy of the mix and store it somewhere separate and safe.
- Store separate masters in different places (disaster control).

Titles and Acknowledgments

- Use a working title until the film is fully edited.
- Double-check contractual obligations for special wording.
- Double-check spelling, particularly that of people's names.
- Shoot plenty of title, just in case.
- Keep onscreen title lengths short and sweet.
- Hold each title card onscreen for one-and-a-half times as long as it takes to read out loud.
- Make sure you have credited any music correctly.
- Never assume titles can be done quickly and accurately. They are Murphy's last refuge.
- Remember to register the copyright of your film.

CAREER TRACK

Part 8 deals with

- Planning ahead for education and a future career
- Alternative paths of learning
- Finding an education
- Building bridges to employment while in school
- Developing proposals and following your fascinations
- Applying for work or making a job for yourself

How and where you learn documentary filmmaking is greatly affected by your economic circumstances, learning style, and what you want. A few people each year write me to say that they have just won an award or sold a film, and that this book was their main teacher, so you may be holding an academy in your hands. However, it is much easier to go to a school or college where there are peers to work with, equipment, and a structured educational path. Choosing one, and making the most of your education, is the subject of this part.

If you cannot go to film school you can, if determined, still work your way toward professional abilities. The same cannot be said for fiction filmmaking, for which formal schooling seems unavoidable.

Whatever you do, it is very important to begin laying the groundwork for your career from the beginning. Make use of the facilities over and above what the college demands for a passing grade, and get experience and put a show reel together that will prove your employability once you need work. You should research festivals and decide what films you could make as entries. Festival awards are your future identity, and they won't happen unless you plan to make it so. The rest of this part is about leveraging yourself into employment.

For further information on issues arising in Part 8, use the Index or go to the Bibliography.

CHAPTER 39

EDUCATION

This chapter deals with

- Approaches to developing a career
- Researching film schools
- Self-help and working with others
- Developing a craft specialty
- Lists of film schools associated with the University Film and Video Association (UFVA) and Centre International de Liaison de Cinéma et de Télévision (CILECT), The International Association of Film and Television Schools

PLANNING A CAREER

How do you get started in any kind of documentary filmmaking? And after, say, 3 to 5 years of professional work, where can you expect to be? These questions deserve answers, especially the last, which indicates a perilous misunderstanding. The plain fact is that making documentaries is not like banking or retail management; it has no career ladder with predictable promotion rates. All filmmaking is a branch of the entertainment industry. How far you get and how long you take to get there depend on your ability, energy, flair, and persistence. Luck plays a part too, but not much. Persistence is mostly what you need.

If you have strong ties to family, community, and affluence, then becoming a filmmaker may meet antagonism at home because the documentary industry is unpredictable, informally structured, and assumes a driving entrepreneurial initiative in the individual. If, on the other hand, you are interested in people, social phenomena, and politics, then making your individual voice heard may be worth a long, uphill, and poorly paid struggle. You will probably like the documentarian's way of life and you won't have to wonder, like so many do, why you go to work every day.

LEARNING ON THE JOB

Taking the "industry route" and getting into a ground-level apprenticeship situation—always supposing one is to be had—initially looks very attractive but can be fraught with frustration. Knowing nothing about this, the ill-prepared youngster who is weary of "more school" gratefully takes the first job that comes along. Little does he know that his boss wanted cheap labor. Five years later he wonders why he is still driving the company station wagon and answering the phones. Simple: most employers live pressured lives and do not consider preparing the individual for more responsibility as a part of the job. Know-how and experience are earning power in the freelance world, so people *avoid* enlightening their juniors. The employee won't rise without arriving prepared to assume more complex duties whenever an opportunity arises. Schooling is a good preparation, and better than this is determined, never-ending self-education superimposed on a good education. Self-education is slower but quite possible for making documentaries.

The on-the-job film training I got, and my 3 decades of teaching, leave me certain of the value in education. A single example should tell you why: students in a 15-week editing class can absorb techniques and insights that took me 10 years on the job to discover for myself. A good schooling gives you

- A cultural and intellectual perspective on the medium
- Knowledge and history, and some ideas about your role in the medium
- Technical training in the use of the tools, techniques, and concepts
- Help in uncovering your talents, abilities, and energies
- A safe environment in which to experiment at expressing individual vision
- Aspirations to use your professional life to its fullest extent and for the widest good
- Collaborators with whom to face adversity, of which there is plenty in school and after it

Schools of course cater to the common denominator—frustrating for anyone who learns unusually fast or who is unusually motivated. A good film school has a structured program of learning, technical facilities, enthusiastic expertise, and contemporaries with whom to collaborate. By going through all the stages of making a film—no matter how badly—you determine what role in the process you are best at. You see the faults or strengths in your own and others' work. A good school encourages you to experiment and lets you learn from the kind of ambitious failures that are suicidal in the commercial arena. From this, students acquire confidence, self-knowledge, and the ability to remain true to themselves under pressures and criticism. The benefits surface not just during your first job but far into your career and for years afterward.

If schooling is out of the question, use this book and get on with it. Try to team up with other enthusiasts. Self-education is the best education because you never forget your lessons.

FINDING THE RIGHT SCHOOL

Many schools, colleges, and universities have film courses. No serious study of film is wasted, but be careful and critical before committing yourself to an extended course of study. Depending on its interests and traditions, a school teaching "documentary" may specialize in electronic journalism, visual anthropology, social documentary, or some other form of nonfiction filmmaking. Be careful you know what any school that interests you teaches. Following are some types of school and some thoughts on each.

Short courses: These can be useful as an initial exposure and for deciding if the work is really what you want to do. In the United States, the Maine Workshops, now the International Film and Television Workshops, is the best-known facility (www.theworkshops.com/filmworkshops/), but there is a heavy emphasis on the trappings of professionalism. Britain has many short film and television courses, and something similar probably exists in many countries. Expect short courses to be equipment or procedure oriented rather than conceptual. There are as yet few facilities specializing in documentary, and a short course at its best can do little more than introduce and inspire you.

Communications departments: Many large universities offer generalist communications programs whose film departments—if they have them—may prove neither adequately equipped nor expertly taught. Film studies are necessary to a liberal education and good for sharpening the perceptions, but divorced from production they are film appreciation, not film creation. Avoid departments whose course structure shows no commitment to field production and whose faculty make no films.

Fine arts schools: Be cautious about film departments in fine arts schools. They are apt to undervalue craftsmanlike control of the medium and overvalue exotic form presented as personal vision. Fine art student filmmakers may see themselves as reclusive soloists like the painters and sculptors around them. This encourages gimmicky, egocentric production without the control over the medium that comes from a team. If you leave school without work of professional standard, developing a career will be next to impossible.

Trade schools: Trade schools are technically disciplined but less therapeutic. The atmosphere is commercial and industry oriented, concerned with drilling students to carry out narrowly defined technical duties for a standardized industrial product. Union and apprenticeship schemes tend to follow these lines, technically superb but often intellectually arid. They do sometimes lead to jobs, unlike the hastily assembled school of communications, which offers the illusion of a quick route to a TV station job. For every occupation there is always a diploma mill. In the TV version expect to find a private, unaffiliated facility with a primitive studio where students are run through the rudiments of equipment operation. Needless to say, nobody but the much-hyped few ever find the career they hope for.

Large versus small film schools: Smaller institutions or departments, unless costly, may lack resources. This means less choice of coursework, fewer faculty among whom to find the right mentor, and less forms of filmmaking available. A curriculum may be limited to generalist courses and the classes may be overenrolled. The small school can be an ideal community with inspired teaching or, if dominated by the wrong personalities, may have become a dysfunctional family. Only careful research reveals what a school is really like. Always visit, and always talk to a range of students.

A large school like my own (Columbia College Chicago, see www.filmatcolumbia.com) though intimidating to the newcomer, usually offers a diversity of education at reasonable cost. Watch out that class sizes are reasonable; for production, you want 15 or so. Any large film school should run a core curriculum that fans out into a comprehensive array of specialization tracks. After hands-on basic experience, the student is able to choose a professional specialty such as screenwriting, cinematography, audio, editing, directing, producing, documentary, alternative forms, animation, or critical studies.

My college happens to start everyone out in fiction. Those who elect to specialize in documentary do so after a fiction cinema training, which has the benefits of giving you some familiarity with the control of language that is unique to fiction. Starting all undergraduate students in fiction is currently under review. Incidentally, take a look at the Semester in Los Angeles Program, an extension unit of Columbia College Chicago located on the CBS lot in Studio City. Those in the fiction program who specialize in writing and producing can study with professionals and take up internships in Hollywood. Because many documentaries are made in Los Angeles, there should eventually be a documentary arm of that program. If you want information, write—not to me as I have retired from everyday college life—to Columbia College Chicago by following the directions at our Web site, www.filmatcolumbia.com. It has a mass of information, but if there are other questions you need answered, the department will be delighted to help.

High-profile film schools: Be warned that some high-reputation film schools make students compete for whose work gets produced. You may enter to study directing, then find after some years of study that your work proposal didn't get enough peer or faculty votes. You wind up recording sound for the winner. Schools in the long shadow of Hollywood tend to promote (or are unable to prevent) pernicious ideas about success that blight some students' potential. The moral? A hard-to-enter, expensive school is not necessarily a good school, nor is it one that necessarily fits your profile. Look long before you leap.

International film schools: There is a long list of international schools listed later in the chapter. Most are state subsidized, very selective, and small. Many, such as those in Australia and the Scandinavian countries, are very good. Prague runs excellent short courses in English for foreigners and has a fine tradition of cinematography and animation. The Documentary Filmmakers' Group Web site offers guidance to resources in Britain (www.dfglondon.com/links.php).

Graduate schools: These are usually small and selective in their intake. Many are new and totally unproved. Students get lots of personal attention, but the school may suffer from small school syndrome, in which a few personalities dominate and a combination of airlessness and high expectations puts undue pressures on the students. The best indicator of quality is whose films are winning awards at festivals. Columbia College Chicago, New York University (NYU), Stanford, Temple University, University of Texas at Austin, and University of Southern California (USC) are best known for documentary.

How to recognize the school for you: Aspiring students shop for schools by assessing their equipment, but this is shortsighted. Faculty, morale, and the curriculum are paramount. A good film school balances a strong conceptual, aesthetic, and historical coursework with sound production expectations. Of course there must be a respectable amount of professional-level equipment as well as enough basic cameras and editing equipment to support the beginning levels. Students should prove their knowledge not in theory but in practical ways, as you would expect in an arts education, before being allowed to make anything. A good school is an enthusiastic film-producing community where students routinely support and crew for each other.

When a metropolitan film school has been in existence for a while, successful former students give visiting lectures and return as teachers. They often employ, or give vital references to, the most promising students. In this networking process, the lines separating school from professional filmmaking are being crossed in both directions. The school filmmaking community tapers off into the young (and not so young) professional community to mutual advantage. In the reverse flow, mentors give advice, steer projects, and exemplify the way of life that students are trying to make their own. Personal recommendation by your teacher is important: even in the largest cities the film and video community operates like a village where personal recommendation is everything.

To locate good teaching, attend student film festivals and note where the films you really like are being made. A sure sign of energetic and productive teaching, even in a small facility, is when student work is receiving awards. The measure of a film school is what the students and faculty produce, what festival awards their films win, and what work its students get after graduating.

School guides: Although there is *Gardner's Guide to Colleges for Multimedia and Animation* (Washington, DC: Garth Gardner, 2002) there is nothing current for live action filmmaking. A history of film schools and information about the issues affecting graduate study can be gained from Karin Kelly and Tom Edgar's *Film School Confidential: The Insider's Guide to Film Schools* (New York: Berkeley Publishing Group, 1997), but it is angled toward feature filmmaking, is very out of date, and the opinions offered come from perilously small samples. Its Web site is www.lather.com/fsc/fsc1.html.

Research: There is no substitute for doing your own research, for which the Internet is most helpful. Make comparisons and decide on a department's emphasis. A rousing statement of philosophy may be undercut when you scan equipment holdings and the program structure. Sometimes a department has evolved under the chairmanship of a journalist or radio specialist, so film and television production is a poorly resourced lure within an all-purpose communications department.

Nicholas Jarecki's *Breaking In: How 20 Movie Directors Got Their First Start* (New York: Broadway Books, 2001) interviews fiction directors. The interviews usefully reiterate the common values underpinning any career in film but won't reveal where the rungs of a reliable career ladder are. The fact is that in fiction or documentary you make them for yourself. The prime attribute of a documentary director is the ability to research a situation and put a picture together from multiple sources of information. Following are some considerations to help you do this with schooling.

- How extensive is the department and what does its structure reveal?
  - Number of courses? (More is better.)
  - How regularly are upper-level courses offered? (Some listed may have been given once, several years ago.)
  - Number of students? (More may not seem better but does enable variety of courses and multiplicity of potential mentors.)
  - Subjects taught by senior and most influential faculty?
  - Average class size?
  - Ratio of full-time to part-time faculty?
- How long is the program? (See model syllabus; less than 2 or 3 years is suspiciously short.)
- Where is the school located, and what amenities does the setting offer?
- How much specialization is possible, and do upper-level courses strive for a professional level of specialization?
- How much equipment is there, what kind, and who gets to use it? (This is a real giveaway.)
- How wide is the introduction to different technologies?
  - At what level and by whom is film used?
  - Is the school using up to date technology? (Faculties are sometimes dominated by film diehards.)
  - How evenhanded is the use of technologies?
  - What kind of backgrounds do the faculty members have?
  - What have they produced?
  - Are they still producing, or are they resting on past laurels?
  - Does the institution support its faculty in producing?
- How experienced are those teaching beginning classes? (Many schools have to use their graduate students to teach lower-end classes before they have developed independent expertise.)
- From tuition and class fees:
  - How much equipment and materials are supplied?
  - How much is the student expected to supply along the way?
  - Does the school have competitive funds or scholarships to assist in production costs?
  - Who owns the copyright to student work? (Many schools retain copyright of their students' work.)
  - How expensive is local accommodation and how available are dormitories?
  - What proportion of those wanting to direct actually do so? (Some schools, under the guise of teaching professionalism, make students compete for top artistic roles and sideline the losers.)
- What does the department say about its attitudes and philosophy?

- How much hype can you detect? For instance:
  - Are the famous names cited (if any are) truly connected with the institution? (Some schools shamelessly list persons who have no regular relationship with them.)
  - When a school lists its famous alumni, how many are recent graduates and how many from decades earlier? Are they still actively involved with the school?
- What does the place feel like? (Visit at all costs.)
- How do the students regard the place? (Speak to your own choice of senior students.)
- How much are your particular interests treated as a specialty? (Speak to students studying in this area.)
- If you already have a BA, what kind of graduate program do they offer?
  - An MFA (a good qualification for production and teaching)
  - A PhD (signifies a scholarly emphasis that generally precludes production)
  - What is the degree's focus?
  - What work do most students go on to do after graduation?
- If the degree conferred is a BA or BFA, how many hours of general studies are you expected to complete, and how germane are they to your focus in film or video?
- What kind of internship and job placement program do they offer?

Film school is like medical school. It takes several years of hard learning to come out with something useful. Filmmaking is an intense, shared experience that leaves few aspects of relationship untouched. Lifelong friendships and partnerships develop out of it, but not without flaws emerging in your own and other people's characters as the pressure mounts. With determination everyone can improve.

International study: Many intending to study internationally come from European, Latin American, or Southern Hemisphere countries and are used to education being free. Of course it should be, but ideals should not stop you from investing in your future if you are able to, because one life is all we get. You, rather than a government, should have some say in this. Some of the film schools in Latin America may have little equipment, but there is a wonderful and spirited education going on and excellent documentaries somehow being made. The University of Buenos Aires, Argentina, and the University of São Paolo, Brazil, are two such schools. The International School of Film and Television in Cuba, the Communications University in Santiago, Chile, and the Mexico City schools are all well equipped and thriving centers of filmmaking.

Some of the larger and well-recognized film/video schools in the United States are listed later. Many allow students in good standing to work for their tuition within the department, so study abroad may not be out of reach. Because many of this book's users will live in other parts of the globe, I have listed the major international film schools affiliated with Centre International de Liaison de Cinéma et de Télévision (CILECT), The International Association of Film and

Television Schools, which is based in Brussels. Most have very competitive entry requirements.

People sometimes assume that work and study abroad are easily arranged and will be an extension of conditions in their own country. Since the attacks on September 11, international study has become even more complicated than it was, and self-support through part-time work usually is illegal. Immigration policies everywhere exclude foreign workers when natives are underemployed. That situation changes only when you have special, unusual, and proven skills to offer. Check local conditions carefully before committing yourself. Also check the length of the visa granted and the average time it takes students to graduate—occasionally the times are not compatible.

National film schools: These hothouse institutions usually are handsomely funded and well connected to their film industry. They can be first rate, or they can be a mixed blessing—that's if you can get in. Entry examining procedures, as for any conservatory, can be lengthy and excruciating, and the tiny proportion of students who pass them, though smart academically or in other ways, are the handpicked choices of a particular faculty. Intakes may be tiny, and courses of study may be long and taught by brilliant filmmakers who are erratic or just plain terrible as teachers. The school atmosphere can be a competitive pressure cooker so that whole intakes occasionally turn into a dysfunctional family. War between students, the institution, and its leadership is not unusual and sometimes is justified.

Most national film schools are predicated on scholarships and what the national film industry thinks it needs. Taking five documentary students every year from a population of five million does not seem a very productive approach, but it's what governments decide is rational. Do not be discouraged if your national film school has rejected you. Mike Figgis was rejected by his, but he found another way and so can you. People accomplish what matters to them. If literature or popular music got its recruits via academe, there would be no books to put in libraries and no music to go in record stores. National film schools feed a system, while private schools are more likely to cater to students' appetite to try oneself out in an art form. Parents often ask, "Is this responsible, when there are so few positions in filmmaking?" The answer is that there will be as many positions as there are exceptional film artists. Filmmakers are seers and entertainers in an entertainment industry, and there is no finite quantity to what a society needs. Many artists come from the wrong side of the tracks and are refused conventional education. When they succeed it is because they won't have their lives decided by an establishment.

State-funded education unfortunately encourages a mind-set of dependency that is averse to risk taking and that makes people docile. But nobody can predict who will do well or badly in filmmaking unless they watch that person trying to make films. In our open admissions college, the one thing we learned is that, with the usual obvious exceptions, *you cannot predict who will grow and flourish while learning to make films.* Education, self-administered or institutional, is your investment in your future. By definition any investment involves commitment and risk. If you can scrape together the funds to buy half a car, you can own the equipment to make documentaries or go to film school for a year. With determination you can prove for yourself what your abilities are.

SELF-HELP AS A REALISTIC ALTERNATIVE

Let us take the worst case and assume you can afford neither time nor money to go to school. You must acquire knowledge and experience another way, or put your trust in reincarnation. Werner Herzog once said in my hearing that anyone wanting to make films should waste no more than a week learning film techniques. Even with his flair for overstatement, this period would appear a little short, but fundamentally I share his attitude. Making films is practical and experiential, like dance and swimming, and it can be tackled by a group of motivated do-it-yourselfers. This book is intended to encourage such people to learn from making films, to learn through doing, and, if absolutely necessary, through doing so in relative isolation. By doing the exercises in this book you will learn a huge amount.

Self-education in the arts, however, is different from that in a technology, because the arts are not finite and calculable. They are based upon shared tastes and perceptions that at an early stage call for the criticism and participation of others. Even the painter, novelist, poet, photographer, or animator—artists normally considered to create alone—is incomplete until he or she engages with society and experiences its reaction. Nowhere is public acceptance more important than with film, the preeminent audience medium.

THE PROS AND CONS OF COLLABORATION

If you use this book to begin active filmmaking, you will recognize that it is a social art, one that will be stillborn without a keen spirit of collaboration. You will need other people as technicians and artistic collaborators if you are to do any sophisticated shooting, and you will need to earn the interest of other people in your end product. If you are unused to working collaboratively—and, sad to say, conventional education teaches students to compete for honors instead of gaining them cooperatively—then you have an inspirational experience ahead.

Somewhere along the way you will need a special mentor or two, people to give knowledgeable and objective criticism of your work and to help solve the problems that arise. Do not worry if none is in the offing right now, for the beginner has far to go. It is a law of nature in any case that you find the right people when you truly need them.

PLANNING A CAREER TRACK DURING YOUR EDUCATION

Whether you are self-educated or whether you pursued a formal education, how people receive your finished work will confirm whether you have developed the vision to be accepted as a sophisticated director. Chances are that you belong with the vast majority for whom directing professionally is still very far off. To prepare for this likelihood, *you must develop a craft specialty in order to make yourself marketable and gain a foothold in the industry.* These aspects are elaborated in Chapter 40: Getting Work.

FILM SCHOOLS AND CHECKING CREDENTIALS

There is no special accreditation for film schools and none even for teachers. So it's caveat emptor, as I have warned. The schools listed later are affiliated with professional associations but you should use all your research powers to establish what a school's reputation is and what you can expect to get from its education. Some film departments, such as the excellent film school at NYU, do not for some reason involve themselves in educational associations and appear in neither the North American nor the international list, but do not discount them.

A way to check reputations is the Web site www.filmmaker.com, which includes some lengthy and often pungent comments on particular film schools. These comments are made by students, so scan them gingerly for common denominators and peripheral information. Discount anything by those who don't bother with spelling or punctuation. Being free and anonymous, it is a great place for malcontents to unload spleen, but frequent and similar complaints about a school may head you off from a costly mistake.

The first list is of mostly North American schools affiliated with the UFVA, so you can see if there is a school near you. The latest version can be seen at www.ufva.org/ under "About UFVA."

All reputable film schools have Web sites that you can find quickly by entering the school name and its location in an Internet search engine such as Google. They usually give a great deal of pertinent information as well as e-mail inquiry addresses. Their facilities and expertise will vary hugely. Most won't offer either production or documentary as a specialization.

FILM SCHOOLS AFFILIATED WITH THE UNIVERSITY FILM AND VIDEO ASSOCIATION

Allan Hancock College, Santa Maria, California
Baylor University, Waco, Texas
Bob Jones University, Greenville, South Carolina
Boston University, Boston, Massachusetts
Brigham Young University, Provo, Utah
Brighton Film School, East Sussex (United Kingdom)
Brooks Institute, Ventura, California
California Institute of the Arts, Valencia, California
California State University, Fullerton, California
California State University, Long Beach, California
California State University, Los Angeles, California
California State University, Northridge, California
Carnegie Mellon University, Pittsburgh, Pennsylvania
Central Missouri State University, Warrensburg, Missouri
Chapman University, Orange, California
Colorado College, Colorado Springs, Colorado
Digital Filmmaking Institute, Albuquerque, New Mexico
Drexel University, Philadelphia, Pennsylvania
Duke University, Durham, North Carolina
Fairleigh Dickinson University, Madison, New Jersey
Florida State University, Tallahassee, Florida
Framingham State College, Framingham, Massachusetts

Georgia State University, Atlanta, Georgia
Grand Valley State University, Allendale, Michigan
Haywood Community College, Clyde, North Carolina
Hellenic Cinema and Television School, Athens (Greece)
Hofstra University, Hempstead, New York
Houston Community College Southwest, Stafford, Texas
Humboldt State University, Arcata, California
Ithaca College, Ithaca, New York
Lamar University, Beaumont, Texas
Lawrence College, Inc., Saint John's, Newfoundland (Canada)
Long Island University–Brooklyn Campus, Brooklyn, New York
Loyola Marymount University, Los Angeles, California
Mel Oppenheim–School of Cinema, Concordia University, Montreal (Canada)
Messiah College, Grantham, Pennsylvania
Mills College, Oakland, California
Montana State University, Bozeman, Montana
Montclair State University, Upper Montclair, New Jersey
Morehead State University, Morehead, Kentucky
Morningside College, Sioux City, Iowa
North Carolina School of the Arts, Winston-Salem, North Carolina
Northwest Nazarene University, Nampa, Idaho
Northwestern College, Orange City, Iowa
Northwestern University, Evanston, Illinois
Nova Scotia Community College, Halifax, Nova Scotia (Canada)
Ohio University School of Film, Athens, Ohio
Piedmont Community College, Roxboro, North Carolina
Pittsburgh Filmmakers, Inc., Pittsburgh, Pennsylvania
Quinnipiac University, Hamden, Connecticut
Rhode Island School of Design, Providence, Rhode Island
Rochester Institute of Technology, Rochester, New York
Rock Valley College, Rockford, Illinois
Rockport College, Rockport, Maine
San Antonio College, San Antonio, Texas
San Francisco State University, San Francisco, California
San Jose State University, San Jose, California
Smith College, Northampton, Massachusetts
Southern Alberta School of Technology, Calgary, Alberta (Canada)
Southern Illinois University, Carbondale, Illinois
Syracuse University, Syracuse, New York
Temple University, Philadelphia, Pennsylvania
Texas A&M University, Corpus Christi, Texas
Towson University, Towson, Maryland
Universidad de Artes, Ciencias y Comunicación (UNIACC)-La Universidad
    de las Comunicaciones, Santiago (Chile)
University at Buffalo, Buffalo, New York
University of Arizona, Tucson, Arizona
University of California, Los Angeles (UCLA), Los Angeles, California
University of Chicago, Chicago, Illinois
University of Colorado, Boulder, Colorado

University of Hartford, West Hartford, Connecticut
University of Iowa, Iowa City, Iowa
University of Kansas, Lawrence, Kansas
University of Michigan, Ann Arbor, Michigan
University of Missouri-Kansas City, Kansas City, Missouri
University of Nebraska, Lincoln, Nebraska
University of New Orleans, Lakefront, New Orleans, Louisiana
University of North Carolina, Greensboro, North Carolina
University of North Carolina, Wilmington, North Carolina
University of North Texas, Denton, Texas
University of Oklahoma, Norman, Oklahoma
University of Southern California, Los Angeles, California
University of Southern Mississippi, Hattiesburg, Mississippi
University of Texas-Arlington, Arlington, Texas
University of Texas-Austin, Austin, Texas
University of Toledo, Toledo, Ohio
University of Toronto, Toronto, Ontario (Canada)
University of Windsor, Windsor, Ontario (Canada)
Valencia Community College, Orlando, Florida
Vassar College, Poughkeepsie, New York
Wayne State University, Detroit, Michigan
Widener University, Chester, Pennsylvania
William Patterson University, Wayne, New Jersey

WORLDWIDE FILM SCHOOLS AFFILIATED WITH CENTRE INTERNATIONAL DE LIAISON DE CINÉMA ET DE TÉLÉVISION, THE INTERNATIONAL ASSOCIATION OF FILM AND TELEVISION SCHOOLS

This list of schools affiliated with CILECT, the International Association of Film and Television Schools, can be found in its latest version on CILECT's Web site (www.cilect.org/) organized by country. Clicking on a film school will give you either a standard form that cross-lists information or links you direct to the school's own Web site. The + sign before a phone or fax number indicates the overseas telephone code that you must first dial in your own country to make an international call. Most schools do not specialize in documentary, but many are adding documentary as a specialization. You can bypass CILECT's Web site by using a search engine to find the school direct via the Internet.

ARGENTINA
Carrera de Diseño de Imagen y Sonido
Facultad de Arquitectura, Diseño y Urbanismo
Universidad de Buenos Aires
Pabellón 3
Cuidad Universitaria
1248 Buenos Aires
  Tel: +54 11 4789 6279
  Fax: +54 11 4576 3205

Escuela de Experimentación y de Realización Cinematográfica
Moreno 1199
1191 Buenos Aires
  Tel/Fax: +54 11 43 84 67 04

Universidad del Cine
Pasaje Giuffra 330
1064 Buenos Aires
  Tel: +54 11 4300 1407
  Fax: +54 11 4300 0674

AUSTRALIA
Australian Film and Television School (AFTRS)
Corner Balaclava Road & Epping Highway
Box 126, North Ryde
N.S.W. 2113
  Tel: +61 2 9805 6401
  Fax: +61 29805 6563

Victorian College of the Arts (VCA)
School of Film & Television
234 St. Kilda Road
Melbourne, Victoria 3004
  Tel: +61 3 9685 9000
  Fax: +61 3 9685 9001

AUSTRIA
Universität für Musik und Darstellende Kunst Wien
Abteilung "Film und Fernsehen"
Metternichgasse 12
1030 Wien
  Tel: +43 171155 2902
  Fax: +43 171155 2999

BELGIUM
Erasmus Hogeschool Brussel
Departement RITS
Moutstraat 15
1000 Brussel
  Tel: +32 2 507 14 11
  Fax: +32 2 507 14 56

Hogeschool Sint-Lukas Brussel
Paleizenstraat 70
1030 Brussel
  Tel: +32 2 250 11 00
  Fax: +32 2 250 11 11

Institut des Arts de Diffusion (IAD)
Rue des Wallons, 77
1348 Louvain-la-Neuve
  Tel: +32 10 47 80 20
  Fax: +31 10 45 11 74

Institut National Supérieur des Arts du Spectacle (INSAS)
Rue Thérésienne
1000 Bruxelles
  Tel: +32 2 511 9286
  Fax: +32 2 511 0279

BRAZIL

Escola de Comunicações e Artes
Universidad de São Paulo
Av. Prof. Lucio Martins Rodrigues, 443
Cidade Universitaria CEP 05508-900
São Paulo
  Tel: +55 11 818 4020
  Fax: +55 11 211 2752

Universidade Estadual de Campinas (UNICAMP)
Programa de Pós-Graduação em Multimeios
Instituto de Artes
CP6159
13083-970 Campinas/SP
  Tel: See CILECT Web site
  Fax: See CILECT Web site

BULGARIA

Nacionalna Academia za Teatralno i Folmovo Izkoustvo (NATFIZ)
"Krustyo Sarafov"-Sofia
Rakovski Street 108a
Sofia 1000
  Tel: +359 2 87 98 66
  Fax: +359 2 89 98 66

New Bulgarian University
Department of Mass Communications
21 Montevideo Str.
1635 Sofia
  Tel: +359 2 558 309
  Fax: +359 2 957 1629

BURKINA FASO

Programme de Formation à l'Image et au Son (PROFIS)
Direction de la Cinématographie Nationale
01 BP 647 Ouagadougou 01

Tel: +226 30 17 85
Fax: +226 30 17 84

CANADA
The School of Image Arts
Ryerson Polytechnic University
350 Victoria Street
Toronto, Ontario M5B 2K3
 Tel: +1 416 979 5167
 Fax: +1 416 979 5139

Université du Québec à Montréal (UQAM)
Module de Communications
Case Postale 8888, Succursale A
Montréal (Québec) H3C 3P8
 Tel: +1 514 987 3759
 Fax: +1 514 987 4650

York University
Faculty of Fine Arts
Department of Film & Video
4700 Keele Street
North York, Ontario M3J 1P3
 Tel: +1 416 736 5149
 Fax: +1 416 736 5710

Institut National de l'image et du Son (INIS)
301 Boul. De Maisonneuve Est
Montréal (Québec) H2X 1K1
 Tel: +1 514 285 1840
 Fax: +1 514 285 1953

CHILE
Universidad de Artes, Ciencias y Comunicación (UNIACC)-La Universidad de
las Comunicaciones
School of Audiovisual Communications
Avda. Salvador 1200
Providencia, Santiago
 Tel: +56 2 640 6000
 Fax: +56 2 640 6200

CHINA
Beijing Broadcasting Institute
No. 1 Ding Fu Zhang Dong Jie
Chao Yang District
Beijing 100024
 Tel: +86 10 6577 9359
 Fax: +86 10 6577 9138

Beijing Film Academy (BFA)
Xi Tu Cheng Lu 4
Haidian District
Beijing 100088
  Tel: +86 10 8204 8899-295
  Fax: +86 10 8204 2132

The Hong Kong School for Performing Arts
School of Film and Television
1 Gloucester Road
GPO Box 12288
Wanchai, Hong Kong
  Tel: +852 2584 8679
  Fax: +852 2802 4372

Hong Kong Baptist College
School of Communication
Department of Cinema & Television
Kowloon Tong, Hong Kong
  Tel: +852 2339 7395
  Fax: +852 2339 7821

Zhejiang Radio and Television College
22 East Zhoushan Road
Hangzhou 310015
  Tel: +86 571 8801 0127
  Fax: +86 571 8801

CROATIA
Akedemija Dramske Umjetnosti (ADU)
Trg Maršala Tita 5
10 000 Zagreb
  Tel: +385 1 482 85 06
  Fax: +385 1 482 85 08

CUBA
Escuela Internacional de Cine y TV (EICTV)
Ap. Aéreo 40/41
San Antonio de los Baños
  Tel: +53 7 335 196
  Fax: +53 7 335 341

CZECH REPUBLIC
Akedemie Múzických Umeni (FAMU)
Filmová a Televisni Fakulta
Smetanovo Nábr. 2
116 65 Prague 1
  Tel: +420 2 24 22 91 76
  Fax: +420 2 24 23 02 85

DENMARK
Den Danske Filmskole
Theodor Christensens Plads 1
DK 1437 Copenhagen K
  Tel: +45 32 68 64 00
  Fax: +45 32 68 64 10

The European Film College
Carl Th. Dreyersvej 1
8400 Ebeltoft
  Tel: +45 86 34 08 55
  Fax: +45 86 34 05 35

EGYPT
Academy of Arts
High Cinema Institute
Pyramids Road
Gamal El Din El Afghany Str.
Giza
  Tel: +202 58 68 203
  Fax: +202 561 1034

FINLAND
Arcada Nylands Svenska Yrkeshögskola
Institutionen för Media
Skogsmansgränden 3,
02130 Esbo
  Tel: +358 9 52 53 21
  Fax: +358 9 52 53 2333

Lahti Polytechnic
Institute of Design, Department of Film and TV
Pl 92 Saimaankatu 11
15141 Lahti
  Tel: +358 3 82 82 855
  Fax: +358 3 82 82 854

University of Art and Design Helsinki (UIAH)
Media Centre LUME
Department of Film and TV
Hämeentie 135 C
00560 Helsinki
  Tel: +358 9 756 30111
  Fax: +358 9 634 303

Turku Polytechnic, Arts Academy
Turun ammattikorkeakoulu, Taideakatemia
Linnankatu 54
20100 Turku

Tel: +358 1055350
Fax: +358 105535202

FRANCE

Ecole Nationale Supérieure Louis Lumière
7 Allée de Promontoire
B.P. 22
Marne-la-Vallée
93161 Noisy-le-Grand Cédex
Tel: +33 1 48 15 40 10
Fax: +33 1 43 05 63 44

Ecole Nationale Supérieure des Métiers de L'Image et du Son (FEMIS)
6 rue Francoeur
75018 Paris
Tel: +33 1 53 41 21 00
Fax: +33 1 53 41 02 80

Institut Internationale de l'Image et du Son (IIIS)
Parc de Pissaloup
F-78190 Trappes
Tel: +33 1 30 69 00 17
Fax: +33 1 30 50 43 63

Atelier de Réalisation Cinématographique (VARAN)
6 Impasse Mont-Louis
75011 Paris
Tel: +33 1 43 56 64 04
Fax: +33 1 43 56 2902

Ecole Supérieure d'Audiovisuel (ESAV)
Université Toulouse Le Mirail
5 Allées Antonio Machado
31058 Toulouse Cédex
Tel: +33 5 61 50 44 46
Fax: +33 5 61 50 49 34

GEORGIA

The Georgian State Institute of Theatre and Film
Film and TV Department
Rustaveli Avenue 19
380008 Tbilisi
Tel/Fax: +995 32 99 73 88

GERMANY

Filmstudium Universität Hamburg
Institut für Theater, Musiktheater und Film
Friedensallee 9

22765 Hamburg
  Tel: +49 40 42838 4143
  Fax: +49 40 42838 4168

Deutsche Film-und Fernsehakademie Berlin (DFFB)
Potsdamer Strasse 2
10785 Berlin
  Tel: +49 30 25759-0
  Fax: +49 30 25759-161

Filmakademie Baden-Württemberg
Mathildenstraße 20
71638 Ludwigsburg
  Tel: +49 (0)7141 969 0
  Fax: +49 (0)7141 969 299

Hochschule für Fernsehen und Film
Frankenthalerstr. 23
D-81539 München
  Tel: +49 89 689 57-0
  Fax: +49 89 689 57 339

Hochschule für Fernsehen und Film "Konrad Wolf"
Marlene-Dietrich Allee 11
14482 Potsdam-Babelsberg
  Tel: +49 331 6202-0
  Fax: +49 331 6202-199

Kunsthochschule für Medien Köln
Television and Film Department
Peter-Weller Platz 2
D-50676 Köln
  Tel: +49 221 201 890
  Fax: +49 221 201 89124

GHANA
National Film & Television Institute (NAFTI)
Private Mail Bag-GPO
Accra
  Tel: +233 21 71 76 10
  Fax: +233 21 77 71 59

GREECE
Hellenic Cinema and Television School Stavrakos
65 Patission Str.
104 33 Athens
  Tel: +30 1 8230 124
  Fax: +30 1 8211 651

HUNGARY
Szinház-es Filmmüvészeti Egyetem
Szentkirályi U. 32/a
1088 Budapest
  Tel/Fax: +36 1 318 5533

INDIA
Film and Television Institute of India (FTII)
Law College Road
Pune 411 004
  Tel: +91 20 543 10 10
  Fax: +91 20 543 04 16

INDONESIA
Institut Kesenian Jakarta (IKJ)
Fakultas Film dan Televisi
Jl. Cikini Raya No. 73
Jakarta 10330
PO Box 4014
Jakarta 10001
  Tel: +62 21 324 807
  Fax: +62 21 323 603

IRELAND
DunLaoghaire Institute of Art, Design & Technology
Kill Avenue
DunLaoghaire
Co. Dublin
  Tel: +353 1 214 4655 GMT +0
  Fax: +353 1 280 3345

ISRAEL
Camera Obscura
School of Art
5 Rival Street
Tel Aviv 67778
  Tel: +972 6368430
  Fax: +972 3 688 1025

Ma'ale School of Television, Film and the Arts
20 Shivtey Israel St.
Jerusalem 95105
  Tel: +972 2 6277366
  Fax: +972 2 6277331

The Sam Spiegel Film & Television School-Jerusalem
4 Yad Harutzim St.
Talpiot Industrial Zone

Jerusalem 91103
  Tel: +972 2 6731950
  Fax: +972 2 6731949

Tel Aviv University
Film and Television Department
The Yolanda and David Katz Faculty of the Arts
Ramat-Aviv-Tel Aviv 69978
  Tel: +972 3 640 9483
  Fax: +972 3 640 9935

ITALY

Scuolo del Cinema e di Televisione
Via Ariberto 14
20123 Milano
  Tel: +39 02 89408858
  Fax: +39 02 89408857

Nuova Università del Cinema e della Televisione
Via Tiburtina 521
00159 Rome
  Tel: +39 06 43599892
  Fax: +39 06 43599859

Scuola Nazionale di Cinema
Via Tuscolana 1524
00173 Rome
  Tel: +39 06 722 94247
  Fax: +39 06 72 11 619

Zelig
School of Documentary, Television and New Media
Via Carducci, 15a
I-39 100 Bolzano
  Tel: +39 0471 977930
  Fax: +39 0471 977931

JAPAN

Japan Academy of Moving Images
1-16-30 Manpukuji
Kawasaki-shi
Kanagawa 245
  Tel: +81 44 951 2511
  Fax: +81 44 951 2681

Nihon University
College of Art
Department of Cinema

2-42-1 Asahigaoka
Nerima-Ku
Tokyo 176-8525
  Tel: +81 3 5995 8220
  Fax: +81 3 5995 8229

KENYA

Kenya Institute of Mass Communication (KIMC)
Film Production Training Department
PO Box 42422
Nairobi
  Tel: +254 2 540 820
  Fax: +254 2 554 566

LEBANON

Université St. Joseph
Institut d'Etudes Scéniques, Audiovisuelles et Cinématographiques
Damascus Road
Beyrouth
  Tel: +961 1 611456
  Fax: +961 1 611362

MEXICO

Centro de Capacitación Cinematográfica (CCC)
Czda. de Tlalpan 1670 Esq Rio Churubusco
México 21, D.F. 04220
  Tel: +52 5 420 44 90
  Fax: +52 5 420 44 92

Centro Universitario de Estudios Cinematográficos (CUEC)
Universidad Nacional Autónoma de México
Adolfo Prieto 721 (Colonia del Valle)
México D. F. 03100
  Tel: +52 5 687 3862 / 5288
  Fax: +52 5 536 17 99

NETHERLANDS

Nederlandse Film en Televisie Academie
Markenplein 1
1011 MV Amsterdam
  Tel: +31 20 527 73 33
  Fax: +31 20 527 73 55

NIGERIA

The National Film Institute
7 Gbadamosi Close
PO Box 693
Jos, Plateau State

Tel: +234 73 463 625
Fax: +234 73 561 233

NORWAY

Den Norske Filmskolen
Pb. 1004
2626 Lillehammer
  Tel: +47 61 28 80 00 (Switchboard)
  Fax: +47 61 28 81 10

PHILIPPINES

University of the Philippines
Film Center
UP Film Center
Magsaysay Avenue
PO Box 214
Diliman
Quezon City 1101
  Tel: +63 2 92 63640/50286
  Fax: +63 2 92 62722

POLAND

Pa'nstwowa Wy'zsza
Szkola Filmova i Teatralna (PWSFTV i T)
Targowa 61/63
90-323 Kód'z
  Tel: +48 42 674 39 43
  Fax: +48 42 674 81 39

PORTUGAL

Escola Superior de Teatro e Cinema
Departamento de Cinema
Av. Marquês de Pombal 22-B
2700-571 Armadora
  Tel: +351 21 498 94 00
  Fax: +351 21 493 76 20

Universidade Católica Portuguesa
Departamento de Som e Imagem
Rua Diego Botelho 1327
4150 Porto
  Tel: +351 22 619 62 95/351 22 619 62 00
  Fax: +351 22 619 62 91

ROMANIA

Universitatea de Arta Teatrala si Cinematografica I.L. Caragiale (UATC)
Facultatea de Film si TV
Str. Matei Voievod 75-77

73224 Bucuresti
  Tel/Fax: +40 1 252 58 81

RUSSIA

Russian State Institute of Cinematography (VGIK)
Wilhelm Pieck Str. 3
Moscow 129226
  Tel: +7 095 181 3868
  Fax: +7 095 187 7174

St. Petersburg Institute of Cinema and Television (SPIC&T)
Pravda Str. 13
191126 St. Petersburg
  Tel: +7 812 315 72 85
  Fax: +7 812 315 01 72

SINGAPORE

Ngee Ann Polytechnic
School of Film and Media Studies
535 Clementi Road
Singapore 599489
  Tel: +65 460 6992
  Fax: +65 462 5617

SLOVAKIA

Vysoka Skola Muzickych Umeni (VSMU)
Filmová a televisna fakulta
Ventúrska 3
813 01 Bratislava
  Tel: +421 2 59 301 461
  Fax: +421 2 544 321 82

SLOVENIA

Akademija za Glendalisce Radio Rilm in Televizijo (AGRFT)
University of Ljubljana
Nazorjeva 3
1000 Ljubljana
  Tel: +386 1 2510 412
  Fax: +386 1 2510 450

SPAIN

Escuela des Artes Visuales
Fuencarral 45, 4°
28004 Madrid
  Tel: +34 91 523 17 01
  Fax: +34 91 523 17 63

Escuela de Cinematografía y del Audiovisual de la Comunidad de Madrid (ECAM)
Juan de Orduña 3
Ciudad de la Imagen
Pozuelo de Alarcón
28223 Madrid
  Tel: +34 915 12 10 60
  Fax: +34 915 12 10 70

Escola Superior de Cinema i Audiovisuals de Catalunya (ESCAC)
Immaculada 25-35
08017 Barcelona
  Tel: +34 3 212 15 62
  Fax: +34 3 417 26 01

Escuela de Cine y Video (ESKIVI)
Avda. Ama Kandida s/n.
20140 Andoain (Guipúzcoa)
  Tel: +34 943 59 41 90
  Fax: +34 943 59 15 62

SWEDEN
Dramatiska Intitutet (DI)
University College of Film, Radio, Television, and Theatre
Borgvägen 5
Box 27090
102-51 Stockholm
  Tel: +46 8 665 13 00
  Fax: +46 8 662 14 84

Göteborg University
School of Photography and Film
Konstepidemins Väg 2A
Box 540
SE 40530 Göteborg
  Tel: +46 31 773 43 44
  Fax: +46 31 773 18 37

SWITZERLAND
Ecole Cantonale d'art de Lausanne
Département Audiovisuel
46 rue de l'Industrie
1030 Bussigny
  Tel: +41 21 702 92 15/01
  Fax: +41 21 702 92 09

Ecole Supérieure des Beaux Arts
2 Rue Général Dufour

Genève 1204
  Tel: +41 22 311 05 10
  Fax: +41 22 310 46 36

Hochschule für Gestaltung und Kunst Zürich
Studienbereich Film/Video
Limmatstrasse 65
8005 Zürich
PO Box 8031
Zurich
  Tel: +41 1 446 23 57
  Fax: +41 1 446 23 55

TAIPEI (CHINA)

National Taiwan University of Arts
No. 59 Section 1 Da-Kuan Road
Pan-Chiao
Taipei, Taiwan 220
  Tel: +886 2 2272 2181 x354
  Fax: +886 2 2968 7563

UNITED KINGDOM

National Film and Television School (NFTS)
Beaconsfield Film Studios
Station Road
Beaconsfield, Bucks HP9 1LG
  Tel: +44 1494 731472
  Fax: +44 1494 671213

The Leeds School of Art, Architecture and Design
Film and Moving Image Production
Leeds Metropolitan University
2 Queen Square
Leeds LS2 8AF
  Tel: +44 113 283 1900
  Fax: +44 113 283 1901

London Film School (LFS)
24 Shelton Street
London WC2H 9UB
  Tel: +44 207 836 9642
  Fax: +44 207 497 3718

National Association for Higher Education in the Moving Image(NAHEMI)
London Guildhall University
Department of Communications
31 Jewry Street
London EC3N 2EY

Tel: +44 208 566 5673
Fax: +44 208 320 3009

University of Westminster
School of Communication, Design and Media
Harrow Campus Studios
Northwick Park
Harrow HA 1 3TP
  Tel: +44 207 911 5000
  Fax: +44 207 911 5943

UNITED STATES OF AMERICA

American Film Institute (AFI)
PO Box 27999
2021 North Western Avenue
Los Angeles, CA 90027
  Tel: +1 323 856 7711
  Fax: +1 213 856 7884

California Institute of the Arts (CALARTS)
24700 McBean Parkway
Valencia, CA 91355
  Tel: +1 661 253 7825
  Fax: +1 661 253 7824

Chapman University
School of Film & TV
One University Drive
Orange, CA 92866
  Tel: +1 714 997 6715
  Fax: +1 714 997 6572

Columbia College Chicago
Film/Video Department, Columbia College
600 S. Michigan Avenue
Chicago, IL 60605-1996
  Tel: +1 312 344 6701
  Fax: +1 312 344 8044

Columbia University
Film Division
513 Dodge Hall, School of the Arts
116th Street and Broadway
New York, NY 10027
  Tel: +1 212 854 2815
  Fax: +1 212 854 7702

Florida State University
School of Motion Picture, Television and Recording Arts
A3102 University Center
Tallahassee, FL 32306-2350
   Tel: +1 850 644 8968
   Fax: +1 850 644 2626

Loyola Marymount University
School of Film and Television
7900 Loyola Boulevard
Los Angeles, CA 90045-8230
   Tel: +1 310 338 7532
   Fax: +1 310 546 2363

New York University (NYU)
Tisch School of the Arts
Maurice Kanbar Institute of Film and Television
721 Broadway
New York, NY 10003-6807
   Tel: +1 212 998-1800
   Fax: +1 212 995 4040

North Carolina School of the Arts
School of Filmmaking
1533 S. Main Street
Winston Salem, NC 27117
   Tel: +1 336 770 1330
   Fax: +1 336 770 1339

Stanford University [documentary program only]
Department of Communication
McClatchy Hall
Stanford, CA 94305-2050
   Tel: +1 650 723 4700
   Fax: +1 650 725 2472

University of California, Los Angeles (UCLA)
School of Theater, Film and Television
Department of Film & Television
East Melnitz
405 Hilgard Avenue
Los Angeles, CA 90095
   Tel: +1 310 825 7741
   Fax: +1 310 206 1686

University of Southern California (USC)
School of Cinema and Television
University Park Campus

850 West 34th Street, Lucas 209
Los Angeles, CA 90089-2211
   Tel: +1 213 743 2804
   Fax: +1 213 740 7682

VIETNAM

The Hanoi Academy of Theatre and Cinema
Truong Dai Hoc San Khau Va Dien Anh
Mai Dich
Caugiay
Hanoi
   Tel: +84 4 764 33 97
   Fax: +84 4 8348732

YUGOSLAVIA (SERBIA, MONTENEGRO)

Fakultet Dramskih Umetnosti (FDU)
Bulevar umentnosti 20
11070 Beograd
   Tel: +381 11 140 419
   Fax: +381 11 130 862

CHAPTER 40

GETTING WORK

LOOKING AHEAD WHILE YOU'RE IN FILM SCHOOL

Many people do not know how they want to specialize as a future professional. Trade journals are a mine of local and technical information (see later). Reading them for insight into specialties that interest you is the first move. Read *The Independent, International Documentary, American Cinematographer, Filmmaker*, and *DV* for news of the independent documentary making, cinematography, and postproduction, respectively. *Variety* will tell you much more than you want to know about the commercial film industry. Astute reading and a good memory enable you to handle yourself as though you are already an insider.

The European Documentary Network (http://tv.oneworld.net/community/index.shtml) is representative of many special interest Web sites that can be very informative. By entering a combination of words that interest you (such as *documentary, festival, production, proposal, pitch, funding*, and *center*) you can locate an enormous body of information on the Internet. Not all of it is accurate or valuable, of course. For the countries of Latin America, some of which now have thriving documentary-making cultures, there are foundations such as the John D. and Catherine T. MacArthur Foundation, which underwrites projects on subjects they wish to see covered, such as human and community development and global security and development. Take a look at the MacArthur Web site, www.macfound.org/programs/index.htm.

In addition to your directing aspirations, you must emerge from school with one or more well-developed *craft skills* so that you can expect to make a living. Useful specialties in addition to your ability to direct are

- Camera operating, lighting, gaffer skills
- Sound recordist and/or microphone operator, sound design
- Editor
- Producer, production manager, production secretary, or assistant director

If your school has a producing track, try to set up a partnership with a keen producer. Developing and marketing future projects will need solid producer skills, and it is debilitating (though often necessary) to do it yourself. You must develop a strategy early in your schooling to amass the necessary sample work and survival skills for when you graduate. You also must decide what films you might enter in which festivals and begin planning your way toward making them. Films do not happen when you are ready to make them; they happen because you make it so.

INTERNSHIPS

Well-established schools such as mine (Columbia College Chicago) tend to have an internship office that places students who have demonstrated their competency with local media employers. A temporary (and usually unpaid) position often turns into your first paying job. My college also has an extension in the CBS studios and thus has many connections in Los Angeles, where a great many documentary series are made.

A steady flow of seniors and recent graduates get work as a grip, assistant editor, production assistant, or camera assistant via an internship where an employer can, at low risk, try you out in places where you can't do much harm. This will happen only if you have also developed the appropriate social skills and utter reliability. To gain acceptance anywhere you will need *professional level skills*, *professional discipline*, and *good references*. Initially the latter will come from your teachers.

ON GRADUATING

Let's fast-forward to a point where you have knowledge and some experience in filmmaking. Graduation is on the horizon, and the scary world of work is hurtling toward you. How else can you make the transition from student to paid worker in the medium?

You must have a respectable *portfolio* of work that makes your production skills manifest. You have entered several projects in many festivals and ideally will have won some awards. These, as credentials in your résumé, are worth their weight in gold. With the crewing skills and contacts made in film school, you should be able to earn short-term money at crewing while you deploy a longer-term plan to slowly get established as a director.

Aspiring documentary directors almost never find positions awaiting them; they have to make jobs for themselves. Your degree will count for nothing in the world of production, but your production work, if good, will help you get *job interviews* and, especially if you have won awards, maybe some modest commissioned work or better.

The film and television industries are downsizing their permanent staffs and employing freelancers, so, in principle, there are now more opportunities for small, self-starter companies. However, work goes to those with a track record of accomplishment, which is catch-22 for the beginner. The films you make at your own expense are your investment in your own future.

If you strike lucky and get commissioned directing straight from school, it will probably still be too sporadic and ill paid to initially cover your bills. So while you pursue your own projects you will need paid crewing work, and this requires building up your résumé with film-related jobs.

CRAFT WORKER

Unless you are lucky enough to be studying in a national film school with assured jobs at graduation, you will have to enter the marketplace as a freelancer. There are regional and national differences to the film and television industries, but developing a track record as a freelancer is similar everywhere. To find openings, you will need to *network* through friends, associates, and any professional contacts acquired during your schooling and internships.

At the beginning, and perhaps for long after, your work probably will be fulfilling mundane commercial needs; expending lots of imagination and effort crewing for industrial, training, or medical films; or shooting conferences and weddings. Learning to do this reliably, well, and inventively will teach you a great deal. A training like this served Robert Altman and many another director well.

If you do good work that is on time, within the projected cost, and with a good spirit, your reputation as an OK person slowly spreads through the grapevine. Such work ethic requisites don't impede creative work, but they do exclude the undisciplined and immature personality who imagines that emerging from film school means a place awaits him or her. It doesn't. You may have become somebody big in film school, but you remain nothing and nobody in the working world until your work and a lengthening track record prove otherwise. So at the start you should be ready to do any kind of work, cheerfully and reliably, so that you are well placed when "something opens up."

Your aim should be to make a living as a freelance crew person and invest any spare time and cash in making films with contemporaries who, like you, are struggling to gain experience and recognition. Each level of accomplishment as a group equips you to seek more interesting and demanding work. By developing your talent together to a point where you have concrete, proven results, you then have something to offer an employer, fund, or sponsor. Festival awards are far and away the most valuable calling card.

If the emphasis on becoming known and fitting in seems like the slipway to fatal compromise, it need not be. The great films that drew you to filmmaking were all produced for profit and were good art by any standards. The whole of cinema and television has its roots in commerce, and each new venture is predicated on the commercial success of the last. Documentaries are no exception to this universal law.

THE SEARCH FOR SUBJECTS AND A MARKET

The market for documentaries is evolving nicely, with cable stations being particularly interested and audience enjoyment of documentaries climbing proportionately. Television networks, especially in Europe, are relying more on co-productions to spread the high cost of making big documentaries over larger audiences. At the same time, desktop digital production even in high definition is now of broadcast quality and available at relatively modest cost. The proliferation of production will produce still more change and democratization in production. This also produces more filmmakers and more competition.

To compete, you must find subjects that interest a sizable audience. This need not be a cynically conceived or fixed commodity, however. On the one hand, there is a subject, and on the other, there is *a way of seeing*. How a film sees may be more important than *what* it sees. Creativity in form is as important, or more so, than finding unique content.

The best way to find subjects is to uncover what deeply interests you and then to pitch it to filmmaking colleagues, argue it out, and discover all its possibilities, depths, and difficulties. Pitch your ideas to non-filmmakers too; they need only be the kind of people for whom discussion of the world's affairs is a necessary part of living. Pitching means bringing a film idea to an audience and getting an immediate reaction. It speeds up the evolution of your projects and doesn't cost a dime. Go through distributors' Web sites looking for your own areas of interest, and make your own market study to see where holes exist in the existing commercial structure.

FESTIVALS

Most important, attend festivals and conferences so that you find out what others are producing, how they present themselves publicly, and what TV networks and distributors seem interested in buying that you could do well. The Independent Feature Project (IFP) Web site is a mine of information on all aspects of producing as an "indie" (www.ifp.org), especially the financial aspects.

At pitching sessions, such as International Documentary Film Festival Amsterdam (IDFA, www.idfa.nl/iprof_home.asp) holds annually, hopeful producers present proposals orally and are publicly grilled by a panel of commissioning editors who may or may not buy into the project. Bear in mind that there is a separation between producers and buyers/backers akin to that between authors and publishers. Without a proven track record you are unlikely to get distributors' or television money for a film in the planning stages. As a newcomer you can only expect funds from a distributor if you already have a commercially marketable product. However, if you have the rights to a "hot" subject, you may get offers of partnership from established concerns, which can be a very good deal.

THE DOCUMENTARY PROPOSAL

With films of your own to show, particularly if you have won awards and have had your work screened or distributed, you have a visible identity and are in a good position to approach the various funds. Naturally competition is keen, but you would be surprised how poorly most prospective filmmakers represent themselves on paper and how often they don't follow the fund's guidelines. Would you give money to someone who can't follow a few simple rules?

Carefully read the sections of this book on proposal writing, draft and redraft your proposal until it is perfect, and try your luck. Remember, you are what you write.

FUNDS

When funding organizations make awards they usually grant no more than 50% of a budget. The proposal has to be well written, focused in the fund or foundation's special area, unusually interesting, and very businesslike. With your application, send a specially edited sample reel of around 5 minutes. This is a trailer showing your best and most applicable work, or sections from material already shot for the proposed film. If your subject is character driven, you should show material to establish your central character as interesting and unusual. The IFP is a useful Web site for funding ideas and information (www.ifp.org/).

In the United States, there is a complex and shifting system of *federal, state,* and *private funding agencies.* Each has guidelines and a track record in funding some special area. Usually nobody will fund student work or first films, and if they do it will be strictly local organizations. Fund money is good money because you usually are not required to pay it back, so making use of local or national funds is an important means of financing documentary filmmaking. As a general rule, private grant funds prefer to give completion money to films that are shot and may be viewed, whereas government agencies are a little more likely to fund research and preproduction.

If your track record is slender (perhaps a short film that has won some festival awards) and you are seeking either preproduction, production, or completion money, you should investigate your *state* or *city arts council.* Each state in the United States has a *state humanities committee,* which works in association with the *National Endowment for the Humanities* (NEH). This agency works to fund groups of accredited individuals (usually academics) producing work in the humanities. National guidelines can be obtained from The National Endowment for the Humanities, 1100 Pennsylvania Avenue, Room 406, Washington, DC 20506 (www.neh.fed.us/). The Web site is a mine of information on state humanity and other funds.

Many states and big cities have a *film commission* or *bureau* that exists to encourage and facilitate filmmaking (because it's good business). These bureaus (see www.blm.gov/nhp/what/commercial/filming/commissions.html) develop formal and informal relationships with the whole local filmmaking community and can be an excellent source of information on all aspects of local production. A full list of those in the United States, as well as a wealth of other documentary-related information, is in the International Documentary Association (IDA) *Membership Directory and Survival Guide,* which can be obtained from the IDA (see under Journals and Associations).

In 2003 Congress authorized $365 million to the Corporation for Public Broadcasting (CPB). CPB redistributes the money to a number of funds, including the Independent Television Service (ITVS, www.itvs.org/). You can see how the CPB money was recently distributed by going to www.aivf.org/resources/IndiePubMoneyGuide.pdf. This is a site of the Association of Independent Video and Filmmakers (AIVF), an organization that is especially useful to the independent filmmaker. Using a search engine such as Google on the Internet can bring up vast quantities of useful information. Enter the words you want associated together in an article, such as *documentary, fund, festival, pitching, proposal,* and *investors.*

Survey organizations exist to help you find the appropriate private fund or charity to approach. Chicago has the Donors Forum, a clearinghouse that periodically publishes local information (www.donorsforum.org/). New York has the Foundation Center (http://fdncenter.org/), which serves as a center for nationwide reference collections for study by those wishing to approach donors and donor organizations.

JOURNALS AND ASSOCIATIONS

The IDA is based in Los Angeles and has a strong program of events in that area. It publishes *International Documentary*, an important quarterly journal with featured articles on new films, filmmakers, trends, festivals, and technology. At the back is a directory of upcoming festivals and competitions, funding, jobs and opportunities, classes/seminars/workshops, distributors looking for new films, new publications, and classifieds. The IDA also publishes a superb *Membership Directory and Survival Guide*. Contact the International Documentary Association, 1201 West 5th Street, Suite M320, Los Angeles, CA 90017-1461 (www.documentary.org/).

Another good move is to take out a subscription to *American Cinematographer*, a monthly publication mainly for feature fiction workers, but which publishes articles on documentaries and keeps you abreast of the latest methods and technical innovations (see www.theasc.com). The journal includes news, interviews, and a great deal of useful "who's doing what" information. Contact *American Cinematographer*, American Society of Cinematographers, Inc., PO Box 2230, Hollywood, CA 90078.

Videomaker is an excellent monthly magazine that reviews new equipment in the prosumer range (i.e., high-end consumer, low-end professional) and is particularly good for its accessible explanations of techniques and technical principles (see www.videomaker.com/, where you may even be able to get a free copy of the magazine sent to you). For subscription info by snail mail contact PO Box 3780, Chico, CA 95927.

JOB INFORMATION

The Internet makes a good labor exchange, and an example of a film job search site is www.media-match.com. You should, of course, always bear in mind that such sites exist to make money for the site organizers and aren't necessarily a passport to employment. You may, however, be the only filmmaking ornithologist or vulcanologist in your area and have a combination of skills that may get you work. Most career guides focus on Hollywood, but information about the general structure and expectations of the film and television industries are available from the following:

Bone, Jan and Julie Rigby. *Opportunities in Film Careers*. Lincolnwood, IL: NTC Publications, 1999.

Horwin, Michael. *Careers in Film and Video Production*. Boston: Focal Press, 1990.

Wiese, Michael. *The Independent Filmmaker's Guide*, 2nd ed. Studio City, CA: Michael Wiese Productions, 1997.

Wiese, Michael and Deke Simon. *Film and Video Budgets*, 3rd ed. Studio City, CA: Michael Wiese Productions, 2001.

With case histories and examples, these works represent a lot of information. Wiese's *The Independent Film and Videomaker's Guide*, dealing as it does specifically with documentaries, is particularly valuable. He corrects the myth that any worthy film can be sold to the Public Broadcasting System (PBS) and tells how Byzantine this sprawling, bureaucratic organization is. "If you have the idea that PBS is a benevolent network serving public and education interests," warns Wiese in an earlier version of the book, "a renewed study is suggested." You can see what PBS expects of its producers by going to www.pbs.org/producers/. If you are intimidated by the expression "business plan," now is the time to hunt down the information to educate yourself.

FESTIVAL AWARDS AND PRESENTING YOURSELF

A professionally laid out résumé is a must when you seek work, and the very best recommendations you can have, apart from letters from established filmmakers, are awards won at festivals. The IDA (www.documentary.org/) and the American Film Institute (AFI, www.afi.com) list upcoming festivals, and you should enter your work in as many as you can afford. Most entries are far from great, so it is realistic to hope to win if you do good work. Awards are inordinately important in swinging votes during a funding application process or in securing an interview.

Whomever you plan to approach, learn all you can about the business, organization, and individual that you are approaching. People who deal with job seekers distinguish rapidly between the hardworking realist and the dreamer adrift in alien seas. This judgment is made not on who you are but on how you present yourself, both on paper and in person. You will do this well only if your homework includes resourceful reading and lots of networking on the phone.

When you send your résumé to an individual or company, send a brief, carefully composed, *individual* cover letter that describes your goals and how you might best contribute to the organization. Call up after a few days and ask if you might have a brief chat with someone in case a position opens up in the future. If you are called for an interview, dress conservatively, be punctual, know what you want, and show you are willing to do any kind of work to get there. Let the interviewer ask the questions, and when you reply, be brief and to the point. Say concisely what skills and qualities you have to offer. This is where you can demonstrate your knowledge of (and therefore commitment to) the interviewer's business. Interviewers often ask if you have any questions, so have two or three good ones ready so that you can again demonstrate your knowledge of the company or group.

If shyness holds you back, do something about it now. Get assertiveness training or join a theater group and force yourself to act, preferably in improvisational material. You alone can do what it takes to start believing in yourself.

Almost all human problems boil down to a matter of courage. Courage, like power, is not given but taken.

MAKING A JOB FOR YOURSELF

I don't remember ever seeing an advertisement for a documentary filmmaker, but this does not mean there are no jobs. It simply means that you must find or create a job rather than expect one ready made. As any actor will tell you, selling your services is initially a grisly business. Rejections hurt, but they help make you better at what's unavoidable: talking people into letting you use their money to make your films.

Some interesting facts emerged in a colloquium given by former students at my institution. All were now working in various capacities in the film industry. It transpired that everyone

- Took about the same (long) time to get established and to begin to earn a reasonable amount of money
- Had moved up the ladder of responsibility at roughly the same (slow) pace
- Found that greater responsibility came suddenly and without warning
- Was scared stiff when it came, feeling they were conning their way into an area beyond their competence
- Grew into their new levels of responsibility
- Loved their work and said they felt privileged to be working in such an important area of public life

A PERSONAL MESSAGE

Documentary is a growing field in which the levels of inventiveness, humor, courage, and humanism are all going up. As I said at the beginning of this book, documentary people are remarkable for their conviviality and helpfulness, and you'll experience this at your first conference or festival. They have chosen documentary film—be it political, humanitarian, or celebratory—as the work that matters to them most in all the world. May you, dear reader, join this community and use the wonderful art of the screen to work for a better world.

Thank you most sincerely for using this book, and if you have any comments that can help me make the next edition better, write either via the Film/Video Department, Columbia College Chicago, 600 S. Michigan, Chicago, IL 60605-1996, USA, or via e-mail to mrabiger@aol.com. I will try to reply; if I don't it is probably because, although I am retired, I am often out on the road giving workshops or seminars. Please don't send unsolicited proposals or films—I simply don't have time to review them (or to do lots of other good things).

May you have good luck, good filming, and good friends.

PART 9

OTHER INFORMATION

APPENDIX 1

PROJECTS: OUTCOMES ASSESSMENT CRITERIA

The outcomes assessments given here can be used as is or adapted either for these or other projects. They are guides, not the final word. Photocopy them, or alter them after downloading them as Microsoft Word files from the book's Web site (go to www.elsevier.com, then enter the book title in the search window). Do develop your own criteria for any and every project.

Students like outcomes assessments because they make expectations for a project evident and encourage a better project from the outset. Forms also let everyone, not just the instructor, assess every project shown in class. You can contribute much by critiquing someone else's work and learn a lot too as you develop constructive critical language. Great films come from honest alliances rather than secretive, competing individuals.

Simply circle the appropriate number when using the ratings. Because they are grouped by areas (directing, camera, sound, editing, etc.), the scores become a bar graph registering weakness or strength in particular areas. As you amass more projects and more assessments, you will easily see where you need to improve and where your strengths as a future professional may lie.

Rate each criterion statement by degree of agreement, scoring thus:

> 5 = Outstandingly true
> 4 = Considerably true
> 3 = True
> 2 = Somewhat true
> 1 = Minimally true
> 0 = Not true/applicable

OVERVIEW AND SCORECARD

Name_____

Project	Project Title	Score	Out of
Critical Writing Projects			
9-1	Analyzing a Documentary for Structure and Style		
9-2	Assessing a Director's Thematic Vision		
	Subtotal		
Camera Handling Projects			
14-3	(Tripod) Interview, One Subject		
14-4	(Handheld) Tracking on Static Subject		
14-5	(Handheld) Tracking Forward on Moving Subject		
14-6	(Handheld) Tracking Backward with Moving Subject		
	Subtotal		
Production Projects			
28-1	Dramatizing a Location		
28-2	Three-Person Conversation (Interior)		
28-3	Covering a Process for Ellipsis Editing		
28-4	Covering a Conversation (Exterior)		
28-5	Mobile Coverage of Complex Action		
28-6	Interview In Depth		
28-7	Two Person Conversation with Conflict		
28-8	Unbroken Five-Minute Story		
28-9	A One-Shot, Catalyzed Event		
28-10	*Vox Populi* Interviews and Metaphoric Counterpoint		
28-11	Self-Portrait		
28-12	Observing the Observer		
28-13	Story, Question, and Suggestion		
28-14	Making History		
28-15	National Anthem		
28-16	Video Letter		
28-17	The Final Project		
	Subtotal		
Postproduction Projects			
38-1	Interview, Varying Image Sizes		
38-2	Conversation, Two or More Persons		
38-3	Editing for Ellipsis		
38-4	Complex Editing Project		
	TOTAL		

CRITICAL WRITING ASSESSMENT CRITERIA
For Project 9-1: Analyzing a Documentary for Structure and Style

Film title _____ Name _____ Date _____

Criteria	Rating
Writer shows well why film subject is central to his/her interests	0 1 2 3 4 5
Presents coherent sequence log in Film Analysis Form, Appendix 2	0 1 2 3 4 5
Sequence tag descriptions, lengths, and functions all well accomplished	0 1 2 3 4 5
Makes a compelling analysis of film's structure	0 1 2 3 4 5
Makes convincing argument for origins of film's organization	0 1 2 3 4 5
Makes a coherent division of film into acts	0 1 2 3 4 5
Gives convincing discussion re sequence lengths vs what each contributes	0 1 2 3 4 5
Intelligent discussion of film's style and what determined it	0 1 2 3 4 5
Good discussion of film's thematic impact and overall effectiveness	0 1 2 3 4 5
Describes well what film made him/her feel	0 1 2 3 4 5
Writes convincingly about what he/she learned from seeing the film	0 1 2 3 4 5
Well-argued views on whether others should see film	0 1 2 3 4 5
Good presentation (literacy, layout, drafts numbered)	0 1 2 3 4 5
Structure of paper was excellent	0 1 2 3 4 5
Writing style makes ideas easily accessible	0 1 2 3 4 5
Demonstrated hidden dimensions in film	0 1 2 3 4 5
Quotations aptly used to support arguments	0 1 2 3 4 5
Examples from films cited to support views	0 1 2 3 4 5
Writing illuminated by original values/perceptions	0 1 2 3 4 5
TOTAL	_____

CRITICAL WRITING ASSESSMENT CRITERIA
For Project 9-2: Assessing a Director's Thematic Vision

Film title _____ Name _____ Date _____

Films chosen _____ & _____

Directed by _____ (dir) Paper draft # _____

Criteria	Rating
Orients reader to content of two chosen films	0 1 2 3 4 5
Orients reader to director's emphases and where two films fit in	0 1 2 3 4 5
Well-structured argument concerning how themes expressed	0 1 2 3 4 5
Critical context and biography thoroughly researched	0 1 2 3 4 5
Sources of ideas and quotations well footnoted/endnoted	0 1 2 3 4 5
Quotations aptly used to support arguments	0 1 2 3 4 5
Examples from films cited to support views	0 1 2 3 4 5
Writing illuminated by original values/perceptions	0 1 2 3 4 5
Deals successfully with director's themes and vision	0 1 2 3 4 5
Deals successfully with other criteria that writer chose	0 1 2 3 4 5
Assesses own changing attitudes to subject	0 1 2 3 4 5
Good presentation (literacy, layout, drafts numbered)	0 1 2 3 4 5
Writing style makes ideas easily accessible	0 1 2 3 4 5
Paper delivers memorable impact	0 1 2 3 4 5
TOTAL	_____

CAMERA HANDLING ASSESSMENT CRITERIA

For Project 14-3: (Tripod) Interview, One Subject

Film title _____ Name _____ Date _____

Criteria	Rating
DIRECTING. Effective because interviewee is at ease	0 1 2 3 4 5
Tends to use wide shot for new subject matter	0 1 2 3 4 5
Tends to cover moments of intensity in big close-up	0 1 2 3 4 5
Interviewee's story has good exposition of information	0 1 2 3 4 5
Interviewing produces moving testimony from interviewee	0 1 2 3 4 5
SOUND good and no mike visible	0 1 2 3 4 5
CAMERA work effective, compositional proportions match at cuts	0 1 2 3 4 5
Zooming and recomposing happen simultaneously and smoothly	0 1 2 3 4 5
EDITING maintains natural rhythm of speaker's speech	0 1 2 3 4 5
Interviewee's body position and expression match between cuts	0 1 2 3 4 5
Interviewer's voice successfully eliminated	0 1 2 3 4 5
Interview successfully restructured to develop meaningfully	0 1 2 3 4 5
Story builds to a climactic or pivotal moment	0 1 2 3 4 5
Story arrives at a resolution	0 1 2 3 4 5
Story told with intensity throughout	0 1 2 3 4 5
Story has an impact	0 1 2 3 4 5
Film leaves a sense of meaning and purpose	0 1 2 3 4 5
TOTAL	_____

CAMERA HANDLING ASSESSMENT CRITERIA

For Project 14-4: (Handheld) Tracking on Static Subject

Film title _____ Name _____ Date _____

Criteria	Rating
CAMERA holds stationary shot	0 1 2 3 4 5
Makes smooth start forward from "hold"	0 1 2 3 4 5
Stays upright throughout	0 1 2 3 4 5
Maintains 45-degree angle to the wall	0 1 2 3 4 5
Maintains 3-foot distance from wall	0 1 2 3 4 5
Camera does not bob or sway in relation to wall	0 1 2 3 4 5
Shot comes to rest on a smooth static "hold"	0 1 2 3 4 5
TOTAL	_____

CAMERA HANDLING ASSESSMENT CRITERIA
For Project 14-5: (Handheld) Tracking Forward on Moving Subject

Film title _____ Name _____ Date _____

Criteria	Rating
CAMERA "in sync" with subject	0 1 2 3 4 5
Stays at appropriate closeness	0 1 2 3 4 5
Subject is steady in frame	0 1 2 3 4 5
Composition adapts to subject changes	0 1 2 3 4 5
Background is meaningful and interesting	0 1 2 3 4 5
Operator handles discovery by subject well	0 1 2 3 4 5
TOTAL	_____

CAMERA HANDLING ASSESSMENT CRITERIA
For Project 14-6: (Handheld) Tracking Backward with Moving Subject

Film title _____ Name _____ Date _____

Criteria	Rating
DIRECTING. Person looks relaxed and unselfconscious	0 1 2 3 4 5
No stumbles or lurches	0 1 2 3 4 5
CAMERA glides as if on wheels	0 1 2 3 4 5
Wide shot well framed	0 1 2 3 4 5
Medium shot well framed	0 1 2 3 4 5
Big close-up well composed	0 1 2 3 4 5
Lead space proportions consistent from shot to shot	0 1 2 3 4 5
Backgrounds used effectively	0 1 2 3 4 5
The two cuts look natural	0 1 2 3 4 5
Has tried intercutting different camera-to-subject axes for assessment	0 1 2 3 4 5
TOTAL	_____

PRODUCTION PROJECT ASSESSMENT CRITERIA
For Project 28-1: Dramatizing a Location

Film title _____ Name _____ Date _____

Criteria	Rating
DIRECTING. Location's geography is well shown	0 1 2 3 4 5
Engaging characters with dimension emerge	0 1 2 3 4 5
Shows typical life cycles of the place	0 1 2 3 4 5
Shows unexpected detail	0 1 2 3 4 5
Piece has humor and wit	0 1 2 3 4 5
Piece has impact and makes a statement	0 1 2 3 4 5
CAMERA work is nicely controlled and secure	0 1 2 3 4 5
Visually imaginative shooting throughout	0 1 2 3 4 5
Sets a strong mood	0 1 2 3 4 5
SOUND effects and atmospheres stimulate imagination	0 1 2 3 4 5
EDITING. Passage of time is shown well	0 1 2 3 4 5
Music enhances mood	0 1 2 3 4 5
Choice of music is fresh and interesting	0 1 2 3 4 5
Form in the music echoed in the form of the film	0 1 2 3 4 5
Music drives use of transitions and accents in the visuals	0 1 2 3 4 5
Piece is exactly 5 minutes in duration	0 1 2 3 4 5
Film transcends limitations of project to say something original	0 1 2 3 4 5
TOTAL	_____

PRODUCTION PROJECT ASSESSMENT CRITERIA

For Project 28-2: Three-Person Conversation (Interior)

Film title _____ Name _____ Date _____

Criteria	Rating
DIRECTING. Director's voice eliminated when side coaching	0 1 2 3 4 5
Participants are at ease and not intimidated by camera	0 1 2 3 4 5
Directing has evoked an interesting conversation with real tension	0 1 2 3 4 5
CAMERA Composition proportions are appropriate from shot to shot	0 1 2 3 4 5
Zooming and recomposing happen simultaneously and smoothly	0 1 2 3 4 5
Tends to use wide shot for new subject matter	0 1 2 3 4 5
Tends to cover moments of intensity in big close-up	0 1 2 3 4 5
SOUND is good and no mike is visible	0 1 2 3 4 5
EDITING maintains rhythm of speaker's speech patterns	0 1 2 3 4 5
Cutaways used successfully to eliminate some camera transitions	0 1 2 3 4 5
Conversation successfully restructured to develop meaningfully	0 1 2 3 4 5
Conversation has impact and intensity throughout	0 1 2 3 4 5
Film transcends limitations of project to say something original	0 1 2 3 4 5
TOTAL	_____

PRODUCTION PROJECT ASSESSMENT CRITERIA

For Project 28-3: Covering a Process for Ellipsis Editing

Film title _____ Name _____ Date _____

These criteria are for dailies viewed in their entirety. Use Project 38-3 to assess edited version, which must be precisely 2 minutes long.

Criteria	Rating
DIRECTING. Whole action is adequately covered	0 1 2 3 4 5
All major steps of the action are clearly shown	0 1 2 3 4 5
CAMERA. Interesting framings and compositions are used	0 1 2 3 4 5
Compositions integrate and juxtapose elements of the action	0 1 2 3 4 5
Camera is absolutely steady between necessary movements	0 1 2 3 4 5
Camera movements are positive and controlled	0 1 2 3 4 5
Camera movements are motivated by the subject	0 1 2 3 4 5
Camera movements are in rhythm with the subject's movements	0 1 2 3 4 5
There is good balance between close-ups and longer shots	0 1 2 3 4 5
Transitions between stages are clearly shown	0 1 2 3 4 5
Film transcends limitations of project to say something original	0 1 2 3 4 5
TOTAL	_____

PRODUCTION PROJECT ASSESSMENT CRITERIA

For Project 28-4: Covering a Conversation (Exterior)

Film title _____ Name _____ Date _____

Criteria	Rating
DIRECTING. Participants look spontaneous and natural	0 1 2 3 4 5
Camera moves in rhythm with conversation	0 1 2 3 4 5
Why they are waiting is visually explained	0 1 2 3 4 5
Two different characters emerge	0 1 2 3 4 5
Topic of conversation evolves interestingly	0 1 2 3 4 5
Film has high overall impact	0 1 2 3 4 5
SOUND. Recording yields good sound	0 1 2 3 4 5
CAMERA. Visuals set an interesting mood	0 1 2 3 4 5
Camera movements are properly motivated	0 1 2 3 4 5
Compositions are well framed	0 1 2 3 4 5
Compositions create depth	0 1 2 3 4 5
Close-ups come when speakers are most intense	0 1 2 3 4 5
Over-the-shoulder shots are well composed, properly complementary	0 1 2 3 4 5
Low-angle shot(s) are motivated	0 1 2 3 4 5
Camera does not cross the line (or scene axis)	0 1 2 3 4 5
EDITING. Cutaways and reactions are motivated and functional	0 1 2 3 4 5
Eyeline shifts are exploited in cutting	0 1 2 3 4 5
Extra inserts, cutaways, and reaction shots function well	0 1 2 3 4 5
"Any-sync" shots included to aid editing	0 1 2 3 4 5
Length requirement (4-minute maximum) is observed	0 1 2 3 4 5
Sound levels effectively matched from shot to shot	0 1 2 3 4 5
Film transcends limitations of project to say something original	0 1 2 3 4 5
TOTAL	_____

PRODUCTION PROJECT ASSESSMENT CRITERIA

For Project 28-5: Mobile Coverage of Complex Action

Film title _____ Name _____ Date _____

Criteria	Rating
DIRECTING. Subject informally tells entertaining tale	0 1 2 3 4 5
CAMERA. Good framing is used throughout shot	0 1 2 3 4 5
Solves getting out of house door	0 1 2 3 4 5
Shows person's face as he/she walks	0 1 2 3 4 5
Solves getting into car	0 1 2 3 4 5
Camera is on driver as car gathers speed	0 1 2 3 4 5
Pans to straight ahead	0 1 2 3 4 5
Camera is steady throughout	0 1 2 3 4 5
Camera moves in sync with events	0 1 2 3 4 5
Compositions are appropriate	0 1 2 3 4 5
SOUND is consistently OK (no expletives, bumps, crashes etc.)	0 1 2 3 4 5
Film transcends limitations of project to say something original	0 1 2 3 4 5
TOTAL	_____

PRODUCTION PROJECT ASSESSMENT CRITERIA
For Project 28-6: Interview In Depth

Film title _____ Name _____ Date _____

Criteria	Rating
DIRECTING. Interviewee is at ease, speaks freely and interestingly	0 1 2 3 4 5
Interviewer nowhere overlapped the interviewee	0 1 2 3 4 5
Relevant facts about the event are supplied	0 1 2 3 4 5
Relevant facts about the interviewee are supplied	0 1 2 3 4 5
Gave a personal, emotional perspective of the event	0 1 2 3 4 5
Interviewee revealed his/her own change and development	0 1 2 3 4 5
Interviewee faced a substantial issue for the very first time	0 1 2 3 4 5
No questions or narration are necessary to make sense of the answers	0 1 2 3 4 5
CAMERA. Different image sizes edit well together compositionally	0 1 2 3 4 5
All camera moves were made smoothly and are usable	0 1 2 3 4 5
SOUND quality is clear and intimate in quality	0 1 2 3 4 5
EDITING Interview structured like a story, with beginning, middle, and end	0 1 2 3 4 5
Climactic moments are well placed	0 1 2 3 4 5
Film was high overall impact	0 1 2 3 4 5
Film transcends limitations of project to say something original	0 1 2 3 4 5
TOTAL	_____

PRODUCTION PROJECT ASSESSMENT CRITERIA

For Project 28-7: Two-Person Conversation with Conflict

Film title _____ Name _____ Date _____

Criteria	Rating
DIRECTING. Pair is interesting, well chosen	0 1 2 3 4 5
Event is well defined	0 1 2 3 4 5
The stages of the event are clear, and so is its significance to each	0 1 2 3 4 5
Sharply differing perceptions are recorded	0 1 2 3 4 5
Sequence builds to a climax	0 1 2 3 4 5
Climax is well placed in sequence	0 1 2 3 4 5
Resolution is interesting	0 1 2 3 4 5
Sequence has natural end	0 1 2 3 4 5
Length of sequence is appropriate	0 1 2 3 4 5
SOUND is good quality throughout	0 1 2 3 4 5
CAMERA. People creatively placed, not just arranged on a couch	0 1 2 3 4 5
Setting creates a mood	0 1 2 3 4 5
Lighting augments mood	0 1 2 3 4 5
Compositions create depth and perspective	0 1 2 3 4 5
Camera movements are smooth and unobtrusive	0 1 2 3 4 5
Camera follows psychological center of the action and reveals subtext	0 1 2 3 4 5
Compositions are well framed	0 1 2 3 4 5
Framings cut together well	0 1 2 3 4 5
Imaginative, well-shot inserts, reactions, and cutaways are present	0 1 2 3 4 5
EDITING. These used in motivated, creative way	0 1 2 3 4 5
Listener reactions used effectively	0 1 2 3 4 5
Editing rhythm is smooth	0 1 2 3 4 5
Mike positions are on different tracks and whole now sounds seamless	0 1 2 3 4 5
Mix is good for level and equalization	0 1 2 3 4 5
There's a discernible point of view by the filmmakers	0 1 2 3 4 5
Film has high overall impact	0 1 2 3 4 5
Film transcends limitations of project to say something original	0 1 2 3 4 5
TOTAL	_____

PRODUCTION PROJECT ASSESSMENT CRITERIA
For Project 28-8: Unbroken Five-Minute Story

Film title _____ Name _____ Date _____

Criteria	Rating
DIRECTING. Story comes out at exactly 5 minutes	0 1 2 3 4 5
Film is well structured for information and development	0 1 2 3 4 5
Storyteller produces an interesting story	0 1 2 3 4 5
Film is emotionally engaging	0 1 2 3 4 5
Content seems natural, spontaneous, and unrehearsed	0 1 2 3 4 5
Time allotment is used in good proportions	0 1 2 3 4 5
Story is told naturally and without forced or slack moments	0 1 2 3 4 5
Story has a natural, well-situated climax	0 1 2 3 4 5
Film makes an impact	0 1 2 3 4 5
CAMERA moves inventively with or around storyteller	0 1 2 3 4 5
Good framing and compositions are found throughout	0 1 2 3 4 5
Camera movements are smooth and motivated	0 1 2 3 4 5
SOUND is good and consistent	0 1 2 3 4 5
Film transcends limitations of project to say something original	0 1 2 3 4 5
TOTAL	_____

PRODUCTION PROJECT ASSESSMENT CRITERIA
For Project 28-9: A One-Shot, Catalyzed Event

Film title _____ Name _____ Date _____

Criteria	Rating
DIRECTING. Film covers its ground in 7 to 10 minutes	0 1 2 3 4 5
There is an interesting build and denouement	0 1 2 3 4 5
The protagonist keeps events moving	0 1 2 3 4 5
There are no flat spots	0 1 2 3 4 5
There are no unduly forced moments	0 1 2 3 4 5
The premise to the film was original	0 1 2 3 4 5
The film makes a socially critical point	0 1 2 3 4 5
The film has a strong impact	0 1 2 3 4 5
CAMERA is where it should be throughout	0 1 2 3 4 5
The camera handles the unexpected with aplomb	0 1 2 3 4 5
SOUND is well recorded throughout	0 1 2 3 4 5
Film transcends limitations of project to say something original	0 1 2 3 4 5
TOTAL	_____

PRODUCTION PROJECT ASSESSMENT CRITERIA

For Project 28-10: *Vox Populi* Interviews and Metaphoric Counterpoint

Film title _____ Name _____ Date _____

Criteria	Rating
DIRECTING. Good *vox pop* topic is used	0 1 2 3 4 5
Good hypothesis is used, evident on screen	0 1 2 3 4 5
Genuine differences of opinion are expressed	0 1 2 3 4 5
Visual metaphor is organic to *vox pop*'s world	0 1 2 3 4 5
Is truly metaphoric and not just illustration or visual diversion	0 1 2 3 4 5
Sequence makes socially critical statement	0 1 2 3 4 5
Conflicting views are well exploited	0 1 2 3 4 5
Participants are stimulated and at ease	0 1 2 3 4 5
Interestingly different types and socioeconomic groups represented	0 1 2 3 4 5
Ideas and participants are ethically handled	0 1 2 3 4 5
CAMERA. Compositional backgrounds are interesting and pertinent	0 1 2 3 4 5
Good framing, composition, and steadiness are seen	0 1 2 3 4 5
Variety of image sizes and angles are shown	0 1 2 3 4 5
Depth created in compositions	0 1 2 3 4 5
SOUND. Good sound is heard	0 1 2 3 4 5
EDITING. Film is entertaining, lively in pace	0 1 2 3 4 5
Good developmental arc of ideas is presented	0 1 2 3 4 5
Work is crisply and intelligently edited	0 1 2 3 4 5
Length is well judged	0 1 2 3 4 5
Delivers emotional impact	0 1 2 3 4 5
Contains surprises and leaves you thinking	0 1 2 3 4 5
Film transcends limitations of project to say something original	0 1 2 3 4 5
TOTAL	_____

PRODUCTION PROJECT ASSESSMENT CRITERIA
For Project 28-11: Self-Portrait

Film title _____ Name _____ Date _____

Criteria	Rating
DIRECTING. Gives factually coherent autobiographical portrait	0 1 2 3 4 5
Gives insight into at least one formative event	0 1 2 3 4 5
Portrays some credible family tensions	0 1 2 3 4 5
Avoids self-indulgence	0 1 2 3 4 5
Is bearably self-critical	0 1 2 3 4 5
Avoids self-censure	0 1 2 3 4 5
Is not overprotective of self or family	0 1 2 3 4 5
Addresses some difficulties of autobiography	0 1 2 3 4 5
Seems trustworthy	0 1 2 3 4 5
Is entertaining and memorable	0 1 2 3 4 5
Film uses its time well	0 1 2 3 4 5
Film is between 5 to 8 minutes as required	0 1 2 3 4 5
Has acquitted him/herself well in this very difficult form	0 1 2 3 4 5
Film transcends limitations of project to say something original	0 1 2 3 4 5
TOTAL	_____

PRODUCTION PROJECT ASSESSMENT CRITERIA
For Project 28-12: Observing the Observer

Film title _____ Name _____ Date _____

Criteria	Rating
DIRECTING. Material to analyze is well chosen	0 1 2 3 4 5
Approach to examining feels motivated and unforced	0 1 2 3 4 5
Speculative comments are informal and un–self-conscious	0 1 2 3 4 5
Analysis yields interesting insights into specific moments	0 1 2 3 4 5
Film reveals one or more genuine ethical dilemmas	0 1 2 3 4 5
Avoids self-congratulation	0 1 2 3 4 5
Avoids self-mortification	0 1 2 3 4 5
Avoids being over-earnest	0 1 2 3 4 5
Avoids avoidance humor	0 1 2 3 4 5
Critique neither belittles nor aggrandizes human subjects	0 1 2 3 4 5
Shows empathy and insight into at least one participant	0 1 2 3 4 5
Film is gripping	0 1 2 3 4 5
Acquits him/herself well in this difficult form	0 1 2 3 4 5
Film transcends limitations of project to say something original	0 1 2 3 4 5
TOTAL	_____

PRODUCTION PROJECT ASSESSMENT CRITERIA

For Project 28-13: Story, Question, and Suggestion

Film title _____ Name _____ Date _____

Criteria	Rating
DIRECTING. Participant "casting" is good	0 1 2 3 4 5
Good story is evoked by astute choice of question	0 1 2 3 4 5
Story provokes reflection on its implied values, dilemmas	0 1 2 3 4 5
Director has spotted all the ambiguities in second layer "thoughts tape"	0 1 2 3 4 5
Final layer shows multiple reflexivity	0 1 2 3 4 5
Final layer provokes thought about first impressions	0 1 2 3 4 5
Final layer provokes thought about afterthoughts and follow-ups	0 1 2 3 4 5
Two people's adjustments to each other are visible	0 1 2 3 4 5
Layers are distinct and experiencing them is not confusing	0 1 2 3 4 5
Each added layer earns its presence in the film	0 1 2 3 4 5
Each layer is well judged in length	0 1 2 3 4 5
Subsequent layers are increasingly complex but not confusingly so	0 1 2 3 4 5
Some wit and irony show through	0 1 2 3 4 5
Participant does not emerge as exploited	0 1 2 3 4 5
Film emerges as a worthwhile dialogue	0 1 2 3 4 5
EDITING. Developmental arc is consistent and satisfying	0 1 2 3 4 5
Film keeps within 8 to 10 minutes and uses its screen time well	0 1 2 3 4 5
Film transcends limitations of project to say something original	0 1 2 3 4 5
TOTAL	_____

PRODUCTION PROJECT ASSESSMENT CRITERIA

For Project 28-14: Making History

Film title _____ Name _____ Date _____

Criteria	Rating
DIRECTING. Interesting historical episode was chosen	0 1 2 3 4 5
Imagery is inherently interesting	0 1 2 3 4 5
Text is acted convincingly so it sounds authentic	0 1 2 3 4 5
TEXT is inherently interesting	0 1 2 3 4 5
Text and images go together well	0 1 2 3 4 5
Tells a story with characters and situations	0 1 2 3 4 5
Develops some narrative tension	0 1 2 3 4 5
DRAMATIC ARC. Character learns something, is changed by experience	0 1 2 3 4 5
Developmental arc of the piece is well judged	0 1 2 3 4 5
EDITING. Sets a compelling mood (using music and effects, perhaps)	0 1 2 3 4 5
Holds the viewer's interest throughout	0 1 2 3 4 5
Pacing is appropriate, nothing rushed or dragging	0 1 2 3 4 5
Words and images counterpointed interestingly	0 1 2 3 4 5
Speech rhythms used to pace the cutting	0 1 2 3 4 5
At the end you wished there was more	0 1 2 3 4 5
Film transcends limitations of project to say something original	0 1 2 3 4 5
TOTAL	_____

PRODUCTION PROJECT ASSESSMENT CRITERIA

For Project 28-15: National Anthem

Film title _____ Name _____ Date _____

Criteria	Rating
DIRECTING. Images make their own narrative	0 1 2 3 4 5
Visually the piece has a beginning, middle, and end	0 1 2 3 4 5
Makes ironic use of anthem's words	0 1 2 3 4 5
Has something memorable to say about your country today	0 1 2 3 4 5
Works on our emotions	0 1 2 3 4 5
Has a sense of humor or irony	0 1 2 3 4 5
Leaves us thoughtful	0 1 2 3 4 5
CAMERA. Is imaginatively used	0 1 2 3 4 5
Camerawork is controlled and well composed	0 1 2 3 4 5
EDITING. Is keyed to musical rhythm and transitions	0 1 2 3 4 5
Film transcends limitations of project to say something original	0 1 2 3 4 5
TOTAL	_____

PRODUCTION PROJECT ASSESSMENT CRITERIA

For Project 28-16: Video Letter

Film title _____ Name _____ Date _____

Criteria	Rating
DIRECTING. The video letter's narrative method was effective	0 1 2 3 4 5
Facts and necessary information were included	0 1 2 3 4 5
It gave voice to more than one person	0 1 2 3 4 5
It accurately reflected important parts of our reality	0 1 2 3 4 5
It showed some of our activities as "newsreel" material	0 1 2 3 4 5
Some of the letter directly addresses the other group	0 1 2 3 4 5
Some of our satisfactions were well addressed	0 1 2 3 4 5
We included some of our frustrations and difficulties	0 1 2 3 4 5
Included philosophy and beliefs about why we make documentaries	0 1 2 3 4 5
It showed where we study, our equipment, and facilities	0 1 2 3 4 5
We asked good questions and can expect an interesting response	0 1 2 3 4 5
We learned something about ourselves while putting this together	0 1 2 3 4 5
Film transcends limitations of project to say something original	0 1 2 3 4 5
TOTAL	_____

PRODUCTION PROJECT ASSESSMENT CRITERIA

For Project 28-17: The Final Project

Film title _____ Name _____ Date _____

Criteria	Rating
DIRECTING. "Corner of nature" seen well "through a temperament"	0 1 2 3 4 5
Successfully exploits visually interesting situations	0 1 2 3 4 5
Demonstrates mastery of director's catalyst function	0 1 2 3 4 5
Demonstrates masterful use of observational cinema techniques	0 1 2 3 4 5
Demonstrates mastery of reflexive techniques	0 1 2 3 4 5
Demonstrates mastery of controlled filming situations	0 1 2 3 4 5
Demonstrates mastery of filming uncontrollable situations	0 1 2 3 4 5
Theme of film is discernibly original	0 1 2 3 4 5
Participants stimulated yet at ease	0 1 2 3 4 5
Participants challenged hard when necessary	0 1 2 3 4 5
Director took necessary risks to evoke profound material	0 1 2 3 4 5
CAMERA work controlled and secure	0 1 2 3 4 5
Demonstrates mastery of tripod camerawork	0 1 2 3 4 5
Demonstrates mastery of handheld camerawork	0 1 2 3 4 5
Demonstrates excellent use of lighting and set arrangement	0 1 2 3 4 5
Strong visual moods in different parts of the film	0 1 2 3 4 5
EDITING. Demonstrates use of words and images in masterly way	0 1 2 3 4 5
Sound composition is aurally rich	0 1 2 3 4 5
Sound mix is well judged	0 1 2 3 4 5
Sound track makes one imagine	0 1 2 3 4 5
Editing feels secure and well judged	0 1 2 3 4 5
Pacing varies but always feels right	0 1 2 3 4 5
Overall length feels right	0 1 2 3 4 5
DRAMATIC FORM. Structure of film works well	0 1 2 3 4 5
Thematic development is well paced	0 1 2 3 4 5
Film handles conflicting forces	0 1 2 3 4 5
Film brings conflicting forces into confrontation	0 1 2 3 4 5
Film shows something/someone change	0 1 2 3 4 5
Film has memorable resolution	0 1 2 3 4 5
Film has high overall impact	0 1 2 3 4 5
Film transmits participants' point(s) of view effectively	0 1 2 3 4 5
AUTHORSHIP. Distinct, individual storytelling "voice" emerges	0 1 2 3 4 5
Film achieves a meaningful outcome	0 1 2 3 4 5
Authorship shows authority and evidence of passion	0 1 2 3 4 5
Film transcends limitations of project to say something original	0 1 2 3 4 5
TOTAL	_____

POSTPRODUCTION PROJECT ASSESSMENT CRITERIA
For Project 38-1: Interview, Varying Image Sizes

Film title _____ Name _____ Date _____

Criteria	Rating
EDITING. Interview is well structured	0 1 2 3 4 5
Head and body positions are well matched at cutting points	0 1 2 3 4 5
Speaker's rhythms sound natural	0 1 2 3 4 5
Interview is a "transparent," smooth, uninterrupted monologue	0 1 2 3 4 5
There is no evidence of the interviewer	0 1 2 3 4 5
SOUND track is cleanly cut, with no clipped breaths or sounds	0 1 2 3 4 5
Sound levels are consistent throughout	0 1 2 3 4 5
Sound mix rendered sound track seamless and undistracting	0 1 2 3 4 5
OVERALL the film has high overall impact	0 1 2 3 4 5
TOTAL	_____

POSTPRODUCTION PROJECT ASSESSMENT CRITERIA
For Project 38-2: Conversation, Two or More Persons

Film title _____ Name _____ Date _____

Criteria	Rating
EDITING. Conversation develops logically	0 1 2 3 4 5
Emotional high points are well structured	0 1 2 3 4 5
Head and body positions are well matched at cutting points	0 1 2 3 4 5
Speakers' rhythms sound natural	0 1 2 3 4 5
Listeners' reactions are indicated through cutaways	0 1 2 3 4 5
Inner lives of characters are somewhat developed through editing	0 1 2 3 4 5
Additional detail is supplied in motivated cutins	0 1 2 3 4 5
Visual rhythm feels balanced throughout	0 1 2 3 4 5
SOUND track is cleanly cut, with no clipped breaths or sounds	0 1 2 3 4 5
Sound levels are consistent throughout	0 1 2 3 4 5
OVERALL. As a piece of editing the film has high overall impact	0 1 2 3 4 5
TOTAL	_____

POSTPRODUCTION PROJECT ASSESSMENT CRITERIA
For Project 38-3: Editing for Ellipsis

Film title _____ Name _____ Date _____

Criteria	Rating
EDITING. Solves the problem of compressing time	0 1 2 3 4 5
Begins and ends appropriately	0 1 2 3 4 5
Each necessary stage of the action is shown or indicated	0 1 2 3 4 5
Stages that can be inferred are left out	0 1 2 3 4 5
Each stage of the process is onscreen for an appropriate time	0 1 2 3 4 5
Rhythms of actions and any speech look natural	0 1 2 3 4 5
Process/conversation develops comprehensibly	0 1 2 3 4 5
Sequence uses narratively consistent screen language	0 1 2 3 4 5
Uses available angles effectively	0 1 2 3 4 5
Makes cutaways and cut-ins look motivated	0 1 2 3 4 5
SOUND. Uses sound and sound transitions creatively	0 1 2 3 4 5
Sound mix renders track seamless and effective	0 1 2 3 4 5
OVERALL. Length is appropriate	0 1 2 3 4 5
As a piece of editing it has high overall impact	0 1 2 3 4 5
TOTAL	_____

POSTPRODUCTION PROJECT ASSESSMENT CRITERIA
For Project 38-4: Complex Editing Project

Film title _____ Name _____ Date _____

Criteria	Rating
EXPOSITION. Successfully develops exposition of facts and situation	0 1 2 3 4 5
TRANSITIONS. Successfully uses action match cuts	0 1 2 3 4 5
Uses subject motion to motivate cuts	0 1 2 3 4 5
Cuts make use of camera movements	0 1 2 3 4 5
Uses eyeline shifts or verbal cues to motivate cuts, inserts, or cutaways	0 1 2 3 4 5
Successful use of overlap cuts, sound precedes its sync picture	0 1 2 3 4 5
Successful use of overlap cuts, track overhangs into next shot	0 1 2 3 4 5
RHYTHMS. Uses verbal rhythms and operative words	0 1 2 3 4 5
Dialogue cutting and pacing always feel natural	0 1 2 3 4 5
Has superior feeling for visual rhythms	0 1 2 3 4 5
Has superior feeling for musical rhythms	0 1 2 3 4 5
DRAMATIC ARC. Piece develops issues in Act I	0 1 2 3 4 5
Complications develop in Act II	0 1 2 3 4 5
Film reaches crisis in which major issue comes to a head	0 1 2 3 4 5
Shows resolution in Act III	0 1 2 3 4 5
Film has memorably effective ending	0 1 2 3 4 5
CHARACTERS. Good factual/ emotional perspectives of characters	0 1 2 3 4 5
MOODS. Uses visuals well to create mood	0 1 2 3 4 5
Uses sound effects, etc., well to help create mood	0 1 2 3 4 5
MUSIC. Choice of music for mood is original and effective	0 1 2 3 4 5
Editing reflects rhythm and texture of music	0 1 2 3 4 5
SOUND. Counterpoint and tension developed between words and images	0 1 2 3 4 5
Dialogue broken into separate tracks according to mike position	0 1 2 3 4 5
Makes effective use of voice-over or narration	0 1 2 3 4 5
Sound mix is well balanced and effective	0 1 2 3 4 5
OVERALL. Length is well judged	0 1 2 3 4 5
As a piece of editing has a high overall impact	0 1 2 3 4 5
TOTAL	_____

APPENDIX 2

USEFUL FORMS

This Appendix contains the following forms for you to photocopy and use:

- **Form and Aesthetics Questionnaire.** This functions as a checklist for what you do (or don't yet) have assembled in preparation to shoot your film.
- **Film Analysis Form.** Use this to make flow charts of your film in the different editing stages or to help you break any film down into its component parts during an analysis.
- **Film Camera Log.** Can be used either with a film camera or a video camera being used in double-system recording.
- **Sound Recorder Log.** For use with any sound recorder when making either a film or video double-system recording.
- **Video Log.** For single-system recording using a camcorder.

FORM AND AESTHETICS QUESTIONNAIRE

Name _____

Film Working Title _____

Phone # _____ E-mail _____

Fill out this form to see how much you know about your film. Take the time to refine your answers and fill out as many spaces as you can. Notice how the questionnaire encapsulates the artistic process by starting with your major belief. It then moves through information about your film and its characters and ends with how you want to act on your audience.

1. Statistics

My film will be _____ minutes long, will be shot on _____ (format), and is expected to take _____ shooting days and to cost $ _____. So far I have (check what applies):

A rough idea, incomplete ☐   A thematic statement ☐   All participants ☐

Complete but rough idea ☐   A proposal ☐   A treatment ☐

A beginning ☐   A middle ☐   An end ☐

Producer ☐   All funds ☐   _____% funds raised ☐

Production manager ☐   Director of $_____ still to raise ☐
                         photography ☐

2. Personal philosophy that inspired the making of this film

In life I believe that _____

_____

_____

3. Premise

The film explores my convictions by showing (here briefly write your film's premise) _____

_____

_____

4. Genre

The genre (type or family) of this film is _____, and my film only departs from this genre in that it _____

_____

_____

5. Main characters and their characteristics (most important first)

Character A _____ mainly wants _____

_____

Dominant traits _____

_____

Major conflict _____

_____

Character B _____ mainly wants _____

Dominant traits _____

_____

Major conflict _____

_____

Character C _____ mainly wants _____

Dominant traits _____

_____

Major conflict _____

_____

Character D _____ mainly wants _____

Dominant traits _____

_____

Major conflict _____

_____

Character E _____ mainly wants _____

Dominant traits _____

_____

Major conflict _____

_____

Character F _____ mainly wants _____

Dominant traits _____

_____

Major conflict _____

_____

More characters? Add on separate sheet.

6. Major situation affecting the main characters

The major situation in which the characters find themselves is _____

_____

_____

_____

7. Point of view

(A) The point-of-view character is _____ and his/her biased way

of seeing means that _____

_____

_____

_____

(B) Subsidiary characters are _____ and their way

of seeing, by contrast, means that _____

_____

_____

_____

(C) The Storyteller's characteristics are _____

_____

and this makes him/her see in a particular way that is _____

_____

_____

8. The film's main conflict

The major forces at conflict in this film are between _____

and _____

9. The confrontation

The story's main conflict is finally played out between _____ and

_____ in _____ scene.

10. Story resolution

The resolution to the characters' struggle is _____

_____

_____

11. Intended impact

After they have seen my film I want my audience to

(A) Feel _____

_____

(B) Think _____

_____

(C) Tell their friends to go and see the film because _____

_____

_____

12. Anything important not included above

_____

_____

_____

_____

_____

_____

FILM ANALYSIS FORM

Film Title _____   Page # _____

Sequence Content	Sequence Establishes	Style or Other Notes
Seq #_____ Begins with Ends with Length ____ min ____ sec		
Seq #_____ Begins with Ends with Length ____ min ____ sec		
Seq #_____ Begins with Ends with Length ____ min ____ sec		
Seq #_____ Begins with Ends with Length ____ min ____ sec		
Seq #_____ Begins with Ends with Length ____ min ____ sec		

FILM CAMERA LOG Production Title_____

_____

Operator:_____ Camera # _____ Magazine # _____ Camera Roll # _____
Location _____ Film Type _____ Date _____

Setup	Take	Comments	Footage

Notes:

Camera Assistant _____ (Phone # _____)

SOUND RECORDER LOG Production Title_____

Mike Operator:_____ Recorder # _____ Tape Type _____ Roll # _____
Location _____ Date _____

Setup	Take	Comments/Mike Types	Sync/Wild

Notes:

Sound Recordist _____ (Phone # _____)

VIDEO LOG Production Title_____

_____

Camera Operator _____ Camera _____ Cassette # _____
Location _____ Date _____

Setup	Take	Comments	Timecode

Notes:

Camera Assistant _____ (Phone # _____)

BIBLIOGRAPHY

SCREENWRITING

Biro, Yvette and Marie-Geneviéve Ripeau. *To Dress a Nude: Exercises in Imagination*. Dubuque, IA: Kendall/Hunt, 1998.

Richardson, Robert. *Literature and Film*. New York: Garland, 1985.

Rosenthal, Alan. *Writing Docudrama: Dramatizing Reality for Film and Television*. Boston: Focal Press, 1995.

Vogler, Christopher. *The Screenwriter's Journey: Mythic Structures*. Studio City, CA: Michael Wiese Productions, 1998.

DIRECTING

Bresson, Robert. *Notes on the Cinematographer*. Los Angeles: Green Integer Books, 1997.

Katz, Steven D. *Film Directing Shot by Shot*. Boston: Focal Press in association with Michael Wiese Production, 1991.

Lumet, Sidney. *Making Movies*. New York: Knopf/Random House, 1996.

Mamet, David. *On Directing Film*. Penguin, 1991.

Rabiger, Michael. *Directing: Film Techniques and Aesthetics*, 3rd ed. Boston: Focal Press, 2003.

Sherman, Eric. *Directing the Film: Film Directors on their Art*. Los Angeles: Acrobat Books, 1988.

LIGHTING

Box, Harry. *The Set Lighting Technician's Handbook: Film Lighting Equipment, Practice, and Electrical Distribution*, 2nd ed. Boston: Focal Press, 1997.

Carlson, Verne and Sylvia Carlson. *Professional Lighting Handbook*, 2nd ed. Boston: Focal Press, 1991.

Ferncase, Richard K. *Film and Video Lighting Terms and Concepts*. Boston: Focal Press, 1995.

Ferncase, Richard K. *Basic Lighting Worktext for Film and Video*. Boston: Focal Press, 1992.

Fitt, Brian. *A-Z of Lighting Terms*. Boston: Focal Press, 1998.

Gloman, Chuck and Tom LeTourneau. *Placing Shadows: Lighting Techniques of Video Production*, 2nd ed. Boston: Focal Press, 2000.

Millerson, Gerald. *Lighting for TV and Film*, 3rd ed. Boston: Focal Press, 1999.

Samuelson, David W. *Motion Picture Camera and Lighting Equipment: Choice and Technique*. Boston: Focal Press, 1986.

Uva, Michael G. and Sabrina Uva. *The Grip Book*. Boston: Focal Press, 1997.

Viera, John David and Dave Viera. *Lighting for Film and Electronic Cinematography*. Belmont, CA: Wadsworth, 1992.

CINEMATOGRAPHY AND MOTION PICTURE TECHNIQUES

Arijon, Daniel. *Grammar of the Film Language*. Los Angeles, CA: Silman-James, 1991.

Ascher, Steven and Edward Pincus. *The Filmmakers Handbook*. New York: Plume, 1999.

Beacham, Frank, ed. *American Cinematographers Video Manual*. Hollywood, CA: American Society of Cinematographers, 1994.

Carlson, Sylvia and Verne Carlson. *Professional Cameraman's Handbook*, 4th ed. Boston: Focal Press, 1994.

Detmers, Fred, ed. *American Cinematographer's Handbook*. Hollywood, CA: American Society of Cinematographers, 1990.

Ettedgui, Peter. *Cinematography*. Boston: Focal Press, 1999.

Hines, William E. *Operating Cinematography for Film and Video: A Professional and Practical Guide*. Los Angeles, CA: Ed-Venture Films/Books, 1997.

Hirschfeld, Gerald and Julia Tucker. *Image Control: Motion Picture and Video Camera Filters and Lab Techniques*. Boston: Focal Press, 1993.

Laszlo, Andrew and Andrew Quicke. *Every Frame a Rembrandt: Art and Practice of Cinematography*. Boston: Focal Press, 2000.

Lobrutto, Vincent. *Principal Photography: Interviews with Feature Film Cinematographers*. Westport, CT: Greenwood, 1999.

Malkiewicz, J. Kris and Jim Fletcher. *Cinematography: A Guide for Film Makers and Film Teachers*, 2nd ed. New York: Simon & Schuster, 1992.

Malkiewicz, J. Kris, Leonard Konopelski, and Barbara Gryboski. *Film Lighting: Talks With Hollywood's Cinematographers and Gaffers*. New York: Simon & Schuster, 1986.

Mascelli, Joseph. *The Five C's of Cinematography: Motion Picture Filming Technique*. Los Angeles, CA: Silman-James Press, 1998.

PRODUCTION MANAGEMENT

Cleve, Bastian. *Film Production Management*, 2nd ed. Boston: Focal Press, 1999.

Gates, Richard. *Production Management for Film and Video*, 3rd ed. Boston: Focal Press 1999.

Maier, Robert G. *Location Scouting and Management Handbook*. Boston: Focal Press, 1994.

Patz, Deborah S. *Surviving Production: The Art of Production Management for Film and Video*. Studio City, CA: Michael Wiese Productions, 1997.

Silver, Alain and Elizabeth Ward. *The Film Director's Team*. Los Angeles, CA: Silman-James, 1992.

MICROPHONES, RECORDING, AND SOUND

Bartlett, Bruce and Jenny Bartlett. *Practical Recording Techniques*, 2nd ed. Boston: Focal Press, 1998.

Bartlett, Bruce and Jenny Bartlett. *On Location Recording Techniques*. Boston: Focal Press, 1999.

Borwick, John. *Sound Recording Practice*, 4th ed. Oxford & New York: Oxford University Press, 1994.

Huber, David Miles. *Modern Recording Techniques*, 5th ed. Boston: Focal Press, 2001.

Lyver, Des and Graham Swainson. *Basics of Video Sound*, 2nd ed. Boston: Focal Press, 1999.

Nisbett, Alec. *The Sound Studio*, 6th ed. Boston: Focal Press, 1994.

Pendergast, Roy M. *Film Music: A Neglected Art*, 2nd ed. New York: W.W. Norton, 1992.

Rumsey, Francis. *The Audio Station Handbook*. Boston: Focal Press, 1996.

Rumsey, Francis. *Sound and Sound Recording: An Introduction*, 3rd ed. Boston: Focal Press, 1997.

Watkinson, John. *The Art of Digital Recording*, 2nd ed. Oxford: Focal Press, 1993.

Watkinson, John. *An Introduction to Digital Audio*. Boston: Focal Press, 2001.

White, Glenn D. *The Audio Dictionary*. Seattle, WA: University of Washington Press, 1991.

EDITING

Anderson, Gary H. *Video Editing and Post Production: A Professional Guide*, 4th ed. Boston: Focal Press, 1998.

Bayes, Steve. *The Avid Handbook. Techniques for the Avid Media Composer and Avid Express*, 3rd ed. Boston: Focal Press, 2000.

Browne, Steven E. *Nonlinear Editing Basics: Electronic Film and Video Editing*. Boston: Focal Press, 2001.

Burder, John. *The Technique of Editing 16mm Films*. Boston: Focal Press, 1990.

Collins, Mike. *ProTools: Practical Recording, Editing, and Mixing for Music Production*. Boston: Focal Press, 2001.

Dancyger, Ken. *The Technique of Film and Video Editing: Theory and Practice*, 3rd ed. Boston: Focal Press, 2001.

Murch, Walter. *In the Blink of an Eye: A Perspective on Film Editing*. Los Angeles, CA: Silman-James, 2001.

Ohanian, Thomas A. *Digital Nonlinear Editing: Editing Film and Video on the Desktop*, 2nd ed. Boston: Focal Press, 1998.

Oldham, Gabriella. *First Cut: Conversations with Film Editors*. Berkeley, CA: University of California Press, 1995.

Reisz, Karel and Gavin Millar. *The Technique of Film Editing*, 2nd ed. Boston: Focal Press, 1995.

Rosenblum, Ralph. *When the Shooting Stops, the Cutting Begins*. New York: Penguin, 1981.

Rubin, Michael. *Nonlinear: A Guide to Digital Film and Video Editing*, 4th ed. Gainesville, FL: Triad Publications, 2000.

Solomons, Tony. *The Avid Digital Editing Room Handbook*. Los Angeles, CA: Silman-James, 1999.

MUSIC

Russell, Mark and James Young. *Film Music*. Boston: Focal Press, 2000.

FINANCE, PRODUCTION, AND DISTRIBUTION

Cones, John W. *Film Finance and Distribution: A Dictionary of Terms*. Los Angeles, CA: Silman-James, 1992.

Gates, Richard. *Production Management for Film and Video*, 2nd ed. Boston: Focal Press, 1995.

Houghton, Buck. *What a Producer Does: The Art of Moviemaking (Not the Business)*. Los Angeles, CA: Silman-James, 1991.

Koster, Robert J. *The On Production Budget Book*. Boston: Focal Press, 1997.

Lazarus, Paul N, III. *The Film Producer*. New York: St. Martin's Press, 1992.

Levison, Louise. *Filmmakers and Financing: Business Plans for Independents*, 3rd ed. Boston: Focal Press, 2001.

Litwak, Mark. *Dealmaking in the Film and Television Industry from Negotiations to Final Contracts*, 2nd ed. Los Angeles, CA: Silman-James, 2002.

Ohanian, Thomas A. and Michael E. Phillips. *Digital Filmmaking: The Changing Art and Craft of Making Motion Pictures*, 2nd ed. Boston: Focal Press, 2000.

Rosen, David. *Off-Hollywood: The Making and Marketing of Independent Films*. New York: Grove/Atlantic, 1990.

Russo, John. *How to Make and Market Your Own Feature Movie for $10,000 or Less*. New York: Barclay House, 1994.

Singleton, Ralph. *Film Budgeting*. Los Angeles, CA: Lone Eagle, 1994.

Wiese, Michael. *Film and Video Financing*. Boston: Focal Press, 1992.

Wiese, Michael. *Film and Video Marketing*. Studio City, CA: Michael Wiese Productions, 1989.

Wiese, Michael. *The Independent Filmmakers' Guide*, 2nd ed. Studio City, CA: Michael Wiese Productions, 1997.

Wiese, Michael and Deke Simon. *Film and Video Budgets*, 3rd ed. Studio City, CA: Michael Wiese Productions, 2001.

EDUCATION AND CAREER POSSIBILITIES

Bayer, William. *Breaking Through, Selling Out, Dropping Dead*. New York: Limelight Editions, 1989.

Bone, Jan and Kathy Siebel. *Film Careers*. Lincolnwood, IL: NTC Publications, 1998.

Bone, Jan and Julie Rigby. *Opportunities in Film Careers*. Lincolnwood, IL: NTC Publications, 1999.

Horwin, Michael. *Careers in Film and Video Production*. Boston: Focal Press, 1990.

Kelly, Karen and Tom Edgar. *Film School Confidential: The Insider's Guide to Film Schools*. New York: Berkley Publishing Group, 1997.

Laskin, Emily, ed. *Getting Started in Film*. New York: Prentice-Hall, 1992.

Lazarus, Paul. *Working in Film*. New York: St. Martin's Press, 1993.

O'Donnell, Gail & Michele Travolta, eds. *Making It In Hollywood*. Naperville, Illinois: Sourcebooks, 1994.

Peterson's Guides to Graduate Programs in the Humanities. Stamford, CT: Petersons (a division of Thomson Corporation), 2002.

USEFUL WEBSITES

ORGANIZATIONS

www.aivf.org	Association of Independent Video and Film Makers; great information source for the low budget independent filmmaker
www.afionline.org	American Film Institute; a center for archives, film studies, and film education
www.bfi.org.uk	British Film Institute; archives, publications, and screenings
www.cilect.org	CILECT (Centre International de Liaison des Ecoles de Cinéma et de Télévision); Brussels-based organization of international film schools; always has an interesting range of special projects going
www.cinematography.com	Professional motion picture camera people, news, and resources
www.facets.org	Facets Cinémathèque; has 35,000 films of every kind for sale on tape or DVD. A helpful and knowledgeable organization with a passion for international and minority interest movies. Be sure to check that they have the tape you want in the format you can play. Consider banishing compatibility problems by getting a VHS international player, such as the AIWA HV MX-100, which will play any VHS PAL, SECAM, or NTSC format through any television set. When you want to record it will also convert NTSC to PAL or vice versa.
www.focalpress.com	Focal Press; Web site for the newest books on media
www.lcweb.loc.gov	Library of Congress
www.soc.org	Society of Camera Operators; information, book lists, and links to other professional societies around the world
www.ufva.org	University Film and Video Association, an organization for North American screen educators

INFORMATIONAL DATABASES

www.allmovie.com	Large movie database
www.boxofficeguru.com	Box office and other statistics
www.cineweb.com	Cineweb is a film production resource

www.us.imdb.com	Gargantuan movie database that enables every imaginable kind of production research, down to the careers of obscure technicians

SCREENWRITING RESOURCES

www.cinestory.com	Screenwriters' resource
www.newcenturywriter.org	New Century writer awards
www.screenplay.com	Screenwriting software download site
www.screenstyle.com	Screenplay software center
www.screenwriting.com	Screenwriters' resource with many links
www.writersstore.com	Everything for writers including software

PERIODICALS

www.dv.com	*Digital Video* magazine; excellent for software and equipment reviews and for keeping up to date with developments in the digital world
www.filmlinc.com	*Film Comment* magazine
www.theasc.com/magazine	*American Cinematographer*
www.variety.com	*Variety*, the show business oracle; get ready to learn a whole new vocabulary
www.videomaker.com	*Videomaker Magazine*; lots of good basic information

FILMOGRAPHY OF DIRECTOR MICHAEL RABIGER

BBC "Breakaway" series

Au Pair to Paris (1968)   (30 min, GB [Great Britain] and France)

Kibbutzniks (1968)   (30 min, GB and Israel)

BBC "Faces of Paris" series

Gerard et Regine (1968)   (30 min, France and Austria)

César (1969)   (30 min, France)

BBC "Yesterday's Witness" series

Prisoners of Conscience (1969)   (30 min, ×2, GB)
The Cramlington Train Wreckers (1969)   (30 min, GB)
Breaking the Silence (1969)   (30 min, GB)
Tolstoy Remembered by His Daughter (1969) (30 min, USA)
The Battle of Cable Street (1970)   (45 min, GB)
A Remnant of a Feudal Society (1970)   (30 min, GB)
A Cause Worth Fighting For (1972)   (45 min, GB)
Charlie Smith at 131 (1973)   (30 min, USA)

BBC "One Pair of Eyes" series

Dr. Spock: We're Heading for Destruction (1969)   (45 min, USA)

Idries Shah: The Dreamwalkers (1971)	(45 min, GB)
Leonardo Ricci: Cities of the Future (1971)	(45 min, Italy/Sicily)

BBC "Voices of the Seventies" series

Our Time Is Coming Now (1970)	(30 min, GB)

BBC "Cameron Country" series

Prejudice: On the Face of It (1970)	(45 min, GB)
Patriotism (1971)	(45 min, GB)

BBC "In the Limelight" series

Ronald Fraser: Having a Lovely Time (1972)	(30 min, GB)
Barry Took: Working Men's Clubs (1972)	(30 min, GB)

Independently Produced

Can You Live Like That? (1971)	(45 min, GB, Krishnamurti Foundation)
Gravity Is the Therapist (1974)	(53 min, USA, Rolf Foundation)
The Memorial Day Massacre (1975)	(20 min, USA)
The Temptation of Charles C. Charley (1978)	(26 min, USA, fiction pilot)
Bishop Hill Celebrates (1981)	(30 min, USA, DePaul University)
Portrait of a Director (1982)	(30 min, USA, Columbia College)
Ro Raises His Roof (1993)	(30 min, USA)
A Child's Journey Through Auschwitz (1994)	(58 min, USA)
Lotte on Lotte (1996)	(13 min, Norway)
Australian Cousins (2004?)	(Australia, work in progress)

GLOSSARY

Further information can be found via the Index.

A

A & B rolls Two or more rolls of film camera-original from which release prints are struck.

Acetate sheet Clear plastic sheet used in making titles or animation cels.

Action match cut Cut made between two different angles of the same action using the subject's movement as the transition.

AD Assistant director.

Adaptation The unique way each person adapts to the changing obstacles that prevent him or her from gaining his or her ends. In drama a prime component in externalizing his or her conflicts.

ADR Automatic dialogue replacement. *See* Postsynchronization.

Aerial shot Shot taken from the air.

AFI American Film Institute.

Ambient sound Sound naturally occurring in any location. Even an empty, quiet room has its own special atmosphere because no space is truly silent.

Analog recording Any sound or picture recording that records its waveforms as an analog representation, rather than digitally, when the waveform is registered by digital numbers, as in the coordinates for a graph.

Angle of acceptance The height and width of the subject filmed by a particular lens at a given distance, expressed in a lens table either in degrees or as measurements. Photographed image also depends on aspect ratio of the format in use. Wide-screen formats have longer horizontal measurement.

Anticipating When an actor (and a documentary participant who is temporarily in the role of actor) speaks or acts in advance of the appropriate moment.

Anticipatory sound Sound brought in ahead of its accompanying picture.

Aspect ratio The size of a screen format expressed as the ratio of the width in relation to the height. Films made for television are photographed at a ratio of 1.33:1. *See also* Angle of acceptance.

Atmosphere track Sound track providing a particular atmosphere (cafe, railroad, beach, rain, for example).

Attack (sound) The beginning portion of any sound.

Audio sweetening The level and equalization adjustment process that accompanies sound mixing.

Auteur theory The concept that one mind controls the creative identity of a film.

Axis *See* Scene axis.

B

Baby legs A miniature tripod for low-angle shots.

Back lighting Lighting from behind the subject.

Back story The events stated or implied to have happened prior to the period covered in the screenplay or documentary.

Bars Standard color bars generated in video systems, usually by the camera.

BCU Big close-up.

Beat Point in a situation where a buildup of pressure produces a major and irreversible change in one or more characters' consciousness(es) (theater term).

Behalfer Someone who makes a film on behalf of someone else and elects to speak for those supposedly without a voice of their own.

BFI British Film Institute.

BG Background.

Blocking Choreographic arrangement of movements by participants and camera in relation to the location.

Body copy Nondialogue descriptive portion of screenplay, usually consisting of stage directions and physical description.

Boom Support pole suspending the microphone close to the speakers but just out of shot.

Boxcar cutting Crude method of assembling sound and action segments as level-cut segments for speed and convenience.

Broad lighting Lighting that produces a broad band of highlight on a face or other three-dimensional object.

Butt splice Taped film splice made without the overlap necessary to cement splicing.

Buzz track *See* Presence.

C

Camera left/right Method of specifying movement or the placement of objects in relation to the camera: "Davy turns away from camera and walks off camera left." Also expressed as *screen right* or *left*.

Camera motivation A shot or a camera movement must be motivated within the terms of the scene or story if it is not to look alien and imposed. Camera motivation is often answered by asking, "What is the point of view here?"

Camera-to-subject axis The invisible line drawn between the camera and the subject in the composition. *See also* Scene axis.

Capturing *See* Digitizing.

Cement splice A film splice made by cementing two overlapping portions of film together.

Character generator An electronic device for producing video titles.

Cheating The practice of moving participants, furniture, or other objects in relation to each other to minimize shadows or other impediments. When such adjustments become evident, you are no longer cheating effectively.

Checkerboarding The practice, during conforming, of alternating film scenes with black leader in each A & B roll of camera original. Sound tracks prior to mixing are likewise alternated between two or more channels, with silence separating sound segments. Both black frame and silence allow the operator a grace period in which to adjust printer or sound channel settings before the arrival of the next segment.

Cinéma vérité Documentary shooting method in which the camera is subservient to an actuality that is sometimes instigated by the director.

Clapper board Marker board used at the beginning of takes whose bar closing permits separate sound to be synchronized. Also called the *slate*.

Climax The dramatic apex or turning point of a scene.

Closed question A question that manipulates the person replying into a certain form of answer.

Color bars Standard electronic video color test, usually generated by the camera.

Color chart Chart attached to film slate board as color reference for laboratory processing technicians.

Color temperature Light color quality is measured in degrees Kelvin (K). Common light sources in moviemaking contain a different mix of colors. The eye compensates effortlessly, but film and video cameras (or lighting itself) must be adjusted to prevailing color temperature if white objects are to be rendered as white onscreen. Mixing daylight (around 5,400 K) and studio lights (3,200 K) in the same scene leads to an unnatural lighting effect. One source must be filtered to make its output match the other, and the camera must likewise be filtered or electronically color balanced for all scene colors to be rendered faithfully.

Comm Commentary.

Complementary shot A shot compositionally designed to intercut with another.

Composite print A film print combining sound and picture.

Compression Sound with a wide dynamic range can be proportionately compressed so that the loudest and softest sounds are closer in volume. All TV transmissions and most radio transmissions, with the exception of high-fidelity music stations, are compressed. Cinemas usually give you the authentic range between whispers and the roar of battle.

Concept The dramatic *raison d'être* underlying the whole screenplay.

Conforming The process in which the film camera original is edited in conformity with the fine-cut workprint prior to making release prints.

Confrontation Bringing into final collision those people or forces representing the dramatic situation's main conflict.

Connotation Any images, words, or sounds used poetically to evoke ideas and feelings rather than to simply denote what something actually is. *See also* Denotation.

Contingency percentage A percentage, usually between 3% and 5%, superadded to a budget to provide for the unforeseeable.

Contingency planning Scheduling alternative shooting for any scenes threatened by weather or other imponderables.

Continuity Consistency of physical detail between shots intended to match.

Continuity script Script made after postproduction as record of film contents. Useful in proving piracy or censorship.

Continuity supervisor *See* Script supervisor.

Contrast Difference in brightness between highlight and deep shadow areas in an image.

Contrast ratio Ratio of lightest to darkest areas in an image.

Controlling point of view The psychological perspective (a character's or the storyteller's) from which a particular scene is shown.

Counterpoint The juxtaposing of antithetical elements, perhaps between sound and picture, to create a conflict of impressions for the audience to resolve.

Coverage The different angles from which a given scene is covered in order to allow variations of viewpoint in editing.

Crab dolly Wheeled camera support platform that can roll in any direction.

Craning A boom supporting the camera that can be raised or lowered during the shot.

Crash zoom Very fast zoom in or zoom out.

Crib notes Director's notes listing intentions and "don't forgets" for a scene.

Crossing the line Moving the camera across the scene axis. Can be problematical.

CS Close shot.

CU Close-up.

Cutaway A shot, often a character's physical point of view, that allows us to cut away momentarily from the main action.

Cut-in *See* Insert.

D

Dailies The film unit's daily output, processed and ready to be viewed. Also called *rushes* because of the rush involved in readying them.

DAT recorder Digital audio tape recorder.

Day for night Special photography that allows a sunlit day shot to pass as moonlit night.

Decay The tapering away of a concluding sound.

Deep focus Photography that holds objects both near and far in sharp focus.

Degradation A picture, either video or photo, becomes degraded when it passes through several generations of analog copying.

Denotation The process of signifying what something actually is. *See also* Connotation.

Depth of field Depth of the picture that is in acceptably sharp focus. Varies widely according to lens and f-stop in use.

Diegetic sound Sound that belongs in the natural world we see in the picture.

Diffused light Light composed of disorganized rays that casts an indistinct shadow.

Digitizing Process of turning an analog signal, whether audio or video, into a digital record (also known as *capturing*). This usually involves using an algorithmic formulation to compress the information and avoid wasteful recording of similarities from one frame to the next. *See also* JPEG and MPEG.

Direct cinema A low-profile observational documentary style of shooting that disallows any directorial intrusion to shape or instigate incidents.

Dissolve Transitional device in which one image cross fades into another. Also called a *lap dissolve*. One sound can dissolve into another.

DOF Depth of field.

Dolby A proprietary electronic recording system that produces low-noise sound recording, that is, having a lowered systemic hiss.

Dolly shot Any shot on a wheeled camera support.

Double-system recording Camera and sound recorder are separate instruments.

DP Director of photography.

Dramatic dynamics The ebb and flow of dramatic pressure through the length of a scene or of a whole film.

Dramatic tension The unresolved knowledge, hopes, fears, and expectations that keep us wanting to know "And what happens next?." Waiting, wondering, fearing, and hoping are vital when you experience good storytelling. Wilkie Collins said, "Make them laugh, make them cry, but make them wait."

Dub To copy from one electronic medium to another. Can be sound or video picture.

Dutch angle Shot made with camera deliberately tilted out of horizontal.

DV Digital video, or video and sound recorded digitally. Tape may be as small as 6 mm wide.

DVD Digital video disk.

Dynamic character definition Defining a participant like a dramatic character—by what he or she wants and is trying to accomplish.

Dynamic composition Pictorial composition as it changes within a moving shot.

E

Echo Sound reflections that return after a constant delay time. *See also* Reverberation.

Edge numbers Code numbers imprinted on the edge of camera original film and printing through to the workprint.

Edit decision list Sound and picture edit decisions in a movie, defined as a list of timecode or Keycode™ numbers. Taking camera originals and a standard edit decision list to a postproduction facility allows the making of a clean facsimile of the workprint.

EDL *See* Edit decision list.

Effects Sounds specially laid to augment the sound track of a film.

Ellipsis In filmmaking, the editing out of superfluous steps in a lengthy process in order to produce a shorthand version whose missing parts can be inferred by the audience (e.g., car stops at garage, gas pump nozzle into gas tank, money given to clerk, car rejoins road).

EQ *See* Equalizing.

Equalizing Using sound filters to reduce the discrepancy between sound tracks that are supposed to match and sound seamless. Abbreviated as EQ.

Establishing shot A shot that establishes a scene's geographical and human contents.

Exposition The part of a scene or a story in which basic information is relayed to the audience. Good exposition is buried within the action and goes unnoticed.

Expressionism A mode in art in which verisimilitude is laid aside in favor of techniques that evoke the subjective vision, either of a character or of the storyteller.

Ext Exterior.

External composition The compositional relationship between two images (shots) at the point of transition between them, usually a cut.

Eyeline The visual trajectory of a character in a scene.

F

Fade down Lower sound level.

Fade to white Fade an image to white instead of black.

Fade up Raise sound level.

Falling action *See* Resolution.

FG Foreground.

FI Fade in.

Fill light Diffused light used to raise light level in shadows cast by key light.

Flash forward Moving temporarily forward in time; the cinematic equivalent of the future tense. This quickly becomes a new form of present.

Flashback Moving temporarily backwards in time; a cinematic past tense that soon becomes an ongoing present.

Floor plan *See* Ground plan.

FO Fade out.

Focal distance Distance between camera and subject.

Focus (acting) In acting it means seeing, hearing, thinking in character. When a documentary participant loses focus, he or she becomes self-conscious and aware of participating in a make-believe world.

Foley Generic name for a stage where sound is recreated to picture.

Foreshadowing A somewhat fatalistic narrative technique by which an outcome is hinted at in advance. Helps to raise expectant tension in the audience.

Form The means and arrangement chosen to present a story's content.

Freeze frame A single frame arrested and held as a still picture.

Frontal lighting Key light coming from the direction of the camera and showing the subject virtually without shadows.

FTs Footsteps. Sometimes recreated for stylized documentaries.

FX Sound effects.

G

Generation Camera original (in film or video) is the first generation, and copies become subsequent numbered generations. Each in analog recording will have increased degradation of the original's fidelity. Many digital generations are possible before degradation sets in.

Genre A kind or type of film (essay, reflexive, direct cinema in documentaries, for example, and horror, sitcom, cowboy, domestic drama, etc., in fiction).

Grading *See* Timing.

Graduated tonality An image composed of midtones and having neither very bright nor very dark areas.

Gray scale Test chart useful to camera and lab technicians that shows the range of gray tones and includes absolute black and white.

Grip Location technician expert in handling lighting, set construction equipment, and camera dolly movements.

Ground plan Diagram showing placement of objects and movements of actors on a floor plan. Also called *floor plan.*

Gun/rifle mike Ultradirectional microphone useful for minimizing the intrusiveness of ambient noise.

H

Hard light *See* Specular light.

Headroom Compositional space left above heads.

High angle Camera mounted high, looking down.

High contrast Image with large range of brightnesses.

High down Camera mounted high, looking down.

High-key picture Image that is overall bright with few areas of shadow.

Highlight Brightest areas in picture.

Hi-hat Ultralow camera support resembling a metal top hat.

I

Improv Improvisation. A dramatic interaction that deliberately permits an outcome to emerge spontaneously. Improvs can involve different degrees of structure or may set a goal to be reached by an undetermined path. Improv drama and documentary directing methods are often interchangeable.

Insert A close shot of detail to be inserted in a shot containing more comprehensive action.

Int Interior.

Interior monologue The interior thoughts—voice an actor will sustain to help himself or herself stay in character and in focus.

Internal composition Composition internal to the frame as opposed to the compositional relationship existing between adjacent shots, called *external composition.*

Irony The revelation of a reality different from that initially apparent.

J

Jam sync Refers to videotape copying method that transfers not only all video and audio data but timecode data as well, with frame-to-frame accuracy.

JPEG An electronic algorithm standard used to compress video up to a 20:1 ratio for recording. Each frame is discrete, unlike MPEG compression, which achieves up to 100:1 compression while maintaining quality. JPEG allows editing to any particular frame; MPEG may not.

Jump cut Transitional device in which two similar images taken at different times are cut together so that the elision of intervening time is apparent. From this the audience infers that time has passed.

Juxtaposition The placing together of different pictorial or sound elements to invite comparison, inference, and heightened thematic awareness on the part of the audience.

K

Keycode™ Kodak's proprietary system for bar coding each camera's original film frame. This facilitates digitizing by assigning each frame its own timecode. Later, after digital editing, the coding permits negative cutting (conforming) from a digitally produced edit decision list.

Key light A scene's apparent source of illumination and the one creating the intended shadow pattern.

Key numbers *See* Edge numbers.

Keystone distortion The distortion of parallel lines that results from photographing an object from an off-axis position.

L

LA Low angle.

Lap dissolve *See* Dissolve.

Lapel Mike *See* Lavalier.

Lavalier mike Any neck or chest microphone.

Lead space The additional compositional space allowed in front of a figure or moving object photographed in profile.

Legal release A legally binding release form signed by a participant in a film that gives permission to use footage taken.

Leitmotiv Intentionally repeated element (sound, shot, dialogue, music, etc.) that helps unify a film by reminding the viewer of its earlier appearance.

Lens speed How fast a lens is depends on its maximum aperture and is a measure of light-transmitting capacity.

Level Sound volume.

Lighting ratio The ratio of highlight brightness to shadow illumination.

Limiter Electronically applied upper sound limit, useful for preventing momentary transient sounds, such as a door slamming, from distortion through over-recording.

Line of tension Invisible dramatic axis, or line of awareness, that can be drawn between protagonists and important elements in a scene.

Lip sync Recreated speech that is in complete sync with the speaker. Singers often lip sync to their recordings and fake a singing performance on television.

Longitudinal study A study that follows its subjects and their development over an appreciable length of time, possibly decades.

Looping *See* ADR.

Lose focus *See* Focus.

Low angle Camera looking up at subject.

Low-contrast image Image with small differences of brightness between highlight areas and shadow.

Low-key picture A scene that may have high contrast but that is predominantly dark overall.

LS Long shot.

M

Magazine Removable lightproof film container for a film camera.

Mannerisms An actor or participant's idiosyncratic and repeated details of behavior. Very hard to change or suppress.

Master mix Final mixed sound, first generation.

Master shot Shot that shows most or all of the scene and most or all of the characters.

Match cut *See* Action match cut.

MCS Medium close shot.

Memory stick A solid-state memory, about the size of a stick of chewing gum, that is plugged into a camera to store settings, information, or even whole images.

Metaphor A verbal or visually implied analogy that ascribes to one thing the qualities associated with another (e.g., the shop assistant, catlike behind her potted plants).

MIDI (Musical Instrument Digital Interface) A standardized digital control for electronic music.

Midtones The intermediate shades of gray lying between the extremes of black and white.

Mise en scène The totality of lighting, blocking, camera use, and composition that produces the dramatic image on film.

Mix The mixing together of sound tracks.

Mix chart Cue chart that functions like a musician's score to assist in the sound mix.

MLS Medium long shot.

Modulations Any electrical or electronic waveforms by which sound or picture are relayed and recorded.

Montage Originally meant editing in general, but now refers to the kind of sequence that shows a process or the passage of time.

Montage sequence *See* Montage.

MOS *Mit Out Sound*, which is what the German directors in Hollywood called for when they intended to shoot silent. In Britain this shot is called *mute*.

Motif Any formal element repeated from film history, or from the film itself, whose repetition draws attention to an unfolding thematic statement. *See also* Leitmotiv.

Motivation Whatever logic (in drama, of the plot) that impels a character to act or react in a particular way, usually a combination of psychological make-up and external pressures.

MPEG An electronic algorithm standard used to compress, by up to a $100:1$ ratio, large amounts of video into a smaller amount of information. Each frame is not discrete, like JPEG compression, but achieves greater compression while maintaining quality. MPEG may not allow editing to any particular frame.

MS Medium shot.

Murphy's Law "Whatever can go wrong will go wrong." Applies also to people.

Mus Music.

Music sync points Places in a film's action where music must exactly fit. Also called *picture pointing* and can be overdone.

Mute shot *See* MOS.

N

Narr Narration.

Narrative compression Storytelling techniques used to highlight narrative essentials through abridging time and space.

Narrow lighting Lighting that in portraiture produces a narrow band of highlight on a face.

Negative cutting *See* Conforming.

Networking The process of going from person to person, using the roots and branches of human networks, in search of particular information or contacts. In relation to this, a journalist friend used to say, "Nobody in the world is further away than five phone calls."

Noise Noise inherent in a sound recording system itself.

Noise reduction Recording and playback technique that minimizes system noise. *See also* Dolby.

Normal lens A lens of a focal length that, in the format being used, renders distances between foreground and background as recognizably normal.

O

Obligatory moment In documentary, as in drama, the moment of maximum dramatic intensity in a scene, for which the whole scene exists.

Offline edit Video editing in low-resolution form. *See also* Online edit.

Omniscient point of view A storytelling mode in which the audience is exposed to the author's capacity to see or know anything going on in the story, to move at will in time and space, and to freely comment upon meanings or themes.

Online edit Video editing assisted by a computer that is in highest resolution form.

Open question A question that is value neutral and that does not indicate the reply you expect. *See* Closed question for its opposite.

Operative words In editing, when language is set against images, the word hitting the beginning of each new image tends to play a big part in how we interpret it. A trained editor will pick important words in speech or narration and make cuts against them, knowing that they have a reinforcing effect.

Optical Any visual device, such as a fade, dissolve, wipe, iris wipe, ripple dissolve, matte, superimposition, etc.

Optical house A company specializing in visual special effects.

Optical track A sound track photographically recorded.

OS Offscreen.

Overlap cut Any cut in which picture and sound transitions are staggered instead of level cut.

P

Parallel storytelling The intercutting of two separate stories proceeding in parallel through time. Useful for abridging each and for making ironic contrasts.

Pan Short for Panorama. Horizontal camera movement.

Participant Someone who takes part in a documentary who would, in a fiction film, be an actor playing a character.

Perspective The size differential between foreground and background objects that causes us to infer receding space. Perspective that is obviously distorted makes us attribute subjectivity to the point of view being expressed.

Picture pointing Making music fit picture events. Walt Disney films used the device so much that its overuse is called *Mickey Mousing.*

Picture texture This can be hard or soft. A hard image has large areas in sharp focus and tends toward contrastiness, whereas a soft image has areas out of focus and lacks contrast.

Pitching The oral presentation of a film proposal in a brief, comprehensive, and attractive form to a committee or interested party. Comes from the idea of the sales pitch.

Playwriting In drama, one actor's tendency to take control of a scene, particularly in improv work, and to manipulate other actors into a passive relationship. Happens in documentaries too.

Plot In drama, the arrangement of incidents and the logic of causality in a story. Plot should create a sense of momentum and credibility, and act as a vehicle for the thematic intention of the piece. Same architecture of logic is necessary in documentaries.

PM Production manager.

Point of view Sometimes literally what a character sees (e.g., a clock approaching midnight) but more usually signifies the outlook and sensations of a character within a particular environment. This can be the momentary consciousness of an unimportant character or that of a main character *(see* Controlling point of view). It can also be the storyteller's point of view (*see* Omniscient point of view).

Postsynchronization Dialogue or effects shot in sync with existing action. Abbreviated as *postsync. See* ADR.

POV Point of view. When thus abbreviated, it can mean a shot reproducing a character's eyeline view.

Practical Any light source visible in the frame as part of the set.

Premise *See* Concept.

Premix A preliminary pass in which subsidiary sound elements are mixed together in preparation for the final mix.

Preroll The amount of time a camcorder or video-editing rig needs to reach running speed prior to recording or making a cut.

Presence Specially recorded location atmosphere to authentically augment "silent" portions of track. Every space has its own unique presence.

Prop Property, or physical object seen in picture.

Property Physical object handled by participants or present for authenticity in a set. A term also used to describe a script or proposal to which someone has secured the rights.

Psychoacoustics A term for the effect on us of a particular sound, as opposed to its literal cause. A sound can have emotional and cultural associations that go far beyond its cause.

R

Rack focus Altering focus between foreground and background during a shot. Prompts or accommodates an attention shift (e.g., a figure enters a door at the back of the room).

Radio microphone A microphone system that transmits its signal by radio to the recorder and is therefore wireless.

Raise the stakes Expression borrowed from betting games to signify raising the importance of whatever a protagonist is struggling to get, do, or accomplish.

Reconnaissance Careful examination of locations prior to shooting. Also called "scouting."

Reflexive cinema Type of film that includes evidence of its own process and the effect, say, on the participants of the filmmaking process.

Release print Final print destined for audience consumption.

Research Library work and observation of real life in search of authentic detail to fill out your knowledge of participants, situations, historical events, or anything else you must know to direct knowledgeably.

Resistance Human evasion mechanisms that show up in actors under different kinds of stress. Similar situations happen in shooting documentary.

Resolution The wind-down events following the film's climax that form the final phase of its development. Also called *falling action*.

Reverberation Sound reflections returning in a disorganized pattern of delay.

Rising action The documentary story developments, including complication and conflict, that lead to a scene or a film's climax.

Risk Whatever makes the protagonist's journey more difficult (and therefore more interesting) or whatever makes the film more challenging to its makers (which lends it more dramatic tension).

Room tone *See* Presence.

Rushes Unedited raw footage as it appears after shooting. Also called *dailies*.

Rushes book Log of important first reactions to rushes footage.

S

Scene axis The invisible line in a scene representing the scene's dramatic polarization. In a labor dispute scene, this might be drawn between the main protagonists, the plant manager, and the union negotiator. Coverage is shot from one side of this line to preserve consistent screen directions for all participants. Complex scenes involving multiple characters and physical regrouping may have more than one axis. *See also* Crossing the line.

Scene breakdown or **crossplot** In fiction, a chart displaying the locations, characters, and script pages necessary to each scene. Used in complex re-enacted documentaries or in any film using actors.

Scene dialectics The forces in opposition in a scene, which in documentary are likely to be externalized through body language, action, and behavior. A sense of the pressures in each scene, even one lacking human presence, is invaluable to documentary makers.

Scene geography The physical layout of the location and the placing of the participants. *See also* Master shot and Blocking.

Scout *See* Reconnaissance.

Screen direction The orientation or movement of characters and objects relative to the screen (screen left, screen right, upscreen, downscreen).

Screen left/right Movement or direction specifications. *See also* Screen direction.

Screenplay Standard script format showing dialogue and stage direction but no camera or editing instructions.

Script supervisor Also called *continuity supervisor*, this is the person who notes the physical details of each scene and the actual dialogue used so that complementary shots, designed to cut together, will match. Seldom used in documentary unless re-creation and actors are being used.

Segue (pronounced "seg-way") Sound transition, often a dissolve.

Set light A light whose function is to illuminate the set.

Setup, camera The combination of particular lens, camera placement, and composition to produce a particular shot.

Setup, narrative The sequence of events by which the characters have arrived at their present circumstances.

SFX Sound effects.

Shooting ratio The ratio of material shot for a scene in relation to its eventual edited length; 8:1 is a not unusual ratio for dramatic film, 20:1 or above is common for documentary.

Shooting script Screenplay with scenes numbered and amended to show intended camera coverage and editing. Used only in docudrama.

Side coaching In drama the director, during breaks in a scene's dialogue, quietly feeds directions to the actors, who incorporate these instructions without breaking character. Rarely used in documentary, but everything is possible.

Sightlines Lines that can be drawn along each character's main lines of vision that influence the pattern of coverage so that it reproduces the feeling of each main character's consciousness.

Silhouette lighting Lighting in which the subject is a dark outline against a light background.

Single shot A shot containing only one character.

Single-system recording Sound recording made on film or video that also carries the picture. *See also* Double-system recording.

Slate *See* Clapper board.

Slate number Setup and take number shown on the slate, or clapper, which identifies a particular take.

Social Actor *See* Participant.

Soft light Light that does not produce hard-edged shadows.

Sound dissolve One sound track dissolving into another.

Sound effects Nondialogue recordings of sounds intended either to intensify a scene's realism or to give it a subjective heightening.

Sound mix The mixing together of sound elements into a sound composition that becomes the film's sound track.

Sound perspective Apparent distance of sound source from the microphone. Lavalier mikes, for instance, give no change of perspective when characters move or turn because they remain in a fixed relationship to the wearer.

Specular light Light composed of parallel rays that casts a comparatively hard-edged shadow.

Split-page format A script format that places action on the left-hand side of the page and its accompanying sound on the right. This format allows an extremely precise transcription of relationship between words, sounds, and images.

Stage directions In drama and docudrama, nondialogue screenplay instructions, also known as *body copy*.

Stand-in In drama and docudrama, someone who takes the place of an actor during setup time or for shots that involve special skills, such as horseback riding, fights, etc.

Static character definition Giving a character fixed attributes instead of defining him or her in terms of dynamic volition.

Static composition The composition elements in a static image.

Steadicam Proprietary body brace camera support that uses counterbalance and gimbal technology so that the camera can float while the operator walks.

Step outline Synopsis of a screenplay expressed as a series of numbered steps and preferably including a definition of each step's function in the whole.

Sting Musical accent to heighten a dramatic moment.

Storyboard Series of key images sketched to suggest what a series of shots will look like, somewhat like a comic strip.

Strobing The unnatural result onscreen caused by the interaction of camera shutter speed with a patterned subject, such as the rotating spokes of a wheel or panning across a picket fence.

Structure The formal organization of the elements of a film, story, or any kind of discourse, principally the handling of time, and the arrangement of these elements into a dramatically satisfying development that includes a climax and resolution.

Style An individual stamp on a film, the elements in a film that issue from its makers' own artistic identity.

Subjective camera angle An angle that implies the physical point of view of one of the characters.

Subtext The hidden, underlying meaning to what is said or done. It is supremely important and the director must usually search for it.

Superobjective In drama, the overarching thematic purpose of the director's dramatic interpretation. Documentarians make the same identifications from life.

Surrealism Concerned with the free movement of the imagination, particularly as expressed in dreams, where the dreamer has no conscious control over events. Often associated with helplessness. Also a movement in art and literature.

Sync coding Code marks to help a film editor keep sound and action in sync.

T

Tag An irreducibly brief description useful for its focus upon essentials.

Take One filmed attempt from one setup. Each setup may have several takes.

Telephoto lens Long or telescopic lens that foreshortens the apparent distance between foreground and background objects.

Tense, change of Temporary change from present to either past, future, or conditional tenses in a film's narrative flow. Whatever tense a film invokes speedily becomes a new, ongoing present. For this reason, screenwriting is always in the present tense.

Tension *See* Dramatic tension.

Thematic purpose The overall interpretation of a complete work that is ultimately identified and decided by the director. *See also* Superobjective.

Theme A dominant idea made concrete through its representation by the characters, action, and imagery of the film.

Three-shot/3S Shot containing three people.

Thumbnail character sketch Brief character description useful either in screenwriting or in writing documentary proposals.

Tilt Camera swiveling in a vertical arc, for example, tilting up and down to show the height of a flagpole.

Timebase correction Electronic stabilization of the video image, particularly necessary to make it compatible with the sensitive circuitry used in transmission over the air.

Timecode Electronic code number unique to each video frame.

Timing The process of examining and grading a negative for color quality and exposure prior to printing. Also called *grading*.

Tracking shot Moving camera shot in which the camera dolly often runs on tracks, like a miniature railroad.

Transition Any visual, sound, or dramatic screen device that signals a jump to another time or place.

Transparent film One that never lets participants look at camera and minimizes evidence that anyone knew they were being filmed. Transparent documentary is rather like the invisible wall between players and audience in the theater. *See also* Reflexive cinema.

Treatment Usually a synopsis in present-tense, short-story form of an intended documentary. It summarizes expected dialogue and describes only what an audience would see and hear. Can also be a puff piece designed to sell the script rather than to give comprehensive information about content.

Trucking shot Moving camera shot that was originally shot from a truck. The term is used interchangeably with *tracking*.

Two-shot/2S Shot containing two people.

U

Unit The whole group of people shooting a film.

Unreliable narrator The narrative convention in which the point of view character's observations are of limited reliability owing to youth, age, bias, emotion, or inexperience, etc. The diametric opposite is the authoritative, omniscient narrator, whose views we are supposed to trust.

V

VCR Video cassette recorder.

Verbal action In drama as in life, words conceived and delivered so as to act upon the listener and instigate a result.

Video assist A video feed taken from the film camera's viewfinder and displayed on a monitor, usually for the director to watch during shooting.

Visual rhythm Each image, depending on its action and compositional complexity, requires a different duration onscreen to look right and to occupy the same audience concentration as its predecessor. A succession of images, when sensitively edited, exhibits a rhythmic constancy that can be slowed or accelerated like any other kind of rhythm.

VO Voice-over.

Volition The will of a character to accomplish something. This leads to constant struggle of one form or another, a concept vital in making dramatic characters come to life. Important concept to a documentary director as he or she struggles to see more deeply into the characters and situations being filmed.

VT Videotape.

W

WA Wide angle.

Whip pan Very fast panning movement.

White balance Video camera setup procedure in which circuitry is adjusted to the color temperature of the lighting source so that a white object is rendered as white onscreen.

Wide-angle lens A lens with a wide angle of acceptance. Its effect is to increase the apparent distance between foreground and background objects.

Wild Nonsync.

Wild track A sound track shot alone and with no synchronous picture.

Window dub A transfer made from a timecoded video camera original that displays each frame's timecode number in an electronic window, usually near the bottom of frame.

Wipe Optical transition between two scenes that appears onscreen as a line moving across the screen. An *iris wipe* makes the new scene appear as a dot that enlarges to fill the screen. Optical effects are overused on the TV screen.

Wireless mike *See* Radio microphone.

WS Wide shot.

WT Wild track.

X

XLS Extra long shot.

Z

Zoom lens A lens whose focal length is infinitely variable between two extremes.

Zoom ratio The ratio of the longest to the widest focal lengths. A 10 to 100 mm zoom would be a 10 : 1 zoom.

FILM SOURCES

FINDING DOCUMENTARIES

Many documentaries are available for purchase at the American sources listed here. Anything you can't find in distribution can often be located via enthusiasts or even the film's maker, whom you find through the Internet. Use a search engine such as Google and enter the title or person's name between quotes (as in "joris ivens" or "night and fog"). This ensures a search for those word groupings, not the words scattered throughout an article, which happens when you omit the quotes. Be aware that in the United States, tapes are NTSC and DVDs are zone 1. Material can only be seen on compatible players. For explanations and alternatives, see beginning of Chapter 2.

Reasonably priced, well-stocked video libraries in the United States are as follows:

Facets Multimedia, Inc. (670 documentaries, 970-page catalogue)
Address: 1517 West Fullerton Avenue, Chicago, IL 60614
Phone: 1-312-281-9075, or toll-free 1-800-331-6197
E-mail: sales@facets.org
Web site: www.facets.org. Scholarly Web site with 20 years of research available via a search facility. Tapes can even be rented by mail.

Movies Unlimited (980 nonfiction films, 800-page catalogue)
Address: 3015 Darnell Road, Philadelphia, PA 19154
Phone: 1-800-4-MOVIES, 24-hour service
E-mail: movies@moviesunlimited.com.
Web site: www.moviesunlimited.com. A more populist source of information.

Netflix is a website service (www.netflix.com). In North American (and maybe elsewhere) you can, for a modest monthly fee, choose from a list of 15,000 DVDs and make a "queue" list of films you want to see. As each becomes available they will mail up to 3 to your home. As you see them, each goes back in its prepaid envelope, and magically a replacement DVD arrives from your queue. The faster you see them, the faster they come. No limit!

Amazon.com (www.amazon.com), the well-known Internet bookstore, and **Barnes** and **Noble** in both its brick and cyberspace manifestations (www. barnesandnoble.com), carry thousands of films, including documentaries. The Web sites offer interesting film combinations at special prices and a list of other films that might interest you. Amazon.com, with its international outlets, offers its films in the local television standard. Comparison shop whenever buying films or books by mail. Prices vary greatly, and used copies are sometimes available.

BIBLIOGRAPHY

DOCUMENTARY THEORY, HISTORY, AND CRITICISM

Andrew, Dudley. *Concepts in Film Theory*. New York: Oxford University Press, 1984.

Barbash, Ilisa and Lucien Taylor. *Cross-Cultural Filmmaking: A Handbook for Making Documentary and Ethnographic Films and Videos*. Berkeley, CA: University of California Press, 1997.

Barsam, Richard Meran. *Nonfiction Film: A Critical History*, 2nd ed. Bloomington, IN: Indiana University Press, 1992.

Barsam, Richard Meran. *The Vision of Robert Flaherty: The Artist as Myth and Filmmaker*. Bloomington, IN: Indiana University Press, 1988.

Barnouw, Erik. *Documentary: A History of Non-Fiction Film*, 3rd ed. New York: Oxford University Press, 1993.

Bordwell, David and Kristin Thompson. *Film Art: An Introduction*, 7th ed. New York: McGraw Hill, 2003.

Bruzzi, Stella. *New Documentary: A Critical Introduction*. London: Routledge, 2000.

Burton, Julianne, ed. *The Social Documentary in Latin America*. Pittsburgh, PA: University of Pittsburgh Press, 1990.

Coles, Robert. *Doing Documentary Work*. New York: Oxford University Press, 1997.

Corrigan, Timothy. *Short Guide to Writing About Film*, 5th ed. London: Pearson Longman, 2003.

Corner, John. *The Art of Record*. New York: St. Martin's Press, 1996.

Gaines, Jane and Michael Renov. *Collecting Visible Evidence*. **Minneapolis**, MN: University of Minnesota, 1999.

Grant, Barry Keith, et al. *Documenting the Documentary: Close Readings of Documentary Film and Video*. **Detroit**, MI: Wayne State University Press, 1998.

Hardy, Forsyth. *John Grierson: A Documentary Biography*. London: Faber, 1979.

Jacobs, Lewis. *The Documentary Tradition: From Nanook to Woodstock*, 2nd ed. New York: Norton, 1979.

Levin, G. Roy. *Documentary Explorations: Fifteen Interviews with Filmmakers.* Garden City, NY: Doubleday, 1971.

Lorentz, Pare. *Lorentz on Film: Movies 1927–1941.* Norman, OK: University of Oklahoma Press, 1986.

Nichols, Bill. *Representing Reality: Issues and Concepts in Documentary.* Bloomington, IN: Indiana University Press, 1991.

Nichols, Bill. *Introduction To Documentary.* Bloomington, IN: Indiana University Press, 2001.

Peyton, Patricia, ed. *Reel Change: A Guide to Social Issue Films.* San Francisco, CA: Film Fund, 1979.

Renov, Michael, ed. *Theorizing Documentary.* New York: Routledge, 1993.

Rosenthal, Alan. *The New Documentary in Action.* Berkeley, CA: University of California Press, 1971.

Rosenthal, Alan. *The Documentary Conscience: A Casebook in Filmmaking.* Berkeley, CA: University of California Press, 1980.

Rosenthal, Alan. *New Challenges for Documentary.* Berkeley, CA: University of California Press, 1988.

Rosenthal, Alan. *Writing Docudrama: Dramatizing Reality for Film and Television.* Boston: Focal Press, 1994.

Rosenthal, Alan. *Why Docudrama? Fact-Fiction on Film and TV.* **Carbondale**, IL: Southern Illinois Press, 1999.

Rosenthal, Alan. *Writing, Directing, and Producing Documentary Films and Videos*, 3rd ed. **Carbondale**, IL: Southern Illinois Press, 2002.

Rotha, Paul. *Documentary Film.* London: Faber & Faber, 1939.

Ruby, Jay. *Picturing Culture: Exploration of Film and Anthropology.* Chicago: University of Chicago Press, 2000.

Stott, William. *Documentary Expression and Thirties America.* Chicago: University of Chicago Press, 1986.

Tobias, Michael. *The Search for "Reality": The Art of Documentary Filmmaking.* Studio City, CA: Michael Wiese Productions, 1998.

Winston, Brian. *Lies, Damn Lies, and Documentaries.* London: British Film Institute, 2000.

CINEMATOGRAPHY AND MOTION PICTURE TECHNIQUES

Arijon, Daniel. *Grammar of the Film Language.* Los Angeles, CA: Silman-James, 1991.

Ascher, Steven and Edward Pincus. *The Filmmakers Handbook.* New York: Plume, 1999.

Beacham, Frank, ed. *American Cinematographers Video Manual.* Hollywood, CA: American Society of Cinematographers, 1994.

Carlson, Sylvia and Verne Carlson. *Professional Cameraman's Handbook*, 4th ed. Boston: Focal Press, 1994.

Detmers, Fred, ed. *American Cinematographer's Handbook.* Hollywood, CA: American Society of Cinematographers, 1990.

Ettedgui, Peter. *Cinematography.* Boston: Focal Press, 1999.

Hines, William E. *Operating Cinematography for Film and Video: A Professional and Practical Guide.* Los Angeles, CA: Ed-Venture Films/Books, 1997.

Hirschfeld, Gerald and Julia Tucker. *Image Control: Motion Picture and Video Camera Filters and Lab Techniques.* Boston: Focal Press, 1993.

Laszlo, Andrew and Andrew Quicke. *Every Frame a Rembrandt: Art and Practice of Cinematography.* Boston: Focal Press, 2000.

Lobrutto, Vincent. *Principal Photography: Interviews with Feature Film Cinematographers.* Westport, CT: Greenwood, 1999.

Malkiewicz, J. Kris and Jim Fletcher. *Cinematography: A Guide for Film Makers and Film Teachers*, 2nd ed. New York: Simon & Schuster, 1992.

Malkiewicz, J. Kris, Leonard Konopelski, and Barbara Gryboski. *Film Lighting: Talks With Hollywood's Cinematographers and Gaffers.* New York: Simon & Schuster, 1986.

Mascelli, Joseph. *The Five C's of Cinematography: Motion Picture Filming Technique.* Los Angeles, CA: Silman-James Press, 1998.

LIGHTING

Box, Harry. *The Set Lighting Technician's Handbook: Film Lighting Equipment, Practice, and Electrical Distribution*, 2nd ed. Boston: Focal Press, 1997.

Carlson, Verne and Sylvia Carlson. *Professional Lighting Handbook*, 2nd ed. Boston: Focal Press, 1991.

Ferncase, Richard K. *Film and Video Lighting Terms and Concepts.* Boston: Focal Press, 1995.

Ferncase, Richard K. *Basic Lighting Worktext for Film and Video.* Boston: Focal Press, 1992.

Fitt, Brian. *A-Z of Lighting Terms.* Boston: Focal Press, 1998.

Gloman, Chuck and Tom LeTourneau. *Placing Shadows: Lighting Techniques of Video Production*, 2nd ed. Boston: Focal Press, 2000.

Millerson, Gerald. *Lighting for TV and Film*, 3rd ed. Boston: Focal Press, 1999.

Samuelson, David W. *Motion Picture Camera and Lighting Equipment: Choice and Technique.* Boston: Focal Press, 1986.

Uva, Michael G. and Sabrina Uva. *The Grip Book.* Boston: Focal Press, 1997.

Viera, John David and Dave Viera. *Lighting for Film and Electronic Cinematography.* Belmont, CA: Wadsworth, 1992.

SOUND RECORDING AND MICROPHONES

Bartlett, Bruce and Jenny Bartlett. *Practical Recording Techniques*, 2nd ed. Boston: Focal Press, 1998.

Bartlett, Bruce and Jenny Bartlett. *On Location Recording Techniques.* Boston: Focal Press, 1999.

Borwick, John. *Sound Recording Practice*, 4th ed. Oxford & New York: Oxford University Press, 1994.

Huber, David Miles. *Modern Recording Techniques*, 5th ed. Boston: Focal Press, 2001.

Lyver, Des and Graham Swainson. *Basics of Video Sound*, 2nd ed. Boston: Focal Press, 1999.

Nisbett, Alec. *The Sound Studio*, 6th ed. Boston: Focal Press, 1994.

Pendergast, Roy M. *Film Music: A Neglected Art*, 2nd ed. New York: W.W. Norton, 1992.

Rumsey, Francis. *The Audio Station Handbook*. Boston: Focal Press, 1996.

Rumsey, Francis. *Sound and Sound Recording: An Introduction*, 3rd ed. Boston: Focal Press, 1997.

Watkinson, John. *The Art of Digital Recording*, 2nd ed. Oxford: Focal Press, 1993.

Watkinson, John. *An Introduction to Digital Audio*. Boston: Focal Press, 2001.

White, Glenn D. *The Audio Dictionary*. Seattle, WA: University of Washington Press, 1991.

PRODUCTION MANAGEMENT

Cleve, Bastian. *Film Production Management*, 2nd ed. Boston: Focal Press, 1999.

Gates, Richard. *Production Management for Film and Video*, 3rd ed. Boston: Focal Press, 1999.

Maier, Robert G. *Location Scouting and Management Handbook*. Boston: Focal Press, 1994.

Patz, Deborah S. *Surviving Production: The Art of Production Management for Film and Video*. Studio City, CA: Michael Wiese Productions, 1997.

Silver, Alain and Elizabeth Ward. *The Film Director's Team*. Los Angeles, CA: Silman-James, 1992.

EDITING

Anderson, Gary H. *Video Editing and Post Production: A Professional Guide*, 4th ed. Boston: Focal Press, 1998.

Bayes, Steve. *The Avid Handbook. Techniques for the Avid Media Composer and Avid Express*, 3rd ed. Boston: Focal Press, 2000.

Browne, Steven E. *Nonlinear Editing Basics: Electronic Film and Video Editing*. Boston: Focal Press, 2001.

Burder, John. *The Technique of Editing 16mm Films*. Boston: Focal Press, 1990.

Collins, Mike. *ProTools: Practical Recording, Editing, and Mixing for Music Production*. Boston: Focal Press, 2001.

Dancyger, Ken. *The Technique of Film and Video Editing: Theory and Practice*, 3rd ed. Boston: Focal Press, 2001.

Murch, Walter. *In the Blink of an Eye: A Perspective on Film Editing*. Los Angeles, CA: Silman-James, 2001.

Ohanian, Thomas A. *Digital Nonlinear Editing: Editing Film and Video on the Desktop*, 2nd ed. Boston: Focal Press, 1998.

Oldham, Gabriella. *First Cut: Conversations with Film Editors*. Berkeley, CA: University of California Press, 1995.

Reisz, Karel and Gavin Millar. *The Technique of Film Editing*, 2nd ed. Boston: Focal Press, 1995.

Rosenblum, Ralph. *When the Shooting Stops, the Cutting Begins*. New York: Penguin, 1981.

Rubin, Michael. *Nonlinear: A Guide to Digital Film and Video Editing*, 4th ed. Gainesville, FL: Triad Publications, 2000.

Solomons, Tony. *The Avid Digital Editing Room Handbook*. Los Angeles, CA: Silman-James, 1999.

MUSIC

Russell, Mark and James Young. *Film Music*. Boston: Focal Press, 2000.

FINANCE, PRODUCTION, LEGAL, AND DISTRIBUTION

Cones, John W. *Film Finance and Distribution: A Dictionary of Terms*. Los Angeles, CA: Silman-James, 1992.

Donaldson, Michael C. *Clearance and Copyright: Everything the Independent Filmmaker Nees to Know*, 2nd ed. Los Angeles, CA: Silman James Press, 2003.

Gates, Richard. *Production Management for Film and Video*, 2nd ed. Boston: Focal Press, 1995.

Houghton, Buck. *What a Producer Does: The Art of Moviemaking (Not the Business)*. Los Angeles, CA: Silman-James, 1991.

Koster, Robert J. *The On Production Budget Book*. Boston: Focal Press, 1997.

Lazarus, Paul N, III. *The Film Producer*. New York: St. Martin's Press, 1992.

Levison, Louise. *Filmmakers and Financing: Business Plans for Independents*, 3rd ed. Boston: Focal Press, 2001.

Litwak, Mark. *Dealmaking in the Film and Television Industry from Negotiations to Final Contracts*, 2nd ed. Los Angeles, CA: Silman-James, 2002.

Ohanian, Thomas A. and Michael E. Phillips. *Digital Filmmaking: The Changing Art and Craft of Making Motion Pictures*, 2nd ed. Boston: Focal Press, 2000.

Rosen, David. *Off-Hollywood: The Making and Marketing of Independent Films*. New York: Grove/Atlantic, 1990.

Russo, John. *How to Make and Market Your Own Feature Movie for $10,000 or Less*. New York: Barclay House, 1994.

Singleton, Ralph. *Film Budgeting*. Los Angeles, CA: Lone Eagle, 1994.

Wiese, Michael. *Film and Video Financing*. Boston: Focal Press, 1992.

Wiese, Michael. *Film and Video Marketing*. Studio City, CA: Michael Wiese Productions, 1989.

Wiese, Michael. *The Independent Filmmakers' Guide*, 2nd ed. Studio City, CA: Michael Wiese Productions, 1997.

Wiese, Michael and Deke Simon. *Film and Video Budgets*, 3rd ed. Studio City, CA: Michael Wiese Productions, 2001.

EDUCATION AND CAREER POSSIBILITIES

Bone, Jan and Kathy Siebel. *Film Careers*. Lincolnwood, IL: NTC Publications, 1998.

Bone, Jan and Julie Rigby. *Opportunities in Film Careers*. Lincolnwood, IL: NTC Publications, 1999.

Horwin, Michael. *Careers in Film and Video Production*. Boston: Focal Press, 1990.

Kelly, Karen and Tom Edgar. *Film School Confidential: The Insider's Guide to Film Schools*. New York: Berkley Publishing Group, 1997.

Laskin, Emily, ed. *Getting Started in Film*. New York: Prentice-Hall, 1992.

Lazarus, Paul. *Working in Film*. New York: St. Martin's Press, 1993.

Peterson's Guides to Graduate Programs in the Humanities. Stamford, CT: Petersons (a division of Thomson Corporation), 2002.

PERIODICALS

American Cinematographer journal	(www.theasc.com/magazine)
Digital Video (DV) magazine	Excellent for software, equipment reviews, and keeping up to date with developments in the digital world (www.dv.com)
Documentary Box	English language journal based in Japan, with wide-ranging documentary issues (www.city.yamagata.yamagata.jp/yidff/docbox/docbox-e.html)
DOX magazine	The journal of the European Documentary Network (http://www.edn.dk/index00.html)
Filmmaker	The journal of the Independent Filmmakers Project (IFP), a not-for-profit service organization dedicated to providing resources, information, and avenues of communication for its members (www.ifp.org)
Film Comment	Magazine for New York's Film Society of Lincoln Center, which includes documentary in its showings (www.filmlinc.com)
The Independent Film & Video Monthly	(www.aivf.org/independent/index.html)
International Documentary	The journal of the Los Angeles based international Documentary Association (www.documentary.org)
Variety	The show business oracle; get ready to learn a whole new vocabulary (www.variety.com)
Videomaker magazine	Lots of good basic information (www.videomaker.com)

USEFUL WEBSITES

ORGANIZATIONS

www.aivf.org	**Association of Independent Video and Film Makers**; great information source for the low-budget independent filmmaker
www.afionline.org	**American Film Institute**; center for archives, film studies, and film education
www.asdafilm.org.au	**Australian Screen Directors Association**; has a strong interest in documentary, which thrives in Australia
www.bfi.org.uk	**British Film Institute**; archives, publications, and screenings
www.cilect.org	**CILECT** (Centre International de Liaison des Ecoles de Cinéma et de Télévision); Brussels-based organization of international film schools; always has an interesting range of special projects going
http://www.edn.dk/index00.html	**European Documentary Network**; important source of information
www.facets.org	**Facets Cinémathèque**; has 50,000 films of every kind for sale on tape or DVD; helpful and knowledgeable organization with a passion for international and minority interest movies
www.focalpress.com	**Focal Press**; Web site for the newest books on media
www.documentary.org	**International Documentary Association**; important for all aspects of news, producing, and exhibiting

www.lcweb.loc.gov	**Library of Congress**
www.soc.org	**Society of Camera Operators;** information, book lists, and links to other professional societies around the world
www.ufva.org	**University Film and Video Association;** organization for North American screen educators

INFORMATIONAL DATABASES

www.allmovie.com	Large movie database
www.boxofficeguru.com	Box office and other statistics
www.cinematography.com	Professional motion picture camera people, news, and resources
www.cineweb.com	Cineweb is a film production resource
www.us.imdb.com	Gargantuan movie database that enables every imaginable kind of production research, down to the careers of obscure technicians

INDEX